MATCHING BOOKS TO READERS

Using Leveled Books in Guided Reading, K–3

Irene C. Fountas and Gay Su Pinnell

HEINEMANN
Portsmouth, NH

Heinemann
A division of Reed Elsevier Inc.
361 Hanover Street
Portsmouth, NH 03801-3912

Offices and agents throughout the world

© 1999 by Irene C. Fountas and Gay Su Pinnell

The author and publisher thank those who generously
gave permission to reprint borrowed material:

Cover illustration by Ellen Childers from "Peaches
the Pig" by Kana Riley in *Guided Reading*
Collection from *Houghton Mifflin Reading: Invitations
to Literacy* by Pikulski, et al. Copyright © 1995 by
Houghton Mifflin Company. Reprinted by permission
of Houghton Mifflin Company. All rights reserved.

Library of Congress Cataloging-in-Publication Data
CIP is on file with the Library of Congress.
ISBN 0-325-00193-6

Editor: Lois Bridges
Production: Melissa L. Inglis
Cover design: Darci Mehall/Aureo Design
Manufacturing: Louise Richardson

Printed in the United States of America on acid-free paper
03 02   EB   5

We dedicate this book to the many teams of teachers who contributed their time and expertise to analyzing and leveling the books in this collection. Without their willingness to read, talk, and interact with children around these texts, this book list could not have been created.

Contents

Acknowledgments

Creating these chapters and the list of books involved long hours of reading, discussing, analyzing, and recording. Most important, we thank the hundreds of teachers who have provided input and feedback as to the characteristics and levels of text difficulty of thousands of books. They have helped in selecting the books, reviewing the leveling process, selecting prototypes, and constantly engaging in the revision of our thinking. We are especially grateful to Pat Prime, Amy Davis, Stephanie Ripley, Flo Metcalf, Kristen Thomas, Susan Sullivan, Mark Canner, Carol Won, Rebecca Goodman, Barbara Butterworth, Norma Sokolowsky, Amy Callen, and Joanne Goughan. They are teachers who are generously committed to children and to their colleagues in ways that make us all proud to be part of the profession.

The construction of this book list would not have been possible without the technical skills of Ron Melhado. For his technical contribution and his personal encouragement and moral support, as well as his endless patience, we owe a tremendous debt. His work has been key to producing *Matching Books to Readers* and we acknowledge his efforts with love and gratitude.

We also acknowledge Jennifer Rassler's expert assistance on the computer and Heather Kroll, Jennifer Gleason, and Sarah Szezcypniak for their support with a myriad of essential details. We also thank Sharon Freeman for her detailed scrutiny of our list. Our Literacy Collaborative colleagues at Lesley University and The Ohio State University have provided continuous support and encouragement that means a great deal to our professional lives.

We also thank those teachers who have encouraged us to love books and to think about their potential for bringing joy and knowledge into children's lives. Charlotte Huck, a master of children's literature, has helped us understand the contribution of books to learning to read and beyond learning to read. Martha King and Moira McKenzie have helped us realize the full potential of text as a support for learning and for thinking about life, and we thank them.

A skilled and insightful editor helps a writer communicate clearly and powerfully. Our editor, Lois Bridges, certainly assists us very well in that role. But she also advises us on critical aspects of text such as organization and sense of audience. She is a sounding board, a provider of feedback, and a good friend. As always, we express our gratitude to her generosity and expertise throughout this project.

To the "dream team" at Heinemann, we are ever grateful for your acceptance of our many challenges, your "can do" posture, and your belief in our work. Mike Gibbons has listened and advised with vision and honesty. Melissa Inglis has carefully guided the production details with her extraordinary skills and cheerful support. Abby Heim has assisted us throughout with care. Renee Le Verrier has brought continuous energy and spirit along with her talent to make our project a reality.

Introduction

All teachers want their students to be successful, confident readers. This process begins with sensitive, responsive reading instruction, an understanding of how books support the "learning to read" process, and access to a sufficient quantity of high-quality books at appropriate instructional levels. A well-organized book collection is essential to successful instruction. In our book *Guided Reading: Good First Teaching for All Children* (1996), we described the key elements and procedures of guided reading. In that volume we provided a list of books, organized alphabetically by title and level, to guide teachers in matching books to readers. *Matching Books to Readers* extends that work by providing an expanded and revised book list arranged in two ways, by title and by level, along with ten chapters that feature practical suggestions to help teachers implement guided reading in primary classrooms. We include descriptions of the list, suggestions for organizing and using it, guides for creating classroom and school collections, and suggestions for acquiring books, including grant proposals.

This book list is intended for use in the instruction of children in grades K–3. It provides for the wide range of achievement levels of children who are learning how to read in any primary grade classroom. Within any classroom, teachers encounter the challenge of matching books to a wide range of readers who reflect varying levels of reading ability. We wrote *Matching Books to Readers* to help you make these critical instructional decisions.

This book list is designed to support primary-level guided, independent, and home reading. Many other books will be part of a rich classroom literacy program—books to read aloud, books to support research and investigation, and books for wide reading and in-depth discussion. We think of book collections in schools and classrooms as continually evolving. As with any precious collection, you think carefully about each addition and you discard items that have not proved their value. The books in this list are organized in a gradient of difficulty for particular purposes. Our goal is to support teachers in finding "just right" texts for readers. When developing readers are matched with the right book, they extend and refine their reading abilities as they read.

The books we suggest are listed at an appropriate level for children to read in guided-reading groups. What does this mean for you and your children? To make each book more accessible, you will carefully select and introduce it. Your children will read the book and, with your support, learn how to solve a few problems. That same book is probably too difficult for the child to pick up on his own and read independently. A lower-level book may be more appropriate for independent and home reading.

We have included many sets of books and series books that are designed to support early readers along a progression of difficulty. We also have included many trade books because we want quality children's literature to be as much a part of guided reading as possible as children become more proficient readers. We place value on variety. Where appropriate, we have included many different kinds of texts—simple one-sentence caption books, realistic narratives, informational books, folktales, and fairy tales. The longer books for more experienced readers involve character development and more complex episodes over several chapters.

Our list of individual titles comes from a variety of publishers. Rather than simply ordering sets, you need to choose each title critically from those available on the market. Every publisher has some high-quality books and others of less quality (or at least less appropriate for guided-reading purposes). Also, some high-quality books may be excellent for other purposes, such as reading aloud or literature discussion, but do not meet the needs of children in guided-reading groups.

The ten chapters that precede the list are designed to assist you in using the list as a support for instruction. In the first chapter, we provide a rationale for matching books to readers, and in Chapter 2 we discuss the role of leveled books within a balanced literacy program. Children become literate as they participate in a wide range of learning contexts. Reading books at appropriate instructional levels is essential to support learning. For your own collection, you may want to include additional books not on this list. In Chapter 3 we present the concept of a leveled collection, along with a general description of characteristics to consider when leveling books.

Chapter 4 provides comparisons of the structure of this book list with other leveled systems, including basal reading material. We present equivalent levels for several different reading systems. We also describe benchmarks and how to coordinate them with the leveled reading collection to create a rigorous assessment system.

In Chapter 5 we describe how to use a leveled book collection to support guided reading, which entails small-group instruction for children who exhibit similar reading behaviors. In Chapters 6 and 7 we focus on organizing and using book collections. We provide estimates for the numbers of books needed and the costs of classroom collections at each grade level. We provide the same information for a school book collection. We also describe the organization and use of a school book room.

In Chapters 8 and 9 we focus on acquiring more books. In Chapter 8, we describe a variety of ways to increase the book collection for a classroom or school. In Chapter 9, we provide specific guidance for writing proposals for grants to support your collection. Finally, Chapter 10 provides a description of how this list is organized, including level-by-level descriptions of the characteristics of text. The Appendixes for this book provide ordering information, including lists of publishers and addresses, as well as a response sheet for teacher feedback on books and future testing of books in classrooms.

Matching Books to Readers in a High Quality Literacy Program

Children arrive at school with varying experiences in the world of literacy. Some have heard many stories and noticed critical aspects of print; others are just beginning to realize that language is represented by print that can be read again and again. This wide range of preschool literacy learning means that teachers must meet children where they are, addressing each individual's knowledge and experience. And this challenge does not diminish as children progress through school. In fact, the differences grow, so we are always in the position of matching books to readers.

Matching books to readers depends on three interrelated sets of understandings, all of which are critical to effective teaching:

I Knowing the readers.
I Knowing the texts.
I Understanding the reading process.

In this book we will provide information that will help you know the texts that children read as part of an effective instructional program in literacy. But we must always consider these texts in relation to the readers and the processes they are learning.

Importance of Matching Books and Readers

Why is matching books to readers so important? The young children we teach are building the network of understandings that make up a reading process. Children develop successful processing strategies as they learn to read for meaning. When children are reading a book that they *can* read, they are able to use many different sources of information from the text in a smoothly operating system. While focusing on the meaning of the story, they might:

I Make predictions about what will happen next.

I Interpret characters and form opinions about their nature.

I Notice language patterns that please them and/or language patterns that represent a new "style" that may challenge their understanding.

I Notice a word that is unfamiliar or that they don't see very often and solve it—that is, think about its meaning or how to pronounce it (often ignored in silent reading).

I Return to the text to confirm information that is essential to understanding the rest of the text.

■ Connect the text to others they have read or to their own life experiences.

Texts in Relation to Readers

Terms like "hard" and "easy" are always relative. "Hard" for whom? "Easy" for which readers? When we use those terms in reference to books, we are always thinking from the perspective of the readers. A book is easy or difficult only in terms of a particular reader or even a group of readers. So, when we know the readers, we can think of any text as "hard," "easy," or "just right." Each kind of text has important implications for the behavior of the reader and the potential to learn.

Hard Texts

Think about reading a text that is very difficult for you as an adult reader. It might be a legal document, a technical manual (such as the tax code), or a novel by an author with an unusual style completely unfamiliar to you. How would reading that difficult text limit your ability to bring what you know to the process of reading? Your understanding might be impaired; if you attempted to read it aloud you might even stumble over some words or use expressions in awkward ways. You might find yourself reading some sections over and over, as you attempt to make sense of them. You might even skip some words altogether because you are unsure of pronunciation, of meaning, or of both. If you have to skip too many words, you may become confused. Chances are, after a while you would not continue to read. You would simply discard the novel or seek the information in some other way.

In a sense, our beginning readers are exactly in the same position with the too-hard texts they encounter in school. If they are struggling, these young readers are unable to use what they know in efficient, strategic ways. In fact, forcing young readers to read too-hard texts has devastating results:

■ Children begin to think that reading is simply a matter of saying one individual word after another. Their reading may, in fact, sound like the laborious reading of a list of isolated words.

■ Children lose the meaning of the text and may conclude that reading doesn't have to make sense.

■ Children find it difficult to bring their knowledge of language structure to the process and may not recognize larger units, such as phrases. They cannot anticipate the next word because they are unaware that reading should sound like language.

■ Children practice inappropriate reading behaviors, such as the laborious "sounding out" of words in a way that makes no sense.

■ Children become frustrated with reading and avoid it altogether.

Easy Texts

What about books that readers find easy? How do such books fit into a reading program? Easy reading is actually beneficial for young readers, just as it is for adults. Reading a book that is very easy for you requires less intensity and energy. Most of what you do is fully automatic. You read quickly and easily. You feel in control. You are probably in a very relaxed state, and you can simply enjoy the reading experience. You are able to enjoy faraway places—almost as though you are there. You can anticipate events in the text; you enjoy thinking about the plot and characters. You may become completely engaged, blocking out everything around you. You meet few problems in terms of words, and you understand the text with little effort. Many of us use this "easy reading" to while away the time in airports or to help us fall asleep at night.

Easy reading is also beneficial for children who are just learning to read. In the first place, it allows them to enjoy reading and to use what they know in a smoothly operating system. With harder books, children may be reading text accurately but not processing it in a smooth, fluent way. With easy books, they are unhindered by the demands of reading because they automatically—or almost automatically—use the skills they control.

Easy books also allow children to focus on the meaning and enjoy humor or suspense. They can ask questions and find answers. They can think in a deeper way about aspects of text such as characters, settings, or plots. They may encounter challenging issues that offer a foundation for discussion after the reading.

Easy reading gives children "mileage" as readers and builds confidence. They process a great many words and build up rapid word recognition as well as fluency in processing. Easy reading frees them to attend to new aspects of print and thus engage in new learning. They can read for meaning and use language in an orchestrated way.

So, texts that are easy to read are appropriate for some aspects of literacy instruction. We recommend that in the classroom children have the opportunity to engage every day in a large amount of easy reading. But to help young readers learn more about *how* to read, we need more than easy reading.

"Just Right" Texts

Our purpose in literacy education is to help readers learn more—to nudge them beyond their current development and help them expand their skills. We want to support their efforts to stretch as readers—to successfully meet the challenges of more demanding texts.

To help young readers build an effective network of reading strategies, teachers must select texts that allow individuals to read for meaning, draw on the skills they already control, and expand their current processing strategies. In other words, the text used for learning "how to read" must have the right mixture of support and challenge.

The reader must be able to process or read the text well. That means

■ Using knowledge of what makes sense, sounds right, and looks right—simultaneously—in a smoothly operating system.

■ Knowing or solving most of the words quickly with a high level of accuracy (above 90 percent).

■ Reading at a good rate with phrasing and intonation (that is, putting words together in groups so they sound more like oral expression) but also slowing down occasionally to engage in successful problem solving (independently and/or supported by the teacher).

The texts you choose for new learning must both support and challenge your students because children—like adults—learn best when the task is well within their control. By matching books to readers, you make it possible even for young children to use their strengths and extend their control of the reading process.

The text should be just demanding enough to enable the readers to work out problems or learn a new strategy. The goal is not just about learning new words and adding them to a reading vocabulary, although that will inevitably happen. It's about the processing, the "working out," that helps readers learn the skills and strategies that will make them independent—strategies that they can apply again and again as they read other texts. The "just right" book provides the context for successful reading work and enables readers to strengthen their "processing power."

Readers in Relation to Texts

Meeting children where they are developmentally requires that we assess their understandings of print and the strategies they are beginning to use to make sense of print. As teachers of children in grades K–3 we encounter a wide range of readers, from those who are just beginning to learn about print to those who can read just about anything we give them.

As we observe children's behavior we need to keep in mind a broad continuum of learning. As we accompany and guide children's literacy development, we need to be ever-mindful of definitive characteristics and behaviors. The goal is to support children in using what they already know to get to what they do not yet know. That means knowing our learners and working "on the edge" of their learning. In Figure 1-1, we have described general characteristics of readers at five levels.

These categories are generally useful in helping us think about the broad characteristics of readers. No one child will exactly fit one of these categories, and many children will evidence behaviors in more than one.

This is the art of teaching: we observe and describe children's reading behavior and, in so doing, build a working understanding of each child as a reader at a particular point in time. In this way, we can trace changes in behavior as children learn and grow and plan sensitive instruction that supports them every step of the way.

Books, Readers, and the Reading Process

The purpose of matching books to readers is to provide the right books—those that provide reading opportunities that will help children develop an effective reading process. There are many opportunities in the school day for children to choose their own books, for example in independent reading time, but in guided reading the teacher does the matching. Our goal for children is to help them develop the kind of processing system that makes it possible to learn a great deal more—a system that extends itself (Clay 1991). As indicated in Figure 1-1, "self-extending" readers use many different sources of information in an orchestrated way. A competent reader reads the words and does so with great accuracy, but processing a text involves much more.

Reading is a complex process that brings together a reader and a text. Competent readers bring everything they know to the process, including:

■ Language knowledge (an aural and reading vocabulary, the structure or syntax, and the subtle nuances of language and how it is interpreted).

■ Background knowledge (from life experiences that include both direct and vicarious learning through books, film, television, etc.).

■ Literary experiences (the books and other print materials they have read throughout their history as readers). Readers are active, in that they are constantly accessing information from this experiential base, which they connect to the text at hand.

Moreover, a self-extending system means that you possess the strategies you need to learn from your reading. And you learn two kinds of information simultaneously. You gain the information or content of the reading material, and you learn more about the reading process itself—you *extend* the knowledge and skill of the reading simply by engaging in the act. Adults control a self-extending system; children develop the system. From the moment we hand a young reader a book, our teaching goal is to help the reader develop a self-extending system. Not surprisingly, independence and confidence are highly related to the development of such a system.

Knowledge of the reading process is a critical element in matching books to readers in guided reading. This knowledge helps us examine texts from two perspectives: (1) we note the demands of the text on the reader; (2) we consider what the particular reader knows how to do with a text. With this information we can begin to make a match:

■ If we know the challenges in a text, and we understand the reading process, then we can think about what this particular text challenges readers to do.

■ If we know what readers control, and we understand the reading process, then we can also think about what they need to learn how to do next.

■ Finally, we can intervene and teach to support new learning while children are reading a text.

Characteristics of Readers: Changes Over Time

Emergent

Emergent readers rely on language and meaning as they read simple texts with only one or two lines of print. They are just beginning to control early behaviors such as matching spoken words one by one with written words on the page, recognizing how print is arranged on pages, and moving left to right in reading. They are just figuring out what a word really is, how letters go together, and how letters are different from each other. They may know a few high-frequency words that can be used as anchors as they learn to focus their attention on specific aspects of print. As they read, they notice aspects of print such as first letters of words, and they begin to pay closer attention to letters and sounds.

Early

Early readers have achieved control of early behaviors such as directionality and word-by-word matching. Their eyes are beginning to control the process of reading, so they do some of their reading without pointing. They have acquired a small core of high-frequency words that they can read and write, and they use these words to monitor their reading. They can read books with several lines of print, keeping the meaning in mind as they use some strategies to solve unfamiliar words. They have developed systems for learning words in reading and can use simple letter-sound relationships in coordination with their own sense of language. They consistently monitor their reading to make sure that it makes sense and sounds like language. Early readers use several sources of information to check on themselves.

Transitional

Transitional readers have the early behaviors well under control. They can read texts with many lines of print. While they notice pictures and enjoy them, they do not need to rely heavily on illustrations as part of the reading process. They read fluently with some expression, using multiple sources of information while reading for meaning. They have a large core of frequently used words that they can recognize quickly and easily. They are working on how to solve more complex words through a range of word analysis techniques.

Self-extending

Self-extending readers use all sources of information flexibly in a smoothly orchestrated system. They can apply their strategies to reading texts that are much longer and more complex. They have a large core of high-frequency words and many other words that they can quickly and automatically recognize. Self-extending readers have developed systems for learning more about the process as they read so that they build skills simply by encountering many different kinds of texts with a variety of new words. Self-extending readers can analyze and make excellent attempts at new, multisyllable words. They are still building background knowledge and learning how to apply what they know to longer and more difficult texts.

Advanced

Students who are advanced in reading have moved well beyond the early "learning to read" phases of literacy learning. They are still learning and developing their strategies while they have varied experiences in reading. Through using reading for many different purposes, they acquire important tools for learning. There is virtually no text that an advanced reader cannot "read," but using prior knowledge, sophisticated word-solving strategies, and understanding the nuances of a complex text are still under development. Advanced readers sustain their interest and understanding of long texts over extended periods of time.

FIGURE 1–1   Characteristics of Readers: Changes Over Time

When we match books to readers, we become more effective teachers. A good match enables young readers to engage in the successful processing that builds the self-extending system—the network of understandings that all competent readers control.

Action Plan

Work with colleagues to explore text difficulty in relation to children's diverse needs.

1. Select a book that children at your grade level typically read.

2. Using the same book, take running records on six different children.

3. Bring the running records to a meeting with colleagues. Discuss the challenges in the book. It will be an easy text for some children, a "just right" text for other children, and a hard text for still others. Talk about text difficulty in relation to the six individual readers.

4. Using the Characteristics of Readers chart, discuss what you have learned about each reader from the running records. Ask:

∎ Which readers did you learn the most about?

∎ What happened when the text was too hard? Or too easy?

5. Talk, in general, about applying your knowledge of individual readers to the creation and use of a gradient of text.

The Role of Leveled Books Within an Effective Literacy Program

An effective literacy program rests on a foundation of good materials, and those materials are largely books: that is, books to be used by the knowledgeable teacher. Classroom libraries that brim with books foster a multitude of learning opportunities. Libraries should include a variety of fiction and informational books, poetry, and children's magazines. They should also include some baskets or pots of books arranged by difficulty level to guide children to books for independent reading.

If we are serious about high literacy achievement, then we must be certain that our classroom materials offer the richest learning opportunities possible. That goal leads us back to books. Books are a one-time expense. They are less costly than many of the commercial literacy "kits" or sets of materials we typically find on the market that quickly become outdated. Teachers can use and adapt books in multiple ways. Books are always available to the young learner and do not require additional equipment or mechanical maintenance. Moreover, the enjoyment that children derive from exploring books sets the stage for a lifetime love of reading.

Our goal is to help teachers develop and use a set of "leveled" books, books that have been analyzed in terms of how they support and challenge young readers as they learn how to read and that have been organized in a gradient of difficulty. They are an important component of the materials teachers need to support literacy learning.

The Classroom Collection

The classroom collection refers to all of the books that are housed in the classroom—either permanently or on a temporary basis. That collection makes up the children's literary exposure for the year, so it must be carefully considered and constructed. Children need experience with books that form the basis for literature discussion, that they can extend through the arts, and that they can use to explore their world. They need books they can select to read or to look at, and they need to revisit good books read aloud by the teacher. Finally, they need good books that are especially selected and chosen for them to support their learning of a reading process, books that have been leveled with the developing reader in mind. Selecting books to support children's reading is a complex task; we find it easier when we are working with a leveled collection.

Not all books in the classroom collection are "leveled." In this chapter we describe, in broad strokes, the classroom collection and the role of leveled books within it. We present three categories of books:

1. Books to expand children's literary experiences.
2. Books to support research and inquiry.
3. Leveled books to support children's reading development.

Books in the first two categories are not leveled, though you would want to be sure they are appropriate and interesting for the age and grade. Of course, a particular book may be on the leveled book list to be used for reading instruction or independent reading, and it may also fit into the first or second category. As the teacher, you decide how to use any particular text based on your knowledge of your students and your curricular goals.

1. Books to Expand Children's Literary Experiences

Through books, children learn more about themselves and their world, and they learn to think in new ways. By providing a richly varied classroom collection, in addition to the instructional books that are leveled in a gradient of difficulty, you open up new language and content learning for your students. In addition, children can enjoy all the vicarious experiences books offer, such as learning about people who are distant in time and space.

There is no substitute for a varied and rich collection of books, and we believe that many of the books should be hardcover editions so that children can fully appreciate beautiful literature. Through the classroom collection, children receive their first lessons in selecting, organizing, and caring for books. Many beautifully illustrated editions of favorite traditional stories and wonderful new stories are currently available. Once purchased, and with proper care, these sturdy editions last for many years. It is easy and affordable to order clear plastic covering from library supply catalogs and to cover all of the books. The clear plastic keeps the book jacket from becoming tattered but does not detract from the appearance of the book.

The classroom library should include a sufficient number of informational texts, including beautifully illustrated picture books, as well as journals and magazines like *Cobblestone*, *Cricket*, *Ranger Rick*, and *Zoo Books*. In Figure 2-1, you can see how one teacher has created an inviting classroom library for young children. Notice the organized baskets of books as well as the clearly defined labels.

A rich exposure to literature constantly nourishes background knowledge, which is a critical factor in successful reading. The more you already know about the content of a text, the more you can understand and appreciate as you read the text. If you have heard the language before, if you've heard the vocabulary, if you're familiar with the ideas, then it is easier to construct meaning and, at the same time, to solve any unfamiliar words you may encounter.

By providing a wider variety of texts in the classroom collection, we are building up a language and knowledge base that will help children as readers much later. Children learn how different authors and illustrators communicate ideas, and they are then able to bring these understandings to their own writing. We are also fostering children's interest in books and ideas. We make this classroom collection available in several different ways, as described in the following section.

Reading Aloud

The texts you read to children are usually those that are more difficult than they can read on their own. You often read aloud books that offer children rich opportunities for discussion and new learning. Books to read aloud may be fiction, including fantasy, poetry, realistic stories, traditional tales, and other kinds of books. Or they may be nonfiction, including biography, autobiography, "how to do it" books, or books on specific topics such as social studies, science, or the arts. There are many informational picture

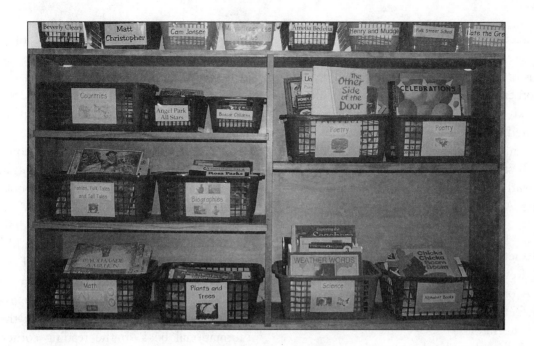

FIGURE 2–1   *Classroom Library*

books that capture the interests of young children, and the variety of these rich texts grows for second and third graders.

When children hear written language read aloud, they can focus on the meaning and ideas and enjoy the language. For young children, the reading demonstration itself is important. They learn that each book always contains the same words and phrases, no matter how often it is read. You can show them that you read the print and use the illustrations to build new meaning. You can demonstrate to children what phrased, fluent reading sounds like. They will hear you group words together, pause at commas, stop at periods, and vary the stress and pitch. Often, children enjoy hearing favorite books read many times over; in this way, they become familiar with the specific language of that story, attending to new aspects of the text each time they hear them.

Reading to children is the most effective literacy demonstration you can provide. As you read aloud, you demonstrate how to think and act like a reader; you also provide insights into writing because you are sharing a coherent, meaningful piece of written language that an author has constructed.

Shared Reading

In shared reading, the teacher and children read together from the same enlarged text. Usually the texts are big books or large-print charts, though there are some small read-aloud books with very large print that can be used for shared reading. Some publishers make little books that match the big books so that children can hold their own copies while reading together. Sharing the task enables even very young children to participate in the act of reading and to learn critical concepts about how print works, such as matching one spoken word to one cluster of letters on a page. Many children come to school with knowledge about concepts such as turning pages, looking at the print, and moving the eyes left to right. Others have had few experiences with "lap stories," in which they hear the story and have opportunities to see and touch pictures and print. Using large-print texts for shared reading helps everyone in the class enter the world of reading even before they know the specifics of recognizing or sounding out words. They engage in successful reading of a text with the support of the adult (see Fountas and Pinnell 1996, 1998; Holdaway 1979).

Individual Reading

Every child needs to develop his or her own tastes as a reader. A well-supplied reading corner or library will include many different kinds of books so that children, at a designated time, can browse and select books to examine or read. Often, we find that children will select books that they have previously heard read aloud or have used in shared reading. As individual readers they:

❚ Learn how to make choices.
❚ Get interested in a variety of books.
❚ Revisit favorite books.
❚ Compare books.
❚ Get to know favorite authors or illustrators.
❚ Talk with each other about books.

Many of the books in the classroom reading corner are not leveled but may be organized in many different ways—by author, subject, illustrator, genre, character, theme, or other aspect of text. The idea is to capture children's interest and make it easy for them to explore books in multiple ways. The books are often arranged face-front in colorful baskets, bins, or pots labeled by category. Beautiful hardcover books, standing upright for full show, grace the bookshelves. This friendly, inviting arrangement beckons young readers.

In the reading corner, it is helpful to have some books that are leveled and arranged in terms of difficulty. We've seen too many children select only books that are too difficult for them to read. When this happens, they are deprived of a rich, meaningful reading experience. The option to draw from leveled books as well as from unleveled books gives them just enough guidance to make good decisions; at the same time, they learn how to find books that are just right for them.

2. Books to Support Research and Inquiry

Informational texts are nonfiction books that expand children's understandings in specific content areas. Many informational books are appropriate for reading aloud to children. In recent years, the supply of informational picture books on focused topics has greatly expanded. Children often find the content fascinating, and they can access content through the text, detailed illustrations, charts, diagrams, and maps.

Through these beginning informational books, children acquire new information and expand their knowledge. These books offer a way to help children learn how expository texts are organized and how to draw information from a text. Hearing a book like *Animal Dads* (Collard 1997) read aloud enables children to enter into discussion on the topic, using language in ways that extend their learning. Should they revisit the informational book in the reading corner, they may engage in conversation about the topic that extends beyond the text.

You can use other informational books as references or as guides for exploring a topic with individual students or in cooperative learning groups. Because these books are not meant to be read from beginning to end, they are not appropriate as part of a reading lesson and are therefore not leveled. However, these books are still essential to the classroom. To help children learn that they can access information in many different ways, try placing content books in work centers where projects are underway (see Figure 2-2). For example, you might include books on leaves and insects in the science center. You might feature books on construction, such as those by David Macaulay, in the building area. Even if children cannot read every word of the informational books, they can use the pictures as a basis for discussion. Often, they can read labels or some parts of the texts. These books raise questions that can become part of the group discussion and can motivate teacher and children to work together to seek information.

3. Leveled Books to Support Children's Reading Development

The leveled collection of multiple copies is organized by the teacher for particular in-

FIGURE 2–2   *Center with Manipulatives and Books*

structional purposes and is kept separate from the books in the reading corner or in centers. In Figure 2-3 we present one teacher's leveled classroom collection.

You will be selecting books from the leveled collection to:

▌ Use in small group guided reading instruction.

▌ Stock leveled baskets in the reading corner or "browsing boxes" of leveled books that children are required to read as part of their independent work.

▌ Supply books for home reading that you want to be sure are on the right level for the individual child to read independently.

Like all books used in the classroom, leveled books should be those that:

▌ Are interesting to children.
▌ Represent many genres.
▌ Are multicultural.
▌ Feature quality illustrations.
▌ Represent changes in challenges of length, language, format, and story structures.

Leveled books are organized in a gradient of difficulty so that you can use the collection as a foundation for moving children along in their development of a reading process. The books are carefully graded according to text features that offer challenge and support to particular readers at particular points in time. Having a leveled collection does not mean simply "moving through" a series of books. You will want to carefully select books for particular groups of children, and gear your teaching actions and decisions to the strengths and needs of individual readers within each group. Each reader is different from the others in the group, though they are similar enough to benefit from a text at a particular level.

Guided Reading

The primary use for the leveled book collection is instructional reading. Guided reading is an instructional setting in which a teacher has brought together a small group of children who are similar in their reading behaviors at a particular point in time (Fountas and Pinnell 1996). The teacher selects a text that enables them to use what they already know how to do as readers and extends their "processing power" with a few new challenges. Through reading with teaching support, they become more effective processors of text.

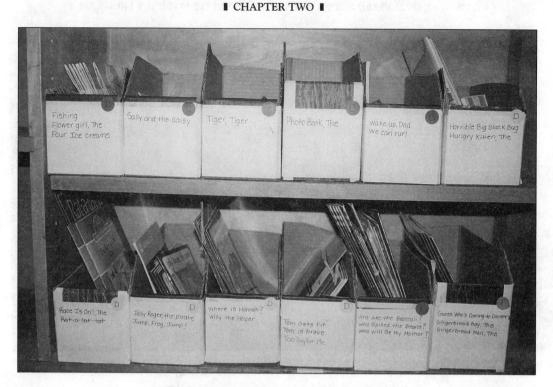

FIGURE 2–3   Teacher's Leveled Classroom Collection

After the teacher selects an appropriate text, she "fine-tunes" the selection with a brief story introduction. Then, members of the group read the whole text softly or silently to themselves. They read simultaneously at their own pace, not in chorus. During reading the teacher observes behavior and interacts with individuals to reinforce or support effective problem-solving behaviors. Afterwards, the teacher engages the readers in a discussion of the story and makes several teaching points based on observation of the children's strengths and needs.

Successful implementation of guided reading depends on selecting appropriate instructional texts day after day. If you are beginning to use small-group reading instruction in your classroom, you will find it very helpful to have books organized in a gradient of difficulty. Having a leveled book collection does not take the place of thoughtful text selection, but it does make it easier.

A leveled book set has several advantages, including the following:

■ An organized set of books makes it easier to select appropriate books for specific groups of children.

■ A gradient of text provides a way to assess children's progress over time.

■ The collection does not need to be replaced but simply revised and expanded over time.

■ As the book collection expands, exposure to the variety of texts will provide many opportunities for children to increase their reading power.

Independent Reading

Independent reading is an extension of the good instruction provided in guided reading. Independent reading with leveled texts enables children to practice and become fluent in their use of effective reading strategies. Fluent reading may be accomplished best on texts that are easy for the child, offering only a few problems to solve while reading for meaning. Students should not be trying to use newly acquired strategies on texts that are too difficult. Often, the teacher creates baskets or tubs of books, sometimes called "browsing boxes," that guide children from particular groups to appropriate texts for independent reading. These boxes may contain books that children have previously read in guided reading, as well as new texts that are easier, perhaps from one or two levels lower than instructional levels (see Chapter 9 in Fountas and Pinnell 1996). Another suggestion is to organize baskets of books as part of the classroom library to support independent reading. It is not necessary for these baskets to have level labels on them; we do not want readers to think of themselves as "level D or E." You can use sticky notes to suggest which boxes are right for particular students, or you can use colors to refer a child to a particular set.

Home Reading

Home reading emerges from children's experiences in guided and independent reading at school. When you send a book home with a child, you want to be sure that parents understand its purpose. If you want children to read books for themselves at home, you must be sure the books are well within their control. You want to avoid at all costs making reading a struggle for parent and child at home. In that situation, reading becomes a negative, unpleasant experience, and both parent and child may avoid it in the future. The leveled collection makes it possible for children to read each book easily and enjoy the experience as a result. Typically, teachers send home books that children have previously read at school. Resealable plastic freezer bags or cloth bags with the child's name facilitate the task of sending books home for reading.

Making Decisions About Texts

In this chapter, we have stressed that your knowledge and skill will enable you to choose effective books to accomplish the goals of a rich literacy program. Some books in the collection enrich children's linguistic and experiential resources, which are important for future learning and developing literacy. Others support the expansion of children's current literacy skills. While we are focusing here on leveled texts that support reading instruction and home reading, we must not forget that the literacy program is broad-based and includes a wide range of resources.

Action Plan

Many different kinds of books are needed for a complete literacy program. Take one classroom in your school and consider the collection of books as a whole. You might work on your own classroom or a group of colleagues might select a well-provisioned classroom as a laboratory.

1. Think about the three categories of books mentioned in this chapter:
   - ▌ Books to expand children's literary experiences.
   - ▌ Books to support research and inquiry.
   - ▌ Leveled books to support children's reading development.

2. Together, sort books into the three various categories, discussing their use:
   - ▌ Which books offer rich literary experiences and should be reserved to read aloud to students or for literature discussion?
   - ▌ Which books are useful for reference or for learning content or for browsing in centers of interest?
   - ▌ Which books are useful for guided reading lessons?
   - ▌ Which books would be good to place in browsing boxes for children to choose for independent reading?

3. You may also want to think about:
   - ■ What is the balance between genre in the books that support literary experiences (for example, biography, poetry, fantasy, realistic fiction)?
   - ■ Could you add journals or magazines to the collection?

4. Chances are, some books fit well into two or more categories, especially when you think about the diversity of the children in the class. Talk about how you would use books in flexible ways.

A Leveled
Book Collection

A leveled book collection is a large set of books organized by level of difficulty—from very easy books appropriate for emergent readers to longer, complex books for advanced readers in the intermediate grades. The book levels represent categories into which books are sorted by teachers. Placing a book within a level means considering a "cluster" of characteristics—many different aspects of the text that support and challenge readers. A level is only an approximation and there is some variability expected within it. The individual levels are described in detail in Chapter 10.

Within a level there are a variety of texts, which will expand at increasing levels of difficulty. In some schools, the collection is housed in a central area, such as a closet, a small room, or a section of the school library. There are multiple copies of many books; there might be about ten levels for grades K–1, and three or four more levels for each grade after that. Books in a leveled collection are selected because they attract children's interest and make them want to read, and because they support children's ability as readers to use multiple sources of information in text.

Matching Books to Readers catalogues a leveled book collection from kindergarten through grade three. We provide sixteen levels, represented not by grade level but by an alphabet letter (A–P). Books are listed by title and by level. We have provided author/series, word count (for most books), and publisher information. We aimed to make the list easy to access and use.

In this chapter we describe a leveled book collection and address some frequently asked questions about leveled book lists.

Book Levels

When we say that books are organized according to "level," we mean that they have been categorized according to characteristics that are related to the supports and challenges in the text for young readers. That means that, even for beginners, it is more helpful to have a book that has a simple language structure rather than a book that has one- or two-word phrases or labels. For beginners, leveled books that support reading should have an increasing number of high-frequency words, natural language, and familiar content.

A gradient of difficulty refers to "levels" designated by alphabet letters. The level is an approximation of difficulty because each child responds to a book differently.[1] Each succeeding alphabet letter indicates in-

---

[1] It is important to note a level designation assumes that teaching will support the child's reading of a text.

creasing difficulty. So, books in a set are always "leveled" in relation to each other. Level B is a little bit harder than level A, and so on. In our leveling system, the gradients—the steps in difficulty—are finer at the earlier levels than at the later levels. We believe that smaller steps are needed at first. Differences in text, such as one line or three lines of print, can make a big difference for a young reader; on the other hand, the layout of print is not as much a factor for more experienced readers who can handle a variety of lines. Additionally, at more advanced levels, there is more variety in genre and format.

Creating a Leveled Book Collection

You may create a leveled collection simply by gathering a large number of books and working with your colleagues to discuss the characteristics of the texts. Using your experiences in teaching children, you will find that you can discuss the supports and challenges to place books along a continuum of difficulty. Of course, your beginning categorizations should be tested as you work with children in guided reading over a period of time. Gradually, categories will become more stable.

Many groups of teachers have worked with their collections over several years, periodically coming together to discuss the books, revise levels, and add new books. They have used running records[2] with children of varying levels to assess text difficulty. As you discuss the books, you will discover that you are talking about more than the texts. You will be talking about the children and their reading behavior. You will be getting to know the books *and* getting to know the readers.

Another way to create a leveled collec-

tion is to begin with a set of books that have already been analyzed and organized along a gradient of difficulty and then to add to the collection. The set should be one that you have found reliable in the past. If you select a collection from a particular publisher, it should be one that you have used with children over time and with which you are familiar. You might begin with the book list we have provided here, but we advise you to go beyond it in developing your own knowledge and skill. *As always, you are considering difficulty based on your experience with children, so don't hesitate to occasionally "re-level" texts that, in your judgment, present particular challenges or are easy for the children you teach.* Then, as you acquire them, add new books from many different publishers to the levels. Selecting a few books on each level that "typify" the range of characteristics for that level will give you something to use in comparison with new texts. Soon, you will have a rich and varied collection.

In creating our book list, we engaged in a process that involved working with a large number of teachers over many years:

1. We discussed the way texts support young children in the development of a reading process. We explored the use of texts with young readers and observed their behavior with running records.

2. We worked with many teams of teachers to gather a beginning collection of books that were appropriate for use in guided reading, K–3. We considered teachers' descriptions of the ways in which they used the books, and we observed guided reading lessons. We examined running records of individual children reading many of these

---

[2]The running record (Clay 1993a) is a tool for recording the details of reading behavior. The teacher sits beside the child, both looking at the text that the child is reading. A coding system is used to record reading behavior, including significant behaviors such as repetition, substitution, and successive attempts at words. For more information about how to take and use running records, see Clay (1993a, 1993b); Fountas and Pinnell (1996); and Johnston (1997).

books and reflected on their reading in relation to their literacy performance in other areas.

3. For this beginning collection of books, we looked at the characteristics of texts in relation to what we know about young children's development of a reading process. For example, for emergent readers, we looked at factors such as number of lines of text, accessible content, picture support, high-frequency words, language, and print layout. For more advanced readers, we looked at factors such as language complexity, content, vocabulary, and text structure.

4. With various teams of teachers, we grouped books with similar characteristics and placed them along a continuum according to their level of complexity.

5. We described the characteristics of text at each level, A through P (for descriptions see Fountas and Pinnell [1996], and Chapters 9 and 10 of this volume).

6. We worked with many teachers to field test the book collection with guided reading groups. As we learned more about the books, we revised the levels.

7. We added new books to the collection by carefully estimating their appropriate levels and then inviting teachers to use the books and running records to assess text difficulty. Again, we revised our levels accordingly.

8. We expanded the list to include other published books based on their similarity to books that exemplified the levels.

Many of the books on this list have been field tested; others are in the process of field testing. Levels are continually revised as they are used over time with varying groups of children and as we receive feedback from teachers. Your input (see Appendix 1) is welcomed; the list is ever-changing based on wide experience with the books and readers.

Text Characteristics to Consider

No one aspect or characteristic of text can be used to place a book on a level in the gradient. Reading is a complex act, and, as we stated in Chapters 1 and 2, we are always considering the readers in relation to the difficulty of a text. We always consider the multiple aspects of every text, each of which has implications for its reading. A sample list of characteristics to consider is presented in Figure 3-1. This list does not represent a simple formula because characteristics are always considered in relation to each other. For example, a short text with only one line of print can focus on complex or technical ideas, thus making it more difficult than the length would indicate. Conversely, a longer text on the same level might have many high-frequency words, contain some repetition, and focus on a familiar topic, making it a long but easier text. Some texts are very uneven; for example, a particular text may in general be easy to read but also have some much more difficult parts.

You might want to use this grid as a guide when you examine and analyze texts in the leveled collection you begin to use. Also, since you will continually add new books to the collection, you will want to consider this range of characteristics in your beginning analysis. You will notice that we have included traditional features such as number of words, number of lines, and difficulty of vocabulary. Those are important characteristics to consider; however, other features, such as theme, also make a difference in the level of challenge offered a young reader. For children who are learning to read, it is very important to select books carefully; making that decision requires us to recognize the complexity and conformation of text characteristics.

Selection also requires that we teachers know the books very well. Talking about texts, along a range of criteria, will help you become an "expert" on the books you are using. In fact, if you are just starting to use

Characteristics to Consider in Examining and Leveling Texts

TEXT FEATURE	GUIDE TO ANALYSIS	TREND IN DIFFICULTY
BOOK AND PRINT FEATURES		
Length	• Number of pages. • Number of words. • Number of lines on the page.	• From shorter texts with fewer lines to longer texts with complete pages of print. • From presentation of fewer words to texts with a large number of words. • From one line of print to full pages of print.
Print	• Type of font • Size of print • Spaces between words and between lines.	• From larger, clear print with distinctive spaces to smaller print and spaces. • From well-defined spaces between lines to little spaces between lines.
Layout	• Placement of phrases. • Placement of sentences. • Placement of print and pictures in space; consistency of layout. • Use of organizational features such as chapters, headings, contents, index.	• From placement of phrases to support reading to no formula for phrase placement. • From sentences consistently beginning on left to sentences that begin in the middle of lines and/or carry over to next page. • From texts with layouts that are consistently the same to texts that have flexible layouts. • From texts with no headings to longer texts with many organizational features.
Punctuation	• Range of punctuation.	• From simple texts that require basic punctuation, such as periods and question marks, to long texts with complex sentences that require a full range of punctuation.
Illustrations	• Number of illustrations. • Relationship of illustrations and print in conveying meaning.	• From illustrations on every page to few or no illustrations. • From a large number of illustrations that give clear clues to the meaning and text to only a few illustrations designed to enhance interpretation.
CONTENT, THEMES, IDEAS		
Content	• Familiarity of subject matter. • Technical nature of subject matter.	• From content close to the experience of readers to more complex and/or technical topics.
Themes	• General sophistication of the theme of the book or story. • General sophistication of the historical event or political issue.	• From themes that involve everyday events to more sophisticated and mature themes. • From a single, clear theme to multiple interrelated themes. • From obvious, concrete themes to subtle, abstract themes.
Ideas	• Complexity of the ideas presented in the text.	• From simple to more complex ideas.
TEXT STRUCTURE		
Narrative Texts	• Predictability of story structure. • Description of setting. • Character development. • Plot complexity. • Episodic structure. • Genre.	• From texts about a simple idea to texts with a well-developed story structure (problems, climax, resolution). • From explicit ideas to ideas developed implicitly. • From simple plots with few characters to more complex plots with many characters who change and develop. • From texts in which setting is relatively unimportant to texts where settings are fully described and important to understandings of the text.

FIGURE 3–1   Characteristics to Consider in Examining and Leveling Texts

		• From simple texts with one or two episodes, organized chronologically, to longer, complex texts with many sequences of action and devices such as flashbacks or stories within stories. • From generic story elements to specialized elements associated with particular genres.
Expository Texts	• Presentation of information and ideas. • Organization of information and ideas. • Level of information or ideas.	• From straightforward (even narrative) style in presenting information to complex ways of presenting information, including figures, charts, and diagrams. • From simple and obvious organizational patterns (such as chronological) to more complex patterns such as categories linking events or kinds of information. • From observable phenomena to abstract and complex topics.
LANGUAGE AND LITERARY FEATURES		
Perspective	• Point of view of author and/or characters.	• From simple narratives from the point of view of one character or the author to several different points of view. • From stories that reveal the point of view of one character to stories in which many characters are revealed in different ways—through thoughts, words, and actions. • From texts that are straightforward in interpretation to texts that require inference and analysis.
Language Structure	• Phrases and sentences. • Paragraph/chapter structure.	• From simple sentences to longer, more complex sentences with embedded clauses. • From no need for paragraphs to long texts organized into paragraphs, chapters, and sections.
Literary Language/ Devices	• Particular use of words or phrases in literary ways.	• From simple, straightforward texts much like oral language to the use of literary language and devices such as metaphor, simile, onomatopoeia, and poetic language.
Vocabulary	• Range and variety of words used in the text. • Specificity of words to convey particular meanings.	• From a limited set of high-frequency words and words generally used in oral language, to a broader repertoire of high-frequency words, incorporating some words typical of spoken language, to specialized and unusual vocabulary, including many words not generally used in spoken language. • From a narrow group of high-frequency and familiar content words to specially selected words that convey subtle and specific meanings.
Words	• Number and range of high-frequency words. • Number and range of interest words. • Number of multisyllable words. • Difficulty of words in terms of problem solving.	• From texts with a few interest words to texts with many interest words. • From texts with a large number of easy high-frequency and one- or two-syllable words to texts with many multisyllable and technical words. • From texts with many easy-to-solve words (regular spelling patterns) to texts with many words that require complex word analysis.

FIGURE 3–1 *continued*

leveled books, it is probably more important to know a smaller collection of books in detail—and to have thought deeply about the supports and challenges in relation to your students—than it is to use a much larger collection with which you are unfamiliar. Your knowledge of books and your expertise in analyzing, leveling, selecting, and introducing them will grow over time.

Working Together

Creating a leveled book collection requires careful planning, time, and thoughtful analysis. But, every moment you spend getting to know the books and organizing them will pay off in terms of supporting children's development of a reading process. Creating the collection is not a mechanical process; rather, it is a stimulating learning process for us as professional educators. As mentioned earlier, it is most advantageous for teachers to get together to discuss the text materials they use to help children become more effective readers. Leveling works best when you compare texts, adjust levels, discard texts you consider inappropriate, become more knowledgeable about the limitations and opportunities in texts, and get to know the texts that you will use with children. Through our professional conversations with our colleagues, we help each other become literacy experts.

Action Plan

Work with grade-level colleagues or as a primary team to learn more about using the characteristics of text.

1. Pool the collection of books that you have selected as appropriate for guided reading.

2. Using the information in this chapter, arrange books along a gradient of text.

3. You will have several "piles" of books. Look at each pile and judge whether the books are similar to each other. Are there any books that you want to move to a lower or higher pile?

4. Select books that you like and use often. Discuss these books in relation to the characteristics of text listed in this chapter (Figure 3-1). The goal here is to begin to internalize your knowledge of the characteristics by looking closely at books that you know and have used.

5. Notice where you have "gaps" in your collection and where you have a large number of appropriate books. That information will guide future purchases so you can use resources wisely.

Understanding Leveled Collections and Reading Systems

Texts have been sorted by levels in different ways for many years. Each way of controlling and sequencing text reveals underlying beliefs about how children learn to read. In this chapter, we compare and contrast across leveling systems—grade levels, basal levels, publishers' guided reading systems, Reading Recovery levels, and our book leveling system. We also describe how to establish and use benchmark texts to form the backbone of an assessment system.

Ways of Controlling Texts

Texts can be controlled for difficulty by limiting and repeating the words, by limiting and repeating the spelling patterns or "phonograms," and/or by using rhyme and repetition of words, phrases, and sentences. They can also be controlled by examining a variety of complex characteristics, as we described in the previous chapter. When it comes to placing texts in a gradient of difficulty, all ways have both drawbacks and advantages.

Control of Words: Basal Systems

Many of us learned to read using a traditional basal system, which presents a series of books in a precise sequence. In the past, these books were controlled so that only a few new words were introduced with each story, reflecting the underlying assumption that learning to read is a process of accumulating a reading vocabulary. As young readers accumulated more words, they were introduced to longer stories with more varied language. While the word difficulty was controlled, the text difficulty sometimes varied considerably. The repetitive language of some basal readers was actually more difficult to read than the natural language of many books; no doubt as some children tackled their basal readers, they thought they were simply reading a list of words. In basal systems in those days, texts like the following six-word "story" were typical.

> I see Mark.
> I see Susan.
> I see Mark run.
> I see Susan run.
> I see Mark and Susan run.
> Run, Mark, run.
> Run, Susan, run.
> Run, run, run.

These texts helped children learn to read words, and most children also learned that texts make sense and sound like language. It is obvious, however, that this sort of text does not fully support the development of a reading process that includes using multiple sources of information contained in a meaningful text. It made reading especially hard for children who had a difficult time relating oral and written language. They often read like robots rather than readers who were engaging with a text to construct meaning. Most of these series have changed a great deal in recent years, some of them abandoning any kind of control to support early readers; however, control in the use of words may become popular again as opinions change.

Control of Spelling Patterns: "Decodable" Texts

Books for young readers can be controlled by writing around and featuring many regular letter-sound patterns, reflecting the assumption that reading is a matter of recognizing and using spelling patterns to decode words. Control is achieved by using a few high-frequency words and creating sentences made up of words that illustrate regular spelling patterns. For example, the *at* pattern is explicitly taught in a lesson before children are expected to read words with the pattern in subsequent texts. Texts are sequenced so that the reader can eventually decode words using all possible letter-sound associations. Since a more natural language structure is not part of the equation, the end result may be distorted language, creating problems for some developing readers who expect the text to "make sense" and do not recognize the patterns involved.

A sequence of difficulty based on decodable spelling patterns might give us a text like this:

> Pat has a hat.
> The hat is Pat's.
> Pat sat on the hat.
> Pat's hat is flat.
> Pat has a flat hat.

Aside from the high-frequency words *a, is, on,* and *the,* all the reader has to know are letter-sound relationships and the phonograms *at* and *as.* Of course, the reader also must understand the substitution principle—that is, how to manipulate the parts of words.

Control by Repetition and Rhyme: Predictable Texts

Some texts draw on repetition and language patterns to control and support reading; these texts recognize that reading is a language process. Children enjoy reading these texts again and again, and the repeated words and phrases assist their efforts. As a rule, a specific sequence of texts is not prescribed, but general levels are presented to assist in placing readers. Repetition and rhyme are the sources of predictability rather than the natural redundancy of language and the meaning of the text. Here, too, there is some unevenness in the gradient of difficulty, which we can trace to tricky language patterns and some difficult words. A "predictable" text containing repetition might look something like this:

> I like to eat bananas.
> I like to eat oranges.
> I like to eat apples.
> What fruit do you like to eat?

Rhyme is also used in many of the books, which makes language patterns harder for beginners to predict. In order for rhyme to be an advantage in reading, the reader needs to understand the concept of rhyme, know the particular rhyme, or at least be able to hear it. In this case, we also caution that the reader might simply be using the rhyme to get the word right and might not be learning how to use multiple sources of information simultaneously, including the print. Rhyming texts reflect a sentence structure that differs from oral language or other literary language. Also, rhyming texts may lack a consistent repetition of high-frequency words so that children sometimes encounter easy but different words from one text to another.

Repetition and rhyme enhance the pleasure of reading for most readers because they have strengths that compensate for potential weaknesses in the texts. Overusing any one kind of text may create difficulty for children who are just beginning to accumulate a reading vocabulary and who are finding reading somewhat difficult. If children are not attending to print information and learning how to use letter-sound information in a strong early reading process, they may over-rely on repetition and rhyme, memorizing them and gaining little "processing power" for reading texts they have never read before. The best texts are those that offer the reader the opportunity to learn to use all sources of information—the meaning, language, and print.

Works of Children's Literature

Finally, children's literature selections are often used for reading instruction. These books are organized in very broad bands, usually centering on grade level. The newer basal systems present literary stories that are bound together into anthologies. Sometimes, many or all of the original illustrations have been omitted, and this procedure makes the text more difficult to read. Fortunately, some current basals include literature texts in their original form, complete with full illustrations. Many beautiful children's books are available in paperback editions, and these may be used for guided reading instruction.

While literary texts provide a rich experience for children, the vocabulary and conceptual load can make them difficult to read. In literary basal instruction, it is not uncommon to find selections in the first-grade books that very few of the children can read. The sequence of stories is sometimes uneven in difficulty; for example, a relatively easy text can be followed by one that demands a large leap in reading ability. In general, these "literature-based" basals do not offer enough practice reading books at any level. And, literature selections are often linked to the rest of the curriculum (e.g., to themes in science or social studies), so teachers need to use them with the whole class simultaneously. While the material is high in quality, it cannot provide a match to all the readers at the same point in time.

A Universal Gradient of Text Difficulty

So how are we to deal with the enormous variety of texts that are available to us today? We can organize many different kinds of high-quality books into a leveled collection and create our own sequences for the children we teach. By examining the supports and challenges in a great variety of books, we can organize them in relation to each other, to how they support the developing reader, and, as they become more difficult, to how they place more demands on the reader. Texts that don't fit for guided reading purposes can be used for reading aloud, literature discussion, shared reading, or placed in a center where children can hear them on tape.

For each type of text control, there are better books and weaker books. Most good books do not fit extreme examples in any category. The best books to support developing literacy:

▌ Have natural and literary language patterns with some predictability but not a singsong repetitious pattern.

▌ Include an increasing number of high-frequency words.

▌ Have some literary merit.

▌ Are interesting and engaging for children.

▌ Integrate an opportunity to notice and use spelling patterns within a quality text.

Finding the best books is a continuous task. The collection is always under revision because you will be adding excellent books as you find them and removing books that are less appropriate for reading instruction but can be used in other ways.

We have attempted to create a universal gradient of difficulty in our book list, one that combines many different kinds of books that may be used as a foundation for reading instruction. Encountering variety makes the reader flexible. A variety of excellent texts makes it easier for you to create a supportive sequence for any particular group of readers. The books on our list are leveled on multiple factors that are related to children's literacy learning.

Grade Level Equivalents

As shown in Figure 4-1, the book levels in our collection correspond in an approximate way to grade levels.

Notice that no rigid division between grade levels exists. Also, grade levels may vary according to school district or geographic region. Matching texts to children is more important than precise definitions of

grade levels. As children become more sophisticated in processing texts, many of them can read books well beyond their present grade levels; the key is understanding and ability to learn from text. As we move up in our text gradient we need broader levels, with many more books and a variety of books, so other factors will enter into the process. Some children may need to spend more time reading at a particular level to build experience and fluency even when they are reading with high accuracy.

Different publishers have based their materials on different book features, but they do not necessarily use the same book characteristics. Some use controlled vocabulary, for example; others use phonics elements; still others use stages of reading development. In this book list, we have attempted to create a universal gradient that incorporates a variety of factors related to readability for younger

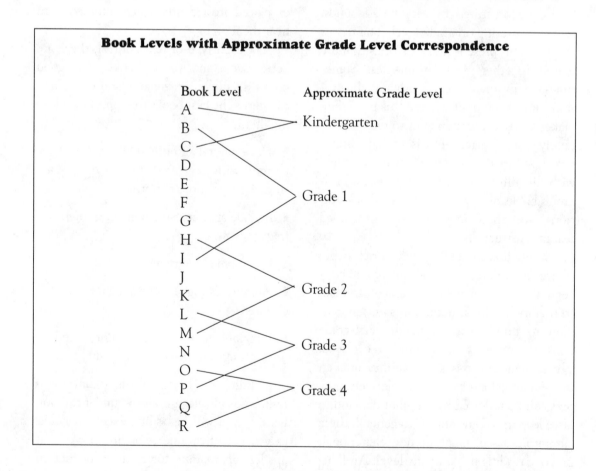

FIGURE 4–1   Book Levels with Approximate Grade Level Correspondence

readers. (See Chapters 3 and 10 for a list of factors and descriptions of characteristics.) Our list includes books from more than fifty different publishers. You will find that many publishers have devised number or letter systems of their own, but they are not consistent with our characteristics. Many publishers have started to use the levels in this book list in their catalogs and have referenced *Guided Reading: Good First Teaching for All Children* (Fountas and Pinnell 1996) as the source for the levels for new books. This kind of coordination is helpful but it is always wise to carefully analyze each new text yourself and to try it with children before assigning it a level.

Basal Levels

Figure 4-2 indicates an approximate correspondence between the levels in this book list and basal reader levels. We have used the terminology of older basal systems that may still be in use. Instead of using the words "preprimer" and "primer," the newer basal systems may simply refer to grade level: early, middle, and late.

Many schools use basal systems. Using this book list does not require discarding all of your present reading materials. Stories appropriate for guided reading may be selected from basal anthologies, for example, and leveled for use. You might get together with colleagues at your grade level or across grade levels and talk about the characteristics of the stories in your basal or anthology, comparing them to the materials we have provided here. Chances are you have used the stories or selections many times with children—this, of course, is an advantage! Pencil in approximate guided reading levels and consider using them in a different sequence.

You may encounter some stories that you will not choose for guided reading but that you can read aloud to children or use for shared reading. If you want the entire class to experience a particular selection that might be related to curriculum themes, you can read selections aloud. You can also do shared reading with some students, use the selection for guided reading with others, and have a third group of children read it on their own. Some stories, currently used at one grade level, might be more appropriate for another grade level. Advanced readers in second grade, for example, might enjoy reading appropriate selections from the third-grade basal. After you pencil in a level in the table of contents, try the stories with groups, and meet again with colleagues to refine and solidify your judgments.

Guided Reading Systems

Many guided reading systems are organized by stages or phases in the acquisition of reading. On the far left column of the equivalence chart, you will notice broad descriptors that correspond to our chart in Figure 1-1, "Characteristics of Readers," discussed in Chapter 1. We are not advocating a stage theory of reading; as noted earlier, these broad categories help in using reading behaviors as a guide for matching books to readers. No one child precisely fits a category, but it helps to have clusters of characteristics in mind. We also caution against checklists, which limit our thinking; we may check characteristics on a list but possess varying understandings of the checklist phrases, or we may rely on the checklist instead of our much more important observations of children's behavior.

Many publishers' guided reading systems offer somewhat different categories and labels for phases of reading. We encourage you to examine publishers' materials critically, looking at children's behaviors as examples to guide your decision-making process.

Reading Recovery Levels

A finely leveled collection of books is used in the Reading Recovery tutorial program for first graders (Clay 1993b). The last column on the equivalence chart provides approximate correlations between classroom levels and the levels used in Reading Recovery. These corre-

Book Level Equivalence Chart[1]

	Grade	Classroom Level[2]	Basal Level	Reading Recovery
Emergent	Kindergarten Grade One	A	Readiness	1
Early	Kindergarten Grade One	B		2
	Kindergarten Grade One	C	PP1	3 & 4
	Grade One	D	PP2	5 & 6
	Grade One	E	PP3	7 & 8
	Grade One	F	Primer	9 & 10
	Grade One	G		11 & 12
Transitional	Grade One	H	Grade One	13 & 14
	Grade One Grade Two	I		15, 16, 17
	Grade Two	J	Grade Two	18, 19, 20
	Grade Two	K		
	Grade Two	L		
	Grade Two Grade Three	M		
Self-extending	Grade Three	N	Grade Three	
	Grade Three	O		
	Grade Three Grade Four	P		
	Grade Four	Q	Grade Four	
	Grade Four	R		
Advanced	Grade Four	S		

[1] All levels and equivalencies are approximations and are subject to revision.
[2] Source: Fountas and Pinnell 1996.

FIGURE 4–2 Book Level Equivalence Chart

lations will be helpful to classroom teachers as they place Reading Recovery children in guided reading groups. Consultation between the classroom teacher and the Reading Recovery teacher is important in this process.

Reading Recovery is a one-to-one tutorial program for first-grade children who are having extreme difficulty in learning to read and write (see Clay 1993a; Fountas and Pinnell 1996, Chapter 15). They are generally confused about aspects of reading and are lagging behind others. Books recommended for use in

Reading Recovery are organized into a very fine gradient, labeled from 1 to 20. Small steps are very important; the goal is accelerated progress. These levels are appropriate approximately from the beginning of grade one in the United States to the beginning of grade two. Based on careful diagnostic information collected every day, the teacher selects one book for one particular child, introduces the book, and supports the child's reading.

Instruction in Reading Recovery is different from instruction in a classroom. In creating our gradient of text for guided reading, we returned to the books themselves. We thought about them in relation to classroom reading instruction, necessary to accommodate the small range of differences within *groups of children*, allowing for slightly more variability within a level as the gradient progresses.

Some variability within a text level is needed to accommodate the minor differences of children within groups. There are some books that we would use in the classroom with groups of children who are going to engage in discussion *that we would not recommend for use in Reading Recovery*. Our gradient of text also incorporates books at much higher levels than needed for a first-grade tutorial. *The characteristics we used were different in many ways from the criteria used for Reading Recovery.*

Benchmark Books for Assessment Purposes

Implementing an effective guided reading program requires a systematic way of documenting children's progress. One way to accomplish this goal is to create an assessment system utilizing benchmark books that are coordinated with the reading levels.

Definition of a Benchmark Book
A benchmark book is a book that is a reliable exemplar (or prototype) for a particular level in the gradient of difficulty. It will be a readable text (can be read at or above 90 percent accuracy) for most of the children who demonstrate similar reading behaviors

at a particular point in time. In other words, the benchmark book is one about which you'll say, for example, "That's a perfect Level C. Children who are consistently reading that level just about always read that book at 90 percent to 95 percent accuracy. And, there are some challenges in the book that help them learn."

Creating a Benchmark Book Set
To create a benchmark book set, you first need to work with a large variety of books at each of the levels. It helps for a group of teachers to collaborate on this process. You get to know the books at a level very well, and you get to know the variety within a level.

1. Have the teachers select five books each that they consider to be reliable at a level. Compare the selections and reach consensus on about five books to try out with individual readers. Use your experience from informal observation as well as your systematic running records, which offer a more objective measure because while the child was reading you were observing in a very neutral way. You were not teaching or actively supporting the reading, so you can be sure that the child was processing the text independently.

2. Try out the five books for each level by taking running records on a group of children, all of whom are reading well but still finding some challenge in books on the particular level.

3. Meet again with the group, compare the running records, and select the three most reliable benchmarks for each level.

4. Continue to work with the benchmarks over time. You may find that as you use them with children, some will prove to be less reliable and you will need to make substitutions. This system works best if teachers engage in a continual dialogue.

Introductions for Benchmark Books
To make the benchmark assessment systematic, you will want to create short,

standardized introductions for each bench-mark book. Remember, you will be working with children individually for this assessment. Introductions consist of two or three sentences that focus on the main idea of the book and use some of the language, which might include the names of characters, specific or technical vocabulary, or other unusual language. Glue or tape the introductions to the front cover of the book so that you can read it aloud to the child before he or she reads it. Include the book's level and the number of running words (to help with running records). Two examples are shown in Figure 4-3.

Using the Benchmark Books to Determine Instructional Level

Benchmark books are used to place children in initial groups and to document their reading progress over time. When assessing instructional level at the beginning of the year, you read the introduction aloud and then the child reads the story. Since the child does not read the text beforehand, you should expect it to be more difficult for him than if he had read the text once before. If the child reads the text at about 90 percent accuracy or above with good processing, it is a good instructional level for the child. If it is read below 90 percent accuracy, it was probably too difficult. You will want to try an easier benchmark text. The goal is to find a "just right" level for each child.

Using the Benchmark System

A group of colleagues who were working together in an elementary school created an efficient way to use the benchmark system. A description of their process follows.

Preparing the Benchmark Books for Assessment

Teachers selected books and wrote introductions for each. They typed the introductions to be read to the child, as well as the title, level, number of words, and number of errors a reader can make before the score goes below 90 percent accuracy. They duplicated the material onto sticky-backed paper, and then stuck them onto the outside front cover of each book (see Figure 4-4). You can purchase label printing software and sheets of labels at office supply stores.

They placed a collection of the benchmark books, one at each level, in a two-gallon resealable plastic bag to create a set for each primary teacher. Each teacher used her benchmark bag several times over the year to measure children's reading progress. Several other benchmark books were identified on each level to serve as a resource so that teachers would have alternatives if they needed them.

Introductions for Two Benchmark Books

At the Zoo
written by Catherine Peters

Level B
RW 54
E 4

In this book a little girl tells a story about all of the animals at the zoo. On each page she says that she likes the animal and the animal likes her.

The Hole in Harry's Pocket
written by Robin Bloksberg

Level I
RW 279
E 27

This story is about a little boy whose mother gives him some money to go to the store to buy some milk. He puts the money in his pocket along with his toys and then he has a big problem when he gets to the store.

FIGURE 4–3 Introductions for Two Benchmark Books

Level E
RW = 120
E = 12

Peaches the Pig
by Kana Riley

Peaches is the name of a little pig. She
wanted to play, so she kept asking
other animals to play with her. Read
to find out what happened.

FIGURE 4–4 *Peaches the Pig* with Introduction

Using Benchmark Books

In September of the school year, each primary teacher took running records (on unseen text) with each child using the benchmark books to determine instructional level. This assessment formed the basis for the initial guided reading groups. The assessment was repeated in January and May to provide grade-level and across-grade-level documentation of progress each year. Between the summative assessment points, teachers used running records with the leveled texts to regroup children on a regular basis so that members of groups would be similar enough to make group instruction effective.

Making Connections to Enrich the Collection

We hope this chapter helped you make connections between all of the reading materials in your classroom and this universal leveling system. Once you internalize characteristics of texts as you work with a leveled collection of books, you can easily analyze almost any materials that come to you in any form. With the skills that you build over time, you can create a dynamic and rich collection that will enable you to teach reading in more effective and powerful ways.

Action Plan

Create a beginning set of benchmark books for your school:

1. Carry out the activities suggested in this chapter, beginning on page 28.

2. Try out your selected benchmark books with children in your class. Record your data.

3. Come back together and talk about how you will use the information from benchmark books to establish beginning levels for instruction. If you have groups already established in your class, talk about how this benchmark assessment has helped you rethink your grouping.

4. You may want to readminister the assessment at mid-year or year-end to provide objective standardized assessment data.

Using Leveled Books in a Guided Reading Program

Guided reading is an instructional approach. Within its instructional setting, teachers select and introduce books to children as they take into account the children's current reading abilities. The following characteristics define guided reading practice:

▌ A teacher works with a small group of children who are similar in their development of a reading process at a particular point in time.

▌ Children in the group exhibit similar reading behaviors and can read, with high accuracy and good problem solving, texts that are about the same level.

▌ Teachers introduce the books to the children and then observe and guide them while they read; teachers also provide some additional teaching after the reading if needed.

▌ The teacher's role in guided reading is to determine how best to help the child, who is extending and refining her in-the-head strategies for accessing and processing information from the text.

▌ At the same time, each child reads the whole text or a unified part of it rather than just a page or sentence (unlike traditional round-robin reading, in which children take turns reading aloud while others listen).

▌ Children are grouped together because they are similar, but as they learn and change, they are regrouped in a dynamic process that involves systematic, ongoing assessment.

▌ The emphasis in guided reading is on reading many books along a gradient of increasing complexity and challenge.

▌ The goal of guided reading is for children to read independently and silently.

Using Running Records to Place Children in Initial Groups for Teaching

The best way to determine an appropriate reading level for a child is to observe reading behavior. Select leveled books (for example, benchmark books) to get started. We strongly encourage you to learn to take a running record of reading behavior because it is the most powerful and objective tool you can find (see footnote on page 16). A general guide is that the child must be reading a text at about 90 to 94 percent accuracy, with evidence of successful processing to determine an instructional level. Take a running record on the entire text if a book has less than two hundred words. If there are more than two hundred words, you will want to take the running record on between 100 and 150 words of text to get a good sampling of the child's processing on a text at that level. You will want to continue to have the child read texts at increasingly difficult levels until you determine the instructional level. This will be a "readable" text, one that will be just right for "learning how to read."

In this book list, we provide the number of words that are read in the text (running words) for most books that include less than 250 words. Generally, books with more than 250 words are indicated by 250+. (We didn't provide a count for some of the books that we leveled previously because they were no longer available to us.) We have included some widely used out-of-print books because you may already have them in your school. For those books, new books you acquire, and segments of longer books, you will simply need to count the words. As you build your collection, you will want to pencil in the word count on the inside cover or put the number of running words on a sticky label on the front or back of the book itself. Having the word count makes it much easier to take a running record and quickly calculate the accuracy and self-correction ratios (see Clay 1991).

You will acquire many new books that are not listed here and will also use titles for which we did not provide word counts. We do not advise conducting "marathon" sessions in which you label and count all of the words in all of the new books at once. Every time you take a running record on a new book, simply count the words and mark the number on the cover. Soon, you will have many more books with word counts indicated.

To standardize the process of counting words, here are some guidelines:

1. Start with the first page of the text, counting each word. Do not include the title page or cover page because these items are not typically in sentence form.

2. Count hyphenated (*jack-o'-lantern*) and compound words (*butterfly*) as one word.

3. Count number words (*twenty-one*) as one word.

4. Do not count numerals (*10*) as words.

5. Count animal noises (*woof-woof*) as one word.

6. When sounds are represented (as in *Mmmmm*), do not count them as words.

When you are a taking a running record on a longer text, you may select the segment to be assessed from anywhere in the text. You do not have to begin on the first page. The goal of the running record is to sample the processing at that level.

Using the Gradient to Help in the Selection of Texts

A gradient of text is not a precise sequence in which children read books in a specific order. In fact, children who are making rapid progress will not even read books on every level; they may skip levels. The goal in guided reading is to select and introduce texts that are "just right" for readers at a point in time and to continue to select books at that level until the processing is going very well. You can take advantage of the breadth of each level if you decide that children need to read at about the same level of difficulty for some time, building fluency and effective strategies. But, if children are finding books very easy and there is no opportunity for the readers to learn something new about processing text, you should move them to another level. (Children will sometimes change very quickly, making leaps in learning, so you may want to skip a level.) Remember, you will need to provide strong teaching at every level to enable the children to develop and change over time.

Using Running Records with Book Levels

Decisions about using the gradient of text are based on careful observation of children. While benchmark books are used to help in initial placement, continuous running records are used to capture progress over time. Take these running records on any book that the child has read in the guided reading group. They are an effective tool for assessing what children can do in reading without teacher support. This ongoing process of taking running records on "seen" text (a text that has been read before) differs from using benchmark books to take a running record on unseen text for the purpose of periodic interval assessment (see Chapter 4). Here are some general guidelines for using running records as part of the guided reading instruction.

❚ Find a time to take two or three running records per day on a systematic basis. It might be just at the beginning of the day while children are independently engaged in reading or writing. It might be at the beginning or end of the group's reading lesson.

❚ Take more frequent records on children who are having difficulty or are lagging behind and less frequent records on high-progress readers. The number of records may vary from one per week to one per month or even to one per quarter on a given child. The assessment folder, though, will contain a sufficient number of running records to document every child's reading behaviors over time. This collection of running records serves as a resource for you as you make ongoing decisions about grouping and regrouping children as well as about text selection.

❚ Take the running record on a book that has been introduced to the child and that the student has read only once, preferably the day before (seen text). Keeping a list of children with a schedule for taking records will help you standardize your procedures and schedules for taking running records.

❚ Sit beside the child, recording the precise reading behavior.

❚ Afterwards, calculate the accuracy rate and the self-correction rate. Self-corrections do not count as errors, but the self-correction rate indicates what ratio of the total number of errors were self-corrected.

❚ Analyze the errors and self-corrections. This qualitative look at the child's reading behavior can give you important insights. For example, a child might read a selection with high accuracy but the errors indicate that he is not noticing errors or that he is neglecting important sources of information, such as letter-sound relationships. This analysis is quite helpful in making teaching moves as well as in deciding whether a text is appropriate. (For further information, see Clay 1993b; Fountas and Pinnell 1996).

❚ Write a brief comment about the child's fluency and phrasing to indicate whether the reading was choppy or smooth, fast or laborious, phrased or read in a robotic way. This information can help you decide whether the text was too easy, too hard, or just right and can guide teaching emphases.

❚ Periodically, reflect on the running records of a group of children, comparing their responses to books and their reading behaviors. Use this reflection as a basis for deciding the kind of texts to select for the group and whether to choose more difficult texts.

These running records will prove to be an invaluable resource when making decisions such as moving children from one group to another, deciding when to change the book level for instructing a particular group, or considering a suggestion to change a text level in the collection.

Changing Book Levels

Decisions about changing the text level at which children are reading are based on continuous, careful observation of children. The observation can be informal (notes and records) or more systematic (using running records). When an individual child is processing well on a level and has had enough experience at a level, move the child to another level. The child may need to change groups, or the entire group may be ready to move forward. Select a book from the next (or even higher) level, introduce it, and observe children's reading. That observation, plus running records taken over the next several days, will give you immediate feedback. If necessary, simply move back and select another book from a lower level and, again, observe behavior carefully. Remember that *text characteristics and opportunities to solve problems* are as important as *level* in selecting a book.

Using the Book Gradient to Document Progress Over Time

In Chapter 1 we described a continuum of learning from emergent to advanced categories of reading behavior. As noted, these categories are not neat and separate but simply help us think about continuous progress. We expect students to change and expand their repertoires of strategies and skills; accordingly, the materials and teaching we provide will change over time. During the primary years it is especially important to closely document children's progress. The book level gradient provides one way of monitoring progress over time. The Record of Book-Reading Progress (fully described in Fountas and Pinnell 1996) provides a picture of one child's journey to literacy. (See Figure 5–1.)

The record provides documentation for reading progress in grades K to 3. Along the top, note the book title, accuracy rate, and self-correction rate. Record about one running record from a child's reading folder at time intervals (e.g., 4–6 weeks); this docu-

mentation is sufficient to create a picture of progress over time. You can use a running record taken as a regular part of your instructional schedule, so you do not need to devote mornings or days to assessment in order to use this graph. The reading is recorded by placing a dot in the box under the date. An open dot (O) indicates that the reading was above 90 percent accuracy, while a closed dot (●) indicates below 90 percent.

A quick glance at the graph in Figure 5–1 shows that Sarah's kindergarten experience enabled her to read the simple texts in levels A, B, and C very well, and she moved on to first grade as a reader. During first grade, she made steady progress, working at levels G and H for a longer time as she learned to orchestrate sources of information and became more skilled at analyzing words. Through second grade, she enjoyed reading longer chapter books and diversified her reading, entering third grade reading comfortably at levels L and M. Of course, many other ways of assessing Sarah's progress—writing samples, spelling tasks, comprehension assessments, and fluency assessments—were part of the total picture of her work in the primary grades. This reading graph, however, provides an overall picture.

The first levels of our reading gradient are more finely drawn; that is, a change in level means a smaller step. As children begin to read, it is necessary to provide these small steps to support growth because they are taking on many different kinds of learning in reading and generally do not know how to put it all together. As the levels increase, more complexity within each level is required, and children are expected to read longer texts. The levels are broader and involve more diversity in reading. As children move through second and third grade, for example, we don't simply think about moving "up" a level, and children don't change levels as frequently. Within a level we want to increase flexibility and the ability to read many different kinds of texts—biography, autobi-

Record of Book-Reading Progress

Child's Name: Sarah

Grade(s): ✓ K ✓ 1 ✓ 2 ____ 3

Title of Book, Accuracy Rate, SC Rate (○ = above 90%   ● = below 90%)

Title of Book	Accuracy Rate	SC Rate	Book Level	Date
Dad	100%	nil	A	2/15/98
At the Zoo	89%	1:6	B ●	3/16/98
Go-Carts	92%	1:2	B	4/18/98
Tiger, Tiger	94%	1:3	C	5/12/98
Homes	89%	1:5	C	9/20/98
Nighttime	96%	1:4	C	11/1/98
No, No	93%	1:4	D	12/20/98
Peaches the Pig	94%	1:3	E	1/27/99
After the Flood	90%	1:3	G	2/20/99
Noise	87%	1:6	G ●	3/15/99
T.J.'s Tree	90%	1:2	G	4/15/99
Surprise Visit	92%	1:3	H	5/3/99
Come And See	95%	1:2	H	5/28/99
Let's Bake	93%	1:2	H	6/15/99
Fox on Wheels	90%	1:3	J	9/16/99
Henry & Mudge	96%	1:2	J	10/30/99
Brave Tailor	92%	1:2	K	11/29/99
Pinky and Rex	97%	1:3	L	1/6/00
Say Cheese	98%	1:2	L	2/27/00
Arthur Makes the Team	98%	1:2	M	3/20/00

Book Level axis (top to bottom): S R Q P O N M L K J I H G F E D C B A

FIGURE 5–1   Record of Book-Reading Progress

ography, fantasy, realistic stories, historical fiction, and all kinds of informational texts.

We also want to be sure that children are interested in what they are reading, that they find characters that reflect our multicultural society. Children need to understand and identify with characters. By the end of second grade, good readers know most of the words and can "decode" just about anything, but we do not want the situation where children are reading but do not fully understand what they are reading. Moving up a level in our guided reading system implies understanding and fluency at every level.

Using the Gradient of Text in Guided Reading and Beyond

Regrouping children, changing text levels, and documenting progress over time are critical elements of an effective guided reading program. The gradient of text is a teacher's tool in accomplishing all of those goals. It is also helpful in supporting wide reading. Think about what happens to the texts used in guided reading.

■ You can place books in a browsing box for children to read again. This practice is especially helpful for children reading levels A through I. They enjoy reading the shorter stories again, experiencing the characters and reveling in the feel of reading fluently with phrasing. Younger children are willing to read simply to enjoy the act as they become more and more competent; just as they enjoy hearing favorite stories read aloud several times, they like rereading books for themselves. As they grow in reading ability and read longer chapter books, they may still like to reread some favorites, especially series books with memorable characters. At this point, they will not reread every book.

■ You can send books home so that children can enjoy them with caregivers and their families. A book that a child takes home to read must be one that is easy to read. Ideal

for home reading are those books that have been introduced, read in guided reading groups, and perhaps read again a couple of times. Books at easier levels that have not yet been read may also be appropriate.

■ The leveled book collection is also helpful in guiding selection of titles for independent reading in the classroom. If a group of children are reading on a certain level, you can select a range of appropriate books that they can read for themselves. Place these books in browsing boxes or in the reading corner. In this way, children will be able to select books that they can successfully process.

A leveled book collection is designed to help you create a classroom context that fosters extensive and intensive reading. It matters *how much* reading children do; it matters *what* they read. Successful processing is essential to building the self-extending system. We believe it is the right of every child to read "just right" and easier books every day. The leveled book collection, together with good teaching, makes it possible.

Action Plan

1. Children will change very quickly, making leaps in learning. Select one or two children to follow intensively for three weeks. You will be focusing on how to match books to these children's current reading abilities, which will help you become more skillful at matching children's reading behaviors with texts.

2. Every day, observe the child in reading activities. Take running records on as many books as you can over the three-week period.

■ Which books are at an appropriate level for the child in guided reading?

■ What supports and challenges do these books offer?

■ Which books are appropriate for the child to read independently, with very little support? What are the characteristics of these books?

3. Is there a change during this time period? What changes did you make in matching books?

4. Get together with colleagues to share the results of your observations.

5. What are some general things you have learned about matching books to readers that you can apply in your work in guided reading?

6. If possible, do a similar round of observation on the same children in a month or two. This process will help you develop an understanding of using a gradient of text to support readers.

Getting Started: Creating a Classroom Collection

The organization of the book collection is the key to efficient use. In this chapter we provide sample charts to guide the purchase of a collection of books for single classrooms at each grade level. Our examples are based on a class size of twenty-five, so you will want to adjust the number of copies proportionately if you have a smaller or larger class.

You do not need a complete classroom collection before you begin to explore guided reading as an instructional approach. If you have a limited amount of money to spend, reduce the approximate cost by one fourth or by half. Purchase some of the titles the first year; build the collection over time. The estimates we provide are based on not-discounted retail prices. Most general suppliers of trade books will provide a 20 percent discount for schools. Other publishers may give discounts for large orders. Search for the best prices and ask for discounts at least on shipping and handling costs.

We provide examples of both starter book collections and basic book collections. A starter collection provides the minimal resources needed to support a guided reading program. Purchase this collection to begin your program. If you have very small classes, it may be sufficient. A basic collection provides more variety in the collection, and books will also be available for independent and home reading.

To effectively implement a daily guided-reading program, you do need a collection of books that you know in detail. Your first step, then, is to collect all copies of all of the books in your classroom that you think will be effective in guided reading.

Multiple Copies

You will need multiple copies of the texts—at least four to begin. Ideally, you will want six to eight copies so you can place one or two copies in a box for children to reread as independent work. Sometimes teachers acquire multiple copies of a text by exchanging and pooling copies with their colleagues. You can break down kits or sets of books and reorganize them according to the classroom reading levels.

Storage and Retrieval

What is the best way to store your books? Use shoe boxes or magazine boxes on a bookshelf. A low-cost alternative is cut-down cereal boxes covered with contact paper or colored paper. The collection for guided reading is not one that children will use on their own, so locate it in a place that is convenient for teacher book selection. Arrange the books alphabetically (by title) within each level. You will have several boxes of books for each level.

Label the boxes with the title and label each book with a level (on the inside or outside cover) so it is easy to return books to the boxes (see Figure 6-1). It's also convenient to write the number of running words on the label or on the inside cover.

You may want to keep multiple copies in resealable plastic storage bags. The gallon size is big enough to contain multiple copies of most books. Some teachers feel that bags make it easy to select and return books and also reduce wear and tear. It's not necessary to label the bags. As an alternative to bags, you can use rubber bands to keep multiple copies together.

Use of Time

We recommend allowing about ninety minutes per day for guided reading and independent work. During that time, you can work with three to four groups of children for an average of fifteen to twenty minutes each while the other children engage in independent reading, writing, and listening activities. You can spend part of the time taking running records on individual children's reading, encouraging and helping children with their independent reading and writing, and observing children as they work in centers.

The successful implementation of guided reading begins with efficiency and effective use of time. Try to keep story introductions brief, and carefully select the texts so that children can read at a reasonable pace during the lesson. Your organized storage and retrieval system for books will also save you precious time during the instructional day.

Number of Books

Teachers frequently ask, "How many books do I need?" The answer is related to the grade level you teach, the number of children in the class, and the time available for guided reading. If you have ninety minutes per day for guided reading, children in

FIGURE 6–1   Book Box with Label

kindergarten through the middle of second grade will be reading about one new book per day, and you can meet with each group at least four times per week. Accounting for holidays, testing days, and special events, and with long texts taking two days, you can expect children to read about 100 to 125 books during the school year in a first-grade classroom. For older children, who average about three to five days to read a longer book, you might plan on 50 to 75 books for the year.

Remember that reading a book means much more than just going through the motions of reading and checking the book off. As you introduce the book, children engage in a discussion about it. Then they read it and discuss it some more. You directly teach specific reading strategies before, during, and after the reading of every book. Sometimes you extend exploration of story meaning through talk, art, drama, or writing. The idea is not just to read the book but to understand it and to learn from it and through it.

Kindergarten

The number of books needed for guided reading in kindergarten depends on how many children are ready to work in a small group and to read a book for themselves. Based on ongoing assessment of their students' understandings about print, alphabet letters, writing, and so forth, kindergarten teachers typically begin to bring together small groups of readers about the middle of the school year. Some children may be ready for group reading earlier and some much later. By the end of the year, however, we would expect all the children in the kindergarten to be able to read levels A, B, or C with some teacher support. Children do not need to know all the letters of the alphabet or all the sounds, but before they are involved in guided reading they should have a good grounding in activities with high group support, such as shared reading and interactive writing, and they should have some understandings of how print works.

For kindergarten, we suggest a range of levels available from A to E, though a few children will be reading beyond these levels. You will not need to fully provision the leveled book collection to provide for unusually advanced readers because you can simply borrow books from other teachers or use the children's literature collection. Movement up levels will not be the only goal for advanced readers; discussion and opportunities for writing about reading will be even more important.

In the charts presented in Figures 6-2 through 6-5, we provide recommendations for a starter collection and a basic collection of guided reading books for kindergarten. A starter collection provides the minimal resources needed to support a guided reading program—purchase this collection to begin your program. Estimates for the number of books have been based on a class of twenty-five children; half-day kindergarten represents one class. If you have a limited amount of money to spend, just purchase a few of the titles each year, and build the collection over time. As illustrated in the figures, you might want to purchase more titles at the earlier levels and fewer titles at higher levels. We have provided information on collections with four copies or six copies of each title.

You will probably be working with groups of three to six children on any given level. Smaller groups of three or four are more effective with kindergartners who are just beginning to read for themselves because you need to observe behaviors very closely and prompt them to support their early reading strategies (for example, pointing to assist one-to-one matching). Guided reading sessions will be quite short in time; you may have two or more groups on the same level.

You will want to take into account typical reading patterns across your group of children. For example, if a large number of children typically enter your kindergarten with rich literacy experiences, you'll still need copies of books at level A, but children may move quickly to B, C, and even D levels.

Example of a Starter Book Collection for a Kindergarten Classroom with Four Copies of Each Title			
Levels	Number of Titles Each Level	Number of Books	Estimated Average Cost @ $4.00
A	10	40	160
B	15	60	240
C	15	60	240
D	5	20	80
E	5	20	80
TOTALS	50	200	$800

FIGURE 6–2   Example of a Starter Book Collection for a Kindergarten Classroom with Four Copies of Each Title

Example of a Starter Book Collection for a Kindergarten Classroom with Six Copies of Each Title			
Levels	Number of Titles Each Level	Number of Books	Estimated Average Cost @ $4.00
A	10	60	240
B	15	90	360
C	15	90	360
D	5	30	120
E	5	30	120
TOTALS	50	300	$1,200

FIGURE 6–3   Example of a Starter Book Collection for a Kindergarten Classroom with Six Copies of Each Title

Example of a Basic Book Collection for a Kindergarten Classroom with Four Copies of Each Title

Levels	Number of Titles Each Level	Number of Books	Estimated Average Cost @ $4.00
A	20	80	320
B	20	80	320
C	20	80	320
D	5	20	80
E	5	20	80
TOTALS	70	280	$1,120

FIGURE 6–4   Example of a Basic Book Collection for a Kindergarten Classroom with Four Copies of Each Title

Example of a Basic Book Collection for a Kindergarten Classroom with Six Copies of Each Title

Levels	Number of Titles Each Level	Number of Books	Estimated Average Cost @ $4.00
A	20	120	480
B	20	120	480
C	20	120	480
D	5	30	120
E	5	30	120
TOTALS	70	420	$1,680

FIGURE 6–5   Example of a Basic Book Collection for a Kindergarten Classroom with Six Copies of Each Title

If you have a large number of children who need many first experiences with simple books, you'll want a large number of titles at levels A and B, so that your students can firm up early behaviors such as word-by-word matching and moving left to right. These early books are also helpful in establishing a core reading vocabulary of high-frequency words, and they make it possible for inexperienced children to notice critical aspects of words, such as letter-sound relationships and spelling patterns. Thus, you'll need to fine-tune our example not only in terms of the numbers of children you have but also in terms of their needs. Books on levels A and B can also be used for shared reading, with children having their own copies, a frequently used teaching approach used as a transition to guided reading. Remember that as teaching becomes more effective, needs for books at higher levels will increase.

First Grade

At first grade, we estimate that you will need a span of at least eleven levels (A through K). You will have some children reading beyond level K, but for that small group you can borrow books and use trade books to enrich their experience. The bulk of reading for first grade, typically, is at levels C through J. A good standard is to have all first graders reading independently at level I by the end of the year. The charts presented in Figures 6-6 through 6-9 provide an estimate of the number and costs of guided reading books for a starter collection and a basic collection, with four or six copies of each title, for the first grade. Make adjustments for the average reading levels of children as they enter reading, at mid-year, and at the end of the year. Remember that as teaching becomes more effective across grade levels, reading levels will increase.

Example of a Starter Book Collection for a First-Grade Classroom with Four Copies of Each Title

Levels	Number of Titles Each Level	Number of Books	Estimated Average Cost @ $4.00 [A–J] and $5.00 [K]
A	5	20	80
B	5	20	80
C	6	24	96
D	6	24	96
E	6	24	96
F	6	24	96
G	6	24	96
H	6	24	96
I	6	24	96
J	5	20	80
K	5	20	100
TOTALS	62	248	$1,012

FIGURE 6–6   Example of a Starter Book Collection for a First-Grade Classroom with Four Copies of Each Title

Example of a Starter Book Collection for a First-Grade Classroom with Six Copies of Each Title

Levels	Number of Titles Each Level	Number of Books	Estimated Average Cost @ $4.00 [A–J] and $5.00 [K+]
A	5	30	120
B	5	30	120
C	6	36	144
D	6	36	144
E	6	36	144
F	6	36	144
G	6	36	144
H	6	36	144
I	6	36	144
J	5	30	120
K	5	30	150
TOTALS	62	372	$1,518

FIGURE 6–7   Example of a Starter Book Collection for a First-Grade Classroom with Six Copies of Each Title

Example of a Basic Book Collection for a First-Grade Classroom with Four Copies of Each Title

Levels	Number of Titles Each Level	Number of Books	Estimated Average Cost @ $4.00 [A–J] and $5.00 [K]
A	8	32	128
B	8	32	128
C	10	40	160
D	10	40	160
E	10	40	160
F	10	40	160
G	10	40	160
H	10	40	160
I	10	40	160
J	8	32	128
K	5	20	100
TOTALS	99	396	$1,604

FIGURE 6–8   Example of a Basic Book Collection for a First-Grade Classroom with Four Copies of Each Title

Levels	Number of Titles Each Level	Number of Books	Estimated Average Cost @ $4.00 [A–J] and $5.00 [K+]
A	8	48	192
B	8	48	192
C	10	60	240
D	10	60	240
E	10	60	240
F	10	60	240
G	10	60	240
H	10	60	240
I	10	60	240
J	8	48	192
K	5	30	150
TOTALS	99	594	$2,406

Example of a Basic Book Collection for a First-Grade Classroom with Six Copies of Each Title

FIGURE 6–9   Example of a Basic Book Collection for a First-Grade Classroom with Six Copies of Each Title

If children enter first grade with very little experience with print, you will need more books at level A; however, with daily instruction and strong teaching to establish early behaviors and concepts, they will move quickly to levels B and C. For children who are having difficulty reading levels A and B, the school will need to provide supplementary one-to-one tutoring, such as Reading Recovery, in addition to daily guided reading in the classroom. Typically, children make rapid progress in the tutorial program, so communication about the child's instructional reading level is essential between the Reading Recovery teacher and the classroom teacher.

Second Grade

The reading for most second graders will be from about levels H through M, with some children reading well beyond those levels. In the charts presented in Figures 6-10 through 6-13, we provide an example of a starter collection and a basic collection, with four or six copies of each title, for second grade.

Being able to read level L or M with fluency and understanding is a good standard for independent reading at the end of second grade. You may have some second graders who require intensive teaching at lower levels (perhaps D, E, and F). You will want to meet with those children in guided reading groups every day, and they will likely need some additional help.

As children read longer chapter books, they will spend more time in silent, independent reading. A guided reading lesson will involve introducing the book and asking children to read a unified part of it—not necessarily a chapter but simply a manageable amount of text that will form the basis for later discussion. Children can read together at the same location or at their own desks and come together again to talk about the parts that they have read. It will be necessary to allocate time for them to perform this individual reading. We estimate that

Example of a Starter Book Collection for a Second-Grade Classroom with Four Copies of Each Title

Levels	Number of Titles Each Level	Number of Books	Estimated Average Cost @ $4.00 [A–J] and $5.00 [K+]
E	5	20	80
F	5	20	80
G	5	20	80
H	5	20	80
I	8	32	128
J	8	32	128
K	8	32	160
L	8	32	160
M	5	20	100
N	5	20	100
O	5	20	100
TOTALS	67	268	$1,196

FIGURE 6–10   Example of a Starter Book Collection for a Second-Grade Classroom with Four Copies of Each Title

Example of a Starter Book Collection for a Second-Grade Classroom with Six Copies of Each Title

Levels	Number of Titles Each Level	Number of Books	Estimated Average Cost @ $4.00 [A–J] and $5.00 [K]
E	5	30	120
F	5	30	120
G	5	30	120
H	5	30	120
I	8	48	192
J	8	48	192
K	8	48	240
L	8	48	240
M	5	30	150
N	5	30	150
O	5	30	150
TOTALS	67	402	$1,794

FIGURE 6–11   Example of a Starter Book Collection for a Second-Grade Classroom with Six Copies of Each Title

Example of a Basic Book Collection for a Second-Grade Classroom with Four Copies of Each Title

Levels	Number of Titles Each Level	Number of Books	Estimated Average Cost @ $4.00 [A–J] and $5.00 [K+]
E	5	20	80
F	10	40	160
G	10	40	160
H	10	40	160
I	12	48	192
J	12	48	192
K	12	48	240
L	10	40	200
M	5	20	100
N	5	20	100
O	5	20	100
TOTALS	96	384	$1,684

FIGURE 6–12   Example of a Basic Book Collection for a Second-Grade Classroom with Four Copies of Each Title

Example of a Basic Book Collection for a Second-Grade Classroom with Six Copies of Each Title

Levels	Number of Titles Each Level	Number of Books	Estimated Average Cost @ $4.00 [A–J] and $5.00 [K+]
E	5	30	120
F	10	60	240
G	10	60	240
H	10	60	240
I	12	72	288
J	12	72	288
K	12	72	360
L	10	60	300
M	5	30	150
N	5	30	150
O	5	30	150
TOTALS	96	576	$2,526

FIGURE 6–13   Example of a Basic Book Collection for a Second-Grade Classroom with Six Copies of Each Title

fewer titles will be needed at levels N and O, but there may well be a group of children who are more advanced and will like to read books at that level. Make adjustments for the average reading levels of children as they enter reading, at mid-year, and at the end of the year. Remember that as teaching becomes more effective across grade levels, reading levels will increase.

Third Grade

Third graders should be reading chapter books and a variety of informational books. Remember that at this grade level it is very important for children to experience a wide variety of texts. Each level has many longer books; we are more concerned about providing a variety of genres. It is particularly important for children to learn how to read informational books.

Explicit teaching is needed to help students understand how informational texts of various kinds are organized. You will be teaching them how to learn from many different kinds of texts. In Figure 6-14 and Figure 6-15 we have provided examples of a starter collection for third grade, and in Figure 6-16 and Figure 6-17 we have provided examples of a basic collection for third grade. We have provided information on collections with six or eight copies of each title.

All books may be used for guided reading lessons, but you also will want to promote a great deal of independent reading on the part of individual students. You will want a variety of titles to choose from for guided reading lessons. It will be important not only to choose books that support the kinds of advanced strategies these readers need but also to pay closer attention to their growing tastes and interests. Guided reading is a setting in which you can broaden children's interests by introducing the kinds of texts they would not generally select on their own. The leveled collection can also

Example of a Starter Book Collection for a Third-Grade Classroom with Six Copies of Each Title			
Levels	Number of Titles Each Level	Number of Books	Estimated Average Cost @ $4.00 [A–J] and $5.00 [K+]
J	5	30	120
K	5	30	150
L	5	30	150
M	6	36	180
N	6	36	180
O	6	36	180
P	6	36	180
Q	5	30	150
R	5	30	150
S	5	30	150
TOTALS	54	324	$1,590

FIGURE 6–14   Example of a Starter Book Collection for a Third-Grade Classroom with Six Copies of Each Title

Example of a Starter Book Collection for a Third-Grade Classroom with Eight Copies of Each Title			
Levels	Number of Titles Each Level	Number of Books	Estimated Average Cost @ $4.00 [A–J] and $5.00 [K+]
J	5	40	160
K	5	40	200
L	5	40	200
M	6	48	240
N	6	48	240
O	6	48	240
P	6	48	240
Q	5	40	200
R	5	40	200
S	5	40	200
TOTALS	54	432	$2,120

FIGURE 6–15   Example of a Starter Book Collection for a Third-Grade Classroom with Eight Copies of Each Title

Example of a Basic Book Collection for a Third-Grade Classroom with Six Copies of Each Title			
Levels	Number of Titles Each Level	Number of Books	Estimated Average Cost @ $4.00 [A–J] and $5.00 [K+]
J	5	30	120
K	8	48	240
L	8	48	240
M	10	60	300
N	10	60	300
O	10	60	300
P	10	60	300
Q	10	60	300
R	5	30	150
S	5	30	150
TOTALS	81	486	$2,400

FIGURE 6–16   Example of a Basic Book Collection for a Third-Grade Classroom with Six Copies of Each Title

Example of a Basic Book Collection for a Third-Grade Classroom with Eight Copies of Each Title			
Levels	Number of Titles Each Level	Number of Books	Estimated Average Cost @ $4.00 [A–J] and $5.00 [K+]
J	5	40	160
K	8	64	320
L	8	64	320
M	10	80	400
N	10	80	400
O	10	80	400
P	10	80	400
Q	10	80	400
R	5	40	200
S	5	40	200
TOTALS	81	648	$3,200

FIGURE 6–17   Example of a Basic Book Collection for a Third-Grade Classroom with Eight Copies of Each Title

be a resource to guide children's selection of books for their independent reading.

Make adjustments for the average reading levels of children as they enter reading, at mid-year, and at the end of the year. Remember that as teaching becomes more effective across grade levels, reading levels will increase.

Sharing and Expanding Classroom Book Collections

At first glance it may seem impossible to bring together the kind of collection you need to support guided reading in your classroom, but the goal is reachable in time. Simply purchase some books each year, and build the collection over several years. It is not even desirable to acquire all of the books at once because you need to get to know the books over time and to make decisions based on the needs of the children. The approach

is highly cost effective because the collection is reusable for many years, only requiring some replacement books on occasion.

First, take an inventory of your existing books to see what you already have on the levels you need. Don't forget that the stories in your basal readers, if appropriate for guided reading, can be leveled and used. With the explosion of reading material in the last few years, you may already have a pretty good range of books; the problem will be multiple copies. If another teacher in your building is interested in guided reading, work out an informal sharing arrangement. With some preliminary investigation and organization, you can work together to get started.

The development of an effective book collection is an ongoing professional responsibility and undertaking, one that offers strong support for your teaching and your students' learning. For this reason, it's a goal well worth achieving.

Action Plan

Evaluate and organize your classroom collection so that you can get started:

1. Make an inventory of the books you currently have in your classroom.

2. Using the list, write the guided reading levels on the inside cover of books or write them on a sticker on the front or back. Indicate the number of words on the label or inside cover so that it will be accessible to you when taking running records. (If you do not have the word count, simply add the word count the first time you take a running record on that book with a child.)

3. Organize the books in labeled boxes or baskets.

4. Locate a good place in your classroom for your collection. This collection should be easily accessible to you but not to the children. (Books for independent reading may be drawn from this collection and placed in boxes or baskets, but they will eventually be returned to the guided reading collection.)

5. Make a list of levels you need to add to your collection as you acquire the resources.

Getting Started: Creating and Using a School Book Room

While the cost and time entailed in creating a leveled book collection may seem daunting, we can offer a strategic tip that will make all the difference: Work with your colleagues! The most efficient and cost-effective system for acquiring and using a collection involves a group of colleagues sharing books that are housed in a school book room or closet. In this chapter, we describe ways that you and your colleagues, working together, can create a valuable resource for the children in your school.

Planning a school book room will undoubtedly mean purchasing a large number of books; however, you will want to approach the task strategically and acquire the books over time. Acquiring a guided reading collection depends on the:

∎ Number of classrooms and number of children in the school.

∎ Number of teachers sharing the collection.

∎ Typical reading levels for the majority of children at each grade level at different points in time.

∎ Books you already have.

∎ Financial resources available from year to year.

You may not have all the answers immediately; accordingly, we do not advise buying the guided reading collection in its entirety the first year. Also, if you have a limited amount of money to spend, you can limit your purchases to one-fourth or one-third of the titles the first year, or start with a sample of lower levels and build the collection over time.

So how should you proceed? First, take an inventory of all of the books you already have and organize them in levels, noting the gaps. You will also want to adjust for the average reading levels of children as they enter reading, at mid-year, and at the end of the year.

Second, start collecting a minimal number of books the first year, using running records and reading graphs to record progress. Then, direct your purchases during the second and third years to filling the gaps. You will know at what levels you need more books. Of course, as you work with guided reading over time, the profile of reading achievement will change and you may need more books at the higher levels.

What about the cost of the books? For books at levels A through J, we estimate the average cost at $4.00, while the average cost of books at higher levels is $5.00. But remember—these prices reflect retail costs. We've discovered that most trade book suppliers will provide paperback books at a 20 percent discount, especially for large orders from schools. Other publishers will sometimes give discounts for larger orders or offer free shipping. Don't hesitate to ask for these discounts!

The School Book Room

Let's consider now where you might house the books. The school book room may fit into a closet, but you'll want to choose a large, well-lighted one. The teachers' workroom or any other large space is another possibility, as long as the room is large enough to place books in boxes on shelves so you can easily store and retrieve them. In some schools, a section of the school library is reserved for the school collection. The photograph in Figure 7-1 depicts the guided reading section of the school library in the American International School of Brussels, Belgium.

Children do not use this section, but teachers can browse there while the children are in their library period. Some advantages to housing a book collection in the school library are that teachers may take their children to the school library quite often, so books are more likely to be returned on a timely basis. Also, the librarian would be instrumental in acquiring books and organizing the book room.

Place all books for each guided reading level consecutively together by level so that when you and your colleagues look at the shelves you have an instant visual picture of your total collection for a level. This display makes selecting books easier and more efficient. Over a period of months and even years, you will have invested many hours in getting to know the books, so just a glance at the titles or a quick exploration of the book will call to mind the text characteristics.

Keeping your book room neat and well-organized is a must. You may want to try a variety of organizational systems before settling on one that works best for your school. For suggestions, refer to the section

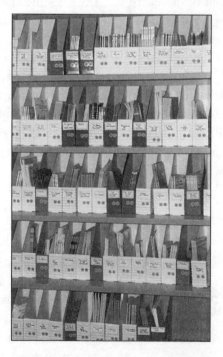

FIGURE 7–1   School Book Room: American International School

titled "Storage and Retrieval" in the previous chapter.

Using the Book Room

Once your book room is organized, you will want to create some way of recording when you take copies of a title from the book box. Some schools give each teacher a tub of clothespins with his or her name on each pin. After taking multiple copies of a book, the teacher simply attaches a clothespin to the box containing the books. That way, everyone knows who has books from that box. Other schools rely on a card system. Cards are pre-made, and the teacher simply places a card with her or his name on it in the box. Some schools have a notebook in which teachers write titles and their names and then cross them out upon return. Some school staffs have found that a complete honor system, with no documentation, works best for them. We have observed some schools that have included guided reading books in the school library resources and they are checked out like other books on loan. You and your colleagues will need to find the system that works best for you.

In addition to developing a system for using the book room, you'll want to consider ways to care for the book room. Everyone should agree on procedures for putting away the books and keeping the room neat and orderly. Post the guidelines for using the book room on the wall so that everyone can be reminded. Schedule a regular meeting or take part of your regular faculty meeting to look around the room and assess how well things are going. You can also use this time to discuss each level of your collection and determine which levels need additional titles or have worn and tattered titles. Add titles that need replacing to a replacement list.

Volunteers (especially parents) can be very helpful in caring for the book room. They can label books, replace books in boxes, and monitor the collection. Furthermore, your book room volunteers may be willing to help in fund-raising to increase the collection.

Coordinating Between the Classroom and the Book Room

In one school we visited, each teacher had a plastic basket with a handle to help collect and carry books to and from the book room. When they returned to their classrooms, the teachers kept the books for guided reading in the basket. They also had a particular spot in the classroom for storing the basket. Over several days, the teachers used the basket to gather the books that had been used in their classrooms and needed to be returned to the book collection. Then, they carried the basket to the book room and exchanged the books they had used for new books.

How long should teachers keep particular titles in their classroom? This is another decision you and your colleagues will need to make. We have found that a return cycle of about two to three weeks seems to work best.

After your students have read and enjoyed a particular title, you might want to keep one or two copies for your browsing box and return the others to the book room. One of the reasons we recommend having about eight copies of each book is to enable the classroom teacher to keep one or two in the browsing box for a few weeks. Eventually, all copies will be returned. In well-provisioned classrooms, one or two copies of the more frequently used titles might be available in a personal collection for the teacher. Then, teachers can use these copies to plan book selection and introductions as well as for independent reading.

Estimated Costs of the School Book Room Collection

We have prepared an estimate of numbers of books and costs to support a K–3 guided reading program. Estimates are based on two classes of twenty-five children at each grade level (K, 1, 2, 3), for a total of two hundred children. If you have one class at each grade level, divide by half. If you have three classes, increase by 50 percent; if you have four classes, double the estimated costs.

The charts in Figures 7-2 through 7-7 provide an estimate of numbers and costs for school book collections with eight or twelve copies of each title. We have provided three levels of book acquisition. Figures 7-2 and 7-3 describe a starter collection with minimal resources available. Purchase this collection to begin your program. If you have very small classes, it may be sufficient.

The cost for a school with eight primary classrooms is about $6,600 (eight copies of each title) to $9,900 (twelve copies of each title). A basic collection, described in Figures 7-4 and 7-5, includes more variety and will cost approximately $11,600 (eight copies of each title) to $17,400 (twelve copies of each title). A basic collection provides more variety within the collection, and books will also be available for independent and home reading. An expanded collection, detailed in Figures 7-6 and 7-7, provides an excellent variety and supply of books. Prices can range from $14,600 (eight copies of each title) to $21,900 (twelve copies of each title). These costs do not reflect possible discounts. Chances are, you already have quite a few books that can be integrated into the beginning collection, so your costs will be less. Also, you may be able to get some free books and others at a good discount. We recommend starting with something like the minimum or adequate collections, adjusting for numbers of students. After working with the collection for about a year, you will have a better idea of how to strategically increase the collection so that you have sufficient books at the levels you need.

Depending on your resources, try to purchase a fourth or half of the books each year for several years. You will see that the cost per child, as the collection expands and is used for many years, compares well

with the purchase of whole reading programs, which become outdated. For example, the Expanded Collection cost for 200 children (K–3) is about $100 per child for four years of instruction ($25.00 per year), or actually about $12.50 per child per year given the collection will be usable for many more years (e.g., eight years). When you conduct this kind of analysis, you can find out how cost effective book programs are for schools.

Advantages of a School Book Room

While creating a school collection requires more time and a great deal of cooperation, you will find it well worth the time and effort for the following reasons:

❙ The system is far more economical than individual classroom collections because all levels can be available all of the time, instead of many copies being stored in individual classrooms without availability to others.

❙ Replacing worn titles and adding new ones is a continual process.

❙ A larger variety of titles is available at each level.

❙ Working together to select and care for the book collection promotes collaboration and a shared vision for continuous achievement in the school.

❙ The book collection is an integral part of the ongoing assessment system.

❙ The book collection creates a feeling of sharing in the school, and people are more willing to work together to pool resources and acquire more funds for books.

❙ The book room is a gathering place for casual but important conversation about books and learning.

❙ All teachers become familiar with the full range of books being used in the primary grades.

Example of a Starter Book Collection for a School Book Room
(Grades K–3 with Eight Copies of Each Title)

Levels	Number of Titles Each Level	Number of Books	Estimated Average Cost @ $4.00 [A–J] and $5.00 [K+]
A	10	80	320
B	10	80	320
C	10	80	320
D	10	80	320
E	10	80	320
F	10	80	320
G	10	80	320
H	10	80	320
I	10	80	320
J	10	80	320
K	10	80	400
L	10	80	400
M	10	80	400
N	10	80	400
O	10	80	400
P	10	80	400
Q	10	80	400
R	10	80	400
S	5	40	200
TOTALS	185	1,480	$6,600

FIGURE 7–2   Example of a Starter Book Collection for a School Book Room (Grades K–3 with Eight Copies of Each Title)

	Example of a Starter Book Collection for a School Book Room (Grades K–3 with Twelve Copies of Each Title)		
Levels	Number of Titles Each Level	Number of Books	Estimated Average Cost @ $4.00 [A–J] and $5.00 [K+]
A	10	120	480
B	10	120	480
C	10	120	480
D	10	120	480
E	10	120	480
F	10	120	480
G	10	120	480
H	10	120	480
I	10	120	480
J	10	120	480
K	10	120	600
L	10	120	600
M	10	120	600
N	10	120	600
O	10	120	600
P	10	120	600
Q	10	120	600
R	10	120	600
S	5	60	300
TOTALS	185	2,220	$9,900

FIGURE 7–3   Example of a Starter Book Collection for a School Book Room (Grades K–3 with Twelve Copies of Each Title)

**Example of a Basic Book Collection for a School Book Room
(Grades K–3 with Eight Copies of Each Title)**

Levels	Number of Titles Each Level	Number of Books	Estimated Average Cost @ $4.00 [A–J] and $5.00 [K+]
A	20	160	640
B	20	160	640
C	20	160	640
D	20	160	640
E	20	160	640
F	20	160	640
G	20	160	640
H	20	160	640
I	20	160	640
J	20	160	640
K	15	120	600
L	15	120	600
M	15	120	600
N	15	120	600
O	15	120	600
P	15	120	600
Q	15	120	600
R	15	120	600
S	10	80	400
TOTALS	330	2,640	$11,600

FIGURE 7–4   Example of a Basic Book Collection for a School Book Room (Grades K–3 with Eight Copies of Each Title)

Example of a Basic Book Collection for a School Book Room
(Grades K–3 with Twelve Copies of Each Title)

Levels	Number of Titles Each Level	Number of Books	Estimated Average Cost @ $4.00 [A–J] and $5.00 [K+]
A	20	240	960
B	20	240	960
C	20	240	960
D	20	240	960
E	20	240	960
F	20	240	960
G	20	240	960
H	20	240	960
I	20	240	960
J	20	240	960
K	15	180	900
L	15	180	900
M	15	180	900
N	15	180	900
O	15	180	900
P	15	180	900
Q	15	180	900
R	15	180	900
S	10	120	600
TOTALS	330	3,960	$17,400

FIGURE 7–5   Example of a Basic Book Collection for a School Book Room (Grades K–3 with Twelve Copies of Each Title)

	Example of an Expanded Book Collection for a School Book Room (Grades K–3 with Eight Copies of Each Title)		
Levels	Number of Titles Each Level	Number of Books	Estimated Average Cost @ $4.00 [A–J] and $5.00 [K+]
A	25	200	800
B	25	200	800
C	25	200	800
D	25	200	800
E	25	200	800
F	25	200	800
G	25	200	800
H	25	200	800
I	25	200	800
J	25	200	800
K	20	160	800
L	20	160	800
M	20	160	800
N	20	160	800
O	20	160	800
P	20	160	800
Q	15	120	600
R	15	120	600
S	15	120	600
TOTALS	415	3,320	$14,600

FIGURE 7–6   Example of an Expanded Book Collection for a School Book Room (Grades K–3 with Eight Copies of Each Title)

	Example of an Expanded Book Collection for a School Book Room (Grades K–3 with Twelve Copies of Each Title)		
Levels	Number of Titles Each Level	Number of Books	Estimated Average Cost @ $4.00 [A–J] and $5.00 [K+]
A	25	300	1,200
B	25	300	1,200
C	25	300	1,200
D	25	300	1,200
E	25	300	1,200
F	25	300	1,200
G	25	300	1,200
H	25	300	1,200
I	25	300	1,200
J	25	300	1,200
K	20	240	1,200
L	20	240	1,200
M	20	240	1,200
N	20	240	1,200
O	20	240	1,200
P	20	240	1,200
Q	15	180	900
R	15	180	900
S	15	180	900
TOTALS	415	4,980	$21,900

FIGURE 7–7   Example of an Expanded Book Collection for a School Book Room (Grades K–3 with Twelve Copies of Each Title)

❙ Teachers at lower grade levels become more aware of what children will be expected to read in the later grades.

❙ Rather than regarding books as "belonging" only to one grade level, teachers have visible evidence of a continuum of reading achievement.

❙ The book collection is highly cost effective.

Teaching becomes easier and children learn more when both teachers and children have plentiful access to high-quality books. Enlist the assistance of administrators and community members in building this invaluable resource for children. With the system we have presented here, a child from kindergarten to third grade will read more than two hundred different books in guided reading, independent reading, and home reading. This type of resourcing makes good sense. Children become effective readers only if they spend lots of time reading at school and at home. Our cherished goal, always, is more reading, and a rich book collection in a school will make it possible.

Action Plan

As described in this chapter, work as a team to organize your book room. Use the book list at the back of this volume as a resource.

1. Make a work plan.
2. Decide whether you need parent or volunteer help.
3. Complete an inventory of books at each level.
4. Make a list of levels at which you need more books.

Acquiring Books: Book Clubs, Gifts, and Cost-Effective Planning

There are never enough books to supply classrooms where children love to read. You'll find that even after you conduct an inventory of your current supply and spend as much money as you can on the initial collection, you will want to acquire still more books. In this chapter, we briefly describe some approaches to bolstering your collection that have worked for many teachers.

Know the Books You Want Before Ordering

Our general policy is not to refuse any gift of books; those that are not appropriate for guided reading can probably be used for another purpose. However, if you have a chance to make selections, you want to be ready. Therefore, we recommend that you work with your colleagues and organize a group that is continually on the lookout for good books and the resources needed to acquire them. Besides monetary resources, you may also receive free books or other supplies that help augment your collection.

Is There a Recommended Starter Set?

Only the teachers in a given school can decide what specific books will be right for the book collection. In this volume we have listed a very wide range of books because we want to assist you in incorporating books you have already and to provide a wide foundation for choice. Decision-making about the collection is an ongoing process as the books are continually evaluated.

How Can I Decide Whether to Order a Book?

We recognize that it is sometimes difficult to make decisions about ordering books when you have not had a chance to examine them. Looking at the pictures in the catalogs is not sufficient. You will want to make the most of your money, so try not to order any books without looking at them first.

There are many ways to arrange review sessions to examine and discuss books before you commit yourself to a purchase. First, involve a wide representation of your staff in making the decisions. It is impossible for one person to choose for everyone. Ask your colleagues to make some time commitments to purchasing books.

Invite sales representatives to your school with individual samples of all the books available for purchase. Be sure to invite many different sales representatives (although not all at one time), as a collection based on what one publisher offers will not be sufficient to develop readers who are flexible and can engage with a wide variety of texts. Ask all interested staff members to attend the review sessions.

With a few colleagues, visit bookstores that display trade books and make a list of your preferred trade titles. Ask your colleagues to fill out a card on each book with an evaluation and/or a level. That way, you will learn how the provision of books from trade publishers fits with what you already have.

Another way to examine books is to send school staff members to local, state, or regional conferences of the International Reading Association, the National Council of Teachers of English, the National Association for the Education of Young Children, or the Reading Recovery Council of North America. Typically, you can count on an annual conference in your own state. Go to the exhibits, and instead of just walking through, spend time looking at books. Hold your work session right there. You can pick up a copy of the publisher's catalog and write your evaluations right in the margins. When you return home, you will have a record of the books you think are best.

Another idea is to spend some "venture capital" by working with book clubs, bookstores, and publishers to purchase a large number of single copies (or sets of four) of as many titles as possible. It is useful to have a "master collection" for reference, or these books can later be integrated into the collection. Look at the single copies to see which books merit purchasing eight to twelve copies. The payoff in terms of better decision-making may make this initial investment worthwhile.

Finally, visit a school that has a well-provisioned book room. Spend some time in the book room; note the titles that seem to be in frequent use. Interview the principal and teachers and ask which books and book sets they have found to be particularly good.

You can also ask them how they were able to obtain the books.

What About Sets That Are Organized by Level?

In general, we recommend purchasing single titles whenever possible. Many publishers sell certain books only in kits that contain multiple copies of selected titles. Some of the sets are good, but we offer this advice:

▌ Ask the sales representative if you can purchase by title. If the answer is no, encourage the representative to work with the publisher to make single titles available in the future.

▌ Look at all of the books in the set. How many are appropriate for guided reading? Don't buy the set unless you will use the great majority of books. Consider whether books that you will not use for guided reading will be useful in other ways.

▌ Calculate the cost per book within the set. Is it cost effective?

▌ In general, ignore the levels publishers have placed on the set. Simply level the books according to the system you are using. You may find a correlation between our levels and some publishers' levels. In any case, you will be tailoring the leveling process to the general experience of your students.

▌ Unless the commercial set containers fit your system, recycle them or use them in another way. Integrate the set into your entire book collection.

Work Together for Creative Solutions

Acquiring quality books and building up your collection is a continual challenge. You may want to begin by gathering your staff and interested parents or community members for a brainstorming session on acquiring books. At first, just invite the group to be creative. Generate as many ideas as possible even if they do not seem practical. Don't criticize any idea. Record them all on large sheets of chart paper. You never know when an impractical idea may spark a very practical one, and soon you will have a long list of constructive suggestions.

Select an idea from the list that you can do right away—one that also fits with your goals and priorities. Select additional ideas that will take longer to implement. Divide into work groups and make a plan for accomplishing the approaches you select. For each task on the work plan, identify a specific person who will be responsible for seeing it through to successful completion or who will head up a committee to get it done. Also, establish time lines both for short-term ideas and long-term projects. And once the big day arrives and you are ready to open your book room, arrange for a special lunch to celebrate the grand opening and thank all who made it possible.

Use Book Clubs

Children's book clubs, which have become very popular in recent years, are a very important source of free and reasonably priced books (see Figure 8–1). Using book clubs accomplishes two purposes:

❚ Children get to purchase books of their own at reasonable prices.
❚ Teachers get free books to use in classrooms!

Get on the mailing list for one or two book clubs that you like. Typically, a flier arrives and you simply send it home with the children. Parents and caregivers have the option of purchasing books. The teacher gets a free book for the classroom collection when children buy a certain number of books. Book clubs often feature volumes "on sale." It is not difficult to coordinate with your colleagues the selection of free books, thus obtaining multiple copies for the book collection.

Hold Book Fairs at the School

Local representatives and children's bookstores are often willing to provide a "book fair" for the school. They bring paperback books to the school, and children are invited to browse the books and purchase them, often at greatly discounted prices. Again, you can negotiate for low prices or free books for the book room.

Work with Parents to Hold Bake Sales and Auctions

Bake sales, auctions, and other fund-raising events can generate resources for a surprising number of books. For example, as indicated on our charts in the previous chapters, about $300 will supply one "level" of the collection. Working toward a goal like this makes the task of building a collection seem more achievable.

Make Gifts Possible

Many teachers have been very creative about making it possible for individuals to give gifts to the school. For example, in one school teachers have suggested to parents that on their child's birthday, they purchase a book for the school collection in honor of their child. The child's name is written on the book's title page as an acknowledgment of the gift. With paperbacks for guided reading, a gift can be a set of a title. You can even provide a master list of titles from which parents can choose.

Ask a Local Business to "Adopt" the School

The adopt-a-school program is quite popular in many cities. Sometimes, owners of a business or corporation are not sure what to do to help the school. Employees of the business get involved to greater and lesser degrees. Sometimes they will be willing to serve as volunteers; they can help organize the collection or listen to children read. Other employees may be more interested in sponsoring a child in reading by providing the cost of the books a child will read for one year.

Providing resources for a school book collection is a visible contribution that can

Children's Book Clubs	
Scholastic Book Club Call 1-800-SCHOLASTIC (1-800-724-6527) Scholastic.com	• Bonus points are accumulated; use bonus points to order free books from catalogs.
Club **Level**	
Firefly Preschool	• Paperback and hardcover • Beginning readers
See-Saw K–1	• Paperback picture books • Beginning readers • Math and science books
Lucky 2–3	• Fiction and nonfiction titles • Picture books • Early chapter books • Junior novels
Arrow 4–5–6	• Award-winning titles • Fiction, history, and nonfiction • Variety of themes
Club de Lectura Pre-K–5	• Spanish and bilingual books • Spanish cassettes • From picture books and beginning readers to chapter books • Translations and original literature in Spanish
Troll Book Club Call 1-800-541-1097 1-888-99-TROLL (1-888-998-7655) Fax: 1-888-71-TROLL (1-888-718-7655) Troll Book Clubs 2 Lethbridge Plaza Mahwah, NJ 07843 www.troll.com [call 800 number for password]	• Use bonus points to order any selection in catalogs • Paperback selections at different grade levels • Selections range from picture books to longer chapter books • Select grade level: Pre-K–K, K–1, 2–3, 4–6

FIGURE 8–1   Children's Book Clubs

be publicized. Provide exact cost figures to your adopting business so that managers and employees can realize exactly what they have contributed. Have children write thank-you notes, perhaps talking about a favorite book. It is very important to help your adopting companies understand the far-ranging positive impact of their gifts.

Find Ways to Save Money

We have advised looking for discounts, sales, and free shipping. The second- and third-grade collections will be easier to buy at bargain rates because most of the books can be purchased through trade book publishers. Also, if many schools in your district are interested in establishing book collections, it is possible to buy in large volume, making discounts even better. Teachers from several schools can meet together to decide on a basic starter set. Remember that if you do not ask for good prices and discounts, you will not receive them. Our motto: It never hurts to ask!

When you save money in some areas, you have more to spend in others. Careful use of resources can yield surprising results. You may be able to purchase more books than you thought possible. And, these books will be around for a long time.

Here are some ways that we have found to save resources:

❚ Carefully monitor the photocopying in your school. Often it is not necessary to do as much duplication as many schools typically do. Reducing duplication by half can yield hundreds of dollars. When children are spending time reading, they need fewer worksheets.

❚ Eliminate unnecessary consumable materials. Sometimes reading and language arts series have workbooks that you purchase every year. Can you accomplish the same instructional goals through word study, reading, and writing? If so, you will save a substantial sum on materials. (See Pinnell and Fountas [1998] for help in active study of phonics and spelling.)

❚ Look for free materials such as paper, pencils, markers, containers, and so forth to free up more resources to buy books.

Keep Your Eye on the Goal

In many of the actions we've described, you will reduce the expenditure of funds for consumable resources (some of which have no research-documented educational value), and pour those funds into books that chil-

dren will read and enjoy again and again for years to come. Reading high-quality books at appropriate levels of difficulty *does* have documented value in terms of reading achievement. Moreover, reading has high value in terms of raising the quality of life for the children you teach. When you make it possible for a child to read successfully every day, you open doors to the future.

Action Plan

First, figure out what you need.

1. Working from the inventory of books (at classroom or school levels), note the number of:
   ❚ Titles at each level.
   ❚ Copies you have of each title.

2. Compare your current inventory with recommendations for numbers of titles and copies of titles in Chapters 6 and 7. Think about the size of your school and the level that children are reading.

3. Then, set goals for:
   ❚ The number of additional titles you need at each level.
   ❚ The number of copies you need of each additional title.

   ❚ The number of additional copies you need of titles that you currently have.

4. Using the variety of suggestions in this chapter, create an action plan.

5. Decide which of the activities you are going to use and which staff members will be responsible for each.

6. Establish a time line for accomplishing your goals.

7. Decide what help you need in accomplishing your goals.

Acquiring More Books: A Practical Guide for Writing Grant Proposals

When you write a proposal for a grant, you are seeking funding from an organization to support your work. Two elements are essential:

▊ You need a good idea. In this case, bolstering your leveled book collection will provide high-quality reading materials for children with the goal of raising reading achievement.

▊ You need to relate your idea to a problem that it solves. Here, the problem is related to the reading achievement and/or quality of reading for the primary children in your school.

For companies and organizations that will consider funding your book collection, it is not enough simply to explain that you need books or that having books is a good idea. You need to clearly and explicitly state your problem and then discuss how increasing the number of books will help to solve the problem. Finally, you need to have a simple, clear statement of what you need, what you will do with the funds, and how you will be accountable.

Remember, a proposal is a persuasive document. Your goal is to attract the attention of your readers and persuade them that:

▊ A good supply of books is essential to supporting the reading achievement of children in your school.

▊ Your plan is logical and well-conceived.

▊ Your plan will work in an efficient and economical way.

▊ The plan is cost effective.

▊ The persons who will implement the plan (staff, parents, or others) are knowledgeable, competent, and committed to the project.

▊ You have acquired some support from additional organizations or community agencies (for example, libraries, stores, churches, community centers, clubs).

▊ The project will have great impact and far-reaching benefit for children.

▊ You are prepared to evaluate whether or not you are successful and report the results.

Sources of Funding

In this chapter we refer to funding agencies in a general way. A funding agency can be just about any organization or individual who is willing to back you with needed funds. Your local public library will have listings of foundations, and you can also find a great deal of information on the Internet. Funding a book collection will not usually be of interest to large nationally active foundations, so you may want to investigate more local philanthropic organizations that are interested in benefiting children in a particular state, city, or even neighborhood.

The Federal Register, a document published by the U.S. Office of Education that describes federal programs and how they are funded, will have listings of funds that are available to support schools in improving achievement. Again, try your local public library or any university library for copies of the Federal Register. Government agencies put out Requests for Proposals (RFPs) regularly. These RFPs will indicate who is eligible to apply for funds, the approximate range of the amount that will be provided, and the guidelines for writing the proposal. Some states have their own register and also put out RFPs. Acquisition of books may well be part of a more comprehensive school reform proposal for your school.

Another source of funding is the private foundation. There are many different kinds of foundations. Family or independent foundations are usually established for particular purposes. The activities they seek to fund fit within those priorities, so it is important to examine the foundation documents before making any contact with the foundation personnel. Usually, if your goals fit within the foundation's priorities, it is appropriate to write a letter or two-page concept paper describing your project. If there is interest, you will be invited to submit a more detailed proposal or to meet with a representative of the foundation.

Many large companies or corporations also establish foundations. Sometimes these foundations are interested in supporting the particular region where the company does business, does manufacturing (employing many people), or has headquarters. Look at the large companies in your area and find out whether they have a philanthropic arm. There are also community foundations, which are established by gifts from many individuals. They are usually run by a board that represents the community. The community foundation is an excellent organization to approach for a project like a book collection.

Sometimes individuals have established a reputation for supporting education in a community. If you know an individual interested in literacy who makes a practice of supporting special projects in schools, start with a courteous letter to ask if there is interest in your project. In general, some sources of funding are:

- Government sources
- Federal government
- State government
- Charitable organizations
- Service clubs
- Parent-teacher associations
- Junior leagues
- Lions Club
- Kiwanis
- Companies that "adopt" a local school
- Headquarters for large companies that may be in your area
- Businesses in your neighborhood
- Employee associations of companies
- Local bookstores and office supply stores
- Private foundations
- Family or independent foundations
- Corporate or company-sponsored foundations
- Community foundations
- Individuals

Length of the Proposal and Abstract

Writing a proposal does not need to be a lengthy or tedious process. Many proposals start with a letter or short summary of the proposed project. Most funding agencies prefer to respond to a concise statement. Many limit proposals to just a few pages, so it is important to state your exact position as succinctly as possible. If funding agencies are interested in providing resources for you, they will most likely invite you to a meeting or visit your school.

Length of Proposal

The longest proposals will be in response to federal or state RFPs. Usually those grants would cover a much wider range of activity than simply creating a book room, but you might find that your goals for the book collection fit into larger plans. If you have received an RFP from a funding agency, be careful to follow the precise guidelines in terms of length. Sometimes there are length guidelines for each section of the proposal; in some cases, the proposal will not even be considered if length guidelines are violated or any section is missing. Writing a long proposal takes a great deal of time and effort. You will want to assemble a work team, and the whole process may take several weeks or months.

Abstract

For any proposal that's more than a couple pages long, you should probably include an abstract. The abstract is a short summary statement that allows the reader to quickly determine the nature of the proposed project. The abstract is important because it must capture attention and communicate very precisely. Here is an example of an abstract:

We propose to increase the reading opportunities, and as a result the reading achievement, of children in Peters School by increasing the numbers of books available for reading instruction. In this proposal we describe a plan of action for establishing an efficient, high-quality book collection for the school. This book collection will be used as reading material for a program of explicit instruction that ensures that children read appropriate material daily. The goal is to provide high-quality instruction that will result in all children becoming effective readers by the end of grade three. This plan of action will

provide more than five thousand books to be used in instruction and will impact the reading achievement of four hundred children over the next eight years. The effectiveness of the project will be evaluated through documenting the number of books read and collecting scores on tests of reading for all children involved.

This abstract is 150 words and would provide a summary for a proposal of about three to eight pages. For longer proposals (nine or more pages), you might need a one- or two-page abstract. Succinctness is highly valued in the abstract. Also, have many people read it to ensure that it communicates necessary information and, overall, communicates a powerful message.

Writing Style for a Proposal

For effective proposal writing, rely on plain language. Avoid educational jargon. Think about communicating with someone outside the field of education. Here are some examples of "inside" words that many people do not use as a matter of course and that you should avoid in your proposal:

- Text-based
- Decoding and encoding
- Basal
- SSSR and "DEAR" time
- Workboard
- Browsing boxes
- Cognitive strategies
- Running records
- Reading process

If people do not know what you mean, they will not fund your project. Don't be afraid to use the words that they understand, such as "reading skills." If you use an "inside" word, such as "guided reading" or "running records," do so because you think it is absolutely vital to your proposal. If you must use an educational term, be sure to define it briefly in plain language so the reader can understand it.

Another mistake many proposal writers make is to use sweeping, general statements that are not supported by any specific information. The more you can provide backup for general statements, the more successful your proposal will be. In Figure 9-1, we provide examples of general and supported statements.

Making supported statements is especially important when you are talking about the problems and issues in your school. If you have evidence that you have investigated a problem, you will be more likely to convince the funding agency that your plan is a sound one.

Writing an Introductory Letter

In writing a proposal for a school book collection, you are actually seeking a relatively small grant—probably $2,000 to $5,000. It takes around $6,000 to establish a beginning collection. Remember that funding agencies can choose to provide a percentage of the funds you need rather than the whole amount. You will have inventoried the books you have. You are probably also planning to allocate some school book money to support your plan. Say so! Funding agencies

find proposals more credible if people in the school have used their own resources as part of the plan. It is generally held that when a project is totally funded by the outside party, it may not survive after the funding ends. Be careful to state that school staff, for example, have contributed time to the effort and that all current resources are being used. The funding agency will know that your plan is a top priority for everyone.

It is likely that you will begin with a letter requesting funds. Letters to several local businesses could be constructed based on the example provided in Figure 9-2. If you can, avoid sending out letters to unknown people at corporations or businesses. There are many networks of communication within a school community. Members of the school staff or parents of children in the school may know someone connected with the company who can find out who should receive the letter. If possible, make a personal contact before sending the letter.

Components of Proposals

Proposals have some general components that are almost always present. The components will vary from proposal to proposal. As

---

Examples of Supported Statements

General Statement	Supported Statement
The students in our school do not read well enough.	A recent school assessment indicated that 63 percent of our third graders do not meet nationally established standards for reading performance at the end of third grade.
Our students are falling behind in reading.	This year, we found that 78 percent of children entering second grade could read end-of-year levels established for first grade; our concern is to help all children meet the standard.
Children do not read enough.	An analysis of our current reading program indicated that first-grade children read an average of only twenty-eight books for the year. Since reading practice is so important, we propose to increase that number to 110 books during that important year.

FIGURE 9–1   Examples of Supported Statements

Components of a Letter Proposing a School Book Collection

Component	Example of Statement
Introduce the idea.	As a group of parents and staff, we write to request support to increase the reading achievement of students at Peters Elementary School.
Recognize the funding agency. (Indicate previous contributions of any kind.)	We recognize and greatly appreciate the contributions of your company to education in our community. Parents at our school are especially appreciative of the contribution you made to the sporting goods fund last year.
Provide background information. (Discuss relevant characteristics and data on your school.)	Peters serves a population of 565 children, 230 of whom are in grades K to 3. Our school is located in an urban area where high unemployment exists. More than 85 percent of the children in our school currently receive free lunch. Parent support for our educational program is high; last month a parent program was attended by more than 350 people.
State the problem or issue to be resolved. (Be specific in documenting the problem or problems.)	While a large percentage of the students in our school read very well, a growing number of children do not have the home and school reading they need to achieve nationally established standards. An assessment of primary children this year revealed that 29 percent of third graders and 31 percent of second graders are beginning the year unable to read the required texts. Moreover, a recent survey of parents indicated that only 27 percent voluntarily engage in reading at home.
Propose the solution. (Make a clear summary statement of what you propose to do. Support with research if appropriate.) Cite research in the text, in footnotes, or in endnotes.	To become good readers, children need massive opportunities to read. Research[1] shows that the more children read, the better readers they become, especially if the materials they read offer an appropriate level of challenge.
Describe a plan of action. (Describe in general terms your plan of action. If the recipient wants a more detailed plan, you can provide it later.)	We propose to establish a guided reading program that combines effective, explicit teaching with a large amount of reading. Implementing guided reading requires a school book collection, shared among teachers at grades K, 1, 2, and 3. This collection, used in an efficient, economical way, will ensure that every child has group reading instruction as well as independent reading every day. The collection represents a one-time purchase, with additional books and replacement books during subsequent years.
Establish your credibility. (Document any previous accomplishments, awards, or extra effort put forth by staff or parents. Persuade the funding agency that you can do the job.)	Members of the teaching staff are fully prepared to put the plan into action. The entire primary team (K–3 teachers) and the principals attended a one-week institute on teaching reading last summer and have been working to refine their skills all year, meeting in regular after-school sessions. Parents have formed a volunteer group and are prepared to help in organizing the book collection and to provide extra support in classrooms to listen to children read.

[1]See Adams 1990; Allington 1983; Durkin 1996; Pinnell, Pikulski, Wixson, Campbell, Gough, and Beatty 1995.

FIGURE 9–2   Components of a Letter Proposing a School Book Collection

Component	Example of Statement
Indicate "in-kind" contributions. (Show that the school community has already taken steps and is willing to make contributions.)	Through the PTA, parents have already contributed three hundred books to the collection. A local office supply store has agreed to donate thirty cardboard library book boxes. Staff and parents have agreed to donate their time for two Saturdays to work on the collection.
Talk about measuring the outcomes. (Persuade the funding agency that you intend to measure the outcomes, to gather data to document whether your plan works. If appropriate, promise a report.)	We expect the full implementation of the research-based instructional program in reading to have positive outcomes in reading achievement. We will measure children's achievement using a rigorous assessment system that is consistent with national standards. This systematic assessment will document the number of children who reach the standard at the end of kindergarten, and the beginning and end of grades, 1, 2, and 3. In grade 4, we administer the state proficiency tests. Scores of students who have participated in the reading program will be compiled and reported each year.
End with a summary statement about impact. (Let the funding agency know just how much impact a relatively small investment can have for children.)	This project, if funded, will affect the reading achievement of more than 200 children during the next year; however, this book collection will continue to serve children for many years to come. For example, if the collection is used for eight years, the cost per child is only about $17 per child. This investment will make it possible to ensure that in reading instruction a child reads almost two hundred books during the year and many more in home reading and independent reading. We hope that your company's priorities include this positive contribution to children's reading.

FIGURE 9–2   *continued*

previously indicated, you will want to follow specific guidelines if they are available. The chart in Figure 9-3 presents very basic components of a proposal.

Introduction and Rationale

In the introduction, capture the reader's attention and provide a clear statement about existing problems and issues. State the need for the book collection, and provide some specific information about the children in your school. State that more reading materials, accompanied by good instruction, can solve the problem. Present information to support your arguments.

Children to Be Served

You need to be clear about who will benefit from the funds, if awarded. State which grades, which school, and how many children the funds from this project will serve.

Purpose

Make a clear statement of purpose for the project, such as "to raise reading achievement in the school by providing high-quality instruction that involves having children read a large amount of appropriate reading material."

Goals and Objectives

State the major goals for the project. Goals are related to the overall purpose. They are more specific but still broad in nature. You will not want to have very many goals for this proposal; one or two will be enough.

Objectives are much more specific than goals. They are measurable, short-term statements of attainment. Neither goals nor objectives are the "methods" that you are proposing. In other words, your *objective* is not to get books. Acquiring more books is a way to

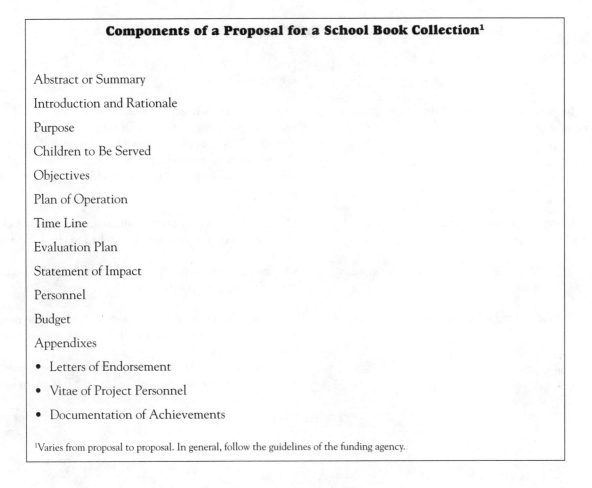

Components of a Proposal for a School Book Collection[1]

Abstract or Summary

Introduction and Rationale

Purpose

Children to Be Served

Objectives

Plan of Operation

Time Line

Evaluation Plan

Statement of Impact

Personnel

Budget

Appendixes

• Letters of Endorsement

• Vitae of Project Personnel

• Documentation of Achievements

[1]Varies from proposal to proposal. In general, follow the guidelines of the funding agency.

FIGURE 9–3   Components of a Proposal for a School Book Collection

get to the objective of increasing the amount of reading and raising reading achievement scores. Not every proposal will require lists of specific goals and objectives, but you should have them in mind. Think about what you would answer if someone asked you to state precisely what you plan to accomplish by establishing this book collection. The answer is your true objective. An example of goals and objectives is shown in Figure 9-4.

Plan of Operation
In this section of the proposal, you describe your methods—*what* you plan to do. Be as specific as possible and use plain language. You want the readers to be able to understand your plan of action, step by step, and to be confident that you really can do what you say. You cannot make every decision in advance because members of the staff must be in-

volved in things like book selection. But you can be specific about how you will involve the staff or how a smaller representative group will be established to do some of the work.

Time Line
A time line is not only helpful to the funding agency; it will be of great value to you and your colleagues as you conceptualize the work ahead. Creating a time line helps you think of the steps you need to address if you are to accomplish your plan. We encourage you to make your time line as detailed as possible and to assign tasks. The time line will provide a road map to accomplishing your goals (see Figure 9-5).

Evaluation Plan
Every time you ask for resources from a funding agency, make it clear that you will evaluate the results. Sometimes evaluation

Goals and Objectives of Establishing a School Book Collection

Goals	Objectives
Goal 1: To increase the amount of reading for primary children at your school.	*Objective 1:* To increase the number of books read during reading instruction at all grade levels. *Objective 2:* To increase the number of books children read during independent reading time. *Objective 3:* To increase the number of books children take home to read.
Goal 2: To improve reading instruction in grades K–3 at your school.	*Objective 1:* To improve the quality of instruction by ensuring that materials are appropriately matched to children's reading skills. *Objective 2:* To increase the number of high-quality texts that are used in reading instruction.
Goal 3: To raise reading achievement of children at your school.	*Objective 1:* To increase the number of children who meet established grade-level standards for reading at the end of grades K, 1, 2, and 3. *Objective 2:* To increase the reading scores of third-grade students on the Gates-McGinitie Reading Test, including Reading Comprehension and Total Reading.

FIGURE 9–4   Goals and Objectives of Establishing a School Book Collection

can be quite informal. In the case of a school book collection, you will want to conduct an evaluation to be sure that the system is working efficiently and that the selections you have made are appropriate. This kind of evaluation is called "formative," because it allows you to make changes and refine or "reform" your system.

You will also want to have some "summative" evaluation so that at the end of the project you can show if it worked or not. That is, there will be a time to "sum up" your achievements. Some informal ways to gather data to document the effects of a school book room are:

▌ Conduct a telephone interview with parents to ask whether and how much students are reading books at home.

▌ Document the number of books each child reads for reading instruction throughout the year.

▌ Document the number of books children read at home.

▌ Conduct interviews with students in grades 2 and 3 to see how they like the books they are reading.

▌ Systematically observe and analyze reading instruction to determine quality, pace, and appropriateness of reading materials.

▌ Ask teachers to complete an evaluation of the book collection after using it for a year.

▌ Interview teachers about the use of the book collection to support their instruction.

More formal evaluation involves a rigorous assessment system within which data are periodically collected on children's achievement. Benchmark books, described in Chapter 4, can be used to compile data on a whole cohort of children. Systemati-

Sample Time Line for Establishing a Book Room

Tasks	Date Started	Date Completed	Personnel Responsible
Analyze current collection.	April 1	April 15	Primary literacy team[1]
Make lists of books needed.	April 15	May 1	Primary literacy team
Contact publisher representatives.	April 15	May 1	Principal
Make final selections and order books.	May 1	May 15	Primary literacy team
Involve total staff to provide input.	May 1	May 10	Have staff look at samples of books and catalogues.
Plan staff training.	May 1	May 30	Primary literacy team with input from whole staff
Label books and organize book room.	June 15	August 15	All staff: 3 work days Volunteers
Create system for using collection.	August 15	August 20	School staff developer
Train staff: Assessment and book room.	August 26, 27, 28	August 26, 27, 28	Primary literacy team: all teachers involved
Train volunteers to assist in book room.	August 29	August 29	School staff developer
Implement instructional program.	September 5	June 5	All staff and volunteers
Assess children's reading.	September 5 January 15 May 15	September 15 February 1 June 1	All staff
Meet staff for evaluation.	Monthly	Monthly	All staff
Project evaluation meeting	June 5	June 5	All staff

[1]The primary literacy team consists of one teacher from each grade level (K, 1, 2, 3), the principal, the school staff developer, and the Reading Recovery teacher and/or special education teacher.

FIGURE 9–5 Sample Time Line for Establishing a Book Room

cally collected running records can be analyzed for case studies of a random sample of children. A standardized test can also be used; however, you will want to be sure that test scores are examined over several years, and that you have fully implemented, in a high-quality way, reading *instruction* using the book collection. Do not expect a book collection alone to increase reading achievement. Since you will not be working with control groups in an experimental way, treat all evaluation results with caution.

Impact
You may want to write a summary statement that describes the total impact funding this project would have. How many children will be affected? In what way?

Personnel
A complete proposal usually includes a description of the personnel who will imple-

ment the plan of action. The qualifications and "track record" of personnel are very important to the funding agency. You may choose to write short paragraphs about key staff members who will bear the major responsibility for the project. You may also want to include a more extensive vita for the project director, which can be included in the appendix. Here's an example of a short biographical sketch:

Sandra Adams currently serves as the literacy coordinator for the school. She teaches in a second-grade classroom for half of the school day and provides ongoing teacher training and coaching during the other half of the day. Ms. Adams has received B.A. and M.A. degrees from The Ohio State University, with a specialty in literacy education. Beyond that, she has received a full year of post-M.A. training in literacy and staff development. She has extensive experience in classroom teaching at grades K, 2, and 3. She has developed particular expertise in using running records and benchmark books to assess reading achievement. Ms. Adams will serve as the project coordinator.

Budget

For a proposal that seeks funds to build a leveled book collection, it will be essential to demonstrate that almost all of the project funds will be used to purchase the books that children will read. Large administrative or staff costs will undermine the potential success of the proposal. Use the guidelines in Chapter 7 to help you calculate costs. Other expenses might be related to the storage of books or to staff training. Include "in-kind" contributions made by the school, such as donated time, materials, or space.

Appendixes

You may want to acquire letters of support from the principal, the president of the parents' association, or a community member. Place these letters in the appendixes instead of within the body of the proposal. Consider also including the full vitae of staff members as well as documentation of special recognition your school may have won. You might also include the evaluation reports of previous projects, but don't go overboard on the appendixes. Evaluate each item carefully before you decide to include it.

Steps in Writing a Proposal for a Grant to Buy Books

Figure 9-6 includes a description of the steps in writing a proposal for a grant to acquire books. Writing a proposal is a project in itself. First, write out some clear statements about what you plan to do and why. This process will help you organize your thinking, and it will provide a basis for the introduction and rationale for your proposal.

Cast a wide net to identify funding sources. Some businesses and corporations may be very pleased to be asked to provide even a small amount of support for such a worthy project. If there are guidelines for your prospective funding agency, you will need to acquire them before going further. In addition, you will need to be sure that you have accurate information on your school. Conduct some research to find out:

■ What is the average income for your community?
■ How many children receive free or reduced-price lunch?
■ What are the educational needs of children in your school?
■ How many children are in the school at each grade level?

Approaching a funding agency without this kind of basic information is not a good idea.

A proposal will go through several drafts. A general rule of thumb is never to send a proposal to a funding agency without asking several knowledgeable outside parties to read it first. If you are sending the proposal to a large corporation, for example, ask a few acquaintances who are business executives to

Steps in Writing a Proposal for a Grant to Buy Books

1. Prepare some clear statements about:

   • What you need.

   • Why you need it.

   • What problem it addresses.

   • How it will solve the problem.

   • Specific details such as number of books.

   • Total costs and costs per child.

2. Identify local, state, and federal funding sources.

3. Select one funding source to begin.

4. Research and obtain guidelines if available.

5. Read the guidelines to determine the priorities of the funding agency.

6. Using the guidelines and your prepared statements, generate ideas, design the proposal, and outline the budget.

7. Develop a work plan for writing the proposal; share jobs.

8. Perform research needed to write the proposal.

9. Write the first draft of the proposal.

10. Complete the budget.

11. Assemble attachments, if appropriate.

12. Complete forms for the funding agency, if applicable.

13. Review and edit the draft, involving several outside people who can give feedback.

14. Prepare final copy, being sure that it is business-like, professional, and attractive.

15. Write a cover letter.

16. Submit proposal by deadline.

FIGURE 9–6   Steps in Writing a Proposal for a Grant to Buy Books

read the proposal critically. Have them underline messages that they don't understand or that sound "jargony." Then make revisions. Finally, it is most important for your proposal to have a highly professional appearance. A proposal with typographical errors, misspelled words, or fragmented sentences will not be funded and will reflect badly on your school. Ask someone who is an excellent copyeditor to read the proposal. In addition, be sure that the final polished proposal is neatly and professionally formatted.

Keep Trying, and Recognize Contributors

There are many organizations that want to contribute dollars to worthwhile endeavors. Nothing is more important than children's literacy. If you pool your efforts and persevere, you and your colleagues stand a strong chance of accomplishing your goals; after all, funding agencies will recognize the tangible value of a school book collection. Consider inviting your funding agencies to come and see children and teachers using it. You might even consider a plaque recognizing contributors; place it right in the book room or in the entry to the school. Another recognition plan is to stamp each book with an acknowledgment of the contributor. What individual or organization wouldn't be proud to be associated with children's daily reading and enjoyment of high-quality materials and with rising reading achievement?

Action Plan

1. Form teams to write proposals for support in acquiring new books. Follow the suggestions for letters, concept papers, and grant proposals provided in this chapter.

2. Review each other's proposals and make suggestions for improvement.

3. Celebrate together if any of your grants or applications is funded!

How to Use This Book List

I n this final chapter we provide a description of the book list and suggestions for using it. We also share our thinking about the text characteristics at each level.

Contents of the List

This book list includes more than seven thousand paperback books for children in grades K through 3, complete with word counts for most books and publisher information. A similar book list, appropriate for grades 3 through 6, will be available in the future.

In preparing this list, we included many books that you most likely have in your classrooms already; some, at this time, may be out of print but still available for use. We decided to provide an inclusive list rather than a highly selective one. We would not want to ignore books that you may already have. We believe that you are the decision makers, and you need a resource that is as comprehensive as possible. It is up to you and your colleagues to select a quality collection of books that will be right for you and the children you teach. In general, all of the books listed here can be used with skillful teaching.

Information on Levels

The sixteen levels, identified by letters of the alphabet A–P, are organized along a continuum of increasing difficulty as described in Chapter 1. A level is not an absolute designation; not all books on a level are precisely alike.[1] Not only is there variability within each level, but when individual children read the books, they bring their own strengths and knowledge to the process, leading to even more variability. We encourage you to adjust levels as you find differences for your particular population. We also encourage you to share your feedback with us on the response form provided in Appendix 1.

Remember, working with your colleagues to browse, review, and discuss books and their characteristics will enhance the effectiveness of your teaching. Use our list to initiate the process of labeling/leveling your own books, but be sure you understand the underlying features we considered in leveling books. In a general way, we addressed these features in Chapter 3. We also refer you to Fountas and Pinnell (1996), Chapters 9 and 10. In those chapters, we described the

---

[1] A level presupposes that teaching (guided reading, for example) will accompany the reading of the book. Books for reading independently (without teacher support) are best selected from a lower level.

levels, provided examples of page layouts for books on each level, and listed behaviors to notice and support for each level.

Here, we provide a level-by-level description of the books on this list. No description can fully capture every book included in a level, but these summaries should guide you in leveling new books as you acquire them.

Level A

The collection in level A provides the very easiest books for young children to read. We begin using level A books for guided reading after children have participated in unison reading of enlarged texts, heard many stories read aloud, tried writing for themselves, and become familiar with print. Before you begin guided reading, gather some evidence that children have some basic understandings about written language (for example, that you read the print rather than the pictures and that you begin on the left and move to the right). Be sure that they can point to words along a simple line of print—perhaps three or four words—in a familiar text.

Children do not need to have full control of basic concepts about print, nor do they need to know all of the names of the alphabet letters and related sounds before they begin to read the simple books on level A. They will learn a great deal more as they read these simple books.

Most level A books have only one line of print and just a few words in the line. This feature enables young children to focus on the print and read left to right, gradually increasing their knowledge of a few high-frequency words such as *I*, *the*, or *is*. In general, these books feature easy-to-see print with ample space between words. It is important that the letters are clear and that it is easy to notice the individual words. Be careful of books in which the print is bold or thick, with letters that are close together and little space between words. Be equally careful of books with thin letters set close together. Those styles of print make it hard for children to discern the word. The font size should be large, but not so large that it is hard to see the whole word at once. Below are examples of appropriate font sizes.

Here comes the bus.

Here comes the bus.

Here comes the bus.

The sentence structure in level A books is very close to children's own natural language and sentences are not too long. Children have to be able to understand and hold in their heads the meaning of the whole sentence while at the same time pointing at the words, moving left to right, and recognizing and checking words. Many of the books are about eight pages.

The language of the text in many books consists of a repeating pattern, using the same words over and over again or building several different ideas using the same sentence structure. Most of the words are very easy high-frequency words (*a*, *the*, *an*, *is*) and/or content words that are cued by the pictures. Print placement is highly consistent. For example, some books have print always on the left page with the picture on the right. Others have print appearing always at the bottom of the page.

There is a clear distinction between print and pictures, so that children can easily find the place to read. Simple punctuation is used, including periods, question marks, and exclamation points. Since there are few lists, commas do not appear often. The pictures provide a very high level of support, illustrating almost precisely the meaning of the text. Books focus on topics that are very familiar to most children. Often, these books are built around a single idea. The books provide an easy, supportive context within which children can practice their early reading behaviors.

Level B

Level B books are similar to level A in that they provide a context for practicing early reading behaviors, but the task is slightly more challenging. Like level A, books tend to focus on a single idea or present a simple story line. They feature clear, easy-to-read print (similar font to A) with noticeable spaces between words. For the most part, level B books contain two or more lines of print, so readers are required to sweep back to the left after reading a line.

Sentences are longer; however, natural language patterns are present to support the reader. Books may have repeating words or sentence patterns, although more variety is observed than in level A. Simple punctuation, including more commas, is used. Very simple dialogue may be included (for example, "I am here," said Mom.). There is a direct correspondence between text and pictures; and, like level A, topics are generally very familiar to most children. Sentences include more easy high-frequency words and some words with *ing*, *ed*, and *s* endings. The characters in books are family members, friends, or people who would be familiar to children. Animal characters behave very much like people. Stories are set in the "here and now;" setting is suggested but seldom important to the plot. Stories are straightforward, not requiring interpretation, and tend to be a string of events or actions rather than story episodes.

Benchmark: We would expect almost all kindergarten children to be able to read, with control of early behaviors, level B books by the end of the school year.

Level C

Books at level C present simple story lines or topics that are, in general, familiar for most children. Familiar topics are explored in a variety of ways that offer new viewpoints to the reader. Stories are longer with more action; there are still very few characters. Characters and story plots are straightforward and require little interpretation. Characters tend not to change or develop during the short story.

While most books are about children, families, and everyday life, there are also animal fantasies and books that we would call "experiential." These books are the precursor of information books because they deal with the events and artifacts of everyday life (for example, animals at the zoo), but they do not require the reader to learn some new piece or body of information.

Sentences are longer and may include some embedded clauses. Some sentences are conjoined using *and*. Dialogue is frequently included, and punctuation reflects more complex sentence structure, to include all ending marks, quotation marks, and commas. Some books have repeating language patterns; others do not. There is more variation among the texts. At level C, children are required to pay closer attention to print because the patterns they encounter are too complex for them to simply remember in two or even three readings. There are more words and more lines of print on each page so the text requires more time to read.

There will be some compound words (*into*, *something*, etc.) as well as many easy high-frequency words. Some words have endings such as *ing* and *s*. Print is still in a clear, readable font with noticeable spaces between words. Most books are still about eight pages, but the number of words on a page has greatly increased.

Illustrations provide a high level of meaning support to the reader but there are many more words to be solved. Children cannot depend on illustrations or sentence pattern to read the book with accuracy. There is opportunity to encounter, notice, and solve words with regular spelling patterns.

Level D

Books at level D include slightly longer and more complex stories than at previous levels. For example, there may be several elaborate episodes within a simple plot line. Topics are generally familiar to most children, but some books include abstract or unfamiliar ideas. Language structures may vary from natural sounding language to phrases with a literary quality. It is not uncommon for texts to contain compound sentences, usually conjoined by *and*.

Text layout is easy to follow. Since there is more printed text, there is a greater variety in the size of print, with some books using smaller fonts. It is still important to evaluate the clarity of the print and layout. Some texts include sentences that are carried over to the next page or over several pages. Interesting new punctuation may appear, such as dashes or ellipses (. . .). Illustrations are supportive but they are moving to a new role— that of enhancing and extending meaning rather than providing all or most of the information needed. In most books, however, the illustrations are still important.

Texts have a large number of easy, high-frequency words as well as words that have a variety of inflectional endings (*ed, ing, s, es*), and there are more compound words and multisyllable words. A greater variety of high-frequency words is included. There are more opportunities to solve words using regular spelling patterns. Many books are longer, ranging from about ten to twenty pages.

Level E

At level E, texts introduce more complex language and ideas. Topics range beyond the familiar and the types of text may include realistic stories, fantasy, and very simple informational books. It is best to be careful that informational books do not introduce too much technical vocabulary because it is difficult for children to use reading to learn new content while still developing a beginning reading process. For example, learning the technical names for parts of flowers or leaves may make a seemingly easy book quite difficult.

Sentences include more embedded phrases and clauses and there is more variety in language. Literary language is common. Books are generally longer, with either more pages or more lines of text on each page. The placement of print ranges widely from smaller fonts to print about the size of

level A. It is still important to be sure that the print is not too small, but readers can tolerate much more variety. Most books range from ten to twenty pages. Shorter books (about eight pages) with a great deal of print on the page may be more difficult for readers.

The text structure for most books is more complex, with stories that often have several simple but repeated episodes. Picture support is moderate. Books have more characters, and, although characters do not develop a great deal, readers may be called on to empathize with them or learn what they are like.

The number of words and lines of print generally increases, as does the variety of high-frequency words. There is frequent use of dialogue and a full range of punctuation. The vocabulary is more interesting; some books introduce less-regular spelling patterns and have more multisyllable words.

Level F

Books at level F require close attention to print and sustaining meaning over longer texts. Most books range from ten to thirty pages. The language reflects patterns that are more characteristic of written language than spoken language. A full range of punctuation is presented and used to enhance meaning. Concepts are more distant from local knowledge or the everyday world. Themes of books include realistic stories of everyday life, human and animal fantasy, simple folktales, and some very simple informational books. In general, children at this level are not yet ready to read biographies or histories because of the time concepts and background information required.

The variety of high-frequency words expands and there is greater variety in vocabulary. Texts are slightly longer by including longer sentences and/or more lines on a page. Some texts may be short but have unusual language patterns or technical words, thus making them more difficult than earlier levels. Some texts have abstract ideas that will require discussion.

Level G

Up to this point in the gradient, many texts have had repeating language patterns, at least in some parts of the text. Level G offers little support through repetition, although there will be some repeating episodes that support the reader in predicting what will happen next.

Texts, in general, have several episodes and a variety of characters. Characters require more understanding and their actions require interpretation. Sentences are longer, with many embedded clauses. There are many easy high-frequency words; a larger number of more difficult high-frequency words is introduced. There are opportunities to solve words with regular spelling patterns and there are the challenges of many words with irregular patterns. A greater quantity of multisyllable words is noticeable.

Books offer challenge in ideas and vocabulary; some include technical words or language that is specific to a place or process (such as fishing or cooking).

Books at level G exhibit a much greater variety of styles of print and text layout. Spacing and font are not critical issues since most children will have achieved control of early strategies; however, it is always helpful to have clear, readable text. Illustrations support and extend the meaning but the story line is completely carried by the text. Since texts are longer, readers are required to remember information and action over a longer reading time.

Level H

At level H, readers are required to apply skills to read longer and more varied texts. The content of texts moves away from highly familiar experiences, although children still enjoy reading longer texts that relate to their own lives. The size and placement of print varies widely and calls for flexibility on the part of readers.

Stories are long (from ten to thirty pages) unless they are short texts with difficult content. Font size varies, but because there are more lines of text, layout becomes important in helping the reader. For example, many texts feature new sentences starting on the left margin.

Many texts feature literary language and text structure; some have poetic language. Texts offer a greater range of vocabulary, including frequent use of multisyllable words and a large number of the full range of high-frequency words. The featured events and language structures of each text are not repetitious, although, as in level G, there may be repeating episodes or events. Picture support is moderate but is still important to enhance meaning and arouse interest. Pictures appear on most pages of the texts.

Most of the books at level H can be categorized as realistic fiction, fantasy, folktales, and informational books that present content that is either within children's experience or adds only a little new information. Characters in stories tend to learn and change; events require interpretation.

Level I

Most books at level I can still be categorized as narrative, although there are more informational books. In general, informational texts are shorter because the content is more difficult. The list of books includes realistic fiction, fantasy, and folktales.

For narratives, there is usually one main plot with a solution. The episodes or events in the text are more highly elaborated, and there are multiple events to understand and follow. Characters and story events require interpretation and offer an interesting focus for discussion.

Books are about the same as levels G and H, but the font size is generally smaller and there are more words on each page. Some books are a little longer, for example thirty to forty pages. Layout varies widely, and there are some texts that have unusual layout features such as maps and charts. Texts use a great deal of dialogue, which is clearly indicated by the identification of speakers and sometimes by spaces between speakers. Sometimes, for texts with many lines of print, new sentences begin on the left margin. Others are signaled by clear spaces after a period or other ending punctuation within a line.

Illustrations enhance meaning but provide little support for precise word solving and meaning. There are still illustrations on almost every page. Complex word solving is required; texts have more multisyllable words and these are embedded within longer sentences and paragraphs. At level I, readers are making the transition to texts that may call for sustaining interest and meaning over several reading periods. There may be a few "chapter-like" books.

Benchmark: At the end of the year, we would expect almost all first graders to be able to independently read, with understanding and fluency, books at level I.

Level J
Stories at level J have characteristics similar to level I but texts are generally longer. Some books are over fifty pages. At this level, children will experience reading their first chapter books. They will begin to meet characters in series books that will expand their interest in reading and the amount of time they spend reading.

Books contain a great deal of dialogue. Speakers are usually identified and there may be spaces between speakers. A full range of punctuation is present and there are many longer and more complex sentences. Many adjectives and adverbs are included, which makes sentences more complicated and requires more interpretation on the part of the reader.

Most books have one main plot with several episodes that take place at different points in time, although most books or chapters in books cover the period of only one day. Word solving requires automatic recognition of a large number of words and quick solving of new words, including words with three or four syllables.

Types of books include realistic fiction, fantasy, and informational texts. For guided reading, be cautious about using a large number of informational texts that are short but very difficult in content. At level J, children need the opportunity to process a large number of longer texts.

Level K
Level K includes longer, slightly more complex chapter books with more characters. Books are usually between fifteen and seventy-five pages long. Some shorter books are placed at this level because of difficult vocabulary, challenging content, or more complex themes. Types of books include realistic fiction, fantasy, and informational texts. Children may read some historical fiction that does not require extensive background to understand. Some fables or legends may also be included. Informational books may contain technical language and harder vocabulary words. Themes may require readers to understand concepts that are well outside their own experiences. Readers will also be required to deal with different writers' styles. Stories in level K have multiple episodes related to a single plot but may cover a longer time period.

The variety of vocabulary continues to expand, and at this level, children will be encountering words that they do not usually use in their spoken language. They will also be exploring the various connotations of words and analyzing language for humor or to discover the varied perspectives of characters.

Texts contain a great deal of dialogue. While speakers are usually identified by name or pronoun, it is not uncommon for several different characters to be talking on one page. The reader is required to follow the dialogue to determine what is going on in the plot.

Texts at level K have illustrations at many places in the text. These are often black and white and children will not need them in order to read the text with high accuracy; however, illustrations play an important role in enhancing enjoyment and helping children visualize characters, setting, and action.

Level L

Level L may include some longer picture books, which guided reading groups can use for discussion. Through common reading of these books, children can be introduced to a new genre or learn new ways of interpreting text. In general, these complex picture books should be used for particular purposes rather than become the norm in guided reading. This level also includes many chapter books. Texts include illustrations, as in level K, but readers are less dependent on them.

The types of text include a full range of genres, from realistic fiction to biography and fantasy. For historical fiction or biography, it may be necessary for students to read or talk about necessary background information. Readers are required to understand several different characters and to follow their actions and interactions. Some stories have abstract or symbolic themes.

Chapter books feature more sophisticated plots with characters that are developed throughout the text. Stories take place over longer periods of time. Events in the story build upon each other, requiring the reader to recall and keep track of information. More characters are speaking and dialogue is not always assigned. Books, in general, require a higher level of conceptual understanding.

Most chapter books are about seventy to eighty pages long, with chapters ranging from five to fifteen pages each. Many conventions of text are introduced, including ellipses, italics, use of all capitals, indentations, and bold letters. Some unusual formats (such as letters within texts) may be used. Sentences are complex and contain many multisyllable and technical words. Vocabulary support may be required because of content specific vocabulary or

words that are not familiar to students. Words are used for a range of connotative meanings. Print size is more varied and often much smaller.

Benchmark: At the end of the year, we would expect almost all second graders to read independently a variety of books at level L with understanding and fluency.

Level M

Level M books present a variety of formats, with many different conventions used to organize the text and convey meanings. Topics vary widely, from familiar subjects to a diverse offering of brand new subjects. Longer chapter books may feature everyday adventures while shorter books are more literary or contain new information. Literary selections have complex language and require interpretation. Themes are more complex; for example, issues such as respect for differences, loneliness, seeking independence, and the ethical treatment of animals may be introduced in a straightforward manner. More biographies are included and these usually have photographs.

Chapter books are longer texts with few pictures; they range from about sixty to one hundred pages in length, with short chapters (five to fifteen pages). Informational books are generally shorter (between fifteen and thirty pages). Many books display lots of text in small print with narrower word spacing. Vocabulary is greatly expanded. Texts have subtle meanings that require interpretation and more background knowledge, and many require an understanding of character development and more complex and expanded plots.

Vocabulary includes words that are specific to context. The connotative meaning of words depends on text interpretation in many cases. Vocabulary may be introduced to create feeling or mood instead of simply laying out the plot. The writer's style may be clearly marked by use of words, sentence structure, descriptions of characters, or humor. There may be text features such as indexes, glossaries, time lines, and historical information. Dialogue is not always assigned.

Level N

Level N includes chapter books that are about one hundred pages and sometimes more, with short chapters (five to fifteen pages). There are more complex and sophisticated themes; for example, immigration, death, slavery. Non-fiction titles are generally shorter and may present social issues.

Longer chapter books present memorable characters; writers use devices such as irony and whimsy to create interest and communicate the nature of characters. Some books offer opportunities to experience mystery and suspense. Some complex picture books may be used like short stories to illustrate themes and build experience in character interpretation or analyzing text structure. In general, picture books are more appropriate for literature discussions than for guided reading. There is more emphasis on reading a variety of informational books.

There is more demand on the reader to use a variety of strategies to understand the plot and theme and to learn the meaning of new vocabulary words. Most books still have one main plot and an episodic structure. Episodes take place over time.

Vocabulary continues to expand and topics go well beyond children's own experience. Vocabulary is more challenging, often requiring the reader to attend to word meanings in new ways. Many books require a cultural or historical context for interpretation. Children are beginning to use books to gain the vicarious experiences that will help them understand their world.

Level O

Level O includes longer chapter books that present a range of problems. Themes are sophisticated and require more interpretation and understanding. Books have multiple characters whose development is shown through what they say and what they do rather than simply through narrative. Chil-dren continue to expand their experiences through empathizing with characters and learning about the lives of others.

The types of books include realistic and historical fiction, biography, science fiction, humor, and traditional literature such as legends and fables. Readers will experience the same themes (for example, sibling relationships, death, etc.) being conveyed through a variety of genres. Previously read texts figure strongly into children's interpretation of what they are reading. Most chapter books have between fifty and two hundred pages with some black and white illustrations in the text.

The vocabulary is sophisticated and varied. Most words will be known or within children's control; however, interpretations of meaning will be required. Many new, multisyllable words are included. Highly complex sentences require a full range of punctuation, which is often important to understanding the meaning of the text. Readers are required to quickly analyze many new words, both simple and multisyllable, while maintaining a focus on meaning.

Benchmark: At the end of the year, we would expect almost all third graders to read independently a variety of books at level O with understanding and fluency.

Level P

Level P includes a variety of literary and informational texts, including history and biography. These books offer an opportunity for students to learn how the different texts are organized, as well as how to gain information from a variety of structures. Chapter books explore the problems of preadolescents and early adolescents, which will interest more advanced third-grade readers. In general, books have more text and more complex ideas and language with a more sophisticated vocabulary. Texts contain many longer descriptive narratives, typically one or two paragraphs long. Often, texts must be read on a literal and figurative level to truly understand them.

Many texts are long, requiring readers to sustain interest and meaning over many days. At this point, since most books are long (with a maximum of about two hundred pages), length is not as important in calculating the difficulty of the text. Instead, the complexity of the text structure, the sophistication of the theme, and the amount of background experience required to understand the text are factors to consider. Longer, more complex texts require readers to retain and recall information to support ongoing comprehension of the text. More sophisticated language, including figurative language and plays on words, is also involved in level P texts. Metaphor and simile, for example, are used but are often explained within the text.

Organization of the List

The list is sorted in two ways. In Figure 10–1 we illustrate the five-column page that we use in the list.

❚ The first column indicates the title of the book. The book is placed alphabetically using the first word of the title—unless it is *a*, *the*, or *an*, in which case the article follows the title. Titles beginning with a numeral are placed at the beginning of the list.

❚ The second column indicates the level of the book, from A to P.

❚ The third column provides the number of running words in the text, generally for books with no more than 250 words. If we could not provide the word count and you are using the book to take a running record, simply count the words the first time you use it and record the number on your book and on your book list (see Chapter 5 for guidelines on counting words). We would be pleased if you would share missing word counts with us so it can benefit readers in the future; to do so, please use the form in Appendix 1.

❚ The fourth column provides the name of the author or series.

❚ The fifth column indicates the publisher's or distributor's name. Addresses and phone numbers for each publisher are provided in Appendix 2 so that you may order a complete set of catalogs. Trade books are available from a variety of general paperback distributors. When a book is distributed by more than one company, information for both is given.

Using Sections of the List

The book list is organized into two sections. Each is designed to be used in a different way. Notice the two dark-edged tabs placed along the side of the book. These tabs make it possible to quickly turn to the section that you want to use.

❚ *Title*. Locate the book by title using the first word—unless it is an article such as *a*, *the*, or *an*. Titles that begin with numerals are located at the beginning of the list. Use this section to support your organization of the collection in your classroom or school. You can find the title, its level, and the number of running words (if they are less than 250 words). You can also find the author, series, publisher, and distributor information for each title. If you notice that a particular title is out of sequence, this is because the level has been updated as a result of teacher input and student use.

❚ *Level*. Titles are listed at each of the levels, A through P, and alphabetically within the level. If you are interested in finding all of the books at a particular level, you can simply turn to that level and browse through the list to generate books you might explore purchasing.

Make This List Your Own List

The best way to use this list is to make it your own. First, integrate your own books into the list by checking them here or

Organization of Book List				
Title	Level	Running Words	Author/Series	Publisher/Distributor
Abby	M	250+	Hanel, Wolfram	North/South Books
Abe Lincoln's Hat	M	250+	Brenner, Martha	Random House
Above and Below	F	128	Sunshine	Wright Group
Abracadabra	L	372	Reading Unlimited	Celebration Press
Abraham Lincoln	L	235	Pebble Books	Grolier, Capstone

FIGURE 10–1   Organization of Book List

adding new titles to the bottoms of pages or in the back. Get to know the books in your collection, and use this list to find others. Make notes or designate particularly good books for instruction as well as potential benchmark books.

Finally, as you use books, notice the ones that you and the children particularly enjoy. Reading is not about "work" or "practice." As adults, we certainly don't read simply for the purpose of getting better at reading. We read to relax, to enter other worlds, and to acquire useful or interesting information. Reading is about enjoying good books and using literacy as a powerful tool to enhance your life.

You'll want to hold a staff development session just to read good books for guided reading and discuss their qualities. The books that you find interesting and enjoyable will usually be the same books that children like. As you introduce and discuss these books with your students, your enthusiasm will captivate and inspire them to read the books, too.

As you observe children reading and talk with them about books, you will discover and internalize a great number of books that are of special appeal to the children in your school. You will find this "short list" of their favorites immensely valuable. When students enjoy reading, they become good readers and acquire a skill that will enhance their lives in immeasurable ways. And it all begins with good teaching and access to quality books.

Evaluation Response for Text Gradient

Directions: Since any text gradient is always in the process of construction as it is used with varying groups of children, we expect our list to change every year. We encourage you to try the levels with your students and to provide feedback based on your own experiences. Please suggest changes to existing book levels and suggest new books for the list. Please provide the information requested below.

Name: _____ Grade Level You Teach: _____

Telephone: (   )_____ E-mail Address: _____

Address (street, city, state): _____

Book evaluated:

Book Title: _____

Level: A   B   C   D   E   F   G   H   I   J   K   L   M   N   O   P   Q   R   S

Author: _____

Publisher: _____

This book is:

_____ A book listed on the gradient that I have evaluated by using it with my class.
(Complete SECTION A and make comments in SECTION C.)

_____ A book listed on the gradient that I am recommending as a benchmark for a level.
(Complete SECTION A and make comments in SECTION C.)

_____ A new book that I suggest adding to the collection.
(Complete SECTION B and make comments in SECTION C.)

SECTION A: (For an evaluation of a book currently included in the list)

Is it appropriately placed on the level (explain)? _____

To what level should the book be moved?

A   B   C   D   E   F   G   H   I   J   K   L   M   N   O   P   Q   R   S

Are there points of difficulty that make it harder than it seems? _____

_____

Is the text supportive in ways that might not be noticeable when examining the superficial characteristics? _____

_____

SECTION B: (For the recommendation of a new book)   Indicate recommended level: _____

How does this book support readers at this level? _____

_____

What challenges does it offer? _____

_____

SECTION C: Please place additional comments on the back or on another sheet.

Mail this form to:

Irene Fountas, Lesley College, 29 Everett Street, Cambridge, Massachusetts 02140.
Fax: (617) 349-8490   E-mail: ifountas@mail.lesley.edu

Gay Su Pinnell, The Ohio State University, 200 Ramseyer Hall, 29 W. Woodruff Avenue, Columbus, Ohio 43210.
Fax: (614) 292-4260   E-mail: pinnell.l@osu.edu

93

©1999 by Irene C. Fountas & Gay Su Pinnell from *Matching Books to Readers*. Portsmouth, NH: Heinemann

APPENDIX 1: Evaluation Response for Text Gradient

Publishers/Distributors

Some companies publish their own titles, while others distribute series books from a variety of sources. Ordering information on series books is available from the following sources:

Benchmark Education
629 Fifth Avenue
Pelham, NY 10803
Phone 1-877-236-2465
Fax 1-914-738-5063
Benchmark@aol.com
www.benchmarkeducation.com

Capstone Press
151 Good Counsel Drive
P.O. Box 669
Mankato, MN 56002-0669
Phone 1-800-747-4992
Fax 1-888-262-0705
www.capstonepress.com

Creative Teaching Press
P.O. Box 2723
Huntington Beach, CA 92647
Phone 1-800-444-4287
Fax 1-800-229-9929

Dominie Press, Inc.
1949 Kellogg Avenue
Carlsbad, CA 92008
Phone 1-800-232-4570
Fax 1-760-431-8777
www.dominie.com
info@dominie.com

Educational Insights
19560 S. Ranch Way
Dominguez Hills, CA 90220
Phone 1-800-933-3277
Fax 1-800-995-0506
www.educationalinsights.com

Greg Michaels Associates
4332 Old William Penn Highway
Monroeville, PA 15146
Phone 1-800-869-1467
Fax 1-412-374-9363

Grolier Press
90 Sherman Turnpike
Danbury, CT 06816
Phone 1-800-621-1115
Fax 1-203-797-3197
www.grolier.com

Hampton Brown
P.O. Box 369
Marina, CA 93933
Phone 1-800-333-3510
Fax 1-831-384-8940
hamptonbrown.com

Houghton Mifflin
181 Ballardvale Street
P.O. Box 7050
Wilmington, MA 01887-7050
Phone 1-800-334-3284
Fax 1-800-733-2098
houghtonmifflin.com

Kaeden Books
P.O. Box 16190
Rocky River, OH 44116
Phone 1-800-890-READ
Fax 1-440-356-5081
www.kaeden.com

Michaels Associates
409 Beatty Road, Suite 100
Moroeville, PA 15146
Phone: 1-800-869-1467
Fax: 1-412-374-9363

Modern Curriculum Press
4350 Equity Drive
P.O. Box 2649
Columbus, OH 43216
Phone 1-800-321-3106
Fax 1-800-393-3156
www.msschool.com

Mondo Publishing
980 Avenue of the Americas
New York, NY 10018
Phone 1-888-88-MONDO
Fax 1-888-532-4492
E-mail mondopub@aol.com
www.mondopub.com

Newbridge Educational Publishing
P.O. Box 1270
Littleton, MA 01460
Phone 1-800-867-0307
Fax 1-800-456-2419

Oxford University Press
2001 Evans Road
Cary, NC 27513
Phone 1-800-451-7556
Fax 1-919-677-1303
www.oup.co.uk.com

Pacific Learning
15342 Graham Street
Huntington Beach, CA 92649
Phone 1-800-279-0737
Fax 1-714-895-5087

Peguis Publishing Ltd.
100-318 McDermot Road
Winnipeg, Manitoba
Canada R3A OA2
Phone 1-800-667-9673
Fax 1-204-947-0080
books@peguis.com
www.peguis.com

Pioneer Valley Educational Press
P.O. Box 9375
North Amherst, MA 01059
Phone: 1-413-548-3906
Fax 1-413-548-4914
www.pvep.com

Richard C. Owen Publishers
P.O. Box 585
Katonah, NY 10536
Phone 1-800-336-5588
Fax 1-914-232-3977
www.rcowen.com

Rigby
P.O. Box 797
Crystal Lake, IL 60039-0797
Phone 1-800-822-8661
Fax 1-800-620-7501
www.rigby.com

Sadlier-Oxford
9 Pine Street, 2nd Floor
New York, NY 10005-1002
Phone: 1-800-221-5175
Fax: 1-212-312-6080
www.sadlier-oxford.com

Scholastic Inc.
P.O. Box 7502
Jefferson City, MD 65102-9968
Phone 1-800-724-6527
Fax 1-800-223-4011
www.scholastic.com

School Zone Publishing
1819 Industrial Drive
P.O. Box 777
Grand Haven, MI 49417
Phone 1-800-253-0564
Fax 1-616-846-6181
www.schoolzone.com

Seedling Publications
4522 Indianola Avenue
Columbus, OH 43214
Phone 1-614-267-7333
Fax 1-614-267-4205
www.seedlingpub.com
sales@seedlingpub.com

SRA/McGraw Hill
220 East Danieldale Road
DeSoto, TX 75115-2490
Phone 1-888-772-4543
Fax 1-972-228-1982
www.sra4kids.com

Steck Vaughn
P.O. Box 690789
Orlando, FL 32819-0789
Phone 1-800-531-5015
Fax 1-800-699-9459
www.steck.vaughn.com

Sundance
P.O. Box 1326
234 Taylor Street
Littleton, MA 01460
Phone 1-800-343-3204
Fax 1-800-456-2419
www.sundancepub.com

Tott Publications
513 Land Drive
Dayton, OH 45440
Phone 1-937-426-7638
Fax 1-937-426-7638
www.tottpublications.com

Troll Publications
100 Corporate Drive
Matwah, NJ 07430
Phone 1-800-526-5289
Fax 1-800-979-8765
www.troll.com

University of Maine
Center for Early Literacy
5766 Shibles Hall
Orono, ME 04469-5766
Phone 1-207-581-2418
Fax 1-207-581-2438
www.maine.edu

Wright Group/McGraw-Hill
19201 120th Avenue NE
Bothell, WA 98011-9512
Phone 1-800-523-2371
Fax 1-800-543-7323
www.wrightgroup.com

Trade Book Publishers

Books published by these companies can be ordered through paperback suppliers, many of which offer a flat paperback discount to schools.

Aladdin
Albert Whitman & Co.

Alfred A. Knopf
Atheneum

Avon Books

Avon Camelot

Bantam Doubleday Dell

Bantam Skylark

Barron's Educational

Beach Tree Books

Blue Sky Press

Bodley

Boyds Mills Press

Bradbury/Trumpet

Bullseye Books

Candlewick Press

Carolrhoda Books

Checkerboard

Children's Press

Clarion

Creative Edge

Crowell

Crown

Cypress

Delacorte

Dell Yearling

Dial

Donovan

Dutton

Farrar, Straus & Giroux

Four Winds

Golden

Greenwillow

Grosset & Dunlop

Gulf Publishing

Harcourt Brace

Harper & Row

HarperCollins

HarperTrophy

Hearst

Henry Holt & Co.

Holiday House

Houghton Mifflin

Hyperion

Ladybird Books

Little, Brown & Co.

Longman/Bow

Lothrop

Macmillan

North/South Books

Orchard

Pantheon

Penguin Group

Philomel

Pocket Books

Prentice-Hall

Puffin Books

Putnam

Random House

Scribner

Seal Books

Secret Passage Press

Simon & Schuster

Tom Doherty

Viking

Whitman

Wm. Morrow & Co.

Yearling

Guided reading book list
organized by title

Title	Level	Words	Author/Series	Publisher/Distributor
1 Is for One	E	82	Book Shop	Mondo Publishing
1, 2, Kangaroo	C	54	Reading Corners	Dominie
20 Pennies	E	212	Teacher's Choice Series	Dominie
89th Kitten, The	O	250+	Nilsson, Eleanor	Scholastic
Abby	M	250+	Hanel, Wolfram	North-South Books
Abe Lincoln's Hat	M	250+	Brenner, Martha	Random House
Above and Below	F	128	Sunshine	Wright Group
Abracadabra	L	372	Reading Unlimited	Pacific Learning
Abraham Lincoln	L	235	Pebble Books	Grolier, Capstone
Abraham Lincoln: President of a Divided Country	N	250+	Rookie Biographies	Children's Press
Absent Author, The	N	250+	Roy, Ron	Random House
Accident, The	H	313	Foundations	Wright Group
Accidents	D	35	Visions	Wright Group
Acid Rain	L	368	Wonder World	Wright Group
Across the Seasons	C	75	Early Connections	Benchmark Education
Across the Stream	F	94	Ginsburg, Mirra	Morrow
Adam Joshua Capers, The: Halloween Monster	N	250+	Smith, Janice Lee	HarperTrophy
Adam Joshua Capers, The: Monster in the Third	N	250+	Smith, Janice Lee	HarperTrophy
Adam Joshua Capers, The: Nelson in Love	N	250+	Smith, Janice Lee	HarperCollins
Adam Joshua Capers, The: Superkid!	N	250+	Smith, Janice Lee	HarperTrophy
Adam Joshua Capers, The: Turkey Trouble	N	250+	Smith, Janice Lee	HarperTrophy
Addie's Bad Day	J	566	Robins, Joan	HarperTrophy
Addition Annie	G	30	Rookie Readers	Children's Press
Adios, Anna	N	250+	Giff, Patricia Reilly	Bantam Doubleday Dell
Adventures of a Kite	L	33	Jellybeans	Rigby
Adventures of Ali Baba Bernstein, The	O	250+	Hurwitz, Johanna	Scholastic
Adventures of Max and Ned, The	N	250+	Little Celebrations	Pearson Learning
Adventures of Ratman	M	250+	Weiss & Freidman	Random House
Adventures of Snail at School	J		Stadler, John	HarperTrophy
Adventures of the Buried Treasure, The	L	250+	McArthur, Nancy	Scholastic
After School	D	58	Sunshine	Wright Group
After School	H	199	Foundations	Wright Group
After the Flood	G	210	PM Extensions-Green	Rigby
Afternoon on the Amazon	L	250+	Osborne, Mary Pope	Random House
Against the Odds	P	250+	Layden, Joe	Scholastic
Agua, Agua, Agua	H	94	Little Celebrations	Pearson Learning
Ah Liang's Gift	J	352	Sunshine	Wright Group
Ah-choo!	I	291	Little Books	Sadlier-Oxford
Airplane, The	B	21	Sunshine	Wright Group
Airplanes	F	60	Pebble Books	Grolier, Capstone
Airport	I	116	Barton, Byron	HarperCollins
Aladdin & the Magic Lamp	J	851	Traditional Tales	Dominie
Albert the Albatross	I	191	Hoff, Syd	HarperCollins
Aldo Ice Cream	O	250+	Hurwitz, Johanna	The Penguin Group
Aldo Peanut Butter	O	250+	Hurwitz, Johanna	The Penguin Group
Alexander and the Wind-Up Mouse	L	250+	Lionni, Leo	Scholastic
Alexander Ant Cools Off	F	76	Little Books	Sadlier-Oxford

Title	Level	Words	Author/Series	Publisher/Distributor
Alfie's Gift	L	250+	Literacy 2000	Rigby
Alien at the Zoo	E	85	Sunshine	Wright Group
Alien, The	H	177	Windmill Books	Rigby
Aliens Don't Wear Braces	M	250+	Dadey, Debbie & Jones, Marcia	Scholastic
Aliens for Breakfast	M	250+	Etra, Jonathan & Spinner, Stephanie	Random House
Aliens for Dinner	M	250+	Spinner, Stephanie	Random House
Aliens for Lunch	M	250+	Spinner, Stephanie & Etra, Jonathan	Random House
Aliens on the Lawn	H	175	Windmill Books	Rigby
Ali's Story	D	236	Sunshine	Wright Group
Alison Wendlebury	J	250+	Literacy 2000	Rigby
Alison's Puppy	K	250+	Bauer, Marion Dane	Hyperion
Alison's Wings	K	250+	Bauer, Marion Dane	Hyperion
All About Bats	J	250+	Ready Readers	Pearson Learning
All About Dinosaurs	C	34	Teacher's Choice Series	Dominie
All About Plants	L	250+	Home Connection Collection	Rigby
All About Sam	O	250+	Lowry, Lois	Houghton Mifflin
All About Stacy	L	250+	Giff, Patricia Reilly	Bantam Doubleday Dell
All About Things People Do	K	250+	Rice, Melanie & Chris	Scholastic
All About You	G	250+	Anholt, Catherine & Laurence	Scholastic
All By Myself	E	105	Foundations	Wright Group
All By Myself	E	157	Mayer, Mercer	Golden
All Dressed Up	B	38	Visions	Wright Group
All Dressed Up	H	137	Voyages	SRA/McGraw-Hill
All Fall Down	C	72	Wildsmith, Brian	Oxford University Press
All Join In	D	38	Literacy 2000	Rigby
All Kinds of Eyes	I	128	Pacific Literacy	Pacific Learning
All Kinds of Eyes	K	250+	Discovery World	Rigby
All Kinds of Food	D	72	Learn to Read	Creative Teaching Press
All Kinds of Things	B	24	Pacific Literacy	Pacific Learning
All Kinds of Wheels	E	76	Pair-It Books	Steck-Vaughn
All Mixed Up	G	105	Little Books	Sadlier-Oxford
All Night Long	E	65	Visions	Wright Group
All of Me	B	25	Literacy 2000	Rigby
All Over Me!	B	24	Pair-It Books	Steck-Vaughn
All Over the World	E	82	Jones, D.	Seedling
All-Pro Biographies: Dan Marino	P		Stewart, Mark	Children's Press
All-Pro Biographies: Gwen Torrence	P		Stewart, Mark	Children's Press
All Pull Together	D	69	Home Connection Collection	Rigby
All Star Fever	M	250+	Christopher, Matt	Little, Brown & Co.
All Through the Week with Cat and Dog	C	91	Learn to Read	Creative Teaching Press
All Through the Year	F	261	Visions	Wright Group
All Tutus Should Be Pink	I	243	Brownrigg, Sheri	Scholastic
All Wet	B	28	Ready Readers	Pearson Learning
Allen Jay and the Underground Railroad	O	250+	Brill, Marlene Targ	Carolrhoda Books
Allie's Basketball Dream	J	250+	Barber, Barbara & Ligasan, Darryl	Scholastic
Alligator Shoes	G	122	Dorros, Arthur	Dutton
Alligators All Around	I	59	Sendak, Maurice	HarperCollins
Along Came Greedy Cat	G	166	Pacific Literacy	Pacific Learning
Along Comes Jake	D	86	Sunshine	Wright Group
Alphabet Game, The	H	272	Story Basket	Wright Group
Alphabet Race, The	C	7	Visions	Wright Group
Alroy's Very Nearly Clean Bedroom	N	250+	Orr, Wendy	Sundance

Title	Level	Words	Author/Series	Publisher/Distributor
Am I Ready Now?	C	41	Visions	Wright Group
Amalia and the Grasshopper	K	392	Tello, Jerry & Krupinski, Loretta	Scholastic
Amanda Pig and Her Big Brother Oliver	L	250+	Van Leeuwen, Jean	Puffin Books
Amanda's Bear	G	154	Reading Corners	Dominie
Amazing But True Sports Stories	P	250+	Hollander, Phyllis & Zander	Scholastic
Amazing Eggs	J	250+	Discovery World	Rigby
Amazing Fish, The	G	167	Pair-It Books	Steck-Vaughn
Amazing Magnets	C	53	Twig	Wright Group
Amazing Maze, The	J	334	Foundations	Wright Group
Amazing Popple Seed, The	G	113	Read Alongs	Rigby
Amazing Race, The	A	28	Smart Starts	Rigby
Amazing Trains	L	482	Pair-It Books	Steck-Vaughn
Amber Brown Goes Fourth	N	250+	Danziger, Paula	Scholastic
Amber Brown Is Feeling Blue	N	250+	Danziger, Paula	Scholastic
Amber Brown Is Not a Crayon	N	250+	Danziger, Paula	Scholastic
Amber Brown Sees Red	N	250+	Danziger, Paula	Scholastic
Amber Brown Wants Extra Credit	N	250+	Danziger, Paula	Scholastic
Ambulance	I	116	Pebble Books	Grolier, Capstone
Amelia Bedelia	L	250+	Parish, Peggy	Harper & Row
Amelia Bedelia and the Baby	L	250+	Parish, Peggy	Harper & Row
Amelia Bedelia and the Surprise Shower	L	250+	Parish, Peggy	Harper & Row
Amelia Bedelia and the Surprise Shower	L	250+	Little Readers	Houghton Mifflin
Amelia Bedelia Goes Camping	L	250+	Parish, Peggy	Avon Camelot
Amelia Bedelia Helps Out	L	250+	Parish, Peggy	Avon Camelot
Amelia Bedelia's Family Album	L	250+	Parish, Peggy	Avon Books
Amelia Earhart	P	250+	Parlin, John	Bantam Doubleday Dell
Amy Loves the Snow	F	127	Hoban, Julia	Scholastic
Amy Loves the Sun	F	122	Hoban, Julia	Scholastic
Amy Loves the Wind	F	116	Hoban, Julia	Scholastic
Anansi's Narrow Waist	I	157	Little Readers	Houghton Mifflin
Anansi's Narrow Waist	I	157	Little Celebrations	Pearson Learning
And Billy Went Out to Play	I	227	Book Shop	Mondo Publishing
And Grandpa Sat on Friday	K	250+	Marshall & Tester	SRA/McGraw-Hill
And I Mean It Stanley	J	184	Bonsall, Crosby	HarperCollins
And the Teacher Got Mad	H	109	City Kids	Rigby
And the Teacher Smiled	H	86	City Kids	Rigby
And Then What Happened, Paul Revere?	O	250+	Fritz, Jean	Scholastic
Andi's Wool	H	107	Books for Young Learners	Richard C. Owen
Angel Park Hoopstars: Nothing but Net	O	250+	Hughes, Dean	Alfred A. Knopf, Inc.
Angel Park Hoopstars: Point Guard	O	250+	Hughes, Dean	Alfred A. Knopf, Inc.
Angel Park Soccer Stars: Backup Goalie	O	250+	Hughes, Dean	Random House
Angel Park Soccer Stars: Defense!	O	250+	Hughes, Dean	Alfred A. Knopf, Inc.
Angel Park Soccer Stars: Psyched!	O	250+	Hughes, Dean	Random House
Angel Park Soccer Stars: Total Soccer	O	250+	Hughes, Dean	Alfred A. Knopf, Inc.
Angel Park Soccer Stars: Victory Goal	O	250+	Hughes, Dean	Alfred A. Knopf, Inc.
Angels Don't Know Karate	M	250+	Dadey, Debbie & Jones, Marcia	Scholastic
Angry Bull and Other Cases, The	O	250+	Simon, Seymour	Avon Books
Angry Old Woman, The	E	126	Adventures in Reading	Dominie
Angus and the Cat	I	250+	Flack, Marjorie	Viking
Animal Actions	I	190	Home Connection Collection	Rigby
Animal Babies	E	114	Rookie Readers	Children's Press
Animal Babies	F	131	Twig	Wright Group

Title	Level	Words	Author/Series	Publisher/Distributor
Animal Builders	I	148	Little Celebrations	Pearson Learning
Animal Coverings	E	153	Early Connections	Benchmark Education
Animal Fibers	I	440	Science	Wright Group
Animal Habitats	B	73	Little Celebrations	Pearson Learning
Animal Habitats	C	73	Little Red Readers	Sundance
Animal Homes	B	48	Little Red Readers	Sundance
Animal Homes	B	48	Early Connections	Benchmark Education
Animal Homes	K	257	Pair-It Books	Steck-Vaughn
Animal Inventions	G	80	Sunshine	Wright Group
Animal Legs	B	37	Discovery World	Rigby
Animal Messengers	I	116	Discovery Links	Newbridge
Animal Reports	L	277	Little Red Readers	Sundance
Animal Shapes	D	14	Wildsmith, Brian	Oxford University Press
Animal Shelters	N	586	Book Shop	Mondo Publishing
Animal Sounds	C	21	Visions	Wright Group
Animal Stretches	C	35	Little Celebrations	Pearson Learning
Animal Tracks	D	152	Wonder World	Wright Group
Animal Tracks	L	250+	Dorros, Arthur	Scholastic
Animals	A	28	Smart Starts	Rigby
Animals	D	70	Foundations	Wright Group
Animals and Their Babies	D	166	Early Connections	Benchmark Education
Animals and Their Teeth	K	510	Sunshine	Wright Group
Animals and Their Young	N	484	Wonders	Hampton-Brown
Animals at Night	I	215	First Start	Troll
Animals at the Mall	D	39	Teacher's Choice Series	Dominie
Animals at the Zoo	F	158	First Start	Troll
Animals Build	H	129	Discovery Links	Newbridge
Animals Eat	C	27	We Do, Too Series	Dominie
Animals' Eyes and Ears	K	411	Early Connections	Benchmark Education
Animals from Long Ago	G	141	Discovery Links	Newbridge
Animals Grow	I	152	Wonder World	Wright Group
Animals Have Babies	C	42	We Do, Too Series	Dominie
Animals Have Homes	C	31	We Do, Too Series	Dominie
Animals Hide	D	55	Discovery Links	Newbridge
Animals Hide and Seek	C	56	Twig	Wright Group
Animals in Danger	M	250+	Pair-It Books	Steck-Vaughn
Animals in the Desert	D	31	Carousel Readers	Dominie
Animals in the Fall	E	34	Pebble Books	Grolier, Capstone
Animals Keep Warm	C	25	We Do, Too Series	Dominie
Animals Love the Fair	E	43	Literacy 2000	Rigby
Animals Make Noises	C	19	We Do, Too Series	Dominie
Animals of the Tundra	N	250+	Little Celebrations	Pearson Learning
Animals on the Move	K	145	Planet Earth	Rigby
Animals Play	C	27	We Do, Too Series	Dominie
Animals That Work	A	14	Foundations	Wright Group
Animals Went to Bed, The	B	32	Smart Starts	Rigby
Anna, Grandpa, and the Big Storm	N	250+	Stevens, Carla	The Penguin Group
Annabel	H	251	Story Basket	Wright Group
Anna's Sandwich	C	33	Windmill Books	Rigby
Anna's Tree	I	213	Windmill Books	Rigby
Annie Bananie Moves to Barry Avenue	L	250+	Komaiko, Leah	Bantam Doubleday Dell

Title	Level	Words	Author/Series	Publisher/Distributor
Annie's Pet	J	250+	Brenner, Barbara	Bantam Doubleday Dell
Annie's Secret Diary	M	250+	Little Celebrations	Pearson Learning
Another Day, Another Challenge	L	250+	Literacy 2000	Rigby
Another Point of View	P	250+	Wildcats	Wright Group
Ant and the Dove, The	I	173	New Way Blue	Steck-Vaughn
Ant and the Grasshopper, The	I	231	Aesop's Fables	Dominie
Ant and the Grasshopper, The	L	250+	Little Celebrations	Pearson Learning
Ant City	J	393	PM Story Books-Turquoise	Rigby
Ant, The	E	97	Ready Readers	Pearson Learning
Ants	B	16	Discovery Links	Newbridge
Ants	E	50	Pebble Books	Grolier, Capstone
Ants	G	94	Wonder World	Wright Group
Ants and Grasshoppers, The	G	144	New Way Blue	Steck-Vaughn
Ants Everywhere	C	24	Visions	Wright Group
Ants Love Picnics Too	B	27	Literacy 2000	Rigby
Ants on a Picnic	C	35	Joy Readers	Dominie
Ants, Ants, Ants	E	131	Sunshine	Wright Group
Apple Farm, The	E	95	Ready Readers	Pearson Learning
Apple Pie Family, The	E	72	Pair-It Books	Steck-Vaughn
Apple Tree	I	110	Book Bank	Wright Group
Apple Tree Apple Tree	G	340	Blocksma, Mary	Children's Press
Apple Tree, The	J	160	Sunshine	Wright Group
Apple Trees	D	62	Pebble Books	Grolier, Capstone
Apples	C	45	Williams, Deborah	Kaeden Books
Apples and More Apples	E	97	Pair-It Books	Steck-Vaughn
Apples and Pumpkins	I	185	Rockwell, Ann	Scholastic
Appointment with Action	P	250+	Wildcats	Wright Group
Aquarium, The	B	24	KinderReaders	Rigby
Aquarium, The	C	18	Kloes, Carol	Kaeden Books
Archaeologists Dig for Clues	N	250+	Duke, Kate	Scholastic
Are We Hurting the Earth?	K	363	Early Connections	Benchmark Education
Are We There Yet?	F	127	Teacher's Choice Series	Dominie
Are You a Ladybug?	F	116	Sunshine	Wright Group
Are You Afraid of...?	B	18	Little Celebrations	Pearson Learning
Are You My Mommy?	F	112	Dijs, Carla	Simon & Schuster
Are You My Mother?	I	250+	Eastman, Philip D.	Random House
Are You the New Principal?	E	120	Teacher's Choice Series	Dominie
Are You There, Bear?	F		Maris, Ron	Greenwillow
Arguments	K	398	Read Alongs	Rigby
Armies of Ants	O	250+	Retan, Walter	Scholastic
Around My School	E	60	Exploring History & Geography	Rigby
Around the Neighborhood	E	74	Pair-It Books	Steck-Vaughn
Art Around the World	J	239	Early Connections	Benchmark Education
Art Around the World	M	250+	Discovery World	Rigby
Art Lesson, The	M	246	DePaola, Tomie	Putnam
Arthur Accused!	M	250+	Brown, Marc	Little, Brown & Co.
Arthur and the Crunch Cereal Contest	M	250+	Brown, Marc	Little, Brown & Co.
Arthur and the Lost Diary	M	250+	Brown, Marc	Little, Brown & Co.
Arthur and the Popularity Test	M	250+	Brown, Marc	Little, Brown & Co.
Arthur and the Scare-Your-Pants-Off Club	M	250+	Brown, Marc	Little, Brown & Co.
Arthur Makes the Team	M	250+	Brown, Marc	Little, Brown & Co.

Title	Level	Words	Author/Series	Publisher/Distributor
Arthur Rocks with BINKY	M	250+	Brown, Marc	Little, Brown & Co.
Arthur's Back to School Day	K	250+	Hoban, Lillian	HarperTrophy
Arthur's Camp-Out	K	250+	Hoban, Lillian	HarperTrophy
Arthur's Christmas Cookies	K	250+	Hoban, Lillian	HarperTrophy
Arthur's Funny Money	K	250+	Hoban, Lillian	HarperTrophy
Arthur's Great Big Valentine	K	250+	Hoban, Lillian	HarperTrophy
Arthur's Honey Bear	K	250+	Hoban, Lillian	HarperCollins
Arthur's Loose Tooth	K	250+	Hoban, Lillian	HarperCollins
Arthur's Mystery Envelope	M	250+	Brown, Marc	Little, Brown & Co.
Arthur's Pen Pal	K	250+	Hoban, Lillian	HarperCollins
Arthur's Prize Reader	K	250+	Hoban, Lillian	HarperTrophy
Artist, The	F	83	Books for Young Learners	Richard C. Owen
As Fast as a Fox	D	69	Ready Readers	Pearson Learning
Ashes for Gold	L	250+	Folk Tales	Mondo Publishing
Ashley's World Record	L		Little Celebrations	Pearson Learning
Ask Mr. Bear	J	613	Flack, Marjorie	Macmillan
Ask Nicely	F	110	Literacy 2000	Rigby
Asleep	C	26	Joy Readers	Dominie
Asteroid, The	M	752	PM Story Books-Gold	Rigby
Astronaut	B	22	Hoenecke, Karen	Kaeden Books
Astronaut, The	B	30	Sunshine	Wright Group
Astronauts	I	171	Wonder World	Wright Group
Astronauts, The	F	112	Foundations	Wright Group
At Christmas	C	26	Visions	Wright Group
At Grandma's House	D	66	Teacher's Choice Series	Dominie
At My School	B	43	Little Books for Early Readers	University of Maine
At Night	D	21	Literacy 2000	Rigby
At School	A	12	Rise & Shine	Hampton-Brown
At School	A	28	Little Books for Early Readers	University of Maine
At School	B	23	Sunshine	Wright Group
At the Barbershop	E	179	Visions	Wright Group
At the Beach	B	30	Discovery Links	Newbridge
At the Beach	E	85	Oxford Reading Tree	Oxford University Press
At the Car Wash	E	143	Visions	Wright Group
At the Edge of the Sea	M	693	Sunshine	Wright Group
At the Fair	A	14	Little Books for Early Readers	University of Maine
At the Fair	C	58	Rise & Shine	Hampton-Brown
At the Fair	D	116	Little Red Readers	Sundance
At the Fair	D	175	Sunshine	Wright Group
At the Farm	C	52	Little Red Readers	Sundance
At the Horse Show	D	24	Books for Young Learners	Richard C. Owen
At the Lake	C	23	KinderReaders	Rigby
At the Library	C	69	PM Starters	Rigby
At the Library	F	31	Little Celebrations	Pearson Learning
At the Museum	B	28	Ready Readers	Pearson Learning
At the Ocean	A	29	Little Books for Early Readers	University of Maine
At the Park	D	37	Hoenecke, Karen	Kaeden Books
At the Park	D	74	Teacher's Choice Series	Dominie
At the Park	D	91	Little Red Readers	Sundance
At the Park	E	29	Oxford Reading Tree	Oxford University Press
At the Pet Store	I	177	Foundations	Wright Group
At the Playground	B	54	Little Books for Early Readers	University of Maine

Title	Level	Words	Author/Series	Publisher/Distributor
At the Playground	C	25	Visions	Wright Group
At the Playground	C	86	Little Red Readers	Sundance
At the Playground	G	151	Discovery Links	Newbridge
At the Pool	C	64	Foundations	Wright Group
At the Pool	F	87	Oxford Reading Tree	Oxford University Press
At the Science Center	H	158	Discovery Links	Newbridge
At the Seaside	E	85	Oxford Reading Tree	Oxford University Press
At the Store	B	21	Read-More Books	Dominie
At the Store	C	14	Visions	Wright Group
At the Supermarket	C	60	Little Readers	Houghton Mifflin
At the Supermarket	D	29	Read-More Books	Dominie
At the Toyshop	D	41	Home Connection Collection	Rigby
At the Track	E	122	Ready Readers	Pearson Learning
At the Truckstop	C	25	Kloes, Carol	Kaeden Books
At the Water Hole	K	236	Foundations	Wright Group
At the Wildlife Park	B	34	Little Red Readers	Sundance
At the Zoo	A	29	Kloes, Carol	Kaeden Books
At the Zoo	B	40	PM Starters	Rigby
At the Zoo	B	54	Little Readers	Houghton Mifflin
At the Zoo	C	73	Little Red Readers	Sundance
At the Zoo	D	37	Little Celebrations	Pearson Learning
At the Zoo	D	116	Predictable Storybooks	SRA/McGraw-Hill
Attaboy Sam	P	250+	Lowry, Lois	Bantam Doubleday Dell
Aunt Eater Loves a Mystery	K	250+	Cushman, Doug	HarperTrophy
Aunt Eater's Mystery Christmas	K	250+	Cushman, Doug	HarperTrophy
Aunt Eater's Mystery Vacation	K	250+	Cushman, Doug	HarperTrophy
Aunt Flossie's Hats (and Crab Cakes Later)	M	250+	Howard, Elizabeth	Scholastic
Aunt Jessie	G	114	Literacy 2000	Rigby
Aunt Louisa Is Coming for Lunch	G	118	Windmill Books	Rigby
Auntie Maria and the Cat	D	215	Sunshine	Wright Group
Aunts	D	49	Pebble Books	Grolier, Capstone
Autumn	J	225	Pebble Books	Grolier, Capstone
Autumn Leaves	A	17	Pebble Books	Grolier, Capstone
Away Went the Hat	I	260	New Way Green	Steck-Vaughn
Awful Mess, The	H		Rockwell, Anne	Four Winds
Awful Waffles	G	296	Williams, D. H.	Seedling
Awww	C	35	Little Celebrations	Pearson Learning
Baba Yaga	K	250+	Literacy 2000	Rigby
Baba Yaga: A Russian Folktale	N	250+	Phinney, Margaret Y.	Mondo
Baby	A	28	Little Books for Early Readers	University of Maine
Baby Animal Zoo	O	250+	Martin, Ann M.	Scholastic
Baby Animals	B	44	Reading Corners	Dominie
Baby Animals	D	41	Discovery Links	Newbridge
Baby Animals	D	78	Foundations	Wright Group
Baby Animals at Home	C	64	Twig	Wright Group
Baby at Our House, The	H	93	Foundations	Wright Group
Baby Bear Goes Fishing	E	112	PM Story Books	Rigby
Baby Bear's Present	F	206	PM Story Books	Rigby
Baby Birds	D	51	Pebble Books	Grolier, Capstone
Baby Chimp	A	14	Twig	Wright Group
Baby Elephant Gets Lost	D	90	Foundations	Wright Group

Title	Level	Words	Author/Series	Publisher/Distributor
Baby Elephant's New Bike	G	187	Foundations	Wright Group
Baby Elephant's Sneeze	F	78	Foundations	Wright Group
Baby Gets Dressed	A	16	Sunshine	Wright Group
Baby Hippo	D	117	PM Extensions-Yellow	Rigby
Baby in the Cart	C	84	Foundations	Wright Group
Baby Island	P	250+	Brink, Carol R.	Simon & Schuster
Baby Lamb's First Drink	C	64	PM Story Books	Rigby
Baby Monkey, The	I	250+	Reading Unlimited	Pacific Learning
Baby Owls, The	C	90	PM Extensions-Red	Rigby
Baby Says	C	26	Steptoe, John	Morrow
Baby Sister for Frances, A	K	250+	Hoban, Lillian	Scholastic
Baby Writer	I	182	Stepping Stones	Nelson/Michaels Assoc.
Baby, The	E	60	Burningham, John	Crowell
Baby's Birthday	D	53	Literacy 2000	Rigby
Baby's Dinner	E	26	Literacy 2000	Rigby
Babysitter, The	H	243	PM Extensions-Green	Rigby
Baby-Sitter, The	E	69	Oxford Reading Tree	Oxford University Press
Baby-Sitter's Club Mystery, #2 Beware Dawn!	O	250+	Martin, Ann M.	Scholastic
Baby-Sitter's Club, #110 Abby the Bad Sport	O	250+	Martin, Ann M.	Scholastic
Baby-Sitter's Club, #116 Abby and the Best Kid	O	250+	Martin, Ann M.	Scholastic
Baby-Sitter's Club, #128 Claudia and the Little Liar	O	250+	Martin, Ann M.	Scholastic
Baby-Sitter's Club, #14 Hello, Mallory	O	250+	Martin, Ann M.	Scholastic
Baby-Sitter's Club, #19 Claudia and the Bad Joke	O	250+	Martin, Ann M.	Scholastic
Baby-Sitter's Club, #27 Jessi and the Superbrat	O	250+	Martin, Ann M.	Scholastic
Baby-Sitter's Club, #31 Dawn's Wicked Stepsister	O	250+	Martin, Ann M.	Scholastic
Baby-Sitter's Club, #67 Dawn's Big Move	O	250+	Martin, Ann M.	Scholastic
Baby-Sitter's Club, #68 Jessi and the Bad Baby-Sitter	O	250+	Martin, Ann M.	Scholastic
Baby-Sitter's Club, #98 Dawn and Too Many Sitters	O	250+	Martin, Ann M.	Scholastic
Baby-Sitter's Little Sister, #107 Karen's Copycat	O	250+	Martin, Ann M.	Scholastic
Baby-Sitter's Little Sister, #69 Karen's Big Sister	O	250+	Martin, Ann M.	Scholastic
Baby-Sitter's Little Sister, #73 Karen's Dinosaur	O	250+	Martin, Ann M.	Scholastic
Baby-Sitter's Little Sister, #79 Karen's Big Fight	O	250+	Martin, Ann M.	Scholastic
Baby-Sitter's Little Sister, #81 Karen's Accident	O	250+	Martin, Ann M.	Scholastic
Back to the Dentist	M	199	City Kids	Rigby
Backyard Zoo	G	167	Ready Readers	Pearson Learning
Bad Day for Benjamin, A	L	250+	Reading Unlimited	Pacific Learning
Bad Day, The	D	93	Teacher's Choice Series	Dominie
Bad Dream, The	E	88	Teacher's Choice Series	Dominie
Bad Hair Day	E	113	Teacher's Choice Series	Dominie
Bad Spell for the Worst Witch, A	P	250+	Murphy, Jill	Puffin Books
Bad-Luck Penny, The	L	250+	O'Connor, Jane	Grosset & Dunlap
Bags, Cans, Pots, and Pans	C	56	Ready Readers	Pearson Learning
Baked Potatoes	D	73	Book Bank	Wright Group
Baking Day	C	35	Windmill Books	Rigby
Balancing	C	46	Twig	Wright Group
Balcony Garden	G	258	Storyteller Nonfiction	Wright Group/ McGraw-Hill
Bald Bandit, The	N	250+	Roy, Ron	Random House

Title	Level	Words	Author/Series	Publisher/Distributor
Ball Bounced, The	D	33	Tafuri, Nancy	Morrow
Ball Game	B	16	Literacy 2000	Rigby
Ball Game, A	D	72	Carousel Readers	Dominie
Ball Games	B	44	PM Starters	Rigby
Ball, The	C	40	KinderReaders	Rigby
Ballad of Robin Hood, The	M	250+	Literacy 2000	Rigby
Ballerina Girl	D	77	My First Reader	Grolier Press
Balloon, The	D	64	Carousel Readers	Dominie
Balloons	B	55	Early Emergent	Pioneer Valley
Balloons!	D	56	Storyteller-First Snow	Wright Group/ McGraw-Hill
Balloons, The	A	19	Sunshine	Wright Group
Ballyhoo!	F	124	Story Basket	Wright Group
Banana Monster, The	D	54	Joy Readers	Dominie
Banana Shake	C	44	Book Bank	Wright Group
Band, The	C	31	Voyages	SRA/McGraw-Hill
Bandages	F	139	Moskowitz, Ellen	Kaeden Books
Bang	F	55	Literacy 2000	Rigby
Barbecue, The	A	14	Sunshine	Wright Group
Bare Feet	B	40	Visions	Wright Group
Bargain for Frances, A	K	250+	Hoban, Russell	HarperTrophy
Barn Dance	C	47	Story Box	Wright Group
Barnaby's New House, The	G	135	Literacy 2000	Rigby
Barney's Horse	I	250+	Hoff, Syd	HarperTrophy
Barney's Lovely Lunch	K	330	Windmill Books	Rigby
Barnyard Baseball	C	19	Pair-It Books	Steck-Vaughn
Barrel of Gold, A	K	251	Story Box	Wright Group
Barry and Bennie	H		Little Celebrations	Pearson Learning
Baseball	B	14	Sunshine	Wright Group
Baseball Ballerina	K	250+	Cristaldi, Kathryn	Random House
Baseball Fever	O	250+	Hurwitz, Johanna	William Morrow & Co.
Baseball Flyhawk	M	250+	Christopher, Matt	Little, Brown & Co.
Baseball Fun	E	51	Geddes, Diana	Kaeden Books
Baseball Game, The	I	211	Foundations	Wright Group
Baseball Heroes, The	M	250+	Schultz, Irene	Wright Group
Baseball Megastars	O	250+	Weber, Bruce	Scholastic
Baseball Pals	M	250+	Christopher, Matt	Little, Brown & Co.
Baseball Pitching Challenge and Other Cases, The	O	250+	Simon, Seymour	Avon Books
Baseball Saved Us	O	250+	Mochizuki, Ken	Scholastic
Baseball's Best, Five True Stories	O	250+	Gutelle, Andrew	Random House
Baseball's Greatest Pitchers	P	250+	Kromer, S. A.	Random House
Basket Counts, The	M	250+	Christopher, Matt	Little, Brown & Co.
Basket Full of Surprises, A	B	43	Little Books	Sadlier-Oxford
Basketball	B	20	Wonder World	Wright Group
Basketball	C	23	Visions	Wright Group
Basketball	I	159	Ready Readers	Pearson Learning
Bat Bones and Spider Stew	K	250+	Poploff, Michelle	Bantam Doubleday Dell
Bath Day for Brutus	K	347	Little Red Readers	Sundance
Bath for a Beagle	D	102	First Start	Troll
Bath for Patches, A	E	89	Carousel Readers	Dominie
Bath Time	C	23	Wonder World	Wright Group

Title	Level	Words	Author/Series	Publisher/Distributor
Bath, The	A	14	Ready Readers	Pearson Learning
Bath, The	B	28	Smart Starts	Rigby
Bats	K	250+	PM Animal Facts-Gold	Rigby
Bats	M	250+	Literacy 2000	Rigby
Bats at Bat	D	36	Pair-It Books	Steck-Vaughn
Bats, Bats, Bats	E	33	Pair-It Books	Steck-Vaughn
Bats, The	C	21	Twig	Wright Group
Batter Up	G	183	Adventures in Reading	Dominie
Bay Run, The	C	80	Foundations	Wright Group
Be a Clown	C	29	The Candid Collection	Dominie
Be Careful, Matthew!	F	80	Sunshine	Wright Group
Be Quiet	A	25	Literacy 2000	Rigby
Be Quiet	B	25	Smart Starts	Rigby
Be Ready at Eight	K	250+	Parish, Peggy	Simon & Schuster/Aladdin
Beach Creatures	H	231	Pair-It Books	Steck-Vaughn
Beach, The	A		Little Celebrations	Pearson Learning
Beach, The	D	38	Book Bank	Wright Group
Beaks	G	125	Discovery Links	Newbridge
Bean Bag That Mom Made, The	I	270	Tadpoles	Rigby
Beans	B	35	Pebble Books	Grolier, Capstone
Beans on the Roof	L	250+	Byars, Betsy	Bantam Doubleday Dell
Bear at the Beach	K	250+	Carmichael, Clay	North-South Books
Bear Escape, The	D	42	Pair-It Books	Steck-Vaughn
Bear Facts	E	41	Pair-It Books	Steck-Vaughn
Bear for Miguel, A	K	250+	Alphin, Elaine Marie	HarperTrophy
Bear Goes to Town	K	250+	Browne, Anthony	Doubleday
Bear Lived in a Cave, A	D	102	Little Red Readers	Sundance
Bear Shadow	J	489	Asch, Frank	Simon & Schuster
Bear, The	B	17	Carousel Earlybirds	Dominie
Bears	C	59	Storyteller Nonfiction	Wright Group/McGraw-Hill
Bears	D	56	Joy Readers	Dominie
Bears' Picnic	M	250+	Berenstain, Stan & Jan	Random House
Bear's Bargain	J	250+	Asch, Frank	Scholastic
Bear's Bicycle, The	I	185	McLeod, Emilie	Little, Brown & Co.
Bears' Christmas	M	250+	Berenstain, Stan & Jan	Random House
Bear's Diet	L	652	PM Story Books-Gold	Rigby
Bears in the Night	D	108	Berenstain, Stan & Jan	Random House
Bears on Hemlock Mountain, The	M	250+	Dalgliesh, Alice	Aladdin
Bears on Wheels	D	89	Berenstain, Stan & Jan	Random House
Bears' Picnic, The	D	61	Story Box	Wright Group
Bears, Bears Everywhere	D	52	Rookie Readers	Children's Press
Bears, Bears, Bears	D	76	Step-By-Step Series	Dominie
Bears, Bears, Bears	I	250+	Little Readers	Houghton Mifflin
Beast and the Halloween Horror	M	250+	Giff, Patricia Reilly	Bantam Doubleday Dell
Beast in Ms. Rooney's Room, The	M	250+	Giff, Patricia Reilly	Bantam Doubleday Dell
Beat This	D	79	Ready Readers	Pearson Learning
Beauregard the Cat	M	876	Book Shop	Mondo Publishing
Beautiful Flowers	B	28	Wonder World	Wright Group
Beautiful Pig	J	423	Read Alongs	Rigby

Title	Level	Words	Author/Series	Publisher/Distributor
Beauty and the Beast	J	250+	PM Traditional Tales-Orange	Rigby
Beauty and the Beast	K	250+	Sunshine	Wright Group
Beaver Tale, A	E	228	Twig	Wright Group
Beavers	J	1193	Book Shop	Mondo Publishing
Beavers Beware!	K	250+	Brenner, Barbara	Bantam Doubleday Dell
Because a Little Bug Went Ka-Choo	I	250+	Stone, Rosetta	Random House
Because Daddy Did My Hair	I	214	Teacher's Choice Series	Dominie
Because I'm Little	B	51	Home Connection Collection	Rigby
Beds	C	44	Interaction	Rigby
Bedtime at Aunt Carmen's	K	250	Ready Readers	Pearson Learning
Bedtime for Frances	K	250+	Hoban, Russell	Scholastic
Bedtime Story, A	K	335	Book Shop	Mondo Publishing
Bee My Valentine!	H	250+	Cohen, Miriam	Bantam Doubleday Dell
Bee, The	C	26	Story Box	Wright Group
Beekeeper, The	M	250+	Literacy 2000	Rigby
Beep, Beep	F	51	Gregorich, Barbara	School Zone
Beetles	D	39	Pebble Books	Grolier, Capstone
Beezus and Ramona	O	250+	Cleary, Beverly	Avon Books
Before I Go to School	B	71	Storyteller-First Snow	Wright Group/ McGraw-Hill
Behind the Couch	N	250+	Gerstein, Mordicai	Hyperion
Behind the Rocks	E	50	Wonder World	Wright Group
Behind the Scenes with Sammy	N	250+	Little Celebrations	Pearson Learning
Ben and the Bear	I	250+	Riddell, Chris	Harper & Row
Ben Ate It	E	130	Teacher's Choice Series	Dominie
Ben the Bold	C	71	Literacy 2000	Rigby
Benjamin Franklin: A Man with Many Jobs	N	250+	Rookie Biographies	Children's Press
Benji's Pup	I	439	Evangeline Nicholas Collection	Wright Group
Benny Bakes a Cake	I		Rice, Eve	Greenwillow
Benny's Baby Brother	E	89	Start to Read	School Zone
Benny's School Trip	G	217	Pair-It Books	Steck-Vaughn
Ben's Banana	C	60	Foundations	Wright Group
Ben's Dad	E	102	PM Story Books	Rigby
Ben's Fun Box	D	63	New Way Red	Steck-Vaughn
Ben's New Trick	F	219	Ready Readers	Pearson Learning
Ben's Pets	C	30	Ready Readers	Pearson Learning
Ben's Red Car	B	49	PM Starters	Rigby
Ben's Teddy Bear	D	68	PM Story Books	Rigby
Ben's Tooth	H	197	PM Story Books	Rigby
Ben's Treasure Hunt	D	72	PM Story Books	Rigby
Berenstain Bear Scouts Ghost Versus Ghost, The	P	250+	Berenstain, Stan & Jan	Scholastic
Berenstain Bears & the Missing Honey	M	531	Berenstain, Stan & Jan	Random House
Berlioz the Bear	N	250+	Brett, Jan	Scholastic
Bertie the Bear	I	250+	Allen, Pamela	Coward
Best Birthday Mole Ever Had, The	E	252	Ready Readers	Pearson Learning
Best Birthday Present, The	K	250+	Literacy 2000	Rigby
Best Cake, The	F	162	PM Story Books	Rigby
Best Children in the World, The	F	148	Story Box	Wright Group
Best Enemies	P	250+	Leverich, Kathleen	Beech Tree Books
Best Enemies Again	P	250+	Leverich, Kathleen	Alfred A. Knopf, Inc.
Best Enemies Forever	P	250+	Leverich, Kathleen	William Morrow & Co.

Title	Level	Words	Author/Series	Publisher/Distributor
Best Friends	D	68	Little Readers	Houghton Mifflin
Best Friends	E	31	Fitros, Pamela	Kaeden Books
Best Friends for Frances	K	250+	Hoban, Russell	Scholastic
Best Guess, The	I	241	Foundations	Wright Group
Best Little Monkeys in the World, The	J	250+	Standiford, Natalie	Random House
Best Nest	J	250+	Eastman, Philip D.	Random House
Best Older Sister, The	L	250+	Choi, Sook Nyul	Bantam Doubleday Dell
Best Place, The	C	61	Literacy 2000	Rigby
Best Places, The	D	68	Ready Readers	Pearson Learning
Best Teacher in the World, The	K	250+	Chardiet, Bernice & Maccarone, Grace	Scholastic
Best Thing About Food, The	F	132	Twig	Wright Group
Best Way to Play, The	K	250+	Cosby, Bill	Scholastic
Best Worst Day, The	L	250+	Graves, Bonnie	Hyperion
Best-Loved Doll, The	L	250+	Caudill, Rebecca	Henry Holt & Co.
Betsy the Babysitter	F	115	First Start	Troll
Better Than TV	J	250+	Miller, Sara Swan	Bantam Doubleday Dell
Between the Tides	E	52	Wonder World	Wright Group
Bicycle, The	C	29	Story Box	Wright Group
Biff's Aeroplane	E	64	Oxford Reading Tree	Oxford University Press
Big Al	L	250+	Yoshi, Andrew C.	Scholastic
Big and Green	D	12	Wonder World	Wright Group
Big and Little	B	21	Foundations	Wright Group
Big and Little	B	24	KinderReaders	Rigby
Big and Little	B	40	Carousel Earlybirds	Dominie
Big and Little	C	36	Sunshine	Wright Group
Big and Little	D	92	Joy Readers	Dominie
Big and Little Dinosaurs	E	50	Planet Earth	Rigby
Big Bad Rex	I	176	Erickson, Betty	Seedling
Big Balloon Festival, The	L	625	PM Story Books-Gold	Rigby
Big Balloon Race, The	K	250+	Coerr, Eleanor	HarperTrophy
Big Barn, The	C	81	Teacher's Choice Series	Dominie
Big Bed, The	I	346	Pacific Literacy	Pacific Learning
Big Beet, The	L	250+	Ready Readers	Pearson Learning
Big Bird's Copycat Day	F	232	Lerner, Sharon	Random House
Big Boo Bird, The	C	66	Joy Readers	Dominie
Big Box, The	G	183	New Way Green	Steck-Vaughn
Big Bulgy Fat Black Slugs	M	250+	Stepping Stones	Nelson/Michaels Assoc.
Big Cat, The	D	41	Ready Readers	Pearson Learning
Big Chase, The	A	14	Foundations	Wright Group
Big Chief of the Neverwoz, The	H		Little Celebrations	Pearson Learning
Big Crocodile, The	G	61	Little Celebrations	Pearson Learning
Big Dog, Little Dog	I	265	Eastman, Philip D.	Random House
Big Eggs	E	103	Coxe, Molly	Random House
Big Enough	C	49	Visions	Wright Group
Big Fat Worm, The	G	250+	Van Laan, Nancy	Random House
Big Fish Little Fish	K	250+	Folk Tales	Wright Group
Big Fish, The	M	301	Yukish, Joe	Kaeden Books
Big Friend, Little Friend	E		Greenfield, Eloise	Houghton Mifflin
Big Game, The	H	69	Pacific Literacy	Pacific Learning
Big Green Caterpillar, The	J	161	Literacy 2000	Rigby

Title	Level	Words	Author/Series	Publisher/Distributor
Big Hill, The	D	19	Story Box	Wright Group
Big Hungry Bear, The	I	148	Wood, Don & Audrey	Scholastic
Big Kick, The	C	67	PM Story Books	Rigby
Big Laugh, The	I	152	Sunshine	Wright Group
Big Long Animal Song	C	29	Little Celebrations	Pearson Learning
Big Mama and Grandma Ghana	J	250+	Shelf Medearis, Angela	Scholastic
Big Max	J	250+	Platt, Kin	HarperTrophy
Big Pig, Little Pig	E	54	Little Celebrations	Pearson Learning
Big Prize, The	K	401	Adventures in Reading	Dominie
Big Red Apple, The	H	250+	Momentum Literacy Program	Troll
Big Red Fire Engine	G	158	First Start	Troll
Big Rocks, Little Rocks	E	180	Early Connections	Benchmark Education
Big Roundup, The	G	121	Wonder World	Wright Group
Big Seed, The	E	83	New Way	Steck-Vaughn
Big Sister	C	44	Visions	Wright Group
Big Sneeze, The	D	112	Foundations	Wright Group
Big Sneeze, The	K	131	Brown, Ruth	Lothrop
Big Surprise, The	H	123	Pacific Literacy	Pacific Learning
Big Things	A	33	PM Starters	Rigby
Big Toe, The	E	123	Read-Togethers	Wright Group
Big, Big Box, A	B	35	Ready Readers	Pearson Learning
Big, Brown Box, The	E	93	Voyages	SRA/McGraw-Hill
Bigfoot Doesn't Square Dance	M	250+	Dadey, Debbie & Jones, Marcia	Scholastic
Bigger and Bigger	C	49	Twig	Wright Group
Bigger or Smaller?	F	112	Sunshine	Wright Group
Bigger Than? Smaller Than?	D	123	Early Connections	Benchmark Education
Biggest Bear in the Woods, The	K	250+	Little Celebrations	Pearson Learning
Biggest Cake in the World, The	F	120	Ready to Read	Pacific Learning
Biggest Cake in the World, The	F	120	Pacific Literacy	Pacific Learning
Biggest Fish, The	I	254	PM Story Books-Orange	Rigby
Biggest Sandwich Ever, The	E	87	Pair-It Books	Steck-Vaughn
Bike Lesson	I	250+	Berenstain, Stan & Jan	Random House
Bike Parade, The	A	16	Literacy 2000	Rigby
Bike Ride, The	D	100	Emergent	Pioneer Valley
Bike That Spike Likes, The	E	91	Ready Readers	Pearson Learning
Bike, The	A	14	Twig	Wright Group
Bikes	D	156	Foundations	Wright Group
Bikes	F	133	Discovery Links	Newbridge
Bill	J	166	Sunshine	Wright Group
Bill and Ted at the Store	D	50	Joy Readers	Dominie
Bill Clinton: Forty-Second President of the U.S.	N	250+	Rookie Biographies	Children's Press
Billie's Book	F	110	Sunshine	Wright Group
Bill's Baby	E	41	Tadpoles	Rigby
Billy Goats Gruff	F	381	Hunia, Fran	Ladybird Books
Billy Magee's New Car	J	391	Foundations	Wright Group
Billy the Ghost and Me	L	250+	Greer, Greg & Ruddick, Bob	HarperTrophy
Bird Barn, The	I	241	Foundations	Wright Group
Bird Beaks	I	180	Wonder World	Wright Group
Bird Behavior: Living Together	M	631	Sunshine	Wright Group
Bird Eggs	F	50	Pebble Books	Grolier, Capstone
Bird Families	F	60	Pebble Books	Grolier, Capstone

Title	Level	Words	Author/Series	Publisher/Distributor
Bird Feeder, The	C	31	Storyteller-First Snow	Wright Group/ McGraw-Hill
Bird Feeder, The	D	55	Coulton, Mia	Kaeden Books
Bird Nests	F	78	Pebble Books	Grolier, Capstone
Bird Song	I	99	Storyteller-Night Crickets	Wright Group/ McGraw-Hill
Bird Table, The	H	166	Book Bank	Wright Group
Bird Talk: Kok, Kok	B	42	Little Celebrations	Pearson Learning
Birds	F	50	Literacy 2000	Rigby
Birds	F	54	Birds Series	Dominie
Birds Need Trees	D	63	Teacher's Choice Series	Dominie
Birds' Nests	J	111	Wonder World	Wright Group
Birds of Prey	O	250+	Woolley, M. & Pigdon, K.	Mondo
Birds of the City	M	840	Sunshine	Wright Group
Birds, Bees, and Sailing Ships	I	243	Sunshine	Wright Group
Bird's-Eye View	J	393	PM Story Books-Turquoise	Rigby
Birthday Balloons	F	182	PM Extensions-Blue	Rigby
Birthday Bike for Brimhall, A	K	250+	Delton, Judy	Bantam Doubleday Dell
Birthday Bird, The	F	82	Books for Young Learners	Richard C. Owen
Birthday Book, The	D	86	Book Bank	Wright Group
Birthday Cake	D	27	Literacy 2000	Rigby
Birthday Cake for Ben, A	C	59	PM Extensions-Red	Rigby
Birthday Cake, The	A	22	Sunshine	Wright Group
Birthday Cake, The	H	201	Story Box	Wright Group
Birthday Candles	C	52	Carousel Readers	Dominie
Birthday Celebrations	E	111	Early Connections	Benchmark Education
Birthday for Frances, A	K	250+	Hoban, Russell	Scholastic
Birthday in the Woods, A	F	199	Salem, Lynn & Stewart, J.	Seedling
Birthday Party, A	C	47	Early Emergent	Pioneer Valley
Birthday Party, The	A	15	Sunshine	Wright Group
Birthday Party, The	A	16	Rise & Shine	Hampton-Brown
Birthday, A	C		New Way	Steck-Vaughn
Birthday, The	A	23	Little Books for Early Readers	University of Maine
Birthdays	C	59	Foundations	Wright Group
Birthdays	I	147	Sunshine	Wright Group
Biscuit	G		Capucilli, Alyssa Satin	HarperTrophy
Biscuit Finds a Friend	G	114	Capucilli, Alyssa Satin	HarperTrophy
Black and White	C	32	Voyages	SRA/McGraw-Hill
Black and White	D	77	Storyteller Nonfiction	Wright Group/ McGraw-Hill
Black Bears	E	50	Pebble Books	Grolier, Capstone
Black Elk: A Man with a Vision	N	250+	Rookie Biographies	Children's Press
Black Swan's Breakfast	G	147	Book Bank	Wright Group
Blackberries	D	107	PM Story Books	Rigby
Blackberries in the Dark	N	250+	Jukes, Mavis	Alfred A. Knopf, Inc.
Blackbird's Nest	G	71	Ready to Read	Pacific Learning
Blackbird's Nest	G	71	Pacific Literacy	Pacific Learning
Blackboard Bear	J	117	Alexander, Martha	The Penguin Group
Blanket, The	E	65	Burningham, John	Crowell
Blast Off!	F	95	Ready Readers	Pearson Learning
Blind Man and the Elephant, The	K	250+	Backstein, Karen	Scholastic

Title	Level	Words	Author/Series	Publisher/Distributor
Blind Pony, The	O	250+	Betancourt, Jeanne	Scholastic
Blocks	C	60	Early Emergent	Pioneer Valley
Blue Bug and the Bullies	D	18	Poulet, Virginia	Children's Press
Blue Bug Goes to School	D	57	Poulet, Virginia	Children's Press
Blue Bug Goes to the Library	F		Poulet, Virginia	Children's Press
Blue Bug's Book of Colors	E	49	Poulet, Virginia	Children's Press
Blue Bug's Vegetable Garden	D	27	Poulet, Virginia	Children's Press
Blue Day	C	35	Literacy 2000	Rigby
Blue Jay, The	H	173	Little Readers	Houghton Mifflin
Blue Lollipops	G	250	Stepping Stones	Nelson/Michaels Assoc.
Blue Ribbon Blues	M	250+	Spinelli, Jerry	Random House
Blue Sue	G	121	Ready Readers	Pearson Learning
Blueberries for Sal	M	250+	McCloskey, Robert	Scholastic
Blueberries from Maine	A	28	Little Books for Early Readers	University of Maine
Blueberry Muffins	D	191	Story Box	Wright Group
BMX Billy	G	93	Literacy 2000	Rigby
Bo Peep's Sheep	C	39	Pair-It Books	Steck-Vaughn
Boat Trip, The	D	70	Carousel Earlybirds	Dominie
Boat, The	A	14	Pacific Literacy	Pacific Learning
Boat, The	A	28	Sunshine	Wright Group
Boats	C	100	Pebble Books	Grolier, Capstone
Boats	D	57	Twig	Wright Group
Boats	G	84	Rockwell, Anne	The Penguin Group
Boats Afloat	M	752	Sunshine	Wright Group
Boats, Boats, Boats	D	44	My First Reader	Grolier Press
Bobbie's Airplane	E	64	Oxford Reading Tree	Oxford University Press
Bobby's Zoo	E	54	Rookie Readers	Children's Press
Bobo's Magic Wishes	L	250+	Little Readers	Houghton Mifflin
Body Battles	P	250+	Gelman, Rita G.	Scholastic
Body Numbers	K	250+	Discovery World	Rigby
Bogeymen Don't Play Football	M	250+	Dadey, Debbie & Jones, Marcia	Scholastic
Boggywooga	I	274	Sunshine	Wright Group
Bogle's Card	H	244	Sunshine	Wright Group
Bogle's Feet	I	280	Sunshine	Wright Group
Bonnie on the Beach	H	198	Little Readers	Houghton Mifflin
Bony-Legs	K	250+	Cole, Joanna	Scholastic
Boogie-Woogie Man, The	D	101	Story Box	Wright Group
Boogly, The	E	61	Literacy 2000	Rigby
Boo-Hoo	E	149	Story Box	Wright Group
Book About Planets and Stars, A	O	250+	Reigot, Betty P.	Scholastic
Book About Your Skeleton, A	M	250+	Gross, Ruth Belov	Scholastic
Book of Black Heroes from A to Z	P	250+	Hudson, Wade & Wilson	Scholastic
Book Week	E	71	Oxford Reading Tree	Oxford University Press
Books	B	21	Smart Starts	Rigby
Books	B	29	Sunshine	Wright Group
Bookstore Cat	I	207	Little Readers	Houghton Mifflin
Boonsville Bombers, The	N	250+	Herzig, Alison	Puffin Books
Boots	C	57	Schreiber, Anne & Doughty, A.	Scholastic
Boots and Shoes	E	68	Cooper, Anne	Kaeden Books
Boots for Toots	C	41	Ready to Read	Pacific Learning
Boots for Toots	C	41	Pacific Literacy	Pacific Learning

Title	Level	Words	Author/Series	Publisher/Distributor
Bootsie Barker Ballerina	K	250+	Bottner, Barbara	HarperTrophy
Boring Old Bed	I	211	Sunshine	Wright Group
Boris Bad Enough	G		Kraus, Robert	Simon & Schuster
Borreguita and the Coyote	O	250+	Aardema, Verna	Scholastic
Boss	C	48	Foundations	Wright Group
Bossy Bettina	F	97	Literacy 2000	Rigby
Bottle Garden, A	E	52	Wonder World	Wright Group
Bottles, Boxes, and Bins	C	36	Twig	Wright Group
Boundless Grace	M	250+	Hoffman, Mary	Scholastic
Bouquet, The	A	38	Carousel Earlybirds	Dominie
Box Can Be Many Things, A	E	51	Rookie Readers	Children's Press
Boxcar Children Return, The	O	250+	Warner, Gertrude Chandler	Scholastic
Boxcar Children, The	O	250+	Warner, Gertrude Chandler	Scholastic
Boxcar Children: Benny Uncovers a Mystery	O	250+	Warner, Gertrude Chandler	Albert Whitman & Co.
Boxcar Children: The Amusement Park Mystery	O	250+	Warner, Gertrude Chandler	Albert Whitman & Co.
Boxcar Children: The Animal Shelter Mystery	O	250+	Warner, Gertrude Chandler	Albert Whitman & Co.
Boxcar Children: The Bicycle Mystery	O	250+	Warner, Gertrude Chandler	Albert Whitman & Co.
Boxcar Children: The Black Pearl Mystery	O	250+	Warner, Gertrude Chandler	Albert Whitman & Co.
Boxcar Children: The Blue Bay Mystery	O	250+	Warner, Gertrude Chandler	Albert Whitman & Co.
Boxcar Children: The Bus Station Mystery	O	250+	Warner, Gertrude Chandler	Albert Whitman & Co.
Boxcar Children: The Camp-Out Mystery	O	250+	Warner, Gertrude Chandler	Albert Whitman & Co.
Boxcar Children: The Canoe Trip Mystery	O	250+	Warner, Gertrude Chandler	Albert Whitman & Co.
Boxcar Children: The Castle Mystery	O	250+	Warner, Gertrude Chandler	Albert Whitman & Co.
Boxcar Children: The Cereal Box Mystery	O	250+	Warner, Gertrude Chandler	Albert Whitman & Co.
Boxcar Children: The Deserted Library Mystery	O	250+	Warner, Gertrude Chandler	Albert Whitman & Co.
Boxcar Children: The Dinosaur Mystery	O	250+	Warner, Gertrude Chandler	Albert Whitman & Co.
Boxcar Children: The Disappearing Friend Mystery	O	250+	Warner, Gertrude Chandler	Albert Whitman & Co.
Boxcar Children: The Firehouse Mystery	O	250+	Warner, Gertrude Chandler	Albert Whitman & Co.
Boxcar Children: The Ghost Ship Mystery	O	250+	Warner, Gertrude Chandler	Albert Whitman & Co.
Boxcar Children: The Growling Bear Mystery	O	250+	Warner, Gertrude Chandler	Scholastic
Boxcar Children: The Haunted Cabin Mystery	O	250+	Warner, Gertrude Chandler	Albert Whitman & Co.
Boxcar Children: The Lighthouse Mystery	O	250+	Warner, Gertrude Chandler	Albert Whitman & Co.
Boxcar Children: The Mountain Top Mystery	O	250+	Warner, Gertrude Chandler	Albert Whitman & Co.
Boxcar Children: The Mystery at the Dog Show	O	250+	Warner, Gertrude Chandler	Albert Whitman & Co.
Boxcar Children: The Mystery at the Fair	O	250+	Warner, Gertrude Chandler	Albert Whitman & Co.
Boxcar Children: The Mystery Bookstore	O	250+	Warner, Gertrude Chandler	Scholastic
Boxcar Children: The Mystery Cruise	O	250+	Warner, Gertrude Chandler	Albert Whitman & Co.
Boxcar Children: The Mystery in the Cave	O	250+	Warner, Gertrude Chandler	Scholastic
Boxcar Children: The Mystery in the Old Attic	O	250+	Warner, Gertrude Chandler	Scholastic
Boxcar Children: The Mystery in the Sand	O	250+	Warner, Gertrude Chandler	Albert Whitman & Co.
Boxcar Children: The Mystery of the Hidden Beach	O	250+	Warner, Gertrude Chandler	Albert Whitman & Co.
Boxcar Children: The Mystery of the Lost Mine	O	250+	Warner, Gertrude Chandler	Scholastic
Boxcar Children: The Mystery of the Lost Village	O	250+	Warner, Gertrude Chandler	Scholastic
Boxcar Children: The Mystery of the Missing Cat	O	250+	Warner, Gertrude Chandler	Albert Whitman & Co.
Boxcar Children: The Mystery of the Mixed-Up Zoo	O	250+	Warner, Gertrude Chandler	Albert Whitman & Co.
Boxcar Children: The Mystery of the Stolen Boxcar	O	250+	Warner, Gertrude Chandler	Scholastic
Boxcar Children: The Mystery of the Stolen Music	O	250+	Warner, Gertrude Chandler	Scholastic
Boxcar Children: The Mystery on Stage	O	250+	Warner, Gertrude Chandler	Albert Whitman & Co.
Boxcar Children: The Mystery on the Train	O	250+	Warner, Gertrude Chandler	Scholastic

Title	Level	Words	Author/Series	Publisher/Distributor
Boxcar Children: The Outer Space Mystery	O	250+	Warner, Gertrude Chandler	Scholastic
Boxcar Children: The Pizza Mystery	O	250+	Warner, Gertrude Chandler	Albert Whitman & Co.
Boxcar Children: The Schoolhouse Mystery	O	250+	Warner, Gertrude Chandler	Albert Whitman & Co.
Boxcar Children: The Snowbound Mystery	O	250+	Warner, Gertrude Chandler	Albert Whitman & Co.
Boxcar Children: The Soccer Mystery	O	250+	Warner, Gertrude Chandler	Scholastic
Boxcar Children: The Surprise Island	O	250+	Warner, Gertrude Chandler	Scholastic
Boxes	E	103	Foundations	Wright Group
Boxes	H	153	Literacy 2000	Rigby
Boxes, Boxes, Boxes	E	63	Stewart, J. & Salem, Lynn	Seedling
Boy and His Donkey, A	K	250+	Literacy 2000	Rigby
Boy and the Lion, The	H	166	Aesop	Wright Group
Boy and the Wolf, The	I	200	Book Bank	Wright Group
Boy in the Doghouse, A	N	250+	Douglas, Ann	Simon & Schuster
Boy Named Boomer, A	K	250+	Esiason, Boomer	Scholastic
Boy Who Cried Wolf, The	H	324	Sunshine	Wright Group
Boy Who Cried Wolf, The	J	140	Littledale, Freya	Scholastic
Boy Who Cried Wolf, The	K	460	Aesop's Fables	Dominie
Boy Who Cried Wolf, The	L	250+	Literacy 2000	Rigby
Boy Who Stretched to the Sky, The	M	463	Book Bank	Wright Group
Boy Who Tried to Hide, The	I	219	Storyteller-Night Crickets	Wright Group/ McGraw-Hill
Boy Who Turned into a T.V. Set, The	L	250+	Manes, Stephen	Avon Camelot
Boy Who Went to the North Wind, The	L	250+	Literacy 2000	Rigby
Bozo	H	94	Wonder World	Wright Group
Bozo the Clone	N	250+	Greenburg, Dan	Grosset & Dunlap
Brachiosaurus in the River	L	200	Wesley & the Dinosaurs	Wright Group
Brad and Butter Play Ball!	M	250+	Hughes, Dean	Random House
Braids	D	24	Visions	Wright Group
Brain-in-a-Box	M	250+	Matthews, Steve	Sundance
Brand New Butterfly, A	L	186	Literacy 2000	Rigby
Brave Ben	K	162	Literacy 2000	Rigby
Brave Father Mouse	E	92	PM Story Books	Rigby
Brave Little Tailor, The	K	250+	PM Trad. Stories & Tales	Rigby
Brave Maddie Egg	M	250+	Standiford, Natalie	Random House
Brave Triceratops	G	178	PM Story Books	Rigby
Bravo Amelia Bedelia!	L	250+	Parish, Herman	Avon Books
Bread	D	69	Sunshine	Wright Group
Bread and Jam for Frances	K	250+	Hoban, Russell	Scholastic
Bread, Bread, Bread	F	95	Morris, Ann	Scholastic
Breakfast	C	35	Foundations	Wright Group
Breakfast	C	37	Little Books for Early Readers	University of Maine
Breakfast in Bed	C	10	Voyages	SRA/McGraw-Hill
Breakfast in Bed	G	36	Tadpoles	Rigby
Breakfast on the Farm	D	73	Storyteller Nonfiction	Wright Group/ McGraw-Hill
Breakfast with John	C	29	Books for Young Learners	Richard C. Owen
Breathing	L	106	Book Shop	Mondo Publishing
Breathing Under Water	C	39	Sunshine	Wright Group
Bremen Town Musicians, The	K	863	Gross & Kent	Scholastic
Brenda's Birthday	A	18	Story Box	Wright Group
Brenda's Private Swing	K	250+	Chardiet, Bernice & Maccarone, Grace	Scholastic

Title	Level	Words	Author/Series	Publisher/Distributor
Bridge, The	B	32	Story Box	Wright Group
Brigid Beware	L	250+	Leverich, Kathleen	Random House
Brigid Bewitched	L	250+	Leverich, Kathleen	Random House
Brigid the Bad	L	250+	Leverich, Kathleen	Random House
Bringing the Sea Back Home	L	250+	Literacy 2000	Rigby
Brith the Terrible	M	250+	Literacy 2000	Rigby
Broken Plate, The	I	198	Foundations	Wright Group
Broken Window	G	136	New Way Blue	Steck-Vaughn
Broken Window and Other Cases, The	O	250+	Simon, Seymour	Avon Books
Brothers	B	36	Pebble Books	Grolier, Capstone
Brothers	E	65	Talk About Books	Dominie
Brown Bear, Brown Bear	C	185	Martin, Bill	Holt, Henry & Co.
Brown Bears	E	45	Pebble Books	Grolier, Capstone
Brown Bears	K	250+	PM Animals in the Wild-Yellow	Rigby
Bruno's Birthday	E	32	Literacy 2000	Rigby
Brushing Well	D	42	Pebble Books	Grolier, Capstone
Bubble Gum	B	21	Carousel Readers	Dominie
Bubble Gum	H	66	City Kids	Rigby
Bubble Gum Can Be Trouble	D	147	Visions	Wright Group
Bubbles	C	31	Sunshine	Wright Group
Bubbles	C	33	Literacy 2000	Rigby
Bubbles	C	34	Discovery Links	Newbridge
Bubbles Everywhere	C	41	Twig	Wright Group
Bubbling Crocodile	K	250+	Ready to Read	Pacific Learning
Buckle My Shoe	C	31	Sunshine	Wright Group
Buffalo Bill and the Pony Express	K	250+	Coerr, Eleanor	HarperTrophy
Buffy	B	28	Literacy 2000	Rigby
Buffy's Tricks	G	97	Literacy 2000	Rigby
Bug Off!	L	250+	Dussling, Jennifer	Grosset & Dunlap
Bug Party	F	131	Twig	Wright Group
Bug Watching	B	25	Twig	Wright Group
Bug, a Bear, and a Boy, A	F	250+	McPhail, David	Random House
Buggy Riddles	I	221	Little Books	Sadlier-Oxford
Bugs	O	250+	Parker, N. & Wright, R.	Scholastic
Bugs!	C	32	Rookie Readers	Children's Press
Build, Build, Build	M	470	Sunshine	Wright Group
Building a House	H	83	Barton, Byron	Morrow
Building Things	F	24	Sunshine	Wright Group
Building with Blocks	A	20	Sunshine	Wright Group
Buildings on My Street	F	109	Foundations	Wright Group
Bulldozer, The	D	48	Sunshine	Wright Group
Bull's-eye!	F	87	Oxford Reading Tree	Oxford University Press
Bumble Bee	D	53	Ready to Read	Pacific Learning
Bumble Bee	D	53	Pacific Literacy	Pacific Learning
Bumble Bees	E	56	Pebble Books	Grolier, Capstone
Bump!	C	12	KinderReaders	Rigby
Bump, Bump, Bump	D	51	Cat on the Mat	Oxford University Press
Bumper Cars, The	C	94	PM Extensions-Red	Rigby
Bumpity, Bumpity, Bump	F	62	Parker, C.	Seedling
Bumps in the Night	K	250+	Allard, Harry	Bantam Doubleday Dell

Title	Level	Words	Author/Series	Publisher/Distributor
Bun, The	I	421	Storyteller-Moon Rising	Wright Group/ McGraw-Hill
Bunnicula	P	250+	Howe, James	Avon Camelot
Bunny Hop, The	I		Slater, Teddy	Scholastic
Bunny Opposites	B	14	Pair-It Books	Steck-Vaughn
Bunny Runs Away	K	250+	Chardiet, Bernice & Maccarone, Grace	Scholastic
Bunny, Bunny	D	40	My First Reader	Grolier Press
Bunny's Recess	A	35	Little Books for Early Readers	University of Maine
Buried Eye, The	M	250+	Schultz, Irene	Wright Group
Burning Questions of Bingo Brown	P	250+	Byars, Betsy	Scholastic
Burrows	E	51	Storyteller-Setting Sun	Wright Group/ McGraw-Hill
Bus Ride, The	C	164	Little Celebrations	Pearson Learning
Bus Ride, The	C	175	Reading Unlimited	Pacific Learning
Bus Ride, The	F	99	Storyteller-Setting Sun	Wright Group/ McGraw-Hill
Bus Stop, The	G		Hellen, Nancy	Orchard
Bus, The	C	46	Twig	Wright Group
Bush Bunyip, The	J	396	Book Shop	Mondo Publishing
Buster	C	36	Twig	Wright Group
Buster McCluster	E	71	Wonder World	Wright Group
Buster's Dino Dilemma	M	250+	Brown, Marc	Little, Brown & Co.
Busy Beavers, The	I	362	PM Story Books-Orange	Rigby
Busy Bird	A	14	Pacific Literacy	Pacific Learning
Busy Buzzing Bumblebees	I	250+	Schwartz, Alvin	HarperTrophy
Busy Buzzing Bumblebees and Other Tongue Twisters	I	250+	Schwartz, Alvin	HarperTrophy
Busy Guy, A	K	72	Rookie Readers	Children's Press
Busy Mosquito, The	C	112	Foundations	Wright Group
Busy People	C	40	Little Celebrations	Pearson Learning
Busy Street	E	67	Traditional Tales & More	Rigby
Busy Week, A	D	49	Pair-It Books	Steck-Vaughn
Busybody Nora	N	250+	Hurwitz, Johanna	The Penguin Group
But Granny Did	D	58	Voyages	SRA/McGraw-Hill
But I Knew Better	H	242	Home Connection Collection	Rigby
Butch, the Outdoor Cat	E	65	Carousel Readers	Dominie
Butterflies	E	41	Pebble Books	Grolier, Capstone
Butterfly Colors	F	52	Pebble Books	Grolier, Capstone
Butterfly Eggs	F	57	Pebble Books	Grolier, Capstone
Button Soup	K	250+	Orgel, Doris	Bantam Doubleday Dell
Buzby	J	250+	Hoban, Julia	HarperTrophy
Buzz Is Part of a Bee, A	E	56	Rookie Readers	Children's Press
Buzz Said the Bee	G	62	Lewison, Wendy	Scholastic
Buzz, Buzz, Buzz	H	162	Barton, Byron	Macmillan
Buzzing Flies	C	45	Sunshine	Wright Group
By the Stream	E	73	Oxford Reading Tree	Oxford University Press
By the Tree	D	75	Ready Readers	Pearson Learning
Cabbage Caterpillar	I	221	Sunshine	Wright Group
Cabbage Princess, The	K	250+	Literacy 2000	Rigby
Cabin in the Hills, The	J	349	PM Story Books-Turquoise	Rigby

Title	Level	Words	Author/Series	Publisher/Distributor
Cactus Town	C	43	Sunshine	Wright Group
Cake for Mom, A	D	63	Home Connection Collection	Rigby
Cake That Mack Ate, The	H	189	Robart, Rose & Kovalski, Maryann	Little, Brown & Co.
Cake, The	M	250+	Read Alongs	Rigby
Calico Cat at School	G		Charles, Donald	Children's Press
Calico Cat at the Zoo	F		Charles, Donald	Children's Press
Calico Cat Meets Bookworm	G		Charles, Donald	Children's Press
Calico Cat's Rainbow	E		Charles, Donald	Children's Press
Calico the Cat	F		Charles, Donald	Children's Press
Call 911	C	22	Twig	Wright Group
Cam Jansen and the Chocolate Fudge Mystery	L	250+	Adler, David	Puffin Books
Cam Jansen and the Ghostly Mystery	L	250+	Adler, David	Puffin Books
Cam Jansen and the Mystery at the Haunted House	L	250+	Adler, David	Puffin Books
Cam Jansen and the Mystery at the Monkey House	L	250+	Adler, David	Puffin Books
Cam Jansen and the Mystery of Flight 54	L	250+	Adler, David	Puffin Books
Cam Jansen and the Mystery of the Babe Ruth Baseball	L	250+	Adler, David	Puffin Books
Cam Jansen and the Mystery of the Carnival Prize	L	250+	Adler, David	Puffin Books
Cam Jansen and the Mystery of the Circus Clown	L	250+	Adler, David	Puffin Books
Cam Jansen and the Mystery of the Dinosaur	L	250+	Adler, David	Puffin Books
Cam Jansen and the Mystery of the Dinosaur Bones	L	250+	Adler, David	Puffin Books
Cam Jansen and the Mystery of the Gold Coins	L	250+	Adler, David	Puffin Books
Cam Jansen and the Mystery of the Monster Movie	L	250+	Adler, David	Puffin Books
Cam Jansen and the Mystery of the Stolen Corn Popper	L	250+	Adler, David	Puffin Books
Cam Jansen and the Mystery of the Stolen Diamonds	L	250+	Adler, David	Puffin Books
Cam Jansen and the Mystery of the Television Dog	L	250+	Adler, David	Puffin Books
Cam Jansen and the Mystery of the U.F.O.	L	250+	Adler, David	Puffin Books
Cam Jansen and the Triceratops Pops Mystery	L	250+	Adler, David	Puffin Books
Camel Called Bump-Along, A	K	373	Evangeline Nicholas Collection	Wright Group
Camouflage	J	154	Sunshine	Wright Group
Camp Big Paw	J	250+	Cushman, Doug	HarperTrophy
Camp Knock Knock	K	250+	Douglas, Ann	Bantam Doubleday Dell
Camp Knock Knock Mystery, The	K	250+	Douglas, Ann	Bantam Doubleday Dell
Camp Sink or Swim	M	250+	Davis, Gibbs	Random House
Camping	B	19	Literacy 2000	Rigby
Camping	C	49	Foundations	Wright Group
Camping	D	64	Hooker, Karen	Kaeden Books
Camping	E	264	Sunshine	Wright Group
Camping Out	E	141	Visions	Wright Group
Camping Outside	F	95	Book Bank	Wright Group
Camping with Claudine	K	250+	Literacy 2000	Rigby
Can a Cow Hop?	D	40	Ready Readers	Pearson Learning
Can Do, Jenny Archer	M	250+	Conford, Ellen	Random House
Can I Have a Dinosaur?	L	250+	Literacy 2000	Rigby
Can I Have a Lick?	C	69	Carousel Readers	Dominie
Can I Play Outside?	H	121	Literacy 2000	Rigby
Can You Find It?	B	34	Ready Readers	Pearson Learning
Can You Find the Pattern?	D	113	Visions	Wright Group

Title	Level	Words	Author/Series	Publisher/Distributor
Can You Fly?	C	51	Foundations	Wright Group
Can You See Me?	C	48	Foundations	Wright Group
Can You See the Eggs?	C	87	PM Starters	Rigby
Canary Caper, The	N	250+	Roy, Ron	Random House
Candle-Light	G	231	PM Story Books	Rigby
Candy Corn Contest, The	L	250+	Giff, Patricia Reilly	Bantam Doubleday Dell
Cannonball Chris	L	250+	Marzollo, Jean	Random House
Can't You Make Them Behave, King George?	O	250+	Fritz, Jean	Scholastic
Can't You See We're Reading?	D	71	Stepping Stones	Nelson/Michaels Assoc.
Caps for Sale	K	675	Slobodkina, Esphyr	Harper & Row
Captain B's Boat	G	158	Sunshine	Wright Group
Captain Bumble	L	510	Story Box	Wright Group
Captain Cat	H	250+	Hoff, Syd	HarperTrophy
Car Accident, The	F	161	Foundations	Wright Group
Car Ride, The	A	41	Little Red Readers	Sundance
Car Trouble	L	724	PM Story Books-Gold	Rigby
Careful Crocodile, The	I	271	PM Story Books-Orange	Rigby
Caring	C	47	Interaction	Rigby
Caring for Our Pets	C	74	Early Connections	Benchmark Education
Carla Gets a Pet	I	250+	Ready Readers	Pearson Learning
Carla's Breakfast	G	225	Harper, Leslie	Kaeden Books
Carla's Ribbons	G	212	Harper, Leslie	Kaeden Books
Carlita Ropes the Twister	L	363	Pair-It Books	Steck-Vaughn
Carnival, The	F	82	Oxford Reading Tree	Oxford University Press
Carrot Seed, The	G	101	Krauss, Ruth	Harper & Row
Carrots	B	51	Pebble Books	Grolier, Capstone
Carrots Don't Talk!	J	250+	Ready Readers	Pearson Learning
Carrots, Peas, and Beans	F	142	Sunshine	Wright Group
Carry-Out Food	D	56	Tadpoles	Rigby
Cars	A	18	Pebble Books	Grolier, Capstone
Cars	B	30	Little Readers	Houghton Mifflin
Cars	F	72	Rockwell, Anne	Dutton
Case for Jenny Archer, A	M	250+	Conford, Ellen	Random House
Case of Hermie the Missing Hamster, The	N	250+	Preller, James	Scholastic
Case of the Cat's Meow, The	K	250+	Bonsall, Crosby	HarperTrophy
Case of the Christmas Snowman, The	N	250+	Preller, James	Scholastic
Case of the Cool-Itch Kid, The	L	250+	Giff, Patricia Reilly	Bantam Doubleday Dell
Case of the Dirty Bird, The	O	250+	Paulsen, Gary	Bantam Doubleday Dell
Case of the Double Cross, The	K	250+	Bonsall, Crosby	HarperTrophy
Case of the Dumb Bells, The	K	250+	Bonsall, Crosby	HarperTrophy
Case of the Elevator Duck, The	M	250+	Brends, Polly Berrien	Random House
Case of the Furry Thing, The	G	267	Ready Readers	Pearson Learning
Case of the Hungry Stranger, The	M	1358	Bonsall, Crosby	HarperTrophy
Case of the Scaredy Cats, The	K	250+	Bonsall, Crosby	Harper & Row
Case of the Secret Valentine, The	N	250+	Preller, James	Scholastic
Case of the Spooky Sleepover, The	N	250+	Preller, James	Scholastic
Case of the Two Masked Robbers, The	K	250+	Hoban, Lillian	HarperTrophy
Cass Becomes a Star	L	250+	Literacy 2000	Rigby
Castle	E	37	Exploring History & Geography	Rigby
Cat and Dog	C	71	Learn to Read	Creative Teaching Press
Cat and Dog	G		Minarik, Else H.	HarperCollins

Title	Level	Words	Author/Series	Publisher/Distributor
Cat and Mouse	B	75	PM Starters	Rigby
Cat and the King	D	30	Literacy 2000	Rigby
Cat and the Mice, The	I	526	Book Bank	Wright Group
Cat Burglar, The	M	250+	Krailing, Tessa	Barron's Educational
Cat Came Back, The	B	22	Ready Readers	Pearson Learning
Cat Came Back, The	I		Little Celebrations	Pearson Learning
Cat Chat	F	85	Ready Readers	Pearson Learning
Cat Concert	J	250+	Literacy 2000	Rigby
Cat Goes Fiddle-i-fee	F	333	Galdone, Paul	Houghton Mifflin
Cat in the Hat	J	250+	Seuss, Dr.	Random House
Cat in the Tree, A	F	79	Oxford Reading Tree	Oxford University Press
Cat on the Mat	B	37	Wildsmith, Brian	Oxford University Press
Cat Prints	C	25	Pair-It Books	Steck-Vaughn
Cat Tails	D	40	Books for Young Learners	Richard C. Owen
Cat That Broke the Rules, The	G	192	Ready Readers	Pearson Learning
Cat Traps	D	93	Coxe, Molly	Random House
Cat Who Loved Red, The	D	63	Salem, Lynn & Stewart, J.	Seedling
Cat Who Wore a Pot on Her Head, The	N	250+	Slepian, Jon & Seidler, A.	Scholastic
Cat with No Tail, The	I	137	Books for Young Learners	Richard C. Owen
Cat, The	A	42	Little Books for Early Readers	University of Maine
Cat, The	C	23	Smart Starts	Rigby
Catch It, Marvin	E	61	Windmill Books	Rigby
Catch That Frog	E	131	Reading Unlimited	Pacific Learning
Catch That Pass!	M	250+	Christopher, Matt	Little, Brown & Co.
Catch the Cookie	J		Little Celebrations	Pearson Learning
Catcher with a Glass Arm	M	250+	Christopher, Matt	Little, Brown & Co.
Catcher's Mask, The	M	250+	Christopher, Matt	Little, Brown & Co.
Catching	B	35	Teacher's Choice Series	Dominie
Caterpillars	F	54	Pebble Books	Grolier, Capstone
Caterpillars	M	114	Book Shop	Mondo Publishing
Caterpillar's Adventure	F	69	Story Box	Wright Group
Catherine the Counter	E	86	Sunshine	Wright Group
Cats	C	45	Williams, Deborah	Kaeden Books
Cats	E	137	Wonder World	Wright Group
Cats	I	250+	PM Animal Facts: Pets-Orange	Rigby
Cats and Kittens	F	51	Reading Unlimited	Pacific Learning
Cats and Mice	H	51	Gelman, Rita	Scholastic
Cats' Burglar, The	K		Parish, Peggy	Hearst Corp.
Cat's Day, A	B	23	Twig	Wright Group
Cat's Meow, The	O	250+	Soto, Gary	Scholastic
Cats of the Night	K	379	Book Bank	Wright Group
Cat's Trip	G	158	Ready Readers	Pearson Learning
Cats, Cats, Cats	B	14	Pair-It Books	Steck-Vaughn
Cats, Cats, Cats	G	217	Story Basket	Wright Group
Catten	K	769	Jellybeans	Rigby
Caught in the Storm	H	250+	Home Connection Collection	Rigby
Cave, The	C	67	Book Bank	Wright Group
Caves	M	250+	Discovery World	Rigby
Celebrations	G	107	Storyteller-Moon Rising	Wright Group/ McGraw-Hill
Cells	J	96	Wonder World	Wright Group

Title	Level	Words	Author/Series	Publisher/Distributor
Cement Tent	G	358	First Start	Troll
Center Court Sting	M	250+	Christopher, Matt	Little, Brown & Co.
Centerfield Ballhawk	M	250+	Christopher, Matt	Little, Brown & Co.
Cesar Chavez	L	262	Pebble Books	Grolier, Capstone
Chair for My Mother, A	M	250+	Williams, Vera B.	Scholastic
Chalk Box Kid, The	N	250+	Bulla, Clyde Robert	Random House
Chalk Talk	C	69	Storyteller-First Snow	Wright Group/ McGraw-Hill
Challenge at Second Base	M	250+	Christopher, Matt	Little, Brown & Co.
Champions	C	13	Twig	Wright Group
Change for Zoe, A	K	250+	Home Connection Collection	Rigby
Changing Caterpillar, The	G	56	Books for Young Learners	Richard C. Owen
Changing Colors	B	16	Pair-It Books	Steck-Vaughn
Changing Land, The	I	64	Pacific Literacy	Pacific Learning
Chang's Paper Pony	L	250+	Coerr, Eleanor	HarperTrophy
Charlie	L	250+	Literacy 2000	Rigby
Charlie Needs a Cloak	J	187	DePaola, Tomie	Prentice-Hall
Chase, The	F	85	Oxford Reading Tree	Oxford University Press
Cheerful King, The	K	351	Little Books	Sadlier-Oxford
Cherries and Cherry Pits	M	250+	Williams, Vera B.	Houghton Mifflin
Chester the Wizard	M	250+	Reading Unlimited	Pacific Learning
Chew, Chew, Chew	C	24	Literacy 2000	Rigby
Chicago Winds	K	173	Evangeline Nicholas Collection	Wright Group
Chick and the Duckling, The	D	112	Ginsburg, Mirra	Macmillan
Chicken Feed	E	67	Joy Readers	Dominie
Chicken for Dinner	C	27	Story Box	Wright Group
Chicken in the Middle of the Road	J	478	Book Shop	Mondo Publishing
Chicken Licken	I	346	Sunshine	Wright Group
Chicken Little	I	250+	PM Traditional Tales-Orange	Rigby
Chicken Little	L	587	Traditional Tales & More	Rigby
Chicken Pox	H	220	Little Readers	Houghton Mifflin
Chicken Soup	B	38	Fitros, Pamela	Kaeden Books
Chicken Soup with Rice	M	310	Sendak, Maurice	HarperCollins
Chicken Sunday	M	250+	Polacco, Patricia	Scholastic
Chickens	B	24	Pebble Books	Grolier, Capstone
Chickens	D	23	Books for Young Learners	Richard C. Owen
Chickens	G	105	Book Shop	Mondo Publishing
Chickens Aren't the Only Ones	K	250+	Heller, Ruth	Scholastic
Chick's Walk	A	14	Story Box	Wright Group
Children	C	45	Pebble Books	Grolier, Capstone
Children as Young Scientists	K	393	Early Connections	Benchmark Education
Children of Sierra Leone, The	J	142	Books for Young Learners	Richard C. Owen
Child's Day, A	C	34	Sunshine	Wright Group
Chinese Kites	A	15	Twig	Wright Group
Chinese New Year	D	33	Pacific Literacy	Pacific Learning
Chipmunk at Hollow Tree Lane	K	250+	Sherrow, Victoria	Scholastic
Chocolate Cake, The	B	23	Story Box	Wright Group
Chocolate Chip Cookies	B	32	Ready Readers	Pearson Learning
Chocolate Fever	O	250+	Smith, Robert	Bantam Doubleday Dell
Chocolate, Chocolate, Chocolate	E	106	Visions	Wright Group
Chocolate-Chip Muffins	J	204	Sunshine	Wright Group

Title	Level	Words	Author/Series	Publisher/Distributor
Chook, Chook	E	42	Sunshine	Wright Group
Choose Me	H	204	Reading Corners	Dominie
Choosing a Puppy	E	158	PM Extensions-Yellow	Rigby
Christmas Santa Almost Missed, The	G	158	First Start	Troll
Christmas Shopping	E	48	Literacy 2000	Rigby
Christmas Surprise	G	145	First Start	Troll
Christmas Tree, The	F	163	PM Books	Dominie
Christopher Columbus: A Great Explorer	N	250+	Rookie Biographies	Children's Press
Chug the Tractor	F	203	PM Extensions-Blue	Rigby
Church	B	17	Visions	Wright Group
Cinco de Mayo	E	120	Fiesta Holiday Series	Dominie
Cinderella	I	580	Traditional Tales	Dominie
Cinderella	I	250+	PM Traditional Tales & Plays	Rigby
Cinderella	K	250+	Once Upon a Time	Wright Group
Circle of Gold	P	250+	Boyd Dawson, Candy	Scholastic
Circus	B	20	Twig	Wright Group
Circus Clown, The	D	31	Literacy 2000	Rigby
Circus Fun	G	219	Momentum Literacy Program	Troll
Circus Mystery, The	M	250+	Schultz, Irene	Wright Group
Circus Train, The	A	48	Little Red Readers	Sundance
Circus, The	C	31	Literacy 2000	Rigby
Circus, The	D	42	Wonder World	Wright Group
Cities Around the World	M	250+	Pair-It Books	Steck-Vaughn
City Buildings	G	133	Discovery Links	Newbridge
City Bus, The	B	21	Visions	Wright Group
City Cat and the Country Cat, The	E	152	Ready Readers	Pearson Learning
City Lights	B	16	Visions	Wright Group
City Mouse and Country Mouse	D	87	Learn to Read	Creative Teaching Press
City Mouse-Country Mouse	J	198	Aesop	Scholastic
City Mouse-Country Mouse	J	250+	Wallner, John	Scholastic
City Scenes	E	24	Pacific Literacy	Pacific Learning
City Senses	C	85	Twig	Wright Group
City Sounds	G	142	Marzollo, Jean	Scholastic
City Storm	E	180	Twig	Wright Group
Clap Your Hands!	B	22	Pair-It Books	Steck-Vaughn
Clara and the Bookwagon	K	250+	Levinson, Nancy Smiler	HarperTrophy
Class Clown	O	250+	Hurwitz, Johanna	Scholastic
Class Play, The	J	250+	Little Readers	Houghton Mifflin
Class President	O	250+	Hurwitz, Johanna	Scholastic
Claudine's Concert	L	250+	Literacy 2000	Rigby
Clean House for Mole and Mouse, A	H	201	Ziefert, Harriet	Scholastic
Clean Up Your Room	B	35	Visions	Wright Group
Cleaning My Room	I	189	Early Connections	Benchmark Education
Cleaning Teeth	C	37	Wonder World	Wright Group
Cleaning Up the Park	H	153	Home Connection Collection	Rigby
Clever Bird	K	250+	Little Celebrations	Pearson Learning
Clever Hamburger	K	560	Jellybeans	Rigby
Clever Happy Monkey	C	28	Joy Readers	Dominie
Clever Little Bird	D	73	Storyteller-Setting Sun	Wright Group/ McGraw-Hill
Clever Mr. Brown	K	397	Story Box	Wright Group

Title	Level	Words	Author/Series	Publisher/Distributor
Clever Penguins, The	G	174	PM Story Books	Rigby
Click	E	41	Books for Young Learners	Richard C. Owen
Click	G	288	Foundations	Wright Group
Clifford, the Big Red Dog	K	241	Bridwell, Norman	Scholastic
Clifford, the Small Red Puppy	K	499	Bridwell, Norman	Scholastic
Climbing	B	48	PM Starters	Rigby
Climbing	C	34	Literacy 2000	Rigby
Cloak of the Wind	O	250+	Voyages in…	Wright Group
Clock That Couldn't Tell Time	H	310	Carousel Readers	Dominie
Clocks and More Clocks	J	374	Hutchins, Pat	Scholastic
Close Your Eyes	E	131	Foundations	Wright Group
Closer and Closer	A	13	Twig	Wright Group
Closet in the Hall, The	D	84	Wonder World	Wright Group
Clothes	C	25	Interaction	Rigby
Clothes	D	63	Voyages	SRA/McGraw-Hill
Clothes	F	103	Talk About Books	Dominie
Clothes	O	386	Wonder World	Wright Group
Cloud Book, The	N	250+	DePaola, Tomie	Scholastic
Clouds	B	42	Voyages	SRA/McGraw-Hill
Clouds	H	108	Sunshine	Wright Group
Clouds	H	132	Twig	Wright Group
Clouds	I	249	Pebble Books	Grolier, Capstone
Clouds	J	246	Early Connections	Benchmark Education
Clouds	M	250+	Literacy 2000	Rigby
Clouds of Terror	L	250+	Welsh, Catherine A.	Carolrhoda Books
Clouds, Rain and Fog	K	488	Sunshine	Wright Group
Cloudy with a Chance of Meatballs	M	250+	Barrett, Judi	Atheneum
Clown and Elephant	C	38	Story Box	Wright Group
Clown Face	A	14	Twig	Wright Group
Clown in the Well, The	D	140	Story Box	Wright Group
Clown, The	A	13	Smart Starts	Rigby
Clown, The	B	29	Urmston, Kathleen & Evans, Karen	Kaeden Books
Clubhouse, The	K	659	PM Story Books-Gold	Rigby
Clue at the Zoo, The	L	250+	Giff, Patricia Reilly	Bantam Doubleday Dell
Clue in the Castle, The	M	250+	Schultz, Irene	Wright Group
Clyde Klutter's Room	I	146	Sunshine	Wright Group
Coat Full of Bubbles, A	G	72	Books for Young Learners	Richard C. Owen
Cobwebs, Elephants, and Stars	M	779	Sunshine	Wright Group
Cock-A-Doodle Do	F		Brandenberg, Franz	Greenwillow
Coconut Lunches	I	564	Sunshine	Wright Group
Cold Day, The	F	80	Oxford Reading Tree	Oxford University Press
Collecting Badges	J	250+	Stepping Stones	Nelson/Michaels Assoc.
Collecting Cones	I	127	Wonder World	Wright Group
Collecting Leaves	K	250+	Stepping Stones	Nelson/Michaels Assoc.
Collecting Shapes	J	250+	Stepping Stones	Nelson/Michaels Assoc.
Color Wizard, The	J	250+	Brenner, Barbara	Bantam Doubleday Dell
Colorful Ghost, The	E	135	TOTTS	Tott Publications
Colors	D	198	Foundations	Wright Group
Colors at the Zoo	B	59	Little Books	Sadlier-Oxford
Colors in the City	B	61	Urmston, Kathleen & Evans, Karen	Kaeden Books
Come and Have Fun	A	49	KinderReaders	Rigby

Title	Level	Words	Author/Series	Publisher/Distributor
Come and Have Fun	I		Hurd, Edith Thacher	HarperCollins
Come and Play	B	34	Interaction	Rigby
Come and Play, Sarah!	D	49	Sunshine	Wright Group
Come and See!	G	134	Foundations	Wright Group
Come Back, Amelia Bedelia	L	250+	Parish, Peggy	Harper & Row
Come for a Swim!	F	129	Sunshine	Wright Group
Come Meet Some Seals	I	118	Little Books	Sadlier-Oxford
Come on Mom	D		New Way	Steck-Vaughn
Come on Up	A	16	KinderReaders	Rigby
Come On!	B	22	Sunshine	Wright Group
Come On, Tim	G	198	PM Story Books	Rigby
Come Out and Play Little Mouse	H	198	Kraus, Robert	Morrow
Come to My House	C	56	Joy Readers	Dominie
Come to My House!	F	131	Sunshine	Wright Group
Come with Me	C	25	Story Box	Wright Group
Come! Sit! Speak!	H	57	Rookie Readers	Children's Press
Comeback Challenge, The	M	250+	Christopher, Matt	Little, Brown & Co.
Commander Toad and the Big Black Hole	K	250+	Yolen, Jane	Putnam & Grosset
Commander Toad and the Dis-Asteroid	K	250+	Yolen, Jane	Putnam & Grosset
Commander Toad and the Intergalactic Spy	K	250+	Yolen, Jane	Putnam & Grosset
Commander Toad and the Planet of the Grapes	K	250+	Yolen, Jane	Putnam & Grosset
Commander Toad and the Space Pirates	K	250+	Yolen, Jane	Putnam & Grosset
Commander Toad and the Voyage Home	K	250+	Yolen, Jane	Putnam & Grosset
Communities	D	42	Pebble Books	Grolier, Capstone
Communities	E	59	Wonder World	Wright Group
Community Jobs	I	207	Early Connections	Benchmark Education
Computers Are for Everyone	K	464	Sunshine	Wright Group
Concert Night	K	250+	Literacy 2000	Rigby
Connie's Dance	M	361	Windmill Books	Rigby
Conversation Club, The	L	250+	Stanley, Diane	Aladdin
Coo Coo Caroo	G	57	Books for Young Learners	Richard C. Owen
Cookie Jar, The	G	106	Sunshine	Wright Group
Cookies	A	15	Twig	Wright Group
Cookies	D	18	Little Celebrations	Pearson Learning
Cookies to Share	E	45	Pair-It Books	Steck-Vaughn
Cookie's Week	F	84	Ward, Cindy	Putnam
Cooking at School	G	68	City Kids	Rigby
Cooking Pot, The	F	132	Sunshine	Wright Group
Cooking Spaghetti	I	150	City Kids	Rigby
Cook-Out, The	E	78	Oxford Reading Tree	Oxford University Press
Cool Off	C	37	Book Shop	Mondo Publishing
Cooling Off	D	104	Reading Corners	Dominie
Copper Lady, The	M	250+	Ross, Alice & Kent	Carolrhoda Books
Copycat	C	54	Story Box	Wright Group
Coral	J	253	Marine Life for Young Readers	Dominie
Coral Reef, The	H	186	Discovery Links	Newbridge
Corals	G	51	Pebble Books	Grolier, Capstone
Corduroy	K	250+	Freeman, Don	Scholastic
Corn: An American Indian Gift	M	690	Pair-It Books	Steck-Vaughn
Corn: From Table to Table	H	171	Discovery Links	Newbridge
Costume Party	A	32	Joy Readers	Dominie

Title	Level	Words	Author/Series	Publisher/Distributor
Costume Party, The	A	15	Sunshine	Wright Group
Costume Party, The	J	145	City Kids	Rigby
Costumes	C	23	Oxford Reading Tree	Oxford University Press
Costumes	C	36	Pebble Books	Grolier, Capstone
Could It Be?	J	250+	Oppenheim, Joanne	Bantam Doubleday Dell
Could We Be Friends? Poems for Pals	L	1717	Book Shop	Mondo Publishing
Count with Me	A	49	Little Books	Sadlier-Oxford
Count Your Money with the Polk Street School	M	250+	Giff, Patricia Reilly	Bantam Doubleday Dell
Counterfeit Tackle, The	M	250+	Christopher, Matt	Little, Brown & Co.
Counting Insects	K	230	Early Connections	Benchmark Education
Counting One to Five	B	64	Early Connections	Benchmark Education
Counting Seeds	C	63	Early Connections	Benchmark Education
Cousins	D	41	Pebble Books	Grolier, Capstone
Covers	E	30	Little Celebrations	Pearson Learning
Cow in the Garden, The	E	158	New Way Green	Steck-Vaughn
Cow Up a Tree	H	215	Read Alongs	Rigby
Cowboy Jake	I	174	Sunshine	Wright Group
Cowboy, The	C	35	Step-By-Step Series	Dominie
Cowpokes and Desperadoes	O	250+	Paulsen, Gary	Bantam Doubleday Dell
Cows in the Garden	G	163	PM Story Books	Rigby
Coyote Plants a Peach Tree	I	233	Books for Young Learners	Richard C. Owen
Crab at the Bottom of the Sea, The	H	141	Literacy 2000	Rigby
Crabbing Time	I	75	Books for Young Learners	Richard C. Owen
Crabs	E	46	Pebble Books	Grolier, Capstone
Crabs	M	272	Wonder World	Wright Group
Crabs	M	501	Sunshine	Wright Group
Crabs, Shrimp, & Lobsters	M	322	Marine Life for Young Readers	Dominie
Cracker Jack, The	D	25	Sunshine	Wright Group
Crackerjack Halfback	M	250+	Christopher, Matt	Little, Brown & Co.
Crafty Jackal	L	250+	Folk Tales	Wright Group
Crane Wife, The	M	620	Pair-It Books	Steck-Vaughn
Crawl, Caterpillar, Crawl!	C	24	Pair-It Books	Steck-Vaughn
Crazy Cats	A	42	Little Books for Early Readers	University of Maine
Crazy Quilt, The	G	148	Little Readers	Houghton Mifflin
Crazy Quilt, The	G	148	Little Celebrations	Pearson Learning
Creature from Beneath the Ice and Other Cases, The	O	250+	Simon, Seymour	Avon Books
Creatures of the Night	O	250+	Murdoch, K. & Ray, S.	Mondo
Creep Show	L	250+	Dussling, Jennifer	Grosset & Dunlap
Creepy Caterpillar	E	118	Little Readers	Houghton Mifflin
Creepy Crawlies	B	38	Carousel Earlybirds	Dominie
Crickets	D	48	Pebble Books	Grolier, Capstone
Crickets on the Go	D	56	Little Celebrations	Pearson Learning
Crinkum Crankum	M	250+	Ready to Read	Pacific Learning
Critter Race	G		Reese, Bob	Children's Press
Crocodile in the Library	M	250+	Ready to Read	Pacific Learning
Crocodile Lake	K	322	Pacific Literacy	Pacific Learning
Crocodile's Christmas Jandles	M	250+	Ready to Read	Pacific Learning
Crosby Crocodile's Disguise	K	250+	Literacy 2000	Rigby
Cross Country Race, The	H	246	PM Story Books	Rigby
Cross-Country Race	C	33	Windmill Books	Rigby

©1999 by I. C. Fountas & G. S. Pinnell from *Matching Books to Readers*. Portsmouth, NH: Heinemann. May not be reproduced without written permission of the publisher.

Title	Level	Words	Author/Series	Publisher/Distributor
Crow and the Pitcher, The	I	265	Aesop's Fables	Dominie
Crowded Dock and Other Cases, The	O	250+	Simon, Seymour	Avon Books
Crunchy Munchy	G	189	Book Shop	Mondo Publishing
Crying Rocks and Other Cases, The	O	250+	Simon, Seymour	Avon Books
Cubby's Gum	J	250+	Ready Readers	Pearson Learning
Culpepper's Canyon	O	250+	Paulsen, Gary	Bantam Doubleday Dell
Cunning Creatures	K	250+	Home Connection Collection	Rigby
Cupboard Full of Summer, A	J	234	Pacific Literacy	Pacific Learning
Cupid Doesn't Flip Hamburgers	M	250+	Dadey, Debbie & Jones, Marcia	Scholastic
Curious Cat	E	95	Little Celebrations	Pearson Learning
Curious George and the Ice Cream	J	250+	Rey, Margaret	Scholastic
Curse of the Cobweb Queen, The	L	250+	Hayes, Geoffrey	Random House
Curse of the Squirrel, The	M	250+	Yep, Laurence	Random House
Custard	E	82	Wonder World	Wright Group
Cyberspace	P	250+	Wildcats	Wright Group
Cyclops Doesn't Roller-Skate	M	250+	Dadey, Debbie & Jones, Marcia	Scholastic
Dabble Duck	K	250+	Leo Ellis, Anne	HarperTrophy
Dad	A	24	PM Starters	Rigby
Dad	B	21	Little Readers	Houghton Mifflin
Dad and I	C	59	Rise & Shine	Hampton-Brown
Dad and the Mosquito	I	246	Sunshine	Wright Group
Dad Cooks Breakfast	H	195	Windmill Books	Rigby
Dad Didn't Mind at All	F	134	Literacy 2000	Rigby
Daddy Works Out	D	39	Visions	Wright Group
Dad's Bike	E	52	Literacy 2000	Rigby
Dad's Garden	D	25	Literacy 2000	Rigby
Dad's Headache	F	86	Sunshine	Wright Group
Dad's New Path	F	218	Foundations	Wright Group
Dad's Shirt	F	38	Joy Readers	Dominie
Dad's Surprise	J	202	Foundations	Wright Group
Daisy	J	250+	Stepping Stones	Nelson/Michaels Assoc.
Dan Gets Dressed	B	42	Story Box	Wright Group
Dan Goes Home	E	153	Story Basket	Wright Group
Dan the Dunce	J	539	Tales from Hans Andersen	Wright Group
Dan the Flying Man	C	60	Read-Togethers	Wright Group
Dance with Rosie	N	250+	Giff, Patricia Reilly	The Penguin Group
Dances We Do, The	G	131	Twig	Wright Group
Dancin' Down	I	193	Evangeline Nicholas Collection	Wright Group
Dancing	C	38	Visions	Wright Group
Dancing Dinosaurs	E	45	Little Celebrations	Pearson Learning
Dancing Dragon, The	I	236	Book Shop	Mondo Publishing
Dancing Shoes	B	23	Literacy 2000	Rigby
Dancing with Jacques	P	250+	Voyages in…	Wright Group
Dancing with the Indians	M	250+	Medearis, Angela	Scholastic
Dancing with the Manatees	K	250+	McNulty, Faith	Scholastic
Dandelion, The	E	99	Sunshine	Wright Group
Danger	C	66	Story Box	Wright group
Danger Guys	N	250+	Abbott, Tony	HarperTrophy
Danger Guys Blast Off	N	250+	Abbott, Tony	HarperTrophy
Danger Guys on Ice	N	250+	Abbott, Tony	HarperTrophy

Title	Level	Words	Author/Series	Publisher/Distributor
Dangerous Comet and Other Cases, The	O	250+	Simon, Seymour	Avon Books
Daniel	L	161	Literacy 2000	Rigby
Daniel Boone: Man of the Forests	N	250+	Rookie Biographies	Children's Press
Daniel's Basketball Team	E	80	Carousel Readers	Dominie
Daniel's Dog	K	250+	Bogart, Jo Allen	Scholastic
Daniel's Duck	K	250+	Bulla, Clyde Robert	HarperTrophy
Danny and the Dinosaur	J	250+	Hoff, Syd	Scholastic
Danny and the Dinosaur Go to Camp	H	250+	Hoff, Syd	HarperTrophy
Danny's Dollars	D	88	Reading Corners	Dominie
Darcy and Gran Don't Like Babies	K	250+	Cutler, Jane	Scholastic
Daring Rescue of Marlon the Swimming Pig, The	P	250+	Saunders, Susan	Random House
Dark, Dark Tale, A	F	115	Brown, Ruth	The Penguin Group
Daughter of the Sun	H	210	Storyteller-Night Crickets	Wright Group/ McGraw-Hill
Day and Night	D	102	Twig	Wright Group
Day and Night	G	115	Discovery Links	Newbridge
Day at School, A	C	38	Sunshine	Wright Group
Day at the Races, A	H	85	Bauer, Roger	Kaeden Books
Day Buzzy Stopped Being Busy, The	G	147	First Start	Troll
Day for J.J. and Me, A	M	371	Evangeline Nicholas Collection	Wright Group
Day I Had to Play with My Sister, The	G	139	Bonsall, Crosby	HarperCollins
Day I Lost My Bus Pass, The	J	131	City Kids	Rigby
Day I Tore My Shorts, The	I	209	City Kids	Rigby
Day in Space, A	L	250+	Lord, Suzanne & Epstein, Jolie	Scholastic
Day in Town, A	L	206	Story Box	Wright Group
Day Jimmy's Boa Ate the Wash, The	K	250+	Noble, Trinka, H.	Scholastic
Day of Ahmed's Secret, A	M	250+	Heide, Florence & Gilliland, Judith	Scholastic
Day of the Dragon King	M	250+	Osborne, Mary Pope	Random House
Day of the Rain, The	L	250+	Cowley, Joy	Dominie
Day of the Snow, The	L	250+	Cowley, Joy	Dominie
Day of the Wind, The	L	250+	Cowley, Joy	Dominie
Day Shopping, A	E	157	Foundations	Wright Group
Day the Gorilla Came to School, The	I	293	Sunshine	Wright Group
Day with My Dad, A	C	88	Fiesta Series	Dominie
Days of Adventure	E	47	Book Shop	Mondo Publishing
Days with Frog and Toad	J	250+	Lobel, Arnold	HarperTrophy
Dayton and the Happy Tree	M	1237	Sunshine	Wright Group
Deadly Dungeon, The	M	250+	Roy, Ron	Random House
Dear Grandma	M	264	Storyteller Nonfiction	Wright Group/ McGraw-Hill
Dear Mabel!	H		Little Celebrations	Pearson Learning
Dear Santa	B	50	Literacy 2000	Rigby
Dear Tom	H	153	Wonder World	Wright Group
Dear Zoo	F	115	Campbell, Rod	Macmillan
Debra's Dog	H	157	Tadpoles	Rigby
December Secrets	L	250+	Giff, Patricia Reilly	Bantam Doubleday Dell
Dede and the Dinosaur	K	232	Wonders	Hampton-Brown
Dee and Me	G	189	Ready Readers	Pearson Learning
Deep in the Woods	E	164	Carousel Readers	Dominie
Deep Sea, The	G	152	Ready Readers	Pearson Learning
Deer and the Crocodile, The	G	178	Literacy 2000	Rigby

Title	Level	Words	Author/Series	Publisher/Distributor
Definitely, Positively, Absolutely NO!	D	147	Story Basket	Wright Group
Dentist, The	G	201	PM Nonfiction-Blue	Rigby
Deputy Dan and the Bank Robbers	L	250+	Rosenbloom, Joseph	Random House
Deputy Dan Gets His Man	L	250+	Rosembloom, Joseph	Random House
Desert Dance	G	184	Little Celebrations	Pearson Learning
Desert Day	C	23	Twig	Wright Group
Desert Giant: The World of the Saguaro Cactus	L	250+	Bash, Barbara	Scholastic
Desert Machine, The	K	202	Sunshine	Wright Group
Desert Treasure	M	250+	Pair-It Books	Steck-Vaughn
Desert, The	C	34	Carousel Readers	Dominie
Detective Dinosaur	J	250+	Skofield, James	HarperTrophy
Detective Max	D	32	Pair-It Books	Steck-Vaughn
Diamond Champs, The	M	250+	Christopher, Matt	Little, Brown & Co.
Diamond of Doom, The	M	250+	Schultz, Irene	Wright Group
Diana Made Dinner	E	81	Carousel Readers	Dominie
Diary of a Honeybee	L	250+	Literacy 2000	Rigby
Did You Carry the Flag Today, Charley	M	250+	Caudill, Rebecca	Bantam Doubleday Dell
Did You Hear Wind Sing Your Name?	N	182	Book Shop	Mondo Publishing
Did you Say "Fire?	G	158	Ready to Read	Pacific Learning
Did you say, "Fire"?	G	158	Pacific Literacy	Pacific Learning
Diego Rivera: An Artist's Life	L	250+	Pair-It Books	Steck-Vaughn
Different Dragons	O	250+	Little, Jean	The Penguin Group
Difficult Day, The	J	304	Read Alongs	Rigby
Dig	C	20	KinderReaders	Rigby
Dig, Dig	A	12	Cat on the Mat	Oxford University Press
Digby	I	250+	Little Readers	Houghton Mifflin
Digging to China	H	108	Books for Young Learners	Richard C. Owen
Dinner	A	21	KinderReaders	Rigby
Dinner by Five	F	215	Ready Readers	Pearson Learning
Dinner!	A	19	Sunshine	Wright Group
Dinosaur Babies	L	250+	Penner, Lucille Recht	Random House
Dinosaur Chase, The	I	240	PM Story Books-Orange	Rigby
Dinosaur Dance, The	B	52	Little Books	Sadlier-Oxford
Dinosaur Days	K	250+	Ready Readers	Pearson Learning
Dinosaur Days	L	250+	Milton, Joyce	Random House
Dinosaur Detective	P	250+	Wildcats	Wright Group
Dinosaur Fan, The	F	125	Windmill Books	Rigby
Dinosaur Fun Facts	E	84	Pair-It Books	Steck-Vaughn
Dinosaur Hunt, The	G	131	Windmill Books	Rigby
Dinosaur Hunters	L	250+	McMullan, Kate	Random House
Dinosaur in Trouble	G	121	First Start	Troll
Dinosaur on the Motorway	K	231	Wesley & the Dinosaurs	Wright Group
Dinosaur Party	B	27	Smart Starts	Rigby
Dinosaur Reports	L	324	Little Red Readers	Sundance
Dinosaur Show and Tell	G	212	Pair-It Books	Steck-Vaughn
Dinosaur Time	K	250+	Parish, Peggy	Harper & Row
Dinosaur Times	D	43	Sunshine	Wright Group
Dinosaur Who Lived in My Backyard, The	I	250+	Hennessy, Brendan G.	Scholastic
Dinosaur, The	A	14	Sunshine	Wright Group
Dinosaur, The	F	131	Joy Readers	Dominie
Dinosaurs	H	117	Sunshine	Wright Group

Title	Level	Words	Author/Series	Publisher/Distributor
Dinosaurs	K	193	Book Shop	Mondo Publishing
Dinosaurs & Other Reptiles	I	123	Planet Earth	Rigby
Dinosaurs Before Dark	M	250+	Osborne, Mary Pope	Random House
Dinosaurs Dance	E	17	Rookie Readers	Children's Press
Dinosaurs Galore	D	34	Eaton, Audrey & Kennedy, Jane	Seedling
Dinosaurs, Dinosaurs	G	96	Barton, Byron	HarperCollins
Diplidocus in the Garden, A	K	210	Wesley & the Dinosaurs	Wright Group
Dirt Bike Racer	M	250+	Christopher, Matt	Little, Brown & Co.
Dirt Bike Runaway	M	250+	Christopher, Matt	Little, Brown & Co.
Dirty Beasts	O	250+	Dahl, Roald	The Penguin Group
Dirty Larry	D	53	Rookie Readers	Children's Press
Disappearing Cookies and Other Cases, The	O	250+	Simon, Seymour	Avon Books
Disappearing Ice Cream and Other Cases, The	O	250+	Simon, Seymour	Avon Books
Disappearing Snowball and Other cases, The	O	250+	Simon, Seymour	Avon Books
Discovering Dinosaurs	K	335	Little Books	Sadlier-Oxford
Dishy-Washy	E	92	Story Basket	Wright Group
Distant Stars and Other Cases, The	O	250+	Simon, Seymour	Avon Books
Ditching School	J	128	City Kids	Rigby
Dive In!	F	133	Ready Readers	Pearson Learning
Diver, The	B	30	Sunshine	Wright Group
Divers, The	C	25	Wonder World	Wright Group
Dizzy Lizzy	E	37	Literacy 2000	Rigby
Do Ladybugs Go to School?	E	75	Visions	Wright Group
Do Not Open This Book!	F	134	Story Basket	Wright Group
Do You Like Cats?	K	250+	Oppenheim, Joanne	Bantam Doubleday Dell
Do You Remember When?	D	198	Visions	Wright Group
Do You Want to be My Friend?	A	8	Carle, Eric	The Penguin Group
Doctor Boondoggle	C	51	Story Box	Wright Group
Doctor Green	G	141	Little Readers	Houghton Mifflin
Doctor Has the Flu, The	H	106	Ready Readers	Pearson Learning
Doctor, The	G	179	PM Nonfiction-Blue	Rigby
Doctor's Office, The	K	272	Pebble Books	Grolier, Capstone
Dog	B	37	Ready to Read	Pacific Learning
Dog	B	37	Pacific Literacy	Pacific Learning
Dog and Cat	E	62	My First Reader	Grolier Press
Dog and Cat	E	62	Fehner, C.	Children's Press
Dog and Cat	E	73	Story Basket	Wright Group
Dog Called Mischief, A	D	42	Cat on the Mat	Oxford University Press
Dog Day!	A	21	Smart Starts	Rigby
Dog School	A	11	TOTTS	Tott Publications
Dog Show, The	F	131	Foundations	Wright Group
Dog That Pitched a No-Hitter, The	L	250+	Christopher, Matt	Little, Brown & Co.
Dog That Stole Football Plays, The	L	250+	Christopher, Matt	Little, Brown & Co.
Dog That Stole Home, The	L	250+	Christopher, Matt	Little, Brown & Co.
Dog Went for a Walk	D	51	Voyages	SRA/McGraw-Hill
Dog Who Wanted to Be a Tiger!, The	M		Little Celebrations	Pearson Learning
Dog, The	G		Burningham, John	Crowell
Dog-Gone Hollywood	L	250+	Sharmat, M. Weinman	Random House
Dogs	I	116	Hutchins, Pat	Wright Group
Dogs	I	250+	PM Animal Facts: Pets-Orange	Rigby
Dogs at School	F	94	Books for Young Learners	Richard C. Owen

Title	Level	Words	Author/Series	Publisher/Distributor
Dogs at Work	J	250+	Little Readers	Houghton Mifflin
Dog's Best Friend, A	M	647	Pair-It Books	Steck-Vaughn
Dogstar	J		Literacy 2000	Rigby
Doing the Dishes	L	136	City Kids	Rigby
Dolphin	L	250+	Morris, Robert A.	HarperTrophy
Dolphin Adventure	P	250+	Grover, Wayne	Beech Tree Books
Dolphin Treasure	P	250+	Grover, Wayne	Beech Tree Books
Dolphins	J	111	Wonder World	Wright Group
Dolphins at Daybreak	M	250+	Osborne, Mary Pope	Random House
Dolphin's First Day	N	250+	Zoehfeld, Kathleen W.	Scholastic
Dolphins, The	L	721	PM Story Books-Gold	Rigby
Dom's Handplant	L	250+	Literacy 2000	rigby
Donald's Garden	K	250+	Reading Unlimited	Pacific Learning
Donovan's Word Jar	N	250+	DeGross, Monalisa	HarperTrophy
Donkey	M	250+	Literacy 2000	Rigby
Donkey in the Lion's Skin, The	G	56	Aesop	Wright Group
Donkey Rescues	M	250+	Krailing, Tessa	Barron's Educational
Donkey Work	H	129	Wonder World	Wright Group
Donkey's Tale, The	J	250+	Oppenheim, Joanne	Bantam Doubleday Dell
Don't Be My Valentine-A Classroom Mystery	J	250+	Lexau, Joan M.	HarperTrophy
Don't Be Silly	E	76	Teacher's Choice Series	Dominie
Don't Call Me Beanhead!	N	250+	Wojciechowski, Susan	Candlewick Press
Don't Cut Down This Tree	G	129	Voyages	SRA/McGraw-Hill
Don't Eat Too Much Turkey	J	250+	Cohen, Miriam	Bantam Doubleday Dell
Don't Forget Fun	L	250+	Little Celebrations	Pearson Learning
Don't Forget the Bacon	M	174	Hutchins, Pat	Puffin Books
Don't Interrupt!	I	225	Windmill Books	Rigby
Don't Leave Anything Behind!	C	26	Literacy 2000	Rigby
Don't Panic!	E	122	Book Bank	Wright Group
Don't Splash Me!	A	24	Windmill	Rigby, Wright Group
Don't Tell!	G	82	Little Books	Sadlier-Oxford
Don't Throw It Away!	F	90	Wonder World	Wright Group
Don't Touch	I	250+	Kline, Suzy	The Penguin Group
Don't Wake the Baby	B	18	Literacy 2000	Rigby
Don't Worry	J	339	Literacy 2000	Rigby
Don't You Laugh at Me!	E	167	Sunshine	Wright Group
Doorbell Rang, The	J	283	Hutchins, Pat	Greenwillow
Double Dutch	E	191	Visions	Wright Group
Double Play at Short	M	250+	Christopher, Matt	Little, Brown & Co.
Double Trouble	M	250+	Literacy 2000	Rigby
Do-Whacky-Do	H	249	Read Alongs	Rigby
Down at the River	E	51	Pacific Literacy	Pacific Learning
Down at the Billabog	F	93	Voyages	SRA/McGraw-Hill
Down By the Bay	E	121	Little Celebrations	Pearson Learning
Down by the Swamp	F	50	Little Celebrations	Pearson Learning
Down in the Woods	I	155	Storyteller-Moon Rising	Wright Group/ McGraw-Hill
Down the Hill	C	32	KinderReaders	Rigby
Down the Hill	C	94	New Way Red	Steck-Vaughn
Down the Street	E	66	Little Celebrations	Pearson Learning
Down to Town	A	26	Sunshine	Wright Group

Title	Level	Words	Author/Series	Publisher/Distributor
Dozen Dogs, A	F	228	Ziefert, Harriet	Random House
Dr. Jekyll, Orthodontist	M	250+	Greenburg, Dan	Grosset & Dunlap
Dracula Doesn't Drink Lemonade	M	250+	Dadey, Debbie	Scholastic
Dragon	I	161	Pacific Literacy	Pacific Learning
Dragon	I	250+	Story Box	Wright Group
Dragon Bones	O	250+	Hindman, Paul & Evans, Nate	Random House
Dragon Breath	L	250+	O'Connor, Jane	Grosset & Dunlap
Dragon Feet	K	153	Books for Young Learners	Richard C. Owen
Dragon Gets By	I	250+	Pilkey, Dav	Orchard
Dragon Hunt, The	F	53	New Way Red	Steck-Vaughn
Dragon in the Family, A	P	250+	Koller, Jackie French	Pocket Books
Dragon Quest	P	250+	Koller, Jackie French	Pocket Books
Dragon Trouble	P	250+	Koller, Jackie French	Pocket Books
Dragon Who Had the Measles, The	J	250+	Literacy 2000	Rigby
Dragon!	E	68	Wonder World	Wright Group
Dragon, The	C	130	Sunshine	Wright Group
Dragonflies	E	39	Pebble Books	Grolier, Capstone
Dragonflies	G	53	Books for Young Learners	Richard C. Owen
Dragonling, The	P	250+	Koller, Jackie French	Pocket Books
Dragons and Kings	P	250+	Koller, Jackie French	Pocket Books
Dragon's Birthday, The	L	250+	Literacy 2000	Rigby
Dragon's Coming After You, The	H		Voyages	SRA/McGraw-Hill
Dragons Don't Cook Pizza	M	250+	Dadey, Debbie & Jones, Marcia	Scholastic
Dragon's Fat Cat	I	250+	Pilkey, Dav	Orchard
Dragons Galore	K	250+	Wildcats	Wright Group
Dragon's Halloween	I	250+	Pilkey, Dav	Orchard
Dragon's Lunch	F	85	Ready Readers	Pearson Learning
Dragon's Merry Christmas	I	250+	Pilkey, Dav	Orchard Paperbacks
Dragons of Blueland, The	L	250+	Gannett, Ruth Stiles	Random House
Dragons of Krad	P	250+	Koller, Jackie French	Pocket Books
Drawbridge	E	29	Books for Young Learners	Richard C. Owen
Dream Catchers	M	176	Storyteller-Night Crickets	Wright Group/ McGraw-Hill
Dream Horse	C	47	Pair-It Books	Steck-Vaughn
Dream in the Wishing Well	H	250+	Allen, R. V.	SRA/McGraw-Hill
Dream, The	F	54	Oxford Reading Tree	Oxford University Press
Dreaming	B	23	Smart Starts	Rigby
Dreams	E	93	Book Bank	Wright Group
Dreams	G	98	Sunshine	Wright Group
Dress Up	D	80	Carousel Readers	Dominie
Dressed Up Sammy	E	91	Urmston, Kathleen & Evans, Karen	Kaeden Books
Dressing Up	B	25	Smart Starts	Rigby
Dressing Up	C	31	Literacy 2000	Rigby
Dressing Up	H	222	Stepping Stones	Nelson/Michaels Assoc.
Dressing Up	A	12	Sunshine	Wright Group
Dressing Up	A	32	PM Starters	Rigby
Dressing-up Box, The	C	61	Book Bank	Wright Group
Dress-Up Corner, The	H	68	City Kids	Rigby
Drinking Gourd	M	250+	Monjo, Ferdinand N.	HarperTrophy
Drought Marker, The	M	250+	Literacy 2000	Rigby
Drummer, Hoff	J	173	Emberly, Ed	Prentice-Hall

Title	Level	Words	Author/Series	Publisher/Distributor
Drummers, The	H	80	Gould, Carol	Kaeden Books
Dry and Snug and Warm	G	64	Book Bank	Wright Group
Duck in the Gun, The	M	250+	Literacy 2000	Rigby
Duck with the Broken Wing, The	F	189	PM Extensions-Blue	Rigby
Duck, Duck, Goose!	E	92	My First Reader	Grolier Press
Ducks	D	94	Story Box	Wright Group
Dumpsideary Jelly	H	250+	Momentum Literacy Program	Troll
Dynamic Duos	P	250+	Moore, David	Scholastic
E Is for Elisa	O	250+	Hurwitz, Johanna	The Penguin Group
Each Peach Pear Plum	G	115	Ahlberg, Allan & Janet	The Penguin Group
Eagle Flies High, An	G	142	Ready Readers	Pearson Learning
Eagle in the Sky	L	250+	Little Celebrations	Pearson Learning
Ear Book	E		Perkins, Al	Random House
Early in the Morning	D	55	Rise & Shine	Hampton-Brown
Ears	C	37	Rise & Shine	Hampton-Brown
Earth and Moon	G	250	Sunshine	Wright Group
Earthquake	E	40	Wonder World	Wright Group
Earthquake	M	415	Jellybeans	Rigby
Earthworm, The	H	157	Wonder World	Wright Group
Easter	E	112	Fiesta Holiday Series	Dominie
Easter Bunny's Lost Egg	G	174	First Start	Troll
Eat Up!	G	95	Sunshine	Wright Group
Eat Up, Gemma	I	463	Hayes, Sarah	Sundance
Eat Your Peas, Louise	E	83	Rookie Readers	Children's Press
Eat!	M	250+	Kroll, Steven	Hyperion
Eating	A	29	Foundations	Wright Group
Eating Apples	A	17	Pebble Books	Grolier, Capstone
Eating Lunch at School	I	170	City Kids	Rigby
Eating Out	C	31	Sunshine	Wright Group
Ebenezer and the Sneeze	D	77	Story Box	Wright Group
Eddie and the Fire Engine	P	250+	Haywood, Carolyn	Beech Tree Books
Edgar Badger's Balloon Day	L	864	Book Shop	Mondo Publishing
Edward's Night Light	M	622	Reading Corners	Dominie
Effie	K	250+	Allinson, Beverly	Scholastic
Egg	K	250+	Logan, Dick	Cypress
Egg to Chick	J	250+	Selsam, Millicent	HarperTrophy
Egg, The	C	48	Joy Readers	Dominie
Eggs and Baby Birds	M	539	Sunshine	Wright Group
Eggs for Breakfast	D	126	PM Nonfiction-Red	Rigby
Eggs!	B	28	Ready Readers	Pearson Learning
Eggs, Eggs, Eggs	J	188	Wonder World	Wright Group
Eggs, Larvae and Flies	K	450	Sunshine	Wright Group
Eggshell Garden, The	A	14	Sunshine	Wright Group
Eight Friends in All	D	64	Ready Readers	Pearson Learning
Elaine	J	250+	Stepping Stones	Nelson/Michaels Assoc.
Elaine and the Flying Frog	K	250+	Chang, Heidi	Scholastic
Electric Spark and Other Cases, The	O	250+	Simon, Seymour	Avon Books
Electrifying Cows and Other Cases, The	O	250+	Simon, Seymour	Avon Books
Elena Makes Tortillas	A	18	Pacific Literacy	Pacific Learning

Title	Level	Words	Author/Series	Publisher/Distributor
Elephant and Envelope	G	158	Gregorich, Barbara	School Zone
Elephant and the Bad Baby, The	J	250+	Hayes, Sarah	Sundance
Elephant for the Holidays, An	I	118	Sunshine	Wright Group
Elephant in the House, An	J	546	Read Alongs	Rigby
Elephant in Trouble	H	98	First Start	Troll
Elephant Walk	C	44	Sunshine	Wright Group
Elephants	H	224	Foundations	Wright Group
Elephants	K	250+	PM Animals in the Wild-Yellow	Rigby
Elephants Are Coming, The	E	138	Little Readers	Houghton Mifflin
Elephant's Trunk, An	C	31	Little Celebrations	Pearson Learning
Elevator	D	90	Story Box	Wright Group
Eleven Kids, One Summer	O	250+	Martin, Ann M.	Scholastic
Elisa in the Middle	O	250+	Hurwitz, Johanna	The Penguin Group
Eliza the Hypnotizer	M	250+	Granger, Michelle	Scholastic
Elizabeth Blackwell: First Woman Doctor	N	250+	Rookie Biographies	Children's Press
Elizabeth the First: Queen of England	N	250+	Rookie Biographies	Children's Press
Ellen Tebbits	P	250+	Cleary, Beverly	Avon Camelot
Elmer and the Dragon	M	250+	Gannett, Ruth Stiles	Random House
Elves and the Shoemaker, The	K	300	PM Trad. Tales & Plays-Turq.	Rigby
Elves and the Shoemaker, The	K	622	New Way Orange	Steck-Vaughn
Elves Don't Wear Hard Hats, The	M	250+	Dadey, Debbie & Jones, Marcia	Scholastic
Elvis the Turnip…And Me	M	250+	Greenburg, Dan	Grosset & Dunlap
Emil	J	250+	Stepping Stones	Nelson/Michaels Assoc.
Emilio and the River	M	403	Sunshine	Wright Group
Emily Arrow Promises to Do Better This Year	M	250+	Giff, Patricia Reilly	Bantam Doubleday Dell
Emily Dickinson: American Poet	N	250+	Rookie Biographies	Children's Press
Emily Eyefinger	M	250+	Ball, Duncan	Aladdin
Emily Loved Yellow	I	99	Sunshine	Wright Group
Emily's Babysitter	C	67	Emergent	Pioneer Valley
Emily's Runaway Imagination	P	250+	Cleary, Beverly	Avon Camelot
Emma, the Birthday Clown	M	1887	Sunshine	Wright Group
Emma's Problem	H	190	Literacy 2000	Rigby
Emperor's New Clothes, The	J	571	Tales from Hans Andersen	Wright Group
Empty Envelope, The	N	250+	Roy, Ron	Random House
Encyclopedia Brown & Case of Mysterious Handprint	P	250+	Sobol, Donald & Rose	Bantam Doubleday Dell
Encyclopedia Brown & Case of the Disgusting Sneakers	P	250+	Sobol, Donald & Rose	Bantam Doubleday Dell
Encyclopedia Brown Boy Detective	P	250+	Sobol, Donald & Rose	Bantam Doubleday Dell
Encyclopedia Brown Case of the Dead Eagles	P	250+	Sobol, Donald & Rose	Bantam Doubleday Dell
Encyclopedia Brown Case of the Midnight Visitor	P	250+	Sobol, Donald & Rose	Bantam Doubleday Dell
Encyclopedia Brown Case of the Secret Pitch	P	250+	Sobol, Donald & Rose	Bantam Doubleday Dell
Encyclopedia Brown Case of the Treasure Hunt	P	250+	Sobol, Donald & Rose	Bantam Doubleday Dell
Encyclopedia Brown Case of the Two Spies	P	250+	Sobol, Donald & Rose	Bantam Doubleday Dell
Encyclopedia Brown Finds the Clues	P	250+	Sobol, Donald & Rose	Bantam Doubleday Dell
Encyclopedia Brown Gets His Man	P	250+	Sobol, Donald & Rose	Bantam Doubleday Dell
Encyclopedia Brown Keeps the Peace	P	250+	Sobol, Donald & Rose	Bantam Doubleday Dell
Encyclopedia Brown Lends a Hand	P	250+	Sobol, Donald & Rose	Bantam Doubleday Dell
Encyclopedia Brown Saves the Day	P	250+	Sobol, Donald & Rose	Bantam Doubleday Dell
Encyclopedia Brown Shows the Way	P	250+	Sobol, Donald & Rose	Bantam Doubleday Dell
Encyclopedia Brown Solves Them All	P	250+	Sobol, Donald & Rose	Bantam Doubleday Dell

Title	Level	Words	Author/Series	Publisher/Distributor
Encyclopedia Brown Takes the Case	P	250+	Sobol, Donald & Rose	Bantam Doubleday Dell
Encyclopedia Brown Tracks Them Down	P	250+	Sobol, Donald & Rose	Bantam Doubleday Dell
Encyclopedia Brown's Book of Strange But True Crimes	P	250+	Sobol, Donald & Rose	Scholastic
Engelbert the Hero	H		Little Celebrations	Pearson Learning
Engelbert's Exercises	E	23	Little Celebrations	Pearson Learning
Engines	E	81	Sunshine	Wright Group
Enormous Crocodile, The	N	250+	Dahl, Roald	Puffin Books
Enormous Turnip	H	431	Hunia, Fran	Ladybird Books
Enormous Watermelon, The	H	304	Traditional Tales & More	Rigby
Erik and the Three Goats	H	257	Ready Readers	Pearson Learning
Er-Lang and the Suns: A Tale from China	M	250+	Folk Tales	Mondo Publishing
Eruption	P	250+	Wildcats	Wright Group
Escalator, The	A	23	Story Box	Wright Group
Eureka! It's an Airplane	N	250+	Bendick, Jeanne	Scholastic
Eve Shops	F	146	Ready Readers	Pearson Learning
Every Bird Has a Beak	E	49	Birds Series	Dominie
Every Bird Has Feathers	E	50	Birds Series	Dominie
Every Bird has Two Feet	E	46	Birds Series	Dominie
Every Day But Sunday	E	83	Home Connection Collection	Rigby
Every Monday	C	52	Pair-It Books	Steck-Vaughn
Every Morning	A	30	Twig	Wright Group
Every Mother Bird Builds a Nest	E	62	Birds Series	Dominie
Every Shape and Size	G	97	Wonder World	Wright Group
Everybody Cooks Rice	M	250+	Dooley, Norah	Scholastic
Everybody Eats Bread	J	241	Literacy 2000	Rigby
Everybody Says	G	70	Rookie Readers	Children's Press
Everyday Forces	M	250+	Discovery World	Rigby
Everyday Math	D	102	Early Connections	Benchmark Education
Everyone Eats	C	44	Discovery Links	Newbridge
Everyone Knows About Cars	L	176	Book Shop	Mondo Publishing
Everyone Wears Wool	A	21	Pair-It Books	Steck-Vaughn
Everything Changes	K	250+	Discovery World	Rigby
Excuses, Excuses	E	104	Tadpoles	Rigby
Experiment with Movement	N	250+	Murphy, Bryan	Scholastic
Experiment with Water	N	250+	Murphy, Bryan	Scholastic
Explorers: Searching for Adventure	M	250+	Pair-It Books	Steck-Vaughn
Exploring Freshwater Habitats	P	250+	Snowball, Diane	Mondo
Exploring Land Habitats	P	250+	Phinney, Margaret Y.	Mondo
Exploring Saltwater Habitats	P	250+	Smith, Sue	Mondo
Exploring Tree Habitats	P	250+	Seifert, Patti	Mondo
Expressway Jewels	M	368	Evangeline Nicholas Collection	Wright Group
Eye Spy	P	250+	Wildcats	Wright Group
Eyes	C	64	Wonder World	Wright Group
Eyes are Everywhere	E	131	Ready Readers	Pearson Learning
Fables by Aesop	K	250+	Reading Unlimited	Pacific Learning
Fabulous Animal Families	K	250+	Home Connection Collection	Rigby
Fabulous Freckles	K	250+	Literacy 2000	Rigby
Fabulous Fruits	D	121	Fiesta Series	Dominie

Title	Level	Words	Author/Series	Publisher/Distributor
Face in the Dark, The	D	64	Storyteller-Setting Sun	Wright Group/ McGraw-Hill
Face Painting	G	90	Wonder World	Wright Group
Face Sandwich, The	A	16	Sunshine	Wright Group
Face-Off	O	250+	Christopher, Matt	Little, Brown & Co.
Faces	B	27	Sunshine	Wright Group
Faces	D		Little Celebrations	Pearson Learning
Fair Day	J	184	City Kids	Rigby
Falcon's Feathers, the	N	250+	Roy, Ron	Random House
Fall	A	22	Little Books for Early Readers	University of Maine
Fall	B	12	Discovery Links	Newbridge
Fall	E	73	Sunshine	Wright Group
Fall Harvest	A	16	Little Books for Early Readers	University of Maine
Fall Harvest	E	39	Pebble Books	Grolier, Capstone
Families	D	60	Pebble Books	Grolier, Capstone
Families	F	132	Twig	Wright Group
Families	H	160	Early Connections	Benchmark Education
Families	J	184	Storyteller-Night Crickets	Wright Group/ McGraw-Hill
Families	B	49	Interaction	Rigby
Families Are Different	K	250+	Pellegrini, Nina	Scholastic
Family Counts	B	19	Rise & Shine	Hampton-Brown
Family Names	D	36	Visions	Wright Group
Family of Five, A	C	26	Pair-It Books	Steck-Vaughn
Family on Lake Street, The	F	159	Teacher's Choice Series	Dominie
Family Pets	C	37	Pebble Books	Grolier, Capstone
Family Photos	F	106	Literacy 2000	Rigby
Family Reunion	G	243	Visions	Wright Group
Family Soccer	D	55	Geddes, Diana	Kaeden Books
Family Time	B	16	Pair-It Books	Steck-Vaughn
Family Tree, The	G	213	Ready Readers	Pearson Learning
Family, The	E	55	Sunshine	Wright Group
Fancy Dress Parade, The	H	171	Stepping Stones	Nelson/Michaels Assoc.
Fancy Feet	M	250+	Giff, Patricia Reilly	Bantam Doubleday Dell
Fans and Umbrellas	E	107	Joy Readers	Dominie
Fantail, Fantail	D	67	Ready to Read	Pacific Learning
Fantail, Fantail	D	67	Pacific Literacy	Pacific Learning
Fantastic Cake, The	E	169	Story Box	Wright Group
Fantastic Mr. Fox	P	250+	Dahl, Roald	The Penguin Group
Fantastic Water Pot and Other Cases, The	O	250+	Simon, Seymour	Avon Books
Far Away Moon	G	80	Pacific Literacy	Pacific Learning
Farley Frog	B	33	Pair-It Books	Steck-Vaughn
Farm Concert, The	D	74	Story Box	Wright Group
Farm Day	D	36	Little Celebrations	Pearson Learning
Farm in Spring, The	D	69	PM Starters	Rigby
Farm Life Long Ago	L	436	Pair-It Books	Steck-Vaughn
Farm, A	A	28	Little Books for Early Readers	University of Maine
Farm, The	A	14	Smart Starts	Rigby
Farm, The	A	14	Ready Readers	Pearson Learning
Farm, The	A	14	Literacy 2000	Rigby
Farm, The	A	28	Little Books for Early Readers	University of Maine

Title	Level	Words	Author/Series	Publisher/Distributor
Farm, The	B	21	Sunshine	Wright Group
Farm, The	I	228	Pebble Books	Grolier, Capstone
Farmer and His Two Lazy Sons, The	J	250+	Aesop's Fables	Dominie
Farmer Brown's Garden	C	48	Windmill Books	Rigby
Farmer in the Dell	E		Parkinson, Kathy	Whitman
Farmer in the Soup, The	K	250+	Littledale, Freya	Scholastic
Farmer Joe's Hot Day	J	406	Richards, Nancy W.	Scholastic
Farmer's Journey, The	M	250+	Little Celebrations	Pearson Learning
Farms	F	102	Sunshine	Wright Group
Farms	F	153	Foundations	Wright Group
Farms	N	606	Wonders	Hampton-Brown
Farmyard Fiasco, A	H	186	Book Bank	Wright Group
Far-Out Frisbee and Other Cases, The	O	250+	Simon, Seymour	Avon Books
Fasi Sings and Fasi's Fish	I	204	Ready to Read	Pacific Learning
Fast and Funny	K	1499	Story Box	Wright Group
Fast Draw Freddie	D	50	Rookie Readers	Children's Press
Fast Food	D	112	Foundations	Wright Group
Fast Food for Butterflies	I	170	Storyteller-Moon Rising	Wright Group/ McGraw-Hill
Fast Machines	D	146	Foundations	Wright Group
Fast, Faster, Fastest	C	66	Twig	Wright Group
Fastest Gazelle, The	E	146	Literacy 2000	Rigby
Fastest Ketchup in the Cafeteria and Other Cases, The	O	250+	Simon, Seymour	Avon Books
Fat Cat	I	250+	Kent, Jack	Scholastic
Fat Cat Sat on the Mat, The	G	250+	Karlin, Nurit	HarperTrophy
Fat Cat Tompkin	I	196	Voyages	SRA/McGraw-Hill
Father Bear Comes Home	I	331	Minarik, Else H.	HarperCollins
Father Bear Goes Fishing	D	98	PM Story Books	Rigby
Father Bear's Surprise	H	224	PM Extensions-Green	Rigby
Father Who Walked on Hands	K	344	Literacy 2000	Rigby
Fathers	B	26	Pebble Books	Grolier, Capstone
Favorite Greek Myths	N	250+	Osborne, Mary Pope	Scholastic
Feathers and Flight	I	790	Sunshine	Wright Group
Feeding the Baby	C	51	Home Connection Collection	Rigby
Feeding Time	C	55	Carousel Readers	Dominie
Feeding Time at the Zoo	D	73	Windmill Books	Rigby
Feelings	D	39	Rise & Shine	Hampton-Brown
Feet	A	14	Foundations	Wright Group
Feet	D	18	Story Box	Wright Group
Feisty Old Woman Who Lived in the Cozy Cave, The	F	301	Foundations	Wright Group
Felicia the Critic	P	250+	Conford, Ellen	Little, Brown & Co.
Felix, the Very Hungry Fish	C	32	Little Books	Sadlier-Oxford
Fergus and Bridey	K	250+	Little Celebrations	Pearson Learning
Fern and Burt	H	250+	Ready Readers	Pearson Learning
Ferry, The	C	27	Sunshine	Wright Group
Festival, The	D	146	Fiesta Series	Dominie
Fibers from Plants	I	392	Sunshine	Wright Group
Fibers Made by People	M	442	Sunshine	Wright Group
Fiddle and the Gun, The	M	250+	Literacy 2000	Rigby

Title	Level	Words	Author/Series	Publisher/Distributor
Fiesta Time	C	28	Little Celebrations	Pearson Learning
Fight in the Schoolyard, The	K	129	City Kids	Rigby
Fight on the Hill, The	J	336	Read Alongs	Rigby
Fighting Tackle	M	250+	Christopher, Matt	Little, Brown & Co.
Fiji Flood, The	M	250+	Schultz, Irene	Wright Group
Filbert the Fly	C	28	Literacy 2000	Rigby
Finches' Fabulous Furnace, The	O	250+	Drury, Roger	Scholastic
Find a Caterpillar	E	102	Book Bank	Wright Group
Find It	C	63	Carousel Earlybirds	Dominie
Find Yourself a Friend	F	261	Visions	Wright Group
Finding Providence: The Story of Roger Williams	L	250+	Avi	HarperTrophy
Finding the Titanic	P	250+	Ballard, Robert D.	Scholastic
Finger Puppet, The	B	18	Sunshine	Wright Group
Finger Puppets, Finger Plays	I	268	Storyteller-Night Crickets	Wright Group/ McGraw-Hill
Fire and Water	E	127	Story Box	Wright Group
Fire at the Triangle Factory	P	250+	Littlefield, Holly	Carolrhoda Books
Fire at the Zoo, A	I	229	Sunshine	Wright Group
Fire Boats	I	188	Pebble Books	Grolier, Capstone
Fire Cat, The	J	250+	Averill, Esther	HarperTrophy
Fire Engines	I	184	Pebble Books	Grolier, Capstone
Fire Station, The	J	237	Pebble Books	Grolier, Capstone
Fire! Fire!	K	250+	Wildcats	Wright Group
Fire, Fire	E	164	PM Story Books	Rigby
Fireflies	E	49	Pebble Books	Grolier, Capstone
Firehouse Sal	F	52	Rookie Readers	Children's Press
Fireworks	C	29	Joy Readers	Dominie
First and Last	C	44	Teacher's Choice Series	Dominie
First Day Back at School	H	132	City Kids	Rigby
First Day of School	B	16	Visions	Wright Group
First Day of School	D	60	Carousel Readers	Dominie
First Fire, The	K	250+	Little Celebrations	Pearson Learning
First Flight	K	250+	Shea, George	HarperTrophy
First Grade Takes a Test	J	250+	Cohen, Miriam	Bantam Doubleday Dell
First in Line	D	77	Teacher's Choice Series	Dominie
First Things	A	18	Home Connection Collection	Rigby
First Things	N	250+	Stepping Stones	Nelson/Michaels Assoc.
Fish	D	58	Wonder World	Wright Group
Fish	L	298	Marine Life for Young Readers	Dominie
Fish Face	M	250+	Giff, Patricia Reilly	Bantam Doubleday Dell
Fish from the Rainbow	I	239	Sunshine	Wright Group
Fishing	B	41	Little Books for Early Readers	University of Maine
Fishing	C	35	Story Box	Wright Group
Fishing	C	35	KinderReaders	Rigby
Fishing	C	63	PM Starters	Rigby
Fishing	D	48	Yukish, Joe	Kaeden Books
Fishing	E	47	Wonder World	Wright Group
Fishing	G	180	Foundations	Wright Group
Fishing Off the Wharf	M	274	Pacific Literacy	Pacific Learning
Fishy Alphabet Story	F	126	Wylie, Joanne & David	Children's Press
Fishy Color Story	D	142	Wylie, Joanne & David	Children's Press

Title	Level	Words	Author/Series	Publisher/Distributor
Fishy Story, A	C	102	Pair-It Books	Steck-Vaughn
Fitness	C	60	Foundations	Wright Group
Five Brave Explorers	P	250+	Hudson, Wade	Scholastic
Five Ducks	D	89	Joy Readers	Dominie
Five Funny Frights	K	250+	Stamper, Judith Bauer	Scholastic
Five Little Dinosaurs	E	113	Ready Readers	Pearson Learning
Five Little Monkeys	F	81	Book Shop	Mondo Publishing
Five Little Monkeys Going to the Zoo	E	201	Cutteridge's, V's First Grade	Seedling
Five Little Monkeys Jumping on the Bed	E	200	Christelow, Eileen	Houghton Mifflin
Five Little Monsters	D		Learn to Read	Creative Teaching Press
Five Notable Inventors	P	250+	Hudson, Wade	Scholastic
Five Silly Fishermen	E	250+	Edwards, Roberta	Random House
Five True Dog Stories	M	250+	Davidson, Margaret	Scholastic
Five True Horse Stories	M	250+	Davidson, Margaret	Scholastic
Fix It	I	171	McPhail, David	The Penguin Group
Fix It, Fox	E	62	Ready Readers	Pearson Learning
Fizz and Splutter	E	92	Story Box	Wright Group
Flat Hat, The	C	24	KinderReaders	Rigby
Flat Stanley	N	250+	Brown, Jeff	HarperTrophy
Flea Story, A	L	250+	Lionni, Leo	Scholastic
Flies	F	56	Pebble Books	Grolier, Capstone
Flight Deck	C	30	Wonder World	Wright Group
Flight of the Union, The	L	250+	White, Tekla	Carolrhoda Books
Flip Flop	G	70	Books for Young Learners	Richard C. Owen
Flip's Trick	H	134	Ready Readers	Pearson Learning
Floating and Sinking	H	168	Sunshine	Wright Group
Floating and Sinking	J	279	Book Shop	Mondo Publishing
Flood, The	H	237	PM Story Books	Rigby
Flood, The	I	138	Wonder World	Wright Group
Floppy the Hero	F	74	Oxford Reading Tree	Oxford University Press
Floppy's Bath	E	55	Oxford Reading Tree	Oxford University Press
Flora, a Friend for the Animals	J	337	Sunshine	Wright Group
Florence Kelley	P	250+	Saller, Carol	Carolrhoda Books
Flossie and the Fox	O	250+	McKissack, Patricia	Scholastic
Flour	K	174	Wonder World	Wright Group
Flower Box, The	B	14	Twig	Wright Group
Flower Girl, The	C	90	PM Extensions-Red	Rigby
Flower Girls #1: Violet	L	250+	Leverich, Kathleen	HarperTrophy
Flower Girls #2: Daisy	L	250+	Leverich, Kathleen	HarperTrophy
Flower Girls #3: Heather	L	250+	Leverich, Kathleen	HarperTrophy
Flower Girls #4: Rose	L	250+	Leverich, Kathleen	HarperTrophy
Flower of Sheba, The	L	250+	Orgel, Doris & Schecter, Ellen	Bantam Doubleday Dell
Flowers	A	27	Hoenecke, Karen	Kaeden Books
Flowers	L	270	Pebble Books	Grolier, Capstone
Flowers for Mom	E	88	Carousel Readers	Dominie
Flowers for Mrs. Falepau	M	857	Book Bank	Wright Group
Flows & Quakes and Spinning Winds	K	250+	Home Connection Collection	Rigby
Fluffy Chicks	E	50	Book Bank	Wright Group
Flunking of Joshua T. Bates, The	N	250+	Shreve, Susan	Scholastic
Fly Away Home	I	250+	Wonder World	Wright Group
Fly High	B	24	Visions	Wright Group
Fly Trap	L	250+	Anastasio, Dina	Grosset & Dunlap

Title	Level	Words	Author/Series	Publisher/Distributor
Fly, Butterfly	F	49	Discovery Links	Newbridge
Flying	C	26	Story Box	Wright Group
Flying and Floating	B	64	Little Red Readers	Sundance
Flying Fingers	K	250+	Literacy 2000	Rigby
Flying Fish, The	H	215	PM Extensions-Green	Rigby
Flying High	F	250+	Predictable Storybooks	SRA/McGraw-Hill
Flying Trunk, The	M	644	Tales from Hans Andersen	Wright Group
Flying-Saucer People and Other Cases, The	O	250+	Simon, Seymour	Avon Books
Folk Dancer	C	36	The Candid Collection	Dominie
Follow That Fish	K	250+	Oppenheim, Joanne	Bantam Doubleday Dell
Follow the Leader	B	15	Windmill	Rigby, Wright Group
Follow the Leader	D	75	Teacher's Choice Series	Dominie
Food Around the World	I	298	Early Connections	Benchmark Education
Food for Healthy Teeth	E	40	Pebble Books	Grolier, Capstone
Food from the Farm	D	78	Home Connection Collection	Rigby
Food Journey, The	K	116	Home Connection Collection	Rigby
Food to Eat	B	29	Little Readers	Houghton Mifflin
Food Trappers	I	165	Wonder World	Wright Group
Foolish Gretel	O	250+	Armstrong, Jennifer	Random House
Foot Book	E		Seuss, Dr.	Random House
Football	B	28	Visions	Wright Group
Football Fever	H	51	Pacific Literacy	Pacific Learning
Football Friends	L	250+	Marzollo, Jean, Dan, & Dave	Scholastic
Football Fugitive	M	250+	Christopher, Matt	Little, Brown & Co.
Footprints in the Snow	D		Benjamin, Cynthia	Scholastic
For Breakfast	B	22	Visions	Wright Group
Forever Amber Brown	N	250+	Danziger, Paula	Scholastic
Forgetful Fred	E	78	Tadpoles	Rigby
Forgotten Door, The	P	250+	Key, Alexander	Scholastic
Forty-Three Cats	K	232	Sunshine	Wright Group
Four A's, The	P	250+	Wildcats	Wright Group
Four Getters and Arf, The	G	123	Little Celebrations	Pearson Learning
Four Ice Creams	C	61	PM Starters	Rigby
Four on the Shore	K	250+	Marshall, Edward	Puffin Books
Fourth of July, The	F	153	Ready Readers	Pearson Learning
Fourth of July, The	G	120	Fiesta Holiday Series	Dominie
Fox All Week	J	250+	Marshall, Edward	Puffin Books
Fox and His Friends	J	250+	Marshall, Edward	Puffin Books
Fox and the Crow, The	I	250+	Aesop	Wright Group
Fox and the Crow, The	J	250+	Aesop's Fables	Dominie
Fox and the Crow, The	K	250+	Ready Readers	Pearson Learning
Fox and the Goat, The	I	365	Aesop's Fables	Dominie
Fox and the Little Red Hen	L	400	Traditional Tales & More	Rigby
Fox and the Stork	H	149	New Way Blue	Steck-Vaughn
Fox at School	J	250+	Marshall, Edward	Puffin Books
Fox Be Nimble	J	250+	Marshall, James	Puffin Books
Fox in Love	J	250+	Marshall, Edward	Puffin Books
Fox Lives Here, A	I	160	Ready Readers	Pearson Learning
Fox on Stage	J	250+	Marshall, James	Puffin Books
Fox on the Box, The	C	36	Gregorich, Barbara	School Zone
Fox on the Box, The	C	36	Little Readers	Houghton Mifflin

Title	Level	Words	Author/Series	Publisher/Distributor
Fox on the Job	J	250+	Marshall, James	Puffin Books
Fox on Wheels	J	250+	Marshall, Edward	Puffin Books
Fox Outfoxed	J	250+	Marshall, James	Puffin Books
Fox Steals Home, The	M	250+	Christopher, Matt	Little, Brown & Co.
Fox Who Was Foxed, The	H	212	PM Story Books	Rigby
Fox, The	C	24	Books for Young Learners	Richard C. Owen
Foxes	K	250+	PM Animal Facts-Gold	Rigby
Fraidy Cats	J	250+	Krensky, Stephen	Scholastic
Frankenstein Doesn't Plant Petunias	M	250+	Dadey, Debbie	Scholastic
Frankenstein Doesn't Slam Hockey Pucks	M	250+	Dadey, Debbie & Jones, Marcia	Scholastic
Frankenstein Moved on to the 4th Floor	M	250+	Levy, Elizabeth	Harper & Row
Franklin Goes to School	K	250+	Bourgeois, Paulette & Clark, Brenda	Scholastic
Franklin Plays the Game	J	250+	Bourgeois, Paulette & Clark, Brenda	Scholastic
Freckle Juice	M	250+	Blume, Judy	Bantam Doubleday Dell
Fred Said	D	35	Sunshine	Wright Group
Freddie the Frog	D	132	First Start	Troll
Freddie's Spaghetti	F	250+	Doyle, R. H.	Random House
Freddy Frog's Note	H	253	Ready Readers	Pearson Learning
Freddy's Train Ride	K	573	Pair-It Books	Steck-Vaughn
Free to Fly	E	96	Gibson, Kathleen	Seedling
Friend for Dragon, A	I	250+	Pilkey, Dav	Orchard Paperbacks
Friend for Little White Rabbit	E	113	PM Story Books	Rigby
Friend, A	G	57	Literacy 2000	Rigby
Friendly Crocodile, The	I	218	Hiris, Monica	Kaeden Books
Friendly Snowman	F	134	First Start	Troll
Friendly Snowman	F		Joyce, William	Scholastic
Friends	B	36	Little Readers	Houghton Mifflin
Friends	D	57	Book Shop	Mondo Publishing
Friends	D	134	Fiesta Series	Dominie
Friends	G	195	Reading Unlimited	Pacific Learning
Friends	I	313	Early Connections	Benchmark Education
Friends are Forever	K	585	Literacy 2000	Rigby
Friends Forever	I	250+	Ready Readers	Pearson Learning
Friends Go Together	D	36	Pair-It Books	Steck-Vaughn
Friendship Garden, The	K	250+	Little Celebrations	Pearson Learning
Frightened	B	42	Story Box	Wright Group
Frito Jumps In	D	34	Step-By-Step Series	Dominie
Frog Prince, The	H	526	Sunshine	Wright Group
Frog and the Fly, The	D	33	Cat on the Mat	Oxford University Press
Frog and Toad All Year	K	250+	Little Readers	Houghton Mifflin
Frog and Toad are Friends	K	250+	Lobel, Arnold	Harper & Row
Frog and Toad Together	K	1927	Lobel, Arnold	HarperCollins
Frog and Toad Together	K	250+	Little Readers	Houghton Mifflin
Frog or Toad?	I	241	Ready Readers	Pearson Learning
Frog Prince, The	I	572	Traditional Tales	Dominie
Frog Prince, The	K	250+	Tarcov, Edith H.	Scholastic
Frog Princess, The	K	206	Literacy 2000	Rigby
Frog Who Thought He Was a Horse, The	L	250+	Literacy 2000	Rigby
Frog Who Would Be King, The	M	250+	Walker, Kate	Mondo
Froggy Learns to Swim	J	250+	London, Jonathan	Scholastic
Froggy Tale, The	I	250+	Literacy 2000	Rigby

Title	Level	Words	Author/Series	Publisher/Distributor
Frogs	A	13	Twig	Wright Group
Frogs	C	34	Pair-It Books	Steck-Vaughn
Frogs	C	36	Joy Readers	Dominie
Frogs	D	28	Pebble Books	Grolier, Capstone
Frogs	G	100	Storyteller-First Snow	Wright Group/ McGraw-Hill
Frogs	K	311	Wonder World	Wright Group
Frogs	N	1440	Book Shop	Mondo Publishing
Frogs Can Jump	C	41	Book Bank	Wright Group
Frog's Lunch	F	89	Lillgard, Dee & Zimmerman, J.	Scholastic
Frogs on a Log	D	75	Teacher's Choice Series	Dominie
From Blossom to Fruit	E	44	Pebble Books	Grolier, Capstone
From Bud to Blossom	D	40	Pebble Books	Grolier, Capstone
From Rocks to Sand: The Story of a Beach	J	224	Wonder World	Wright Group
From Sky to Sea	H	40	Pacific Literacy	Pacific Learning
From the Air	E	107	Wonder World	Wright Group
From the Earth	J	186	Discovery Links	Newbridge
Frown, The	K	228	Read Alongs	Rigby
Fruit	B	20	Rise & Shine	Hampton-Brown
Fruit Salad	A	15	Literacy 2000	Rigby
Fruit Salad	B	24	Early Emergent	Pioneer Valley
Fruit Salad	D	18	Hoenecke, Karen	Kaeden Books
Fruit Salad	D	37	Wonder World	Wright Group
Fruit Trees	B	24	Visions	Wright Group
Fun	D	45	Yannone, Deborah	Kaeden Books
Fun at Camp	H	178	First Start	Troll
Fun at School	C	50	Foundations	Wright Group
Fun at the Amusement Park	G	176	Frankford, Marilyn	Kaeden Books
Fun Food	C	29	Home Connection Collection	Rigby
Fun in the Mud	G	182	Foundations	Wright Group
Fun Place to Eat, A	E	90	Ready Readers	Pearson Learning
Fun Things to Make and Do	I	250+	Discovery World	Rigby
Fun with Friends	B	18	Rise & Shine	Hampton-Brown
Fun with Hats	B	38	Book Shop	Mondo Publishing
Fun with Mo and Toots	C	41	Ready to Read	Pacific Learning
Fun with Mo and Toots	C	41	Pacific Literacy	Pacific Learning
Funny Bones	J	250+	Ahlberg, Allan & Janet	Viking
Funny Faces and Funny Places	D	45	Ready Readers	Pearson Learning
Funny Fish Story	E	152	Rookie Readers	Children's Press
Funny Man, A	E	244	Jensen, Patricia	Scholastic
Funny Old Man and the Funny Old Woman, The	M	562	Book Shop	Mondo Publishing
Funny Talk and More	I	250+	Book Shop	Mondo Publishing
Fur	D		Mark, Jan	Harper & Row
Fur, Feathers, Scales, Skin	H	173	Discovery Links	Newbridge
Furry	B		Little Celebrations	Pearson Learning
Fuzz, Feathers, Fur	E	131	Twig	Wright Group
Gabby Is Hungry	C	78	Emergent	Pioneer Valley
Gadget War, the	N	250+	Douglas, Ann	The Penguin Group
Gail & Me	L	250+	Literacy 2000	Rigby
Gail Devers: A Runner's Dream	L	250+	Pair-It Books	Steck-Vaughn
Gallo and Zorro	J	369	Literacy 2000	Rigby

©1999 by I. C. Fountas & G. S. Pinnell from *Matching Books to Readers*. Portsmouth, NH: Heinemann. May not be reproduced without written permission of the publisher.

Title	Level	Words	Author/Series	Publisher/Distributor
Game for Jamie, A	M	572	Sunshine	Wright Group
Games	A	28	KinderReaders	Rigby
Garbage	C	51	Wonder World	Wright Group
Garden Colors	B	15	Pair-It Books	Steck-Vaughn
Garden, A	A	40	Foundations	Wright Group
Gardening	D	77	Foundations	Wright Group
Gardens on Green Street, The	I	174	TOTTS	Tott Publications
Gargoyles Don't Drive School Buses	M	250+	Dadey, Debbie & Jones, Marcia	Scholastic
Gasp!	L	529	Book Shop	Mondo Publishing
Gaston the Giant	M	331	New Way Orange	Steck-Vaughn
Gator Girls Book 2, The: Rockin Reptiles	L	250+	Calmenson, Stephanie & Cole	Beech Tree Books
Gator Girls, The	L	250+	Calmenson, Stephanie & Cole	Beech Tree Books
Gecko's Story	F	61	Books for Young Learners	Richard C. Owen
Genies Don't Ride Bicycles	M	250+	Dadey, Debbie & Jones, Marcia	Scholastic
Geoffrey the Dinosaur	D	36	Sunshine	Wright Group
George and Martha	L	250+	Marshall, James	Houghton Mifflin
George and Martha Back in Town	L	250+	Marshall, James	Houghton Mifflin
George and Martha Encore	L	250+	Marshall, James	Houghton Mifflin
George and Martha One Fine Day	L	250+	Marshall, James	Houghton Mifflin
George and Martha Rise and Shine	L	250+	Marshall, James	Houghton Mifflin
George and Martha Round and Round	L	250+	Marshall, James	Houghton Mifflin
George Shrinks	H	114	Joyce, William	Scholastic
George the Drummer Boy	K	250+	Benchley, Nathaniel	HarperTrophy
George Washington	L	270	Pebble Books	Grolier, Capstone
George Washington Carver: Scientist and Teacher	N	250+	Rookie Biographies	Children's Press
George Washington: First President of the U.S.	N	250+	Rookie Biographies	Children's Press
George Washington's Mother	M	250+	Fritz, Jean	Scholastic
George Washington's Socks	O	250+	Woodruff, Elvira	Scholastic
George's Marvelous Medicine	P	250+	Dahl, Roald	Puffin Books
Geraldine's Big Snow	I	250+	Keller, Holly	Scholastic
Gerbilitis	P	250+	Spinner, Stephanie & Weiss, E.	HarperTrophy
Get Lost Becka!	E	102	Start to Read	School Zone
Get Lost!	F	219	Foundations	Wright Group
Getting Around	H	211	Momentum Literacy Program	Troll
Getting Cold! Getting Hot!	K	753	Sunshine	Wright Group
Getting Dressed	A	16	Sunshine	Wright Group
Getting Dressed	B	40	Carousel Earlybirds	Dominie
Getting Fit	C	15	Wonder World	Wright Group
Getting Glasses	G	82	Wonder World	Wright Group
Getting Ready	B	29	Little Books for Early Readers	University of Maine
Getting Ready for School	E	109	Foundations	Wright Group
Getting Ready for the Ball	C	27	Literacy 2000	Rigby
Getting the Mail	G	213	Voyages	SRA/McGraw-Hill
Getting There	B	36	Wonder World	Wright Group
Getting to Know Sharks	K	379	Little Books	Sadlier-Oxford
Get-Up Machine, The	J	115	Sunshine	Wright Group
Ghost Dog	N	250+	Allen, Eleanor	Scholastic
Ghost Fox, The	P	250+	Yep, Laurence	Scholastic
Ghost in Tent 19, The	M	250+	O'Connor, Jim & Jane	Random House
Ghost Named Wanda, A	M	250+	Greenburg, Dan	Grosset & Dunlap
Ghost Pony, The	O	250+	Betancourt, Jeanne	Scholastic
Ghost Town at Sundown	M	250+	Osborne, Mary Pope	Random House

Title	Level	Words	Author/Series	Publisher/Distributor
Ghost Town Treasure	M	250+	Bulla, Clyde Robert	The Penguin Group
Ghost, The	A	26	Story Box	Wright Group
Ghosts Don't Eat Potato Chips	M	250+	Dadey, Debbie & Jones, Marcia	Scholastic
Ghosts' Secret, The	D	79	TOTTS	Tott Publications
Ghosts!	J	250+	Schwartz, Alvin	HarperTrophy
Ghosts! Ghostly Tales from Folklore	J	250+	Schwartz, Alvin	HarperTrophy
Ghouls Don't Scoop Ice Cream	M	250+	Dadey, Debbie & Jones, Marcia	Scholastic
Giant and the Boy, The	C	44	Sunshine	Wright Group
Giant in the Bed, The	H	253	New Way Green	Steck-Vaughn
Giant in the Forest, A	J	250+	Reading Unlimited	Pacific Learning
Giant Jack's Boots	M	420	Book Bank	Wright Group
Giant Jam Sandwich, The	K	250+	Vernon Lord, John	Houghton Mifflin
Giant Pandas	G	72	Pebble Books	Grolier, Capstone
Giant -Sized Day, A	I	245	Ready Readers	Pearson Learning
Giant Soup	J	419	Pacific Literacy	Pacific Learning
Giant, The	A	20	Joy Readers	Dominie
Giant's Boy, The	H	89	Sunshine	Wright Group
Giant's Breakfast, The	B	42	Literacy 2000	Rigby
Giant's Cake	M	250+	Learning Media	Mondo Publishing
Giant's Cake, The	H	162	Literacy 2000	Rigby
Giant's Day Out, The	B	26	Smart Starts	Rigby
Giants Don't Go Snowboarding	M	250+	Dadey, Debbie & Jones, Marcia	Scholastic
Giant's Job, The	H	180	Stewart, J. & Salem, Lynn	Seedling
Giant's Pizza, The	C	28	Joy Readers	Dominie
Giant's Rice, The	C	28	Joy Readers	Dominie
Giant's Stew, The	I	259	Sunshine	Wright Group
Giant-Size Hamburger, A	C	38	Wonder World	Wright Group
Giddy Up	C	49	Cat on the Mat	Oxford University Press
Gift for Mama, A	N	250+	Hautzig, Esther	The Penguin Group
Gift to Share, A	K	544	Pair-It Books	Steck-Vaughn
Gifts for Dad	H	178	Urmston, Kathleen & Evans, Karen	Kaeden Books
Gifts to Make	K	509	Pair-It Books	Steck-Vaughn
Gifts, The	B	34	Story Box	Wright Group
Gigantic Ants and Other Cases, The	O	250+	Simon, Seymour	Avon Books
Gigantic George	H		Little Celebrations	Pearson Learning
Giggle Box, The	E	176	Story Box	Wright Group
Ginger	I	232	Liitle Readers	Houghton Mifflin
Ginger Brown: The Nobody Boy	L	250+	Wyeth, Sharon	Random House
Ginger Brown: Too Many Houses	L	250+	Wyeth, Sharon	Random House
Ginger Pye	O	250+	Estes, Eleanor	Scholastic
Gingerbread Boy	F	137	New Way Red	Steck-Vaughn
Gingerbread Boy, The	L	1097	Galdone, Paul	Clarion
Gingerbread Man	I	250+	Hunia, Fran	Ladybird Books
Gingerbread Man, The	F	180	Little Readers	Houghton Mifflin
Gingerbread Man, The	H	197	Sunshine	Wright Group
Gingerbread Man, The	I	544	Traditional Tales	Dominie
Gingerbread Man, The	I	250+	Rose, Rita	Scholastic
Gingerbread Man, The	J	535	Traditional Tales & More	Rigby
Gingerbread Men, The	D	37	Sunshine	Wright Group
Giraffe and the Pelly and Me, The	P	250+	Dahl, Roald	Puffin Books
Girl Called Al, A	P	250+	Greene, Constance C.	The Penguin Group
Girl Who Climbed to the Moon, The	L	604	Sunshine	Wright Group

Title	Level	Words	Author/Series	Publisher/Distributor
Give Me a Hug	B	28	Sunshine	Wright Group
Give Me Back My Pony	O	250+	Betancourt, Jeanne	Scholastic
Gladys and Max Love Bob	M	459	Book Bank	Wright Group
Glass Slipper for Rosie, A	N	250+	Giff, Patricia Reilly	The Penguin Group
Glasses	D	19	Visions	Wright Group
Glenda	P	250+	Udry, Janice	HarperTrophy
Glenda the Lion	E	88	Ready Readers	Pearson Learning
Gloves	E	103	Story Box	Wright Group
Gluepots	K	205	Book Bank	Wright Group
Go and Hush the Baby	K	250+	Byars, Betsy	Viking
Go Away Dog	I	250+	Nodset, Joan	HarperCollins
Go Back to Sleep	E	74	Literacy 2000	Rigby
Go Dog Go	E		Eastman, Philip D.	Random House
Go Sea It!	A	16	Little Celebrations	Pearson Learning
Go to Bed	D	45	Joy Readers	Dominie
Go, Go, Go	A	17	Story Box	Wright Group
Go, Go, Go	A	23	Little Books for Early Readers	University of Maine
Goat, The	C	17	KinderReaders	Rigby
Gobble, Gobble, Gone	D	58	Little Celebrations	Pearson Learning
Go-cart Day	K	165	City Kids	Rigby
Go-cart, The	E	47	Oxford Reading Tree	Oxford University Press
Go-carts, The	B	46	PM Starters	Rigby
Godzilla Ate My Homework	O	250+	Jones, Marcia	Scholastic
Goes to the Races	H	158	The Monster Bus Series	Dominie
Goggly Gookers	H	100	Story Basket	Wright Group
Goha and His Donkey	I	114	Books for Young Learners	Richard C. Owen
Going Fishing	B	22	Ready Readers	Pearson Learning
Going Fishing	C	30	Visions	Wright Group
Going Fishing	E	26	Literacy 2000	Rigby
Going Fishing	F	26	Voyages	SRA/McGraw-Hill
Going Fishing	I	250+	Momentum Literacy Program	Troll
Going for a Ride	B	40	Little Books for Early Readers	University of Maine
Going for a Ride	C	52	Early Emergent	Pioneer Valley
Going in the Car	B	24	Sunshine	Wright Group
Going on a Field Trip	I	288	Visions	Wright Group
Going Out	A	42	KinderReaders	Rigby
Going Out	D	94	Foundations	Wright Group
Going Places	K	410	Early Connections	Benchmark Education
Going Shopping	D	92	Carousel Readers	Dominie
Going Shopping	F	112	Book Shop	Mondo Publishing
Going Swimming	J	210	City Kids	Rigby
Going to a Football Game	I	131	City Kids	Rigby
Going to Grandpa's	C	37	Frankford, Marilyn	Kaeden Books
Going to Lucy's House	E	151	Sunshine	Wright Group
Going to School	A	21	Smart Starts	Rigby
Going to School	C	43	Story Box	Wright Group
Going to School	C	50	Sunshine	Wright Group
Going to School	F	171	Foundations	Wright Group
Going to the Bank	J	317	Foundations	Wright Group
Going to the Beach	A	30	Ready to Read	Pacific Learning
Going to the Beach	A	30	Pacific Literacy	Pacific Learning
Going to the Beach	C	75	Carousel Readers	Dominie

Title	Level	Words	Author/Series	Publisher/Distributor
Going to the Dentist	F	122	Pebble Books	Grolier, Capstone
Going to the Hairdresser	J	227	Foundations	Wright Group
Going to the Hospital	H	335	Foundations	Wright Group
Going to the Park	C	41	Home Connection Collection	Rigby
Going to the Park with Grandaddy	C	30	Visions	Wright Group
Going to the Pool	D	55	Pair-It Books	Steck-Vaughn
Going to the Symphony	G	132	Twig	Wright Group
Going to the Vet	D	46	Sunshine	Wright Group
Going Up and Down	B	51	Early Emergent	Pioneer Valley
Going Up?	B		Little Celebrations	Pearson Learning
Golden Goose, The	L	731	Sunshine	Wright Group
Golden Goose, The	M	250+	Literacy 2000	Rigby
Golden Lasso, The	H	250+	Home Connection Collection	Rigby
Goldfish	I	250+	PM Animal Facts: Pets-Orange	Rigby
Goldilocks	G	244	Sunshine	Wright Group
Goldilocks & the Three Bears	E		Hunia, Fran	Ladybird Books
Goldilocks and the Three Bears	C	54	Little Books	Sadlier-Oxford
Goldilocks and the Three Bears	G	265	Storyteller Nonfiction	Wright Group/ McGraw-Hill
Goldilocks and the Three Bears	H	250+	Traditional Tales & More	Rigby
Goldilocks and the Three Bears	K	250+	Once Upon a Time	Wright Group
Goldilocks Comes back	F	134	Pair-It Books	Steck-Vaughn
Goldsworthy and Mort Blast Off	L	250+	Little Celebrations	Pearson Learning
Goliath and the Burglar	L	250+	Dicks, Terrance	Barron's Educational
Goliath and the Buried Treasure	L	250+	Dicks, Terrance	Barron's Educational
Goliath and the Cub Scouts	L	250+	Dicks, Terrance	Barron's Educational
Goliath at the Dog Show	L	250+	Dicks, Terrance	Barron's Educational
Goliath at the Seaside	L	250+	Dicks, Terrance	Barron's Educational
Goliath Goes to Summer School	L	250+	Dicks, Terrance	Barron's Educational
Goliath on Vacation	L	250+	Dicks, Terrance	Barron's Educational
Goliath's Birthday	L	250+	Dicks, Terrance	Barron's Educational
Goliath's Christmas	L	250+	Dicks, Terrance	Barron's Educational
Goliath's Easter Parade	L	250+	Dicks, Terrance	Barron's Educational
Golly Sisters Go West, The	K	250+	Byars, Betsy	HarperTrophy
Golly Sisters Ride Again, The	K	250+	Byars, Betsy	HarperTrophy
Gone Fishing	G	180	Long, Erlene	Houghton Mifflin
Gonna Bird, The	H	209	Storyteller-Night Crickets	Wright Group/ McGraw-Hill
Good As New	L	250+	Douglass, Barbara	Scholastic
Good Bad Cat	D	65	Start to Read	School Zone
Good Bad Cat, The	D	65	Little Readers	Houghton Mifflin
Good Boy, Andrew!	E	85	Literacy 2000	Rigby
Good Catch!, A	E	191	New Way Red	Steck-Vaughn
Good Dog, Bonita	N	250+	Giff, Patricia Reilly	Bantam Doubleday Dell
Good Driving, Amelia Bedelia	L	250+	Parish, Peggy	Harper & Row
Good for You	D	44	Sunshine	Wright Group
Good Girl	B	18	Ready Readers	Pearson Learning
Good Grief Third Grade	O	250+	O'Shaughnessy, Colleen	Scholastic
Good Knee for a Cat, A	I	205	Pacific Literacy	Pacific Learning
Good Luck Elephant	I	171	Sunshine	Wright Group
Good Morning Mrs. Martin	K	156	Book Bank	Wright Group
Good News	I	250+	Brenner, Barbara	Bantam Doubleday Dell

Title	Level	Words	Author/Series	Publisher/Distributor
Good Night, Little Brother	F	69	Literacy 2000	Rigby
Good Night, Little Bug	D	54	Ready Readers	Pearson Learning
Good Night, Little Kitten	D	78	My First Reader	Grolier Press
Good Old Mom	C	34	Oxford Reading Tree	Oxford University Press
Good Sports	H	206	Foundations	Wright Group
Good to Eat	B	31	Twig	Wright Group
Good Work, Amelia Bedelia	L	250+	Parish, Peggy	Avon Camelot
Good-bye Perky	E	54	Twig	Wright Group
Good-bye Summer, Hello Fall	H	169	Ready Readers	Pearson Learning
Goodbye, Lucy	D	60	Sunshine	Wright Group
Good-bye, Zoo	D	48	Ready Readers	Pearson Learning
Good-for-Nothing Dog, The	M	250+	Schultz, Irene	Wright Group
Goodness Gracious	I	190	Literacy 2000	Rigby
Goodnight Peter	G	107	Windmill	Wright Group
Goodnight!	D	61	Joy Readers	Dominie
Goodnight, Moon	H	130	Brown, Margaret Wise	HarperCollins
Goodnight, Owl!	I	196	Hutchins, Pat	Macmillan
Gooey Chewy Contest, The	N	1512	Book Shop	Mondo Publishing
Goose Chase	D	43	Ready Readers	Pearson Learning
Goose That Laid the Golden Egg, The	G	73	Aesop	Wright Group
Goose's Gold, The	N	250+	Roy, Ron	Random House
Gorganzola Zombies in the Park	O	250+	Levy, Elizabeth	HarperTrophy
Gotcha Box, The	A	30	Story Box	Wright Group
Grace the Pirate	O	250+	Lasky, Kathryn	Hyperion
Grace's Letter to Lincoln	P	250+	Roop, Peter and Connie	Hyperion
Graffiti	I	168	Sunshine	Wright Group
Grain of Rice, A	N	250+	Pittman, Helena Clare	Bantam Doubleday Dell
Grandad	L	250+	Literacy 2000	Rigby
Grandad's Mask	J	446	PM Story Books-Turquoise	Rigby
Grandfather Horned Toad	K	250+	Little Celebrations	Pearson Learning
Grandfathers	C	41	Pebble Books	Grolier, Capstone
Grandma and the Pirate	F		Lloyd, David	Crown
Grandma Carol's Plant	I	250+	Home Connection Collection	Rigby
Grandma Mixup, The	J	250+	Little Readers	Houghton Mifflin
Grandma Mix-Up, The	J	250+	McCully, Emily Arnold	HarperTrophy
Grandma's Heart	K	90	Wonder World	Wright Group
Grandma's at Bat	J	250+	McCully, Emily Arnold	HarperTrophy
Grandma's at the Lake	K	250+	McCully, Emily Arnold	HarperTrophy
Grandma's Bicycle	G	74	Read-Togethers	Wright Group
Grandma's Bicycle	G	74	Read Alongs	Rigby
Grandma's Letter	D	67	Foundations	Wright Group
Grandma's Memories	F	102	Literacy 2000	Rigby
Grandma's Pictures of the Past	J	250+	Home Connection Collection	Rigby
Grandma's Present	E	191	Foundations	Wright Group
Grandmother	E	60	Joy Readers	Dominie
Grandmother and I	C	53	Home Connection Collection	Rigby
Grandmother Is Tired	C	31	Joy Readers	Dominie
Grandmothers	C	50	Pebble Books	Grolier, Capstone
Grandpa	E	70	Sunshine	Wright Group
Grandpa and I	C	40	Home Connection Collection	Rigby
Grandpa Comes to Stay	K	1083	Lewis, Rob	Mondo Publishing
Grandpa Knits Hats	E	55	Wonder World	Wright Group

Title	Level	Words	Author/Series	Publisher/Distributor
Grandpa Snored	F	51	Literacy 2000	Rigby
Grandpa, Grandma, and the Tractor	H	220	Ready Readers	Pearson Learning
Grandpa, Grandpa	G	122	Read-Togethers	Wright Group
Grandpa's Candy Store	F	65	Books for Young Learners	Richard C. Owen
Grandpa's Cookies	F	193	Little Readers	Houghton Mifflin
Grandpa's Lemonade	G	138	Storyteller Nonfiction	Wright Group/ McGraw-Hill
Grandpa's Special Present	I	286	Foundations	Wright Group
Granny and the Desperadoes	J	250+	Parish, Peggy	Simon & Schuster
Granny Bundle's Boring Walk	H	250+	Stepping Stones	Nelson/Michaels Assoc.
Grass Is for Goats	D	84	Joy Readers	Dominie
Grasshopper and the Ants	K	452	Sunshine	Wright Group
Grasshopper on the Road	L	250+	Lobel, Arnold	HarperTrophy
Grasshoppers	F	50	Pebble Books	Grolier, Capstone
Gravity	D	33	Wonder World	Wright Group
Great Bean Race, The	K	295	Pacific Literacy	Pacific Learning
Great Big Enormous Turnip, The	H	317	Reading Unlimited	Pacific Learning
Great Big Enormous Turnip, The	H	250+	Tolstoi, Aleksei & Nikolaevich, Graf	Watts
Great Bug Hunt, The	G	96	Rookie Readers	Children's Press
Great Car Race, The	E	162	Carousel Readers	Dominie
Great Day for Up	J	180	Seuss, Dr.	Random House
Great Dinosaur Hunt, The	M	250+	Schultz, Irene	Wright Group
Great Enormous Hamburger, The	B	36	Sunshine	Wright Group
Great Ghosts	L	250+	Cohen, Daniel	Scholastic
Great Grumbler and the Wonder	M	250+	Ready to Read	Pacific Learning
Great Little Madison, The	O	250+	Fritz, Jean	Scholastic
Great Race, The	G	250+	McPhail, David	Scholastic
Great Snake Escape, The	J	250+	Coxe, Molly	HarperTrophy
Great White Sharks	F	98	Pair-It Books	Steck-Vaughn
Greatest Binnie in the World, The	M	709	Sunshine	Wright Group
Great-Grandpa	G	130	Voyages	SRA/McGraw-Hill
Great-Grandpa's in the Litter Box	M	250+	Greenburg, Dan	Grosset & Dunlap
Greedy Cat	G	166	Ready to Read	Pacific Learning
Greedy Cat Is Hungry	D	103	Ready to Read	Pacific Learning
Greedy Cat Is Hungry	D	103	Pacific Literacy	Pacific Learning
Greedy Cat's Breakfast	E	53	Story Basket	Wright Group
Greedy Dog, The	H	148	New Way Blue	Steck-Vaughn
Greedy Goat, The	L	451	Book Shop	Mondo Publishing
Greedy Gray Octopus, The	G	195	Tadpoles	Rigby
Green Banana	F	49	Tadpoles	Rigby
Green Dragon, The	I	131	Sunshine	Wright Group
Green Eggs and Ham	J	250+	Seuss, Dr.	Random House
Green Eyes	F	111	Literacy 2000	Rigby
Green Footprints	E	42	Literacy 2000	Rigby
Green Grass	B	26	Story Box	Wright Group
Green Plants	H	213	Foundations	Wright Group
Green Snake, The	D	131	Twig	Wright Group
Green Thumbs, Everyone	N	250+	Giff, Patricia Reilly	Bantam Doubleday Dell
Green, Green	D	114	Little Readers	Houghton Mifflin
Gregor the Grumblesome Giant	G	212	Literacy 2000	Rigby
Gregory, the Terrible Eater	L	250+	Sharmat, M. Weinman	Scholastic
Gregory's Dog	C	23	Cat on the Mat	Oxford University Press

Title	Level	Words	Author/Series	Publisher/Distributor
Gregory's Garden	F	70	Cat on the Mat	Oxford University Press
Greg's Microscope	K	250+	Selsam, Millicent	HarperTrophy
Gremlins Don't Chew Bubble Gum	M	250+	Dadey, Debbie & Jones, Marcia	Scholastic
Griffin, the School Cat	I	160	Sunshine	Wright Group
Grizzly Bears	O	250+	Woolley, M. & Pigdon, K.	Mondo
Grizzly Mistake and Other Cases, The	O	250+	Simon, Seymour	Avon Books
Grizzwold	I	250+	Hoff, Syd	HarperTrophy
Grocery Shopping	D	34	Yannone, Deborah	Kaeden Books
Grow, Seed, Grow	E	36	Discovery Links	Newbridge
Growing	B	23	Windmill	Rigby, Wright Group
Growing a Plant	G	115	Discovery World	Rigby
Growing Older	I	216	Early Connections	Benchmark Education
Growing Radishes and Carrots	I	125	Book Shop	Mondo Publishing
Growing Up Is Fun	C	87	The Candid Collection	Dominie
Growing Up, Up, Up Book	F	120	First Start	Troll
Gruff Brothers, The	I	250+	Hooks, William H.	Bantam Doubleday Dell
Grumbles, Growls, and Roars	F	133	Twig	Wright Group
Grump, The	F	73	Literacy 2000	Rigby
Grumputer, The	G	235	Story Basket	Wright Group
Grumpy Elephant	E	100	Story Box	Wright Group
Guard the House, Sam!	G	46	Rookie Readers	Children's Press
Guess What Kind of Ball	E	219	Urmston, Kathleen & Evans, Karen	Kaeden Books
Guess What!	E	28	Literacy 2000	Rigby
Guess What?	E	120	Foundations	Wright Group
Guess Who?	L	250+	Home Connection Collection	Rigby
Guess Who's Coming to Dinner?	F	130	Literacy 2000	Rigby
Guide Dog, The	K	338	Foundations	Wright Group
Guinea Pig Grass	I	140	Literacy 2000	Rigby
Guinea Pigs	I	250+	PM Animal Facts: Pets-Orange	Rigby
Gulp!	D	103	Story Box	Wright Group
Gum on the Drum	E	41	Gregorich, Barbara	School Zone
Gumby Shop, The	I	359	Read Alongs	Rigby
Habitat Is Where We Live, A	F	132	Twig	Wright Group
Haddie's Caps	D	90	Ready Readers	Pearson Learning
Ha-Ha Party, The	J	250	Sunshine	Wright Group
Hailstorm, The	J	386	PM Story Books-Turquoise	Rigby
Hair	A	32	Carousel Earlybirds	Dominie
Hair	B	37	Foundations	Wright Group
Hair	C	35	Little Celebrations	Pearson Learning
Hair Party, The	J	250+	Literacy 2000	Rigby
Haircut, The	D	27	Hartley, S. & Armstrong, Shane	Scholastic
Hairdresser, The	G	164	PM Nonfiction-Blue	Rigby
Hairy Bear	G	109	Read-Togethers	Wright Group
Half for You, Half for Me	K	399	Literacy 2000	Rigby
Halloween	B	44	Story Box	Wright Group
Halloween	D	32	Visions	Wright Group
Halloween	E	128	Fiesta Holiday Series	Dominie
Halloween Horror and Other Cases, The	O	250+	Simon, Seymour	Avon Books
Halloween Mask for Monster	C		Mueller, Virginia	Whitman
Hamburger	H	49	City Kids	Rigby
Hand Me Downs, The	G	156	Little Readers	Houghton Mifflin

Title	Level	Words	Author/Series	Publisher/Distributor
Hand Tools	M	367	Wonder World	Wright Group
Hand, Hand, Fingers, Thumb	J	250+	Perkins, Al	Random House
Hands	B	15	Twig	Wright Group
Hands	C	39	Literacy 2000	Rigby
Hands, Hands, Hands	B	17	Little Celebrations	Pearson Learning
Hands, Hands, Hands	F	85	Book Shop	Mondo Publishing
Handy Dragon, A	H	159	Literacy 2000	Rigby
Hannah	J	250+	Stepping Stones	Nelson/Michaels Assoc.
Hannah	N	250+	Whelan, Gloria	Random House
Hannah's Halloween	A	14	Little Books for Early Readers	University of Maine
Hannah's Hiccups	G	196	Home Connection Collection	Rigby
Hans Christian Andersen: Prince of Storytellers	N	250+	Rookie Biographies	Children's Press
Hansel and Gretel	G	451	Hunia, Fran	Ladybird Books
Hansel and Gretel	K	250+	Enrichment	Wright Group
Happily Ever After	O	250+	Quindlen, Anna	The Penguin Group
Happy 100th Day!	C	35	Little Celebrations	Pearson Learning
Happy Birthday	C	28	Literacy 2000	Rigby
Happy Birthday	G	130	First Start	Troll
Happy Birthday, Anna,Sorpresa!	N	250+	Giff, Patricia Reilly	Bantam Doubleday Dell
Happy Birthday, Danny and the Dinosaur	D	250+	Little Readers	Houghton Mifflin
Happy Birthday, Danny and the Dinosaur!	D	250+	Hoff, Syd	HarperTrophy
Happy Birthday, Dear Duck	K	250+	Bunting, Eve	Clarion
Happy Birthday, Estela!	D	30	Pacific Literacy	Pacific Learning
Happy Birthday, Frog	C	87	Story Box	Wright Group
Happy Birthday, Martin Luther King	L	250+	Marzollo, Jean	Scholastic
Happy Birthday, Moon	L	345	Asch, Frank	Simon & Schuster
Happy Birthday, Mrs. Boedecker	L	250+	Little Celebrations	Pearson Learning
Happy Birthday, Sam	I	213	Hutchins, Pat	Greenwillow
Happy Egg	E	210	Kraus, Robert	Scholastic
Happy Face, Sad Face	C	77	Foundations	Wright Group
Happy Faces	H	210	Reading Unlimited	Pacific Learning
Happy Holidays	B	27	Teacher's Choice Series	Dominie
Happy Jack	F	99	First Start	Troll
Happy Monkey in the Shed	C	30	Joy Readers	Dominie
Happy Monkey's Peanuts	D	63	Joy Readers	Dominie
Happy Mother's Day!	G	101	Teacher's Choice Series	Dominie
Hard at Work	B	66	Early Emergent	Pioneer Valley
Hard Drive to Short	M	250+	Christopher, Matt	Little, Brown & Co.
Hare and the Tortoise, The	K	250+	Literacy 2000	Rigby
Hare and the Tortoise, The	P	587	Aesop's Fables	Dominie
Harold and the Purple Crayon	K	660	Johnson, Crockett	Harper & Row
Harold's Flyaway Kite	G	166	First Start	Troll
Harry and the Lady Next Door	J	250+	Zion, Gene	HarperTrophy
Harry and Willy and Carrothead	L	250+	Caseley, Judith	Scholastic
Harry Hates Shopping!	K	250+	Armitage, Ronda & David	Scholastic
Harry Takes Bath	F	132	Ziefert, Harriet	The Penguin Group
Harry's Hat	B	45	Little Books	Sadlier-Oxford
Harry's Hats	D	49	Teacher's Choice Series	Dominie
Harry's House	F	83	Medearis, Angela & Keeter, S.	Scholastic
Hat Came Back, The	K	250+	Literacy 2000	Rigby
Hat Trick	C	38	Literacy 2000	Rigby
Hat, The	A	12	Ready Readers	Pearson Learning

Title	Level	Words	Author/Series	Publisher/Distributor
Hatching Chickens at School	H	94	City Kids	Rigby
Hats	B	46	Williams, Deborah	Kaeden Books
Hats	C	27	Twig	Wright Group
Hats	C	35	Joy Readers	Dominie
Hats	C	43	Little Readers	Houghton Mifflin
Hats	F	88	Talk About Books	Dominie
Hats	F	114	Wonder World	Wright Group
Hats Around the World	B	59	Charlesworth, Liza	Scholastic
Hattie and the Fox	I	321	Fox, Mem	Bradbury/Trumpet
Haunted Bike, The	L	250+	Herman, Gail	Grosset & Dunlap
Haunted Halloween, The	M	250+	Schultz, Irene	Wright Group
Haunted House, The	E	77	Story Box	Wright Group
Haunting of Grade Three, The	O	250+	Maccarone, Grace	Scholastic
Have a Cookout	A	21	Little Books for Early Readers	University of Maine
Have You Seen a Javelina?	K	250+	Literacy 2000	Rigby
Have You Seen Joe?	D	57	Home Connection Collection	Rigby
Have You Seen My Cat?	B	93	Carle, Eric	Putnam
Have You Seen My Duckling?	B	28	Tafuri, Nancy	Greenwillow
Have You Seen the Crocodile?	F	150	West, Colin	Harper & Row
Have You Seen the Tooth Fairy?	E	187	Visions	Wright Group
Have You Seen?	C	38	Literacy 2000	Rigby
Having a Haircut	J	298	City Kids	Rigby
Having My Hair Washed	I	171	City Kids	Rigby
Hay for Ambrosia	G	86	Pacific Literacy	Pacific Learning
Hay Making	F	62	Wonder World	Wright Group
He Bear, She Bear	J	250+	Berenstain, Stan & Jan	Random House
He Who Listens	K	250+	Literacy 2000	Rigby
Head Full of Notions: A Story About Robert Fulton	P	250+	Russell Bowen, Andy	Carolrhoda Books
Headache, The	B	20	Oxford Reading Tree	Oxford University Press
Headless Horseman, The	L	250+	Standiford, Natalie	Random House
Heads and Tails	A	29	Windmill Books	Rigby
Healthy Visit, A	E	44	New Way Red	Steck-Vaughn
Heat	I	203	Early Connections	Benchmark Education
Heather's Book	K	250+	Ready Readers	Pearson Learning
Heavy Weight and Other Cases, The	O	250+	Simon, Seymour	Avon Books
Hedgehog Bakes a Cake	J	250+	McDonald, Maryann	Bantam Doubleday Dell
Hedgehog Is Hungry	C	48	PM Story Books	Rigby
Helen Keller	M	250+	Davidson, Margaret	Scholastic
Helen Keller	P	250+	Graff, Stewart & Polly Anne	Bantam Doubleday Dell
Helen Keller's Teacher	N		Davidson, Margaret	Scholastic
Helicopter Over Hawaii	A	21	Twig	Wright Group
Hello	C	63	Story Box	Wright Group
Hello Creatures!	K	250+	Literacy 2000	Rigby
Hello Goodbye	B	29	Literacy 2000	Rigby
Hello Puppet	C	26	Voyages	SRA/McGraw-Hill
Hello, Cat You Need a Hat	I		Gelman, Rita	Scholastic
Hello, Dad!	D	16	Pacific Literacy	Pacific Learning
Hello, First Grade	I		Ryder, Joanne	Troll
Hello, Hello, Hello	E	56	Sunshine	Wright Group
Hello, Peter-Bonjour, Remy	L	250+	Little Celebrations	Pearson Learning
Help Me	D	107	Emergent	Pioneer Valley
Help Me	H	196	Story Box	Wright Group

Title	Level	Words	Author/Series	Publisher/Distributor
Help Me!	C	55	New Way Red	Steck-Vaughn
Help!	C	57	Reading Corners	Dominie
Help! Help!	B	14	Joy Readers	Dominie
Help! I'm Stuck!	J	250+	Little Celebrations	Pearson Learning
Helping	D	79	Joy Readers	Dominie
Helping	F	64	Book Shop	Mondo Publishing
Helping Dad	C	34	Sunshine	Wright Group
Helping My Dad	D	90	Teacher's Choice Series	Dominie
Helping You	D	53	Interaction	Rigby
Henny Penny	H	292	New Way Green	Steck-Vaughn
Henny Penny	I	582	Galdone, Paul	Scholastic
Henry	E	77	Books for Young Learners	Richard C. Owen
Henry and Beezus	O	250+	Cleary, Beverly	Avon Books
Henry and Mudge and the Bedtime Thumps	J	250+	Rylant, Cynthia	Aladdin
Henry and Mudge and the Best Day of All	J	250+	Rylant, Cynthia	Aladdin
Henry and Mudge and the Careful Cousin	J	250+	Rylant, Cynthia	Aladdin
Henry and Mudge and the Forever Sea	J	250+	Rylant, Cynthia	Aladdin
Henry and Mudge and the Happy Cat	J	250+	Rylant, Cynthia	Aladdin
Henry and Mudge and the Long Weekend	J	250+	Rylant, Cynthia	Aladdin
Henry and Mudge and the Wild Wind	J	250+	Rylant, Cynthia	Aladdin
Henry and Mudge Get the Cold Shivers	J	250+	Rylant, Cynthia	Aladdin
Henry and Mudge Get the Cold Shivers	J	250+	Little Readers	Houghton Mifflin
Henry and Mudge in Puddle Trouble	J	250+	Rylant, Cynthia	Aladdin
Henry and Mudge in the Family Trees	J	250+	Rylant, Cynthia	Aladdin
Henry and Mudge in the Green Time	J	250+	Rylant, Cynthia	Aladdin
Henry and Mudge in the Sparkle Days	J	250+	Rylant, Cynthia	Aladdin
Henry and Mudge Take the Big Test	J	250+	Rylant, Cynthia	Aladdin
Henry and Mudge Under the Yellow Moon	J	250+	Rylant, Cynthia	Aladdin
Henry and Mudge: The First Book	J	250+	Rylant, Cynthia	Aladdin
Henry and Mudge: The First Book	J	250+	Little Readers	Houghton Mifflin
Henry and Ribsy	O	250+	Cleary, Beverly	Avon Books
Henry and the Clubhouse	O	250+	Cleary, Beverly	Avon Books
Henry and the Helicopter	D	58	Literacy 2000	Rigby
Henry and the Paper Route	O	250+	Cleary, Beverly	Avon Books
Henry Huggins	O	250+	Cleary, Beverly	Avon Books
Henry's Busy Day	E		Campbell, Rod	The Penguin Group
Henry's Choice	M	527	Reading Unlimited	Pacific Learning
Herbie Jones	O	250+	Kline, Suzy	Puffin Books
Herbie Jones and Hamburger Head	O	250+	Kline, Suzy	Puffin Books
Herbie Jones and the Birthday Showdown	O	250+	Kline, Suzy	Puffin Books
Herbie Jones and the Class Gift	O	250+	Kline, Suzy	Puffin Books
Herbie Jones and the Dark Attic	O	250+	Kline, Suzy	Puffin Books
Herbie Jones and the Monster Ball	O	250+	Kline, Suzy	Puffin Books
Hercules and Other Greek Legends	P	250+	Wildcats	Wright Group
Hercules Doesn't Pull Teeth	M	250+	Dadey, Debbie & Jones, Marcia	Scholastic
Here are My Hands	H		Bobber Book	SRA/McGraw-Hill
Here Comes a Bus	F	171	Ziefert, Harriet	The Penguin Group
Here Comes Annette!	E	143	Voyages	SRA/McGraw-Hill
Here Comes McBroom	O	250+	Fleischman, Sid	Beech Tree Books
Here Comes the Parade!	B	32	Pair-It Books	Steck-Vaughn
Here Comes the Rain!	C	47	Little Books	Sadlier-Oxford
Here Comes the Strike Out	K	250+	Little Readers	Houghton Mifflin

Title	Level	Words	Author/Series	Publisher/Distributor
Here Comes the Strike Out	K	250+	Kessler, Leonard	HarperTrophy
Here Comes Winter	G	134	First Start	Troll
Here Is a Carrot	C	96	Foundations	Wright Group
Here Is...	B	49	Carousel Earlybirds	Dominie
Here We Go Round the Mulberry Bush	D	187	Little Readers	Houghton Mifflin
Here's a House	A	45	Windmill	Wright Group
Here's Bobby's World! How a TV Cartoon Is Made	L	250+	Little Celebrations	Pearson Learning
Here's Skipper	B	28	Salem, Lynn & Stewart, J.	Seedling
Here's What I Made	C	38	Literacy 2000	Rigby
Herman Henry's Dog	I	250+	Little Readers	Houghton Mifflin
Herman the Helper	E	94	Kraus, Robert	Simon & Schuster
Herman the Helper Lends a Hand	F		Kraus, Robert	Windmill
Herman's Tooth	F	210	Foundations	Wright Group
Hermit Crab	E	111	PM Story Books	Rigby
Hermit Crab, The	G	119	Sunshine	Wright Group
Heroes	J	250+	Wildcats	Wright Group
Hey Coach!	C	37	TOTTS	Tott Publications
Hey There, Bear!	C		Little Celebrations	Pearson Learning
Hey, Diddle, Diddle!	D	30	Sunshine	Wright Group
Hey, New Kid!	N	250+	Douglas, Ann	The Penguin group
Hi Dog	D	137	Ready Readers	Pearson Learning
Hiccups	I	268	Book Shop	Mondo Publishing
Hiccups for Elephant	I	250+	Preller, James	Scholastic
Hiccups for Hippo	I	100	Sunshine	Wright Group
Hiccups Would Not Stop, The	H	177	Ready Readers	Pearson Learning
Hickory, Dickory Pizza Clock	C		Little Celebrations	Pearson Learning
Hidden Hand, The	M	250+	Schultz, Irene	Wright Group
Hide & Seek	H	138	Wonder World	Wright Group
Hide and Seek	B	38	Smart Starts	Rigby
Hide and Seek	B	38	Literacy 2000	Rigby
Hide and Seek	D	49	New Way Red	Steck-Vaughn
Hide and Seek	D	63	Brown, R. & Carey, S.	Scholastic
Hide and Seek	D	108	PM Extensions-Red	Rigby
Hide and Seek	E	215	Foundations	Wright Group
Hide to Survive	L	250+	Home Connection Collection	Rigby
Hide, Spider!	G	179	Momentum Literacy Program	Troll
Hide-and-Seek	H	250+	Momentum Literacy Program	Troll
Hide-and-Seek with Grandpa	I	250+	Lewis, Rob	Mondo Publishing
Hi-De-Hi	E	110	Little Celebrations	Pearson Learning
Hiding	A	28	KinderReaders	Rigby
Hiding	D	97	Foundations	Wright Group
Hiding Places	J	250+	Storyteller-Night Crickets	Wright Group/ McGraw-Hill
Hike at Day Camp, The	C	32	Visions	Wright Group
Hiking with Dad	H	189	Wonder World	Wright Group
Hill of Fire	L	1099	Lewis, Thomas P.	HarperCollins
Hippo from Another Planet	M	250+	Little Celebrations	Pearson Learning
Hippo in June's Tub, A	H	85	Little Books	Sadlier-Oxford
Hippopotamus Ate the Teacher, A	J	250+	Thaler, Mike	Avon Books
Hippos	K	250+	PM Animals in the Wild-Yellow	Rigby
Hippo's Hiccups	G	208	Literacy 2000	Rigby

Title	Level	Words	Author/Series	Publisher/Distributor
His Majesty the King	J	250+	Little Celebrations	Pearson Learning
Hit-Away Kid, The	M	250+	Christopher, Matt	Little, Brown & Co.
Ho, Ho, Benjamin, Feliz Navidad	N	250+	Giff, Patricia Reilly	Bantam Doubleday Dell
Hobson Family Vacation, The	H	250+	Momentum Literacy Program	Troll
Hockey Practice	G	134	Geddes, Diana	Kaeden Books
Hogboggit, The	D	65	Ready to Read	Pacific Learning
Hogboggit, The	D	65	Pacific Literacy	Pacific Learning
Hoiho's Chicks	D	38	Ready to Read	Pacific Learning
Hoketichee and the Manatee	I	113	Books for Young Learners	Richard C. Owen
Hole in Harry's Pocket, The	I	250+	Little Readers	Houghton Mifflin
Hole in the Hedge, The	F	188	Sunshine	Wright Group
Home for a Puppy	G	194	First Start	Troll
Home for Little Teddy, A	D	53	PM Extensions-Red	Rigby
Home in the Sky	K	250+	Baker, Jeannie	Scholastic
Home Run, The	E	92	Teacher's Choice Series	Dominie
Home Sweet Home	E		Roffey, Maureen	Bodley
Homes	C	69	Storyteller Nonfiction	Wright Group/ McGraw-Hill
Homes	D	42	Rise & Shine	Hampton-Brown
Homes Are for Living	N	417	Wonders	Hampton-Brown
Homes for People	B	40	Early Connections	Benchmark Education
Honey Bees	D	41	Pebble Books	Grolier, Capstone
Honey Bees	L	250+	Kahkonen, Sharon	Steck-Vaughn
Honey Bees and Flowers	G	67	Pebble Books	Grolier, Capstone
Honey Bees and Hives	E	58	Pebble Books	Grolier, Capstone
Honey Bees and Honey	F	57	Pebble Books	Grolier, Capstone
Honey for Baby Bear	F	200	PM Story Books	Rigby
Honey, My Rabbit	E	56	Voyages	SRA/McGraw-Hill
Honk!	B	36	Book Shop	Mondo Publishing
Hoofprints	D	62	Teacher's Choice Series	Dominie
Hoopstars: Go to the Hoop!	M	250+	Hughes, Dean	Random House
Hooray for Snail	F	102	Stadler, John	HarperCollins
Hooray for the Golly Sisters!	K	250+	Byars, Betsy	HarperTrophy
Hop on Pop	J	250+	Seuss, Dr.	Random House
Hope Not	D	83	Salem, Lynn & Stewart, J.	Seedling
Horace	D	56	Story Box	Wright Group
Horrakapotchkin	M	250+	Ready to Read	Pacific Learning
Horrible Big Black Bug, The	D	50	Tadpoles	Rigby
Horrible Harry and the Ant Invasion	L	250+	Kline, Suzy	Scholastic
Horrible Harry and the Christmas Surprise	L	250+	Kline, Suzy	Scholastic
Horrible Harry and the Dungeon	L	250+	Kline, Suzy	Puffin Books
Horrible Harry and the Green Slime	L	250+	Kline, Suzy	Puffin Books
Horrible Harry and the Kickball Wedding	L	250+	Kline, Suzy	Puffin Books
Horrible Harry and the Purple People	L	250+	Kline, Suzy	Puffin Books
Horrible Harry in Room 2B	L	250+	Kline, Suzy	Puffin Books
Horrible Harry's Secret	L	250+	Kline, Suzy	Puffin Books
Horrible Thing with Hairy Feet	H	208	Read Alongs	Rigby
Horrible Urktar of Or, The	G	143	Sunshine	Wright Group
Horse and the Donkey, The	I	382	New Way Green	Steck-Vaughn
Horse Feathers	D	41	Pair-It Books	Steck-Vaughn
Horse in Harry's Room, The	J	425	Hoff, Syd	HarperCollins
Horses	F	131	Twig	Wright Group

Title	Level	Words	Author/Series	Publisher/Distributor
Horse's Hiccups	F	83	Storyteller-Moon Rising	Wright Group/ McGraw-Hill
Horses of the Air	N	250+	Little Celebrations	Pearson Learning
Hospitals	L	177	Book Shop	Mondo Publishing
Hot Air Balloons	L	479	Pair-It Books	Steck-Vaughn
Hot and Cold Weather	K	922	Sunshine	Wright Group
Hot Dogs	I	196	City Kids	Rigby
Hot Dogs (Sausages)	C	84	PM Story Books	Rigby
Hot Fudge Hero	P	250+	Brink, Carol R.	Henry Holt & Co.
Hot Potato and Cold Potato	C	77	Foundations	Wright Group
Hot Rod Harry	E	66	Rookie Readers	Children's Press
Hot Sidewalks	C	28	Visions	Wright Group
Hour of the Olympics	M	250+	Osborne, Mary Pope	Random House
House	C		Little Celebrations	Pearson Learning
House Cleaning	A	19	Book Bank	Wright Group
House for a Mouse, A	A	21	Pacific Literacy	Pacific Learning
House for Hickory, A	H	174	Book Shop	Mondo Publishing
House for Me, A	C	71	Twig	Wright Group
House in the Tree, The	F	202	PM Story Books	Rigby
House of the Horrible Ghosts	M	250+	Hayes, Geoffrey	Random House
House on Walenska Street, The	N	250+	Herman, Charlotte	The Penguin Group
House that Jack Built, The	I		Cat on the Mat	Oxford University Press
House that Jack Built, The	J	250+	Peppe, Rodney	Delacorte
House That Jack's Friends Built, The	J	254	Pair-It Books	Steck-Vaughn
House that Stood on Booker Hill, The	J	250+	Ready Readers	Pearson Learning
House, A	A	32	PM Starters One	Rigby
House-Hunting	G	223	PM Story Books	Rigby
Houses	C	35	Little Celebrations	Pearson Learning
Houses	C	38	Windmill	Rigby, Wright Group
Houses	C	64	Story Box	Wright Group
Houses	M	279	Wonder World	Wright Group
How a Volcano Is Formed	M	135	Wonder World	Wright Group
How Animals Hide	F	98	Wonder World	Wright Group
How Animals Move	G	132	Discovery Links	Newbridge
How Animals Move	L	250+	Discovery World	Rigby
How Are We the Same?	D	100	Teacher's Choice Series	Dominie
How Bat Learned to Fly	H	168	Storyteller-Night Crickets	Wright Group/ McGraw-Hill
How Birds Live	I	1090	Sunshine	Wright Group
How Can I Help?	D	65	Questions & Answers	Dominie
How Do Fish Live?	I	1242	Sunshine	Wright Group
How Do Frogs Grow?	G	42	Discovery Links	Newbridge
How Do I Feel?	D	64	Questions & Answers	Dominie
How Do I Put It On?	H		Watanabe, Shigeo	The Penguin Group
How Do Plants Get Food?	L	250+	Goldish, Meish	Steck-Vaughn
How Do You Make a Bubble?	G	250+	Hooks, William H.	Bantam Doubleday Dell
How Do You Measure a Dinosaur?	M	257	Pacific Literacy	Pacific Learning
How Does It Breathe?	K	250+	Home Connection Collection	Rigby
How Does It Grow?	L	250+	Home Connection Collection	Rigby
How Far Will I Fly?	F	94	Oyama, Sachi	Scholastic
How Fire Came to Earth	K	250+	Literacy 2000	Rigby
How Flies Live	I	448	Sunshine	Wright Group

Title	Level	Words	Author/Series	Publisher/Distributor
How Grandmother Spider Got the Sun	J	115	Little Readers	Houghton Mifflin
How Have I Grown	G	235	Reid, Mary	Scholastic
How Is a Crayon Made?	N	250+	Charles, Oz	Scholastic
How Kittens Grow	J	250+	Selsam, Millicent	Scholastic
How Machines Help	D	143	Sunshine	Wright Group
How Many Ants?	E	35	Rookie Readers	Children's Press
How Many Are Left?	I	225	Early Connections	Benchmark Education
How Many Bugs in a Box?	D	126	Carter, David	Simon & Schuster
How Many Fish?	B	30	Gossett, R. & Ballinger, Margaret	Scholastic
How Many Hot Dogs?	E	115	Story Box	Wright Group
How Many Kittens?	C	37	Twig	Wright Group
How Many Legs?	B	19	Windmill	Wright Group
How Many Monkeys?	B	16	Pair-It Books	Steck-Vaughn
How Many Pets?	D	37	Book Shop	Mondo Publishing
How Many Seeds?	E	42	Pair-It Books	Steck-Vaughn
How Many?	E	147	Early Connections	Benchmark Education
How Much Does This Hold?	K	179	Coulton, Mia	Kaeden Books
How Much Is That Guinea Pig in the Window?	L	250+	Rocklin, Joanne	Scholastic
How Owl Changed His Hoot	I	227	Sunshine	Wright Group
How Spiders Got Eight Legs	L	884	Pair-It Books	Steck-Vaughn
How Spiders Live	F	145	Sunshine	Wright Group
How the Chick Tricked the Fox	G	167	Ready Readers	Pearson Learning
How the Crystals Grow	P	1234	Book Shop	Mondo Publishing
How the Giraffe Became a Giraffe	M	648	Sunshine	Wright Group
How the Mouse Got Brown Teeth	I	460	Book Shop	Mondo Publishing
How the Rattlesnake Got Its Rattle	L	1006	Pair-It Books	Steck-Vaughn
How the Water Got to the Plains	L	250+	Home Connection Collection	Rigby
How to Be Cool in the Third Grade	N	250+	Douglas, Ann	The Penguin Group
How to Choose a Pet	L	250+	Discovery World	Rigby
How to Clean a Dinosaur	G	208	Windmill Books	Rigby
How to Cook Scones	J		Book Shop	Mondo Publishing
How to Grow a Plant	E	172	Visions	Wright Group
How to Make a Card	G	69	Urmston, Kathleen & Evans, Karen	Kaeden Books
How to Make a Crocodile	H	62	Little Books	Sadlier-Oxford
How to Make a Hen House	B	25	Ready Readers	Pearson Learning
How to Make a Hot Dog	C	48	Story Box	Wright Group
How to Make a Mud Pie	H	127	Little Readers	Houghton Mifflin
How to Make a Mudpie	A	32	Learn to Read	Creative Teaching Press
How to Make a Sandwich	C	27	Visions	Wright Group
How to Make a Sun Hat	E	87	Home Connection Collection	Rigby
How to Make Can Stilts	C	28	Story Box	Wright Group
How to Make Salsa	J	192	Book Shop	Mondo Publishing
How to Make Snack Mix	C	47	Oppenlander, Meredith	Kaeden Books
How to Ride a Giraffe	I	191	Little Readers	Houghton Mifflin
How to Speak Dolphin in Three Easy Lessons	N	250+	Greenburg, Dan	Grosset & Dunlap
How to Weigh an Elephant	K	390	Pacific Literacy	Pacific Learning
How Turtle Raced Beaver	J	182	Literacy 2000	Rigby
Howie Has a Stomachache	E	100	Moore, J. R.	Seedling
Howling at the Hauntly's	M	250+	Dadey, Debbie & Jones, Marcia	Scholastic
Howling Dog and Other Cases, The	O	250+	Simon, Seymour	Avon Books
How's the Weather	B	29	Learn to Read	Creative Teaching Press
Huberta the Hiking Hippo	L	250+	Literacy 2000	Rigby

©1999 by I. C. Fountas & G. S. Pinnell from Matching Books to Readers. Portsmouth, NH: Heinemann. May not be reproduced without written permission of the publisher.

Title	Level	Words	Author/Series	Publisher/Distributor
Hug Bug	F	65	Start to Read	School Zone
Hug Is Warm, A	C	60	Sunshine	Wright Group
Huggles Breakfast	A	14	Sunshine	Wright Group
Huggles Can Juggle	A	15	Sunshine	Wright Group
Huggles Goes Away	A	14	Sunshine	Wright Group
Hugo Hogget	K	528	Wonders	Hampton-Brown
Humpback Whales	E	48	Pair-It Books	Steck-Vaughn
Humpback Whales	F	72	Ready Readers	Pearson Learning
Humpity-Bump	C		Little Celebrations	Pearson Learning
Humpty Dumpty	D		Peppe, Rodney	The Penguin Group
Hundred Dresses, The	O	250+	Estes, Eleanor	Scholastic
Hundred Hugs, A	I	229	Sunshine	Wright Group
Hungry Animals	G	127	Little Readers	Houghton Mifflin
Hungry Bear	C	22	Smart Starts	Rigby
Hungry Giant	F	183	Read-Togethers	Wright Group
Hungry Giant, The	F	183	Story Box	Wright Group
Hungry Giant's Birthday Cake, The	G	241	Story Basket	Wright Group
Hungry Giant's Lunch, The	F	140	Story Box	Wright Group
Hungry Giant's Soup, The	G	42	Story Basket	Wright Group
Hungry Goat, The	C	33	Rise & Shine	Hampton-Brown
Hungry Happy Monkey	E	77	Joy Readers	Dominie
Hungry Horse	E	35	Literacy 2000	Rigby
Hungry Kitten	C	50	Teacher's Choice Series	Dominie
Hungry Kitten, The	D	95	PM Story Books	Rigby
Hungry Monster	I	241	Story Box	Wright Group
Hungry Sea Star, The	I	69	Books for Young Learners	Richard C. Owen
Hungry, Hungry Sharks	L	250+	Cole, Joanna	Random House
Hunt for Clues, A	G	157	Ready Readers	Pearson Learning
Hunt for Pirate Gold, The	M	250+	Schultz, Irene	Wright Group
Hurray for Ali Baba Bernstein	O	250+	Hurwitz, Johanna	Scholastic
Hurricane	D	36	Joy Readers	Dominie
Hurricane Machine and Other Cases, The	O	250+	Simon, Seymour	Avon Books
Hurricanes!	P	250+	Hopping, Jean	Scholastic
Hurry Squirrel!	E	72	Start to Read	School Zone
Hurry Up	D	49	Voyages	SRA/McGraw-Hill
Hush Up!	L		Little Celebrations	Pearson Learning
Huzzard Buzzard	F		Reese, Bob	Children's Press
Hypnotized Frog and Other Cases, The	O	250+	Simon, Seymour	Avon Books
I Am	B	32	Little Readers	Houghton Mifflin
I Am	D	27	Rookie Readers	Children's Press
I Am a Bookworm	C	32	Sunshine	Wright Group
I Am a Dentist	C	20	Read-More Books	Dominie
I Am a Fireman	D	45	Read-More Books	Dominie
I Am a Gypsy Pot	K	220	Evangeline Nicholas Collection	Wright Group
I Am a Photographer	E	32	Read-More Books	Dominie
I Am a Train Driver	D	32	Read-More Books	Dominie
I Am an Explorer	D	32	Rookie Readers	Children's Press
I Am Cold	E	136	Foundations	Wright Group
I Am Frightened	B	41	Story Box	Wright Group
I Am Hot	E	123	Foundations	Wright Group
I Am King!	E	57	My First Reader	Grolier Press

Title	Level	Words	Author/Series	Publisher/Distributor
I Am Not Afraid	K	250+	Mann, Kenny	Bantam Doubleday Dell
I Am Thankful	A	42	Carousel Earlybirds	Dominie
I Am...	A	20	Sunshine	Wright Group
I Bought My Lunch Today	I	90	City Kids	Rigby
I Can	A	21	Carousel Earlybirds	Dominie
I Can	B	40	Ready Readers	Pearson Learning
I Can	B	54	Little Readers	Houghton Mifflin
I Can	B		New Way	Steck-Vaughn
I Can	C	27	Visions	Wright Group
I Can Be Anything	E	242	Pair-It Books	Steck-Vaughn
I Can Dig	C	45	Can You Do This	SRA/McGraw-Hill
I Can Do Anything!	C	21	Sunshine	Wright Group
I Can Do It	I	200	Book Shop	Mondo Publishing
I Can Do It Myself	C	37	Literacy 2000	Rigby
I Can Do It Myself	E	150	Visions	Wright Group
I Can Do It, I Really Can	G	195	Teacher's Choice Series	Dominie
I Can Do Many Things	C	43	Carousel Readers	Dominie
I Can Draw	C	75	Carousel Earlybirds	Dominie
I Can Eat	C	51	Can You Do This	SRA/McGraw-Hill
I Can Fly	A	21	Sunshine	Wright Group
I Can Fly	F	107	Carousel Readers	Dominie
I Can Hear	A	32	TOTTS	Tott Publications
I Can Help	D	65	Teacher's Choice Series	Dominie
I Can Jump	C	40	Sunshine	Wright Group
I Can Make Music	B	41	Little Red Readers	Sundance
I Can Paint	A	35	Book Bank	Wright Group
I Can Play	C	45	Can You Do This	SRA/McGraw-Hill
I Can Read	A	35	Learn to Read	Creative Teaching Press
I Can Read	B	38	Ready to Read	Pacific Learning
I Can Read	B	38	Pacific Literacy	Pacific Learning
I Can Read	C	38	Teacher's Choice Series	Dominie
I Can Read Anything	C	42	Sunshine	Wright Group
I Can Read with My Eyes Shut	J	250+	Seuss, Dr.	Random House
I Can Read! I Can Read!	L	250+	Little Celebrations	Pearson Learning
I Can Ride	C	66	Can You Do This	SRA/McGraw-Hill
I Can See	A	40	Carousel Earlybirds	Dominie
I Can See the Leaves	K	368	Pacific Literacy	Pacific Learning
I Can Spell Dinosaur	F		Predictable Storybooks	SRA/McGraw-Hill
I Can Squeak	E	154	Windmill	Wright Group
I Can Swim	D	61	Ready Readers	Pearson Learning
I Can Taste	C	31	Teacher's Choice Series	Dominie
I Can Use a Computer	D	52	Teacher's Choice Series	Dominie
I Can Wash	C	66	Carousel Earlybirds	Dominie
I Can Write	A	40	Learn to Read	Creative Teaching Press
I Can Write, Can You?	B	30	Stewart, J. & Salem, Lynn	Seedling
I Can!	F	131	Twig	Wright Group
I Can't Said the Ant	M	250+	Cameron, Polly	Scholastic
I Can't See	C	36	Little Celebrations	Pearson Learning
I Can't Sleep	D	71	Learn to Read	Creative Teaching Press
I Can't Wait to Read	H	185	Adventures in Reading	Dominie
I Climb	C	57	This Is the Way	SRA/McGraw-Hill
I Could Be	C	40	Visions	Wright Group

Title	Level	Words	Author/Series	Publisher/Distributor
I Crawl	C	56	This Is the Way	SRA/McGraw-Hill
I Did That!	I	250+	Momentum Literacy Program	Troll
I Do Not Like Peas	D	32	Visions	Wright Group
I Don't Care!	H	250	TOTTS	Tott Publications
I Don't Think It's Fair	G	147	Teacher's Choice Series	Dominie
I Dream	K	583	Sunshine	Wright Group
I Dress Up Like Mama	C	35	Visions	Wright Group
I Eat Leaves	C	47	Book Shop	Mondo Publishing
I Feel Cold	C	57	Home Connection Collection	Rigby
I Feel Hot	C	58	Home Connection Collection	Rigby
I Fixed Breakfast	H	176	Teacher's Choice Series	Dominie
I Fly	C	57	This Is the Way	SRA/McGraw-Hill
I Found a Can	C	33	Twig	Wright Group
I Get Ready for School	C	37	Visions	Wright Group
I Get the Creeps	K	250+	Reading Corners	Dominie
I Get Tired	B	37	Carousel Earlybirds	Dominie
I Go, Go, Go	B	21	Sunshine	Wright Group
I Got a Goldfish	E	92	Ready Readers	Pearson Learning
I Grow Too!	C	30	Start to Read	School Zone
I Hate Camping	M	250+	Petersen, P. J.	The Penguin Group
I Hate English	L	250+	Levine, Ellen	Scholastic
I Hate My Best Friend	L	250+	Rosner, Ruth	Hyperion
I Have a Home	E	79	Sunshine	Wright Group
I Have a Paper Route	I	90	City Kids	Rigby
I Have a Pet	B	35	Reading Corners	Dominie
I Have a Question, Grandma	G	124	Literacy 2000	Rigby
I Have a Watch!	C	60	Williams, Deborah	Kaeden Books
I Have Shoes	C	24	Visions	Wright Group
I Jump	C	56	This Is the Way	SRA/McGraw-Hill
I Know a Lady	L	221	Zolotow, Charlotte	Puffin Books
I Know That Tune!	F	201	Foundations	Wright Group
I Know That!	I	99	Sunshine	Wright Group
I Like	A	24	Sunshine	Wright Group
I Like	C	24	Literacy 2000	Rigby
I Like Balloons	A	27	Reading Corners	Dominie
I Like Books	D		Browne, Anthony	Random House
I Like Fruit	B	18	Visions	Wright Group
I Like Green	C	47	Literacy 2000	Rigby
I Like Me	A	31	Visions	Wright Group
I Like My Picture!	D	160	Teacher's Choice Series	Dominie
I Like Shapes	B	21	Armstrong, Shane	Scholastic
I Like Shopping	M	287	Sunshine	Wright Group
I Like to Count	C	40	Ready Readers	Pearson Learning
I Like to Eat	A	41	Reading Corners	Dominie
I Like to Eat	C	56	Sunshine	Wright Group
I Like to Find Things	C	40	Sunshine	Wright Group
I Like to Help	B	46	Little Books for Early Readers	University of Maine
I Like to Paint	A	29	Reading Corners	Dominie
I Like to Play	C	50	Carousel Readers	Dominie
I Like to Read	B	49	Little Books for Early Readers	University of Maine
I Like to Write	C	62	Carousel Readers	Dominie
I Like Worms!	D	213	Sunshine	Wright Group

Title	Level	Words	Author/Series	Publisher/Distributor
I Live in a House	D	51	Read-More Books	Dominie
I Live in an Apartment	D	41	Read-More Books	Dominie
I Live in an Apartment Building	I	111	City Kids	Rigby
I Live on a Farm	C	42	Read-More Books	Dominie
I Love Bugs	C	40	Book Shop	Mondo Publishing
I Love Camping	B	34	Early Emergent	Pioneer Valley
I Love Camping	E	83	Carousel Readers	Dominie
I Love Cats	E	116	Rookie Readers	Children's Press
I Love Cats	I	104	Book Shop	Mondo Publishing
I Love Chickens	D	67	Story Box	Wright Group
I Love Fishing	D	37	Rookie Readers	Children's Press
I Love Mud and Mud Loves Me	D	121	Stephens, Vicki	Scholastic
I Love Music	C	41	Carousel Readers	Dominie
I Love My Family	B	31	Sunshine	Wright Group
I Love My Family	B	31	Foundations	Wright Group
I Love My Grandma	D	36	Rise & Shine	Hampton-Brown
I Love the Beach	M	250+	Literacy 2000	Rigby
I Love to Sneeze	J	250+	Schecter, Ellen	Bantam Doubleday Dell
I Love You	E	121	Teacher's Choice Series	Dominie
I Need a Book	F	113	Sunshine	Wright Group
I Need a Rest	F	119	Home Connection Collection	Rigby
I Paint	A	22	Literacy 2000	Rigby
I Paint	A	26	Book Shop	Mondo Publishing
I Play Soccer	J	97	City Kids	Rigby
I Read	A	38	Reading Corners	Dominie
I Remember	C	26	Literacy 2000	Rigby
I Run	B	22	Carousel Earlybirds	Dominie
I Run	C	56	This Is the Way	SRA/McGraw-Hill
I Saw a Dinosaur	G	55	Literacy 2000	Rigby
I Saw You in the Bathtub	J	250+	Schwartz, Alvin	HarperTrophy
I See	B	29	Book Shop	Mondo Publishing
I See	C	29	Teacher's Choice Series	Dominie
I See Colors	B	23	Learn to Read	Creative Teaching Press
I See Monkeys	C	39	Williams, Deborah	Kaeden Books
I See Tails!	B	42	Rise & Shine	Hampton-Brown
I See You	C	56	Twig	Wright Group
I Shop with My Daddy	G	131	Maccarone, Grace	Scholastic
I Smell Smoke!	E	49	Sunshine	Wright Group
I Spy	C	25	Literacy 2000	Rigby
I Spy a Fly	I	132	Wonder World	Wright Group
I Swim	C	57	This Is the Way	SRA/McGraw-Hill
I Thought I Couldn't	C	40	Visions	Wright Group
I Want a Pet	C	46	Little Readers	Houghton Mifflin
I Want a Pet	C	46	Gregorich, Barbara	School Zone
I Want a Pony	O	250+	Betancourt, Jeanne	Scholastic
I Want Ice Cream	C	18	Story Box	Wright Group
I Want My Own Room!	C	25	Visions	Wright Group
I Want to be a Ballerina	D	66	Teacher's Choice Series	Dominie
I Want to Be a Clown	F	82	Start to Read	School Zone
I Was So Mad	J	232	Mayer, Mercer	Donovan
I Was Walking Down the Road	H	299	Barchas, Sarah	Scholastic
I Went to the Dentist	K	152	City Kids	Rigby

Title	Level	Words	Author/Series	Publisher/Distributor
I Went to the Movies	J	120	City Kids	Rigby
I Went to Visit a Friend One Day	F		Voyages	SRA/McGraw-Hill
I Went Walking	C	105	Williams, Sue	Harcourt Brace
I Wish I Had a Dinosaur	D	46	Little Celebrations	Pearson Learning
I Wish I Was Sick Too	G		Brandenburg, Franz	Morrow
I Wonder	C	49	Little Celebrations	Pearson Learning
I Wonder	F	67	Sunshine	Wright Group
I Wonder Why	E	73	Foundations	Wright Group
I Wonder Why Snakes Shed their Skins	O	250+	O'Neill, Amanda	Scholastic
I Wonder Why?	F	95	Wonder World	Wright Group
I Write	C	19	Sunshine	Wright Group
Ibis: A True Whale Story	K	250+	Himmelman, John	Scholastic
Ice Cream	C	49	Sunshine	Wright Group
Ice Fishing	H	140	Ready Readers	Pearson Learning
Ice Is ... Whee!	D	59	Rookie Readers	Children's Press
Ice Magic	M	250+	Christopher, Matt	Little, Brown & Co.
Ice-Cream Stick	B	35	Story Box	Wright Group
Icy Question and Other Cases, The	O	250+	Simon, Seymour	Avon Books
If	H	83	Sunshine	Wright Group
If Germs Were Purple	D	53	Carousel Readers	Dominie
If Horses Could Talk!	E	32	Teacher's Choice Series	Dominie
If I Had an Alligator	H		Mayer, Mercer	Dial
If I Had an Elephant	F	90	Teacher's Choice Series	Dominie
If I Were a Penguin	H	159	Goeneil, Heidi	Little, Brown & Co.
If I Were an Ant	I	51	Rookie Readers	Children's Press
If I Were You	E	77	Wildsmith, Brian	Oxford University Press
If You Give a Moose a Muffin	K	250+	Numeroff, Laura Joffe	HarperCollins
If You Give a Mouse a Cookie	K	291	Numeroff, Laura Joffe	HarperCollins
If You Grew Up with Abraham Lincoln	P	250+	McGovern, Ann	Scholastic
If You Like Strawberries, Don't Read this Book	H	101	Literacy 2000	Rigby
If You Lived at the Time of the Civil War	P	250+	Moore, Kay	Scholastic
If You Lived at the Time of the Great San Francisco Earthquake	P	250+	Levine, Ellen	Scholastic
If You Lived in Colonial Times	P	250+	McGovern, Ann	Scholastic
If You Lived in the Time of Martin Luther King	P	250+	Levine, Ellen	Scholastic
If You Lived with the Sioux Indians	P	250+	McGovern, Ann	Scholastic
If You Meet a Dragon	C	31	Story Box	Wright Group
If You Sailed on the Mayflower in 1620	P	250+	McGovern, Ann	Scholastic
If You Traveled on the Underground Railroad	P	250+	Levine, Ellen	Scholastic
If You Were There When They Signed the Constitution	P	250+	Levy, Elizabeth	Scholastic
If Your Name Was Changed at Ellis Island	P	250+	Levine, Ellen	Scholastic
I'll Be a Pirate	E	53	Eifrig, Kate	Kaeden Books
I'll Run Away	D	53	Home Connection Collection	Rigby
I'm a Caterpillar	G	169	Marzollo, Jean	Scholastic
I'm a Good Reader	H	188	Carousel Readers	Dominie
I'm a Little Seed	D	30	Pair-It Books	Steck-Vaughn
I'm Bigger Than You!	D	48	Sunshine	Wright Group
I'm Brave	D	51	Sunshine	Wright Group
I'm Glad I'm Me	F	147	Windmill Books	Rigby
I'm Glad to Say	H	165	Sunshine	Wright Group
I'm Hungry	B	25	Fitros, Pamela	Kaeden Books

Title	Level	Words	Author/Series	Publisher/Distributor
I'm Hungry	C	37	Visions	Wright Group
I'm Hungry	D	84	Tuer, Judy	Scholastic
I'm King of the Castle	F		Watanabe, Shigeo	Philomel
I'm King of the Mountain	G	285	Ready to Read	Pacific Learning
I'm Looking for My Hat	F	89	Book Bank	Wright Group
I'm No One Else But Me	M	1010	Book Bank	Wright Group
I'm Not, I'm Not	C	19	Windmill	Rigby, Wright Group
I'm Out of My Body…Please Leave a Message	M	250+	Greenburg, Dan	Grosset & Dunlap
I'm Sick Today	H	150	Carousel Readers	Dominie
I'm Telling	E	71	Teacher's Choice Series	Dominie
I'm King of the Mountain	G	285	Pacific Literacy	Pacific Learning
Imagine That	J	250+	Story Box	Wright Group
Impossible Bend and Other Cases, The	O	250+	Simon, Seymour	Avon Books
In a New Land	L	378	Sunshine	Wright Group
In a Dark, Dark Room	J	250+	Schwartz, Alvin	HarperTrophy
In a Dark, Dark Wood	E	81	Read-Togethers	Wright Group
In a Faraway Forest	K	347	Wonders	Hampton-Brown
In a Town	E	47	Little Celebrations	Pearson Learning
In City Gardens	L		Little Celebrations	Pearson Learning
In Danger	M	250+	Home Connection Collection	Rigby
In My Backyard	A	18	Visions	Wright Group
In My Bed	C	57	Literacy 2000	Rigby
In My Bucket	F	94	Carousel Readers	Dominie
In My Desert	D	24	Little Celebrations	Pearson Learning
In My Garden	C	36	Carousel Readers	Dominie
In My Garden	I	250+	Momentum Literacy Program	Troll
In My Head	G	74	Voyages	SRA/McGraw-Hill
In My Pocket	E	195	Carousel Readers	Dominie
In My Room	C	44	Literacy 2000	Rigby
In My School	A	27	Little Books for Early Readers	University of Maine
In My Toolbox	B	36	Foundations	Wright Group
In Nonna's Kitchen	D	32	Home Connection Collection	Rigby
In Spring	B	15	Discovery Links	Newbridge
In Summer	D	36	Discovery Links	Newbridge
In the Afternoon	H	156	PM Nonfiction-Green	Rigby
In the Air	B	20	Sunshine	Wright Group
In the Backyard	H		Little Celebrations	Pearson Learning
In the Bathroom	B	24	Smart Starts	Rigby
In the Chicken Coop	D	56	Twig	Wright Group
In the City	C	45	Pasternac, Susana	Scholastic
In the City	C	50	Rise & Shine	Hampton-Brown
In the Clouds	M	250+	Literacy 2000	Rigby
In the Dark Forest	C	24	Pacific Literacy	Pacific Learning
In the Desert	D	62	Sunshine	Wright Group
In the Dinosaur's Paw	M	250+	Giff, Patricia Reilly	Bantam Doubleday Dell
In the Forest	C	42	Twig	Wright Group
In the Forest	G	95	Voyages	SRA/McGraw-Hill
In the Garden	D	90	Literacy 2000	Rigby
In the Hen House	G	82	Oppenlander, Meredith	Kaeden Books
In the Mirror	B	26	Story Box	Wright Group
In the Morning	H	218	PM Nonfiction-Green	Rigby
In the Mountains	A	14	Twig	Wright Group

Title	Level	Words	Author/Series	Publisher/Distributor
In the Park	D	65	Foundations	Wright Group
In the Park	F	96	Literacy 2000	Rigby
In the Rain	B	19	Ready Readers	Pearson Learning
In the Rain Forest	E	57	Twig	Wright Group
In the Rain Forest	P	250+	Wildcats	Wright Group
In the Sea	C	41	Sunshine	Wright Group
In the Shopping Cart	A	24	PM Starters	Rigby
In the Supermarket	A	24	Smart Starts	Rigby
In the Teacup	A	35	KinderReaders	Rigby
In the Treetops	O	250+	Woolley, M. & Pigdon, K.	Mondo
In the Woods	B	48	Book Shop	Mondo Publishing
In the Woods	G	304	Reading Corners	Dominie
In Went Goldilocks	C	30	Literacy 2000	Rigby
Incredible Places	P	250+	Wildcats	Wright Group
Incredible Shrinking Machine and Other Cases, The	O	250+	Simon, Seymour	Avon Books
Indian School, The	P	250+	Whelan, Gloria	HarperTrophy
Indian-Head Pennies and Other Cases, The	O	250+	Simon, Seymour	Avon Books
In-Line Skates, The	F	137	Foundations	Wright Group
Insects	J	171	MacLulich, Carolynn	Scholastic
Insects All Around	K	229	Early Connections	Benchmark Education
Insects That Bother Us	D	87	Foundations	Wright Group
Inside a Rain Forest	M	353	Pair-It Books	Steck-Vaughn
Inside or Outside?	E	57	Literacy 2000	Rigby
Inside School	A	35	Little Books for Early Readers	University of Maine
Inside Story, The	E	43	Teacher's Choice Series	Dominie
Inside, Outside, Upside Down	E		Berenstain, Stan & Jan	Random House
International Day	D	47	Home Connection Collection	Rigby
Interruptions	F	81	Book Shop	Mondo Publishing
Into Space	J	250+	Momentum Literacy Program	Troll
Inventor's Diary, The	M	271	Pacific Literacy	Pacific Learning
Inventors: Making Things Better	M	250+	Pair-It Books	Steck-Vaughn
Invisible	I	111	Read Alongs	Rigby
Invisible Dog, The	M	250+	King-Smith, Dick	Alfred A. Knopf, Inc.
Invisible in the Third Grade	M	250+	Cuyler, Margery	Scholastic
Invisible Spy, The	J	227	Foundations	Wright Group
Invisible Stanley	N	250+	Brown, Jeff	HarperTrophy
Iron Horse, The	A	21	Smart Starts	Rigby
Is a Dollar Enough?	D	75	Visions	Wright Group
Is Anyone Home?	F	65	Maris, Ron	Greenwillow
Is It a Fish?	K	606	Sunshine	Wright Group
Is It Alive?	C	26	Learn to Read	Creative Teaching Press
Is It Floating?	E	146	Sunshine	Wright Group
Is It Time Yet?	G	162	Foundations	Wright Group
Is It Time?	C	52	Campbell, J. G.	Scholastic
Is This a Monster?	C	93	Book Shop	Mondo Publishing
Is This My Dinner?	I		Black/Fry	Whitman
Is This You?	F	250+	Krauss, Ruth	Scholastic
Is Tomorrow My Birthday?	E	87	Blaxland, Wendy	Scholastic
Island Baby	M	250+	Keller, Holly	Scholastic
Island Picnic, The	H	236	PM Story Books	Rigby
Island, The	D	24	Wildsmith, Brian	Oxford University Press
It Came Through the Wall	O	1182	Book Shop	Mondo Publishing

Title	Level	Words	Author/Series	Publisher/Distributor
It Could Be Worse	E	108	Home Connection Collection	Rigby
It Didn't Frighten Me	D	387	Book Shop	Mondo Publishing
It Looked Like Split Milk	E	172	Shaw, Charles	Harper & Row
It Sounds Like Music	D	56	Pair-It Books	Steck-Vaughn
It Takes a Village	N	250+	Cowen-Fletcher, Jane	Scholastic
It Takes Time to Grow	H	57	Sunshine	Wright Group
Itch! Itch!	C	76	Book Shop	Mondo Publishing
Itchy, Itchy Chicken Pox	F	131	Maccarone, Grace	Scholastic
It's a Bit Tricky	G	250+	Home Connection Collection	Rigby
It's a Fiesta, Benjamin	N	250+	Giff, Patricia Reilly	Bantam Doubleday Dell
It's About Time	B	39	Twig	Wright Group
It's About Time	M	481	Storyteller Nonfiction	Wright Group/ McGraw-Hill
It's Alright to Cry	F	138	Teacher's Choice Series	Dominie
It's Football Time	C	24	Geddes, Diana	Kaeden Books
It's Game Day	D	65	Salem, Lynn & Stewart, J.	Seedling
It's George!	H		Cohen, Miriam	Bantam Doubleday Dell
It's Halloween	K	250+	Prelutsky, Jack	Scholastic
It's Hot	D	54	Ready Readers	Pearson Learning
It's Mine!	P	250+	Lionni, Leo	Scholastic
It's My Bread	B	43	Pacific Literacy	Pacific Learning
It's Noisy at Night	E	80	Wonder World	Wright Group
It's Not Easy Being a Bunny	I		Sadler, Marilyn	Random House
It's Not Fair	F	51	Tadpoles	Rigby
It's Raining	E	86	Teacher's Choice Series	Dominie
It's Raining!	C	32	Pair-It Books	Steck-Vaughn
It's Time for Bed	E	126	Visions	Wright Group
It's Time to Get Up	E	143	Visions	Wright Group
It's Valentine's Day	K	250+	Prelutsky, Jack	Scholastic
I've Got New Sneakers	H	111	City Kids	Rigby
I've Lost My Boot	C	18	Windmill	Wright Group
J My Name Is Jess	C	61	Little Books	Sadlier-Oxford
Jace, Mace, and the Big Race	H		Gregorich, Barbara	School Zone
Jack and Chug	I	337	PM Story Books-Orange	Rigby
Jack and Jill	E	51	Sunshine	Wright Group
Jack and the Beanstalk	H	170	Sunshine	Wright Group
Jack and the Beanstalk	I	777	Traditional Tales & More	Rigby
Jack and the Beanstalk	K	901	Hunia, Fran	Ladybird Books
Jack and the Beanstalk	K	250+	Weisner, David	Scholastic
Jack and the Magic Harp	J	250+	PM Traditional Tales & Plays	Rigby
Jack DePert at the Supermarket	G	188	Wonder World	Wright Group
Jackets	C	42	Joy Readers	Dominie
Jackie Robinson and the Story of All-Black Baseball	N	250+	O'Connor, Jim	Random House
Jackie Robinson: Baseball's First Black Major Leaguer	N	250+	Rookie Biographies	Children's Press
Jackie's New Friend	F	168	O'Connor, C. M.	Seedling
Jack-in-the-Box	B	34	Literacy 2000	Rigby
Jack-O-Lantern	B	37	Twig	Wright Group
Jack-O-Lantern	D	47	Pebble Books	Grolier, Capstone
Jacks and More Jacks	F	79	Little Celebrations	Pearson Learning
Jack's Pack	C	22	KinderReaders	Rigby
Jackson's Monster	I	250+	Little Readers	Houghton Mifflin

Title	Level	Words	Author/Series	Publisher/Distributor
Jacob Two-Two Meets the Hooded Fang	P	250+	Richler, Mordecai	Seal Books
Jake	A	35	Little Books for Early Readers	University of Maine
Jake and the Copycats	J	250+	Rocklin, Joanne	Bantam Doubleday Dell
Jake Can Play	B	42	Little Books for Early Readers	University of Maine
Jamaica and Brianna	K	250+	Little Readers	Houghton Mifflin
Jamaica's Find	K	250+	Havill, Juanita	Scholastic
Jamberry	J	111	Degen, Bruce	Harper & Row
James Is Hiding	A	24	Windmill	Rigby, Wright Group
Jan and the Jacket	E	74	Oxford Reading Tree	Oxford University Press
Jan Can Juggle	B	25	Ready Readers	Pearson Learning
Jane Goodall and the Wild Chimpanzees	L	250+	Birnbaum, Bette	Steck-Vaughn
Jane's Car	F	121	PM Story Books	Rigby
Jan's New Fan	C	34	KinderReaders	Rigby
Japan	M	488	Pair-It Books	Steck-Vaughn
Jason and the Aliens Down the Street	O	250+	Greer, Greg & Ruddick, Bob	HarperTrophy
Jason Kidd Story, The	P	250+	Moore, David	Scholastic
Jason's Bus Ride	G	117	Ziefert, Harriet	The Penguin Group
Jazz Pizzazz and the Silver Threads	P	250+	Quattlebaum, Mary	Bantam Doubleday Dell
Jeb's Barn	G	86	Little Celebrations	Pearson Learning
Jellybean Tree, The	H	231	Sunshine	Wright Group
Jenius-The Amazing Guinea Pig	N	250+	King-Smith, Dick	Hyperion
Jennifer Pockets	I	205	Book Bank	Wright Group
Jennifer, Too	L	250+	Havill, Juanita	Hyperion
Jenny and the Cornstalk	L	890	Pair-It Books	Steck-Vaughn
Jenny Archer to the Rescue	M	250+	Conford, Ellen	Little, Brown & Co.
Jenny Archer, Author	M	250+	Conford, Ellen	Little, Brown & Co.
Jenny Lives on Hunter Street	H	141	Book Bank	Wright Group
Jeremy's Cake	F	97	Storyteller-Moon Rising	Wright Group/ McGraw-Hill
Jesse Owens: Olympic Hero	P	250+	Sabin, Francene	Troll
Jessica in the Dark	I	362	PM Story Books-Orange	Rigby
Jessica's Dress Up	F	130	Voyages	SRA/McGraw-Hill
Jessie's Flower	G	132	Read Alongs	Rigby
Jigaree, The	E	128	Story Box	Wright Group
Jillian Jiggs	J	250+	Gilman, Phoebe	Scholastic
Jilly the Kid	M	250+	Krailing, Tessa	Barron's Educational
Jim Meets the Thing	I	250+	Cohen, Miriam	Bantam Doubleday Dell
Jimmy	D	83	Foundations	Wright Group
Jimmy Lee Did It	J	250+	Cummings, Pat	Lothrop
Jimmy's Birthday Balloon	F	95	Foundations	Wright Group
Jimmy's Goal	E	159	Foundations	Wright Group
Jim's Dog Muffins	I	250+	Cohen, Miriam	Bantam Doubleday Dell
Jim's Trumpet	H	304	Sunshine	Wright Group
Jim's Visit to Kim	G	149	Ready Readers	Pearson Learning
Jip the Pirate	F	142	New Way Blue	Steck-Vaughn
Job for Giant Jim, A	J	298	Sunshine	Wright Group
Job for Jenny Archer, A	M	250+	Conford, Ellen	Little, Brown & Co.
Jobs	E	112	Benger, Wendy	Kaeden Books
Jock Jerome	E	99	Voyages	SRA/McGraw-Hill
Joe and Betsy the Dinosaur	J	250+	Hoban, Lillian	HarperTrophy
Joe and the BMX Bike	E	91	Oxford Reading Tree	Oxford University Press
Joe and the Mouse	F	138	Oxford Reading Tree	Oxford University Press

Title	Level	Words	Author/Series	Publisher/Distributor
Joe's Father	E	138	Book Bank	Wright Group
Joey	G	243	PM Extensions-Green	Rigby
Joey's Head	L	250+	Cretan, Gladys	Simon & Schuster
Joey's Rowboat	H	83	Little Books	Sadlier-Oxford
Jog, Frog, Jog	F	72	Gregorich, Barbara	School Zone
Johann Sebastian Bach: Great Man of Music	N	250+	Rookie Biographies	Children's Press
John Chapman: The Man Who Was Johnny Appleseed	N	250+	Rookie Biographies	Children's Press
John Muir: Man of the Wild Places	N	250+	Rookie Biographies	Children's Press
John Philip Sousa: The March King	N	250+	Rookie Biographies	Children's Press
Johnny Appleseed	K	250+	Moore, Eva	Scholastic
Johnny Lion's Book	J	250+	Hurd, Edith Thacher	HarperCollins
Johnny Lion's Rubber Boots	F		Hurd, Edith Thacher	HarperCollins
Johnny Long Legs	M	250+	Christopher, Matt	Little, Brown & Co.
Joke, The	H	186	Little Readers	Houghton Mifflin
Jolly Jumping Jelly Beans	E	121	Sunshine	Wright Group
Jolly Roger, the Pirate	D	138	PM Extensions-Yellow	Rigby
Jonathan Buys a Present	J	353	PM Story Books-Turquoise	Rigby
Jordan Is Hiding	A	24	Little Books for Early Readers	University of Maine
Jordan's Lucky Day	J	466	PM Story Books-Turquoise	Rigby
Josefina Story Quilt	L	250+	Coerr, Eleanor	HarperTrophy
Joshua James Likes Trucks	C	50	Rookie Readers	Children's Press
Josie Cleans Up	I	213	Little Readers	Houghton Mifflin
Joyful Noise: Poems for Two Voices	P	250+	Fleischman, Paul	HarperTrophy
Juan	H	77	City Kids	Rigby
Julian, Dream Doctor	N	250+	Cameron, Ann	Random House
Julian, Secret Agent	N	250+	Cameron, Ann	Random House
Julian's Glorious Summer	N	250+	Cameron, Ann	Random House
Julia's Lists	D	47	Little Celebrations	Pearson Learning
Julie's Mornings	K	250+	Ready Readers	Pearson Learning
Jumbaroo, The	H	173	Story Basket	Wright Group
Jumble Sale, The	E	81	Oxford Reading Tree	Oxford University Press
Jump and Thump!	C	18	Home Connection Collection	Rigby
Jump Right In	D	50	Ready Readers	Pearson Learning
Jump Rope	D	31	Visions	Wright Group
Jump the Broom	L	119	Books for Young Learners	Richard C. Owen
Jump, Frog	C	33	Stewart, J. & Salem, Lynn	Seedling
Jump, Jump, Kangaroo	B	31	Story Box	Wright Group
Jumpers	B	21	Sunshine	Wright Group
Jumping Shoes	C	34	Joy Readers	Dominie
Jungle Parade: A Singing Game	D	105	Little Celebrations	Pearson Learning
Jungle Spots	B	28	Little Celebrations	Pearson Learning
Jungle Tiger Cat	G	120	Frankford, Marilyn	Kaeden Books
Junie B. Jones and a Little Monkey Business	M	250+	Park, Barbara	Random House
Junie B. Jones and Her Big Fat Mouth	M	250+	Park, Barbara	Random House
Junie B. Jones and Some Sneaky Peeky Spying	M	250+	Park, Barbara	Random House
Junie B. Jones and that Meanie Jim's Birthday	M	250+	Park, Barbara	Random House
Junie B. Jones and the Stupid Smelly Bus	M	250+	Park, Barbara	Random House
Junie B. Jones and the Yucky Blucky Fruitcake	M	250+	Park, Barbara	Random House
Junie B. Jones Has a Monster Under Her Bed	M	250+	Park, Barbara	Random House
Junie B. Jones Is a Beauty Shop Guy	M	250+	Park, Barbara	Random House
Junie B. Jones Is a Party Animal	M	250+	Park, Barbara	Random House

Title	Level	Words	Author/Series	Publisher/Distributor
Junie B. Jones Is Not a Crook	M	250+	Park, Barbara	Random House
Junie B. Jones Loves Handsome Warren	M	250+	Park, Barbara	Random House
Junie B. Jones Smells Something Fishy	M	250+	Park, Barbara	Random House
Junior Gymnasts: #2 Katie's Big Move	M	250+	Slater, Teddy	Scholastic
Junk Box, The	C	54	Windmill Books	Rigby
Junkpile Robot, The	L	250+	Ready Readers	Pearson Learning
Just a Mess	I	206	Mayer, Mercer	Donovan
Just a Seed	E	74	Blaxland, Wendy	Scholastic
Just Add Water	C	41	Discovery World	Rigby
Just Enough	G	107	Salem, Lynn & Stewart, J.	Seedling
Just for Fun	J	250+	Literacy 2000	Rigby
Just for You	G	160	Mayer, Mercer	Donovan
Just Grandma and Me	I	186	Mayer, Mercer	Donovan
Just Hanging Around	J	223	Storyteller-Night Crickets	Wright Group/ McGraw-Hill
Just Like Dad	D	44	Hiris, Monica	Kaeden Books
Just Like Daddy	F	93	Asch, Frank	Simon & Schuster
Just Like Everyone Else	I		Kuskin, Karla	HarperCollins
Just Like Grandpa	C	49	Little Celebrations	Pearson Learning
Just Like Grandpa	E	81	Literacy 2000	Rigby
Just Like Me	E	138	Rookie Readers	Children's Press
Just Like Me	F		First Start	Troll
Just Like Me	J	2154	Story Box	Wright Group
Just Like Me!	D	62	Sunshine	Wright Group
Just Like My Grandpa	D	48	Rise & Shine	Hampton-Brown
Just Like Us	E	55	Ready Readers	Pearson Learning
Just Look at You	A	16	Sunshine	Wright Group
Just Me	C	51	Literacy 2000	Rigby
Just Me and My Babysitter	H	182	Mayer, Mercer	Donovan
Just Me and My Dad	H	161	Mayer, Mercer	Donovan
Just Me and My Puppy	H	190	Mayer, Mercer	Donovan
Just My Luck	G	136	Literacy 2000	Rigby
Just One Fish Would Do	I	250+	Home Connection Collection	Rigby
Just One Guinea Pig	I	339	PM Story Books-Orange	Rigby
Just Right for the Night	E		Voyages	SRA/McGraw-Hill
Just Right!	G	105	Sunshine	Wright Group
Just This Once	H	252	Sunshine	Wright Group
Just Us Women	K	250+	Caines, Jeannette	Scholastic
Justin and the Best Biscuits in the World	P	250+	Pitts, Walter & Mildred	Random House
Kangaroo from Wooloomooloo	H	254	Jellybeans	Rigby
Kangaroo in the Kitchen	D	72	Ready Readers	Pearson Learning
Kangaroos	K	250+	PM Animals in the Wild-Yellow	Rigby
Karina	D	40	Step-By-Step Series	Dominie
Kate Shelley and the Midnight Express	M	250+	Wetterer, Margaret	Carolrhoda Books
Katherine Dunham, Black Dancer	N	250+	Rookie Biographies	Children's Press
Katie Couldn't	F	176	Rookie Readers	Children's Press
Katie Did It	G	105	Rookie Readers	Children's Press
Katy and the Big Snow	L	250+	Burton, Virginia L.	Scholastic
Katydids	E	20	Books for Young Learners	Richard C. Owen
Kay's Birthday	C	26	KinderReaders	Rigby
Keelboat Annie	N	250+	Johnson, Janet P.	Troll

Title	Level	Words	Author/Series	Publisher/Distributor
Keep Out!	A	19	Ready Readers	Pearson Learning
Keep the Beat	D	48	Little Celebrations	Pearson Learning
Keep the Lights Burning Abbie	K	250+	Roop, Peter & Connie	Scholastic
Keeping Baby Animals Safe	C	56	Little Books	Sadlier-Oxford
Keeping Cool	C	18	Pacific Literacy	Pacific Learning
Keeping Cool	D	84	Foundations	Wright Group
Keeping Fit!	E	36	Little Celebrations	Pearson Learning
Keeping Score	J	240	Early Connections	Benchmark Education
Keeping Tadpoles	N	250+	Discovery World	Rigby
Keeping Warm! Keeping Cool!	K	946	Sunshine	Wright Group
Kenny and the Little Kickers	J	250+	Mareollo, Claudio	Scholastic
Kerri Strug: Heart of Gold	L	250+	Strug, Kerri & Brown, Greg	Scholastic
Key to the Playhouse, The	O	250+	York, Carol	Scholastic
Key to the Treasure	N	250+	Parish, Peggy	Yearling
Keys	B	31	Ready Readers	Pearson Learning
Kick, Pass, and Run	J	250+	Kessler, Leonard	HarperTrophy
Kick-a-Lot Shoes, The	H	433	Story Box	Wright Group
Kid Next Door, The	N	250+	Smith, Janice Lee	HarperTrophy
Kid Who Only Hit Homers, The	M	250+	Christopher, Matt	Little, Brown & Co.
Kids at Our School	I	107	City Kids	Rigby
Kids in Ms. Colman's Class: Author Day	M	250+	Martin, Ann M.	Scholastic
Kilmer's Pet Monster	L	250+	Dadey, Debbie & Jones, Marcia	Scholastic
Kindergarten	D	118	Carousel Readers	Dominie
King Arthur	M	250+	Brown, Marc	Little, Brown & Co.
King Beast's Birthday	L	250+	Literacy 2000	Rigby
King Midas & the Golden Touch	J	562	Traditional Tales	Dominie
King Midas and the Golden Touch	K	721	PM Story Books-Gold	Rigby
King, the Mice and the Cheese	K	250+	Gurney, Nancy	Random House
King's Equal, The	O	250+	Paterson, Katherine	HarperTrophy
King's Ring, The	C	38	KinderReaders	Rigby
King's Surprise, The	D	54	Stewart, J. & Salem, Lynn	Seedling
Kink the Mink	C	18	KinderReaders	Rigby
Kip and Tip	C	24	KinderReaders	Rigby
Kipper's Birthday	E	64	Oxford Reading Tree	Oxford University Press
Kiss for Little Bear	J	250+	Minarik, Else H.	HarperTrophy
Kiss for Little Bear, A	H	250+	Hoban, Tana	Scholastic
Kitchen Tools	D	104	Foundations	Wright Group
Kite and the Butterflies, The	I	364	Book Bank	Wright Group
Kite That Flew Away, The	H	279	Ready Readers	Pearson Learning
Kite, The	D	59	My First Reader	Grolier Press
Kites	C	41	Joy Readers	Dominie
Kitten Chased a Fly	C	57	Windmill	Rigby, Wright Group
Kittens	C	22	Literacy 2000	Rigby
Kittens	G	107	Discovery Links	Newbridge
Kitty and the Birds	C	64	PM Story Books	Rigby
Kitzikuba	G	198	Story Basket	Wright Group
Knight at Dawn, The	M	250+	Osborne, Mary Pope	Random House
Knights Don't Teach Piano	M	250+	Dadey, Debbie & Jones, Marcia	Scholastic
Knit, Knit, Knit, Knit	J	250+	Literacy 2000	Rigby
Knock! Knock!	K	250+	Carter, Jackie	Scholastic
Knock, Knock	C		Little Celebrations	Pearson Learning
Know-Nothing Birthday, A	K	250+	Spirn, Michelle Sobel	HarperTrophy

Title	Level	Words	Author/Series	Publisher/Distributor
Know-Nothings, The	K	250+	Spirn, Michelle Sobel	HarperTrophy
Koalas	E	36	Literacy 2000	Rigby
Koalas	F	45	Pebble Books	Grolier, Capstone
Koi's Python	P	250+	Moore, Miriam	Hyperion
Korky Paul	M	250+	Discovery World	Rigby
Koya Delaney and the Good Girl Blues	P	250+	Greenfield, Eloise	Scholastic
Kristy and the Walking Disaster	O	250+	Martin, Ann M.	Scholastic
Kwanzaa	K	225	Visions	Wright Group
Kyle's First Kwanzaa	L		Little Celebrations	Pearson Learning
Lad Who Went to the North Wind, The	J	796	Book Shop	Mondo Publishing
Ladybugs	D	42	Pebble Books	Grolier, Capstone
Lake Critter Journal	O		Little Celebrations	Pearson Learning
Larry and the Cookie	E	56	Rookie Readers	Children's Press
Last Chance for Magic	P	250+	Chew, Ruth	Scholastic
Last Look	P	250+	Bulla, Clyde Robert	Puffin Books
Last One in Is a Rotten Egg	J	250+	Kessler, Leonard	HarperTrophy
Last Puppy, The	K	244	Asch, Frank	Simon & Schuster
Late for Soccer (Football)	F	185	PM Story Books	Rigby
Late One Night	D	97	Mader, Jan	Kaeden Books
Later	D	106	Teacher's Choice Series	Dominie
Laughing Cake, The	G	89	Reading Corners	Dominie
Laundromat, The	B	25	Visions	Wright Group
Laundromat, The	D	50	Sunshine	Wright Group
Laura Ingalls Wilder: An Author's Story	L	250+	Pair-It Books	Steck-Vaughn
Laura Ingalls Wilder: Author of the Little House Books	N	250+	Rookie Biographies	Children's Press
Lavender	O	250+	Hesse, Karen	Henry Holt & Co.
Lavender the Library Cat	M	418	Jellybeans	Rigby
Lazy Jackal, The	M	561	Sunshine	Wright Group
Lazy Lions, Lucky Lambs	M	250+	Giff, Patricia Reilly	Bantam Doubleday Dell
Lazy Mary	D	191	Read-Togethers	Wright Group
Lazy Pig, The	C	78	PM Story Books	Rigby
Leaf Rain	F	82	Book Bank	Wright Group
Learning New Things	H	156	Foundations	Wright Group
Learning to Swim	I	234	My World	Steck-Vaughn
Leaves	C	29	Hoenecke, Karen	Kaeden Books
Leaves	I	250+	Momentum Literacy Program	Troll
Leaves	K	236	Pebble Books	Grolier, Capstone
Leaves, Fruits, Seeds, and Roots	C	26	Pacific Literacy	Pacific Learning
Left, Right	G	182	Sunshine	Wright Group
Leftovers, The: Catch Flies!	N	250+	Howard, Tristan	Scholastic
Leftovers, The: Fast Break!	N	250+	Howard, Tristan	Scholastic
Leftovers, The: Get Jammed!	N	250+	Howard, Tristan	Scholastic
Leftovers, The: Reach Their Goal!	N	250+	Howard, Tristan	Scholastic
Leftovers, The: Strike Out!	N	250+	Howard, Tristan	Scholastic
Leftovers, The: Use Their Heads!	N	250+	Howard, Tristan	Scholastic
Legend of the Bluebonnet, The	O	250+	DePaola, Tomie	Scholastic
Legend of the Hummingbird, The	M	250+	Folk Tales	Mondo Publishing
Legend of the Red Bird, The	K	389	Sunshine	Wright Group
Legs	A	21	Twig	Wright Group
Legs	D	21	Literacy 2000	Rigby

Title	Level	Words	Author/Series	Publisher/Distributor
Legs, Legs, Legs	A	15	Gossett, R. & Ballinger, Margaret	Scholastic
Legs, Legs, Legs	C	36	Wonder World	Wright Group
Leo the Late Bloomer	I	164	Kraus, Robert	Simon & Schuster
Leotyne Price: Opera Superstar	N		Williams, Sylvia	Children's Press
Leprechauns Don't Play Basketball	M	250+	Dadey, Debbie & Jones, Marcia	Scholastic
Let Me In	I	1814	Story Box	Wright Group
Let's Bake	G	195	Discovery Links	Newbridge
Let's Be Enemies	J	250+	Sendak, Maurice	Harper & Row
Let's Be Friends	D	23	Pair-It Books	Steck-Vaughn
Let's Build a Tower	B	15	Literacy 2000	Rigby
Let's Celebrate	D	33	Rise & Shine	Hampton-Brown
Let's Eat	E	63	Teacher's Choice Series	Dominie
Let's Get a Pet	F	22	Jellybeans	Rigby
Let's Get Moving	M	250+	Literacy 2000	Rigby
Let's Go	A	32	Reading Corners	Dominie
Let's Go	B	81	Early Connections	Benchmark Education
Let's Go	C	30	Windmill	Wright Group
Let's Go Marching	E	94	Ready Readers	Pearson Learning
Let's Go Shopping	C	34	Rise & Shine	Hampton-Brown
Let's Go, Philadelphia!	M	250+	Giff, Patricia Reilly	Bantam Doubleday Dell
Let's Have a Swim	C	74	Sunshine	Wright Group
Let's Make Something New	G	116	Discovery Links	Newbridge
Let's Move!	B	29	Ready Readers	Pearson Learning
Let's Paint	C	51	Rise & Shine	Hampton-Brown
Let's Play Ball	B	40	Little Books for Early Readers	University of Maine
Let's Play Ball	C	68	New Way Red	Steck-Vaughn
Let's Play Basketball	E	46	Geddes, Diana	Kaeden Books
Let's Pretend	B	40	Home Connection Collection	Rigby
Letter to Amy, A	K	250+	Keats, Ezra Jack	Harper & Row
Letter, The	B	15	Twig	Wright Group
Letters for Mr. James	H	203	Sunshine	Wright Group
Levi Sings	C	29	Teacher's Choice Series	Dominie
Liar, Liar Pants on Fire	I	250+	Cohen, Miriam	Bantam Doubleday Dell
Library, The	C	33	Carousel Readers	Dominie
Library, The	D	96	Emergent	Pioneer Valley
License Plates	J	411	PM Story Books-Turquoise	Rigby
Life in the City	J	307	Early Connections	Benchmark Education
Life in the Desert	M	250+	Pair-It Books	Steck-Vaughn
Life in the Mangroves	I	172	Home Connection Collection	Rigby
Life on a Farm	A	24	Early Connections	Benchmark Education
Lift Off!	G	121	Pair-It Books	Steck-Vaughn
Lift the Sky Up	H	133	Little Readers	Houghton Mifflin
Lift the Sky Up	H	133	Little Celebrations	Pearson Learning
Lift-off!	I	141	Pacific Literacy	Pacific Learning
Light	A	30	Twig	Wright Group
Light	J	250+	Momentum Literacy Program	Troll
Light and Shadow	G	138	Discovery Links	Newbridge
Lighthouse Children, The	I	250+	Hoff, Syd	HarperTrophy
Lighthouse Mermaid, The	M	250+	Karr, Kathleen	Hyperion
Lightning	L	279	Pebble Books	Grolier, Capstone
Lightning Liz	F	41	Rookie Readers	Children's Press

Title	Level	Words	Author/Series	Publisher/Distributor
Lights at Night	C	33	Pacific Literacy	Pacific Learning
Lightweight Rocket and Other Cases, The	O	250+	Simon, Seymour	Avon Books
Like Me	D	20	Book Bank	Wright Group
Like My Daddy	D	129	Visions	Wright Group
Lilacs, Lotuses, and Ladybugs	L	402	Evangeline Nicholas Collection	Wright Group
Lili the Brave	N	250+	Armstrong, Jennifer	Random House
Lili's Breakfast	F	156	Storyteller-Setting Sun	Wright Group/ McGraw-Hill
Lilly-Lolly-Little-Legs	H	129	Literacy 2000	Rigby
Lily and Miss Liberty	M	250+	Stephens, Carla	Scholastic
Lin's Backpack	C	49	Little Celebrations	Pearson Learning
Lion and the Mouse, The	F	115	New Way Red	Steck-Vaughn
Lion and the Mouse, The	G	125	PM Story Books	Rigby
Lion and the Mouse, The	G	250	Traditional Tales & More	Rigby
Lion and the Mouse, The	J	285	Sunshine	Wright Group
Lion and the Mouse, The	J	325	Little Books	Sadlier-Oxford
Lion and the Mouse, The	K	557	Pair-It Books	Steck-Vaughn
Lion and the Mouse, The	M	499	Aesop's Fables	Dominie
Lion and the Rabbit, The	F	99	PM Story Books	Rigby
Lion Dancer: Ernie Wan's Chinese New Year	N	250+	Waters, Kate & Slovenz-Low, Madeline	Scholastic
Lion in the Night, The	J	250+	Momentum Literacy Program	Troll
Lion Roars, The	I	270	Ready Readers	Pearson Learning
Lion Talk	I	216	Storyteller-Night Crickets	Wright Group/ McGraw-Hill
Lion to Guard Us, A	P	250+	Bulla, Clyde Robert	HarperTrophy
Lionel and Amelia	L	702	Book Shop	Mondo Publishing
Lionel and Louise	K	250+	Krensky, Stephen	Puffin Books
Lionel at Large	K	250+	Krensky, Stephen	Puffin Books
Lions	L	644	Pair-It Books	Steck-Vaughn
Lions & Tigers	K	250+	PM Animals in the Wild-Yellow	Rigby
Lions at Lunchtime	M	250+	Osborne, Mary Pope	Random House
Lion's Tail, The	F	147	Reading Unlimited	Pacific Learning
Listen	D	35	Visions	Wright Group
Listen to Me	G	47	Rookie Readers	Children's Press
Listening in Bed	M	116	Book Bank	Wright Group
Litle Mouse's Trail Tale	I	349	Book Shop	Mondo Publishing
Little Bear	D	77	My First Reader	Grolier Press
Little Bear	J	1664	Minarik, Else H.	HarperCollins
Little Bear's Friend	J	250+	Minarik, Else H.	HarperTrophy
Little Bear's Visit	J	250+	Minarik, Else H.	HarperTrophy
Little Bike, The	C	29	Joy Readers	Dominie
Little Bird	E	42	Sunshine	Wright Group
Little Black, a Pony	J	250+	Farley, Walter	Random House
Little Blue and Little Yellow	J	250+	Lionni, Leo	Scholastic
Little Boy Blue	D	32	Sunshine	Wright Group
Little Brother	A	14	Sunshine	Wright Group
Little Brother	C	14	Story Box	Wright Group
Little Brown House	H	266	Jellybeans	Rigby
Little Brown Jay, The: A Tale from India	L	366	Folk Tales	Mondo Publishing
Little Bulldozer Helps Again	F	197	PM Extensions-Blue	Rigby
Little Bulldozer Man	E	170	PM Story Books	Rigby
Little Car	F	181	Sunshine	Wright Group

Title	Level	Words	Author/Series	Publisher/Distributor
Little Chick's Friend Duckling	I	572	Kwitz, Mary Deball	HarperTrophy
Little Chief	K	250+	Hoff, Syd	HarperCollins
Little Cousins' Visit, The	C	123	Emergent	Pioneer Valley
Little Danny Dinosaur	G	195	First Start	Troll
Little Dinosaur Escapes	J	389	PM Story Books-Turquoise	Rigby
Little Elephant	G	192	New Way Blue	Steck-Vaughn
Little Firefighter, The	M	867	Sunshine	Wright Group
Little Fireman	J	250+	Brown, Margaret Wise	HarperCollins
Little Fish that Got Away	I	250+	Cook, Bernadine	Scholastic
Little Frog's Monster Story	E	144	Ready Readers	Pearson Learning
Little Ghost Goes to School	G	210	TOTTS	Tott Publications
Little Ghost's Baby Brother	G	221	TOTTS	Tott Publications
Little Ghost's Vacation	G	118	TOTTS	Tott Publications
Little Girl and Her Beetle, The	I	250+	Literacy 2000	Rigby
Little Gorilla	J	167	Bornstein, Ruth	Clarion
Little Hawk's New Name	K	250+	Bolognese, Don	Scholastic
Little Hearts	C	44	Story Box	Wright Group
Little Hen, The	D	107	Ready Readers	Pearson Learning
Little House	A	14	Ready Readers	Pearson Learning
Little House, The	I	391	Pacific Literacy	Pacific Learning
Little Icicle	O	250+	Szymanski, Lois	Avon Camelot
Little Kid	H	169	Literacy 2000	Rigby
Little Kittens	B	27	Ready Readers	Pearson Learning
Little Knight, The	K	250+	Reading Unlimited	Pacific Learning
Little Leaf's Journey, The	I	564	New Way Orange	Steck-Vaughn
Little Lefty	M	250+	Christopher, Matt	Little, Brown & Co.
Little Meanie's Lunch	D	90	Story Box	Wright Group
Little Miss Muffet	F		Literacy 2000	Rigby
Little Miss Stoneybrook and Dawn	O	250+	Martin, Ann M.	Scholastic
Little Monkey Is Stuck	E	251	Foundations	Wright Group
Little Old Lady Who Danced on the Moon, The	M	711	Sunshine	Wright Group
Little One Inch	K	384	Gibson, A. & Akiyam, M.	Scholastic
Little Overcoat, The	F	237	Book Shop	Mondo Publishing
Little Penguin's Tale	L	250+	Wood, Audrey	Scholastic
Little Pig	C	63	Story Box	Wright Group
Little Polar Bear and the Brave Little Hare	K	250+	DeBeer, Hans	North-South Books
Little Puppy Rap	I	211	Sunshine	Wright Group
Little Rabbit Is Sad	D	97	Williams, Deborah	Kaeden Books
Little Red and the Wolf	I	316	Pair-It Books	Steck-Vaughn
Little Red Bus, The	H	222	PM Story Books	Rigby
Little Red Hen	G	255	New Way Green	Steck-Vaughn
Little Red Hen	I	250+	Hunia, Fran	Ladybird Books
Little Red Hen	K	558	Galdone, Paul	Clarion
Little Red Hen, The	B	87	Windmill	Wright Group
Little Red Hen, The	G	256	Storyteller-Moon Rising	Wright Group/ McGraw-Hill
Little Red Hen, The	H	375	Traditional Tales	Dominie
Little Red Hen, The	I	226	Sunshine	Wright Group
Little Red Hen, The	I	416	Traditional Tales & More	Rigby
Little Red Hen, The	J	250+	Galdone, Paul	Viking
Little Red Pig, The	G	214	Ready Readers	Pearson Learning
Little Red Riding Hood	H	250+	Hunia, Fran	Ladybird Books

Title	Level	Words	Author/Series	Publisher/Distributor
Little Red Riding Hood	J	250+	PM Trad. Tales & Plays-Turq.	Rigby
Little Red Riding Hood	K	250+	Enrichment	Wright Group
Little Runner of the Longhouse	K	250+	Baker, Betty	HarperTrophy
Little Sea Pony, The	P	250+	Cresswell, Helen	Simon & Schuster
Little Seed, A	B	18	Smart Starts	Rigby
Little Sister	C	40	Mitchell, Robin	Scholastic
Little Snowman, The	C	59	PM Extensions-Red	Rigby
Little Soup's Birthday	K	250+	Peck, Robert	Bantam Doubleday Dell
Little Spider, The	L	250+	Literacy 2000	Rigby
Little Swan	M	250+	Geras, Adele	Random House
Little Things	A	33	PM Starters	Rigby
Little Tin Soldier,The	M	766	Tales from Hans Andersen	Wright Group
Little Tuppen	I	250+	Galdone, Paul	Houghton Mifflin
Little Vampire and the Midnight Bear	L	250+	Kwitz, Mary Deball	Puffin Books
Little Walrus Rising	K	250+	Young, Carol	Scholastic
Little Whale, The	M	1057	Sunshine	Wright Group
Little Witch Goes to School	K	250+	Hautzig, Deborah	Random House
Little Witch's Big Night	K	250+	Hautzig, Deborah	Random House
Little Women	M	250+	Bullseye	Random House
Little Yellow Chicken, The	I	322	Sunshine	Wright Group
Little Yellow Chicken's House, The	F	287	Story Basket	Wright Group
Little Zoot	E	33	Little Celebrations	Pearson Learning
Little, Little Man, The	M	741	Book Bank	Wright Group
Littles and the Great Halloween Scare, The	M	250+	Peterson, John	Scholastic
Littles and the Lost Children, The	M	250+	Peterson, John	Scholastic
Littles and the Terrible Tiny Kid, The	M	250+	Peterson, John	Scholastic
Littles and the Trash Tinies, The	M	250+	Peterson, John	Scholastic
Littles Give a Party, The	M	250+	Peterson, John	Scholastic
Littles Go Exploring, The	M	250+	Peterson, John	Scholastic
Littles Go to School, The	M	250+	Peterson, John	Scholastic
Littles Have a Wedding, The	M	250+	Peterson, John	Scholastic
Littles Take a Trip, The	M	250+	Peterson, John	Scholastic
Littles to the Rescue, The	M	250+	Peterson, John	Scholastic
Littles, The	M	250+	Peterson, John	Scholastic
Living in the Sky	K	328	Sunshine	Wright Group
Lizard	E	80	Foundations	Wright Group
Lizard Loses His Tail	D	54	PM Story Books	Rigby
Lizard on a Stick	C	38	Wonder World	Wright Group
Lizards	L	356	Wonder World	Wright Group
Lizards and Salamanders	M	250+	Reading Unlimited	Pacific Learning
Lizard's Grandmother	J	336	Sunshine	Wright Group
Lizzie's Lizard	L	289	Storyteller Nonfiction	Wright Group/ McGraw-Hill
Llama Pajamas	N	250+	Clymer, Susan	Scholastic
Lobster Fishing at Dawn	I	194	Ready Readers	Pearson Learning
Lobstering	A	14	Little Books for Early Readers	University of Maine
Locked in the Library!	M	250+	Brown, Marc	Little, Brown & Co.
Locked Out	G	195	PM Story Books	Rigby
Locked Out!	B	15	Twig	Wright Group
Log Hotel, The	A	22	Little Celebrations	Pearson Learning
Log, The	C	29	New Way Red	Steck-Vaughn
Lola and Miss Kitty	H	250+	Little Readers	Houghton Mifflin

Title	Level	Words	Author/Series	Publisher/Distributor
Lollipop	G		Watson, Wendy	Crowell
Lollipop Please, A	H	73	Literacy 2000	Rigby
Lonely Bull, The	E	116	Pacific Literacy	Pacific Learning
Lonely Dragon, The	J	250+	Momentum Literacy Program	Troll
Lonely Giant, The	K	449	Literacy 2000	Rigby
Long Ago	D	105	Early Connections	Benchmark Education
Long Ago and Far Away	P	250+	Wildcats	Wright Group
Long Grass of Tumbledown Road	M	283	Read Alongs	Rigby
Long Shot for Paul	M	250+	Christopher, Matt	Little, Brown & Co.
Long Walk, A	E	131	Twig	Wright Group
Long Way to a New Land, A	L	250+	Sandin, Joan	HarperTrophy
Long Way Westward, The	L	250+	Sandin, Joan	HarperTrophy
Long, Long Tail, The	B	33	Sunshine	Wright Group
Longest Noodle in the World, The	D	66	Joy Readers	Dominie
Look	A	20	Sunshine	Wright Group
Look Again	C	47	Book Shop	Mondo Publishing
Look at Conor	A	27	Little Books for Early Readers	University of Maine
Look at Dogs, A	M	551	Pair-It Books	Steck-Vaughn
Look at Kyle	B	46	Little Books for Early Readers	University of Maine
Look at Me	A	17	Little Books for Early Readers	University of Maine
Look at Me	B	48	PM Starters	Rigby
Look at Me	D	67	Carousel Readers	Dominie
Look at Me	F	48	Literacy 2000	Rigby
Look at Me!	A	27	KinderReaders	Rigby
Look at Spiders, A	M	785	Pair-It Books	Steck-Vaughn
Look at the Garden	A	43	Windmill Books	Rigby
Look at the Moon	N	405	Book Shop	Mondo Publishing
Look at the Ocean, A	B	50	Little Books for Early Readers	University of Maine
Look at This	B	57	Carousel Earlybirds	Dominie
Look Closer	A	21	Ready Readers	Pearson Learning
Look for Me	D	71	Story Box	Wright Group
Look for Me	G	208	Little Readers	Houghton Mifflin
Look Here!	E	67	Wonder World	Wright Group
Look in Mom's Purse	D	60	Carousel Readers	Dominie
Look Inside	J	168	Storyteller Nonfiction	Wright Group/ McGraw-Hill
Look into Space, A	D	71	Discovery World	Rigby
Look of Snakes, A	M	784	Pair-It Books	Steck-Vaughn
Look Out for Your Tail	J	250+	Literacy 2000	Rigby
Look Out!	B	15	Literacy 2000	Rigby
Look Out!	D	53	Sunshine	Wright Group
Look Out, Dan!	B	34	Story Box	Wright Group
Look Out, Washington D.C.!	O	250+	Giff, Patricia Reilly	Bantam Doubleday Dell
Look Up	E	44	Little Celebrations	Pearson Learning
Look Up, Look Down	D	165	PM Nonfiction-Red	Rigby
Look What I Can Do	A	15	Aruego, Jose	Macmillan
Look Who's Playing First Base	M	250+	Christopher, Matt	Little, Brown & Co.
Look!	C	43	Little Celebrations	Pearson Learning
Looking After Baby	E	143	Storyteller Nonfiction	Wright Group/ McGraw-Hill
Looking After Grandpa	D	91	Foundations	Wright Group
Looking at Baby Animals	E	54	Teacher's Choice Series	Dominie

Title	Level	Words	Author/Series	Publisher/Distributor
Looking at Insects	L	250+	Discovery World	Rigby
Looking Down	C	70	PM Starters	Rigby
Looking Down	E	130	Early Connections	Benchmark Education
Looking for a Letter	F	223	New Way Green	Steck-Vaughn
Looking for Angus	H	99	Ready Readers	Pearson Learning
Looking for Eggs	C	47	Windmill Books	Rigby
Looking for Halloween	C	49	Urmston, Kathleen & Evans, Karen	Kaeden Books
Looking for Patterns	J	160	Early Connections	Benchmark Education
Looking for Shapes	K	289	Early Connections	Benchmark Education
Looking into Space	L	345	Early Connections	Benchmark Education
Loose Laces	L	209	Reading Unlimited	Pacific Learning
Lost	A	29	TOTTS	Tott Publications
Lost	C	38	Story Box	Wright Group
Lost and Found	D	55	New Way Red	Steck-Vaughn
Lost and Found	D	64	Carousel Readers	Dominie
Lost at the Fun Park	F	192	PM Extensions-Blue	Rigby
Lost at the White House: A 1909 Easter Story	L	250+	Griest, Lisa	Carolrhoda Books
Lost Continent and Other Cases, The	O	250+	Simon, Seymour	Avon Books
Lost Glove, The	C	105	Foundations	Wright Group
Lost Hikers and Other Cases, The	O	250+	Simon, Seymour	Avon Books
Lost in the Fog	D	59	Ready Readers	Pearson Learning
Lost in the Forest	I	298	PM Story Books-Orange	Rigby
Lost in the Museum	I	250+	Cohen, Miriam	Bantam Doubleday Dell
Lost Sheep, The	I	219	Little Readers	Houghton Mifflin
Lost Tooth, The	J	632	New Way Orange	Steck-Vaughn
Lost!	B	18	Smart Starts	Rigby
Lot Happened Today, A	I	193	Ready Readers	Pearson Learning
Lots and Lots of stairs	B	33	Little Books for Early Readers	University of Maine
Lots of Caps	I	205	New Way Blue	Steck-Vaughn
Lots of Dogs	C	68	Teacher's Choice Series	Dominie
Lots of Dolls!	C	61	The Candid Collection	Dominie
Lots of Things	A	23	Reading Corners	Dominie
Lots of Toys	B	47	Carousel Earlybirds	Dominie
Lottie Goat & Donny Goat	H	145	Ready Readers	Pearson Learning
Louis Braille: The Boy Who Invented Books for the Blind	N		Davidson, Margaret	Scholastic
Love Is	C	11	Visions	Wright Group
Lucky Baseball Bat, The	M	250+	Christopher, Matt	Little, Brown & Co.
Lucky Day for Little Dinosaur, A	F	135	PM Extensions-Yellow	Rigby
Lucky Duck, The	E	73	Ready Readers	Pearson Learning
Lucky Feather, The	L	250+	Literacy 2000	Rigby
Lucky Goes to Dog School	E	127	PM Story Books	Rigby
Lucky Last Luke	M	250+	Clark, Margaret	Sundance
Lucky Stars	L	250+	Adler, David	Random House
Lucky Stone, The	P	250+	Clifton, Lucille	Bantam Doubleday Dell
Lucky We Have a Station Wagon	F	259	Foundations	Wright Group
Lucy Meets a Dragon	L	250+	Literacy 2000	Rigby
Lucy's Sore Knee	F	93	Windmill	Wright Group
Ludwig van Beethoven: Musical Pioneer	N	250+	Rookie Biographies	Children's Press
Luke's Bully	N	250+	Winthrop, Elizabeth	Puffin Books
Luke's Go-Cart	L	656	PM Story Books-Gold	Rigby
Lulu Goes to Witch School	J	250+	O'Connor, Jane	HarperTrophy

Title	Level	Words	Author/Series	Publisher/Distributor
Lump in My Bed, A	D	48	Book Bank	Wright Group
Lunch	F	156	Urmston, Kathleen & Evans, Karen	Kaeden Books
Lunch at the Pond	E	146	Foundations	Wright Group
Lunch at the Zoo	B	64	Blaxland, Wendy & Brimage, C.	Scholastic
Lunch Bunch, The	I	169	Storyteller-Moon Rising	Wright Group/ McGraw-Hill
Lunch Orders	C	18	Tadpoles	Rigby
Lunch Time	C	69	Carousel Readers	Dominie
Lunchbox, The	H	90	Pacific Literacy	Pacific Learning
Lydia and Her Cat	G	77	Oxford Reading Tree	Oxford University Press
Lydia and Her Garden	G	88	Oxford Reading Tree	Oxford University Press
Lydia and Her Kitten	G	77	Oxford Reading Tree	Oxford University Press
Lydia and the Ducks	G	87	Oxford Reading Tree	Oxford University Press
Lydia and the Present	F	77	Oxford Reading Tree	Oxford University Press
M & M and the Bad News Babies	K	250+	Ross, Pat	The Penguin Group
M & M and the Big Bag	K	250+	Ross, Pat	The Penguin Group
M & M and the Halloween Monster	K	250+	Ross, Pat	The Penguin Group
M & M and the Haunted House Game	K	250+	Ross, Pat	The Penguin Group
M & M and the Mummy Mess	K	250+	Ross, Pat	The Penguin Group
M & M and the Santa Secrets	K	250+	Ross, Pat	Puffin Chapters
M & M and the Super Child Afternoon	K	250+	Ross, Pat	The Penguin Group
Ma and Pa Dracula	O	250+	Martin, Ann M.	Scholastic
Machines	C	36	Little Celebrations	Pearson Learning
Machines	E	44	Twig	Wright Group
Machines at Work	H	101	Little Red Readers	Sundance
Mad Scientist, the Mountain Gorillas	M	250+	Schultz, Irene	Wright Group
Madeline	K	250+	Bemelmans, Ludwig	Scholastic
Madeline's Rescue	K	250+	Bemelmans, Ludwig	Scholastic
Made's Birthday	L	250+	Little Celebrations	Pearson Learning
Mae-Nerd	C	44	Teacher's Choice Series	Dominie
Maggie Moves Away	H	327	Adventures in Reading	Dominie
Magic All Around	L	250+	Literacy 2000	Rigby
Magic Box, The	K	250+	Brenner, Barbara	Bantam Doubleday Dell
Magic Finger, The	N	250+	Dahl, Roald	Puffin Books
Magic Fish	L	870	Littledale, Freya	Scholastic
Magic Fish, The	J	250+	Rylant, Cynthia	Scholastic
Magic Food	C	26	Smart Starts	Rigby
Magic Machine, The	C	163	Sunshine	Wright Group
Magic Money	L	250+	Adler, David	Random House
Magic Pear Tree, The	I		Little Celebrations	Pearson Learning
Magic Porridge Pot, The	I	321	New Way Orange	Steck-Vaughn
Magic Porridge Pot, The	L	497	Sunshine	Wright Group
Magic Ride, The	M	170	Book Bank	Wright Group
Magic School Bus and the Electric Field Trip	P	250+	Cole, Joanna & Degen, Bruce	Scholastic
Magic School Bus at the Waterworks	P	250+	Cole, Joanna & Degen, Bruce	Scholastic
Magic School Bus Blows Its Top	P	250+	Cole, Joanna	Scholastic
Magic School Bus Gets All Dried Up	P	250+	Cole, Joanna & Degen, Bruce	Scholastic
Magic School Bus Gets Ants in Its Pants	P	250+	Cole, Joanna & Degen, Bruce	Scholastic
Magic School Bus Gets Baked in a Cake	P	250+	Cole, Joanna & Degen, Bruce	Scholastic
Magic School Bus Goes Upstream	P	250+	Cole, Joanna & Degen, Bruce	Scholastic
Magic School Bus in the Haunted Museum	P	250+	Cole, Joanna	Scholastic

Title	Level	Words	Author/Series	Publisher/Distributor
Magic School Bus in the Time of the Dinosaurs	P	250+	Cole, Joanna & Degen, Bruce	Scholastic
Magic School Bus Inside a Beehive	P	250+	Cole, Joanna & Degen, Bruce	Scholastic
Magic School Bus Inside a Hurricane	P	250+	Cole, Joanna & Degen, Bruce	Scholastic
Magic School Bus Inside Ralphie	P	250+	Cole, Joanna & Degen, Bruce	Scholastic
Magic School Bus Inside the Earth	P	250+	Cole, Joanna & Degen, Bruce	Scholastic
Magic School Bus Inside the Human Body	P	250+	Cole, Joanna & Degen, Bruce	Scholastic
Magic School Bus Lost in the Solar System	P	250+	Cole, Joanna & Degen, Bruce	Scholastic
Magic School Bus on the Ocean Floor	P	250+	Cole, Joanna & Degen, Bruce	Scholastic
Magic School Bus Plants Seeds	P	250+	Cole, Joanna & Degen, Bruce	Scholastic
Magic School Bus Spins a Web	P	250+	Cole, Joanna	Scholastic
Magic Squad and the Dog of Great Potential	P	250+	Quattlebaum, Mary	Bantam Doubleday Dell
Magic Store, The	J	203	Sunshine	Wright Group
Magic Wand, The	E	100	Start to Read	School Zone
Magic!	A	23	Twig	Wright Group
Magician's Lunch	I	272	Jellybeans	Rigby
Magnets	C	55	Early Connections	Benchmark Education
Magnets	E	52	Discovery Links	Newbridge
Magnets	I	79	Sunshine	Wright Group
Magnifying Glass, The	C	45	Foundations	Wright Group
Magpie's Baking Day	F	132	PM Story Books	Rigby
Magpie's Tail, The	L	543	Pacific Literacy	Pacific Learning
Mai Li's Surprise	F	63	Books for Young Learners	Richard C. Owen
Mail Came Today, The	C	35	Carousel Readers	Dominie
Mail Myself to You	E	60	Little Celebrations	Pearson Learning
Major Jump	B	21	Sunshine	Wright Group
Make a "Talking" Card	H	165	Sunshine	Wright Group
Make a Boat That Floats	I	126	Book Bank	Wright Group
Make a Bottle Orchestra	J	250	Sunshine	Wright Group
Make a Glider	G	57	Storyteller-Setting Sun	Wright Group/ McGraw-Hill
Make a Guitar	J	540	Sunshine	Wright Group
Make a Lei	F	39	Pacific Literacy	Pacific Learning
Make a Pinata	C	16	Little Celebrations	Pearson Learning
Make a Valentine	C	36	Book Shop	Mondo Publishing
Make a Wish, Molly	O	250+	Cohen, Barbara	Bantam Doubleday Dell
Make Dinosaur Eggs	I	188	Sunshine	Wright Group
Make It Spin	D	18	Pacific Literacy	Pacific Learning
Make Masks for a Play	J	540	Sunshine	Wright Group
Make Mini Movies	I	309	Sunshine	Wright Group
Make Prints and Patterns	K	454	Sunshine	Wright Group
Make Room for Elisa	O	250+	Hurwitz, Johanna	Puffin Books
Make Way for Ducklings	L	250+	McCloskey, Robert	Puffin Books
Make Your Own Party	I	314	Sunshine	Wright Group
Making a Garden	A	28	Foundations	Wright Group
Making a Memory	D	53	Ballinger, Margaret	Scholastic
Making a Plate	H	183	Ready Readers	Pearson Learning
Making Caterpillars and Butterflies	I	162	Literacy 2000	Rigby
Making Friends	J	214	Foundations	Wright Group
Making Friends on Beacon Street	M	250+	Literacy 2000	Rigby
Making Mountains	B	35	Ballinger, Margaret & Gossett, R.	Scholastic
Making Movies	F	43	Sunshine	Wright Group
Making Music	C	35	Wonder World	Wright Group

Title	Level	Words	Author/Series	Publisher/Distributor
Making Oatmeal	E	38	Interaction	Rigby
Making Pancakes	D	39	Carousel Readers	Dominie
Making Patterns	C	30	Twig	Wright Group
Making Pictures	B	48	Foundations	Wright Group
Making Things	D	64	Foundations	Wright Group
Malawi-Keeper of the Trees	K	250+	Little Celebrations	Pearson Learning
Malcolm Magpie	G	126	Storyteller-Setting Sun	Wright Group/ McGraw-Hill
Mama Goes to School	D	47	Visions	Wright Group
Mamma Hen, Come Quick!	C	35	Ready Readers	Pearson Learning
Man in the Moon, The	H	173	Pair-It Books	Steck-Vaughn
Man Out at First	M	250+	Christopher, Matt	Little, Brown & Co.
Manatee Winter	K	250+	Zoehfeld, Kathleen Weidnetz	Scholastic
Manly Ferry Pigeon, The	L	375	Sunshine	Wright Group
Manners of a Pig, The	I	299	Book Shop	Mondo Publishing
Manners, Please!	C	27	Pair-It Books	Steck-Vaughn
Many Friends, Many Languages	D	98	Fiesta Series	Dominie
Map Book, The	F	144	Sunshine	Wright Group
Maple Thanksgiving, The	L		Little Celebrations	Pearson Learning
Maple Trees	F	118	Pebble Books	Grolier, Capstone
Maps and Codes	P	250+	Wildcats	Wright Group
Marcella	L	250+	Literacy 2000	Rigby
March Along with Me	D	56	Literacy 2000	Rigby
March for Freedom	G	132	Twig	Wright Group
March, March, Marching	D	60	Teacher's Choice Series	Dominie
Marching Band	B	35	Urmston, Kathleen & Evans, Karen	Kaeden Books
Marco Saves Grandpa	I	232	Foundations	Wright Group
Mare for Young Wolf, A	L	250+	Shefelman, Janice	Random House
Margaret Wise Brown	N	250+	Rookie Biographies	Children's Press
Margarito's Carvings	L	250+	Little Celebrations	Pearson Learning
Maria	I	72	City Kids	Rigby
Maria Goes to School	D	174	Foundations	Wright Group
Marigold and Grandma on the Town	J	250+	Calmenson, Stephanie	HarperTrophy
Mario's Mayan Journey	P	1021	Book Shop	Mondo Publishing
Market Day for Mrs. Wordy	K	177	Sunshine	Wright Group
Market, The	D	48	Joy Readers	Dominie
Marketplace, The	E	58	Visions	Wright Group
Mark's Monster	I		Reading Unlimited	Pacific Learning
Marmalade's Nap	F	57	Wheeler, Cindy	Alfred A. Knopf, Inc.
Marmalade's Snowy Day	F		Wheeler, Cindy	Alfred A. Knopf, Inc.
Martian Goo	E	65	Salem, Lynn & Stewart, J.	Seedling
Martians Don't Take Temperatures	M	250+	Dadey, Debbie & Jones, Marcia	Scholastic
Martin and the Teacher's Pets	K	250+	Chardiet, Bernice & Maccarone, Grace	Scholastic
Martin and the Tooth Fairy	K	250+	Chardiet, Bernice & Maccarone, Grace	Scholastic
Martin Luther King Day	L	250+	Lowery, Linda	Scholastic
Martin Luther King, Jr.	L	290	Pebble Books	Grolier, Capstone
Martin Luther King, Jr., a Man Who Changed Things	N	250+	Rookie Biographies	Children's Press
Martin's Mighty Hit	M	390	Windmill Books	Rigby
Marvella and the Moon	F	303	Book Shop	Mondo Publishing
Marvelous Me	F	29	Literacy 2000	Rigby

Title	Level	Words	Author/Series	Publisher/Distributor
Marvelous Treasure, The	M	481	Sunshine	Wright Group
Marvin Redpost: Alone in His Teacher's House	L	250+	Sachar, Louis	Random House
Marvin Redpost: Is He a Girl?	L	250+	Sachar, Louis	Random House
Marvin Redpost: Kidnapped at Birth?	L	250+	Sachar, Louis	Random House
Marvin Redpost: Why Pick on Me?	L	250+	Sachar, Louis	Random House
Marvin's Manners	E	32	Pair-It Books	Steck-Vaughn
Mary Maroney Hides Out	L	250+	Kline, Suzy	Bantam Doubleday Dell
Mary Marony and the Chocolate Surprise	L	250+	Kline, Suzy	Bantam Doubleday Dell
Mary Marony and the Snake	L	250+	Kline, Suzy	Bantam Doubleday Dell
Mary Marony, Mummy Girl	L	250+	Kline, Suzy	Bantam Doubleday Dell
Mary Wore Her Red Dress	D	170	Peek, Merle	Clarion
Mask, The	E	45	Pair-It Books	Steck-Vaughn
Masks	C	41	Pebble Books	Grolier, Capstone
Masks	E	62	Wonder World	Wright Group
Matchbox Collection, A	K	250+	Stepping Stones	Nelson/Michaels Assoc.
Materials	L	250+	Discovery World	Rigby
Math Is Everywhere	F	95	Sunshine	Wright Group
Matthew Likes to Read	J	144	Ready to Read	Pacific Learning
Matthew's Tantrum	J	250+	Literacy 2000	Rigby
Maui and the Sun	M	359	Pacific Literacy	Pacific Learning
Maui and the Sun	M	250+	Ready to Read	Pacific Learning
Max	J	234	Isadora, Rachel	Macmillan
Max Malone and the Great Cereal Rip-off	N	250+	Herman, Charlotte	Henry Holt & Co.
Max Malone Makes a Million	N	250+	Herman, Charlotte	Henry Holt & Co.
Max Malone the Magnificent	N	250+	Herman, Charlotte	Scholastic
Max Malone, Superstar	N	250+	Herman, Charlotte	Scholastic
Max's Box	B	43	Little Celebrations	Pearson Learning
May I Stay Home Today?	E	73	Tadpoles	Rigby
Maybe I'll Be	D	49	Carousel Readers	Dominie
Maybe Yes, Maybe No, Maybe Maybe	M	250+	Patron, Susan	Bantam Doubleday Dell
McBroom's Wonderful One-Acre Farm	O	250+	Fleischman, Sid	Beech Tree Books
McBungle's African Safari	I	336	Traditional Tales & More	Rigby
Me	A	24	PM Starters	Rigby
Me	C	41	Reading Corners	Dominie
Me (boy)	C	34	Tonon, Terry	Kaeden Books
Me (girl)	C	34	Tonon, Terry	Kaeden Books
Me and My Dog	F	115	Sunshine	Wright Group
Me and My Shadow	H	247	Momentum Literacy Program	Troll
Me Too	K	136	Mayer, Mercer	Donovan
Meanest Thing to Say, The	K	250+	Cosby, Bill	Scholastic
Meanies	F	158	Read-Togethers	Wright Group
Meanies Came to School, The	E	135	Story Basket	Wright Group
Meanie's Trick, The	E	93	Story Box	Wright Group
Meanies' Trick, The	E	158	Story Basket	Wright Group
Measure It	C	56	Twig	Wright Group
Measure Up!	K	303	Early Connections	Benchmark Education
Measuring Time	E	217	Early Connections	Benchmark Education
Meat Eaters, Plant Eaters	K	156	Planet Earth	Rigby
Medal for Nickie, A	M	262	Sunshine	Wright Group
Meet M & M	K	250+	Ross, Pat	Puffin Chapters

Title	Level	Words	Author/Series	Publisher/Distributor
Meet Me at the Water Hole	H	144	Storyteller-Night Crickets	Wright Group/ McGraw-Hill
Meet Mr. Cricket	E	86	Carousel Readers	Dominie
Meet My Mouse	H	135	Little Celebrations	Pearson Learning
Meet the Molesons	L	250+	Bos, Burny	North-South Books
Meet the Octopus	K	701	Book Shop	Mondo Publishing
Meet the Villarreals	K	387	Wonders	Hampton-Brown
Meet Tom Paxton	I		Little Celebrations	Pearson Learning
Meet William Joyce	I		Little Celebrations	Pearson Learning
Meg and Mog	J	236	Nicoll, Helen	Viking
Meg Mackintosh and the Case of the Curious Whale	O	250+	Landon, Lucinda	Secret Passage Press
Meg Mackintosh and the Case of the Missing Babe Ruth	O	250+	Landon, Lucinda	Secret Passage Press
Meg Mackintosh and the Myst. at the Medieval Castle	O	250+	Landon, Lucinda	Secret Passage Press
Meg Mackintosh and the Mystery at Camp Creepy	O	250+	Landon, Lucinda	Secret Passage Press
Meg Mackintosh and the Mystery at the Soccer Match	O	250+	Landon, Lucinda	Secret Passage Press
Meg Mackintosh and the Mystery in the Locked Library	O	250+	Landon, Lucinda	Secret Passage Press
Meg's Eggs	C	38	New Way Red	Steck-Vaughn
Melting	F	69	Book Shop	Mondo Publishing
Melting Snow Sculptures and Other Cases, The	O	250+	Simon, Seymour	Avon Books
Mermaid Island	L	250+	Frith, Margaret	Grosset & Dunlap
Mermaids Don't Run Track	M	250+	Dadey, Debbie & Jones, Marcia	Scholastic
Merry-Go-Round	C	66	Teacher's Choice Series	Dominie
Merry-Go-Round, The	C	45	Ready Readers	Pearson Learning
Merry-Go-Round, The	C	62	Sunshine	Wright Group
Merry-Go-Round, The	C	84	PM Story Books	Rigby
Mess Monster	G	179	Literacy 2000	Rigby
Mess, A	D	34	Ready Readers	Pearson Learning
Mess, The	D	55	My First Reader	Grolier Press
Messy Bessey	I	63	Rookie Readers	Children's Press
Messy Bessey's Closet	K	92	Rookie Readers	Children's Press
Messy Bessey's Garden	I	60	Rookie Readers	Children's Press
Messy Bessey's School Desk	J	104	Rookie Readers	Children's Press
Messy Mark	F	180	First Start	Troll
Messy Monsters, The	G	167	Carousel Readers	Dominie
Messy Moose	C	45	Little Books	Sadlier-Oxford
Mexican Holiday, A	C	24	The Candid Collection	Dominie
Mia's Sun Hat	E	32	Start to Read	School Zone
Mice	H	143	Literacy 2000	Rigby
Mice	I	250+	PM Animal Facts: Pets-Orange	Rigby
Mice and Max	G	169	Carousel Readers	Dominie
Mice at Bat	I	250+	Oechsli, Kelly	HarperTrophy
Mice on Ice	C	34	KinderReaders	Rigby
Michael and the Eggs	G	154	Oxford Reading Tree	Oxford University Press
Michael in the Hospital	E	91	Oxford Reading Tree	Oxford University Press
Michael Jordan	M	250+	Edwards, Nick	Scholastic
Michael's Picture	C	33	Little Celebrations	Pearson Learning
Microscope	C	46	Story Box	Wright Group

Title	Level	Words	Author/Series	Publisher/Distributor
Midge in the Hospital	E	91	Oxford Reading Tree	Oxford University Press
Midnight on the Moon	M	250+	Osborne, Mary Pope	Random House
Mieko and the Fifth Treasure	O	250+	Coerr, Eleanor	Bantam Doubleday Dell
Migration, The	D	45	Wonder World	Wright Group
Mike and Tony: Best Friends	G	171	Ziefert, Harriet	The Penguin Group
Mike Ghost's Delicious Rainbow	F	157	TOTTS	Tott Publications
Mike Swam, Sink or Swim	J	250+	Heiligman, Deborah	Bantam Doubleday Dell
Mike's First Haircut	G	136	First Start	Troll
Mike's New Bike	F	183	First Start	Troll
Mile High, A	K	331	Book Bank	Wright Group
Milking	F	67	Wonder World	Wright Group
Milo's Great Invention	M	250+	Pair-It Books	Steck-Vaughn
Milton the Early Riser	J	148	Kraus, Robert	Simon & Schuster
Milwaukee Cows	E	79	Story Box	Wright Group
Minerva's Dream	M	250+	Pair-It Books	Steck-Vaughn
Mine's the Best	G	104	Bonsall, Crosby	HarperCollins
Minpins, The	P	250+	Dahl, Roald	The Penguin Group
Miracle at the Plate	M	250+	Christopher, Matt	Little, Brown & Co.
Mirror, The	D	112	Story Box	Wright Group
Misfortune Cookie, The	M	250+	Greenburg, Dan	Grosset & Dunlap
Misha Disappears	K	250+	Literacy 2000	Rigby
Mishi-Na	I	217	Sunshine	Wright Group
Miss Geeta's Hair	D	44	Joy Readers	Dominie
Miss Geneva's Lantern	P	1691	Book Shop	Mondo Publishing
Miss McKenzie Had a Farm	J	515	Pair-It Books	Steck-Vaughn
Miss Mouse Gets Married	K	250+	Folk Tales	Wright Group
Miss Muffett and the Spider	I	270	Ready Readers	Pearson Learning
Miss Nelson Has a Field Day	L	250+	Allard, Harry	Scholastic
Miss Nelson Is Missing	L	598	Allard, Harry	Houghton Mifflin
Miss Popple's Pets	A	28	Literacy 2000	Rigby
Missing Fossil Mystery, The	L	250+	Herman, Emily	Hyperion
Missing Necklace, The	H	231	Reading Unlimited	Pacific Learning
Missing Pet, The	K	618	Pair-It Books	Steck-Vaughn
Missing Tooth, The	J	250+	Cole, Joanna	Random House
Misty's Mischief	H	61	Campbell, Rod	Viking
Mitch to the Rescue	I	302	PM Story Books-Orange	Rigby
Mitten, The	M	250+	Brett, Jan	Scholastic
Mix It Up	C	35	Twig	Wright Group
Mix, Make and Munch	J	245	Home Connection Collection	Rigby
Mixed-Up Max	P	250+	King-Smith, Dick	Troll
Mmm...Very Nice	E	91	Home Connection Collection	Rigby
Moana's Island	M	450	Sunshine	Wright Group
Moccasins	A	20	Twig	Wright Group
Model, The	B	18	Smart Starts	Rigby
Mog at the Zoo	L	250+	Nicoll, Helen	The Penguin Group
Mog's Mumps	L	250+	Nicoll, Helen	The Penguin Group
Mollie Whuppie	K	250+	New Way Orange	Steck-Vaughn
Molly the Brave and Me	K	250+	O'Connor, Jane	Random House
Molly's Bracelet	I	250+	Voyages	SRA/McGraw-Hill
Molly's Broccoli	I	233	Ready Readers	Pearson Learning
Molly's Mailbox	F	122	Teacher's Choice Series	Dominie

Title	Level	Words	Author/Series	Publisher/Distributor
Molly's Pilgrim	M	250+	Cohen, Barbara	Bantam Doubleday Dell
Mom	A	24	PM Starters	Rigby
Mom Can Fix Anything	D	74	Learn to Read	Creative Teaching Press
Mom Paints the House	H	220	Foundations	Wright Group
Mommy, Where Are You?	B	64	Ziefert, Harriet & Boon, Emilie	Puffin Books
Momotaro	M	631	Sunshine	Wright Group
Moms and Dads	A	36	PM Starters	Rigby
Mom's Birthday	I	229	Sunshine	Wright Group
Mom's Diet	I	228	Sunshine	Wright Group
Mom's Getting Married	K	376	Sunshine	Wright Group
Mom's Haircut	H	99	Literacy 2000	Rigby
Mom's Hat	C	39	Joy Readers	Dominie
Mom's New Car	D	116	Foundations	Wright Group
Monarch Butterflies	G	56	Pebble Books	Grolier, Capstone
Monarch Butterfly, The	I	152	Foundations	Wright Group
Money in My Pocket	G	133	Twig	Wright Group
Monkey and Fire	J	372	Literacy 2000	Rigby
Monkey Bridge, The	D	66	Sunshine	Wright Group
Monkey Hop, The	C	26	Joy Readers	Dominie
Monkey Moves	B	16	Pair-It Books	Steck-Vaughn
Monkey See, Monkey Do	F	89	Gave, Marc	Scholastic
Monkey Tricks	E	81	Joy Readers	Dominie
Monkey Tricks	J	328	PM Story Books-Turquoise	Rigby
Monkeys	B	27	Canizares, Susan & Chanko, Pamela	Scholastic
Monkeys	G		Reading Unlimited	Pacific Learning
Monkeys & Apes	K	250+	PM Animals in the Wild-Yellow	Rigby
Monkey's Friends	C	36	Literacy 2000	Rigby
Monster	I	201	Read Alongs	Rigby
Monster and the Baby	D		Mueller, Virginia	Puffin Books
Monster at the Beach, The	E	82	Storyteller-Moon Rising	Wright Group/ McGraw-Hill
Monster Bus	H	103	The Monster Bus Series	Dominie
Monster Bus Goes on a Hot Air Balloon Trip	I	254	The Monster Bus Series	Dominie
Monster Bus Goes to Yellowstone Park	I	259	The Monster Bus Series	Dominie
Monster Can't Sleep	D		Mueller, Virginia	Puffin Books
Monster for Hire	M	250+	Wilson, Trevor	Mondo Publishing
Monster from the Sea, The	K	250+	Hooks, William H.	Bantam Doubleday Dell
Monster Manners	J	250+	Cole, Joanna	Scholastic
Monster Math School Time	G	120	Maccarone, Grace	Scholastic
Monster Meals	C	33	Literacy 2000	Rigby
Monster Mop	A	8	Ready Readers	Pearson Learning
Monster Movie	K	250+	Cole, Joanna	Scholastic
Monster of Mirror Mountain, The	K	250+	Literacy 2000	Rigby
Monster Party	A	20	Smart Starts	Rigby
Monster Party	A	25	Literacy 2000	Rigby
Monster Rabbit Runs Amuck!	M	250+	Giff, Patricia Reilly	Bantam Doubleday Dell
Monster Sandwich, A	C	36	Story Box	Wright Group
Monster Under the Bed, The	K	250+	Ready Readers	Pearson Learning
Monster, Monster	C	38	Reading Corners	Dominie
Monster's Party, The	C	92	Story Box	Wright Group
Monsters	C	30	TOTTS	Tott Publications

Title	Level	Words	Author/Series	Publisher/Distributor
Monsters Don't Scuba Dive	M	250+	Dadey, Debbie & Jones, Marcia	Scholastic
Monsters Next Door, The	L	250+	Dadey, Debbie & Jones, Marcia	Scholastic
Monsters!	D	45	My First Reader	Grolier Press
Moon Boy	J	250+	Brenner, Barbara	Bantam Doubleday Dell
Moon Cake, The	E	127	Joy Readers	Dominie
Moon Stories	J	250+	Ready Readers	Pearson Learning
Moon, The	D	139	Joy Readers	Dominie
Moonlight	D	48	Literacy 2000	Rigby
Moonwalk-The First Trip to the Moon	O	250+	Donnelly, Judy	Random House
Moose Is Loose, A	F	120	Little Readers	Houghton Mifflin
More and More Clowns	D	249	Allen, R. V.	SRA/McGraw-Hill
More or Less Fish Story	E		Wylie, Joanne & David	Children's Press
More Spaghetti I Say	G	340	Gelman, Rita	Scholastic
More Stories Huey Tells	N	250+	Cameron, Ann	Alfred A. Knopf, Inc.
More Stories Julian Tells	N	250+	Cameron, Ann	Random House
More Tales of Amanda Pig	K	1939	Van Leeuwen, Jean	The Penguin Group
More Tales of Oliver Pig	K	2052	Van Leeuwen, Jean	The Penguin Group
Morning Dance, The	K	268	Jellybeans	Rigby
Morning Star	J	250+	Literacy 2000	Rigby
Morning, Noon, and Night: Poems to Fill Your Day	J	1132	Book Shop	Mondo Publishing
Morris and Boris at the Circus	J	250+	Wiseman, Bernard	HarperTrophy
Morris Goes to School	J	250+	Wiseman, Bernard	HarperTrophy
Morris the Moose	E	250+	Wiseman, Bernard	HarperTrophy
Mosquito	C	46	Book Bank	Wright Group
Mosquito Buzzed, A	E	133	Little Readers	Houghton Mifflin
Mosquitoes	E	39	Pebble Books	Grolier, Capstone
Most Beautiful Place in the World, The	O	250+	Cameron, Ann	Alfred A. Knopf, Inc.
Most Scary Ghost	H	355	Jellybeans	Rigby
Most Terrible Creature in the World, The	M	340	Pacific Literacy	Pacific Learning
Most Wonderful Doll in the World	O	250+	McGinley, Phyllis	Scholastic
Mother and Me	B	48	Spinelle, Nancy Louise	Kaeden Books
Mother Animals and Baby Animals	A	31	Reading Unlimited	Pacific Learning
Mother Hen	G	205	Book Bank	Wright Group
Mother Hippopotamus	A	7	Foundations	Wright Group
Mother Hippopotamus Gets Wet	J	421	Foundations	Wright Group
Mother Hippopotamus Goes Shopping	C	79	Foundations	Wright Group
Mother Hippopotamus's Dry Skin	D	201	Foundations	Wright Group
Mother Hippopotamus's Hiccups	I	162	Foundations	Wright Group
Mother Sea Turtle	K	240	Foundations	Wright Group
Mother Sun's Rest Day	H	250+	Momentum Literacy Program	Troll
Mothers	B	26	Pebble Books	Grolier, Capstone
Mother's Day	F	128	Fiesta Holiday Series	Dominie
Mother's Helpers	K	250+	Ready Readers	Pearson Learning
Motorbike Race, The	C	48	Joy Readers	Dominie
Mountain Gorillas	N	250+	Connal, Julie	Wright Group
Mountain Gorillas	P	330	Wonder World	Wright Group
Mouse	C	40	Story Box	Wright Group
Mouse and the Elephant, The	J	250+	Little Readers	Houghton Mifflin
Mouse and the Motorcycle, The	O	250+	Cleary, Beverly	Avon Camelot
Mouse Finds a House	D	72	Start to Read	School Zone
Mouse Monster	J	302	Jellybeans	Rigby

Title	Level	Words	Author/Series	Publisher/Distributor
Mouse Party!	M		Little Celebrations	Pearson Learning
Mouse Soup	J	1350	Lobel, Arnold	HarperCollins
Mouse Tales	J	1519	Lobel, Arnold	HarperCollins
Mouse Train	B	48	Story Box	Wright Group
Mouse Who Wanted to Marry, The	J	250+	Orgel, Doris	Bantam Doubleday Dell
Mouse, The	C	26	Pacific Literacy	Pacific Learning
Mouse's Baby Blanket	D	68	Swerdlow Brown, Beverly	Seedling
Mouse's House	D	70	New Way Red	Steck-Vaughn
Move it	E	58	Wonder World	Wright Group
Move Like Us!	H	250+	Home Connection Collection	Rigby
Move Over!	E	118	Story Basket	Wright Group
Moving	B	56	Little Red Readers	Sundance
Moving Day	C	90	Foundations	Wright Group
Moving Day	E		Sunshine	Wright Group
Moving Day	G	215	Momentum Literacy Program	Troll
Moving In	D	82	Foundations	Wright Group
Moving to America	E	81	Carousel Readers	Dominie
Mr. and Mrs. Murphy and Bernard	K	250+	Little Celebrations	Pearson Learning
Mr. Beekman's Deli	H	96	Story Basket	Wright Group
Mr. Beep	M	250+	Read Alongs	Rigby
Mr. Bitter's Butter	H	231	Story Basket	Wright Group
Mr. Brown	C	20	KinderReaders	Rigby
Mr. Bumbleticker	B	28	Foundations	Wright Group
Mr. Bumbleticker Goes Shopping	J	391	Foundations	Wright Group
Mr. Bumbleticker Likes to Cook	I	196	Foundations	Wright Group
Mr. Bumbleticker Likes to Fix Machines	I	142	Foundations	Wright Group
Mr. Bumbleticker's Apples	I	338	Foundations	Wright Group
Mr. Bumbleticker's Birthday	E	110	Foundations	Wright Group
Mr. Clutterbus	H		Voyages	SRA/McGraw-Hill
Mr. Crawford	E	119	Foundations	Wright Group
Mr. Cricket Finds a Friend	G	134	Carousel Readers	Dominie
Mr. Cricket Takes a Vacation	E	165	Carousel Readers	Dominie
Mr. Cricket's New Home	F	121	Carousel Readers	Dominie
Mr. Egg	E	22	Pair-It Books	Steck-Vaughn
Mr. Fin's Trip	E	130	Ready Readers	Pearson Learning
Mr. Fixit	H	196	Sunshine	Wright Group
Mr. Fizzle, the Man Who Went "Boo!"	I	250+	Home Connection Collection	Rigby
Mr. Grump	D	73	Sunshine	Wright Group
Mr. Gumpy's Motor Car	K	250+	Burningham, John	HarperCollins
Mr. Gumpy's Outing	L	283	Burningham, John	Holt, Henry & Co.
Mr. McCready's Cleaning Day	H	119	Shilling, Tracy	Scholastic
Mr. McGrah's New Car	H	119	Book Bank	Wright Group
Mr. Noisy	D	90	Learn to Read	Creative Teaching Press
Mr. Pepperpot's Pet	K	250+	Literacy 2000	Rigby
Mr. Popper's Penguins	O	250+	Atwater, Richard & Florence	Little, Brown & Co.
Mr. Putter and Tabby Bake the Cake	J	250+	Rylant, Cynthia	Harcourt Brace
Mr. Putter and Tabby Fly the Plane	J	250+	Rylant, Cynthia	Harcourt Brace
Mr. Putter and Tabby Pick the Pears	J	250+	Rylant, Cynthia	Harcourt Brace
Mr. Putter and Tabby Pour the Tea	J	250+	Rylant, Cynthia	Harcourt Brace
Mr. Putter and Tabby Walk the Dog	J	250+	Rylant, Cynthia	Harcourt Brace
Mr. Rabbit and the Moon	F	137	New Way Red	Steck-Vaughn

Title	Level	Words	Author/Series	Publisher/Distributor
Mr. Smarty Loves to Party	F	101	Storyteller-Moon Rising	Wright Group/ McGraw-Hill
Mr. Sun and Mr. Sea	I	202	Little Celebrations	Pearson Learning
Mr. Sun and Mr. Sea	L	506	Sunshine	Wright Group
Mr. Verdi's New Path	I	250+	Home Connection Collection	Rigby
Mr. Whisper	H	325	Sunshine	Wright Group
Mr. Wind	F	37	Literacy 2000	Rigby
Mr. Wink	E	86	Ready Readers	Pearson Learning
Mr. Wolf	D	48	Joy Readers	Dominie
Mr. Wumple's Travels	I	259	Read Alongs	Rigby
Mrs. Always Goes Shopping	M	423	Sunshine	Wright Group
Mrs. Barnett's Birthday	J	135	Sunshine	Wright Group
Mrs. Bold	F	94	Literacy 2000	Rigby
Mrs. Brice's Mice	I	250+	Hoff, Syd	HarperTrophy
Mrs. Bubble's Baby	M	250+	Ready to Read	Pacific Learning
Mrs. Cook's Hats	C	31	Mader, Jan	Kaeden Books
Mrs. Grindy's Shoes	I	211	Sunshine	Wright Group
Mrs. Huggins and Her Hen Hannah	K	250+	Dabcovich, Lydia	Dutton
Mrs. Jeepers' Batty Vacation	L	250+	Dadey, Debbie & Jones, Marcia	Scholastic
Mrs. Lunch	B	17	Joy Readers	Dominie
Mrs. McNosh Hangs Up Her Wash	H		Little Celebrations	Pearson Learning
Mrs. Muddle's Mud-Puddle	I	181	Sunshine	Wright Group
Mrs. Murphy's Bears	I	188	Little Readers	Houghton Mifflin
Mrs. Murphy's Crows	H	120	Books for Young Learners	Richard C. Owen
Mrs. Pomelili's Wet Week	G	215	Book Bank	Wright Group
Mrs. Sato's Hens	D	51	Little Readers	Houghton Mifflin
Mrs. Sato's Hens	D	51	Little Celebrations	Pearson Learning
Mrs. Spider's Beautiful Web	H	250+	PM Story Books	Rigby
Mrs. Tuck's Little Tune	F	195	Ready Readers	Pearson Learning
Mrs. Wishy Washy	E	102	Story Box	Wright Group
Mrs. Wishy-Washy's Tub	B	38	Story Box	Wright Group
Much Ado About Aldo	O	250+	Hurwitz, Johanna	Puffin Books
Mud	D		Lewison, Wendy	Random House
Mud Pie	C	14	Literacy 2000	Rigby
Mud Pies	C	56	TOTTS	Tott Publications
Mud Pies	E	143	Start to Read	School Zone
Mud Pony, The	L	764	Sunshine	Wright Group
Mud Puddles	C	24	TOTTS	Tott Publications
Mudskipper	G	132	Twig	Wright Group
Muffy and Fluffy	F	155	First Start	Troll
Muggie Maggie	O	250+	Cleary, Beverly	Avon Camelot
Mummies Don't Coach Softball	M	250+	Dadey, Debbie & Jones, Marcia	Scholastic
Mummies in the Morning	M	250+	Osborne, Mary Pope	Random House
Mummy's Gold, The	L	250+	McMullan, Kate	Grosset & Dunlap
Mumps	D	108	Carousel Readers	Dominie
Mumps	D	112	PM Story Books	Rigby
Munching Mark	G	88	Tadpoles	Rigby
Munching Monster	I	261	Storyteller-Moon Rising	Wright Group/ McGraw-Hill
Mural, The	F	262	Visions	Wright Group
Museum, The	D	41	Sunshine	Wright Group

©1999 by I. C. Fountas & G. S. Pinnell from Matching Books to Readers. Portsmouth, NH: Heinemann. May not be reproduced without written permission of the publisher.

Title	Level	Words	Author/Series	Publisher/Distributor
Mushrooms for Dinner	G	177	PM Story Books	Rigby
Mutt and the Lifeguards	M	754	Sunshine	Wright Group
My Accident	C	46	PM Starters	Rigby
My Apartment	C	20	Visions	Wright Group
My Baby	D	64	Storyteller-First Snow	Wright Group/ McGraw-Hill
My Backyard	A	14	Little Books for Early Readers	University of Maine
My Best Friend	C	63	Carousel Readers	Dominie
My Best Friend	C		Little Celebrations	Pearson Learning
My Best Friend	I		Hutchins, Pat	Greenwillow
My Big Box	D	94	Voyages	SRA/McGraw-Hill
My Big Brother	E	103	PM Nonfiction-Yellow	Rigby
My Big Wheel	C	38	Visions	Wright Group
My Bike	B	42	Foundations	Wright Group
My Bike	D	38	Storyteller-First Snow	Wright Group/ McGraw-Hill
My Bike	D	108	Ready to Read	Pacific Learning
My Bike	D	108	Pacific Literacy	Pacific Learning
My Birthday Party	A	16	Little Readers	Houghton Mifflin
My Birthday Party	C	38	Visions	Wright Group
My Birthday Surprise	G	153	Foundations	Wright Group
My Boat	G	133	Sunshine	Wright Group
My Body	C	47	Discovery World	Rigby
My Body Works	E	131	Twig	Wright Group
My Book	A	17	Maris, Ron	Viking
My Book	C	32	Sunshine	Wright Group
My Box	A	30	Literacy 2000	Rigby
My Brother	D	51	Rise & Shine	Hampton-Brown
My Brother Wants to Be Like Me	D	62	Mader, Jan	Kaeden Books
My Brother, Ant	J	250+	Byars, Betsy	Viking
My Brother, Owen	I	150	Book Bank	Wright Group
My Brother, the Brat	E		Hall, Kirsten	Scholastic
My Brother's Motorcycle	D	45	Visions	Wright Group
My Brown Bear Barney	H		Butler, Dorothy	Morrow
My Brown Cow	D	62	Story Box	Wright Group
My Buddy, My Friend	D	33	Visions	Wright Group
My Bug Box	E	99	Books for Young Learners	Richard C. Owen
My Cat	D	40	Ready Readers	Pearson Learning
My Cat	D	42	Sunshine	Wright Group
My Cat	F		My World	Steck-Vaughn
My Cat	H	79	Taylor, Judy	Macmillan
My Cat Muffin	B	35	Gardner, Marjory	Scholastic
My Cat's Surprise	D	71	New Way Blue	Steck-Vaughn
My Chair	B	24	Pacific Literacy	Pacific Learning
My Circus Family	C	42	Book Shop	Mondo Publishing
My Class	A	14	Stewart, J. & Salem, Lynn	Seedling
My Clock Is Sick	D	45	Ready Readers	Pearson Learning
My Clothes	C	16	Carousel Earlybirds	Dominie
My Clothes	C	86	Foundations	Wright Group
My Computer	F	76	Wonder World	Wright Group
My Dad	E	114	PM Nonfiction-Yellow	Rigby

Title	Level	Words	Author/Series	Publisher/Distributor
My Dad	F	79	Talk About Books	Dominie
My Dad Cooks	C	29	Carousel Readers	Dominie
My Dad Has Asthma	I	138	Wonder World	Wright Group
My Dad Lost His Job	E	76	Carousel Readers	Dominie
My Dad's Truck	E	57	Costain, Meredith	Scholastic
My Day	B	24	Sunshine	Wright Group
My Day	C	44	Rise & Shine	Hampton-Brown
My Day	C	51	Barney, Mike	Kaeden Books
My Dog	C	79	Early Emergent	Pioneer Valley
My Dog	D	38	Visions	Wright Group
My Dog	D	51	Sunshine	Wright Group
My Dog	G	72	Taylor, Judy	Macmillan
My Dog	G		My World	Steck-Vaughn
My Dog Ben	C	19	Voyages	SRA/McGraw-Hill
My Dog Willy	C	71	Little Readers	Houghton Mifflin
My Dog's the Best!	F	175	Calmenson, Stephanie	Scholastic
My Doll	E	86	Yukish, Joe	Kaeden Books
My Dream	C	34	Wildsmith, Brian	Oxford University Press
My Family	B	87	Carousel Earlybirds	Dominie
My Family	A	28	Sunshine	Wright Group
My Family Split Up	H	85	City Kids	Rigby
My Father	J	194	Mayer, Laura	Scholastic
My Father's Dragon	M	250+	Gannett, Ruth Stiles	Random House
My Feet	B	25	Twig	Wright Group
My Feet Are Just Right	G	220	Sunshine	Wright Group
My Fish Bowl	B	29	Foundations	Wright Group
My Fish Does Not Chirp	E	77	Ready Readers	Pearson Learning
My Five Senses	E	142	Early Connections	Benchmark Education
My Fort	A	17	Little Books for Early Readers	University of Maine
My Friend	B	41	Sunshine	Wright Group
My Friend	E	95	Foundations	Wright Group
My Friend Alan	D	65	Carousel Readers	Dominie
My Friend at School	C	30	Visions	Wright Group
My Friend Goes Left	F	72	Gregorich, Barbara	School Zone
My Friend Jess	H	124	Wonder World	Wright Group
My Friend Trent	H	186	Foundations	Wright Group
My Friends	D	58	Little Celebrations	Pearson Learning
My Friends	G	152	Gomi, Taro	Scholastic
My Grandfather's Face	B	27	Literacy 2000	Rigby
My Grandma and Grandpa	E	130	PM Nonfiction-Yellow	Rigby
My Grandpa	F	75	Book Shop	Mondo Publishing
My Hamster, Van	E	73	Ready Readers	Pearson Learning
My Hard-Boiled Egg	F	94	Windmill Books	Rigby
My Helicopter Ride	C	42	Foundations	Wright Group
My Holiday Diary	F	95	Stepping Stones	Nelson/Michaels Assoc.
My Home	A	20	Literacy 2000	Rigby
My Home	B	56	Sunshine	Wright Group
My Home	C	46	Story Box	Wright Group
My Home Is High	B	23	Literacy 2000	Rigby
My Home Is Just Right for Me	G	250+	Momentum Literacy Program	Troll
My House	A	40	Carousel Earlybirds	Dominie
My House	B	25	Voyages	SRA/McGraw-Hill

©1999 by I. C. Fountas & G. S. Pinnell from Matching Books to Readers. Portsmouth, NH: Heinemann. May not be reproduced without written permission of the publisher.

Title	Level	Words	Author/Series	Publisher/Distributor
My House	F	52	Cat on the Mat	Oxford University Press
My House	F	79	My First Reader	Grolier Press
My House	F	126	Literacy 2000	Rigby
My Kitchen	F		Rockwell, Harlow	Morrow
My Kite	C	37	Williams, Deborah	Kaeden Books
My Letter	C	51	Wonder World	Wright Group
My Little Brother	C	59	Windmill	Rigby, Wright Group
My Little Brother Ben	D	35	Books for Young Learners	Richard C. Owen
My Little Dog	C	90	PM Starters	Rigby
My Little Sister	D	44	Joy Readers	Dominie
My Little Sister	E	120	PM Nonfiction-Yellow	Rigby
My Lost Top	E	70	Ready Readers	Pearson Learning
My Lunch	C	70	Early Emergent	Pioneer Valley
My Mama	C	25	Visions	Wright Group
My Messy Room	D		Packard, Mary	Scholastic
My Mom	B	40	Little Books for Early Readers	University of Maine
My Mom	F	91	Talk About Books	Dominie
My Mom and Dad	D	86	Story Box	Wright Group
My Monster and Me	B	37	Ready Readers	Pearson Learning
My Monster Friends	F	94	Literacy 2000	Rigby
My Name Is Maria Isabel	N	250+	Ada, Alma Flor	Aladdin
My Native American School	F	86	Gould, Carol	Kaeden Books
My Nest	C	42	Little Celebrations	Pearson Learning
My Nest Is Best	D	92	Foundations	Wright Group
My New House	C	26	Reading Corners	Dominie
My New Mom	K	282	Sunshine	Wright Group
My New Pet	F	105	Little Readers	Houghton Mifflin
My Old Cat	E	110	Foundations	Wright Group
My Old Cat and the Computer	F	81	Foundations	Wright Group
My Party	C	35	The Candid Collection	Dominie
My Pet	C	18	KinderReaders	Rigby
My Pet	D	65	Salem, Lynn & Stewart, J.	Seedling
My Pet Bobby	E	150	Little Readers	Houghton Mifflin
My Picture	A	23	Story Box	Wright Group
My Picture	C	37	Carousel Readers	Dominie
My Place	A	28	Foundations	Wright Group
My Planet	A	28	Smart Starts	Rigby
My Pony	C	49	Rise & Shine	Hampton-Brown
My Pony Minnie	E	59	Sunshine	Wright Group
My Prairie Summer	M	250+	Pair-It Books	Steck-Vaughn
My Pumpkin	C	52	Teacher's Choice Series	Dominie
My Puppy	B	14	Sunshine	Wright Group
My Puppy	C	33	Little Celebrations	Pearson Learning
My Ride	C	56	Foundations	Wright Group
My Rocket	A	28	KinderReaders	Rigby
My Room	A	14	Ready Readers	Pearson Learning
My Room	A	15	Twig	Wright Group
My Room	A	28	Carousel Earlybirds	Dominie
My Room	C	42	Ready Readers	Pearson Learning
My School	B	34	Little Readers	Houghton Mifflin
My School	C	40	TOTTS	Tott Publications

Title	Level	Words	Author/Series	Publisher/Distributor
My Scrapbook	K	312	Storyteller Nonfiction	Shortland Publications
My Secret Hiding Place	G	155	First Start	Troll
My Secret Place	G	121	Wonder World	Wright Group
My Shadow	A	29	Book Bank	Wright Group
My Shadow	C	35	Sunshine	Wright Group
My Shadow	C	42	Foundations	Wright Group
My Shadow	E	46	Pacific Literacy	Pacific Learning
My Shadow	F	116	Ready Readers	Pearson Learning
My Shoes	B	25	Rise & Shine	Hampton-Brown
My Sister June	H	182	Ready Readers	Pearson Learning
My Sister's Getting Married	K	300	Foundations	Wright Group
My Skateboard	D	89	Carousel Readers	Dominie
My Skateboard	I	81	City Kids	Rigby
My Skin	D	64	Wonder World	Wright Group
My Skin Looks After Me	G	82	Pacific Literacy	Pacific Learning
My Sloppy Tiger	I	211	Sunshine	Wright Group
My Sloppy Tiger Goes to School	J	217	Sunshine	Wright Group
My Son, the Time Traveler	M	250+	Greenburg, Dan	Grosset & Dunlap
My Special Job	E	110	Pacific Literacy	Pacific Learning
My Special Place	E	116	Teacher's Choice Series	Dominie
My Story	A	17	Wonder World	Wright Group
My Teacher Helps Me	C	37	Visions	Wright Group
My Teacher's Leaving	I	154	City Kids	Rigby
My Three-Wheeler	C	38	Visions	Wright Group
My Tiger Cat	E	76	Frankford, Marilyn	Kaeden Books
My Tower	A	15	Windmill	Wright Group
My Toys	A	28	Little Books for Early Readers	University of Maine
My Treasure Garden	J	134	Book Bank	Wright Group
My Twin!	C	40	Ready Readers	Pearson Learning
My Two Homes	E	69	Carousel Readers	Dominie
My Uncle's Truck	C	24	Visions	Wright Group
My Very Hungry Pet	F	334	Reading Corners	Dominie
My Weekly Chores	C	44	Visions	Wright Group
My Wonderful Aunt, Story Five	M	493	Sunshine	Wright Group
My Wonderful Aunt, Story Four	M	436	Sunshine	Wright Group
My Wonderful Aunt, Story One	L	193	Sunshine	Wright Group
My Wonderful Aunt, Story Six	M	432	Sunshine	Wright Group
My Wonderful Aunt, Story Three	M	392	Sunshine	Wright Group
My Wonderful Aunt, Story Two	L	199	Sunshine	Wright Group
My Wonderful Chair	F	109	Windmill	Wright Group
Mysterious Green Swimmer and Other Cases, The	O	250+	Simon, Seymour	Avon Books
Mysterious Tracks and Other Cases, The	O	250+	Simon, Seymour	Avon Books
Mystery Box, The	I	326	New Way Orange	Steck-Vaughn
Mystery in the Night Woods	M	250+	Peterson, John	Scholastic
Mystery of Pony Hollow, The	N	250+	Hall, Lynn	Random House
Mystery of the Blue Ring, The	L	250+	Giff, Patricia Reilly	Bantam Doubleday Dell
Mystery of the Dark Old House, The	M	250+	Schultz, Irene	Wright Group
Mystery of the Missing Dog, The	J	250+	Levy, Elizabeth	Scholastic
Mystery of the Missing Dog, The	M	250+	Schultz, Irene	Wright Group

Title	Level	Words	Author/Series	Publisher/Distributor
Mystery of the Missing Red Mitten, The	H	246	Little Readers	Houghton Mifflin
Mystery of the Phantom Pony, The	N	250+	Hall, Lynn	Random House
Mystery of the Pirate Ghost, The	L	250+	Hayes, Geoffrey	Random House
Mystery of the Stolen Bike, The	M	250+	Brown, Marc	Little, Brown & Co.
Mystery of the Talking Tail, The	M	250+	Clark, Margaret	Sundance
Mystery of the Tooth Gremlin	L	250+	Graves, Bonnie	Hyperion
Mystery on October Road	O	250+	Herzig, Alison C. & Mali, Jane	Scholastic
Mystery Seeds	L	250+	Reading Unlimited	Pacific Learning
Mythical Beasts	P	250+	Wildcats	Wright Group
Name for a Dog, A	I	258	Windmill Books	Rigby
Name for Rabbit, A	H	94	Pacific Literacy	Pacific Learning
Name Garden, A	F	125	Sunshine	Wright Group
Name Is the Same, The	G	115	Ready Readers	Pearson Learning
Nana's in the Plum Tree	M	250+	Ready to Read	Pacific Learning
Nana's Orchard	F	92	Gould, Carol	Kaeden Books
Nana's Place	I	211	Gibson, Akimi & Meyer, K.	Scholastic
Nana's Sweet Potato Pie	E	233	Visions	Wright Group
Nannies for Hire	M	250+	Hest, Amy	William Morrow & Co.
Nanny Goat's Nap	C	96	Ready Readers	Pearson Learning
Nap Time	C	24	KinderReaders	Rigby
Napping House, The	I	268	Wood, Don & Audrey	Harcourt
Nate the Great	K	250+	Sharmat, M. Weinman	Bantam Doubleday Dell
Nate the Great and the Boring Beach Bag	K	250+	Sharmat, M. Weinman	Bantam Doubleday Dell
Nate the Great and the Crunchy Christmas	K	250+	Sharmat, M. Weinman	Bantam Doubleday Dell
Nate the Great and the Fishy Prize	K	250+	Sharmat, M. Weinman	Bantam Doubleday Dell
Nate the Great and the Halloween Hunt	K	250+	Sharmat, M. Weinman	Bantam Doubleday Dell
Nate the Great and the Lost List	K	250+	Sharmat, M. Weinman	Bantam Doubleday Dell
Nate the Great and the Missing Key	K	250+	Sharmat, M. Weinman	Bantam Doubleday Dell
Nate the Great and the Mushy Valentine	K	250+	Sharmat, M. Weinman	Bantam Doubleday Dell
Nate the Great and the Musical Note	K	250+	Sharmat, M. Weinman	Bantam Doubleday Dell
Nate the Great and the Phony Clue	K	250+	Sharmat, M. Weinman	Bantam Doubleday Dell
Nate the Great and the Pillowcase	K	250+	Sharmat, M. Weinman	Bantam Doubleday Dell
Nate the Great and the Snowy Trail	K	250+	Sharmat, M. Weinman	Bantam Doubleday Dell
Nate the Great and the Sticky Case	K	250+	Sharmat, M. Weinman	Bantam Doubleday Dell
Nate the Great and the Stolen Base	K	250+	Sharmat, M. Weinman	Bantam Doubleday Dell
Nate the Great and the Tardy Tortoise	K	250+	Sharmat, M. Weinman	Bantam Doubleday Dell
Nate the Great Goes Down in the Dumps	K	250+	Sharmat, M. Weinman	Bantam Doubleday Dell
Nate the Great Goes Undercover	K	250+	Sharmat, M. Weinman	Bantam Doubleday Dell
Nate the Great Saves the King of Sweden	K	250+	Sharmat, M. Weinman	Bantam Doubleday Dell
Nate the Great Stalks Stupidweed	K	250+	Sharmat, M. Weinman	Bantam Doubleday Dell
Nathan and Nicholas Alexander	K	250+	Delacre, Lulu	Scholastic
Natural History Museum, The	K	250+	Stepping Stones	Nelson/Michaels Assoc.
Nature Hike	C	32	Twig	Wright Group
Nature's Celebration	M	250+	Literacy 2000	Rigby
Naughty Ann, The	G	159	PM Story Books	Rigby
Naughty Happy Monkey	C	33	Joy Readers	Dominie
Naughty Kitten!	A	18	Smart Starts	Rigby
Naughty Patch	D	74	Foundations	Wright Group
Needs and Wants	C	43	Early Connections	Benchmark Education
Neep, Beep, Beep	D	86	Foundations	Wright Group
Neighborhood Clubhouse, The	G	474	Visions	Wright Group

Title	Level	Words	Author/Series	Publisher/Distributor
Neighborhood Party, The	C	60	Pair-It Books	Steck-Vaughn
Neighborhood Picnic, The	F	157	Visions	Wright Group
Nelson the Baby Elephant	J	350	PM Story Books-Turquoise	Rigby
Nest Full of Eggs, A	B	25	Pair-It Books	Steck-Vaughn
Nest, The	C	32	Story Box	Wright Group
Nest, The	C	34	Sunshine	Wright Group
Nesting Place, The	J	356	PM Story Books-Turquoise	Rigby
Nests	C	35	Wonder World	Wright Group
Nests	E	58	Literacy 2000	Rigby
Never Be	D	73	Salem, Lynn & Stewart, J.	Seedling
Never Say Never	G	225	Ready Readers	Pearson Learning
Never Trust a Cat Who Wears Earrings	M	250+	Greenburg, Dan	Grosset & Dunlap
New Baby Calf, The	H	240	Chase, Edith & Reid, Barbara	Scholastic
New Baby, The	E	133	PM Story Books	Rigby
New Balloon, A	E	36	Pacific Literacy	Pacific Learning
New Bike, The	J	526	Sunshine	Wright Group
New Building, The	H	78	Sunshine	Wright Group
New Cat, The	B	29	Ready to Read	Pacific Learning
New Cat, The	B	29	Pacific Literacy	Pacific Learning
New Dog, A	D	52	Oxford Reading Tree	Oxford University Press
New Gym Shoes	F	175	Yukish, Joe	Kaeden Books
New Highway, The	C	67	Foundations	Wright Group
New House for Mole and Mouse, A	G	223	Ziefert, Harriet	The Penguin Group
New House, The	A	15	Sunshine	Wright Group
New Kid in Town	N	250+	Kroll, Stephen	Avon Camelot
New Kind of Magic, The	P	250+	Szymanski, Lois	Avon Camelot
New Nest, A	A	14	Pair-It Books	Steck-Vaughn
New Nest, The	E	207	Foundations	Wright Group
New Pants	B	20	Story Box	Wright Group
New Paper, Everyone!	G	53	Pacific Literacy	Pacific Learning
New Puppy, A	G	250+	Momentum Literacy Program	Troll
New Road, The	D	49	Joy Readers	Dominie
New School, The	J	210	City Kids	Rigby
New Shoes	C	29	Wonder World	Wright Group
New Sneakers	F	34	Oxford Reading Tree	Oxford University Press
New York City Buildings	F	59	Books for Young Learners	Richard C. Owen
Newborn Animals	J	250+	Momentum Literacy Program	Troll
Newspaper for Dad, A	G	192	New Way Green	Steck-Vaughn
Newspaper, The	G	132	Twig	Wright Group
Newt	J	250+	Novak, Matt	HarperTrophy
Next Spring an Oriole	N	250+	Whelan, Gloria	Random House
Next Stop, New York City!	O	250+	Giff, Patricia Reilly	Bantam Doubleday Dell
Next Time I Will	K	250+	Orgel, Doris	Bantam Doubleday Dell
Nibbly Mouse	E		Voyages	SRA/McGraw-Hill
Nice New Neighbors	K	250+	Brandenberg, Franz	Scholastic
Nick Goes Fishing	I	123	Yukish, Joe	Kaeden Books
Nick's Glasses	E	51	Ready to Read	Pacific Learning
Nickels and Pennies	E	53	Williams, Deborah	Kaeden Books
Nick's Glasses	E	51	Pacific Literacy	Pacific Learning
Nick's Pet	E	119	Teacher's Choice Series	Dominie
Nicky Upstairs and Downstairs	G	179	Ziefert, Harriet	The Penguin Group
Nicole Helps Grandma	B	35	Little Books for Early Readers	University of Maine

Title	Level	Words	Author/Series	Publisher/Distributor
Night and Day	E	112	Ready Readers	Pearson Learning
Night Animals	D	56	Ready Readers	Pearson Learning
Night Crossing, The	O	250+	Ackerman, Karen	Alfred A. Knopf, Inc.
Night in the Desert	D	69	Carousel Readers	Dominie
Night Music	P	250+	Voyages in…	Wright Group
Night Noises	G	97	Storyteller-Moon Rising	Wright Group/ McGraw-Hill
Night Noises	G	107	Sunshine	Wright Group
Night of the Ninjas	M	250+	Osborne, Mary Pope	Random House
Night Owls, The	M	368	Wonder World	Wright Group
Night Sky	C	15	Twig	Wright Group
Night Sky, The	G	226	Ready Readers	Pearson Learning
Night the Lights Went Out, The	H	155	Little Readers	Houghton Mifflin
Night Train, The	E	65	Story Box	Wright Group
Night Walk	E	47	Prokopchak, Ann	Kaeden Books
Night Walk	F	51	Books for Young Learners	Richard C. Owen
Night Walk, The	I	667	PM Story Books-Gold	Rigby
Nightingale, The	J	563	Tales from Hans Andersen	Wright Group
Nighttime	C	44	Story Box	Wright Group
Niles Likes to Smile	F	80	Little Books	Sadlier-Oxford
Nine Days of Camping, The	E	254	Twig	Wright Group
Nine Lives of Adventure Cat, The	L	250+	Clymer, Susan	Scholastic
Nine Men Chase a Hen	G	74	Gregorich, Barbara	School Zone
Nine True Dolphin Stories	M	250+	Davidson, Margaret	Scholastic
No Arm in Left Field	M	250+	Christopher, Matt	Little, Brown & Co.
No Ball Games Here	H		Ziefert, Harriet	The Penguin Group
No Copycats Allowed!	L	250+	Graves, Bonnie	Hyperion
No Dinner for Sally	J	340	Literacy 2000	Rigby
No Dogs Allowed	F	73	Books for Young Learners	Richard C. Owen
No Extras	F	90	Literacy 2000	Rigby
No Fighting, No Biting!	K	250+	Minarik, Else H.	HarperTrophy
No Good in Art	I	250+	Cohen, Miriam	Bantam Doubleday Dell
No Luck	F	120	Stewart, J. & Salem, Lynn	Seedling
No Mail for Mitchell	G	250+	Siracusa, Catherine	Random House
No More Monsters for Me!	J	250+	Parish, Peggy	HarperTrophy
No One Else Like Me	D	129	Early Connections	Benchmark Education
No One Is Going to Nashville	O	250+	Jukes, Mavis	Alfred A. Knopf, Inc.
No Room for a Dog	N	250+	Kane Nichols, Joan	Avon Books
No Singing Today	H	419	Book Shop	Mondo Publishing
No Tooth, No Quarter!	K	250+	Buller, Jon	Random House
No Way, Winky Blue!	P	4053	Book Shop	Mondo Publishing
No, No	D	91	Story Box	Wright Group
No, You Can't	D	52	Sunshine	Wright Group
Nobody Knew My Name	G	276	Foundations	Wright Group
Nobody Listens to Andrew	I	250+	Little Readers	Houghton Mifflin
Noggin and Bobbin By the Sea	I		Little Celebrations	Pearson Learning
Noggin and Bobbin in the Garden	E	57	Little Celebrations	Pearson Learning
Noise	G	138	Sunshine	Wright Group
Noises	E	49	Literacy 2000	Rigby
Noises!!!	C	98	Teacher's Choice Series	Dominie
Noisy Breakfast	D		Blonder, Ellen	Scholastic
Noisy Nora	I	204	Wells, Rosemary	Scholastic

© 1999 by I. C. Fountas & G. S. Pinnell from *Matching Books to Readers*. Portsmouth, NH: Heinemann. May not be reproduced without written permission of the publisher.

Title	Level	Words	Author/Series	Publisher/Distributor
Noisy Toys	E	77	Home Connection Collection	Rigby
Nora Plays All Day	B	42	Little Books	Sadlier-Oxford
Norma Jean, Jumping Bean	J	250+	Cole, Joanna	Random House
Nose Book	E		Perkins, Al	Random House
Nose for Trouble, A	P	250+	Wilson, Nancy	Avon Camelot
Noses	E	56	Literacy 2000	Rigby
Not Enough Water	D	84	Armstrong, Shane & Hartley, S.	Scholastic
Not Me, Said the Monkey	G	118	West, Colin	Harper & Row
Not Now! Said the Cow	J	250+	Demares, Chris	Bantam Doubleday Dell
Not What It Seems	P	250+	Wildcats	Wright Group
Notes from Mom	F	99	Salem, Lynn & Stewart, J.	Seedling
Notes to Dad	F	114	Stewart, J. & Salem, Lynn	Seedling
Nothing in the Mailbox	F	73	Books for Young Learners	Richard C. Owen
Nothing to Be Scared About	K	343	Sunshine	Wright Group
Not-So-Dead Fish and Other Cases, The	O	250+	Simon, Seymour	Avon Books
Not-So-Perfect Rosie	N	250+	Giff, Patricia Reilly	The Penguin Group
Not-So-Scary-Scarecrow, The	I	166	Ready Readers	Pearson Learning
Now I Am Five	I	582	Sunshine	Wright Group
Now I Ride	D	63	Carousel Readers	Dominie
Now Listen, Stanley	K		Literacy 2000	Rigby
Now We Can Go	C		Jonas, Ann	Greenwillow
Now You See Me…Now You Don't	M	250+	Greenburg, Dan	Grosset & Dunlap
Nowhere and Nothing	I	143	Sunshine	Wright Group
Number One	J	170	Ready to Read	Pacific Learning
Numbers Are Everywhere	E	125	Early Connections	Benchmark Education
Numbers Are Everywhere	E	131	Twig	Wright Group
Nut Pie for Jud, A	D	46	Ready Readers	Pearson Learning
Oak Tree and Fir Tree	G	102	New Way Red	Steck-Vaughn
Oak Trees	F	132	Pebble Books	Grolier, Capstone
Oatmeal	F	96	Wonder World	Wright Group
Obadiah	G	105	Read-Togethers	Wright Group
Obstacle Course, The	H	211	Foundations	Wright Group
Ocean Animals	J	204	Early Connections	Benchmark Education
Ocean by the Lake, The	N	250+	Little Celebrations	Pearson Learning
Ocean Waves	B	21	Twig	Wright Group
Octopus Goes to School	C	42	Bordelon, Carolyn	Seedling
Octopuses	G	47	Pebble Books	Grolier, Capstone
Octopuses and Squids	N	328	Wonder World	Wright Group
Octopuses, Squid, & Cuttlefish	L	231	Marine Life for Young Readers	Dominie
Odd Socks	G	83	Literacy 2000	Rigby
Odds on Oliver	P	250+	Greene, Carol	Puffin Books
Off to Grandma's House	D	80	Little Celebrations	Pearson Learning
Off to Squintums/The Four Musicians	N	1268	Book Shop	Mondo Publishing
Off to the Shop	H	323	Storyteller-Night Crickets	Wright Group/ McGraw-Hill
Off to Work	B	41	Literacy 2000	Rigby
Off We Go!	A	16	Pacific Literacy	Pacific Learning
Oh a Hunting We Will Go	E	346	Langstaff, John	Macmillan
Oh Boy, Boston!	O	250+	Giff, Patricia Reilly	Bantam Doubleday Dell
Oh Dear	F		Campbell, Rod	Macmillan
Oh No Otis!	E	45	Rookie Readers	Children's Press

Title	Level	Words	Author/Series	Publisher/Distributor
Oh No!	E	127	Book Shop	Mondo Publishing
Oh No!	F	122	Traditional Tales & More	Rigby
Oh, Brother	P	250+	Wilson, Johnnice M.	Scholastic
Oh, Cats!	E	93	Buck, Nola	HarperTrophy
Oh, Jump in a Sack	E	130	Story Box	Wright Group
Oh, No!	C	53	Joy Readers	Dominie
Oh, No!	G	128	Little Celebrations	Pearson Learning
Oh, No, Sherman	E	66	Erickson, Betty	Seedling
Oh, What a Daughter!	L	250+	Literacy 2000	Rigby
Old and New	C	50	Interaction	Rigby
Old Bones	M	848	Sunshine	Wright Group
Old Car, The	F	135	Voyages	SRA/McGraw-Hill
Old Cat, New Cat	G	169	Wonder World	Wright Group
Old Enough for Magic	L	250+	Pickett, A.	HarperTrophy
Old Friends	M	345	Literacy 2000	Rigby
Old Grizzly	H	185	Sunshine	Wright Group
Old Hat, New Hat	H		Berenstain, Stan & Jan	Random House
Old MacDonald Had a Farm	D	505	Rounds, Glen	Holiday House
Old MacDonald Had a Farm	D		Jones, Carol	Houghton Mifflin
Old Man and the Bear, The	M	250+	Hanel, Wolfram	North-South Books
Old Man's Mitten, The	I	378	Book Shop	Mondo Publishing
Old Mother Hubbard	H	117	Literacy 2000	Rigby
Old Oak Tree, The	F	108	Little Celebrations	Pearson Learning
Old Rocking Chair, The	M	250+	Root, Phyllis	Scholastic
Old Steam Train, The	F	43	Literacy 2000	Rigby
Old Teeth, New Teeth	F	53	Wonder World	Wright Group
Old Train, The	F	68	Books for Young Learners	Richard C. Owen
Old Tuatara	C	33	Ready to Read	Pacific Learning
Old Tuatara	C	33	Pacific Literacy	Pacific Learning
Old Woman Who Lived in a Vinegar Bottle, The	M	1161	Book Shop	Mondo Publishing
Old Woman, The	H	69	Sunshine	Wright Group
Oliver	H		Kraus, Robert	Simon & Schuster
Oliver and Amanda's Halloween	L	250+	Van Leeuwen, Jean	Puffin Books
On a Chair	C	30	Story Box	Wright Group
On a Cold, Cold Day	C	33	Tadpoles	Rigby
On a Hill	D	53	Start to Read	School Zone
On a Walk	A	5	Ready Readers	Pearson Learning
On Friday the Giant	K	240	The Giant	Wright Group
On Monday the Giant	K	250+	The Giant	Wright Group
On My Street	H	292	Visions	Wright Group
On Safari	A	28	Smart Starts	Rigby
On Sunday the Giant	K	250+	The Giant	Wright Group
On the Beach	B	28	Smart Starts	Rigby
On the Computer	D	67	Twig	Wright Group
On the Farm	C	18	Literacy 2000	Rigby
On the Go	C	43	Learn to Read	Creative Teaching Press
On the Ground	C	40	Sunshine	Wright Group
On the Move	D	26	Wonder World	Wright Group
On the Open Plains	J	250+	Momentum Literacy Program	Troll
On the Road	C	47	Teacher's Choice Series	Dominie
On the School Bus	F	62	Little Readers	Houghton Mifflin
On This Earth	D	71	Rise & Shine	Hampton-Brown

Title	Level	Words	Author/Series	Publisher/Distributor
On Thursday the Giant	K	250+	The Giant	Wright Group
On Top of Spaghetti	G	105	Little Celebrations	Pearson Learning
On Tuesday the Giant	K	250+	The Giant	Wright Group
On Vacation	D	88	Little Red Readers	Sundance
On Wednesday the Giant	K	250+	The Giant	Wright Group
On with the Show!	M	250+	Pair-It Books	Steck-Vaughn
Once Upon a Time	H	243	Ready Readers	Pearson Learning
Once When I Was Shipwrecked	L	250+	Literacy 2000	Rigby
One Bad Thing About Father, The	M	250+	Monjo, Ferdinand N.	HarperTrophy
One Bear All Alone	H	107	Bucknall, Caroline	Dial
One Bee Got on the Bus	C	43	Ready Readers	Pearson Learning
One Bird Sat on the Fence	C	40	Wonder World	Wright Group
One Chick, One Egg	D	64	Step-By-Step Series	Dominie
One Cold, Wet Night	D	134	Read-Togethers	Wright Group
One Day in the Tropical Rain Forest	P	250+	Craighead George, Jean	HarperTrophy
One Day in the Woods	P	250+	Craighead George, Jean	HarperTrophy
One Drop of Water and a Million More	K	156	Book Bank	Wright Group
One- Eyed Jake	M	547	Hutchins, Pat	Morrow
One for You and One for Me	C	27	Blaxland, Wendy	Scholastic
One for You and One for Me	I	354	Early Connections	Benchmark Education
One Happy Classroom	D	49	Rookie Readers	Children's Press
One Hot Summer Night	I	126	Book Shop	Mondo Publishing
One in the Middle Is the Green Kangaroo, The	M	250+	Blume, Judy	Bantam Doubleday Dell
One Little Elephant	H	174	Sunshine	Wright Group
One Monday Morning	G	180	Shulevitz, Uri	Scribner
One Sock, Two Socks	H	285	Reading Corners	Dominie
One Stormy Night	F	165	Story Basket	Wright Group
One Sun in the Sky	E	120	Windmill	Wright Group
One Thousand Currant Buns	H	213	Sunshine	Wright Group
One, One Is the Sun	B	42	Story Box	Wright Group
One, Two, Three, Four	B	21	KinderReaders	Rigby
One, Two, Three, Four	D	89	Rise & Shine	Hampton-Brown
Onion Sundaes	M	250+	Adler, David	Random House
On-Line Spaceman and Other Cases, The	O	250+	Simon, Seymour	Avon Books
Only an Octopus	H	236	Literacy 2000	Rigby
Oogly Gum Chasing Game, The	K	250+	Literacy 2000	Rigby
Oops!	D		Mayer, Mercer	The Penguin Group
Open It!	D	27	Pacific Literacy	Pacific Learning
Open Wide	G	189	Home Connection Collection	Rigby
Opposite of Pig, The	K	250+	Little Celebrations	Pearson Learning
Optometrist, The	G	191	PM Nonfiction-Blue	Rigby
Orca Song	K	250+	Armour, Michael C.	Scholastic
Orchestra, The	C	33	Foundations	Wright Group
Oscar Otter	J	250+	Benchley, Nathaniel	HarperTrophy
Other Side of the Lake, The	L	250+	Little Celebrations	Pearson Learning
Otto the Cat	J	250+	Herman, Gail	Grosset & Dunlap
Ouch!	A	40	Literacy 2000	Rigby
Our Baby	B	14	Literacy 2000	Rigby
Our Baby	D	70	Voyages	SRA/McGraw-Hill
Our Baby	E	90	PM Nonfiction-Yellow	Rigby
Our Baby	J	128	Foundations	Wright Group
Our Book of Maps	N	250+	Discovery World	Rigby

Title	Level	Words	Author/Series	Publisher/Distributor
Our Busy Bodies	K	144	Home Connection Collection	Rigby
Our Car	C	32	Sunshine	Wright Group
Our Car	G	94	Book Shop	Mondo Publishing
Our Cat	E	99	Foundations	Wright Group
Our Chore Chart	D	65	Storyteller-First Snow	Wright Group/ McGraw-Hill
Our Dog Sam	C	56	Literacy 2000	Rigby
Our Earth	D	33	Discovery Links	Newbridge
Our Eyes	I	869	Sunshine	Wright Group
Our Garage	F	80	Urmston, Kathleen & Evans, Karen	Kaeden Books
Our Garden	B	16	Literacy 2000	Rigby
Our Grandad	C	30	Sunshine	Wright Group
Our Granny	C	41	Sunshine	Wright Group
Our House Had a Mouse	E	102	Worthington, Denise	Seedling
Our Mom	E	107	PM Nonfiction-Yellow	Rigby
Our Money	J	255	Early Connections	Benchmark Education
Our New Principal	K	149	City Kids	Rigby
Our Parents	G	142	PM Nonfiction-Blue	Rigby
Our Playhouse	D	46	Voyages	SRA/McGraw-Hill
Our Polliwogs	I	91	Books for Young Learners	Richard C. Owen
Our Pumpkin	B		Learn to Read	Creative Teaching Press
Our Rocket	B	28	Pacific Literacy	Pacific Learning
Our School	C	46	Twig	Wright Group
Our School	H	98	City Kids	Rigby
Our Senses	D	39	Rise & Shine	Hampton-Brown
Our Senses	F	182	Discovery Links	Newbridge
Our Street	C	40	Sunshine	Wright Group
Our Teacher, Miss Pool	D	62	Ready to Read	Pacific Learning
Our Teacher, Miss Pool	D	62	Pacific Literacy	Pacific Learning
Our Tree House	E	144	Twig	Wright Group
Our Week	C	37	Storyteller-First Snow	Wright Group/ McGraw-Hill
Out After Dark	H	114	Book Bank	Wright Group
Out in the Big Wild World	K	430	Jellybeans	Rigby
Out in the Weather	B	56	PM Starters	Rigby
Out the Door	E	150	Rookie Readers	Children's Press
Outing, An	E	68	Sunshine	Wright Group
Outside and Inside	C	43	Twig	Wright Group
Outside Dog, The	K	250+	Pomerantz, Charlotte	HarperTrophy
Outside, Inside	D	97	Teacher's Choice Series	Dominie
Over in the Meadow	G	242	Little Readers	Houghton Mifflin
Over in the Meadow	L	375	Galdone, Paul	Simon & Schuster
Over the Bridge	B	50	Little Red Readers	Sundance
Over the Marble Mountain	E	92	Voyages	SRA/McGraw-Hill
Over the Oregon Trail	D	131	Twig	Wright Group
Over-Under	E	29	Rookie Readers	Children's Press
Owl and the Pussy Cat	L	215	Lear, Edward	Scholastic
Owl at Home	J	1488	Lobel, Arnold	HarperCollins
Owl Moon	O	250+	Yolen, Jane	Scholastic
Owls	K	250+	PM Animal Facts-Gold	Rigby
Owls in the Family	P	250+	Mowat, Farley	Bantam Doubleday Dell
Owls in the Garden	L	670	PM Story Books-Gold	Rigby

Title	Level	Words	Author/Series	Publisher/Distributor
P.J. Funnybunny Camps Out	G	250+	Sadler, Marilyn	Random House
Pack 109	J	164	Thaler, Mike	Scholastic
Package, The	E	35	Bauer, Roger	Kaeden Books
Packing	B	37	Foundations	Wright Group
Packing My Bag	B	52	PM Starters	Rigby
Paco's Garden	G	118	Books for Young Learners	Richard C. Owen
Paint Brush Kid, The	M	250+	Bulla, Clyde Robert	Random House
Paint the Sky	A	14	Sunshine	Wright Group
Painters	A	23	Twig	Wright Group
Painting	C	24	Story Box	Wright Group
Pajama Party	M	250+	Hest, Amy	William Morrow & Co.
Pajama Party, The	D	46	Sunshine	Wright Group
Palm Trees	I	123	Pebble Books	Grolier, Capstone
Paloma's Party	L	250+	Little Celebrations	Pearson Learning
Pam & Sam at the Park	C	108	Carousel Earlybirds	Dominie
Pam & Sam at the Zoo	C	84	Carousel Earlybirds	Dominie
Pam & Sam Fly Over the City	C	80	Carousel Earlybirds	Dominie
Pam & Sam on the Beach	D	94	Carousel Earlybirds	Dominie
Pancake, The	K	250+	Lobel, Anita	Bantam Doubleday Dell
Pancakes	G	181	Foundations	Wright Group
Pancakes for Breakfast	C	108	Emergent	Pioneer Valley
Pancakes for Supper	H	96	Literacy 2000	Rigby
Pancakes!	F	106	Ready Readers	Pearson Learning
Pancakes, Crackers and Pizza	C	63	Rookie Readers	Children's Press
Pandas in the Mountains	M	735	PM Story Books-Gold	Rigby
Panda's Surprise	H	242	Little Readers	Houghton Mifflin
Papa's Spaghetti	G	248	Literacy 2000	Rigby
Paper Bag Trail	E	67	Schreiber, Anne & Doughty, A.	Scholastic
Paper Birds, The	K	363	Foundations	Wright Group
Paper Patchwork	F	54	Pacific Literacy	Pacific Learning
Paper Route, The	K	314	New Way Green	Steck-Vaughn
Paper Trail, The	I	253	Windmill Books	Rigby
Parachutes	J	145	Storyteller-Moon Rising	Wright Group/ McGraw-Hill
Parades!	C	24	Pair-It Books	Steck-Vaughn
Parakeets	I	250+	PM Animal Facts: Pets-Orange	Rigby
Pardon? Said the Giraffe	F	123	West, Colin	Harper & Row
Parents	C	60	Pebble Books	Grolier, Capstone
Parents' Night Fright	K	250+	Levy, Elizabeth	Scholastic
Parrotfish	G	51	Pebble Books	Grolier, Capstone
Partners	L	159	Home Connection Collection	Rigby
Parts of a Whole	E	165	Early Connections	Benchmark Education
Party Games	J	399	Foundations	Wright Group
Party Time at the Milky Way	I	160	Sunshine	Wright Group
Party, A	A	14	Story Box	Wright Group
Party, The	D	26	Ready Readers	Pearson Learning
Paru Has a Bath	J	242	Ready to Read	Pacific Learning
Paru Has a Bath	J	242	Pacific Literacy	Pacific Learning
Pass the Pasta, Please	D	63	Storyteller-Setting Sun	Wright Group/ McGraw-Hill

Title	Level	Words	Author/Series	Publisher/Distributor
Pass the Present	C	86	Storyteller-First Snow	Wright Group/ McGraw-Hill
Pasta	N	250+	Little Celebrations	Pearson Learning
Pat, Pat, Pat	B	37	Book Bank	Wright Group
Patches	M	250+	Szymanski, Lois	Avon Camelot
Patchwork Patterns	G		Little Celebrations	Pearson Learning
Patrick and the Leprechaun	L	677	PM Story Books-Gold	Rigby
Patrick Doyle Is Full of Blarney	N	250+	Armstrong, Jennifer	Random House
Pat's New Puppy	E	88	Reading Unlimited	Pacific Learning
Pat's Perfect Pizza	C	37	Ready Readers	Pearson Learning
Pat's Train	D	22	KinderReaders	Rigby
Patterns	C	35	Discovery Links	Newbridge
Patterns	E	57	Literacy 2000	Rigby
Patterns All Around	B	55	Early Connections	Benchmark Education
Patty and Pop's Picnic	C	57	Little Books	Sadlier-Oxford
Paul	F	54	Ready to Read	Pacific Learning
Paul and Lucy	J	250+	Stepping Stones	Nelson/Michaels Assoc.
Paul the Pitcher	D	86	Rookie Readers	Children's Press
Paulo the Pilot	F	131	Windmill Books	Rigby
Paul's Day at School	B	38	Little Books for Early Readers	University of Maine
Pea or the Flea?, The	F	66	Start to Read	School Zone
Peaches the Pig	E	120	Little Readers	Houghton Mifflin
Peanut Butter	E	60	Little Celebrations	Pearson Learning
Peanut Butter and Jelly	E	164	Little Readers	Houghton Mifflin
Peanut Butter and Jelly	G	156	Wescott, Nadine B.	The Penguin Group
Peanut Butter Gang, The	K	250+	Siracusa, Catherine	Hyperion
Peas and Potatoes, 1,2,3	B	44	Pair-It Books	Steck-Vaughn
Pedal Power	C	22	Pacific Literacy	Pacific Learning
Pedro's Journal: A Voyage with Christopher Columbus	L	250+	Conrad, Pam	Scholastic
Pee Wee Scouts: A Pee Wee Christmas	L	250+	Delton, Judy	Bantam Doubleday Dell
Pee Wee Scouts: Blue Skies, French Fries	L	250+	Delton, Judy	Bantam Doubleday Dell
Pee Wee Scouts: Bookworm Buddies	L	250+	Delton, Judy	Bantam Doubleday Dell
Pee Wee Scouts: Computer Clues	L	250+	Delton, Judy	Bantam Doubleday Dell
Pee Wee Scouts: Cookies and Crutches	L	250+	Delton, Judy	Bantam Doubleday Dell
Pee Wee Scouts: Eggs with Legs	L	250+	Delton, Judy	Bantam Doubleday Dell
Pee Wee Scouts: Fishy Wishes	L	250+	Delton, Judy	Bantam Doubleday Dell
Pee Wee Scouts: Greedy Groundhogs	L	250+	Delton, Judy	Bantam Doubleday Dell
Pee Wee Scouts: Grumpy Pumpkins	L	250+	Delton, Judy	Bantam Doubleday Dell
Pee Wee Scouts: Halloween Helpers	L	250+	Delton, Judy	Bantam Doubleday Dell
Pee Wee Scouts: Lights, Action, Land-Ho!	L	250+	Delton, Judy	Bantam Doubleday Dell
Pee Wee Scouts: Lucky Dog Days	L	250+	Delton, Judy	Bantam Doubleday Dell
Pee Wee Scouts: Moans & Groans & Dinosaur Bones	L	250+	Delton, Judy	Bantam Doubleday Dell
Pee Wee Scouts: Pedal Power	L	250+	Delton, Judy	Bantam Doubleday Dell
Pee Wee Scouts: Pee Wee Pool Party	L	250+	Delton, Judy	Bantam Doubleday Dell
Pee Wee Scouts: Piles of Pets	L	250+	Delton, Judy	Bantam Doubleday Dell
Pee Wee Scouts: Planet Pee Wee	L	250+	Delton, Judy	Bantam Doubleday Dell
Pee Wee Scouts: Rosy Noses, Freezing Toes	L	250+	Delton, Judy	Bantam Doubleday Dell
Pee Wee Scouts: Send in the Clowns	L	250+	Delton, Judy	Bantam Doubleday Dell
Pee Wee Scouts: Sky Babies	L	250+	Delton, Judy	Bantam Doubleday Dell

Title	Level	Words	Author/Series	Publisher/Distributor
Pee Wee Scouts: Sonny's Secret	L	250+	Delton, Judy	Bantam Doubleday Dell
Pee Wee Scouts: Spring Sprouts	L	250+	Delton, Judy	Bantam Doubleday Dell
Pee Wee Scouts: Stage Frightened	L	250+	Delton, Judy	Bantam Doubleday Dell
Pee Wee Scouts: Super Duper Pee Wee!	L	250+	Delton, Judy	Bantam Doubleday Dell
Pee Wee Scouts: Teeny Weeny Zucchinis	L	250+	Delton, Judy	Bantam Doubleday Dell
Pee Wee Scouts: That Mushy Stuff	L	250+	Delton, Judy	Bantam Doubleday Dell
Pee Wee Scouts: The Pee Wee Jubilee	L	250+	Delton, Judy	Bantam Doubleday Dell
Pee Wee Scouts: Trash Bash	L	250+	Delton, Judy	Bantam Doubleday Dell
Pee Wee Scouts: Tricks and Treats	L	250+	Delton, Judy	Bantam Doubleday Dell
Pee Wee Scouts: Wild, Wild West	L	250+	Delton, Judy	Bantam Doubleday Dell
Pee Wees on First	L	250+	Delton, Judy	Bantam Doubleday Dell
Pee Wees on Parade	L	250+	Delton, Judy	Bantam Doubleday Dell
Pee Wees on Skis	L	250+	Delton, Judy	Bantam Doubleday Dell
PeeWee Scouts	L	250+	Delton, Judy	Yearling
PeeWee's on First	L	250+	Delton, Judy	Yearling
Pencil, The	B	97	PM Starters	Rigby
Penguins	O	250+	Woolley, M. & Pigdon, K.	Mondo
Penguin's Chicks	D	38	Pacific Literacy	Pacific Learning
Penguins on Parade	O	250+	Little Celebrations	Pearson Learning
People Are Living Things	K	250+	Home Connection Collection	Rigby
People at Work	J	250+	Momentum Literacy Program	Troll
People Can Build	E	46	Sunshine	Wright Group
People Dance	E	46	Wonder World	Wright Group
People on the Beach	F	87	Carousel Readers	Dominie
People Use Tools	A	24	Early Connections	Benchmark Education
People Who Help Us	D	62	Foundations	Wright Group
Pepper Goes to School	H	125	Foundations	Wright Group
Pepper Sees Me	A	28	Little Books for Early Readers	University of Maine
Peppers	D	32	Rise & Shine	Hampton-Brown
Pepper's Adventure	H	250+	PM Story Books	Rigby
Percival	I	303	Literacy 2000	Rigby
Perfect Pony, A	O	250+	Szymanski, Lois	Avon Camelot
Perfect the Pig	L	250+	Jeschke, Susan	Scholastic
Pesky Paua, The	H	267	Book Bank	Wright Group
Pet Day at School	I	198	City Kids	Rigby
Pet for Me, A	C	73	Early Emergent	Pioneer Valley
Pet for Pat, A	D	45	Rookie Readers	Children's Press
Pet for You, A	K	531	Pair-It Books	Steck-Vaughn
Pet Parade	C	33	Literacy 2000	Rigby
Pet Parade	O	250+	Giff, Patricia Reilly	Bantam Doubleday Dell
Pet Shop	D	167	Story Box	Wright Group
Pet Shop, The	C	32	Oxford Reading Tree	Oxford University Press
Pet Sitters Plus Five	L	250+	Springstubb, Tricia	Scholastic
Pet Tarantula, The	I	208	Storyteller Nonfiction	Wright Group/ McGraw-Hill
Pet That I Want, The	E		Packard, Mary	Scholastic
Pete Little	G	222	PM Story Books	Rigby
Pete the Parakeet	F	133	First Start	Troll
Peter and the North Wind	K	250+	Littledale, Freya	Scholastic
Peter and the Pennytree	G	119	First Start	Troll
Peter's Chair	J	250+	Keats, Ezra Jack	HarperTrophy
Peter's Move	H	224	Little Readers	Houghton Mifflin

Title	Level	Words	Author/Series	Publisher/Distributor
Peter's Painting	F	147	Book Shop	Mondo Publishing
Pete's Bad Day	G	164	Ready Readers	Pearson Learning
Pete's New Shoes	G	91	Literacy 2000	Rigby
Pete's Story	L	250+	Literacy 2000	Rigby
Pets	A	33	PM Starters	Rigby
Pets	F	56	Literacy 2000	Rigby
Pets	J	90	Ready to Read	Pacific Learning
Pets	J	90	Pacific Literacy	Pacific Learning
Phantoms Don't Drive Sports Cars	M	250+	Dadey, Debbie & Jones, Marcia	Scholastic
Pheasant and Kingfisher	L	910	Book Shop	Mondo Publishing
Philippa and the Dragon	G	137	Literacy 2000	Rigby
Phyllis Wheatley: First African-American Poet	N	250+	Rookie Biographies	Children's Press
Photo Book, The	C	50	PM Story Books	Rigby
Photos, Photos	L	250+	Wildcats	Wright Group
Pick a Pet	C		Little Celebrations	Pearson Learning
Pick Up Nick!	H	219	Ready Readers	Pearson Learning
Picked for the Team	L	709	PM Story Books-Gold	Rigby
Picking Apples and Pumpkins	L	250+	Hutchings, A. & R.	Scholastic
Picking Apples	F	53	Pebble Books	Grolier, Capstone
Picking Up Papers	K	161	City Kids	Rigby
Pickle Puss	L	250+	Giff, Patricia Reilly	Bantam Doubleday Dell
Picnic in the Sand, A	A	14	Ready Readers	Pearson Learning
Picnic in the Sky, The	D	80	Foundations	Wright Group
Picnic Tea	I	224	Stepping Stones	Nelson/Michaels Assoc.
Picnic, The	A	18	Book Bank	Wright Group
Picnic, The	C	48	Teacher's Choice Series	Dominie
Picnic, The	F	122	Wonder World	Wright Group
Picnic, The	G	151	Home Connection Collection	Rigby
Picture Book of Hellen Keller, A	M	250+	Little Readers	Houghton Mifflin
Picture for Harold's Room, A	H	550	Johnson, Crockett	HarperCollins
Picture, A	C	58	Storyteller-First Snow	Wright Group/ McGraw-Hill
Pictures	E	76	Teacher's Choice Series	Dominie
Piece of Cake	I	250+	Home Connection Collection	Rigby
Pied Piper	L	250+	Hunia, Fran	Ladybird Books
Pied Piper of Hamelin, The	K	250+	Hautzig, Deborah	Random House
Pied Piper, The	M	585	Sunshine	Wright Group
Pig That Learned to Jig, The	I	140	Wonder World	Wright Group
Pig William's Midnight Walk	H	354	Book Bank	Wright Group
Piggle	K	250+	Bonsall, Crosby	HarperCollins
Piglet in a Playpen	P	250+	Daniels, Lucy	Barron's Educational
Pignocchio	L	250+	Pair-It Books	Steck-Vaughn
Pigs Peek	C	28	Books for Young Learners	Richard C. Owen
Pile in Pete's Room, The	K	745	Sunshine	Wright Group
Pillow Sale, The	B	26	KinderReaders	Rigby
Pinata Time	D	71	Teacher's Choice Series	Dominie
Pine Trees	H	138	Pebble Books	Grolier, Capstone
Pink Pig	B	23	Ready Readers	Pearson Learning
Pinky and Rex	L	250+	Howe, James	Simon & Schuster
Pinky and Rex and the Bully	L	250+	Howe, James	Simon & Schuster
Pinky and Rex and the Double-Dad Weekend	L	250+	Howe, James	Simon & Schuster
Pinky and Rex and the Mean Old Witch	L	250+	Howe, James	Simon & Schuster

Title	Level	Words	Author/Series	Publisher/Distributor
Pinky and Rex and the New Baby	L	250+	Howe, James	Simon & Schuster
Pinky and Rex and the New Neighbors	L	250+	Howe, James	Simon & Schuster
Pinky and Rex and the Perfect Pumpkin	L	250+	Howe, James	Simon & Schuster
Pinky and Rex and the School Play	L	250+	Howe, James	Simon & Schuster
Pinky and Rex and the Spelling Bee	L	250+	Howe, James	Simon & Schuster
Pinky and Rex Get Married	L	250+	Howe, James	Simon & Schuster
Pioneer Bear	L	250+	Sandin, Joan	Random House
Pioneer Cat	N	250+	Hooks, William H.	Random House
Pip and the Little Monkey	F	112	Oxford Reading Tree	Oxford University Press
Pip at the Zoo	F	70	Oxford Reading Tree	Oxford University Press
Pippa's Pet Pest	D	35	Home Connection Collection	Rigby
Pirate Feast, The	H	172	Story Basket	Wright Group
Pirates Don't Wear Pink Sunglasses	M	250+	Dadey, Debbie & Jones, Marcia	Scholastic
Pirates Past Noon	M	250+	Osborne, Mary Pope	Random House
Pirate's Promise	N	250+	Bulla, Clyde Robert	HarperTrophy
Pirate's Treasure, The	E	63	Joy Readers	Dominie
Pitching Trouble	N	250+	Kroll, Stephen	Avon Camelot
Pitty Pitty Pat	C	45	Little Celebrations	Pearson Learning
Pizza for Dinner	H	164	Literacy 2000	Rigby
Pizza for Everyone	K	251	Pair-It Books	Steck-Vaughn
Pizza Party!	F		Maccarone, Grace	Scholastic
Pizza Pokey	I	280	Pair-It Books	Steck-Vaughn
Pizza, The	D	100	Foundations	Wright Group
Places	C	88	Little Red Readers	Sundance
Plane Ride, The	F	68	Little Red Readers	Sundance
Planets, The	J	101	Wonder World	Wright Group
Planning a Birthday Party	N	1455	Book Shop	Mondo Publishing
Planning Dinner	H	260	Urmston, Kathleen & Evans, Karen	Kaeden Books
Planting a Garden	E	62	Ready Readers	Pearson Learning
Plants	I	250+	Momentum Literacy Program	Troll
Plants and Seeds	I	148	Sunshine	Wright Group
Plants of My Aunt	J	429	Jellybeans	Rigby
Platypus	N	1098	Book Shop	Mondo Publishing
Play Ball	A	7	Book Shop	Mondo Publishing
Play Ball	A	14	Twig	Wright Group
Play Ball!	D	30	Books for Young Learners	Richard C. Owen
Play Ball, Amelia Bedelia	L	250+	Parish, Peggy	Harper & Row
Play Ball, Sherman	F	88	Erickson, Betty	Seedling
Play Dough	C	63	Foundations	Wright Group
Play It Again Sam	I	139	Literacy 2000	Rigby
Playground Fun	D	127	Early Connections	Benchmark Education
Playground Opposites	B	21	Pair-It Books	Steck-Vaughn
Playground, The	A	16	Twig	Wright Group
Playground, The	C	108	Early Emergent	Pioneer Valley
Playhouse for Monster	C		Mueller, Virginia	Whitman
Playhouse, The	K	197	Pacific Literacy	Pacific Learning
Playing	A	39	PM Starters	Rigby
Playing Favorites	N	250+	Kroll, Stephen	Avon Camelot
Playing in the Snow	C	61	Early Emergent	Pioneer Valley
Playing It Safe	F	135	Early Connections	Benchmark Education
Playing Soccer	I	123	Foundations	Wright Group

Title	Level	Words	Author/Series	Publisher/Distributor
Playing with Dad	F	146	Foundations	Wright Group
Playtime	C		Voyages	SRA/McGraw-Hill
Please, Do Not Drop Your Jelly Beans	I	180	Storyteller-Night Crickets	Wright Group/ McGraw-Hill
Plop!	C	30	Story Box	Wright Group
Pocahontas: Daughter of a Chief	N	250+	Rookie Biographies	Children's Press
Pocket for Corduroy, A	K	250+	Freeman, Don	Scholastic
Pockets	D	32	Visions	Wright Group
Polar Bears	F	77	Pebble Books	Grolier, Capstone
Polar Bears	K	276	Wonder World	Wright Group
Polar Bears Past Bedtime	M	250+	Osborne, Mary Pope	Random House
Police Cars	I	177	Pebble Books	Grolier, Capstone
Polka Dots!	F		Little Celebrations	Pearson Learning
Pollution	F	46	Wonder World	Wright Group
Polly's Shop	E	130	Ready Readers	Pearson Learning
Pompeii…Buried Alive!	N	250+	Kunhardt, Edith	Random House
Pond for Tim, A	G		Counters & Seekers	Steck-Vaughn
Pond Party	D	33	Little Celebrations	Pearson Learning
Pond Where Harriet Lives, The	H	151	Storyteller-Night Crickets	Wright Group/ McGraw-Hill
Pond, A	A	14	Discovery Links	Newbridge
Pond, The	C	25	Books for Young Learners	Richard C. Owen
Pond, The	C	54	Joy Readers	Dominie
Pony for Keeps, A	O	250+	Betancourt, Jeanne	Scholastic
Pony in Trouble, A	O	250+	Betancourt, Jeanne	Scholastic
Pony Named Shawney, A	P	3075	Book Shop	Mondo Publishing
Pony to the Rescue	O	250+	Betancourt, Jeanne	Scholastic
Pony Trouble	L	250+	Gasque, Dale Blackwell	Hyperion
Pookie and Joe	K	250+	Literacy 2000	Rigby
Pooped Troop, The	L	250+	Delton, Judy	Bantam Doubleday Dell
Poor Old Polly	F	111	Read-Togethers	Wright Group
Poor Polly Pig	F	57	Start to Read	School Zone
Poor Sore Paw, The	I	244	Sunshine	Wright Group
POP Pops the Popcorn	E	60	Ready Readers	Pearson Learning
Pop…Pop…Popcorn	C	40	Home Connection Collection	Rigby
Popcorn Book, The	K	208	Reading Unlimited	Pacific Learning
Popcorn Shop, The	J	250+	Low, Alice	Scholastic
Poppleton	J	250+	Rylant, Cynthia	Scholastic
Poppleton and Friends	J	250+	Rylant, Cynthia	Blue Sky Press
Poppleton and Friends	J	250+	Rylant, Cynthia	Scholastic
Poppleton Everyday	J	250+	Rylant, Cynthia	Scholastic
Poppleton Forever	J	250+	Rylant, Cynthia	Scholastic
Poppleton in Spring	J	250+	Rylant, Cynthia	Scholastic
Poppy, The	K	152	Pacific Literacy	Pacific Learning
Porcupine, A	D	49	Wonder World	Wright Group
Porcupine's Pajama Party	J	250+	Harshman, Terry Webb	HarperTrophy
Postcard Pest, The	M	250+	Giff, Patricia Reilly	Bantam Doubleday Dell
Postman Pete	J	285	Book Shop	Mondo Publishing
Pot of Gold, The	I	266	Reading Unlimited	Pacific Learning
Pot of Stone Soup, A	L	250+	Ready Readers	Pearson Learning
Potato Chips	I	101	City Kids	Rigby
Potato Harvest Time	A	33	Little Books for Early Readers	University of Maine

Title	Level	Words	Author/Series	Publisher/Distributor
Potatoes on Tuesday	C	28	Little Celebrations	Pearson Learning
Potatoes, Potatoes	H	91	Wonder World	Wright Group
Potter in Fiji, A	P	453	Wonder World	Wright Group
Powder Puff Puzzle, The	L	250+	Giff, Patricia Reilly	Bantam Doubleday Dell
Power of Nature, The	K	274	Early Connections	Benchmark Education
Power of Water, The	L	250+	Home Connection Collection	Rigby
Practice Makes Perfect	D	111	Teacher's Choice Series	Dominie
Praying Mantis, The	D	46	Ready to Read	Pacific Learning
Praying Mantis, The	D	46	Pacific Literacy	Pacific Learning
Prehistoric Record Breakers	N	250+	Discovery World	Rigby
Present from Aunt Skidoo, The	M	250+	Literacy 2000	Rigby
Present, The	E	30	Literacy 2000	Rigby
Presents	D	43	Storyteller-First Snow	Wright Group/ McGraw-Hill
Pretty Good Majic	J	250+	Dubowski, Cathy	Random House
Pride of the Rockets	N	250+	Kroll, Stephen	Avon Camelot
Princess and the Pea, The	I	304	Traditional Tales	Dominie
Princess and the Peas, The	K	250+	Enrichment	Wright Group
Princess and the Wise Woman, The	K	250+	Ready Readers	Pearson Learning
Princess Josie's Pets	L	250+	Macdonald, Maryann	Hyperion
Princess Who Couldn't Cry, The	G	300	Ready Readers	Pearson Learning
Princess, the Mud Pies, and the Dragon, The	I	250+	Little Readers	Houghton Mifflin
Printing Machine, The	G	102	Literacy 2000	Rigby
Priscilla and the Dinosaurs	L	340	Sunshine	Wright Group
Private Notebook of Katie Roberts, Age 11, The	P	250+	Hest, Amy	Candlewick Press
Prize for Purry, A	K	250+	Literacy 2000	Rigby
Processed Food	F	54	Wonder World	Wright Group
Pterodactyl at the Airport	K	185	Wesley & the Dinosaurs	Wright Group
Pterosaur's Long Flight	I	301	PM Story Books-Orange	Rigby
Public Library, The	K	250+	Stepping Stones	Nelson/Michaels Assoc.
Pukeko Morning	G		Ready to Read	Pacific Learning
Pumpkin House, The	J	250+	Literacy 2000	Rigby
Pumpkin That Kim Carved, The	H	149	Little Readers	Houghton Mifflin
Pumpkin, The	E	56	Story Box	Wright Group
Puppet Play, A	C	54	Storyteller-First Snow	Wright Group/ McGraw-Hill
Puppet Show	F	105	First Start	Troll
Puppet Show, The	E	25	Literacy 2000	Rigby
Puppets	J	250+	Little Celebrations	Pearson Learning
Puppets for a Play	D	45	Home Connection Collection	Rigby
Puppy Love	N	250+	Duffy, Betsy	Puffin Books
Puppy Who Wanted a Boy, The	L	250+	Thayer, Jane	Scholastic
Purple Climbing Days	M	250+	Giff, Patricia Reilly	Bantam Doubleday Dell
Purple Is Part of a Rainbow	E	131	Rookie Readers	Children's Press
Purple Walrus and Other Perfect Pets	K	250+	Wildcats	Wright Group
Push!	D	21	Oxford Reading Tree	Oxford University Press
Pussy Cat	F	143	Literacy 2000	Rigby
Put Me in the Zoo	H	250+	Lopshire, Robert	Random House
Puzzle, The	B	32	Smart Starts	Rigby
Puzzle, The	B	28	Storyteller Nonfiction	Wright Group/ McGraw-Hill
Python Caught the Eagle, The	C	60	Voyages	SRA/McGraw-Hill

Title	Level	Words	Author/Series	Publisher/Distributor
Quack, Said the Billy Goat	H	88	Causley, Charles	Harper & Row
Quack!	E	48	Ready Readers	Pearson Learning
Quack, Quack, Quack	D	97	Carousel Readers	Dominie
Quack, Quack, Quack!	I	219	Sunshine	Wright Group
Quarter Story, The	E	99	Williams, Deborah	Kaeden Books
Queen and the Dragon, The	I	243	New Way Green	Steck-Vaughn
Queen on a Quilt	C	26	Ready Readers	Pearson Learning
Queen's Parrot, The: A Play	J	365	Literacy 2000	Rigby
Questions, Questions, Questions	F	190	Visions	Wright Group
Quick, Go Peek!	E	83	Little Celebrations	Pearson Learning
Quiet in the Library!	H	113	Sunshine	Wright Group
Quilt for Kiri, A	K	367	Pacific Literacy	Pacific Learning
Quilt Story, The	L	250+	Johnston, Tony & DePaola, Tomie	Scholastic
Quilt, The	I	165	Jonas, Ann	Morrow
Quilts	C	35	Foundations	Wright Group
Quilts	E	131	Twig	Wright Group
Rabbit Catches the Sun	M	621	Sunshine	Wright Group
Rabbit Stew	L	250+	Literacy 2000	Rigby
Rabbit, The	H	59	Burningham, John	Crowell
Rabbits	M	250+	Literacy 2000	Rigby
Rabbit's Birthday Kite Dell	J	250+	McDonald, Maryann	Bantam Doubleday
Rabbit's Party	G	351	Bunting, Eve & Sloan-Childers, E.	Scholastic
Raccoons	K	250+	PM Animal Facts-Gold	Rigby
Race Is On, The	D	45	New Way Red	Steck-Vaughn
Race to Green End, The	J	506	PM Story Books-Turquoise	Rigby
Race, The	B	34	Windmill	Rigby, Wright Group
Race, The	C	25	Sunshine	Wright Group
Race, The	E	30	Little Celebrations	Pearson Learning
Race, The	F	145	Little Readers	Houghton Mifflin
Race, The	I	451	New Way Green	Steck-Vaughn
Rachel Carson: Friend of Nature	N	250+	Rookie Biographies	Children's Press
Rain	B	52	Reading Corners	Dominie
Rain	C	56	Kalan, Robert	Greenwillow
Rain	D	45	Step-By-Step Series	Dominie
Rain	G	68	Literacy 2000	Rigby
Rain	K	263	Pebble Books	Grolier, Capstone
Rain and the Sun, The	E	45	Wonder World	Wright Group
Rain Forest Adventure	L	482	Pair-It Books	Steck-Vaughn
Rain in the Hills	D	41	Book Bank	Wright Group
Rain or Shine?	C	21	Twig	Wright Group
Rain Puddle	J		Holl, Adelaide	Morrow
Rain! Rain!	D	29	Rookie Readers	Children's Press
Rain, Rain	G	58	Ready to Read	Pacific Learning
Rain, Rain, and More Rain	H	250+	Momentum Literacy Program	Troll
Rain, Snow, and Hail	J	250+	Discovery World	Rigby
Rain, The	G	171	Foundations	Wright Group
Rainbow Bird, A	A	18	Pair-It Books	Steck-Vaughn
Rainbow of My Own	C	268	Freeman, Don	The Penguin Group
Rainbow Somewhere, A	G	201	Ready Readers	Pearson Learning

Title	Level	Words	Author/Series	Publisher/Distributor
Raindrop, A	C	41	Teacher's Choice Series	Dominie
Raindrops	B	34	Book Shop	Mondo Publishing
Raindrops	C	66	Gay, Sandy	Scholastic
Rainy Day Counting	B	30	Twig	Wright Group
Rainy Day, A	D	105	New Way Blue	Steck-Vaughn
Rainy Days at School	H	118	City Kids	Rigby
Ralph S. Mouse	O	250+	Cleary, Beverly	Avon Books
Ramona and Her Father	O	250+	Cleary, Beverly	Avon Books
Ramona and Her Mother	O	250+	Cleary, Beverly	Avon Books
Ramona Forever	O	250+	Cleary, Beverly	Avon Books
Ramona Quimby, Age 8	O	250+	Cleary, Beverly	Avon Books
Ramona the Brave	O	250+	Cleary, Beverly	Avon Books
Ramona the Pest	O	250+	Cleary, Beverly	Avon Books
Rap Party, The	F	300	Foundations	Wright Group
Rapid Robert Roadrunner	H	125	Reese, Bob	Children's Press
Rapunzel	L	250+	Literacy 2000	Rigby
Rashee and the Seven Elephants	M	250+	Little Celebrations	Pearson Learning
Rat-a-tat-tat	E	107	Literacy 2000	Rigby
Rat's Funny Story	C	39	Story Box	Wright Group
Rats on the Range	M	250+	Marshall, James	Puffin Books
Rats on the Range and Other Stories	M	250+	Marshall, James	The Penguin Group
Rats on the Roof	M	250+	Marshall, James	Troll
Rats on the Roof and Other Stories	M	250+	Marshall, James	The Penguin Group
Rats, Bats, and Black Puddings	K	714	Pacific Literacy	Pacific Learning
Rattlesnake Looks for Food, The	E	105	Foundations	Wright Group
Ratty Tatty	H	181	Sunshine	Wright Group
Raven's Gift	L	160	Books for Young Learners	Richard C. Owen
Reaching the Sky	C	46	Sunshine	Wright Group
Reading Is Everywhere	D	53	Sunshine	Wright Group
Reading Robot, The	H	224	Sunshine	Wright Group
Reading Under the Covers	D	25	Visions	Wright Group
Ready for School	C	41	Teacher's Choice Series	Dominie
Ready for School	E	77	Windmill Books	Rigby
Ready Steady Jump	D	25	Ready to Read	Pacific Learning
Ready, Get Set, Go!	G	137	First Start	Troll
Ready, Set, Go	H	250+	Stadler, John	HarperTrophy
Ready, Steady, Jump!	D	25	Pacific Literacy	Pacific Learning
Real-Skin Rubber Monster Mask, The	H		Cohen, Miriam	Bantam Doubleday Dell
Rebecca and the Concert	I	374	PM Story Books-Orange	Rigby
Rebus Bears, The	I	250+	Reit, Seymour	Bantam Doubleday Dell
Recess	B	26	Teacher's Choice Series	Dominie
Recycle It!	G	118	Discovery Links	Newbridge
Recycling Dump	D	48	Little Celebrations	Pearson Learning
Red and Blue and Yellow	D	100	PM Nonfiction-Red	Rigby
Red and Blue Mittens	M	250+	Reading Unlimited	Pacific Learning
Red and I Visit the Vet	F	196	Ready Readers	Pearson Learning
Red Balloon, The	C	34	Joy Readers	Dominie
Red or Blue?	A	13	Ready Readers	Pearson Learning
Red Ribbon Rosie	M	250+	Marzollo, Jean	Random House
Red Rose, The	E	127	Read-Togethers	Wright Group
Red Socks and Yellow Socks	G	155	Sunshine	Wright Group
Red-Tailed Hawk, The	L	197	Books for Young Learners	Richard C. Owen

Title	Level	Words	Author/Series	Publisher/Distributor
Reduce, Reuse, and Recycle	K	326	Early Connections	Benchmark Education
Reflections	I		Jonas, Ann	Morrow
Rent a Third Grader	O	250+	Hiller, Bonnie Bryant	Scholastic
Rescue	O	250+	Wildcats	Wright Group
Rescue!	J	295	Sunshine	Wright Group
Rescue, The	H	155	PM Extensions-Green	Rigby
Rescue, The	L	176	Ready to Read	Pacific Learning
Rescuing Nelson	J	369	PM Story Books-Turquoise	Rigby
Return of Rinaldo, the Sly Fox	M	250+	Scheffler, Ursel	North-South Books
Return of the Home Run Kid	N	250+	Christopher, Matt	Scholastic
Return of the Third-Grade Ghost Hunters	M	250+	Maccarone, Grace	Scholastic
Revolting Rhymes	P	250+	Dahl, Roald	The Penguin Group
Rex's Dance	E	103	Little Readers	Houghton Mifflin
Rhyme Game, The	G	159	Storyteller-Setting Sun	Wright Group/ McGraw-Hill
Rhymes	A	9	Ready Readers	Pearson Learning
Ribbit!	A	7	Little Celebrations	Pearson Learning
Ribbon, The	C	46	Rise & Shine	Hampton-Brown
Ribsy	O	250+	Cleary, Beverly	Avon Books
Rice Cakes	H	332	Literacy 2000	Rigby
Riches from Nature	K	382	Early Connections	Benchmark Education
Richie the Greedy Mouse	I	179	Sunshine	Wright Group
Riddle Book	F		Reading Unlimited	Pacific Learning
Riddle of the Red Purse, The	L	250+	Giff, Patricia Reilly	Bantam Doubleday Dell
Riddles	E	51	Literacy 2000	Rigby
Ride in the Country, A	D	83	Carousel Readers	Dominie
Riding	C	67	Foundations	Wright Group
Riding	H	210	Wonder World	Wright Group
Riding to Craggy Rock	J	386	PM Story Books-Turquoise	Rigby
Rinaldo the Sly Fox	M	250+	Scheffler, Ursel	North-South Books
Ripeka's Carving	J	250+	Literacy 2000	Rigby
Rip-Roaring Russell	M	250+	Hurwitz, Johanna	The Penguin Group
Rise and Shine, Mariko-chan	K		Tomioka, Chiyoko	Scholastic
Rising Stars of the NBA	P	250+	Layden, Joe	Scholastic
Rita Rolls	C	36	Little Celebrations	Pearson Learning
River Grows, The	E	70	Ready Readers	Pearson Learning
River Rapids Ride, The	L	283	Sunshine	Wright Group
River, The	D	42	Foundations	Wright Group
Road Goes By, A	J	250+	Momentum Literacy Program	Troll
Road Work Ahead	I	207	Little Readers	Houghton Mifflin
Roald Dahl's Revolting Rhymes	N	250+	Dahl, Roald	Puffin Books
Robber Pig and the Ginger Bear	M	403	Read Alongs	Rigby
Robber Pig and the Green Eggs	M	250+	Read Alongs	Rigby
Robber, The	B	25	Smart Starts	Rigby
Robber, The	M	1255	Sunshine	Wright Group
Robert Makes a Graph	H	160	Coulton, Mia	Kaeden Books
Robert the Rose Horse	I		Heilbroner, Joan	Random House
Roberto Clemente: Baseball Superstar	N	250+	Rookie Biographies	Children's Press
Roberto's Smile	C	43	Story Box	Wright Group
Robot, The	A	18	Smart Starts	Rigby
Rock Garden, The	H	139	Windmill Books	Rigby
Rock Pools	I	250+	Momentum Literacy Program	Troll

Title	Level	Words	Author/Series	Publisher/Distributor
Rock Pools, The	B	49	PM Starters	Rigby
Rock-a-Bye Moon	H	107	Pair-It Books	Steck-Vaughn
Rockets	C		Little Celebrations	Pearson Learning
Rocking and Rolling Along	I	73	Evangeline Nicholas Collection	Wright Group
Rockity Rock	C	36	KinderReaders	Rigby
Rocks	D	49	Voyages	SRA/McGraw-Hill
Rocks	F	112	Discovery Links	Newbridge
Rocks in the Road, The	J	457	Pacific Literacy	Pacific Learning
Roler Coaster Ride, The	G	106	Carousel Readers	Dominie
Roll Out the Red Rug	E	68	Ready Readers	Pearson Learning
Roll Over	F	220	Gerstein, Mordicai	Crown
Roll Over!	C	201	Peek, Merle	Clarion
Roller Blades, The	F	137	Foundations	Wright Group
Roller Coaster	C	45	Joy Readers	Dominie
Roller Coaster, The	B	34	KinderReaders	Rigby
Roller Coaster, The	I	194	Sunshine	Wright Group
Roller Skates!	J	250+	Calmenson, Stephanie	Scholastic
Rollerama	N	250+	Hinchliffe, Jo	Sundance
Rollo and Tweedy and the Ghost at Dougal Castle	K	250+	Allen, Laura Jean	HarperTrophy
Roly-Poly	I	1227	Story Box	Wright Group
Roof and a Door, A	D	93	PM Nonfiction-Red	Rigby
Rooster and the Weather Vane, The	H	235	First Start	Troll
Rope Swing, The	E	77	Oxford Reading Tree	Oxford University Press
Rosa at the Zoo	H	135	Pacific Literacy	Pacific Learning
Rosa's Tonsils	K	337	Foundations	Wright Group
Rose	F		Wheeler, Cindy	Alfred A. Knopf, Inc.
Rose Rest Home, The	K	304	Sunshine	Wright Group
Roses for Renee	J	395	Evangeline Nicholas Collection	Wright Group
Rosie at the Zoo	H	135	Ready to Read	Pacific Learning
Rosie the Nosy Goat	D	56	Sunshine	Wright Group
Rosie's Big City Ballet	N	250+	Giff, Patricia Reilly	The Penguin Group
Rosie's Button Box	F	233	Stepping Stones	Nelson/Michaels Assoc.
Rosie's House	K		Literacy 2000	Rigby
Rosie's Nutcracker Dreams	N	250+	Giff, Patricia Reilly	The Penguin Group
Rosie's Party	E	111	Little Readers	Houghton Mifflin
Rosie's Pool	G	130	Little Readers	Houghton Mifflin
Rosie's Story	L	840	Book Shop	Mondo Publishing
Rosie's Walk	F	32	Hutchins, Pat	Macmillan
Rotating Rollerblades and Other Cases, The	O	250+	Simon, Seymour	Avon Books
Rotten Reggie	G	232	TOTTS	Tott Publications
Round	C	40	Windmill Books	Rigby
Round and Round	C	38	Story Box	Wright Group
Row Your Boat	C	18	Literacy 2000	Rigby
Row, Row, Row Your Boat	J	250+	O'Malley, Kevin	Bantam Doubleday Dell
Roy and the Parakeet	E	74	Oxford Reading Tree	Oxford University Press
Roy at the Fun Park	G	111	Oxford Reading Tree	Oxford University Press
Roy G. Biv	D	68	Story Box	Wright Group
Royal Baby-Sitters, The	J	435	Sunshine	Wright Group
Royal Drum, The	L	526	Book Shop	Mondo Publishing
Royal Family, The	A	17	Stewart, J. & Salem, Lynn	Seedling
Royal Goose, The	H	198	Ready Readers	Pearson Learning
Ruby the Copycat	K	250+	Rathman, Peggy	Scholastic

Title	Level	Words	Author/Series	Publisher/Distributor
Rules	J	265	Early Connections	Benchmark Education
Rules for Pets	C	54	Joy Readers	Dominie
Rumble, Rumble, Boom!	D	26	Pacific Literacy	Pacific Learning
Rummage Sale, The	E	81	Oxford Reading Tree	Oxford University Press
Rumpelstilskin	J	940	Traditional Tales	Dominie
Rumpelstiltskin	J	250+	PM Traditional Tales & Plays	Rigby
Rumpelstiltskin	M	250+	Once Upon a Time	Wright Group
Rumpelstiltskin	N	250+	Zelinsky, Paul O.	Scholastic
Rumpelstltskin	J	855	Book Shop	Mondo Publishing
Rum-Tum-Tum	E	62	Story Box	Wright Group
Run!	B	28	Sunshine	Wright Group
Run! Run!	C	64	Book Shop	Mondo Publishing
Run, Run, Run	B	19	Joy Readers	Dominie
Runaway Monkey	B	39	Stewart, J. & Salem, Lynn	Seedling
Runaway Pony	O	250+	Betancourt, Jeanne	Scholastic
Runaway Ralph	O	250+	Cleary, Beverly	Hearst
Runaway Wheels, The	B	32	Pair-It Books	Steck-Vaughn
Running	C	39	Foundations	Wright Group
Running	F	185	Visions	Wright Group
Rush, Rush, Rush	E	52	Ready Readers	Pearson Learning
Russell and Elisa	M	250+	Hurwitz, Johanna	The Penguin Group
Russell Rides Again	M	250+	Hurwitz, Johanna	Puffin Books
Russell Sprouts	M	250+	Hurwitz, Johanna	Puffin Books
Sable	M	250+	Hesse, Karen	Henry Holt & Co.
Sack Race, A	E	106	New Way Blue	Steck-Vaughn
Sacks of Gold	I	263	Sunshine	Wright Group
Sadie and the Snowman	L	250+	Morgan, Allen	Scholastic
Safe Place, The	H	147	Ready to Read	Pacific Learning
Safe Place, The	H	147	Pacific Literacy	Pacific Learning
Safety	C	35	Interaction	Rigby
Safety First	C	131	Twig	Wright Group
Saguaro	E	44	Books for Young Learners	Richard C. Owen
Salad	A	36	Carousel Earlybirds	Dominie
Salad Feast, A	D	57	Little Readers	Houghton Mifflin
Salad Vegetables	A	15	Foundations	Wright Group
Salad Vegetables	A	27	Story Box	Wright Group
Sally and the Daisy	C	60	PM Story Books	Rigby
Sally and the Elephant	C	45	Wonder World	Wright Group
Sally and the Sparrows	E	151	PM Extensions-Yellow	Rigby
Sally the Great	H	250+	Home Connection Collection	Rigby
Sally's Beans	D	123	PM Story Books	Rigby
Sally's Friends	F	128	PM Story Books	Rigby
Sally's New Shoes	B	58	PM Starters	Rigby
Sally's Picture	G	125	Literacy 2000	Rigby
Sally's Red Bucket	E	127	PM Story Books	Rigby
Sally's Spaceship	E	86	Ready Readers	Pearson Learning
Salmon Story, A	G	132	Twig	Wright Group
Sam	C	17	KinderReaders	Rigby
Sam and Dasher	G	53	Rookie Readers	Children's Press
Sam and the Firefly	J	250+	Eastman, Philip D.	Random House
Sam the Garbage Hound	G	53	Rookie Readers	Children's Press

Title	Level	Words	Author/Series	Publisher/Distributor
Sam the Minuteman	J	250+	Benchley, Nathaniel	HarperTrophy
Sam the Scarecrow	F	143	First Start	Troll
Sam Who Never Forgets	K	281	Rice, Eve	Morrow
Sam Writes	D	62	Book Bank	Wright Group
Same But Different	I	184	Sunshine	Wright Group
Same Team	C	44	The Candid Collection	Dominie
Sammy at the Farm	C	83	Urmston, Kathleen & Evans, Karen	Kaeden Books
Sammy Gets a Ride	F	91	Evans, Karen & Urmston, Kathleen	Kaeden Books
Sammy the Seal	H	250+	Hoff, Syd	HarperTrophy
Sammy's Moving	F	166	Urmston, Kathleen & Evans, Karen	Kaeden Books
Sammy's Sneeze	D	69	Home Connection Collection	Rigby
Sammy's Supper	I	293	Reading Unlimited	Pacific Learning
Sam's Ball	D	64	Lindgren, Barbro	Morrow
Sam's Big Clean-up	K	287	Windmill Books	Rigby
Sam's Big Day	H	74	Cat on the Mat	Oxford University Press
Sam's Cookie	D	52	Lindgren, Barbro	Morrow
Sam's Glasses	M	250+	Literacy 2000	Rigby
Sam's Mask	E	36	Pacific Literacy	Pacific Learning
Sam's Mask	E	41	Ready to Read	Pacific Learning
Sam's Seasons	E	143	Pair-It Books	Steck-Vaughn
Sam's Solution	K		Literacy 2000	Rigby
Sam's Teddy Bear	D	60	Lindgren, Barbro	Morrow
Sam's Wagon	D	83	Lindgren, Barbro	Morrow
Samuel's Sprout	F	194	Little Celebrations	Pearson Learning
San Francisco Exploratorium, The	O	250+	Little Celebrations	Pearson Learning
Sand	B	32	Voyages	SRA/McGraw-Hill
Sand Castle Contest, The	E	173	Pair-It Books	Steck-Vaughn
Sand Castles	G	80	Wonder World	Wright Group
Sand Picnic, The	E	123	New Way White	Steck-Vaughn
Sandwich Person, A	G	63	Wonder World	Wright Group
Sandwich, The	C	68	Carousel Earlybirds	Dominie
Sandwiches	D		New Way	Steck-Vaughn
Sandwiches, Sandwiches	D	54	Pair-It Books	Steck-Vaughn
Sandy	C	32	Ready Readers	Pearson Learning
Sandy's Suitcase	K		Edwards, Elsy	SRA/McGraw-Hill
Santa Claus Doesn't Mop Floors	M	250+	Dadey, Debbie	Scholastic
Sarah and the Barking Dog	I	328	PM Story Books-Orange	Rigby
Sarah Snail	E	55	Voyages	SRA/McGraw-Hill
Sara's Lovely Songs	I	250+	Ready Readers	Pearson Learning
Saturday Morning	G	180	Ready to Read	Pacific Learning
Saturday Morning Breakfast	E	65	Teacher's Choice Series	Dominie
Saturday Mornings	D	63	Book Shop	Mondo Publishing
Saturday Sandwiches	I	154	Evangeline Nicholas Collection	Wright Group
Save That Trash!	G	181	Ready Readers	Pearson Learning
Save the Manatee	N	250+	Friesinger, Alison	Random House
Save the River!	M	250+	Pair-It Books	Steck-Vaughn
Say "Cheese	L	250+	Giff, Patricia Reilly	Bantam Doubleday Dell
Say Cheese!	F	128	Storyteller-Moon Rising	Wright Group/ McGraw-Hill
Say Goodnight	G		Gregorich, Barbara	School Zone
Say Hello!	A	15	Rise & Shine	Hampton-Brown
Say Hola, Sarah	N	250+	Giff, Patricia Reilly	Bantam Doubleday Dell

Title	Level	Words	Author/Series	Publisher/Distributor
Say It Sign It	G	169	Epstein, Elaine	Scholastic
Scarecrow	C	31	Literacy 2000	Rigby
Scarecrow, The	D	97	Little Red Readers	Sundance
Scarecrows	D	39	Pebble Books	Grolier, Capstone
Scarecrow's Friends	C	56	Start to Read	School Zone
Scared	D	59	Twig	Wright Group
Scaredy Cat	C	85	Learn to Read	Creative Teaching Press
Scaredy Cat Runs Away	D		Learn to Read	Creative Teaching Press
Scaredy Dog	K	250+	Thomas, Jane Resh	Hyperion
Scare-Kid	K		Literacy 2000	Rigby
Scary Larry	G		Rookie Readers	Children's Press
Scary Monster	C	19	Eifrig, Kate	Kaeden Books
Scary Spiders!	J	198	Sunshine	Wright Group
Scat! Said the Cat	D	33	Sunshine	Wright Group
School Bus	D	51	Crews, Donald	Morrow
School Bus, The	E	60	Sunshine	Wright Group
School Lunch	A	14	Ready Readers	Pearson Learning
School Mural, The	L	250+	Pair-It Books	Steck-Vaughn
School Vacation	J	113	City Kids	Rigby
School, The	E	27	Burningham, John	Crowell
Schools Around the World	E	78	Pair-It Books	Steck-Vaughn
School's Out	N	250+	Hurwitz, Johanna	Scholastic
Schoolyard Mystery, The	L	250+	Levy, Elizabeth	Scholastic
Science-Just Add Salt	L	250+	Markle, Sandra	Scholastic
Scientist, The	G	195	Adventures in Reading	Dominie
Scissors	D	51	Storyteller-Setting Sun	Wright Group/ McGraw-Hill
Scit, Scat, Scaredy Cat!	F	59	Sunshine	Wright Group
Scratch My Back	D	66	Foundations	Wright Group
Screech!	D	43	Literacy 2000	Rigby
Scrubbing Machine, The	F	148	Story Box	Wright Group
Scruffy	K	250+	Parish, Peggy	HarperTrophy
Scruffy Messed It Up	G	105	Literacy 2000	Rigby
Scrumptious Sundae	B	18	Literacy 2000	Rigby
Scrunder Goes Wandering	M	250+	Krailing, Tessa	Barron's Educational
Sculpture	L		Little Celebrations	Pearson Learning
Sea Anemones	G	58	Pebble Books	Grolier, Capstone
Sea Horses	F	67	Pebble Books	Grolier, Capstone
Sea Otters	L	406	Storyteller Nonfiction	Wright Group/ McGraw-Hill
Sea Star, A	E	82	Ready Readers	Pearson Learning
Sea Stars	E	63	Pebble Books	Grolier, Capstone
Sea Turtle Night	I	200	Ready Readers	Pearson Learning
Sea Turtles	K	296	Marine Life for Young Readers	Dominie
Sea Urchins	G	51	Pebble Books	Grolier, Capstone
Sea Wall, The	K	251	Foundations	Wright Group
Seagull Is Clever	E	98	PM Story Books	Rigby
Search for the Lost Cave, The	M	250+	Schultz, Irene	Wright Group
Seashells	K	186	Marine Life for Young Readers	Dominie
Season to Season	F	113	Pair-It Books	Steck-Vaughn
Seasons	C	28	Discovery World	Rigby
Seat Belt Song, The	J	505	PM Story Books-Turquoise	Rigby

Title	Level	Words	Author/Series	Publisher/Distributor
Second Chance	N	250+	Kroll, Stephen	Avon Camelot
Second Grade-Friends Again!	M	250+	Cohen, Miriam	Scholastic
Secondhand Star	L	250+	Macdonald, Maryann	Hyperion
Secret at the Polk Street School, The	M	250+	Giff, Patricia Reilly	Bantam Doubleday Dell
Secret Code, The	G	69	Rookie Readers	Children's Press
Secret Friend, The	E	189	Little Readers	Houghton Mifflin
Secret Friend, The	E	196	Little Celebrations	Pearson Learning
Secret Hideaway, The	H	618	PM Story Books-Gold	Rigby
Secret Lives of Mr. And Mrs. Smith, The	I	395	Sunshine	Wright Group
Secret of Foghorn Island, The	K	250+	Hayes, Geoffrey	Random House
Secret of Spooky House,The	J	352	Sunshine	Wright Group
Secret of the Monster Book, The	M	250+	Schultz, Irene	Wright Group
Secret of the Old Oak Trunk, The	M	250+	Schultz, Irene	Wright Group
Secret of the Song, The	M	250+	Schultz, Irene	Wright Group
Secret Soldier, The	L	250+	McGovern, Ann	Scholastic
Secret Soup	E	51	Literacy 2000	Rigby
Secret Valentine	G	223	First Start	Troll
See You in Second Grade	J	250+	Cohen, Miriam	Bantam Doubleday Dell
See You Tomorrow, Charles	J	250+	Cohen, Miriam	Bantam Doubleday Dell
Seed, The	A	51	Wonder World	Wright Group
Seed, The	D	51	Sunshine	Wright Group
Seeds	B	30	Rise & Shine	Hampton-Brown
Seeds	J	210	Pebble Books	Grolier, Capstone
Seeds, Seeds, Seeds	E	96	Sunshine	Wright Group
Seeing the School Doctor	K	167	City Kids	Rigby
Seesaw, The	C	46	Voyages	SRA/McGraw-Hill
Seesaw, The	C	100	Emergent	Pioneer Valley
Selena Who Speaks in Silence	J	311	Evangeline Nicholas Collection	Wright Group
Selfish Giant, The	L		Literacy 2000	Rigby
Selli and Kana' Ti	M	250+	Folk Tales	Mondo Publishing
Sending Messages	B	49	Wonder World	Wright Group
Senses	E	66	Voyages	SRA/McGraw-Hill
Seven Foolish Fishermen	I	250+	PM Traditional Tales & Plays	Rigby
Seven Little Monsters	H	55	Sendak, Maurice	HarperCollins
Shadow Dance	D	66	Little Celebrations	Pearson Learning
Shadow of the Wolf	N	250+	Whelan, Gloria	Random House
Shadow Over Second	M	250+	Christopher, Matt	Little, Brown & Co.
Shadows	D	35	Literacy 2000	Rigby
Shadows	E	190	Visions	Wright Group
Shadows	F	130	Wonder World	Wright Group
Shaggy Sheep, The	G	301	Wonders	Hampton-Brown
Shane and Ned	E	52	Windmill Books	Rigby
Shape Walk	C	25	Little Celebrations	Pearson Learning
Shapes	A	24	Urmston, Kathleen & Evans, Karen	Kaeden Books
Shapes	B	19	Discovery World	Rigby
Shapes	B	40	Early Connections	Benchmark Education
Shapes	C	30	Rise & Shine	Hampton-Brown
Shapes	C	31	Visions	Wright Group
Shapes	D	98	Carousel Readers	Dominie
Shapes in My World	D	47	Visions	Wright Group
Sharing	C	24	Literacy 2000	Rigby
Sharing Danny's Dad	G	89	Little Celebrations	Pearson Learning

Title	Level	Words	Author/Series	Publisher/Distributor
Sharing Time	D	113	Carousel Readers	Dominie
Shark in a Sack	C	65	Sunshine	Wright Group
Shark in School	N	250+	Giff, Patricia Reilly	Bantam Doubleday Dell
Shark Lady: The Adventures of Eugenie Clark	N	250+	McGovern, Ann	Scholastic
Sharks	H	155	Ready Readers	Pearson Learning
Sharks	L	238	Wonder World	Wright Group
Sharks & Rays	L	284	Marine Life for Young Readers	Dominie
She Said	C	35	Ready Readers	Pearson Learning
Sheep in a Jeep	G	83	Shaw, Nancy	Houghton Mifflin
Sheep's Bell	C	37	Ready Readers	Pearson Learning
Sheila Rae, the Brave	K	250+	Henkes, Kevin	Scholastic
Shell Shopping	F	145	Ready Readers	Pearson Learning
SHHH	F	66	Henkes, Kevin	Greenwillow
Shhhh!	G		Kline, Suzy	Whitman
Shine Sun	F		Rookie Readers	Children's Press
Shingo's Grandfather	K	370	Sunshine	Wright Group
Shining Blue Planet and Other Cases, The	O	250+	Simon, Seymour	Avon Books
Shintaro's Umbrellas	I	95	Books for Young Learners	Richard C. Owen
Ships	L	275	Wonder World	Wright Group
Shipwreck Saturday	K	250+	Cosby, Bill	Scholastic
Shoe Grabber, The	I	260	Read Alongs	Rigby
Shoebag	P	250+	James, Mary	Scholastic
Shoes	A	16	Little Celebrations	Pearson Learning
Shoes	D	79	Book Bank	Wright Group
Shoes	F	73	Talk About Books	Dominie
Shoeshine Girl	N	250+	Bulla, Clyde Robert	HarperTrophy
Shoo!	C	37	Sunshine	Wright Group
Shoo, Fly!	B	24	Story Box	Wright Group
Shooting Star, The	M	661	PM Story Books-Gold	Rigby
Shopping	A	15	Sunshine	Wright Group
Shopping	C	41	Interaction	Rigby
Shopping	C	78	Little Red Readers	Sundance
Shopping	D	26	Literacy 2000	Rigby
Shopping	D	41	Sunshine	Wright Group
Shopping	E	45	Read-More Books	Dominie
Shopping	E	101	Storyteller-Setting Sun	Wright Group/ McGraw-Hill
Shopping at the Supermarket	B	46	Foundations	Wright Group
Shopping at the Mall	G	145	Urmston, Kathleen & Evans, Karen	Kaeden Books
Shopping for School	C	33	Visions	Wright Group
Shopping Mall, The	B	44	PM Starters	Rigby
Shopping with a Crocodile	M	250+	Ready to Read	Pacific Learning
Shopping with Dad	C	43	Home Connection Collection	Rigby
Shortest Kid in the World	K	250+	Bliss, Corinne Demas	Random House
Shortstop from Tokyo	M	250+	Christopher, Matt	Little, Brown & Co.
Shorty	M	250+	Literacy 2000	Rigby
Shots	I	90	City Kids	Rigby
Shoveling Snow	F	109	Cummings, Pat	Scholastic
Show and Tell	A	32	Little Books	Sadlier-Oxford
Show and Tell	G	190	First Start	Troll
Show and Tell	I		Little Celebrations	Pearson Learning
Show and Tell	K	201	City Kids	Rigby

Title	Level	Words	Author/Series	Publisher/Distributor
Show Time at the Polk Street School	M	250+	Giff, Patricia Reilly	Bantam Doubleday Dell
Show-and-Tell	J	220	Foundations	Wright Group
Show-and-Tell Frog, The	J	250+	Oppenheim, Joanna	Bantam Doubleday Dell
Show-and-Tell War, The	N	250+	Smith, Janice Lee	HarperTrophy
Shush!	D	29	Pacific Literacy	Pacific Learning
Shut the Door	D	46	Visions	Wright Group
Shy People's Picnic, The	M	250+	Little Celebrations	Pearson Learning
Si Won's Victory	M	250+	Little Celebrations	Pearson Learning
Sick Bear, The	D	61	Joy Readers	Dominie
Sick in Bed	F	109	Little Red Readers	Sundance
Sid and Sam	D	120	Buck, Nola	HarperTrophy
Sidetrack Sam	K	250+	Literacy 2000	Rigby
Sidewalk Story	N	250+	Mathis, Sharon Bell	The Penguin Group
Sideways Stories from Wayside School	O	250+	Sachar, Louis	Avon Books
Signs	B	24	Literacy 2000	Rigby
Signs	C	35	Little Celebrations	Pearson Learning
Signs	C	40	Carousel Earlybirds	Dominie
Signs	E	131	Twig	Wright Group
Silent World, A	L		Literacy 2000	Rigby
Silly Cat Tricks	D	83	Teacher's Choice Series	Dominie
Silly Old Possum	C	41	Story Box	Wright Group
Silly Tilly's Valentine	J	250+	Hoban, Lillian	HarperTrophy
Silly Times with Two Silly Trolls	I	250+	Jewell, Nancy	HarperTrophy
Silly Willy	M	500	Book Shop	Mondo Publishing
Silly Willy and Silly Billy	J	221	Foundations	Wright Group
Silver	N	250+	Whelan, Gloria	Random House
Silvia's Soccer Game	F	138	Ready Readers	Pearson Learning
Simon and the Aliens	N	250+	Mills, Eva	Sundance
Simply Sam	E	69	Voyages	SRA/McGraw-Hill
Sing a Song	E	154	Read-Togethers	Wright Group
Sing to the Moon	K	2448	Story Box	Wright Group
Sione Went Fishing	I	225	Sunshine	Wright Group
Sisters	B	28	Pebble Books	Grolier, Capstone
Sisters	E	77	Talk About Books	Dominie
Sitting	E	46	Literacy 2000	Rigby
Six Cats	C	50	Joy Readers	Dominie
Six Empty Pockets	F	85	Rookie Readers	Children's Press
Six Fine Fish	F	252	Ready Readers	Pearson Learning
Six Foolish Fishermen	L	715	Elkin, Benjamin	Children's Press
Six Go By	C	24	Ready Readers	Pearson Learning
Six Things to Make	L	987	Book Shop	Mondo Publishing
Sizes	C	32	Discovery World	Rigby
Skateboard Tough	M	250+	Christopher, Matt	Little, Brown & Co.
Skates for Luke	I	346	PM Story Books-Orange	Rigby
Skates of Uncle Richard, The	P	250+	Fenner, Carol	Random House
Skating	B	35	Foundations	Wright Group
Skating	C	52	Story Box	Wright Group
Skating on Thin Ice	G	130	First Start	Troll
Skating Whiz	E	40	Visions	Wright Group
Skeleton on the Bus, The	J	250+	Literacy 2000	Rigby
Skeletons Don't Play Tubas	M	250+	Dadey, Debbie & Jones, Marcia	Scholastic

Title	Level	Words	Author/Series	Publisher/Distributor
Ski Lesson, The	H	155	Storyteller-Moon Rising	Wright Group/ McGraw-Hill
Ski School	A	34	Little Books for Early Readers	University of Maine
Skier, The	B	48	PM Starters	Rigby
Skin	F	97	Literacy 2000	Rigby
Skin, Skin	E	44	Wonder World	Wright Group
Skipper's Balloon	E	62	Oxford Reading Tree	Oxford University Press
Skipper's Birthday	E	64	Oxford Reading Tree	Oxford University Press
Skipper's Idea	E	81	Oxford Reading Tree	Oxford University Press
Skipper's Laces	E	66	Oxford Reading Tree	Oxford University Press
Skunks	K	250+	PM Animal Facts-Gold	Rigby
Sky High	L	619	Pair-It Books	Steck-Vaughn
Sky Is Falling Down, The	D	101	Joy Readers	Dominie
Sky Is Falling, The	I	181	Storyteller-Setting Sun	Wright Group/ McGraw-Hill
SkyFire	J	250+	Asch, Frank	Scholastic
Sky's the Limit, The	P	250+	Wildcats	Wright Group
SkyScraper, The	K	252	Little Red Readers	Sundance
Slam Dunk Saturday	M	250+	Marzollo, Jean	Random House
Sleeping	E	43	Literacy 2000	Rigby
Sleeping	I	114	Book Bank	Wright Group
Sleeping Beauty	K	250+	Enrichment	Wright Group
Sleeping Out	D	49	Story Box	Wright Group
Sleep-Over Mouse	D	63	My First Reader	Grolier Press
Sleepy Bear	E	153	Foundations	Wright Group
Sleepy Bear	F	80	Literacy 2000	Rigby
Sleepy Dog	D	118	Ziefert, Harriet	Random House
Slim Shorty and the Mules	L	411	Reading Unlimited	Pacific Learning
Slippery, Sloppery Spaghetti	H	250+	Home Connection Collection	Rigby
Slithery Snakes and Unicorns	I	289	Sunshine	Wright Group
Sloppy Tiger and the Party	I	293	Sunshine	Wright Group
Sloppy Tiger Bedtime	I	320	Sunshine	Wright Group
Slugs and Snails	H	132	Wonder World	Wright Group
Slugs and Snails	J	426	Book Shop	Mondo Publishing
Slump, The	N	250+	Kroll, Stephen	Avon Camelot
Sly Fox and Red Hen	F	314	Hunia, Fran	Ladybird Books
Small Baby Raccoon, A	G	104	Ready Readers	Pearson Learning
Small Pig	I	250+	Lobel, Arnold	HarperTrophy
Small Rabbit Goes Visiting	H	445	Book Bank	Wright Group
Small Wolf	J	250+	Benchley, Nathaniel	HarperTrophy
Small World, A	H	146	Sunshine	Wright Group
Smallest Cow in the World, The	K	250+	Paterson, Katherine	HarperTrophy
Smallest Tree, The	K		Literacy 2000	Rigby
Smarty Pants	E	116	Read-Togethers	Wright Group
Smasher	O	250+	King-Smith, Dick	Random House
Smile! Said Dad	D	66	Pacific Literacy	Pacific Learning
Smile, Baby!	F	165	Little Readers	Houghton Mifflin
Smile, The	D	53	Ready to Read	Pacific Learning
Smile, The	D	53	Pacific Literacy	Pacific Learning
Smile, The	K	253	Read Alongs	Rigby
Smiles	E	366	Visions	Wright Group
Smiling Salad, A	C	32	Pair-It Books	Steck-Vaughn

Title	Level	Words	Author/Series	Publisher/Distributor
Smiling Stan, the Pedicab Man	E	121	Joy Readers	Dominie
Smokie	C	47	Carousel Readers	Dominie
Snack Time	G	59	City Kids	Rigby
Snacks	D	19	Joy Readers	Dominie
Snaggle Doodles	M	250+	Giff, Patricia Reilly	Bantam Doubleday Dell
Snail Girl	H	250+	Momentum Literacy Program	Troll
Snail Saves the Day	G		Stadler, John	HarperCollins
Snails	E	67	Foundations	Wright Group
Snails in School	H	181	Discovery Links	Newbridge
Snake Alarm	M	250+	Krailing, Tessa	Barron's Educational
Snake Slithers, A	H		Reading Unlimited	Pacific Learning
Snake!	M	641	Sunshine	Wright Group
Snakes	E	37	Visions	Wright Group
Snakes	I	208	Momentum Literacy Program	Troll
Snakes	J	448	Sunshine	Wright Group
Snakes	K	259	Foundations	Wright Group
Snakes	L	252	Wonder World	Wright Group
Snake's Sore Head	F	139	Storyteller-Moon Rising	Wright Group/ McGraw-Hill
Snap!	B	31	Sunshine	Wright Group
Snap! Splash!	G	48	Pacific Literacy	Pacific Learning
Snap! Splat!	C	25	Sunshine	Wright Group
Sneakers	K	388	Sunshine	Wright Group
Sneezes	F	36	Literacy 2000	Rigby
Snickers	I	250+	Momentum Literacy Program	Troll
Snip-Snap, Clickety-Click	C		Little Celebrations	Pearson Learning
Snow	B	29	Discovery Links	Newbridge
Snow	B	33	Hoenecke, Karen	Kaeden Books
Snow	H	217	Stepping Stones	Nelson/Michaels Assoc.
Snow Cover	C	29	Little Celebrations	Pearson Learning
Snow Daughter, The	L	505	Sunshine	Wright Group
Snow Day	I	250+	Bliss, Corinne Demas	Random House
Snow Goes to Town	L		Literacy 2000	Rigby
Snow Joe	D	59	Rookie Readers	Children's Press
Snow on the Hill	H	213	PM Extensions-Green	Rigby
Snow Walk	D	32	Reading Corners	Dominie
Snow White and Rose Red	K	250+	Hunia, Fran	Ladybird Books
Snow White and the Seven Dwarfs	I	250+	Enrichment	Wright Group
Snow White and the Seven Dwarfs	J	250+	PM Traditional Tales & Plays	Rigby
Snow, The	D	36	Sunshine	Wright Group
Snow, The	G		Burningham, John	Crowell
Snowball Fight!	D	35	Wonder World	Wright Group
Snowball War, The	K	250+	Chardiet, Bernice	Scholastic
Snowflakes	D	49	Urmston, Kathleen & Evans, Karen	Kaeden Books
Snowman	A	14	Smart Starts	Rigby
Snowman	A	19	Story Box	Wright Group
Snowman	C	21	Sunshine	Wright Group
Snowman, A	C	59	Foundations	Wright Group
Snowman, The	E	76	Oxford Reading Tree	Oxford University Press
Snowshoe Thompson	K	250+	Smiler Levinson, Nancy	HarperTrophy
Snowy Day, The	J	319	Keats, Ezra Jack	Scholastic
Snowy Gets a Wash	F	181	PM Extensions-Yellow	Rigby

©1999 by I. C. Fountas & G. S. Pinnell from Matching Books to Readers. Portsmouth, NH: Heinemann. May not be reproduced without written permission of the publisher.

Title	Level	Words	Author/Series	Publisher/Distributor
Snuggle Up	F	125	Harrison, P. & Worthington, Denise	Seedling
So Do I	D	49	Teacher's Choice Series	Dominie
So Many Birthdays	I	250+	Momentum Literacy Program	Troll
So Many Things to Do	A	21	Home Connection Collection	Rigby
So What?	I	250+	Cohen, Miriam	Bantam Doubleday Dell
So You Want to Move a Building?	M	380	Pacific Literacy	Pacific Learning
So, So Sam	G	107	TOTTS	Tott Publications
Soap Soup and Other Verses	K	250+	Kuskin, Karla	HarperTrophy
Soccer	M		Little Celebrations	Pearson Learning
Soccer at the Park	F	131	PM Extensions-Yellow	Rigby
Soccer Cousins	K	250+	Marzollo, Jean	Scholastic
Soccer Game!	F	63	Maccarone, Grace	Scholastic
Soccer Mania	M	250+	Tamar, Erika	Random House
Soccer Sam	M	250+	Marzollo, Jean	Random House
Socks	A	21	Smart Starts	Rigby
Socks	B	21	Ready Readers	Pearson Learning
Socks	O	250+	Cleary, Beverly	Avon Books
Solo Flyer	L	605	PM Story Books-Gold	Rigby
Solo Girl	M	250+	Pinkey, Andrea Davis	Hyperion
Some Days Are Like That	D	69	Teacher's Choice Series	Dominie
Some Machines are Enormous	J	337	Book Shop	Mondo Publishing
Some People	D	50	Reading Corners	Dominie
Someone Is Following Pip Ramsey	N	250+	Roy, Ron	Random House
Something Everyone Needs	J	250+	Ready Readers	Pearson Learning
Something New	D	72	Little Celebrations	Pearson Learning
Something Noise, The	J	276	Windmill Books	Rigby
Something Queer at the Ball Park	N	250+	Levy, Elizabeth	Bantam Doubleday Dell
Something Queer at the Haunted School	N	250+	Levy, Elizabeth	Bantam Doubleday Dell
Something Queer at the Lemonade Stand	N	250+	Levy, Elizabeth	Bantam Doubleday Dell
Something Queer at the Library	N	250+	Levy, Elizabeth	Hyperion
Something Queer at the Scary Movie	N	250+	Levy, Elizabeth	Hyperion
Something Queer in Outer Space	N	250+	Levy, Elizabeth	Hyperion
Something Queer in the Cafeteria	N	250+	Levy, Elizabeth	Hyperion
Something Queer in the Wild West	N	250+	Levy, Elizabeth	Hyperion
Something Queer Is Going On	N	250+	Levy, Elizabeth	Bantam Doubleday Dell
Something Queer on Vacation	N	250+	Levy, Elizabeth	Bantam Doubleday Dell
Something Soft for Danny Bear	M	493	Literacy 2000	Rigby
Something to Munch	E	58	Ready Readers	Pearson Learning
Something to Share	D	98	Carousel Readers	Dominie
Sometimes	A	25	Wonder World	Wright Group
Sometimes	B	18	Literacy 2000	Rigby
Sometimes I'm Silly	C	24	Visions	Wright Group
Sometimes Things Change	G		Rookie Readers	Children's Press
Sometimes...	B	25	Home Connection Collection	Rigby
Somewhere	J	93	Book Shop	Mondo Publishing
Song Lee and the Hamster Hunt	N	250+	Kline, Suzy	The Penguin Group
Song Lee and the Leech Man	N	250+	Kline, Suzy	The Penguin Group
Song Lee in Room 2B	N	250+	Kline, Suzy	The Penguin Group
Sophie's Chicken	H	107	Tadpoles	Rigby
Sophie's Singing Mother	J	313	Jellybeans	Rigby
Sound, Heat & Light: Energy at Work	L	250+	Berger, Melvin	Scholastic
Sounds	J	200	Early Connections	Benchmark Education

Title	Level	Words	Author/Series	Publisher/Distributor
Sounds all Around	G	153	Discovery Links	Newbridge
Sounds in the Night	E	126	Visions	Wright Group
Soup	A	17	Little Celebrations	Pearson Learning
Soup Can Telephone	I	190	Wonder World	Wright Group
Souvenirs	K	179	Literacy 2000	Rigby
Space	H	100	Sunshine	Wright Group
Space Aliens in Our School	D	45	Joy Readers	Dominie
Space Ark, The	B	20	Sunshine	Wright Group
Space Dog and Roy	L	250+	Standiford, Natalie	Random House
Space Dog and the Pet Show	L	250+	Standiford, Natalie	Random House
Space Dog in Trouble	L	250+	Standiford, Natalie	Random House
Space Dog the Hero	L	250+	Standiford, Natalie	Random House
Space Journey	A	19	Sunshine	Wright Group
Space Quest	O	250+	Discovery World	Rigby
Space Race	J	213	Sunshine	Wright Group
Space Rock	K	250+	Buller, Jon	Random House
Space Shuttle, The	D	45	Sunshine	Wright Group
Space Station Plot and Other Cases, The	O	250+	Simon, Seymour	Avon Books
Spaceship	B	27	Hoenecke, Karen	Kaeden Books
Spaghetti! Spaghetti!	G	85	Book Bank	Wright Group
Sparky's Bone	F	273	Ready Readers	Pearson Learning
Sparrows, The	F	60	Books for Young Learners	Richard C. Owen
Speak Up!	F	194	Sunshine	Wright Group
Special Effects	P	250+	Wildcats	Wright Group
Special Friend, A	F	80	Carousel Readers	Dominie
Special Ride, The	K	647	PM Story Books-Gold	Rigby
Special Things	G	128	Literacy 2000	Rigby
Spectacular Stone Soup	M	250+	Giff, Patricia Reilly	Yearling
Speed Boat, The	C	170	Sunshine	Wright Group
Speeding Sleigh and Other Cases, The	O	250+	Simon, Seymour	Avon Books
Speedy Pasta and Other Cases, The	O	250+	Simon, Seymour	Avon Books
Speedy Snake and Other Cases, The	O	250+	Simon, Seymour	Avon Books
Speedy Soapbox Car and Other Cases, The	O	250+	Simon, Seymour	Avon Books
Spicy-Herby Day, A	G	117	Evangeline Nicholas Collection	Wright Group
Spider	D	43	Sunshine	Wright Group
Spider and the King, The	L		Literacy 2000	Rigby
Spider Can't Fly	G	149	Book Bank	Wright Group
Spider Legs	D	52	Twig	Wright Group
Spider Man	M	250+	Literacy 2000	Rigby
Spider, Spider	D	70	Sunshine	Wright Group
Spiders	E	53	Discovery Links	Newbridge
Spiders	E	75	Wonder World	Wright Group
Spiders	M	447	Book Shop	Mondo Publishing
Spiders Everywhere	D	36	Books for Young Learners	Richard C. Owen
Spiders in Space	I	242	Sunshine	Wright Group
Spider's Web, A	L	323	Wonder World	Wright Group
Spiders, Spiders Everywhere!	D		Learn to Read	Creative Teaching Press
Spinning Snake, A	F	156	Sunshine	Wright Group
Spinning Top	I	182	Wonder World	Wright Group
Spirit of Hope	N	878	Book Shop	Mondo Publishing
Splash	C	34	Foundations	Wright Group
Splash!	D	63	New Way Red	Steck-Vaughn

Title	Level	Words	Author/Series	Publisher/Distributor
Splash!	E	85	Joy Readers	Dominie
Splashing Dad	C	37	Early Emergent	Pioneer Valley
Splish Splash!	B	28	Windmill	Wright Group
Splish! Splash!	D	45	Little Celebrations	Pearson Learning
Splishy-Sploshy	E	127	Story Basket	Wright Group
Splosh	C	47	Story Box	Wright Group
Spoiled Rotten	L	250+	DeClements, Barthe	Hyperion
Spooky Pet	B	24	Smart Starts	Rigby
Spooky Riddles	I		Brown, Marc	Random House
Sports Are Fun	B	21	Pair-It Books	Steck-Vaughn
Sports Bloopers	P	250+	Hollander, Phyllis & Zander	Scholastic
Sports Day	C	24	Home Connection Collection	Rigby
Spots	A	27	Smart Starts	Rigby
Spots	B	31	Visions	Wright Group
Spots	C	41	Sunshine	Wright Group
Spots	E	48	Literacy 2000	Rigby
Spot's Birthday Party	I	97	Hill, Eric	Putnam
Spot's First Walk	G	63	Hill, Eric	Putnam
Spots!	E	55	Oxford Reading Tree	Oxford University Press
Spots, Feathers and Curly Tails	C		Tafuri, Nancy	Morrow
Spray-Paint Mystery, The	P	250+	Medearis, Angela	Scholastic
Spreading the Word	P	250+	Wildcats	Wright Group
Spring	C	47	Carousel Readers	Dominie
Spring	E	58	Sunshine	Wright Group
Spring	I	142	Pebble Books	Grolier, Capstone
Spy Down the Street, The	M	250+	Schultz, Irene	Wright Group
Spy in the Attic, The	M	250+	Scheffler, Ursel	North-South Books
Spy on Third Base, The	M	250+	Christopher, Matt	Little, Brown & Co.
Squanto and the First Thanksgiving	L	250+	Celsi, Teresa	Steck-Vaughn
Squanto: Friend of the Pilgrims	N	250+	Bulla, Clyde Robert	Scholastic
Squares Everywhere	C	26	Discovery Links	Newbridge
Squeaky Car, The	G	200	New Way Green	Steck-Vaughn
Squirrels	F	109	Ready Readers	Pearson Learning
Squirrels	N	460	Storyteller Nonfiction	Wright Group/ McGraw-Hill
Ssh, Don't Wake the Baby	F	135	Voyages	SRA/McGraw-Hill
Sssh!	C	49	Book Bank	Wright Group
Stables Are for Horses	I	66	Windmill	Wright Group
Stacey and the Haunted Masquerade	O	250+	Martin, Ann M.	Scholastic
Stacey and the Missing Ring	O	250+	Martin, Ann M.	Scholastic
Stacey and the Mystery at the Mall	O	250+	Martin, Ann M.	Scholastic
Stacey and the Mystery Money	O	250+	Martin, Ann M.	Scholastic
Stacy Says Good-Bye	M	250+	Giff, Patricia Reilly	Bantam Doubleday Dell
Staircase to the Sky	D	133	Visions	Wright Group
Stallion's Call, The	E	77	Salem, Lynn & Stewart, J.	Seedling
Stamps	G	58	Wonder World	Wright Group
Stan Packs	E	84	Ready Readers	Pearson Learning
Stan the Hot Dog Man	K	250+	Kessler, Ethel & Leonard	HarperTrophy
Stanley	I	250+	Hoff, Syd	HarperTrophy
Stanley and the Magic Lamp	N	250+	Brown, Jeff	HarperTrophy
Star	M	250+	Simon, Jo Ann	Random House
Starfish & Urchins	K	322	Marine Life for Young Readers	Dominie

Title	Level	Words	Author/Series	Publisher/Distributor
Starring First Grade	J	250+	Cohen, Miriam	Bantam Doubleday Dell
Starring Rosie	N	250+	Giff, Patricia Reilly	The Penguin Group
Stars	G	105	Sunshine	Wright Group
Stars	H	181	Discovery Links	Newbridge
Starshine	H	224	Sunshine	Wright Group
Starting School	E		Voyages	SRA/McGraw-Hill
Statue of Liberty, The	L	250+	Penner, Lucille Recht	Random House
Stay Away from Simon!	O	250+	Carrick, Carol	Clarion
Staying with Grandma Norma	F	168	Salem Lynn & Stewart, J.	Seedling
Stella	E	57	Storyteller-Moon Rising	Wright Group/ McGraw-Hill
Stems	K	231	Pebble Books	Grolier, Capstone
Stepping Stones	C	42	Sunshine	Wright Group
Steve's Room	G	171	Ready Readers	Pearson Learning
Stew for Egor's Mom, A	G	162	Ready Readers	Pearson Learning
Sticky Stanley	F	97	First Start	Troll
Stingrays	I	126	Wonder World	Wright Group
Stone Fox	P	250+	Gardiner, John Reynolds	HarperTrophy
Stone Soup	J	932	McGovern, Ann	Scholastic
Stone Soup	J	250+	PM Trad. Tales & Plays-Turq.	Rigby
Stone Works	K	124	Wonder World	Wright Group
Stop	C	54	Story Box	Wright Group
Stop Knitting, Nina!	I	250+	Home Connection Collection	Rigby
Stop That	C	41	Ready Readers	Pearson Learning
Stop That Noise!	A	21	KinderReaders	Rigby
Stop That Noise!	C	41	Pacific Literacy	Pacific Learning
Stop That Rabbit	G	168	First Start	Troll
Stop!	A	12	Ready Readers	Pearson Learning
Stop!	B	90	PM Starters	Rigby
Stop!	C	31	Wonder World	Wright Group
Stop, Stop	M	250+	Hurd, Edith Thacher	HarperCollins
Stores	C	66	Carousel Readers	Dominie
Stories Huey Tells, The	N	250+	Cameron, Ann	Alfred A. Knopf, Inc.
Stories in Stone	M	250+	Pacific Literacy	Pacific Learning
Stories Julian Tells, The	N	250+	Cameron, Ann	Alfred A. Knopf, Inc.
Storm on the Beach, A	I	72	Book Bank	Wright Group
Storm!	E	49	Wonder World	Wright Group
Storm, The	B	19	Sunshine	Wright Group
Storm, The	C	28	Voyages	SRA/McGraw-Hill
Storm, The	C	29	Story Box	Wright Group
Storm, The	D	71	Foundations	Wright Group
Storm, The	E	33	Literacy 2000	Rigby
Storm, The	G	75	Books for Young Learners	Richard C. Owen
Storms!	L	359	Pair-It Books	Steck-Vaughn
Story of Alexander Graham Bell, The	P		Davidson, Margaret	Gareth Stevens
Story of Benjamin Franklin, The	O		Davidson, Margaret	Gareth Stevens
Story of Chicken Licken	I	250+	Ormerod, Jan	Lothrop
Story of Corn, The	H	171	Ready Readers	Pearson Learning
Story of George Washington Carver, The	P	250+	Moore, Eva	Scholastic
Story of Harriet Tubman, The	P	250+	McMullen, Kate	Dell Publishing
Story of Hungbu and Nolbu, The	K	802	Book Shop	Mondo Publishing
Story of Jackie Robinson, Bravest Man in Baseball	P	250+	Davidson, Margaret	Dell Publishing

Title	Level	Words	Author/Series	Publisher/Distributor
Story of Jeans, The	M	250+	Discovery World	Rigby
Story of Ruby Bridges, The	O	250+	Coles, Robert	Scholastic
Story of Thomas Alva Edison, Inventor, The	P	250+	Davidson, Margaret	Scholastic
Story of Walt Disney, Maker of Magical Worlds, The	P	250+	Selden, Bernice	Bantam Doubleday Dell
Story of You, The	M	482	Sunshine	Wright Group
Story Time	C	32	Ready Readers	Pearson Learning
Storytellers	L	506	Storyteller Nonfiction	Wright Group/ McGraw-Hill
Straight Line Wonder, The	J	464	Book Shop	Mondo Publishing
Strange Clues and Other Cases, The	O	250+	Simon, Seymour	Avon Books
Strange Museum and Other cases, The	O	250+	Simon, Seymour	Avon Books
Strange Plants	E	30	Books for Young Learners	Richard C. Owen
Strawberries	C	37	Little Books for Early Readers	University of Maine
Strawberry Jam	E	77	Oxford Reading Tree	Oxford University Press
Strawberry Pop And Soda Crackers	K		Little Celebrations	Pearson Learning
Streak, The	N	250+	Kroll, Stephen	Avon Camelot
Street Action	K	250+	Wildcats	Wright Group
Street Musicians	J	283	Sunshine	Wright Group
Strike Me Down with a Stringbean	L	404	Read Alongs	Rigby
Strike Out!	M	250+	Howard, Tristan	Scholastic
String Food	K	250+	Home Connection Collection	Rigby
String Performers	J	250+	Home Connection Collection	Rigby
Strings	C	53	Storyteller-First Snow	Wright Group/ McGraw-Hill
Strings, Ropes, and Cables	I	250+	Home Connection Collection	Rigby
Striped Ice Cream	N	250+	Lexau, Joan M.	Scholastic
Stripes	A	28	Twig	Wright Group
Strongest Animal, The	F	58	Books for Young Learners	Richard C. Owen
Stuck in the Muck	E	139	Spinelle, Nancy Louise	Kaeden Books
Stuck on an Island	H	181	Sunshine	Wright Group
Sub, The	P	250+	Peterson, P. J.	Puffin Books
Sue Likes Blue	G	131	Gregorich, Barbara	School Zone
Sugar Cakes Cyril	N	4022	Book Shop	Mondo Publishing
Suki and the Case of the Lost Bunnies	K	250+	Ready Readers	Pearson Learning
Sulky Simon	J	246	Windmill Books	Rigby
Summer	E	73	Sunshine	Wright Group
Summer	I	178	Pebble Books	Grolier, Capstone
Summer at Cove Lake	G	288	Ready Readers	Pearson Learning
Summer Camp	J	182	City Kids	Rigby
Summer Fun	E	30	Literacy 2000	Rigby
Summer Sands	M	839	Evangeline Nicholas Collection	Wright Group
Summer Trips	G	272	Visions	Wright Group
Sun Flower, A	B	42	Foundations	Wright Group
Sun, The	E	42	Discovery Links	Newbridge
Sun, The	J	219	Wonder World	Wright Group
Sun, the Wind, & Tashira, The	L	371	Folk Tales	Mondo Publishing
Sunburn	B	48	Prokopchak, Ann	Kaeden Books
Sunburn	J	176	City Kids	Rigby
Sunflower Seeds	D	48	Story Box	Wright Group
Sunflower That Went Flop, The	L	637	Story Box	Wright Group
Sunflowers	D	35	Pebble Books	Grolier, Capstone
Sunflowers	E	33	Books for Young Learners	Richard C. Owen

Title	Level	Words	Author/Series	Publisher/Distributor
Sunny-Side Up	M	250+	Giff, Patricia Reilly	Bantam Doubleday Dell
Sunrise	C	46	Literacy 2000	Rigby
Sunset of the Sabertooth	M	250+	Osborne, Mary Pope	Random House
Sunshine	L	307	Pebble Books	Grolier, Capstone
Sunshine Street	H	110	Sunshine	Wright Group
Sunshine, Moonshine	E	128	Armstrong, Jennifer	Random House
Sunshine, the Black Cat	G	143	Carousel Readers	Dominie
Super Hero	B	33	Sunshine	Wright Group
Super Pig's Adventures	E	133	New Way Blue	Steck-Vaughn
Super Smile Shop, The	H	254	Story Basket	Wright Group
Super Supermarket Plan, The	J	250+	Home Connection Collection	Rigby
Supercharged Infield	M	250+	Christopher, Matt	Little, Brown & Co.
Super-Duper Sunflower Seeds, The	I	389	Book Bank	Wright Group
Superkids	H	165	Sunshine	Wright Group
Supermarket Chase, The	L	438	Sunshine	Wright Group
Supermarket, The	K	255	Pebble Books	Grolier, Capstone
Surfer, The	D	40	Wonder World	Wright Group
Surfing the Information Highway	H	137	Wonder World	Wright Group
Surf's Up	P	250+	Wildcats	Wright Group
Surprise Cake	C	32	Literacy 2000	Rigby
Surprise Dinner, The	L	680	PM Story Books-Gold	Rigby
Surprise for Mom	E	101	Urmston, Kathleen & Evans, Karen	Kaeden Books
Surprise from the Sky	I	295	Windmill Books	Rigby
Surprise Party	K	333	Hutchins, Pat	Macmillan
Surprise Party, The	I	192	New Way Green	Steck-Vaughn
Surprise Party, The	J	250+	Proger, Annabelle	Random House
Surprise Visit, The	G	23	New Way Blue	Steck-Vaughn
Surprise!	D	28	My First Reader	Grolier Press
Surprise!	I		Little Celebrations	Pearson Learning
Surprise, The	A	14	Story Box	Wright Group
Surprise, The	H	124	Literacy 2000	Rigby
Surprises	L	250+	Hopkins, Lee Bennett	HarperTrophy
Survival of Fish, The	M	946	Science	Wright Group
Susie Goes Shopping	F	194	First Start	Troll
Swamp Hen	F	59	Pacific Literacy	Pacific Learning
Swamp of the Hideous Zombies	O	250+	Hayes, Geoffrey	Random House
Swans	D	53	Joy Readers	Dominie
Swat it!	D	46	Bauer, Roger	Kaeden Books
Sweet or Sour?	I	177	Sunshine	Wright Group
Sweet Potato Pie	E	72	Rockwell, Anne	Random House
Sweet to Eat	I	105	Pacific Literacy	Pacific Learning
Swimming	C	65	Carousel Readers	Dominie
Swimming Lessons	I	200	Storyteller Nonfiction	Wright Group/ McGraw-Hill
Swimming Pool, The	C	29	Visions	Wright Group
Swing	A	18	Story Box	Wright Group
Swing, Swing, Swing	C	93	Tuchman, G. & Dieterichs, S.	Scholastic
Sword in the Stone, The	J	250+	Maccarone, Grace	Scholastic
T Shirts	F	112	Pacific Literacy	Pacific Learning
T. J.'s Tree	G	77	Literacy 2000	Rigby
Tabby in the Tree	F	200	PM Story Books	Rigby

Title	Level	Words	Author/Series	Publisher/Distributor
Table for Two	L		Little Celebrations	Pearson Learning
Tails	B	42	Book Bank	Wright Group
Tails	D	52	Wonder World	Wright Group
Tails	E	59	Discovery Links	Newbridge
Tails	F	47	Literacy 2000	Rigby
Tails	F	65	Book Shop	Mondo Publishing
Tails	I	170	Sunshine	Wright Group
Tails and Claws	C	65	Wonder World	Wright Group
Tails Can Tell	I	346	Wonder World	Wright Group
Take a Bite	C	19	Little Celebrations	Pearson Learning
Take a Bow, Jody	D	78	Eaton, Audrey & Kennedy, Jane	Seedling
Take a Guess	C	45	Little Celebrations	Pearson Learning
Take Care of Our Earth	M	250+	Pair-It Books	Steck-Vaughn
Taking Care of Baby	G	159	Discovery Links	Newbridge
Taking Care of Our World	D	137	Visions	Wright Group
Taking Care of Rosie	E	61	Salem Lynn & Stewart, J.	Seedling
Taking Jason to Grandma's	F	118	Book Bank	Wright Group
Taking Our Photos	E	132	Voyages	SRA/McGraw-Hill
Tale of Cowboy Roy, The	H	185	Ready Readers	Pearson Learning
Tale of Peter Rabbit, The	L	250+	Potter, Beatrix	Scholastic
Tale of the Christmas Mouse	H	97	First Start	Troll
Tale of the Turnip, The	I	250+	PM Traditional Tales-Orange	Rigby
Tale of Veruschka Babushka, The	M	250+	Literacy 2000	Rigby
Tales of Amanda Pig	L	250+	Van Leeuwen, Jean	Puffin Books
Tales of Olga da Polga, The	P	250+	Bond, Michael	Houghton Mifflin
Talk! Talk! Talk!	N	50	Little Celebrations	Pearson Learning
Talk, Talk, Talk	C	56	Literacy 2000	Rigby
Talking Yam, The	I	340	Little Readers	Houghton Mifflin
Tall Tale and Other Cases, The	O	250+	Simon, Seymour	Avon Books
Tall Things	D	83	PM Nonfiction-Red	Rigby
Tallest Sunflower, The	I		Counters & Seekers	Steck-Vaughn
Tamika and the Wisdom Rings	O	250+	Yarbrough, Camille	Random House
Tania's Tooth	I	131	Sunshine	Wright Group
Tarantulas are Spiders	F	39	Book Shop	Mondo Publishing
Tasmanian Devils	K	250+	PM Animal Facts-Gold	Rigby
Taste Sensation	D	115	Visions	Wright Group
Tasty Bug, A	D	50	Little Celebrations	Pearson Learning
Taxi, The	C	45	Joy Readers	Dominie
T-Ball	D	35	Visions	Wright Group
Tea	K	267	Wonder World	Wright Group
Tea Party	C	38	Carousel Readers	Dominie
Tea Party, The	C	76	Storyteller-First Snow	Wright Group/ McGraw-Hill
Teach Us, Amelia Bedelia	L	250+	Parish, Peggy	Scholastic
Teacher, The	G	155	PM Nonfiction-Blue	Rigby
Teachers at Our School	I	115	City Kids	Rigby
Teacher's Pet	L	250+	Dicks, Terrance	Scholastic
Teacher's Pet	O	250+	Hurwitz, Johanna	Scholastic
Team Sports	B	23	Twig	Wright Group
Teasing Dad	F	158	PM Extensions-Blue	Rigby
Teddy Bear for Sale	G	152	Herman, Gail	Scholastic
Teddy Bears Cure a Cold	K		Gretz, Susanna	Scholastic

Title	Level	Words	Author/Series	Publisher/Distributor
Ted's Red Sled	D	69	Ready Readers	Pearson Learning
Tee-Ball	C	53	Little Celebrations	Pearson Learning
Teeny Tiny	I	250+	Bennett, Jill	Putnam
Teeny Tiny Tina	C	34	Literacy 2000	Rigby
Teeny Tiny Woman, The	F	250+	O'Connor, Jane	Random House
Teeny Tiny Woman, The	J	369	Seuling, Barbara	Scholastic
Teeter-Totter, The	C	35	Joy Readers	Dominie
Teeth	C	26	Wonder World	Wright Group
Teeth	D	71	Story Box	Wright Group
Teeth	K	470	Sunshine	Wright Group
Tell Me a Story, Grandpa	L		Little Celebrations	Pearson Learning
Ten Apples Up on Top	J	250+	LaSieg, Theo	Random House
Ten Bears in My Bed	G	252	Mack, Stan	Pantheon
Ten Crazy Caterpillars	C	40	Voyages	SRA/McGraw-Hill
Ten Happy Elephants	I	201	Sunshine	Wright Group
Ten Little Bears	G	211	Reading Unlimited	Pacific Learning
Ten Little Caterpillars	F	102	Literacy 2000	Rigby
Ten Little Garden Snails	H	101	PM Story Books	Rigby
Ten Little Men	E	38	Literacy 2000	Rigby
Ten Loopy Caterpillars	I	191	Jellybeans	Rigby
Ten Sleepy Sheep	G		Keller, Holly	Greenwillow
Ten Traveling Tigers	H	165	Little Readers	Houghton Mifflin
Ten True Animal Rescues	O	250+	Betancourt, Jeanne	Scholastic
Tents	I	175	Reading Unlimited	Pacific Learning
Termites	I	130	Books for Young Learners	Richard C. Owen
Terrible Armadillo	I	229	Jellybeans	Rigby
Terrible Fright, A	K	291	Story Box	Wright Group
Terrible Test Mark and Other Cases, The	O	250+	Simon, Seymour	Avon Books
Terrible Tiger, The	G	140	Sunshine	Wright Group
Terrible Twos	E	86	Tadpoles	Rigby
Terrific Shoes	C	19	Ready Readers	Pearson Learning
Tess and Paddy	J	242	Sunshine	Wright Group
Thank You, Amelia Bedelia	L	250+	Parish, Peggy	Harper & Row
Thank You, Amelia Bedelia	L	250+	Little Readers	Houghton Mifflin
Thank You, Nicky!	F	119	Ziefert, Harriet	The Penguin Group
Thanksgiving	F	75	Urmston, Kathleen & Evans, Karen	Kaeden Books
That Cat!	G	146	Ready Readers	Pearson Learning
That Dog!	E	213	Foundations	Wright Group
That Fat Hat	K	250+	Barkan, Joanne	Scholastic
That Fly	C	26	Ready Readers	Pearson Learning
That Pig Can't Do a Thing	F	83	Ready Readers	Pearson Learning
That's a Laugh: Four Funny Fables	M	250+	Literacy 2000	Rigby
That's Dangerous	D	71	Voyages	SRA/McGraw-Hill
That's Not All	G	105	Start to Read	School Zone
That's Really Weird!	K	129	Read Alongs	Rigby
Then and Now	J	250+	Discovery World	Rigby
There are Mice in Our School	I	95	City Kids	Rigby
There Are Spots On…	A	14	Little Books for Early Readers	University of Maine
There Is a Planet	C	52	Sunshine	Wright Group
There Is a Town	D	116	Heiman, Gail	Random House
There Is No Water	I	250+	Home Connection Collection	Rigby
There Was a Crooked Man	E	40	Sunshine	Wright Group

©1999 by I. C. Fountas & G. S. Pinnell from Matching Books to Readers. Portsmouth, NH: Heinemann. May not be reproduced without written permission of the publisher.

Title	Level	Words	Author/Series	Publisher/Distributor
There Was a Mouse	D	77	Books for Young Learners	Richard C. Owen
There's a Dog in the Yard	I	119	City Kids	Rigby
There's a Hippopotamus Under My Bed	J	250+	Thaler, Mike	Avon Books
There's a Mouse in the House	B	42	Book Shop	Mondo Publishing
There's a Nightmare in My Closet	I	153	Mayer, Mercer	The Penguin Group
There's a Rainbow in the River	L	250+	Home Connection Collection	Rigby
There's An Alligator Under My Bed	J	250+	Mayer, Mercer	The Penguin Group
There's No One Like Me!	D	80	Sunshine	Wright Group
There's Something in My Attic	J	258	Mayer, Mercer	The Penguin Group
These Legs	C	42	Foundations	Wright Group
These Old Rags	M	352	Evangeline Nicholas Collection	Wright Group
They Call Me...	D	31	The Candid Collection	Dominie
They Led the Way: 14 American Women	O	250+	Johnston, Joanna	Scholastic
Thing in the Log, The	H		Reading Unlimited	Pacific Learning
Things Change	N	569	Wonders	Hampton-Brown
Things I Can Do	B	36	Little Readers	Houghton Mifflin
Things I Like	C	42	Carousel Earlybirds	Dominie
Things I Like	D		Browne, Anthony	Random House
Things I Like to Do	C	58	Foundations	Wright Group
Things I Like to Do	C	63	Carousel Earlybirds	Dominie
Things on Wheels	C	69	Little Red Readers	Sundance
Things People Do for Fun	E	124	Foundations	Wright Group
Things That Drag Behind	D	42	Teacher's Choice Series	Dominie
Things That Go: A Traveling Alphabet	L	250+	Reit, Seymour	Bantam Doubleday Dell
Things That Help Me	C	18	Pacific Literacy	Pacific Learning
Things That Protect You	D	51	Foundations	Wright Group
Things to Read	A	18	Little Books for Early Readers	University of Maine
Things to See in Maine	A	14	Little Books for Early Readers	University of Maine
Things with Wings	J	267	Storyteller Nonfiction	Wright Group/ McGraw-Hill
Thinking About Ants	L	662	Book Shop	Mondo Publishing
Third Grade Bullies	N	250+	Levy, Elizabeth	Hyperion
Third Grade Stars	P	250+	Ransom, Candice	Troll
This Game	B	63	Carousel Earlybirds	Dominie
This Hat	D	52	Little Celebrations	Pearson Learning
This Is Lobstering	A	27	Little Books for Early Readers	University of Maine
This Is My Family	D	36	Read-More Books	Dominie
This Is My Friend	C	77	Foundations	Wright Group
This Is My Home	C	51	Joy Readers	Dominie
This Is My House	L	250+	Dorros, Arthur	Scholastic
This Is the Bear	I	211	Hayes, Sarah & Craig, H.	Harper & Row
This Is the Place for Me	I	250+	Cole, Joanna	Scholastic
This Is the Plate	D		Little Celebrations	Pearson Learning
This Is the Seed	I	171	Little Celebrations	Pearson Learning
This Mouth	D	64	Wonder World	Wright Group
This Old Car	H		Voyages	SRA/McGraw-Hill
This Room Is a Mess!	I	250+	Ready Readers	Pearson Learning
This Tall	B	41	Foundations	Wright Group
Thomas Jefferson: Author, Inventor, President	N	250+	Rookie Biographies	Children's Press
Three Bears	K	873	Galdone, Paul	Clarion
Three Billy Goats Gruff	I	536	Traditional Tales	Dominie
Three Billy Goats Gruff	K	478	Stevens, Janet	Harcourt Brace

Title	Level	Words	Author/Series	Publisher/Distributor
Three Billy Goats Gruff, The	G	140	Little Readers	Houghton Mifflin
Three Billy Goats Gruff, The	G		New Way Green	Steck-Vaughn
Three Billy Goats Gruff, The	I	450	PM Traditional Tales-Orange	Rigby
Three Billy Goats Gruff, The	I	549	Brown, Marcia	Harcourt Brace
Three Blind Mice Mystery, The	L	250+	Krensky, Stephen	Bantam Doubleday Dell
Three By the Sea	K	250+	Marshall, Edward	Puffin Books
Three Cheers for Hippo	G	90	Stadler, John	HarperCollins
Three Days on a River in a Red Canoe	K	250+	Williams, Vera B.	Scholastic
Three Ducks Went Wandering	K	250+	Roy, Ron	Clarion
Three Goats, The	F	128	Storyteller-Setting Sun	Wright Group/ McGraw-Hill
Three Kittens	G	116	Ginsburg, Mirra	Crown
Three Little Ducks	E	102	Read-Togethers	Wright Group
Three Little Kittens	H	164	Ready Readers	Pearson Learning
Three Little Monkeys	E	36	Sunshine	Wright Group
Three Little Pigs	H	392	New Way Blue	Steck-Vaughn
Three Little Pigs	H		Hunia, Fran	Ladybird Books
Three Little Pigs	L	919	Galdone, Paul	Houghton Mifflin
Three Little Pigs	L	250+	Once Upon a Time	Wright Group
Three Little Pigs and One Big Pig	E	123	Ready Readers	Pearson Learning
Three Little Pigs, The	G	250+	Little Readers	Houghton Mifflin
Three Little Pigs, The	H	276	Reading Unlimited	Pacific Learning
Three Little Pigs, The	H	346	Reading Corners	Dominie
Three Little Pigs, The	I	523	PM Traditional Tales-Orange	Rigby
Three Little Pigs, The	I	568	Traditional Tales	Dominie
Three Little Pigs, The	L	250+	Marshall, James	Scholastic
Three Little Witches	G	189	First Start	Troll
Three Magicians, The	K		Literacy 2000	Rigby
Three Muddy Monkeys	F	180	Foundations	Wright Group
Three Sillies, The	L		Literacy 2000	Rigby
Three Silly Cowboys	H	213	Ready Readers	Pearson Learning
Three Silly Monkeys	D	150	Foundations	Wright Group
Three Silly Monkeys Go Fishing	I	163	Foundations	Wright Group
Three Smart Pals	L	250+	Rocklin, Joanne	Scholastic
Three Stories You Can Read to Your Cat	K	250+	Miller, Sara Swan	Houghton Mifflin
Three Stories You Can Read to Your Dog	K	250+	Miller, Sara Swan	Houghton Mifflin
Three White Sheep	B	20	Ready Readers	Pearson Learning
Three Wishes	H	250+	Ready Readers	Pearson Learning
Three Wishes, The	K	501	Sunshine	Wright Group
Three Wishes, The	L	717	Book Shop	Mondo Publishing
Three-Legged Race, The	H	202	Windmill Books	Rigby
Through Grandpa's Eyes	L	250+	MacLachlan, Patricia	HarperTrophy
Through the Medicine Cabinet	M	250+	Greenburg, Dan	Grosset & Dunlap
Throw-Away Pets	N	250+	Duffy, Betsy	Puffin Books
Thumbelina	K	807	Tales from Hans Andersen	Wright Group
Thumbprint Critters	D	27	Little Celebrations	Pearson Learning
Thumpety-Rah!	G	98	Sunshine	Wright Group
Thurgood Marshall: First Black Supreme Court Justice	N	250+	Rookie Biographies	Children's Press
Tickle-Bugs, The	J		Literacy 2000	Rigby
Tick-Tock	C	53	Story Box	Wright Group
Tides	I	210	Wonder World	Wright Group

Title	Level	Words	Author/Series	Publisher/Distributor
Tidy Titch	I	231	Hutchins, Pat	Morrow
Tiger Dave	G	33	Books for Young Learners	Richard C. Owen
Tiger Is a Scaredy Cat	F	220	Phillips, Joan	Random House
Tiger Runs Away	F	213	PM Extensions-Blue	Rigby
Tiger Tales	O		Little Celebrations	Pearson Learning
Tiger, Tiger	C	55	PM Story Books	Rigby
Tiger's Tummy Ache	I	220	Ready Readers	Pearson Learning
Tight End	M	250+	Christopher, Matt	Little, Brown & Co.
Timber Box, The	M	250+	Enrichment	Wright Group
Time Capsule, The	M	257	Book Bank	Wright Group
Time for a Bath	D	60	Mader, Jan	Kaeden Books
Time for a Change	C	31	Pacific Literacy	Pacific Learning
Time for a Party	F	111	Discovery World	Rigby
Time for Bed	C	28	Smart Starts	Rigby
Time for Bed, Little Bear	I	303	Story Basket	Wright Group
Time for Dinner	A	15	Smart Starts	Rigby
Time for Dinner	B	38	PM Starters	Rigby
Time for Lunch	B	28	Ready Readers	Pearson Learning
Time for Sleep!	D	62	Sunshine	Wright Group
Time Machine and Other Cases, The	O	250+	Simon, Seymour	Avon Books
Time Warp Trio, The: 2095	P	250+	Scieszka, Jon	The Penguin Group
Time Warp Trio, The: The Not-So-Jolly Roger	P	250+	Scieszka, Jon	The Penguin Group
Time Warp Trio, The: Tut Tut	P	250+	Scieszka, Jon	The Penguin Group
Time Warp Trio, The: Your Mother Was a Neanderthal	P	250+	Scieszka, Jon	The Penguin Group
Time Warp Trio, The: The Good, the Bad, and the Goofy	P	250+	Scieszka, Jon	The Penguin Group
Time Warp Trio, The: The Knights of the Kitchen Table	P	250+	Scieszka, Jon	The Penguin Group
Timmy	E	54	Literacy 2000	Rigby
Timmy Tries	C	22	Little Celebrations	Pearson Learning
Timothy's Five-City Tour	M	250+	Pair-It Books	Steck-Vaughn
Tim's Favorite Toy	F	202	PM Extensions-Blue	Rigby
Tim's Paintings	A	33	Literacy 2000	Rigby
Tim's Pumpkin	I	250+	Home Connection Collection	Rigby
Tin Lizzy	M	425	Windmill Books	Rigby
Tiny and the Big Wave	F	163	PM Extensions-Yellow	Rigby
Tiny Christmas Elf, The	G	173	First Start	Troll
Tiny Creatures	J	250+	Discovery World	Rigby
Tiny Little Woman, The	D	74	Joy Readers	Dominie
Tiny Woman's Coat, The	H	147	Sunshine	Wright Group
Tires	E	180	Foundations	Wright Group
Titanic, The	N	250+	Donnelly, Judy	Random House
Titanic, the Lost…and Found	N	250+	Donnelly, Judy	Random House
Titch	G	121	Hutchins, Pat	The Penguin Group
Tittle-Tattle Goose	E	117	Story Box	Wright Group
To Market, to Market	I	393	Read-Togethers	Wright Group
To New York	D	32	Story Box	Wright Group
To School	A	22	Sunshine	Wright Group
To the Beach	D	43	Urmston, Kathleen & Evans, Karen	Kaeden Books
To the Ocean	C	26	Twig	Wright Group

Title	Level	Words	Author/Series	Publisher/Distributor
To the Top!	N	250+	Kramer, Sydelle A.	Random House
To Town	F	148	Read-Togethers	Wright Group
To Work	C	43	Sunshine	Wright Group
Toad for Tuesday, A	N	250+	Erickson, Russell	Beech Tree Books
Toast for Mom	I	250+	Ready Readers	Pearson Learning
Toby and B.J.	I	307	PM Story Books-Orange	Rigby
Toby and the Accident	J	329	PM Story Books-Turquoise	Rigby
Toby and the Big Red Van	I	291	PM Story Books-Orange	Rigby
Toby and the Big Tree	I	298	PM Story Books-Orange	Rigby
Toby Tomato	D	54	Little Celebrations	Pearson Learning
Today I Got Yelled At	J	174	City Kids	Rigby
Toenails	E	83	Voyages	SRA/McGraw-Hill
Together	C	37	Sunshine	Wright Group
Tom and His Tractor	C	27	Cat on the Mat	Oxford University Press
Tom Edison's Bright Idea	M	250+	Keller, Jack	Steck-Vaughn
Tom Gets Fit	D	150	New Way Red	Steck-Vaughn
Tom Is Brave	D	57	PM Story Books	Rigby
Tom the TV Cat	J	250+	Heilbroner, Joan	Random House
Tom, the Dragon	M	522	New Way Orange	Steck-Vaughn
Tomatoes and Bricks	E	126	Windmill	Wright Group
Tommy Snake's Problem	H	328	TOTTS	Tott Publications
Tommy's Treasure	I		Literacy 2000	Rigby
Tommy's Tummy Ache	C	20	Literacy 2000	Rigby
Tom's Rubber Band	E	82	Sunshine	Wright Group
Tom's Trousers	G	173	Storyteller-Night Crickets	Wright Group/ McGraw-Hill
Tongue Twister Prize, The	J	331	Little Books	Sadlier-Oxford
Tongues Are for Tasting, Licking, Tricking	L		Literacy 2000	Rigby
Too Big for Me	D	70	Story Box	Wright Group
Too Busy for Pets!	K	472	Sunshine	Wright Group
Too Fast	A	36	Reading Corners	Dominie
Too High!	D	66	Ready Readers	Pearson Learning
Too Hot to Handle	M	250+	Christopher, Matt	Little, Brown & Co.
Too Late!	G	226	Foundations	Wright Group
Too Little	E	119	Foundations	Wright Group
Too Many Babas	K	250+	Little Readers	Houghton Mifflin
Too Many Babas	K	250+	Croll, Carolyn	HarperTrophy
Too Many Balloons	D	182	Rookie Readers	Children's Press
Too Many Bones	G	125	New Way Blue	Steck-Vaughn
Too Many Clothes	C	24	Literacy 2000	Rigby
Too Many Mice	J	250+	Brenner, Barbara	Bantam Doubleday Dell
Too Many Ponies	O	250+	Betancourt, Jeanne	Scholastic
Too Many Rabbits	J	250+	Parish, Peggy	Bantam Doubleday Dell
Too Many Steps	J	424	Foundations	Wright Group
Too Much	B	27	Teacher's Choice Series	Dominie
Too Much Ketchup	D	30	Ready Readers	Pearson Learning
Too Much Noise	H	340	Literacy 2000	Rigby
Too Much Noise	J	250+	McGovern, Ann	Scholastic
Too Small Jill	J	306	Little Books	Sadlier-Oxford
Tool Box	H	144	Rockwell, Anne	Macmillan
Toot! Toot!	C	21	Joy Readers	Dominie
Toot, Toot	C	47	Wildsmith, Brian	Oxford University Press

Title	Level	Words	Author/Series	Publisher/Distributor
Tooth Fairy, The	D	57	My First Reader	Grolier Press
Tooth Race, The	I	250+	Little Readers	Houghton Mifflin
Toothbrush Tale	G	117	New Way Blue	Steck-Vaughn
Too-Tight Shoes	I	170	Evangeline Nicholas Collection	Wright Group
Tornado	E	37	Spinelle, Nancy Louise	Kaeden Books
Tornado	O	250+	Byars, Betsy	The Penguin Group
Tornadoes!	P	250+	Hopping, Lorraine	Scholastic
Tortillas	E	71	Gonzalez-Jensen	Scholastic
Tossed Salad	C	28	Twig	Wright Group
Totara Tree, The	M	391	Book Bank	Wright Group
Touch	C	39	Twig	Wright Group
Touchdown for Tommy	M	250+	Christopher, Matt	Little, Brown & Co.
Town Mouse and Country Mouse, The	I	172	Aesop	Wright Group
Toy Box, A	A	19	Literacy 2000	Rigby
Toy Box, The	A	14	Ready Readers	Pearson Learning
Toy Farm, The	I	311	PM Story Books-Orange	Rigby
Toy Models	A	40	Early Connections	Benchmark Education
Toy Town	C	36	Home Connection Collection	Rigby
Toys	B	37	Foundations	Wright Group
Toys	E	76	Talk About Books	Dominie
Toys' Party, The	F	48	Oxford Reading Tree	Oxford University Press
Toys with Wheels	C	41	Home Connection Collection	Rigby
Tracks	C	25	Sunshine	Wright Group
Tracks	C	49	Twig	Wright Group
Traffic Jam	B	18	Voyages	SRA/McGraw-Hill
Traffic Jam	E	133	Harper, Leslie	Kaeden Books
Traffic Light Sandwich	H	87	Wonder World	Wright Group
Train Ride, The	C	29	Literacy 2000	Rigby
Train that Ran Away	I	32	Jellybeans	Rigby
Train, The	C	27	Visions	Wright Group
Transportation Museum, The	C	79	Little Red Readers	Sundance
Transportation Time Line, A	P	250+	Discovery World	Rigby
Trapped!	O	250+	Small, Mary	Sundance
Trash	H	130	Sunshine	Wright Group
Trash Can Band, The	J	252	Little Books	Sadlier-Oxford
Travel Money, U.S.A.	I	245	Early Connections	Benchmark Education
Traveling	C	86	Foundations	Wright Group
Traveling Ted's Postcards	C		Little Celebrations	Pearson Learning
Treasure Hunt	A	14	Smart Starts	Rigby
Treasure Hunting	M	250+	Literacy 2000	Rigby
Treasure of the Lost Lagoon	K	250+	Hayes, Geoffrey	Random House
Tree Can Be, A	E	74	Nayer, Judy	Scholastic
Tree Fell Over the River, A	C	72	Little Red Readers	Sundance
Tree House Fun	G	165	First Start	Troll
Tree House, The	B	32	Sunshine	Wright Group
Tree House, The	B	32	Story Box	Wright Group
Tree Is a Home, A	I	135	Pacific Literacy	Pacific Learning
Tree Stump, The	B	34	Little Celebrations	Pearson Learning
Tree, The	F	101	Sunshine	Wright Group
Treehouse Club, The	F	158	Home Connection Collection	Rigby
Treehouse, The	D	43	Hoenecke, Karen	Kaeden Books
Trees	A	28	Twig	Wright Group

Title	Level	Words	Author/Series	Publisher/Distributor
Trees	H	194	Momentum Literacy Program	Troll
Trees	J	124	Literacy 2000	Rigby
Trees	K	388	Early Connections	Benchmark Education
Trees Are Special	I	85	Sunshine	Wright Group
Trees Belong to Everyone	L		Literacy 2000	Rigby
Trek, The	I	158	Jonas, Ann	Greenwillow
Triceratops on the Farm	L	208	Wesley & the Dinosaurs	Wright Group
Trick or Treat Halloween	F	131	First Start	Troll
Trick, The	F	65	New Way Red	Steck-Vaughn
Tricking Tracy	F	125	Tadpoles	Rigby
Trickster Ghost, The	O	250+	Showell, Ellen	Scholastic
Tricky Sticky Problem, The	H	71	Pacific Literacy	Pacific Learning
Trip into Space, A	I	129	Little Red Readers	Sundance
Trip to the Aquarium, A	C	18	Kloes, Carol	Kaeden Books
Trip to the Park, The	F	277	Foundations	Wright Group
Trip to the Video Store, A	H	203	Foundations	Wright Group
Trip to the Zoo, A	C	78	Carousel Readers	Dominie
Trip, The	E	108	Ready Readers	Pearson Learning
Triplet Trouble and the Bicycle Race	L	250+	Dadey, Debbie & Jones, Marcia	Scholastic
Triplet Trouble and the Class Trip	L	250+	Dadey, Debbie & Jones, Marcia	Scholastic
Triplet Trouble and the Cookie Contest	L	250+	Dadey, Debbie & Jones, Marcia	Scholastic
Triplet Trouble and the Field Day	L	250+	Dadey, Debbie & Jones, Marcia	Scholastic
Triplet Trouble and the Field Day Disaster	L	250+	Dadey, Debbie & Jones, Marcia	Scholastic
Triplet Trouble and the Pizza Party	L	250+	Dadey, Debbie & Jones, Marcia	Scholastic
Triplet Trouble and the Red Heart Race	L	250+	Dadey, Debbie & Jones, Marcia	Scholastic
Triplet Trouble and the Runaway Reindeer	L	250+	Dadey, Debbie & Jones, Marcia	Scholastic
Triplet Trouble and the Talent Show	L	250+	Dadey, Debbie & Jones, Marcia	Scholastic
Triplet Trouble and the Talent Show Mess	L	250+	Dadey, Debbie & Jones, Marcia	Scholastic
Trixie and the Cyber Pet	M	250+	Krailing, Tessa	Barron's Educational
Trog	M	432	Sunshine	Wright Group
Trojan Horse, The: How the Greeks Won the War	N	250+	Little, Emily	Random House
Trolley Ride, The	C	87	Tadpoles	Rigby
Trolls Don't Ride Roller Coasters	M	250+	Dadey, Debbie & Jones, Marcia	Scholastic
Trouble	E	113	Teacher's Choice Series	Dominie
Trouble in the Sandbox	F	318	Foundations	Wright Group
Trouble with Buster, The	N	250+	Lorimer, Janet	Scholastic
Trouble with Herbert, The	L	1830	Book Shop	Mondo Publishing
Truck Is Struck, The	B	23	Ready Readers	Pearson Learning
Truck Stop, The	C	25	Kloes, Carol	Kaeden Books
Trucks	A	35	Little Books for Early Readers	University of Maine
Trucks	C	24	Twig	Wright Group
Trucks	C	27	Pebble Books	Grolier, Capstone
Trucks	C	38	Literacy 2000	Rigby
Trucks	E	196	Foundations	Wright Group
Trucks	I	38	Literacy 2000	Rigby
True or False?	G	119	Ready Readers	Pearson Learning
True Stories About Abraham Lincoln	M	250+	Gross, Ruth Belov	Scholastic
True Story of Balto, The	L	250+	Standiford, Natalie	Random House
True Story of Balto: The Bravest Dog Ever	L	250+	Standiford, Natalie	Random House
True-Life Treasure Hunts	N	250+	Donnelly, Judy	Random House
Try Again, Hannah	G	228	PM Extensions-Green	Rigby
Try It!	D	49	Reading Corners	Dominie

Title	Level	Words	Author/Series	Publisher/Distributor
Try to Be a Brave Girl, Sarah	F	102	Windmill	Wright Group
T-Shirt Triplets, The	L	344	Literacy 2000	Rigby
T-Shirts	F	112	Ready to Read	Pacific Learning
Tubes in My Ears: My Trip to the Hospital	K	658	Book Shop	Mondo Publishing
Tug of War	I	250+	Folk Tales	Wright Group
Tummy Ache	J	104	Sunshine	Wright Group
Turkey Trouble	M	250+	Giff, Patricia Reilly	Bantam Doubleday Dell
Turkeys' Side of it, The	M	250+	Smith, Janice Lee	HarperTrophy
Turtle Flies South	K		Literacy 2000	Rigby
Turtle Nest	H	85	Books for Young Learners	Richard C. Owen
Turtle Talk	I	217	Storyteller-Setting Sun	Wright Group/ McGraw-Hill
Turtle, The	D	68	Foundations	Wright Group
Tut's Mummy: Lost and Found	P	250+	Donnelly, Judy	Random House
TweedledeDee Tumbleweed	G		Reese, Bob	Children's Press
Twelve Dancing Princesses	M	250+	Enrichment	Wright Group
Twiddle Twins' Haunted House, The	L	1141	Book Shop	Mondo Publishing
Twisters and Other Wind Storms	P	250+	Wildcats	Wright Group
Twits, The	P	250+	Dahl, Roald	Puffin Books
Two	A	17	Little Celebrations	Pearson Learning
Two	E	84	Carousel Readers	Dominie
Two Bear Cubs	H		Jonas, Ann	Morrow
Two Crazy Pigs	D	250+	Nagel, Karen Berman	Scholastic
Two Eyes, Two Ears	D	83	PM Nonfiction-Red	Rigby
Two Foolish Cats	K		Literacy 2000	Rigby
Two Is a Pair	E	78	Teacher's Choice Series	Dominie
Two Little Chicks	C	32	KinderReaders	Rigby
Two Little Dogs	E	74	Story Box	Wright Group
Two Little Goldfish	I	344	PM Story Books-Orange	Rigby
Two Little Mice, The	I	163	Literacy 2000	Rigby
Two More	A	16	Voyages	SRA/McGraw-Hill
Two Ogres, The	F	116	Joy Readers	Dominie
Two Plus One Goes A.P.E.	L	250+	Springstubb, Tricia	Scholastic
Two Plus Two	E	44	Teacher's Choice Series	Dominie
Two Points	B	40	Kennedy, J. & Eaton, A.	Seedling
Two Runaways, The	M	250+	Schultz, Irene	Wright Group
Two Silly Trolls	J	250+	Jewell, Nancy	HarperTrophy
Two Stupid Cats	G	140	Sunshine	Wright Group
Two Turtles	A	13	Ready Readers	Pearson Learning
Tyler Toad and Thunder	M	250+	Crowe, Robert	Dutton
Tyler's Train	C		Little Celebrations	Pearson Learning
Tyrannosaurus the Terrible	L	182	Wesley & the Dinosaurs	Wright Group
Ugly Duckling, The	J	558	Tales from Hans Andersen	Wright Group
Ugly Duckling, The	K	452	Traditional Tales & More	Rigby
Uh-Oh! Said the Crow	J	250+	Oppenheim, Joanna	Bantam Doubleday Dell
Umbrella	C	73	Story Box	Wright Group
Umbrellas	M	430	Sunshine	Wright Group
Uncle Buncle's House	C	56	Sunshine	Wright Group
Uncle Carlos's Barbecue	H	207	Foundations	Wright Group
Uncle Elephant	J	1784	Lobel, Arnold	HarperCollins

Title	Level	Words	Author/Series	Publisher/Distributor
Uncle Elephant and Uncle Tiger	D	77	Joy Readers	Dominie
Uncle Jim	G	127	Windmill Books	Rigby
Uncle Joe	H	149	Pacific Literacy	Pacific Learning
Uncle Timi's Sleep	G		Ready to Read	Pacific Learning
Uncles	D	36	Pebble Books	Grolier, Capstone
Uncle's Clever Tricks	D	61	Joy Readers	Dominie
Under a Microscope	H	254	Sunshine	Wright Group
Under My Bed	C	49	Little Celebrations	Pearson Learning
Under My Sombrero	F	79	Books for Young Learners	Richard C. Owen
Under the Bed	A	28	Smart Starts	Rigby
Under the Big Top	E	103	Twig	Wright Group
Under the City	K	206	Sunshine	Wright Group
Under the Ground	C	42	Foundations	Wright Group
Under Water	A	35	Twig	Wright Group
Underground	C	31	Twig	Wright Group
Underwater Journey	F	60	Sunshine	Wright Group
Unicorns Don't Give Sleigh Rides	M	250+	Dadey, Debbie & Jones, Marcia	Scholastic
Universal Solvent and Other Cases, The	O	250+	Simon, Seymour	Avon Books
Until We Got Princess	E	94	Book Shop	Mondo Publishing
Unusual Machines	J	229	Little Red Readers	Sundance
Up and Away! Taking a Flight	N	1195	Book Shop	Mondo Publishing
Up and Down	B	25	Little Books for Early Readers	University of Maine
Up and Down	D	92	New Way Red	Steck-Vaughn
Up and Down	E	79	Storyteller-Setting Sun	Wright Group/ McGraw-Hill
Up Close	G	123	Discovery Links	Newbridge
Up in a Tree	C	47	Sunshine	Wright Group
Up in the Air	P	250+	Wildcats	Wright Group
Up the Haystack	H	251	Book Shop	Mondo Publishing
Up the Tree	D	41	New Way Red	Steck-Vaughn
Up They Go	B	30	Ready Readers	Pearson Learning
Up Went Edmond	D	26	Pacific Literacy	Pacific Learning
Up Went the Goat	C	38	Gregorich, Barbara	School Zone
Upside-Down Reader, The	L	250+	Gruber, Wolfram	North-South Books
Use Your Beak!	F	106	Erickson, Betty	Seedling
Using the Library	L	291	Wonder World	Wright Group
Using Tools	C	30	Discovery Links	Newbridge
Using Wheels	G	115	Little Red Readers	Sundance
Vacation Journal, A	M	250+	Discovery World	Rigby
Vacation Under the Volcano	M	250+	Osborne, Mary Pope	Random House
Vacation, The	C	94	Emergent	Pioneer Valley
Vacations	B	22	Smart Starts	Rigby
Vagabond Crabs	J	117	Literacy 2000	Rigby
Valentine Star, The	M	250+	Giff, Patricia Reilly	Bantam Doubleday Dell
Valentine's Checkup	C	45	Little Books	Sadlier-Oxford
Valentine's Day	C	49	Story Box	Wright Group
Valentine's Day	E	132	Fiesta Holiday Series	Dominie
Vampire Trouble	L	250+	Dadey, Debbie & Jones, Marcia	Scholastic
Vampires Don't Wear Polka Dots	M	250+	Dadey, Debbie & Jones, Marcia	Scholastic
Very Big	D	49	Ready Readers	Pearson Learning
Very Busy Spider, The	I	263	Carle, Eric	Philomel

Title	Level	Words	Author/Series	Publisher/Distributor
Very Funny Act, A	H	181	Home Connection Collection	Rigby
Very Greedy Dog, The	H	228	Aesop's Fables	Dominie
Very Happy Birthday, A	M	1017	Jellybeans	Rigby
Very Hungry Caterpillar, The	J	237	Carle, Eric	Philomel
Very Strange Dollhouse, A	L	250+	Dussling, Jennifer	Grosset & Dunlap
Very Strong Baby, The	E	74	Joy Readers	Dominie
Very Thin Cat of Alloway Road, The	L		Literacy 2000	Rigby
Vicar of Nibbleswick, The	O	250+	Dahl, Roald	Puffin Books
Vicky the High Jumper	K		Literacy 2000	Rigby
Victor and the Kite	F	84	Oxford Reading Tree	Oxford University Press
Victor and the Martian	H	109	Oxford Reading Tree	Oxford University Press
Victor and the Sail-cart	H	94	Oxford Reading Tree	Oxford University Press
Victor Makes a TV	H	85	Reading Unlimited	Pacific Learning
Victor the Champion	G	102	Oxford Reading Tree	Oxford University Press
Victor the Hero	H	103	Oxford Reading Tree	Oxford University Press
Viking Ships at Sunrise	M	250+	Osborne, Mary Pope	Random House
Virtual Fred	O	250+	Courtney, Vincent	Random House
Visit to the Doctor, A	A	28	Little Books for Early Readers	University of Maine
Visit to the Library, A	E	109	Foundations	Wright Group
Visiting Grandma and Grandpa	G	136	Carousel Readers	Dominie
Visiting the Vet	H	259	Foundations	Wright Group
Visitors	E	46	Literacy 2000	Rigby
Volcano Goddess Will See You Now, The	M	250+	Greenburg, Dan	Grosset & Dunlap
Voyage, The	M	250+	Pair-It Books	Steck-Vaughn
Vultures on Vacation	C	36	Ready Readers	Pearson Learning
Wacky Jacks	L	250+	Adler, David	Random House
Wagon Ride, The	E	115	Teacher's Choice Series	Dominie
Wagon Wheels	K	250+	Brenner, Barbara	HarperTrophy
Wagon, The	H		Reading Unlimited	Pacific Learning
Wait for Me	C	75	Little Books	Sadlier-Oxford
Wait for Me	D	185	Visions	Wright Group
Wait for Your Turn!	H	141	Teacher's Choice Series	Dominie
Wait Skates	G	58	Rookie Readers	Children's Press
Waiting	A	28	Story Box	Wright Group
Waiting	E	75	Voyages	SRA/McGraw-Hill
Waiting	G	59	Literacy 2000	Rigby
Waiting for a Frog	G	124	Coats, Glenn	Kaeden Books
Waiting for the Rain	J	307	Foundations	Wright Group
Wake Me in Spring	J	301	Preller, James	Scholastic
Wake Up Mom!	C	94	Sunshine	Wright Group
Wake Up, Dad	C	67	PM Story Books	Rigby
Wake Up, Emily, It's Mother's Day	M	250+	Giff, Patricia Reilly	Yearling
Wake Up, Sleepyheads!	F	35	Little Books	Sadlier-Oxford
Wake Up, Sun!	E	250+	Harrison, David	Random House
Wake Up, Wake Up!	D		Wildsmith, B. & R.	Scholastic
Wake-Up, Baby!	J	209	Oppenheim, Joanna	Bantam Doubleday Dell
Walk	G		Reading Unlimited	Pacific Learning
Walk in the Rain, A	B	28	Pair-It Books	Steck-Vaughn
Walk with Grandpa, A	L	388	Read Alongs	Rigby
Walking in the Autumn	H	206	PM Nonfiction-Green	Rigby
Walking in the Spring	H	168	PM Nonfiction-Green	Rigby

Title	Level	Words	Author/Series	Publisher/Distributor
Walking in the Summer	H	233	PM Nonfiction-Green	Rigby
Walking in the Winter	H	251	PM Nonfiction-Green	Rigby
Walking the Road to Freedom	N	250+	Ferris, Jeri	Carolrhoda
Walking to School	C	38	Voyages	SRA/McGraw-Hill
Walking, Walking	C	32	Twig	Wright Group
Wall of Names: The Story of the Viet Vets Memorial	O	250+	Donnelly, Judy	Random House
Walter the Warlock	M	250+	Hautzig, Deborah	Random House
Wanted Dead or Alive: The True Story of H. Tubman	P	250+	McGovern, Ann	Scholastic
Warm Clothes	C	51	Pebble Books	Grolier, Capstone
Warming Up! Cooling Off!	I	553	Sunshine	Wright Group
Wash Day	B	35	Voyages	SRA/McGraw-Hill
Washing	F	150	Foundations	Wright Group
Washing the Dog	G	84	Little Red Readers	Sundance
Washing the Dog	G	84	Little Readers	Houghton Mifflin
Watch Me Zoom	C	45	Windmill Books	Rigby
Watch Out!	C	27	Literacy 2000	Rigby
Watch Out! Man-eating Snake	L	250+	Giff, Patricia Reilly	Bantam Doubleday Dell
Watching Every Drop	M	250+	Home Connection Collection	Rigby
Watching the Game	G	210	Momentum Literacy Program	Troll
Watching the Weather	G	142	Discovery Links	Newbridge
Watching the Whales	L	267	Foundations	Wright Group
Watching TV	B	18	Sunshine	Wright Group
Watching TV	D	89	Foundations	Wright Group
Water	B	24	Little Celebrations	Pearson Learning
Water	B	28	Literacy 2000	Rigby
Water	C	20	Carousel Readers	Dominie
Water	H	94	Wonder World	Wright Group
Water	J	250+	Momentum Literacy Program	Troll
Water Boatman, The	F	44	Ready to Read	Pacific Learning
Water Boatman, The	F	94	Pacific Literacy	Pacific Learning
Water Changes	D	36	Discovery Links	Newbridge
Water Falling	D	41	Literacy 2000	Rigby
Water Fight, The	E	64	Oxford Reading Tree	Oxford University Press
Water for the World	M	250+	Home Connection Collection	Rigby
Water Goes Up! Water Goes Down!	K	299	Early Connections	Benchmark Education
Water! Water!	C	33	Sunshine	Wright Group
Water! Water!	F	186	Story Basket	Wright Group
Waterhole	K	149	Planet Earth	Rigby
Watermelon	E	81	Rise & Shine	Hampton-Brown
Watermelon, The	D	80	Joy Readers	Dominie
Waves	E	70	Voyages	SRA/McGraw-Hill
Waves: The Changing Surface of the Sea	J	204	Wonder World	Wright Group
Waving Sheep, The	H	252	PM Story Books	Rigby
Wax Museum	L	250+	Cook, Donald	Grosset & Dunlap
Way I Go to School, The	B	53	PM Starters	Rigby
Wayside School Gets a Little Stranger	N	250+	Sachar, Louis	Avon Camelot
We All Play Sports	C	26	Pacific Literacy	Pacific Learning
We Are Best Friends	H	629	Aliki	Morrow
We Are Singing	B	26	Ready Readers	Pearson Learning
We Are Twins	A	24	Little Books for Early Readers	University of Maine
We Can	A	21	KinderReaders	Rigby

Title	Level	Words	Author/Series	Publisher/Distributor
We Can Make Pizza	A	30	Little Books for Early Readers	University of Maine
We Can Play	E	58	TOTTS	Tott Publications
We Can Run	C	77	PM Starters	Rigby
We Can Share It	H	140	Little Celebrations	Pearson Learning
We Care for Our School	I	134	Wonder World	Wright Group
We Dance	C	30	Pacific Literacy	Pacific Learning
We Go Out	A	41	PM Starters	Rigby
We Go to School	B	27	Carousel Earlybirds	Dominie
We Just Moved!	I	250+	Krensky, Stephen	Scholastic
We Like	C	42	Foundations	Wright Group
We Like Fish	D	109	PM Starters	Rigby
We Like the Sun	C	30	Pair-It Books	Steck-Vaughn
We Like to Graph	C	48	Coulton, Mia	Kaeden Books
We Love Recess	C	63	Fiesta Series	Dominie
We Make Cookies	E	48	Pair-It Books	Steck-Vaughn
We Make Music	D	44	Literacy 2000	Rigby
We Make Pizza	C	37	Carousel Readers	Dominie
We Need Trees	C	33	Hoenecke, Karen	Kaeden Books
We Ride	B	40	Carousel Earlybirds	Dominie
We Scream for Ice Cream	K	250+	Chardiet, Bernice & Maccarone, Grace	Scholastic
We Ski	B	35	Storyteller-First Snow	Wright Group/ McGraw-Hill
We Use Numbers	J	298	Early Connections	Benchmark Education
We Use Water	C	48	Early Connections	Benchmark Education
We Want That	F	158	Visions	Wright Group
We Went Flying	C	40	Carousel Earlybirds	Dominie
We Went to the Zoo	B	32	Little Red Readers	Sundance
We Wrote to Grandma	H	239	Momentum Literacy Program	Troll
Weather	A	14	Smart Starts	Rigby
Weather	C	54	Chanko, P. & Morton, D.	Scholastic
Weather	E	138	Early Connections	Benchmark Education
Weather Chart, The	B	24	Sunshine	Wright Group
Weather Poems for All Seasons	L	250+	Hopkins, Lee Bennett	HarperTrophy
Weather Watch	N	624	Wonders	Hampton-Brown
Wedding, The	F	50	Literacy 2000	Rigby
Wee Whopper	H	181	Windmill Books	Rigby
Week with Aunt Bea, A	D	62	Book Shop	Mondo Publishing
Well I Never	K	2517	Story Box	Wright Group
Well-fed Bear, The	E	35	Literacy 2000	Rigby
We're Going on a Bear Hunt	I	363	Rosen, Michael	Macmillan
We're in Big Trouble, Black Board Bear	I	250+	Alexander, Martha	Dial
We're Off to Thunder Mountain	L	270	Book Shop	Mondo Publishing
Werewolves Don't Go to Summer Camp	M	250+	Dadey, Debbie & Jones, Marcia	Scholastic
Wet Day at School, A	J	130	Sunshine	Wright Group
Wet Grass	H	188	Story Box	Wright Group
Wet Paint	E	92	Storyteller-Setting Sun	Wright Group/ McGraw-Hill
Whale Watch	B	27	Ready Readers	Pearson Learning
Whale Watchers, The	E	63	Windmill Books	Rigby
Whales	G	150	Foundations	Wright Group
Whales	N	1617	Book Shop	Mondo Publishing

Title	Level	Words	Author/Series	Publisher/Distributor
Whales	O	333	Wonder World	Wright Group
Whales on the Move	N	250+	Little Celebrations	Pearson Learning
Whales-The Gentle Giants	L	250+	Milton, Joyce	Random House
What a Bad Dog!	D	52	Oxford Reading Tree	Oxford University Press
What a Dog!	F	134	First Start	Troll
What a Dog!	H	223	Story Basket	Wright Group
What a Funny Thing to Do	K	236	Stepping Stones	Nelson/Michaels Assoc.
What a Mess	G	124	New Way Blue	Steck-Vaughn
What a Mess!	A	14	Smart Starts	Rigby
What a Mess!	C	51	Story Box	Wright Group
What a Noise!	I	165	Pacific Literacy	Pacific Learning
What a School	F	100	Salem, Lynn & Stewart, J.	Seedling
What a Tale!	C	38	Wildsmith, Brian	Oxford University Press
What a Week!	C	36	Home Connection Collection	Rigby
What Am I Going to Be?	H	111	Storyteller-Moon Rising	Wright Group/ McGraw-Hill
What Am I Made Of?	N	250+	Bennett, David	Scholastic
What Am I?	C	51	Williams, Deborah	Kaeden Books
What Am I?	G	124	Sunshine	Wright Group
What Am I?	I	100	Foundations	Wright Group
What Animal Lives Here?	O	250+	Woolley, M. & Pigdon, K.	Mondo
What Animals Do You See?	C	50	Read-More Books	Dominie
What Animals Eat	E	75	Little Red Readers	Sundance
What Are My Chances	J	393	Early Connections	Benchmark Education
What Are Purple Elephants Good For?	H	136	Reading Corners	Dominie
What Are We Doing?	A	21	KinderReaders	Rigby
What Are You Called?	C	66	Voyages	SRA/McGraw-Hill
What Are You Doing?	D	101	Foundations	Wright Group
What Are You Going to Buy?	F	180	Read Alongs	Rigby
What Are You?	A	27	Literacy 2000	Rigby
What Bear Cubs Like to Do	I	83	Little Books	Sadlier-Oxford
What Came Out of My Bean?	H	158	Book Bank	Wright Group
What Can Change?	G	96	Discovery Links	Newbridge
What Can Float?	B	27	Ready Readers	Pearson Learning
What Can Float?	C	32	Windmill Books	Rigby
What Can Fly?	B	28	Literacy 2000	Rigby
What Can Fly?	B	29	Discovery Links	Newbridge
What Can Fly?	C	33	Joy Readers	Dominie
What Can Hurt?	C	30	Windmill Books	Rigby
What Can I Do?	C	42	Read-More Books	Dominie
What Can I Do?	C	42	Foundations	Wright Group
What Can I Read?	A	28	Carousel Earlybirds	Dominie
What Can I See?	C	42	Foundations	Wright Group
What Can It Be?	F	113	Storyteller-First Snow	Wright Group/ McGraw-Hill
What Can Jigarees Do?	A	22	Story Box	Wright Group
What Can Jump?	A	32	Windmill Books	Rigby
What Can She Do?	A	21	Little Books for Early Readers	University of Maine
What Can Swim?	A	30	Windmill Books	Rigby
What Can This Animal Do?	B	28	Foundations	Wright Group
What Can We Do Today?	G	146	Carousel Readers	Dominie
What Can We Smell?	C	44	Windmill Books	Rigby

Title	Level	Words	Author/Series	Publisher/Distributor
What Can You Do with a Ball of String?	G	250+	Home Connection Collection	Rigby
What Can You Make?	B	22	Ready Readers	Pearson Learning
What Can You See?	C	25	Literacy 2000	Rigby
What Can You Taste?	B	45	Windmill Books	Rigby
What Comes First?	C	56	Book Shop	Mondo Publishing
What Comes from a Cow?	G	85	Sunshine	Wright Group
What Comes in Twos?	D	125	Early Connections	Benchmark Education
What Comes Out at Night?	B	48	Little Red Readers	Sundance
What Could I Be?	C	64	Foundations	Wright Group
What Did Ben Want?	A	28	Smart Starts	Rigby
What Did I Forget?	D	43	Teacher's Choice Series	Dominie
What Did I Use?	D	65	Discovery World	Rigby
What Did Kim Catch?	C	48	Literacy 2000	Rigby
What Did They Want?	C	28	Smart Starts	Rigby
What Did You Bring?	B	23	Ready Readers	Pearson Learning
What Dinosaurs Ate	F	44	Planet Earth	Rigby
What Do I See in the Garden?	F	108	Wonder World	Wright Group
What Do I See?	B	28	Twig	Wright Group
What Do Insects Do?	A	24	Canizares, Susan & Chanko, Pamela	Scholastic
What Do Scientists Do?	B	24	Twig	Wright Group
What Do Scientists Do?	H	79	Discovery Links	Newbridge
What Do We Have to Get?	E	117	Ready Readers	Pearson Learning
What Do We Have?	C	28	Step-By-Step Series	Dominie
What Do You Do?	G	125	Little Celebrations	Pearson Learning
What Do You Have?	C	88	Windmill Books	Rigby
What Do You Hear When Cows Sing?	J	250+	Maestro, Marco & Giulio	HarperTrophy
What Do You Hear?	D	60	Windmill Books	Rigby
What Do You Like to Eat?	D	99	Foundations	Wright Group
What Do You Like to Wear?	D	50	Read-More Books	Dominie
What Do You Like?	B	52	Little Books for Early Readers	University of Maine
What Do You See at the Pet Store?	C	27	Read-More Books	Dominie
What Do You See by the Sea?	A	14	Little Books	Sadlier-Oxford
What Do You See?	C	35	Windmill Books	Rigby
What Do You Think?	L	250+	Wildcats	Wright Group
What Do You Touch?	C	50	Windmill Books	Rigby
What Does a Garden Need?	G	118	Discovery Links	Newbridge
What Does Greedy Cat Like?	C	35	Pacific Literacy	Pacific Learning
What Does Lucy Like?	A	11	Little Books	Sadlier-Oxford
What Else?	I	154	Sunshine	Wright Group
What Feels Cold?	B	30	Windmill Books	Rigby
What Feels Hot?	A	28	Windmill Books	Rigby
What Feels Sticky	B	26	Windmill Books	Rigby
What Fell Out?	D	32	Carousel Readers	Dominie
What Floats?	C	16	Twig	Wright Group
What Game Shall We Play?	H	306	Hutchins, Pat	Sundance
What Gives You Goose Bumps?	H	140	Home Connection Collection	Rigby
What Goes Around and Around?	B	46	Windmill Books	Rigby
What Goes in the Bathtub?	C	31	Literacy 2000	Rigby
What Goes into a Salad?	C	22	Home Connection Collection	Rigby
What Goes Up and Down	C	40	Windmill Books	Rigby
What Goes Up High?	A	38	Windmill Books	Rigby
What Grows on Trees?	E	49	Start to Read	School Zone

Title	Level	Words	Author/Series	Publisher/Distributor
What Hangs from the Tree?	C	42	Questions & Answers	Dominie
What Happens When You Recycle?	K	215	Discovery World	Rigby
What Has Spots?	B	33	Literacy 2000	Rigby
What Has Stripes?	C	25	Ballinger, Margaret	Scholastic
What Has Wheels?	A	28	Hoenecke, Karen	Kaeden Books
What Has Wings?	H	250+	Momentum Literacy Program	Troll
What Helps a Bird to Fly?	F	95	Birds Series	Dominie
What I Left on My Plate	C	54	Teacher's Choice Series	Dominie
What I Like at School	C	64	Little Red Readers	Sundance
What I Like to Wear	D	93	Home Connection Collection	Rigby
What I Would Do	I	173	Read Alongs	Rigby
What I'd Like to Be	F	112	Little Red Readers	Sundance
What If...	E	57	Teacher's Choice Series	Dominie
What If?	C	41	Little Celebrations	Pearson Learning
What Is a Fly?	M	561	Sunshine	Wright Group
What Is a Huggles?	B	41	Sunshine	Wright Group
What Is a Park?	H	138	Discovery World	Rigby
What Is a Reptile?	M	183	Now I Know	Troll
What Is at the Top?	E	197	Ready Readers	Pearson Learning
What Is Bat?	G	136	Literacy 2000	Rigby
What Is Big?	D	72	Armstrong, Shane & Hartley, S.	Scholastic
What Is Blue?	C	31	Carousel Earlybirds	Dominie
What Is Delicious?	C	25	Windmill Books	Rigby
What Is Enormous	B	33	Windmill Books	Rigby
What Is Fast?	A	30	Windmill Books	Rigby
What Is Fierce?	B	32	Windmill Books	Rigby
What Is Fun?	C	34	Windmill Books	Rigby
What Is Green?	B	30	Carousel Earlybirds	Dominie
What Is He Looking For?	A	42	KinderReaders	Rigby
What Is in Space?	C	41	Science	Wright Group
What Is in the Closet?	E	107	Story Box	Wright Group
What Is It Called?	D		Reading Unlimited	Pacific Learning
What Is It?	E	69	Storyteller-First Snow	Wright Group/ McGraw-Hill
What Is It?	F	135	Foundations	Wright Group
What Is Little?	A	22	Rise & Shine	Hampton-Brown
What Is Noisy?	B	31	Windmill Books	Rigby
What Is Old?	C	32	Windmill Books	Rigby
What Is Red?	B	27	Carousel Earlybirds	Dominie
What Is Red?	B	30	Literacy 2000	Rigby
What Is Scary?	B	31	Windmill Books	Rigby
What Is Slippery?	B	26	Windmill Books	Rigby
What Is Slow?	C	29	Windmill Books	Rigby
What Is Soft?	C	30	Windmill Books	Rigby
What Is Tall?	B	30	Windmill Books	Rigby
What Is That?	C	61	Ready Readers	Pearson Learning
What Is That? Said the Cat	F	118	Maccarone, Grace	Scholastic
What Is the Weather Today?	H	250+	Momentum Literacy Program	Troll
What Is This Skeleton?	C	48	Science	Wright Group
What Is This?	A	25	Little Books for Early Readers	University of Maine
What Is This?	A	29	KinderReaders	Rigby
What Is This?	C	28	Ready Readers	Pearson Learning

Title	Level	Words	Author/Series	Publisher/Distributor
What Is Under the Hat?	B	29	Ready Readers	Pearson Learning
What Is White?	B	26	Carousel Earlybirds	Dominie
What Is Yellow?	B	26	Carousel Earlybirds	Dominie
What Is Young?	C	31	Windmill Books	Rigby
What Joy Found	L	250+	Ready Readers	Pearson Learning
What Keeps Them Warm?	L	156	Pacific Literacy	Pacific Learning
What Kind of Babysitter Is This?	L	250+	Johnson, Dolores	Scholastic
What Kind of Dog Am I?	C	21	Twig	Wright Group
What Lays Eggs?	D	56	Storyteller Nonfiction	Wright Group/ McGraw-Hill
What Lays Eggs?	I	216	Momentum Literacy Program	Troll
What Made Teddalik Laugh	M	250+	Folk Tales	Wright Group
What Makes a Bird a Bird?	N	250+	Garelick, May	Mondo
What Makes Light?	F	119	Sunshine	Wright Group
What Mynah Bird Saw	F	90	Sunshine	Wright Group
What Next, Baby Bear?	L	313	Murphy, Jill	Dial
What Next?	F	277	Story Basket	Wright Group
What on Earth?	I	133	Sunshine	Wright Group
What People Do	D	113	Early Connections	Benchmark Education
What People Do	H	148	Little Red Readers	Sundance
What Plays Music?	C	36	Questions & Answers	Dominie
What Rhymes With...	A	9	Ready Readers	Pearson Learning
What Season Is This?	C	24	Wonder World	Wright Group
What Shall I Do?	M	584	Sunshine	Wright Group
What Shall I Wear?	E	58	Book Bank	Wright Group
What Smells Good?	C	26	Windmill Books	Rigby
What Things Go Together	E	26	Literacy 2000	Rigby
What Tommy Did	E	125	Literacy 2000	Rigby
What Was This?	F	53	Wonder World	Wright Group
What Will You Pack?	B	35	Ready Readers	Pearson Learning
What Would the Zoo Do?	D	59	Salem, Lynn	Seedling
What Would You Do?	G	272	Book Bank	Wright Group
What Would You Do?	J	160	Sunshine	Wright Group
What Would You Like?	D	52	Sunshine	Wright Group
Whatever Am I Going to Do Now?	M	250+	Little Celebrations	Pearson Learning
Whatever Will These Become	E	47	Literacy 2000	Rigby
What's Alive?	D	53	Discovery Links	Newbridge
What's Behind This Door?	B	43	Twig	Wright Group
What's Black and White and Moos?	E	78	Twig	Wright Group
What's Cooking	H	287	Book Shop	Mondo Publishing
What's Cooking, Jenny Archer?	M	250+	Conford, Ellen	Little, Brown & Co.
What's for Dinner, Dad?	K	459	Sunshine	Wright Group
What's for Dinner?	B	35	Hoenecke, Karen	Kaeden Books
What's for Dinner?	E	112	Salem, Lynn & Stewart, J.	Seedling
What's for Lunch	E	91	New Way Red	Steck-Vaughn
What's for Lunch?	B	42	Story Box	Wright Group
What's for Lunch?	C	48	Carle, Eric	Scholastic
What's for Lunch?	D	49	Rise & Shine	Hampton-Brown
What's for Lunch?	H	169	Ready Readers	Pearson Learning
What's in the Bag?	E	98	Visions	Wright Group
What's in This Egg?	A	16	Sunshine	Wright Group
What's Inside?	C	47	Hoenecke, Karen	Kaeden Books

Title	Level	Words	Author/Series	Publisher/Distributor
What's Inside?	G	50	Foundations	Wright Group
What's Inside?	K	238	Wonder World	Wright Group
What's It For?	D	47	Visions	Wright Group
What's It Like to Be a Fish?	L	250+	Little Readers	Houghton Mifflin
What's Missing?	K	252	Book Bank	Wright Group
What's on My Farm?	B	38	Rise & Shine	Hampton-Brown
What's on Your T-Shirt?	C	64	Carousel Readers	Dominie
What's Round?	A	14	Discovery Links	Newbridge
What's That Smell?	H	56	Pacific Literacy	Pacific Learning
What's That?	B	28	Sunshine	Wright Group
What's That?	C	27	Carousel Earlybirds	Dominie
What's the Big Idea, Ben Franklin?	O	250+	Fritz, Jean	Scholastic
What's the Matter with Herbie Jones?	O	250+	Kline, Suzy	Puffin Books
What's the Matter, Kelly Beans?	N	250+	Enderle, Judith & Tessler, Stephanie	Candlewick Press
What's the Time Mr Wolf?	C	49	Windmill	Wright Group
What's Under My Bed?	C	18	Visions	Wright Group
What's Under the Ocean	H		Now I Know	Troll
What's Underneath?	K	200	Discovery World	Rigby
What's Up?	B	26	Pacific Literacy	Pacific Learning
Wheel, The	C	102	Joy Readers	Dominie
Wheels	C	27	Literacy 2000	Rigby
Wheels	C	29	Discovery Links	Newbridge
Wheels	C	39	Sunshine	Wright Group
Wheels	D	49	Rise & Shine	Hampton-Brown
Wheels	D	69	Cobb, Annie	Random House
Wheels on the Bus	I	362	Kovalski, Mary Ann	Little, Brown & Co.
When Bob Woke Up Late	G	139	Ready Readers	Pearson Learning
When Dad Came Home	F	46	Literacy 2000	Rigby
When Dad Went to Daycare	H	211	Sunshine	Wright Group
When Do Cars Stop?	C	62	Questions & Answers	Dominie
When Do You Feel	F	132	Twig	Wright Group
When Goldilocks Went to the House of the Bears	F	156	Book Shop	Mondo Publishing
When I Broke the Office Window	L	257	City Kids	Rigby
When I Get Bigger	K	205	Mayer, Mercer	Donovan
When I Go See Gram	G	123	Ready Readers	Pearson Learning
When I Grow Up	C	38	Rise & Shine	Hampton-Brown
When I Look Up	B	55	Foundations	Wright Group
When I Play	C	31	Literacy 2000	Rigby
When I Pretend	C	40	Literacy 2000	Rigby
When I Was Sick	F	53	Literacy 2000	Rigby
When I'm Older	F	156	Literacy 2000	Rigby
When It Rains	C	39	Foundations	Wright Group
When It Rains	E	36	Voyages	SRA/McGraw-Hill
When It Rains	F	106	Frankford, Marilyn	Kaeden Books
When It Snowed	C	33	Home Connection Collection	Rigby
When Itchy Witchy Sneezes	C	39	Sunshine	Wright Group
When Jose Hits That Ball	G	45	Pacific Literacy	Pacific Learning
When Lana Was Absent	F	78	Tadpoles	Rigby
When Lincoln Was a Boy	F	132	Twig	Wright Group
When Mr. Quinn Snored	C	31	Little Books	Sadlier-Oxford
When My Dad Came to School	M	230	City Kids	Rigby
When Robins Sing	H	238	Twig	Wright Group

Title	Level	Words	Author/Series	Publisher/Distributor
When the Circus Comes to Town	A	40	Little Red Readers	Sundance
When the Giants Came to Town	L	250+	Leonard, Marcia	Scholastic
When the King Rides By	J	247	Book Shop	Mondo Publishing
When the Moon Was Blue	I	174	Literacy 2000	Rigby
When the Sun Goes Down	G	109	Wonder World	Wright Group
When the Volcano Erupted	J	262	PM Story Books-Turquoise	Rigby
When Tony Got Lost at the Zoo	L	122	City Kids	Rigby
When We Are Big	E	123	Ready Readers	Pearson Learning
When Will I Read?	I	250+	Cohen, Miriam	Bantam Doubleday Dell
When Will We Be Sisters?	K	250+	Kroll, Virginia	Scholastic
When You Were a Baby	G	104	Jonas, Ann	Morrow
Where Are My Socks?	D	42	Ready to Read	Pacific Learning
Where Are My Socks?	D	42	Pacific Literacy	Pacific Learning
Where Are the Babies?	B	8	PM Starters	Rigby
Where Are the Bears?	K	250+	Winters, Kay	Bantam Doubleday Dell
Where Are the Car Keys?	B	36	Windmill	Wright Group
Where Are the Eggs?	F	152	Discovery Links	Newbridge
Where Are the Seeds?	D	67	Wonder World	Wright Group
Where Are the Sunhats?	D	130	PM Story Books	Rigby
Where Are They Going?	C	42	Story Box	Wright Group
Where Are We?	B	72	Early Emergent	Pioneer Valley
Where Are You Going, Aja Rose?	D	100	Sunshine	Wright Group
Where Are You Going, Little Mouse?	H	148	Kraus, Robert	Greenwillow
Where Are You Going?	B	42	KinderReaders	Rigby
Where Are You Going?	D	66	Learn to Read	Creative Teaching Press
Where Can a Hippo Hide?	D	41	Ready Readers	Pearson Learning
Where Can It Be?	E	83	Jonas, Ann	Morrow
Where Can Kitty Sleep?	B	15	Windmill	Wright Group
Where Can Teddy Go?	E	141	Foundations	Wright Group
Where Can We Go from Here?	F	54	Spinelle, Nancy Louise	Kaeden Books
Where Can We Put an Elephant?	B	48	Windmill	Wright Group
Where Did They Go?	D	102	Teacher's Choice Series	Dominie
Where Do Bugs Live?	D	33	Pair-It Books	Steck-Vaughn
Where Do I Live?	C	29	Visions	Wright Group
Where Do Monsters Live?	C	56	Learn to Read	Creative Teaching Press
Where Do They Live?	C	45	Ready Readers	Pearson Learning
Where Do We Go?	B	22	Ready Readers	Pearson Learning
Where Do You Play?	D	131	Twig	Wright Group
Where Does a Leopard Hide?	C	108	Foundations	Wright Group
Where Does Breakfast Come From?	H	170	Discovery World	Rigby
Where Does It Go?	C	61	Questions & Answers	Dominie
Where Does the Rabbit Hop?	E	71	Ready Readers	Pearson Learning
Where Does the Teacher Sleep?	C	50	Gibson, Kathleen	Seedling
Where Does the Wind Go?	M	95	Book Shop	Mondo Publishing
Where I Live	B	36	Carousel Earlybirds	Dominie
Where in the World Is the Perfect Family?	P	250+	Hest, Amy	The Penguin Group
Where Is Daniel?	E	135	Carousel Readers	Dominie
Where Is Hannah?	D	141	PM Extensions-Red	Rigby
Where Is Happy Monkey?	C	46	Joy Readers	Dominie
Where Is It?	B	21	Ready Readers	Pearson Learning
Where Is Jake?	E	35	My First Reader	Grolier Press
Where Is Kate's Skate?	D	46	KinderReaders	Rigby

Title	Level	Words	Author/Series	Publisher/Distributor
Where Is Lunch?	B	25	Pacific Literacy	Pacific Learning
Where Is Miss Pool?	D	55	Ready to Read	Pacific Learning
Where Is Miss Pool?	D	55	Pacific Literacy	Pacific Learning
Where Is My Bone?	C	42	Sunshine	Wright Group
Where Is My Caterpillar?	H	277	Wonder World	Wright Group
Where Is My Grandma?	C	74	Foundations	Wright Group
Where Is My Pencil?	C	34	Little Celebrations	Pearson Learning
Where Is My Pet?	A	34	Literacy 2000	Rigby
Where Is My Teacher?	B	43	Little Books for Early Readers	University of Maine
Where Is Nancy?	E	56	Literacy 2000	Rigby
Where Is She?	A	35	Little Books for Early Readers	University of Maine
Where Is Skunk?	D	65	Story Box	Wright Group
Where Is Teddy's Head?	A	27	Windmill	Wright Group
Where Is the Bear?	K	250+	Nims, Bonnie	Whitman
Where Is the Cat?	C	28	Read-More Books	Dominie
Where Is the Milk?	D	87	Foundations	Wright Group
Where Is the Queen?	H	109	Ready Readers	Pearson Learning
Where Is the School Bus?	D	40	Carousel Readers	Dominie
Where Is Water?	C	36	Twig	Wright Group
Where Jeans Come From	K	250+	Ready Readers	Pearson Learning
Where People Live	J	259	Early Connections	Benchmark Education
Where the Wild Things Are	J	339	Sendak, Maurice	Harper & Row
Where Will I Sit?	F	78	Teacher's Choice Series	Dominie
Where Will You Sleep Tonight?	C	77	Foundations	Wright Group
Where's Al?	D	49	Barton, Byron	Houghton Mifflin
Where's Baby Tom?	D	91	Book Bank	Wright Group
Where's Bear?	C	41	Windmill	Wright Group
Where's Cupcake?	D	71	Little Readers	Houghton Mifflin
Where's Little Mole?	C	43	Little Celebrations	Pearson Learning
Where's Lulu?	I	250+	Hooks, William H.	Bantam Doubleday Dell
Where's My Backpack?	C	27	Little Celebrations	Pearson Learning
Where's My Daddy?	F		Watanabe, Shigeo	Putnam
Where's Spot?	E	65	Hill, Eric	Putnam
Where's Sylvester's bed?	F	78	Wonder World	Wright Group
Where's the Dog?	B	36	Windmill Books	Rigby
Where's the Egg Cup?	B	25	Windmill	Wright Group
Where's the Fish?	B	39	Gomi, Taro	Morrow
Where's the Frog?	D	46	Discovery Links	Newbridge
Where's the Halloween Treat?	C	102	Ziefert, Harriet	The Penguin Group
Where's the Puppy?	D		Dwight, Laura	Checkerboard
Where's Tim?	C	38	Sunshine	Wright Group
Where's Tony?	J	114	City Kids	Rigby
Where's Your Tooth?	C	53	Learn to Read	Creative Teaching Press
Which Animal Is That?	I	250+	Momentum Literacy Program	Troll
Which Animal?	B	14	Foundations	Wright Group
Which Clothes Do You Wear?	C	49	Foundations	Wright Group
Which Egg Is Mine?	D	65	Rise & Shine	Hampton-Brown
Which Hat Today?	E	94	Ballinger, Margaret & Gossett, R.	Scholastic
Which Is Heavier	D	51	Questions & Answers	Dominie
Which Juice Would You Like?	C	28	Step-By-Step Series	Dominie
Which One Is Which?	G	187	Sunshine	Wright Group
Which Toys?	D	40	Home Connection Collection	Rigby

Title	Level	Words	Author/Series	Publisher/Distributor
Which Way Home?	C	26	Little Celebrations	Pearson Learning
Whipping Boy, The	O	250+	Fleischman, Sid	Troll
Whiskers	A	32	Wonder World	Wright Group
Whisper and Shout	C	92	Twig	Wright Group
Whistle for Willie	L	380	Keats, Ezra Jack	The Penguin Group
Whistle Like a Bird	D	53	Pair-It Books	Steck-Vaughn
Whistle Tooth, The	H	188	Storyteller-Night Crickets	Wright Group/ McGraw-Hill
White Bird	N	250+	Bulla, Clyde Robert	Random House
White Horse, The	K		Literacy 2000	Rigby
White Paw, Black Paw	C	41	KinderReaders	Rigby
White Wednesday	H	321	Literacy 2000	Rigby
Whizz! Click!	L	285	Pacific Literacy	Pacific Learning
Who Am I ?	D	81	Rise & Shine	Hampton-Brown
Who Am I?	E		Christensen, Nancy	Scholastic
Who Are We?	C	30	Home Connection Collection	Rigby
Who Are You?	C	55	Book Bank	Wright Group
Who Ate the Broccoli?	E	42	Little Readers	Houghton Mifflin
Who Ate the Pizza?	C	59	Foundations	Wright Group
Who Came By Here?	C	31	Rise & Shine	Hampton-Brown
Who Came Out?	F	45	Ready Readers	Pearson Learning
Who Can Hop?	C	35	Questions & Answers	Dominie
Who Can See the Camel?	C	70	Story Box	Wright Group
Who Can?	B	35	Book Shop	Mondo Publishing
Who Cried for Pie?	D	86	First Start	Troll
Who Goes Out on Halloween?	G		Alexander, Sue	Bantam Doubleday Dell
Who Has a Tail?	G	186	Ready Readers	Pearson Learning
Who Has Wings?	C	30	Questions & Answers	Dominie
Who Is Coming?	E	28	Rookie Readers	Children's Press
Who Is Ready?	C	36	Ready Readers	Pearson Learning
Who Is the Robot?	C	67	Pacific Literacy	Pacific Learning
Who Is the Tallest?	D	46	Sunshine	Wright Group
Who Is Who?	D	115	Rookie Readers	Children's Press
Who Lays Eggs?	G	132	Twig	Wright Group
Who Likes Ice Cream?	A	15	Literacy 2000	Rigby
Who Likes the Cold?	A	29	Twig	Wright Group
Who Likes to Swim?	D	100	Teacher's Choice Series	Dominie
Who Likes Water?	B	35	KinderReaders	Rigby
Who Lives Here?	C	28	Story Box	Wright Group
Who Lives Here?	C	42	Questions & Answers	Dominie
Who Lives Here?	C	62	Learn to Read	Creative Teaching Press
Who Lives Here?	F	185	Storyteller Nonfiction	Wright Group/ McGraw-Hill
Who Lives Here?	I	230	Little Readers	Houghton Mifflin
Who Lives in a Tree?	B	46	Canizares, Susan & Morton, Daniel	Scholastic
Who Lives in a Tree?	C	43	Discovery Links	Newbridge
Who Lives in the Arctic?	B	48	Canizares, Susan & Chanko, Pamela	Scholastic
Who Lives in the Sea?	B	69	Book Shop	Mondo Publishing
Who Lives in the Woods?	F	110	Pair-It Books	Steck-Vaughn
Who Lives in this Hole?	C	25	Twig	Wright Group
Who Loves Getting Wet?	I	204	Sunshine	Wright Group
Who Made That?	C	31	Ready Readers	Pearson Learning

Title	Level	Words	Author/Series	Publisher/Distributor
Who Made These Tracks?	B	24	Literacy 2000	Rigby
Who Made These Tracks?	D	45	Teacher's Choice Series	Dominie
Who Pushed Humpty?	K		Literacy 2000	Rigby
Who Reads?	B	25	Teacher's Choice Series	Dominie
Who Rides the Bus?	C	19	Little Celebrations	Pearson Learning
Who Sank the Boat?	K	219	Allen Pamela	Coward
Who Says?	C	49	Twig	Wright Group
Who Says?	D	36	My First Reader	Grolier Press
Who Shot the President?	P	250+	Donnelly, Judy	Random House
Who Spilled the Beans?	E	87	Story Basket	Wright Group
Who Took the Farmer's Hat	I	340	Nodset, Joan	Scholastic
Who Uses These Tools?	B	23	Twig	Wright Group
Who Wants One?	I		Serfozo, Mary	Macmillan
Who Wants to Live in My House?	D	60	Book Bank	Wright Group
Who Wants to See the Doctor?	F	116	Adventures in Reading	Dominie
Who Wears This Hat?	B	42	Windmill	Wright Group
Who Will Be My Friends?	F	205	Hoff, Syd	HarperTrophy
Who Will Be My Mother?	E	156	Read-Togethers	Wright Group
Who Will Help Me?	C	53	Home Connection Collection	Rigby
Who Will Help?	B	20	Carousel Readers	Dominie
Who Will Help?	D	93	Learn to Read	Creative Teaching Press
Who Will Help?	F	74	New Way Red	Steck-Vaughn
Who Will Win the Race?	D	53	Sunshine	Wright Group
Who Works Here?	D	57	Questions & Answers	Dominie
Who?	E	46	Storyteller-Setting Sun	Wright Group/ McGraw-Hill
Whoops!	E	49	Little Celebrations	Pearson Learning
Who's a Pest?	J	250+	Bonsall, Crosby	HarperTrophy
Who's Afraid of the Big, Bad Bully?	K	250+	Slater, Teddy	Scholastic
Who's Afraid of the Dark?	I	250+	Bonsall, Crosby	HarperTrophy
Who's Afraid?	I		Reading Unlimited	Pacific Learning
Who's Coming for a Ride?	B	25	Literacy 2000	Rigby
Who's Going to Lick the Bowl?	C	18	Story Box	Wright Group
Who's Hiding?	D	51	Learn to Read	Creative Teaching Press
Who's in Love with Arthur?	M	250+	Brown, Marc	Little, Brown & Co.
Who's in the Jungle?	F	116	Ready Readers	Pearson Learning
Who's in the Nest?	E	75	Start to Read	School Zone
Who's in the Shed?	I	202	Traditional Tales & More	Rigby
Who's Looking After the Baby?	H	127	Foundations	Wright Group
Who's There?	E	92	Story Box	Wright Group
Whose Birthday Is It Today?	C	50	Book Bank	Wright Group
Whose Eggs Are These?	E	125	Sunshine	Wright Group
Whose Forest Is It?	C	45	Learn to Read	Creative Teaching Press
Whose List Is This?	C		Little Celebrations	Pearson Learning
Whose Mouse Are You?	H	98	Kraus, Robert	Macmillan
Whose Shoes?	D	84	Twig	Wright Group
Whose Tracks?	B	14	Little Celebrations	Pearson Learning
Why Can't I Fly	G	449	Gelman, Rita	Scholastic
Why Cats Wash After Dinner	I	128	Pacific Literacy	Pacific Learning
Why Coyote Howls at Night	K	274	Little Books	Sadlier-Oxford
Why Crocodiles Live in Rivers	M	415	Sunshine	Wright Group
Why Cry?	G	121	Sunshine	Wright Group

Title	Level	Words	Author/Series	Publisher/Distributor
Why Do I Feel Safe?	D	61	Questions & Answers	Dominie
Why Do I Need to Know When?	G	198	Visions	Wright Group
Why Elephants Have Long Noses	G	175	Literacy 2000	Rigby
Why the Bear's Tail Is Short	J	431	Sunshine	Wright Group
Why the Kangaroo Hops	K	391	Sunshine	Wright Group
Why the Leopard Has Spots	L	250+	Pair-It Books	Steck-Vaughn
Why the Sea Is Salty	L		Literacy 2000	Rigby
Why There Are Shooting Stars	K	362	Pacific Literacy	Pacific Learning
Why?	D	68	Twig	Wright Group
Wibble Wobble, Albatross	H	101	Ready to Read	Pacific Learning
Wibble Wobble, Albatross!	H	101	Pacific Literacy	Pacific Learning
Wibble-Wobble	H	263	Storyteller-Night Crickets	Wright Group/ McGraw-Hill
Wicked Pirates, The	I	226	Sunshine	Wright Group
Wide Street Club and Molly, The	K	965	Sunshine	Wright Group
Wide Street Club and the Duck Man, The	L	1057	Sunshine	Wright Group
Wide-mouthed Frog, The	E	121	Literacy 2000	Rigby
Wiggly Worm	G	115	Literacy 2000	Rigby
Wiggly, Jiggly, Joggly, Tooth, A	E	61	Little Celebrations	Pearson Learning
Wilbert Took a Walk	H	216	Ready Readers	Pearson Learning
Wild Baby Animals	N	250+	Little Celebrations	Pearson Learning
Wild Bear	A	21	Pacific Literacy	Pacific Learning
Wild Culpepper Cruise, The	O	250+	Paulsen, Gary	Bantam Doubleday Dell
Wild Pony, The	O	250+	Betancourt, Jeanne	Scholastic
Wild Swans, The	L	754	Tales from Hans Andersen	Wright Group
Wild Wet Wellington Wind	I	104	Ready to Read	Pacific Learning
Wild Willie and King Kyle Detectives	N	250+	Joosse, Barbara M.	Bantam Doubleday Dell
Wild, Wooly Child, The	J	315	Read Alongs	Rigby
Wildlife Helpers	G	132	Twig	Wright Group
Will It Rain on the Parade?	H	102	Wonder World	Wright Group
Will You Play with Us?	D	62	Book Shop	Mondo Publishing
William, Where Are You?	F	239	Gerstein, Mordicai	Crown
William's Skateboard	G	100	Windmill	Wright Group
William's Wheelchair Race	K	279	Sunshine	Wright Group
Willie the Slowpoke	G	125	First Start	Troll
Willie's Wonderful Pet	I	315	Cebulash, Mel	Scholastic
Willy the Helper	D	79	Little Readers	Houghton Mifflin
Willy's Hats	E	65	Stewart, J. & Salem, Lynn	Seedling
Wilma's Wagon	D	48	Ready Readers	Pearson Learning
Wind and Storms	K	868	Sunshine	Wright Group
Wind and Sun	G	170	Literacy 2000	Rigby
Wind and Sun	I	238	Sunshine	Wright Group
Wind and the Sun, The	J	250+	New Way Orange	Steck-Vaughn
Wind Blew, The	L	169	Hutchins, Pat	Puffin Books
Wind Blows Strong, The	E	114	Sunshine	Wright Group
Wind Eagle, The	K	370	Wonders	Hampton-Brown
Wind Power	J	103	Ready to Read	Pacific Learning
Wind Power	J	103	Pacific Literacy	Pacific Learning
Wind Surfing	D	224	Sunshine	Wright Group
Wind, The	D	34	Wonder World	Wright Group
Wind, The	E	36	Discovery Links	Newbridge
Wind, The	E	64	Ready to Read	Pacific Learning

Title	Level	Words	Author/Series	Publisher/Distributor
Wind, The	E	64	Pacific Literacy	Pacific Learning
Wind, The	F	84	Voyages	SRA/McGraw-Hill
Wingman	O	250+	Pinkwater, Daniel	Bantam Skylark
Wingman on Ice	M	250+	Christopher, Matt	Little, Brown & Co.
Wings	A	14	KinderReaders	Rigby
Winklepoo the Wicked	M	1614	Sunshine	Wright Group
Winter	C	49	Carousel Readers	Dominie
Winter	C	54	Foundations	Wright Group
Winter	E	56	Discovery Links	Newbridge
Winter	H	172	Storyteller-Setting Sun	Wright Group/ McGraw-Hill
Winter	I	240	Pebble Books	Grolier, Capstone
Winter Fun	C	13	Teacher's Choice Series	Dominie
Winter Is Here	D	55	Weinberger, Kimberly	Scholastic
Winter Sleeps	F	158	Reading Corners	Dominie
Winter Wind, The	H	250+	Momentum Literacy Program	Troll
Winter Woollies	K	289	Storyteller Nonfiction	Wright Group/ McGraw-Hill
Winter's Song	H	233	Ready Readers	Pearson Learning
Wishing for a Horse	D	105	Carousel Earlybirds	Dominie
Wishy-Washy Day	E	65	Story Basket	Wright Group
Witch Hunt: It Happened in Salem Village	N	250+	Krensky, Stephen	Random House
Witches Don't Do Backflips	M	250+	Dadey, Debbie & Jones, Marcia	Scholastic
Witch's Cat	P	250+	Chew, Ruth	Scholastic
Witch's Haircut, The	G	135	Windmill	Wright Group
With My Mom and Dad	C	63	Early Connections	Benchmark Education
Wizard and Wart at Sea	J	250+	Smith, Janice Lee	HarperTrophy
Wizard of Earthsea, The	C		Voyages	SRA/McGraw-Hill
Wizard of Oz, The	L	903	Hunia, Fran	Ladybird Books
Wizards Don't Need Computers	M	250+	Dadey, Debbie & Jones, Marcia	Scholastic
Wobbly Tooth, The	D	102	Literacy 2000	Rigby
Wobbly Tooth, The	F	74	Oxford Reading Tree	Oxford University Press
Wolf and the Seven Little Kids	L	250+	Hunia, Fran	Ladybird Books
Wolfgang Amadeus Mozart: Musical Genius	N	250+	Rookie Biographies	Children's Press
Wolf's First Deer	M	434	Book Bank	Wright Group
Wolves	F	132	Twig	Wright Group
Wolves	I	188	Pair-It Books	Steck-Vaughn
Wolves of Willoughby Chase	L	250+	Aiken, Joan	Bantam Doubleday Dell
Women at Work	G	112	Foundations	Wright Group
Wonder Kid Meets the Evil Lunch Snatcher	M	250+	Duncan, Lois	Little, Brown & Co.
Wonderful Ears	I	1017	Science	Wright Group
Wonderful Eyes	M	1070	Science	Wright Group
Wood	B	26	Twig	Wright Group
Wood and Other Materials	G	97	Discovery World	Rigby
Woods, Irons, and Greens	P	250+	Wildcats	Wright Group
Woof!	C	40	Literacy 2000	Rigby
Wool	F	91	Sunshine	Wright Group
Woolly Sally	I		Ready to Read	Pacific Learning
Wooly, Wooly	E	136	Literacy 2000	Rigby
Woosh!	E	124	Read-Togethers	Wright Group
Word Machine, The	D	33	Sunshine	Wright Group
Words	M	578	Pacific Literacy	Pacific Learning

Title	Level	Words	Author/Series	Publisher/Distributor
Words	M	250+	Ready to Read	Pacific Learning
Words are Everywhere	E	46	Literacy 2000	Rigby
Work	C	65	TOTTS	Tott Publications
Workers	A	16	KinderReaders	Rigby
Worker's Tools, A	F	93	Discovery World	Rigby
Working for Dad	D	31	Visions	Wright Group
Working on Water	L	250+	Home Connection Collection	Rigby
Working Together	C	50	Early Connections	Benchmark Education
Working with Animals	I	250+	Home Connection Collection	Rigby
World's Biggest Baby, The	H	239	Ready Readers	Pearson Learning
World's Greatest Juggler, The	E	105	Little Readers	Houghton Mifflin
World's Greatest Toe Show, The	M	250+	Lamb, Nancy & Singer, Muff	Troll
Worms	D	39	Literacy 2000	Rigby
Worms for Breakfast	I	250+	Little Readers	Houghton Mifflin
Worst Show-and-Tell Ever, The	J	250+	Walsh, Rita	Troll
Worst Witch at Sea, The	P	250+	Murphy, Jill	Candlewick Press
Worst Witch Strikes Again, The	P	250+	Murphy, Jill	Candlewick Press
Worst Witch, The	P	250+	Murphy, Jill	Puffin Books
Would You Like to Fly?	C	52	Twig	Wright Group
Wow! What a Week!	J	364	Wonders	Hampton-Brown
Wrinkles	C	32	Literacy 2000	Rigby
Write Up a Storm with the Polk Street School	M	250+	Giff, Patricia Reilly	Bantam Doubleday Dell
Writer of the Plains: A Story About Willa Cather	P	250+	Streissguth, Tom	Carolrhoda Books
Writer's Work, A	N	481	Wonder World	Wright Group
Wrong Way Around Magic	N	250+	Chew, Ruth	Scholastic
Wrong Way Reggie	J		Little Celebrations	Pearson Learning
Wrong-Way Rabbit, The	J		Slater, Teddy	Scholastic
Yang the Second and Her Secret Admirers	P	250+	Namiaka, Lensey	Bantam Doubleday Dell
Yang the Third & Her Impossible Family	P	250+	Namiaka, Lensey	Bantam Doubleday Dell
Yang the Youngest & His Terrible Ear	P	250+	Namiaka, Lensey	Bantam Doubleday Dell
Yard Sale, The	I	250+	Little Readers	Houghton Mifflin
Year Mom Won the Pennant, The	M	250+	Christopher, Matt	Little, Brown & Co.
Year with Mother Bear, A	I	164	Storyteller Nonfiction	Wright Group/ McGraw-Hill
Yellow	B	32	Literacy 2000	Rigby
Yellow Overalls	L		Literacy 2000	Rigby
Yellow Yarn Mystery, The	B	61	Little Books	Sadlier-Oxford
Yes Ma'am	H	125	Read-Togethers	Wright Group
Yes, I Can	C	30	Teacher's Choice Series	Dominie
Yes, I Can!	D	45	Ready Readers	Pearson Learning
Yes, It Does	D	91	Teacher's Choice Series	Dominie
Yippy-Day-Yippy-Doo!	E	117	Sunshine	Wright Group
Yoo Hoo, Moon!	I	250+	Blocksma, Mary	Bantam Doubleday Dell
You	C	20	Carousel Earlybirds	Dominie
You and Your Teeth	I	1009	Sunshine	Wright Group
You Are Much Too Small	J	250+	Boegehold, Betty	Bantam Doubleday Dell
You Can Always Tell Cathy from Caitlin	K	583	Sunshine	Wright Group
You Can Make Skittles	G	128	Sunshine	Wright Group
You Can't Catch Me	J	250+	Oppenheim, Joanne	Houghton Mifflin
You Can't Eat Your Chicken Pox, Amber Brown	N	250+	Danziger, Paula	Scholastic
You Did It!	G	246	Sunshine	Wright Group

Title	Level	Words	Author/Series	Publisher/Distributor
You Do Ride Well	H	165	Windmill Books	Rigby
You Look Funny	G	180	First Start	Troll
You Might Fall	H	180	Stepping Stones	Nelson/Michaels Assoc.
You Should Try That with a Rhino	E	123	Home Connection Collection	Rigby
You'll Soon Grow into Them Titch	H	191	Hutchins, Pat	Morrow
Young Arthur Ashe: Brave Champion	L	250+	First-Start Biography	Troll
Young Clara Barton: Battlefield Nurse	L	250+	First-Start Biography	Troll
Young Davy Crockett: Frontier Fighter	L	250+	First-Start Biography	Troll
Young Helen Keller: Woman of Courage	L	250+	First-Start Biography	Troll
Young Jackie Robinson: Baseball Hero	L	250+	First Start Biography	Troll
Young Jim Thorpe: All-American Athlete	L	250+	First-Start Biography	Troll
Young Orville and Wilbur Wright: First to Fly	L	250+	First-Start Biography	Troll
Young Reggie Jackson: Hall of Fame Champion	L	250+	First-Start Biography	Troll
Young Rosa Parks: A Civil Rights Heroine	L	250+	First-Start Biography	Troll
Young Squanto: The First Thanksgiving	L	250+	First-Start Biography	Troll
Young Thurgood Marshall: Fighter for Equality	L	250+	First-Start Biography	Troll
Young Tom Edison: Great Inventor	L	250+	First-Start Biography	Troll
Young Wolf's First Hunt	M	250+	Shefelman, Janice	Random House
Youngest in the Family	F	144	Visions	Wright Group
Your Teeth	J	131	Pebble Books	Grolier, Capstone
You're Out	N	250+	Kroll, Stephen	Avon Camelot
You're So Clever	H	188	Voyages	SRA/McGraw-Hill
Yo-yos	G	62	City Kids	Rigby
Yuk Soup	B	25	Sunshine	Wright Group
Yukadoos	I	121	Jellybeans	Rigby
Yum and Yuk	I	125	Story Box	Wright Group
Yummy, Tum, Tum	C		Little Celebrations	Pearson Learning
Yummy, Yummy	F		Grey, Judith	Troll
Zack's Alligator	K	250+	Mozelle, Shirley	HarperTrophy
Zack's Alligator	K	250+	Little Readers	Houghton Mifflin
Zack's Alligator Goes to School	K	250+	Mozelle, Shirley	HarperTrophy
Zap! I'm a Mind Reader	M	250+	Greenburg, Dan	Grosset & Dunlap
Zebra's Yellow Van	C	31	Ready Readers	Pearson Learning
Zero's Slider	M	250+	Christopher, Matt	Little, Brown & Co.
Ziggy and the Cat	E	72	Windmill Books	Rigby
Zippers	C	21	Books for Young Learners	Richard C. Owen
Zip-Zip, Rattle-Bang!	E	141	Story Basket	Wright Group
Zithers	H	55	Little Celebrations	Pearson Learning
Zoe at the Fancy Dress Ball	J		Literacy 2000	Rigby
Zoe's Birthday Presents	D	83	Emergent	Pioneer Valley
Zombies Don't Play Soccer	M	250+	Dadey, Debbie & Jones, Marcia	Scholastic
Zoo Babies	F		Little Celebrations	Pearson Learning
Zoo Food	C	58	Reading Corners	Dominie
Zoo in Willy's Bed, The	E	81	Sturnman Gorman, Kate	Seedling
Zoo Party, A	H	134	Book Bank	Wright Group
Zoo, A	A	14	Literacy 2000	Rigby
Zoo, The	B	31	Wonder World	Wright Group
Zoo, The	C	33	Carousel Readers	Dominie
Zoo-Looking	G	149	Book Shop	Mondo Publishing
Zoom! Zoom!	C	43	Joy Readers	Dominie
Zunid	J	250+	Stepping Stones	Nelson/Michaels Assoc.

©1999 by I. C. Fountas & G. S. Pinnell from Matching Books to Readers. Portsmouth, NH: Heinemann. May not be reproduced without written permission of the publisher.

Guided reading book list organized by level

Title	Level	Words	Author/Series	Publisher/Distributor
Amazing Race, The	A	28	Smart Starts	Rigby
Animals	A	28	Smart Starts	Rigby
Animals That Work	A	14	Foundations	Wright Group
At School	A	12	Rise & Shine	Hampton-Brown
At School	A	28	Little Books for Early Readers	University of Maine
At the Fair	A	14	Little Books for Early Readers	University of Maine
At the Ocean	A	29	Little Books for Early Readers	University of Maine
At the Zoo	A	29	Kloes, Carol	Kaeden Books
Autumn Leaves	A	17	Pebble Books	Grolier, Capstone
Baby	A	28	Little Books for Early Readers	University of Maine
Baby Chimp	A	14	Twig	Wright Group
Baby Gets Dressed	A	16	Sunshine	Wright Group
Balloons, The	A	19	Sunshine	Wright Group
Barbecue, The	A	14	Sunshine	Wright Group
Bath, The	A	14	Ready Readers	Pearson Learning
Be Quiet	A	25	Literacy 2000	Rigby
Beach, The	A		Little Celebrations	Pearson Learning
Big Chase, The	A	14	Foundations	Wright Group
Big Things	A	33	PM Starters	Rigby
Bike Parade, The	A	16	Literacy 2000	Rigby
Bike, The	A	14	Twig	Wright Group
Birthday Cake, The	A	22	Sunshine	Wright Group
Birthday Party, The	A	15	Sunshine	Wright Group
Birthday Party, The	A	16	Rise & Shine	Hampton-Brown
Birthday, The	A	23	Little Books for Early Readers	University of Maine
Blueberries from Maine	A	28	Little Books for Early Readers	University of Maine
Boat, The	A	14	Pacific Literacy	Pacific Learning
Boat, The	A	28	Sunshine	Wright Group
Bouquet, The	A	38	Carousel Earlybirds	Dominie
Brenda's Birthday	A	18	Story Box	Wright Group
Building with Blocks	A	20	Sunshine	Wright Group
Bunny's Recess	A	35	Little Books for Early Readers	University of Maine
Busy Bird	A	14	Pacific Literacy	Pacific Learning
Car Ride, The	A	41	Little Red Readers	Sundance
Cars	A	18	Pebble Books	Grolier, Capstone
Cat, The	A	42	Little Books for Early Readers	University of Maine
Chick's Walk	A	14	Story Box	Wright Group
Chinese Kites	A	15	Twig	Wright Group
Circus Train, The	A	48	Little Red Readers	Sundance
Closer and Closer	A	13	Twig	Wright Group
Clown Face	A	14	Twig	Wright Group
Clown, The	A	13	Smart Starts	Rigby
Come and Have Fun	A	49	KinderReaders	Rigby
Come on Up	A	16	KinderReaders	Rigby
Cookies	A	15	Twig	Wright Group
Costume Party	A	32	Joy Readers	Dominie
Costume Party, The	A	15	Sunshine	Wright Group
Count with Me	A	49	Little Books	Sadlier-Oxford

Title	Level	Words	Author/Series	Publisher/Distributor
Crazy Cats	A	42	Little Books for Early Readers	University of Maine
Dad	A	24	PM Starters	Rigby
Dig, Dig	A	12	Cat on the Mat	Oxford University Press
Dinner	A	21	KinderReaders	Rigby
Dinner!	A	19	Sunshine	Wright Group
Dinosaur, The	A	14	Sunshine	Wright Group
Do You Want to be My Friend?	A	8	Carle, Eric	The Penguin Group
Dog Day!	A	21	Smart Starts	Rigby
Dog School	A	11	TOTTS	Tott Publications
Don't Splash Me!	A	24	Windmill	Rigby, Wright Group
Down to Town	A	26	Sunshine	Wright Group
Dressing Up	A	12	Sunshine	Wright Group
Dressing Up	A	32	PM Starters	Rigby
Eating	A	29	Foundations	Wright Group
Eating Apples	A	17	Pebble Books	Grolier, Capstone
Eggshell Garden, The	A	14	Sunshine	Wright Group
Elena Makes Tortillas	A	18	Pacific Literacy	Pacific Learning
Escalator, The	A	23	Story Box	Wright Group
Every Morning	A	30	Twig	Wright Group
Everyone Wears Wool	A	21	Pair-It Books	Steck-Vaughn
Face Sandwich, The	A	16	Sunshine	Wright Group
Fall	A	22	Little Books for Early Readers	University of Maine
Fall Harvest	A	16	Little Books for Early Readers	University of Maine
Farm, A	A	28	Little Books for Early Readers	University of Maine
Farm, The	A	14	Smart Starts	Rigby
Farm, The	A	14	Ready Readers	Pearson Learning
Farm, The	A	14	Literacy 2000	Rigby
Farm, The	A	28	Little Books for Early Readers	University of Maine
Feet	A	14	Foundations	Wright Group
First Things	A	18	Home Connection Collection	Rigby
Flowers	A	27	Hoenecke, Karen	Kaeden Books
Frogs	A	13	Twig	Wright Group
Fruit Salad	A	15	Literacy 2000	Rigby
Games	A	28	KinderReaders	Rigby
Garden, A	A	40	Foundations	Wright Group
Getting Dressed	A	16	Sunshine	Wright Group
Ghost, The	A	26	Story Box	Wright Group
Giant, The	A	20	Joy Readers	Dominie
Go Sea It!	A	16	Little Celebrations	Pearson Learning
Go, Go, Go	A	17	Story Box	Wright Group
Go, Go, Go	A	23	Little Books for Early Readers	University of Maine
Going Out	A	42	KinderReaders	Rigby
Going to School	A	21	Smart Starts	Rigby
Going to the Beach	A	30	Ready to Read	Pacific Learning
Going to the Beach	A	30	Pacific Literacy	Pacific Learning
Gotcha Box, The	A	30	Story Box	Wright Group
Hair	A	32	Carousel Earlybirds	Dominie
Hannah's Halloween	A	14	Little Books for Early Readers	University of Maine
Hat, The	A	12	Ready Readers	Pearson Learning
Have a Cookout	A	21	Little Books for Early Readers	University of Maine
Heads and Tails	A	29	Windmill Books	Rigby

Title	Level	Words	Author/Series	Publisher/Distributor
Helicopter Over Hawaii	A	21	Twig	Wright Group
Here's a House	A	45	Windmill	Wright Group
Hiding	A	28	KinderReaders	Rigby
House Cleaning	A	19	Book Bank	Wright Group
House for a Mouse, A	A	21	Pacific Literacy	Pacific Learning
House, A	A	32	PM Starters One	Rigby
How to Make a Mudpie	A	32	Learn to Read	Creative Teaching Press
Huggles Breakfast	A	14	Sunshine	Wright Group
Huggles Can Juggle	A	15	Sunshine	Wright Group
Huggles Goes Away	A	14	Sunshine	Wright Group
I Am Thankful	A	42	Carousel Earlybirds	Dominie
I Am...	A	20	Sunshine	Wright Group
I Can	A	21	Carousel Earlybirds	Dominie
I Can Fly	A	21	Sunshine	Wright Group
I Can Hear	A	32	TOTTS	Tott Publications
I Can Paint	A	35	Book Bank	Wright Group
I Can Read	A	35	Learn to Read	Creative Teaching Press
I Can See	A	40	Carousel Earlybirds	Dominie
I Can Write	A	40	Learn to Read	Creative Teaching Press
I Like	A	24	Sunshine	Wright Group
I Like Balloons	A	27	Reading Corners	Dominie
I Like Me	A	31	Visions	Wright Group
I Like to Eat	A	41	Reading Corners	Dominie
I Like to Paint	A	29	Reading Corners	Dominie
I Paint	A	22	Literacy 2000	Rigby
I Paint	A	26	Book Shop	Mondo Publishing
I Read	A	38	Reading Corners	Dominie
In My Backyard	A	18	Visions	Wright Group
In My School	A	27	Little Books for Early Readers	University of Maine
In the Mountains	A	14	Twig	Wright Group
In the Shopping Cart	A	24	PM Starters	Rigby
In the Supermarket	A	24	Smart Starts	Rigby
In the Teacup	A	35	KinderReaders	Rigby
Inside School	A	35	Little Books for Early Readers	University of Maine
Iron Horse, The	A	21	Smart Starts	Rigby
Jake	A	35	Little Books for Early Readers	University of Maine
James Is Hiding	A	24	Windmill	Rigby, Wright Group
Jordan Is Hiding	A	24	Little Books for Early Readers	University of Maine
Just Look at You	A	16	Sunshine	Wright Group
Keep Out!	A	19	Ready Readers	Pearson Learning
Legs	A	21	Twig	Wright Group
Legs, Legs, Legs	A	15	Gossett, R. & Ballinger, Margaret	Scholastic
Let's Go	A	32	Reading Corners	Dominie
Life on a Farm	A	24	Early Connections	Benchmark Education
Light	A	30	Twig	Wright Group
Little Brother	A	14	Sunshine	Wright Group
Little House	A	14	Ready Readers	Pearson Learning
Little Things	A	33	PM Starters	Rigby
Lobstering	A	14	Little Books for Early Readers	University of Maine
Log Hotel, The	A	22	Little Celebrations	Pearson Learning
Look	A	20	Sunshine	Wright Group

Title	Level	Words	Author/Series	Publisher/Distributor
Look at Conor	A	27	Little Books for Early Readers	University of Maine
Look at Me	A	17	Little Books for Early Readers	University of Maine
Look at Me!	A	27	KinderReaders	Rigby
Look at the Garden	A	43	Windmill Books	Rigby
Look Closer	A	21	Ready Readers	Pearson Learning
Look What I Can Do	A	15	Aruego, Jose	Macmillan
Lost	A	29	TOTTS	Tott Publications
Lots of Things	A	23	Reading Corners	Dominie
Magic!	A	23	Twig	Wright Group
Making a Garden	A	28	Foundations	Wright Group
Me	A	24	PM Starters	Rigby
Miss Popple's Pets	A	28	Literacy 2000	Rigby
Moccasins	A	20	Twig	Wright Group
Mom	A	24	PM Starters	Rigby
Moms and Dads	A	36	PM Starters	Rigby
Monster Mop	A	8	Ready Readers	Pearson Learning
Monster Party	A	20	Smart Starts	Rigby
Monster Party	A	25	Literacy 2000	Rigby
Mother Animals and Baby Animals	A	31	Reading Unlimited	Pacific Learning
Mother Hippopotamus	A	7	Foundations	Wright Group
My Backyard	A	14	Little Books for Early Readers	University of Maine
My Birthday Party	A	16	Little Readers	Houghton Mifflin
My Book	A	17	Maris, Ron	Viking
My Box	A	30	Literacy 2000	Rigby
My Class	A	14	Stewart, J. & Salem, Lynn	Seedling
My Family	A	28	Sunshine	Wright Group
My Fort	A	17	Little Books for Early Readers	University of Maine
My Home	A	20	Literacy 2000	Rigby
My House	A	40	Carousel Earlybirds	Dominie
My Picture	A	23	Story Box	Wright Group
My Place	A	28	Foundations	Wright Group
My Planet	A	28	Smart Starts	Rigby
My Rocket	A	28	KinderReaders	Rigby
My Room	A	14	Ready Readers	Pearson Learning
My Room	A	15	Twig	Wright Group
My Room	A	28	Carousel Earlybirds	Dominie
My Shadow	A	29	Book Bank	Wright Group
My Story	A	17	Wonder World	Wright Group
My Tower	A	15	Windmill	Wright Group
My Toys	A	28	Little Books for Early Readers	University of Maine
Naughty Kitten!	A	18	Smart Starts	Rigby
New House, The	A	15	Sunshine	Wright Group
New Nest, A	A	14	Pair-It Books	Steck-Vaughn
Off We Go!	A	16	Pacific Literacy	Pacific Learning
On a Walk	A	5	Ready Readers	Pearson Learning
On Safari	A	28	Smart Starts	Rigby
Ouch!	A	40	Literacy 2000	Rigby
Paint the Sky	A	14	Sunshine	Wright Group
Painters	A	23	Twig	Wright Group
Party, A	A	14	Story Box	Wright Group
People Use Tools	A	24	Early Connections	Benchmark Education

Title	Level	Words	Author/Series	Publisher/Distributor
Pepper Sees Me	A	28	Little Books for Early Readers	University of Maine
Pets	A	33	PM Starters	Rigby
Picnic in the Sand, A	A	14	Ready Readers	Pearson Learning
Picnic, The	A	18	Book Bank	Wright Group
Play Ball	A	7	Book Shop	Mondo Publishing
Play Ball	A	14	Twig	Wright Group
Playground, The	A	16	Twig	Wright Group
Playing	A	39	PM Starters	Rigby
Pond, A	A	14	Discovery Links	Newbridge
Potato Harvest Time	A	33	Little Books for Early Readers	University of Maine
Rainbow Bird, A	A	18	Pair-It Books	Steck-Vaughn
Red or Blue?	A	13	Ready Readers	Pearson Learning
Rhymes	A	9	Ready Readers	Pearson Learning
Ribbit!	A	7	Little Celebrations	Pearson Learning
Robot, The	A	18	Smart Starts	Rigby
Royal Family, The	A	17	Stewart, J. & Salem, Lynn	Seedling
Salad	A	36	Carousel Earlybirds	Dominie
Salad Vegetables	A	15	Foundations	Wright Group
Salad Vegetables	A	27	Story Box	Wright Group
Say Hello!	A	15	Rise & Shine	Hampton-Brown
School Lunch	A	14	Ready Readers	Pearson Learning
Seed, The	A	51	Wonder World	Wright Group
Shapes	A	24	Urmston, Kathleen & Evans, Karen	Kaeden Books
Shoes	A	16	Little Celebrations	Pearson Learning
Shopping	A	15	Sunshine	Wright Group
Show and Tell	A	32	Little Books	Sadlier-Oxford
Ski School	A	34	Little Books for Early Readers	University of Maine
Snowman	A	14	Smart Starts	Rigby
Snowman	A	19	Story Box	Wright Group
So Many Things to Do	A	21	Home Connection Collection	Rigby
Socks	A	21	Smart Starts	Rigby
Sometimes	A	25	Wonder World	Wright Group
Soup	A	17	Little Celebrations	Pearson Learning
Space Journey	A	19	Sunshine	Wright Group
Spots	A	27	Smart Starts	Rigby
Stop That Noise!	A	21	KinderReaders	Rigby
Stop!	A	12	Ready Readers	Pearson Learning
Stripes	A	28	Twig	Wright Group
Surprise, The	A	14	Story Box	Wright Group
Swing	A	18	Story Box	Wright Group
There Are Spots On…	A	14	Little Books for Early Readers	University of Maine
Things to Read	A	18	Little Books for Early Readers	University of Maine
Things to See in Maine	A	14	Little Books for Early Readers	University of Maine
This Is Lobstering	A	27	Little Books for Early Readers	University of Maine
Time for Dinner	A	15	Smart Starts	Rigby
Tim's Paintings	A	33	Literacy 2000	Rigby
To School	A	22	Sunshine	Wright Group
Too Fast	A	36	Reading Corners	Dominie
Toy Box, A	A	19	Literacy 2000	Rigby
Toy Box, The	A	14	Ready Readers	Pearson Learning
Toy Models	A	40	Early Connections	Benchmark Education

Title	Level	Words	Author/Series	Publisher/Distributor
Treasure Hunt	A	14	Smart Starts	Rigby
Trees	A	28	Twig	Wright Group
Trucks	A	35	Little Books for Early Readers	University of Maine
Two	A	17	Little Celebrations	Pearson Learning
Two More	A	16	Voyages	SRA/McGraw-Hill
Two Turtles	A	13	Ready Readers	Pearson Learning
Under the Bed	A	28	Smart Starts	Rigby
Under Water	A	35	Twig	Wright Group
Visit to the Doctor, A	A	28	Little Books for Early Readers	University of Maine
Waiting	A	28	Story Box	Wright Group
We Are Twins	A	24	Little Books for Early Readers	University of Maine
We Can	A	21	KinderReaders	Rigby
We Can Make Pizza	A	30	Little Books for Early Readers	University of Maine
We Go Out	A	41	PM Starters	Rigby
Weather	A	14	Smart Starts	Rigby
What a Mess!	A	14	Smart Starts	Rigby
What Are We Doing?	A	21	KinderReaders	Rigby
What Are You?	A	27	Literacy 2000	Rigby
What Can I Read?	A	28	Carousel Earlybirds	Dominie
What Can Jigarees Do?	A	22	Story Box	Wright Group
What Can Jump?	A	32	Windmill Books	Rigby
What Can She Do?	A	21	Little Books for Early Readers	University of Maine
What Can Swim?	A	30	Windmill Books	Rigby
What Did Ben Want?	A	28	Smart Starts	Rigby
What Do Insects Do?	A	24	Canizares, Susan & Chanko, Pamela	Scholastic
What Do You See by the Sea?	A	14	Little Books	Sadlier-Oxford
What Does Lucy Like?	A	11	Little Books	Sadlier-Oxford
What Feels Hot?	A	28	Windmill Books	Rigby
What Goes Up High?	A	38	Windmill Books	Rigby
What Has Wheels?	A	28	Hoenecke, Karen	Kaeden Books
What Is Fast?	A	30	Windmill Books	Rigby
What Is He Looking For?	A	42	KinderReaders	Rigby
What Is Little?	A	22	Rise & Shine	Hampton-Brown
What Is This?	A	25	Little Books for Early Readers	University of Maine
What Is This?	A	29	KinderReaders	Rigby
What Rhymes With...	A	9	Ready Readers	Pearson Learning
What's in This Egg?	A	16	Sunshine	Wright Group
What's Round?	A	14	Discovery Links	Newbridge
When the Circus Comes to Town	A	40	Little Red Readers	Sundance
Where Is My Pet?	A	34	Literacy 2000	Rigby
Where Is She?	A	35	Little Books for Early Readers	University of Maine
Where Is Teddy's Head?	A	27	Windmill	Wright Group
Whiskers	A	32	Wonder World	Wright Group
Who Likes Ice Cream?	A	15	Literacy 2000	Rigby
Who Likes the Cold?	A	29	Twig	Wright Group
Wild Bear	A	21	Pacific Literacy	Pacific Learning
Wings	A	14	KinderReaders	Rigby
Workers	A	16	KinderReaders	Rigby
Zoo, A	A	14	Literacy 2000	Rigby
Airplane, The	B	21	Sunshine	Wright Group
All Dressed Up	B	38	Visions	Wright Group

Title	Level	Words	Author/Series	Publisher/Distributor
All Kinds of Things	B	24	Pacific Literacy	Pacific Learning
All of Me	B	25	Literacy 2000	Rigby
All Over Me!	B	24	Pair-It Books	Steck-Vaughn
All Wet	B	28	Ready Readers	Pearson Learning
Animal Habitats	B	73	Little Celebrations	Pearson Learning
Animal Homes	B	48	Little Red Readers	Sundance
Animal Homes	B	48	Early Connections	Benchmark Education
Animal Legs	B	37	Discovery World	Rigby
Animals Went to Bed, The	B	32	Smart Starts	Rigby
Ants	B	16	Discovery Links	Newbridge
Ants Love Picnics Too	B	27	Literacy 2000	Rigby
Aquarium, The	B	24	KinderReaders	Rigby
Are You Afraid of...?	B	18	Little Celebrations	Pearson Learning
Astronaut	B	22	Hoenecke, Karen	Kaeden Books
Astronaut, The	B	30	Sunshine	Wright Group
At My School	B	43	Little Books for Early Readers	University of Maine
At School	B	23	Sunshine	Wright Group
At the Beach	B	30	Discovery Links	Newbridge
At the Museum	B	28	Ready Readers	Pearson Learning
At the Playground	B	54	Little Books for Early Readers	University of Maine
At the Store	B	21	Read-More Books	Dominie
At the Wildlife Park	B	34	Little Red Readers	Sundance
At the Zoo	B	40	PM Starters	Rigby
At the Zoo	B	54	Little Readers	Houghton Mifflin
Baby Animals	B	44	Reading Corners	Dominie
Ball Game	B	16	Literacy 2000	Rigby
Ball Games	B	44	PM Starters	Rigby
Balloons	B	55	Early Emergent	Pioneer Valley
Bare Feet	B	40	Visions	Wright Group
Baseball	B	14	Sunshine	Wright Group
Basket Full of Surprises, A	B	43	Little Books	Sadlier-Oxford
Basketball	B	20	Wonder World	Wright Group
Bath, The	B	28	Smart Starts	Rigby
Be Quiet	B	25	Smart Starts	Rigby
Beans	B	35	Pebble Books	Grolier, Capstone
Bear, The	B	17	Carousel Earlybirds	Dominie
Beautiful Flowers	B	28	Wonder World	Wright Group
Because I'm Little	B	51	Home Connection Collection	Rigby
Before I Go to School	B	71	Storyteller-First Snow	Wright Group/ McGraw-Hill
Ben's Red Car	B	49	PM Starters	Rigby
Big and Little	B	21	Foundations	Wright Group
Big and Little	B	24	KinderReaders	Rigby
Big and Little	B	40	Carousel Earlybirds	Dominie
Big, Big Box, A	B	35	Ready Readers	Pearson Learning
Bird Talk: Kok, Kok	B	42	Little Celebrations	Pearson Learning
Books	B	21	Smart Starts	Rigby
Books	B	29	Sunshine	Wright Group
Bridge, The	B	32	Story Box	Wright Group
Brothers	B	36	Pebble Books	Grolier, Capstone
Bubble Gum	B	21	Carousel Readers	Dominie
Buffy	B	28	Literacy 2000	Rigby

Title	Level	Words	Author/Series	Publisher/Distributor
Bug Watching	B	25	Twig	Wright Group
Bunny Opposites	B	14	Pair-It Books	Steck-Vaughn
Camping	B	19	Literacy 2000	Rigby
Can You Find It?	B	34	Ready Readers	Pearson Learning
Carrots	B	51	Pebble Books	Grolier, Capstone
Cars	B	30	Little Readers	Houghton Mifflin
Cat and Mouse	B	75	PM Starters	Rigby
Cat Came Back, The	B	22	Ready Readers	Pearson Learning
Cat on the Mat	B	37	Wildsmith, Brian	Oxford University Press
Catching	B	35	Teacher's Choice Series	Dominie
Cat's Day, A	B	23	Twig	Wright Group
Cats, Cats, Cats	B	14	Pair-It Books	Steck-Vaughn
Changing Colors	B	16	Pair-It Books	Steck-Vaughn
Chicken Soup	B	38	Fitros, Pamela	Kaeden Books
Chickens	B	24	Pebble Books	Grolier, Capstone
Chocolate Cake, The	B	23	Story Box	Wright Group
Chocolate Chip Cookies	B	32	Ready Readers	Pearson Learning
Church	B	17	Visions	Wright Group
Circus	B	20	Twig	Wright Group
City Bus, The	B	21	Visions	Wright Group
City Lights	B	16	Visions	Wright Group
Clap Your Hands!	B	22	Pair-It Books	Steck-Vaughn
Clean Up Your Room	B	35	Visions	Wright Group
Climbing	B	48	PM Starters	Rigby
Clouds	B	42	Voyages	SRA/McGraw-Hill
Clown, The	B	29	Urmston, Kathleen & Evans, Karen	Kaeden Books
Colors at the Zoo	B	59	Little Books	Sadlier-Oxford
Colors in the City	B	61	Urmston, Kathleen & Evans, Karen	Kaeden Books
Come and Play	B	34	Interaction	Rigby
Come On!	B	22	Sunshine	Wright Group
Counting One to Five	B	64	Early Connections	Benchmark Education
Creepy Crawlies	B	38	Carousel Earlybirds	Dominie
Dad	B	21	Little Readers	Houghton Mifflin
Dan Gets Dressed	B	42	Story Box	Wright Group
Dancing Shoes	B	23	Literacy 2000	Rigby
Dear Santa	B	50	Literacy 2000	Rigby
Dinosaur Dance, The	B	52	Little Books	Sadlier-Oxford
Dinosaur Party	B	27	Smart Starts	Rigby
Diver, The	B	30	Sunshine	Wright Group
Dog	B	37	Ready to Read	Pacific Learning
Dog	B	37	Pacific Literacy	Pacific Learning
Don't Wake the Baby	B	18	Literacy 2000	Rigby
Dreaming	B	23	Smart Starts	Rigby
Dressing Up	B	25	Smart Starts	Rigby
Eggs!	B	28	Ready Readers	Pearson Learning
Faces	B	27	Sunshine	Wright Group
Fall	B	12	Discovery Links	Newbridge
Families	B	49	Interaction	Rigby
Family Counts	B	19	Rise & Shine	Hampton-Brown
Family Time	B	16	Pair-It Books	Steck-Vaughn
Farley Frog	B	33	Pair-It Books	Steck-Vaughn

Title	Level	Words	Author/Series	Publisher/Distributor
Farm, The	B	21	Sunshine	Wright Group
Fathers	B	26	Pebble Books	Grolier, Capstone
Finger Puppet, The	B	18	Sunshine	Wright Group
First Day of School	B	16	Visions	Wright Group
Fishing	B	41	Little Books for Early Readers	University of Maine
Flower Box, The	B	14	Twig	Wright Group
Fly High	B	24	Visions	Wright Group
Flying and Floating	B	64	Little Red Readers	Sundance
Follow the Leader	B	15	Windmill	Rigby, Wright Group
Food to Eat	B	29	Little Readers	Houghton Mifflin
Football	B	28	Visions	Wright Group
For Breakfast	B	22	Visions	Wright Group
Friends	B	36	Little Readers	Houghton Mifflin
Frightened	B	42	Story Box	Wright Group
Fruit	B	20	Rise & Shine	Hampton-Brown
Fruit Salad	B	24	Early Emergent	Pioneer Valley
Fruit Trees	B	24	Visions	Wright Group
Fun with Friends	B	18	Rise & Shine	Hampton-Brown
Fun with Hats	B	38	Book Shop	Mondo Publishing
Furry	B		Little Celebrations	Pearson Learning
Garden Colors	B	15	Pair-It Books	Steck-Vaughn
Getting Dressed	B	40	Carousel Earlybirds	Dominie
Getting Ready	B	29	Little Books for Early Readers	University of Maine
Getting There	B	36	Wonder World	Wright Group
Giant's Breakfast, The	B	42	Literacy 2000	Rigby
Giant's Day Out, The	B	26	Smart Starts	Rigby
Gifts, The	B	34	Story Box	Wright Group
Give Me a Hug	B	28	Sunshine	Wright Group
Go-carts, The	B	46	PM Starters	Rigby
Going Fishing	B	22	Ready Readers	Pearson Learning
Going for a Ride	B	40	Little Books for Early Readers	University of Maine
Going in the Car	B	24	Sunshine	Wright Group
Going Up and Down	B	51	Early Emergent	Pioneer Valley
Going Up?	B		Little Celebrations	Pearson Learning
Good Girl	B	18	Ready Readers	Pearson Learning
Good to Eat	B	31	Twig	Wright Group
Great Enormous Hamburger, The	B	36	Sunshine	Wright Group
Green Grass	B	26	Story Box	Wright Group
Growing	B	23	Windmill	Rigby, Wright Group
Hair	B	37	Foundations	Wright Group
Halloween	B	44	Story Box	Wright Group
Hands	B	15	Twig	Wright Group
Hands, Hands, Hands	B	17	Little Celebrations	Pearson Learning
Happy Holidays	B	27	Teacher's Choice Series	Dominie
Hard at Work	B	66	Early Emergent	Pioneer Valley
Harry's Hat	B	45	Little Books	Sadlier-Oxford
Hats	B	46	Williams, Deborah	Kaeden Books
Hats Around the World	B	59	Charlesworth, Liza	Scholastic
Have You Seen My Cat?	B	93	Carle, Eric	Putnam
Have You Seen My Duckling?	B	28	Tafuri, Nancy	Greenwillow

Title	Level	Words	Author/Series	Publisher/Distributor
Headache, The	B	20	Oxford Reading Tree	Oxford University Press
Hello Goodbye	B	29	Literacy 2000	Rigby
Help! Help!	B	14	Joy Readers	Dominie
Here Comes the Parade!	B	32	Pair-It Books	Steck-Vaughn
Here Is...	B	49	Carousel Earlybirds	Dominie
Here's Skipper	B	28	Salem, Lynn & Stewart, J.	Seedling
Hide and Seek	B	38	Smart Starts	Rigby
Hide and Seek	B	38	Literacy 2000	Rigby
Homes for People	B	40	Early Connections	Benchmark Education
Honk!	B	36	Book Shop	Mondo Publishing
How Many Fish?	B	30	Gossett, R. & Ballinger, Margaret	Scholastic
How Many Legs?	B	19	Windmill	Wright Group
How Many Monkeys?	B	16	Pair-It Books	Steck-Vaughn
How to Make a Hen House	B	25	Ready Readers	Pearson Learning
How's the Weather	B	29	Learn to Read	Creative Teaching Press
I Am	B	32	Little Readers	Houghton Mifflin
I Am Frightened	B	41	Story Box	Wright Group
I Can	B	40	Ready Readers	Pearson Learning
I Can	B	54	Little Readers	Houghton Mifflin
I Can	B		New Way	Steck-Vaughn
I Can Make Music	B	41	Little Red Readers	Sundance
I Can Read	B	38	Ready to Read	Pacific Learning
I Can Read	B	38	Pacific Literacy	Pacific Learning
I Can Write, Can You?	B	30	Stewart, J. & Salem, Lynn	Seedling
I Get Tired	B	37	Carousel Earlybirds	Dominie
I Go, Go, Go	B	21	Sunshine	Wright Group
I Have a Pet	B	35	Reading Corners	Dominie
I Like Fruit	B	18	Visions	Wright Group
I Like Shapes	B	21	Armstrong, Shane	Scholastic
I Like to Help	B	46	Little Books for Early Readers	University of Maine
I Like to Read	B	49	Little Books for Early Readers	University of Maine
I Love Camping	B	34	Early Emergent	Pioneer Valley
I Love My Family	B	31	Sunshine	Wright Group
I Love My Family	B	31	Foundations	Wright Group
I Run	B	22	Carousel Earlybirds	Dominie
I See	B	29	Book Shop	Mondo Publishing
I See Colors	B	23	Learn to Read	Creative Teaching Press
I See Tails!	B	42	Rise & Shine	Hampton-Brown
Ice-Cream Stick	B	35	Story Box	Wright Group
I'm Hungry	B	25	Fitros, Pamela	Kaeden Books
In My Toolbox	B	36	Foundations	Wright Group
In Spring	B	15	Discovery Links	Newbridge
In the Air	B	20	Sunshine	Wright Group
In the Bathroom	B	24	Smart Starts	Rigby
In the Mirror	B	26	Story Box	Wright Group
In the Rain	B	19	Ready Readers	Pearson Learning
In the Woods	B	48	Book Shop	Mondo Publishing
It's About Time	B	39	Twig	Wright Group
It's My Bread	B	43	Pacific Literacy	Pacific Learning
Jack-in-the-Box	B	34	Literacy 2000	Rigby
Jack-O-Lantern	B	37	Twig	Wright Group

Title	Level	Words	Author/Series	Publisher/Distributor
Jake Can Play	B	42	Little Books for Early Readers	University of Maine
Jan Can Juggle	B	25	Ready Readers	Pearson Learning
Jump, Jump, Kangaroo	B	31	Story Box	Wright Group
Jumpers	B	21	Sunshine	Wright Group
Jungle Spots	B	28	Little Celebrations	Pearson Learning
Keys	B	31	Ready Readers	Pearson Learning
Laundromat, The	B	25	Visions	Wright Group
Let's Build a Tower	B	15	Literacy 2000	Rigby
Let's Go	B	81	Early Connections	Benchmark Education
Let's Move!	B	29	Ready Readers	Pearson Learning
Let's Play Ball	B	40	Little Books for Early Readers	University of Maine
Let's Pretend	B	40	Home Connection Collection	Rigby
Letter, The	B	15	Twig	Wright Group
Little Kittens	B	27	Ready Readers	Pearson Learning
Little Red Hen, The	B	87	Windmill	Wright Group
Little Seed, A	B	18	Smart Starts	Rigby
Locked Out!	B	15	Twig	Wright Group
Long, Long Tail, The	B	33	Sunshine	Wright Group
Look at Kyle	B	46	Little Books for Early Readers	University of Maine
Look at Me	B	48	PM Starters	Rigby
Look at the Ocean, A	B	50	Little Books for Early Readers	University of Maine
Look at This	B	57	Carousel Earlybirds	Dominie
Look Out!	B	15	Literacy 2000	Rigby
Look Out, Dan!	B	34	Story Box	Wright Group
Lost!	B	18	Smart Starts	Rigby
Lots and Lots of stairs	B	33	Little Books for Early Readers	University of Maine
Lots of Toys	B	47	Carousel Earlybirds	Dominie
Lunch at the Zoo	B	64	Blaxland, Wendy & Brimage, C.	Scholastic
Major Jump	B	21	Sunshine	Wright Group
Making Mountains	B	35	Ballinger, Margaret & Gossett, R.	Scholastic
Making Pictures	B	48	Foundations	Wright Group
Marching Band	B	35	Urmston, Kathleen & Evans, Karen	Kaeden Books
Max's Box	B	43	Little Celebrations	Pearson Learning
Model, The	B	18	Smart Starts	Rigby
Mommy, Where Are You?	B	64	Ziefert, Harriet & Boon, Emilie	Puffin Books
Monkey Moves	B	16	Pair-It Books	Steck-Vaughn
Monkeys	B	27	Canizares, Susan & Chanko, Pamela	Scholastic
Mother and Me	B	48	Spinelle, Nancy Louise	Kaeden Books
Mothers	B	26	Pebble Books	Grolier, Capstone
Mouse Train	B	48	Story Box	Wright Group
Moving	B	56	Little Red Readers	Sundance
Mr. Bumbleticker	B	28	Foundations	Wright Group
Mrs. Lunch	B	17	Joy Readers	Dominie
Mrs. Wishy-Washy's Tub	B	38	Story Box	Wright Group
My Bike	B	42	Foundations	Wright Group
My Cat Muffin	B	35	Gardner, Marjory	Scholastic
My Chair	B	24	Pacific Literacy	Pacific Learning
My Day	B	24	Sunshine	Wright Group
My Family	B	87	Carousel Earlybirds	Dominie
My Feet	B	25	Twig	Wright Group
My Fish Bowl	B	29	Foundations	Wright Group

Title	Level	Words	Author/Series	Publisher/Distributor
My Friend	B	41	Sunshine	Wright Group
My Grandfather's Face	B	27	Literacy 2000	Rigby
My Home	B	56	Sunshine	Wright Group
My Home Is High	B	23	Literacy 2000	Rigby
My House	B	25	Voyages	SRA/McGraw-Hill
My Mom	B	40	Little Books for Early Readers	University of Maine
My Monster and Me	B	37	Ready Readers	Pearson Learning
My Puppy	B	14	Sunshine	Wright Group
My School	B	34	Little Readers	Houghton Mifflin
My Shoes	B	25	Rise & Shine	Hampton-Brown
Nest Full of Eggs, A	B	25	Pair-It Books	Steck-Vaughn
New Cat, The	B	29	Ready to Read	Pacific Learning
New Cat, The	B	29	Pacific Literacy	Pacific Learning
New Pants	B	20	Story Box	Wright Group
Nicole Helps Grandma	B	35	Little Books for Early Readers	University of Maine
Nora Plays All Day	B	42	Little Books	Sadlier-Oxford
Ocean Waves	B	21	Twig	Wright Group
Off to Work	B	41	Literacy 2000	Rigby
On the Beach	B	28	Smart Starts	Rigby
One, One Is the Sun	B	42	Story Box	Wright Group
One, Two, Three, Four	B	21	KinderReaders	Rigby
Our Baby	B	14	Literacy 2000	Rigby
Our Garden	B	16	Literacy 2000	Rigby
Our Pumpkin	B		Learn to Read	Creative Teaching Press
Our Rocket	B	28	Pacific Literacy	Pacific Learning
Out in the Weather	B	56	PM Starters	Rigby
Over the Bridge	B	50	Little Red Readers	Sundance
Packing	B	37	Foundations	Wright Group
Packing My Bag	B	52	PM Starters	Rigby
Pat, Pat, Pat	B	37	Book Bank	Wright Group
Patterns All Around	B	55	Early Connections	Benchmark Education
Paul's Day at School	B	38	Little Books for Early Readers	University of Maine
Peas and Potatoes, 1,2,3	B	44	Pair-It Books	Steck-Vaughn
Pencil, The	B	97	PM Starters	Rigby
Pillow Sale, The	B	26	KinderReaders	Rigby
Pink Pig	B	23	Ready Readers	Pearson Learning
Playground Opposites	B	21	Pair-It Books	Steck-Vaughn
Puzzle, The	B	32	Smart Starts	Rigby
Puzzle, The	B	28	Storyteller Nonfiction	Wright Group/ McGraw-Hill
Race, The	B	34	Windmill	Rigby, Wright Group
Rain	B	52	Reading Corners	Dominie
Raindrops	B	34	Book Shop	Mondo Publishing
Rainy Day Counting	B	30	Twig	Wright Group
Recess	B	26	Teacher's Choice Series	Dominie
Robber, The	B	25	Smart Starts	Rigby
Rock Pools, The	B	49	PM Starters	Rigby
Roller Coaster, The	B	34	KinderReaders	Rigby
Run!	B	28	Sunshine	Wright Group
Run, Run, Run	B	19	Joy Readers	Dominie
Runaway Monkey	B	39	Stewart, J. & Salem, Lynn	Seedling

Title	Level	Words	Author/Series	Publisher/Distributor
Runaway Wheels, The	B	32	Pair-It Books	Steck-Vaughn
Sally's New Shoes	B	58	PM Starters	Rigby
Sand	B	32	Voyages	SRA/McGraw-Hill
Scrumptious Sundae	B	18	Literacy 2000	Rigby
Seeds	B	30	Rise & Shine	Hampton-Brown
Sending Messages	B	49	Wonder World	Wright Group
Shapes	B	19	Discovery World	Rigby
Shapes	B	40	Early Connections	Benchmark Education
Shoo, Fly!	B	24	Story Box	Wright Group
Shopping at the Supermarket	B	46	Foundations	Wright Group
Shopping Mall, The	B	44	PM Starters	Rigby
Signs	B	24	Literacy 2000	Rigby
Sisters	B	28	Pebble Books	Grolier, Capstone
Skating	B	35	Foundations	Wright Group
Skier, The	B	48	PM Starters	Rigby
Snap!	B	31	Sunshine	Wright Group
Snow	B	29	Discovery Links	Newbridge
Snow	B	33	Hoenecke, Karen	Kaeden Books
Socks	B	21	Ready Readers	Pearson Learning
Sometimes	B	18	Literacy 2000	Rigby
Sometimes...	B	25	Home Connection Collection	Rigby
Space Ark, The	B	20	Sunshine	Wright Group
Spaceship	B	27	Hoenecke, Karen	Kaeden Books
Splish Splash!	B	28	Windmill	Wright Group
Spooky Pet	B	24	Smart Starts	Rigby
Sports Are Fun	B	21	Pair-It Books	Steck-Vaughn
Spots	B	31	Visions	Wright Group
Stop!	B	90	PM Starters	Rigby
Storm, The	B	19	Sunshine	Wright Group
Sun Flower, A	B	42	Foundations	Wright Group
Sunburn	B	48	Prokopchak, Ann	Kaeden Books
Super Hero	B	33	Sunshine	Wright Group
Tails	B	42	Book Bank	Wright Group
Team Sports	B	23	Twig	Wright Group
There's a Mouse in the House	B	42	Book Shop	Mondo Publishing
Things I Can Do	B	36	Little Readers	Houghton Mifflin
This Game	B	63	Carousel Earlybirds	Dominie
This Tall	B	41	Foundations	Wright Group
Three White Sheep	B	20	Ready Readers	Pearson Learning
Time for Dinner	B	38	PM Starters	Rigby
Time for Lunch	B	28	Ready Readers	Pearson Learning
Too Much	B	27	Teacher's Choice Series	Dominie
Toys	B	37	Foundations	Wright Group
Traffic Jam	B	18	Voyages	SRA/McGraw-Hill
Tree House, The	B	32	Sunshine	Wright Group
Tree House, The	B	32	Story Box	Wright Group
Tree Stump, The	B	34	Little Celebrations	Pearson Learning
Truck Is Struck, The	B	23	Ready Readers	Pearson Learning
Two Points	B	40	Kennedy, J. & Eaton, A.	Seedling
Up and Down	B	25	Little Books for Early Readers	University of Maine
Up They Go	B	30	Ready Readers	Pearson Learning

Title	Level	Words	Author/Series	Publisher/Distributor
Vacations	B	22	Smart Starts	Rigby
Walk in the Rain, A	B	28	Pair-It Books	Steck-Vaughn
Wash Day	B	35	Voyages	SRA/McGraw-Hill
Watching TV	B	18	Sunshine	Wright Group
Water	B	24	Little Celebrations	Pearson Learning
Water	B	28	Literacy 2000	Rigby
Way I Go to School, The	B	53	PM Starters	Rigby
We Are Singing	B	26	Ready Readers	Pearson Learning
We Go to School	B	27	Carousel Earlybirds	Dominie
We Ride	B	40	Carousel Earlybirds	Dominie
We Ski	B	35	Storyteller-First Snow	Wright Group/ McGraw-Hill
We Went to the Zoo	B	32	Little Red Readers	Sundance
Weather Chart, The	B	24	Sunshine	Wright Group
Whale Watch	B	27	Ready Readers	Pearson Learning
What Can Float?	B	27	Ready Readers	Pearson Learning
What Can Fly?	B	28	Literacy 2000	Rigby
What Can Fly?	B	29	Discovery Links	Newbridge
What Can This Animal Do?	B	28	Foundations	Wright Group
What Can You Make?	B	22	Ready Readers	Pearson Learning
What Can You Taste?	B	45	Windmill Books	Rigby
What Comes Out at Night?	B	48	Little Red Readers	Sundance
What Did You Bring?	B	23	Ready Readers	Pearson Learning
What Do I See?	B	28	Twig	Wright Group
What Do Scientists Do?	B	24	Twig	Wright Group
What Do You Like?	B	52	Little Books for Early Readers	University of Maine
What Feels Cold?	B	30	Windmill Books	Rigby
What Feels Sticky	B	26	Windmill Books	Rigby
What Goes Around and Around?	B	46	Windmill Books	Rigby
What Has Spots?	B	33	Literacy 2000	Rigby
What Is a Huggles?	B	41	Sunshine	Wright Group
What Is Enormous	B	33	Windmill Books	Rigby
What Is Fierce?	B	32	Windmill Books	Rigby
What Is Green?	B	30	Carousel Earlybirds	Dominie
What Is Noisy?	B	31	Windmill Books	Rigby
What Is Red?	B	27	Carousel Earlybirds	Dominie
What Is Red?	B	30	Literacy 2000	Rigby
What Is Scary?	B	31	Windmill Books	Rigby
What Is Slippery?	B	26	Windmill Books	Rigby
What Is Tall?	B	30	Windmill Books	Rigby
What Is Under the Hat?	B	29	Ready Readers	Pearson Learning
What Is White?	B	26	Carousel Earlybirds	Dominie
What Is Yellow?	B	26	Carousel Earlybirds	Dominie
What Will You Pack?	B	35	Ready Readers	Pearson Learning
What's Behind This Door?	B	43	Twig	Wright Group
What's for Dinner?	B	35	Hoenecke, Karen	Kaeden Books
What's for Lunch?	B	42	Story Box	Wright Group
What's on My Farm?	B	38	Rise & Shine	Hampton-Brown
What's That?	B	28	Sunshine	Wright Group
What's Up?	B	26	Pacific Literacy	Pacific Learning
When I Look Up	B	55	Foundations	Wright Group

Title	Level	Words	Author/Series	Publisher/Distributor
Where Are the Babies?	B	8	PM Starters	Rigby
Where Are the Car Keys?	B	36	Windmill	Wright Group
Where Are We?	B	72	Early Emergent	Pioneer Valley
Where Are You Going?	B	42	KinderReaders	Rigby
Where Can Kitty Sleep?	B	15	Windmill	Wright Group
Where Can We Put an Elephant?	B	48	Windmill	Wright Group
Where Do We Go?	B	22	Ready Readers	Pearson Learning
Where I Live	B	36	Carousel Earlybirds	Dominie
Where Is It?	B	21	Ready Readers	Pearson Learning
Where Is Lunch?	B	25	Pacific Literacy	Pacific Learning
Where Is My Teacher?	B	43	Little Books for Early Readers	University of Maine
Where's the Dog?	B	36	Windmill Books	Rigby
Where's the Egg Cup?	B	25	Windmill	Wright Group
Where's the Fish?	B	39	Gomi, Taro	Morrow
Which Animal?	B	14	Foundations	Wright Group
Who Can?	B	35	Book Shop	Mondo Publishing
Who Likes Water?	B	35	KinderReaders	Rigby
Who Lives in a Tree?	B	46	Canizares, Susan & Morton, Daniel	Scholastic
Who Lives in the Arctic?	B	48	Canizares, Susan & Chanko, Pamela	Scholastic
Who Lives in the Sea?	B	69	Book Shop	Mondo Publishing
Who Made These Tracks?	B	24	Literacy 2000	Rigby
Who Reads?	B	25	Teacher's Choice Series	Dominie
Who Uses These Tools?	B	23	Twig	Wright Group
Who Wears This Hat?	B	42	Windmill	Wright Group
Who Will Help?	B	20	Carousel Readers	Dominie
Who's Coming for a Ride?	B	25	Literacy 2000	Rigby
Whose Tracks?	B	14	Little Celebrations	Pearson Learning
Wood	B	26	Twig	Wright Group
Yellow	B	32	Literacy 2000	Rigby
Yellow Yarn Mystery, The	B	61	Little Books	Sadlier-Oxford
Yuk Soup	B	25	Sunshine	Wright Group
Zoo, The	B	31	Wonder World	Wright Group
1, 2, Kangaroo	C	54	Reading Corners	Dominie
Across the Seasons	C	75	Early Connections	Benchmark Education
All About Dinosaurs	C	34	Teacher's Choice Series	Dominie
All Fall Down	C	72	Wildsmith, Brian	Oxford University Press
All Through the Week with Cat and Dog	C	91	Learn to Read	Creative Teaching Press
Alphabet Race, The	C	7	Visions	Wright Group
Am I Ready Now?	C	41	Visions	Wright Group
Amazing Magnets	C	53	Twig	Wright Group
Animal Habitats	C	73	Little Red Readers	Sundance
Animal Sounds	C	21	Visions	Wright Group
Animal Stretches	C	35	Little Celebrations	Pearson Learning
Animals Eat	C	27	We Do, Too Series	Dominie
Animals Have Babies	C	42	We Do, Too Series	Dominie
Animals Have Homes	C	31	We Do, Too Series	Dominie
Animals Hide and Seek	C	56	Twig	Wright Group
Animals Keep Warm	C	25	We Do, Too Series	Dominie
Animals Make Noises	C	19	We Do, Too Series	Dominie
Animals Play	C	27	We Do, Too Series	Dominie

Title	Level	Words	Author/Series	Publisher/Distributor
Anna's Sandwich	C	33	Windmill Books	Rigby
Ants Everywhere	C	24	Visions	Wright Group
Ants on a Picnic	C	35	Joy Readers	Dominie
Apples	C	45	Williams, Deborah	Kaeden Books
Aquarium, The	C	18	Kloes, Carol	Kaeden Books
Asleep	C	26	Joy Readers	Dominie
At Christmas	C	26	Visions	Wright Group
At the Fair	C	58	Rise & Shine	Hampton-Brown
At the Farm	C	52	Little Red Readers	Sundance
At the Lake	C	23	KinderReaders	Rigby
At the Library	C	69	PM Starters	Rigby
At the Playground	C	25	Visions	Wright Group
At the Playground	C	86	Little Red Readers	Sundance
At the Pool	C	64	Foundations	Wright Group
At the Store	C	14	Visions	Wright Group
At the Supermarket	C	60	Little Readers	Houghton Mifflin
At the Truckstop	C	25	Kloes, Carol	Kaeden Books
At the Zoo	C	73	Little Red Readers	Sundance
Awww	C	35	Little Celebrations	Pearson Learning
Baby Animals at Home	C	64	Twig	Wright Group
Baby in the Cart	C	84	Foundations	Wright Group
Baby Lamb's First Drink	C	64	PM Story Books	Rigby
Baby Owls, The	C	90	PM Extensions-Red	Rigby
Baby Says	C	26	Steptoe, John	Morrow
Bags, Cans, Pots, and Pans	C	56	Ready Readers	Pearson Learning
Baking Day	C	35	Windmill Books	Rigby
Balancing	C	46	Twig	Wright Group
Ball, The	C	40	KinderReaders	Rigby
Banana Shake	C	44	Book Bank	Wright Group
Band, The	C	31	Voyages	SRA/McGraw-Hill
Barn Dance	C	47	Story Box	Wright Group
Barnyard Baseball	C	19	Pair-It Books	Steck-Vaughn
Basketball	C	23	Visions	Wright Group
Bath Time	C	23	Wonder World	Wright Group
Bats, The	C	21	Twig	Wright Group
Bay Run, The	C	80	Foundations	Wright Group
Be a Clown	C	29	The Candid Collection	Dominie
Bears	C	59	Storyteller Nonfiction	Wright Group/ McGraw-Hill
Beds	C	44	Interaction	Rigby
Bee, The	C	26	Story Box	Wright Group
Ben the Bold	C	71	Literacy 2000	Rigby
Ben's Banana	C	60	Foundations	Wright Group
Ben's Pets	C	30	Ready Readers	Pearson Learning
Best Place, The	C	61	Literacy 2000	Rigby
Bicycle, The	C	29	Story Box	Wright Group
Big and Little	C	36	Sunshine	Wright Group
Big Barn, The	C	81	Teacher's Choice Series	Dominie
Big Boo Bird, The	C	66	Joy Readers	Dominie
Big Enough	C	49	Visions	Wright Group
Big Kick, The	C	67	PM Story Books	Rigby

Title	Level	Words	Author/Series	Publisher/Distributor
Big Long Animal Song	C	29	Little Celebrations	Pearson Learning
Big Sister	C	44	Visions	Wright Group
Bigger and Bigger	C	49	Twig	Wright Group
Bird Feeder, The	C	31	Storyteller-First Snow	Wright Group/ McGraw-Hill
Birthday Cake for Ben, A	C	59	PM Extensions-Red	Rigby
Birthday Candles	C	52	Carousel Readers	Dominie
Birthday Party, A	C	47	Early Emergent	Pioneer Valley
Birthday, A	C		New Way	Steck-Vaughn
Birthdays	C	59	Foundations	Wright Group
Black and White	C	32	Voyages	SRA/McGraw-Hill
Blocks	C	60	Early Emergent	Pioneer Valley
Blue Day	C	35	Literacy 2000	Rigby
Bo Peep's Sheep	C	39	Pair-It Books	Steck-Vaughn
Boats	C	100	Pebble Books	Grolier, Capstone
Boots	C	57	Schreiber, Anne & Doughty, A.	Scholastic
Boots for Toots	C	41	Ready to Read	Pacific Learning
Boots for Toots	C	41	Pacific Literacy	Pacific Learning
Boss	C	48	Foundations	Wright Group
Bottles, Boxes, and Bins	C	36	Twig	Wright Group
Breakfast	C	35	Foundations	Wright Group
Breakfast	C	37	Little Books for Early Readers	University of Maine
Breakfast in Bed	C	10	Voyages	SRA/McGraw-Hill
Breakfast with John	C	29	Books for Young Learners	Richard C. Owen
Breathing Under Water	C	39	Sunshine	Wright Group
Brown Bear, Brown Bear	C	185	Martin, Bill	Holt, Henry & Co.
Bubbles	C	31	Sunshine	Wright Group
Bubbles	C	33	Literacy 2000	Rigby
Bubbles	C	34	Discovery Links	Newbridge
Bubbles Everywhere	C	41	Twig	Wright Group
Buckle My Shoe	C	31	Sunshine	Wright Group
Bugs!	C	32	Rookie Readers	Children's Press
Bump!	C	12	KinderReaders	Rigby
Bumper Cars, The	C	94	PM Extensions-Red	Rigby
Bus Ride, The	C	164	Little Celebrations	Pearson Learning
Bus Ride, The	C	175	Reading Unlimited	Pacific Learning
Bus, The	C	46	Twig	Wright Group
Buster	C	36	Twig	Wright Group
Busy Mosquito, The	C	112	Foundations	Wright Group
Busy People	C	40	Little Celebrations	Pearson Learning
Buzzing Flies	C	45	Sunshine	Wright Group
Cactus Town	C	43	Sunshine	Wright Group
Call 911	C	22	Twig	Wright Group
Camping	C	49	Foundations	Wright Group
Can I Have a Lick?	C	69	Carousel Readers	Dominie
Can You Fly?	C	51	Foundations	Wright Group
Can You See Me?	C	48	Foundations	Wright Group
Can You See the Eggs?	C	87	PM Starters	Rigby
Caring	C	47	Interaction	Rigby
Caring for Our Pets	C	74	Early Connections	Benchmark Education
Cat and Dog	C	71	Learn to Read	Creative Teaching Press

Title	Level	Words	Author/Series	Publisher/Distributor
Cat Prints	C	25	Pair-It Books	Steck-Vaughn
Cat, The	C	23	Smart Starts	Rigby
Cats	C	45	Williams, Deborah	Kaeden Books
Cave, The	C	67	Book Bank	Wright Group
Chalk Talk	C	69	Storyteller-First Snow	Wright Group/ McGraw-Hill
Champions	C	13	Twig	Wright Group
Chew, Chew, Chew	C	24	Literacy 2000	Rigby
Chicken for Dinner	C	27	Story Box	Wright Group
Children	C	45	Pebble Books	Grolier, Capstone
Child's Day, A	C	34	Sunshine	Wright Group
Circus, The	C	31	Literacy 2000	Rigby
City Senses	C	85	Twig	Wright Group
Cleaning Teeth	C	37	Wonder World	Wright Group
Clever Happy Monkey	C	28	Joy Readers	Dominie
Climbing	C	34	Literacy 2000	Rigby
Clothes	C	25	Interaction	Rigby
Clown and Elephant	C	38	Story Box	Wright Group
Come to My House	C	56	Joy Readers	Dominie
Come with Me	C	25	Story Box	Wright Group
Cool Off	C	37	Book Shop	Mondo Publishing
Copycat	C	54	Story Box	Wright Group
Costumes	C	23	Oxford Reading Tree	Oxford University Press
Costumes	C	36	Pebble Books	Grolier, Capstone
Counting Seeds	C	63	Early Connections	Benchmark Education
Cowboy, The	C	35	Step-By-Step Series	Dominie
Crawl, Caterpillar, Crawl!	C	24	Pair-It Books	Steck-Vaughn
Cross-Country Race	C	33	Windmill Books	Rigby
Dad and I	C	59	Rise & Shine	Hampton-Brown
Dan the Flying Man	C	60	Read-Togethers	Wright Group
Dancing	C	38	Visions	Wright Group
Danger	C	66	Story Box	Wright group
Day at School, A	C	38	Sunshine	Wright Group
Day with My Dad, A	C	88	Fiesta Series	Dominie
Desert Day	C	23	Twig	Wright Group
Desert, The	C	34	Carousel Readers	Dominie
Dig	C	20	KinderReaders	Rigby
Divers, The	C	25	Wonder World	Wright Group
Doctor Boondoggle	C	51	Story Box	Wright Group
Don't Leave Anything Behind!	C	26	Literacy 2000	Rigby
Down the Hill	C	32	KinderReaders	Rigby
Down the Hill	C	94	New Way Red	Steck-Vaughn
Dragon, The	C	130	Sunshine	Wright Group
Dream Horse	C	47	Pair-It Books	Steck-Vaughn
Dressing Up	C	31	Literacy 2000	Rigby
Dressing-up Box, The	C	61	Book Bank	Wright Group
Ears	C	37	Rise & Shine	Hampton-Brown
Eating Out	C	31	Sunshine	Wright Group
Egg, The	C	48	Joy Readers	Dominie
Elephant Walk	C	44	Sunshine	Wright Group

Title	Level	Words	Author/Series	Publisher/Distributor
Elephant's Trunk, An	C	31	Little Celebrations	Pearson Learning
Emily's Babysitter	C	67	Emergent	Pioneer Valley
Every Monday	C	52	Pair-It Books	Steck-Vaughn
Everyone Eats	C	44	Discovery Links	Newbridge
Eyes	C	64	Wonder World	Wright Group
Family of Five, A	C	26	Pair-It Books	Steck-Vaughn
Family Pets	C	37	Pebble Books	Grolier, Capstone
Farmer Brown's Garden	C	48	Windmill Books	Rigby
Fast, Faster, Fastest	C	66	Twig	Wright Group
Feeding the Baby	C	51	Home Connection Collection	Rigby
Feeding Time	C	55	Carousel Readers	Dominie
Felix, the Very Hungry Fish	C	32	Little Books	Sadlier-Oxford
Ferry, The	C	27	Sunshine	Wright Group
Fiesta Time	C	28	Little Celebrations	Pearson Learning
Filbert the Fly	C	28	Literacy 2000	Rigby
Find It	C	63	Carousel Earlybirds	Dominie
Fireworks	C	29	Joy Readers	Dominie
First and Last	C	44	Teacher's Choice Series	Dominie
Fishing	C	35	Story Box	Wright Group
Fishing	C	35	KinderReaders	Rigby
Fishing	C	63	PM Starters	Rigby
Fishy Story, A	C	102	Pair-It Books	Steck-Vaughn
Fitness	C	60	Foundations	Wright Group
Flat Hat, The	C	24	KinderReaders	Rigby
Flight Deck	C	30	Wonder World	Wright Group
Flower Girl, The	C	90	PM Extensions-Red	Rigby
Flying	C	26	Story Box	Wright Group
Folk Dancer	C	36	The Candid Collection	Dominie
Four Ice Creams	C	61	PM Starters	Rigby
Fox on the Box, The	C	36	Gregorich, Barbara	School Zone
Fox on the Box, The	C	36	Little Readers	Houghton Mifflin
Fox, The	C	24	Books for Young Learners	Richard C. Owen
Frogs	C	34	Pair-It Books	Steck-Vaughn
Frogs	C	36	Joy Readers	Dominie
Frogs Can Jump	C	41	Book Bank	Wright Group
Fun at School	C	50	Foundations	Wright Group
Fun Food	C	29	Home Connection Collection	Rigby
Fun with Mo and Toots	C	41	Ready to Read	Pacific Learning
Fun with Mo and Toots	C	41	Pacific Literacy	Pacific Learning
Gabby Is Hungry	C	78	Emergent	Pioneer Valley
Garbage	C	51	Wonder World	Wright Group
Getting Fit	C	15	Wonder World	Wright Group
Getting Ready for the Ball	C	27	Literacy 2000	Rigby
Giant and the Boy, The	C	44	Sunshine	Wright Group
Giant's Pizza, The	C	28	Joy Readers	Dominie
Giant's Rice, The	C	28	Joy Readers	Dominie
Giant-Size Hamburger, A	C	38	Wonder World	Wright Group
Giddy Up	C	49	Cat on the Mat	Oxford University Press
Goat, The	C	17	KinderReaders	Rigby
Going Fishing	C	30	Visions	Wright Group
Going for a Ride	C	52	Early Emergent	Pioneer Valley

Title	Level	Words	Author/Series	Publisher/Distributor
Going to Grandpa's	C	37	Frankford, Marilyn	Kaeden Books
Going to School	C	43	Story Box	Wright Group
Going to School	C	50	Sunshine	Wright Group
Going to the Beach	C	75	Carousel Readers	Dominie
Going to the Park	C	41	Home Connection Collection	Rigby
Going to the Park with Grandaddy	C	30	Visions	Wright Group
Goldilocks and the Three Bears	C	54	Little Books	Sadlier-Oxford
Good Old Mom	C	34	Oxford Reading Tree	Oxford University Press
Grandfathers	C	41	Pebble Books	Grolier, Capstone
Grandmother and I	C	53	Home Connection Collection	Rigby
Grandmother Is Tired	C	31	Joy Readers	Dominie
Grandmothers	C	50	Pebble Books	Grolier, Capstone
Grandpa and I	C	40	Home Connection Collection	Rigby
Gregory's Dog	C	23	Cat on the Mat	Oxford University Press
Growing Up Is Fun	C	87	The Candid Collection	Dominie
Hair	C	35	Little Celebrations	Pearson Learning
Halloween Mask for Monster	C		Mueller, Virginia	Whitman
Hands	C	39	Literacy 2000	Rigby
Happy 100th Day!	C	35	Little Celebrations	Pearson Learning
Happy Birthday	C	28	Literacy 2000	Rigby
Happy Birthday, Frog	C	87	Story Box	Wright Group
Happy Face, Sad Face	C	77	Foundations	Wright Group
Happy Monkey in the Shed	C	30	Joy Readers	Dominie
Hat Trick	C	38	Literacy 2000	Rigby
Hats	C	27	Twig	Wright Group
Hats	C	35	Joy Readers	Dominie
Hats	C	43	Little Readers	Houghton Mifflin
Have You Seen?	C	38	Literacy 2000	Rigby
Hedgehog Is Hungry	C	48	PM Story Books	Rigby
Hello	C	63	Story Box	Wright Group
Hello Puppet	C	26	Voyages	SRA/McGraw-Hill
Help Me!	C	55	New Way Red	Steck-Vaughn
Help!	C	57	Reading Corners	Dominie
Helping Dad	C	34	Sunshine	Wright Group
Here Comes the Rain!	C	47	Little Books	Sadlier-Oxford
Here Is a Carrot	C	96	Foundations	Wright Group
Here's What I Made	C	38	Literacy 2000	Rigby
Hey Coach!	C	37	TOTTS	Tott Publications
Hey There, Bear!	C		Little Celebrations	Pearson Learning
Hickory, Dickory Pizza Clock	C		Little Celebrations	Pearson Learning
Hike at Day Camp, The	C	32	Visions	Wright Group
Homes	C	69	Storyteller Nonfiction	Wright Group/ McGraw-Hill
Hot Dogs (Sausages)	C	84	PM Story Books	Rigby
Hot Potato and Cold Potato	C	77	Foundations	Wright Group
Hot Sidewalks	C	28	Visions	Wright Group
House	C		Little Celebrations	Pearson Learning
House for Me, A	C	71	Twig	Wright Group
Houses	C	35	Little Celebrations	Pearson Learning
Houses	C	38	Windmill	Rigby, Wright Group
Houses	C	64	Story Box	Wright Group

Title	Level	Words	Author/Series	Publisher/Distributor
How Many Kittens?	C	37	Twig	Wright Group
How to Make a Hot Dog	C	48	Story Box	Wright Group
How to Make a Sandwich	C	27	Visions	Wright Group
How to Make Can Stilts	C	28	Story Box	Wright Group
How to Make Snack Mix	C	47	Oppenlander, Meredith	Kaeden Books
Hug Is Warm, A	C	60	Sunshine	Wright Group
Humpity-Bump	C		Little Celebrations	Pearson Learning
Hungry Bear	C	22	Smart Starts	Rigby
Hungry Goat, The	C	33	Rise & Shine	Hampton-Brown
Hungry Kitten	C	50	Teacher's Choice Series	Dominie
I Am a Bookworm	C	32	Sunshine	Wright Group
I Am a Dentist	C	20	Read-More Books	Dominie
I Can	C	27	Visions	Wright Group
I Can Dig	C	45	Can You Do This	SRA/McGraw-Hill
I Can Do Anything!	C	21	Sunshine	Wright Group
I Can Do It Myself	C	37	Literacy 2000	Rigby
I Can Do Many Things	C	43	Carousel Readers	Dominie
I Can Draw	C	75	Carousel Earlybirds	Dominie
I Can Eat	C	51	Can You Do This	SRA/McGraw-Hill
I Can Jump	C	40	Sunshine	Wright Group
I Can Play	C	45	Can You Do This	SRA/McGraw-Hill
I Can Read	C	38	Teacher's Choice Series	Dominie
I Can Read Anything	C	42	Sunshine	Wright Group
I Can Ride	C	66	Can You Do This	SRA/McGraw-Hill
I Can Taste	C	31	Teacher's Choice Series	Dominie
I Can Wash	C	66	Carousel Earlybirds	Dominie
I Can't See	C	36	Little Celebrations	Pearson Learning
I Climb	C	57	This Is the Way	SRA/McGraw-Hill
I Could Be	C	40	Visions	Wright Group
I Crawl	C	56	This Is the Way	SRA/McGraw-Hill
I Dress Up Like Mama	C	35	Visions	Wright Group
I Eat Leaves	C	47	Book Shop	Mondo Publishing
I Feel Cold	C	57	Home Connection Collection	Rigby
I Feel Hot	C	58	Home Connection Collection	Rigby
I Fly	C	57	This Is the Way	SRA/McGraw-Hill
I Found a Can	C	33	Twig	Wright Group
I Get Ready for School	C	37	Visions	Wright Group
I Grow Too!	C	30	Start to Read	School Zone
I Have a Watch!	C	60	Williams, Deborah	Kaeden Books
I Have Shoes	C	24	Visions	Wright Group
I Jump	C	56	This Is the Way	SRA/McGraw-Hill
I Like	C	24	Literacy 2000	Rigby
I Like Green	C	47	Literacy 2000	Rigby
I Like to Count	C	40	Ready Readers	Pearson Learning
I Like to Eat	C	56	Sunshine	Wright Group
I Like to Find Things	C	40	Sunshine	Wright Group
I Like to Play	C	50	Carousel Readers	Dominie
I Like to Write	C	62	Carousel Readers	Dominie
I Live on a Farm	C	42	Read-More Books	Dominie
I Love Bugs	C	40	Book Shop	Mondo Publishing
I Love Music	C	41	Carousel Readers	Dominie

Title	Level	Words	Author/Series	Publisher/Distributor
I Remember	C	26	Literacy 2000	Rigby
I Run	C	56	This Is the Way	SRA/McGraw-Hill
I See	C	29	Teacher's Choice Series	Dominie
I See Monkeys	C	39	Williams, Deborah	Kaeden Books
I See You	C	56	Twig	Wright Group
I Spy	C	25	Literacy 2000	Rigby
I Swim	C	57	This Is the Way	SRA/McGraw-Hill
I Thought I Couldn't	C	40	Visions	Wright Group
I Want a Pet	C	46	Little Readers	Houghton Mifflin
I Want a Pet	C	46	Gregorich, Barbara	School Zone
I Want Ice Cream	C	18	Story Box	Wright Group
I Want My Own Room!	C	25	Visions	Wright Group
I Went Walking	C	105	Williams, Sue	Harcourt Brace
I Wonder	C	49	Little Celebrations	Pearson Learning
I Write	C	19	Sunshine	Wright Group
Ice Cream	C	49	Sunshine	Wright Group
If You Meet a Dragon	C	31	Story Box	Wright Group
I'm Hungry	C	37	Visions	Wright Group
I'm Not, I'm Not	C	19	Windmill	Rigby, Wright Group
In My Bed	C	57	Literacy 2000	Rigby
In My Garden	C	36	Carousel Readers	Dominie
In My Room	C	44	Literacy 2000	Rigby
In the City	C	45	Pasternac, Susana	Scholastic
In the City	C	50	Rise & Shine	Hampton-Brown
In the Dark Forest	C	24	Pacific Literacy	Pacific Learning
In the Forest	C	42	Twig	Wright Group
In the Sea	C	41	Sunshine	Wright Group
In Went Goldilocks	C	30	Literacy 2000	Rigby
Is It Alive?	C	26	Learn to Read	Creative Teaching Press
Is It Time?	C	52	Campbell, J. G.	Scholastic
Is This a Monster?	C	93	Book Shop	Mondo Publishing
Itch! Itch!	C	76	Book Shop	Mondo Publishing
It's Football Time	C	24	Geddes, Diana	Kaeden Books
It's Raining!	C	32	Pair-It Books	Steck-Vaughn
I've Lost My Boot	C	18	Windmill	Wright Group
J My Name Is Jess	C	61	Little Books	Sadlier-Oxford
Jackets	C	42	Joy Readers	Dominie
Jack's Pack	C	22	KinderReaders	Rigby
Jan's New Fan	C	34	KinderReaders	Rigby
Joshua James Likes Trucks	C	50	Rookie Readers	Children's Press
Jump and Thump!	C	18	Home Connection Collection	Rigby
Jump, Frog	C	33	Stewart, J. & Salem, Lynn	Seedling
Jumping Shoes	C	34	Joy Readers	Dominie
Junk Box, The	C	54	Windmill Books	Rigby
Just Add Water	C	41	Discovery World	Rigby
Just Like Grandpa	C	49	Little Celebrations	Pearson Learning
Just Me	C	51	Literacy 2000	Rigby
Kay's Birthday	C	26	KinderReaders	Rigby
Keeping Baby Animals Safe	C	56	Little Books	Sadlier-Oxford
Keeping Cool	C	18	Pacific Literacy	Pacific Learning
King's Ring, The	C	38	KinderReaders	Rigby

Title	Level	Words	Author/Series	Publisher/Distributor
Kink the Mink	C	18	KinderReaders	Rigby
Kip and Tip	C	24	KinderReaders	Rigby
Kites	C	41	Joy Readers	Dominie
Kitten Chased a Fly	C	57	Windmill	Rigby, Wright Group
Kittens	C	22	Literacy 2000	Rigby
Kitty and the Birds	C	64	PM Story Books	Rigby
Knock, Knock	C		Little Celebrations	Pearson Learning
Lazy Pig, The	C	78	PM Story Books	Rigby
Leaves	C	29	Hoenecke, Karen	Kaeden Books
Leaves, Fruits, Seeds, and Roots	C	26	Pacific Literacy	Pacific Learning
Legs, Legs, Legs	C	36	Wonder World	Wright Group
Let's Go	C	30	Windmill	Wright Group
Let's Go Shopping	C	34	Rise & Shine	Hampton-Brown
Let's Have a Swim	C	74	Sunshine	Wright Group
Let's Paint	C	51	Rise & Shine	Hampton-Brown
Let's Play Ball	C	68	New Way Red	Steck-Vaughn
Levi Sings	C	29	Teacher's Choice Series	Dominie
Library, The	C	33	Carousel Readers	Dominie
Lights at Night	C	33	Pacific Literacy	Pacific Learning
Lin's Backpack	C	49	Little Celebrations	Pearson Learning
Little Bike, The	C	29	Joy Readers	Dominie
Little Brother	C	14	Story Box	Wright Group
Little Cousins' Visit, The	C	123	Emergent	Pioneer Valley
Little Hearts	C	44	Story Box	Wright Group
Little Pig	C	63	Story Box	Wright Group
Little Sister	C	40	Mitchell, Robin	Scholastic
Little Snowman, The	C	59	PM Extensions-Red	Rigby
Lizard on a Stick	C	38	Wonder World	Wright Group
Log, The	C	29	New Way Red	Steck-Vaughn
Look Again	C	47	Book Shop	Mondo Publishing
Look!	C	43	Little Celebrations	Pearson Learning
Looking Down	C	70	PM Starters	Rigby
Looking for Eggs	C	47	Windmill Books	Rigby
Looking for Halloween	C	49	Urmston, Kathleen & Evans, Karen	Kaeden Books
Lost	C	38	Story Box	Wright Group
Lost Glove, The	C	105	Foundations	Wright Group
Lots of Dogs	C	68	Teacher's Choice Series	Dominie
Lots of Dolls!	C	61	The Candid Collection	Dominie
Love Is	C	11	Visions	Wright Group
Lunch Orders	C	18	Tadpoles	Rigby
Lunch Time	C	69	Carousel Readers	Dominie
Machines	C	36	Little Celebrations	Pearson Learning
Mae-Nerd	C	44	Teacher's Choice Series	Dominie
Magic Food	C	26	Smart Starts	Rigby
Magic Machine, The	C	163	Sunshine	Wright Group
Magnets	C	55	Early Connections	Benchmark Education
Magnifying Glass, The	C	45	Foundations	Wright Group
Mail Came Today, The	C	35	Carousel Readers	Dominie
Make a Pinata	C	16	Little Celebrations	Pearson Learning
Make a Valentine	C	36	Book Shop	Mondo Publishing
Making Music	C	35	Wonder World	Wright Group

Title	Level	Words	Author/Series	Publisher/Distributor
Making Patterns	C	30	Twig	Wright Group
Mamma Hen, Come Quick!	C	35	Ready Readers	Pearson Learning
Manners, Please!	C	27	Pair-It Books	Steck-Vaughn
Masks	C	41	Pebble Books	Grolier, Capstone
Me	C	41	Reading Corners	Dominie
Me (boy)	C	34	Tonon, Terry	Kaeden Books
Me (girl)	C	34	Tonon, Terry	Kaeden Books
Measure It	C	56	Twig	Wright Group
Meg's Eggs	C	38	New Way Red	Steck-Vaughn
Merry-Go-Round	C	66	Teacher's Choice Series	Dominie
Merry-Go-Round, The	C	45	Ready Readers	Pearson Learning
Merry-Go-Round, The	C	62	Sunshine	Wright Group
Merry-Go-Round, The	C	84	PM Story Books	Rigby
Messy Moose	C	45	Little Books	Sadlier-Oxford
Mexican Holiday, A	C	24	The Candid Collection	Dominie
Mice on Ice	C	34	KinderReaders	Rigby
Michael's Picture	C	33	Little Celebrations	Pearson Learning
Microscope	C	46	Story Box	Wright Group
Mix It Up	C	35	Twig	Wright Group
Mom's Hat	C	39	Joy Readers	Dominie
Monkey Hop, The	C	26	Joy Readers	Dominie
Monkey's Friends	C	36	Literacy 2000	Rigby
Monster Meals	C	33	Literacy 2000	Rigby
Monster Sandwich, A	C	36	Story Box	Wright Group
Monster, Monster	C	38	Reading Corners	Dominie
Monster's Party, The	C	92	Story Box	Wright Group
Monsters	C	30	TOTTS	Tott Publications
Mosquito	C	46	Book Bank	Wright Group
Mother Hippopotamus Goes Shopping	C	79	Foundations	Wright Group
Motorbike Race, The	C	48	Joy Readers	Dominie
Mouse	C	40	Story Box	Wright Group
Mouse, The	C	26	Pacific Literacy	Pacific Learning
Moving Day	C	90	Foundations	Wright Group
Mr. Brown	C	20	KinderReaders	Rigby
Mrs. Cook's Hats	C	31	Mader, Jan	Kaeden Books
Mud Pie	C	14	Literacy 2000	Rigby
Mud Pies	C	56	TOTTS	Tott Publications
Mud Puddles	C	24	TOTTS	Tott Publications
My Accident	C	46	PM Starters	Rigby
My Apartment	C	20	Visions	Wright Group
My Best Friend	C	63	Carousel Readers	Dominie
My Best Friend	C		Little Celebrations	Pearson Learning
My Big Wheel	C	38	Visions	Wright Group
My Birthday Party	C	38	Visions	Wright Group
My Body	C	47	Discovery World	Rigby
My Book	C	32	Sunshine	Wright Group
My Circus Family	C	42	Book Shop	Mondo Publishing
My Clothes	C	16	Carousel Earlybirds	Dominie
My Clothes	C	86	Foundations	Wright Group
My Dad Cooks	C	29	Carousel Readers	Dominie
My Day	C	44	Rise & Shine	Hampton-Brown

Title	Level	Words	Author/Series	Publisher/Distributor
My Day	C	51	Barney, Mike	Kaeden Books
My Dog	C	79	Early Emergent	Pioneer Valley
My Dog Ben	C	19	Voyages	SRA/McGraw-Hill
My Dog Willy	C	71	Little Readers	Houghton Mifflin
My Dream	C	34	Wildsmith, Brian	Oxford University Press
My Friend at School	C	30	Visions	Wright Group
My Helicopter Ride	C	42	Foundations	Wright Group
My Home	C	46	Story Box	Wright Group
My Kite	C	37	Williams, Deborah	Kaeden Books
My Letter	C	51	Wonder World	Wright Group
My Little Brother	C	59	Windmill	Rigby, Wright Group
My Little Dog	C	90	PM Starters	Rigby
My Lunch	C	70	Early Emergent	Pioneer Valley
My Mama	C	25	Visions	Wright Group
My Nest	C	42	Little Celebrations	Pearson Learning
My New House	C	26	Reading Corners	Dominie
My Party	C	35	The Candid Collection	Dominie
My Pet	C	18	KinderReaders	Rigby
My Picture	C	37	Carousel Readers	Dominie
My Pony	C	49	Rise & Shine	Hampton-Brown
My Pumpkin	C	52	Teacher's Choice Series	Dominie
My Puppy	C	33	Little Celebrations	Pearson Learning
My Ride	C	56	Foundations	Wright Group
My Room	C	42	Ready Readers	Pearson Learning
My School	C	40	TOTTS	Tott Publications
My Shadow	C	35	Sunshine	Wright Group
My Shadow	C	42	Foundations	Wright Group
My Teacher Helps Me	C	37	Visions	Wright Group
My Three-Wheeler	C	38	Visions	Wright Group
My Twin!	C	40	Ready Readers	Pearson Learning
My Uncle's Truck	C	24	Visions	Wright Group
My Weekly Chores	C	44	Visions	Wright Group
Nanny Goat's Nap	C	96	Ready Readers	Pearson Learning
Nap Time	C	24	KinderReaders	Rigby
Nature Hike	C	32	Twig	Wright Group
Naughty Happy Monkey	C	33	Joy Readers	Dominie
Needs and Wants	C	43	Early Connections	Benchmark Education
Neighborhood Party, The	C	60	Pair-It Books	Steck-Vaughn
Nest, The	C	32	Story Box	Wright Group
Nest, The	C	34	Sunshine	Wright Group
Nests	C	35	Wonder World	Wright Group
New Highway, The	C	67	Foundations	Wright Group
New Shoes	C	29	Wonder World	Wright Group
Night Sky	C	15	Twig	Wright Group
Nighttime	C	44	Story Box	Wright Group
Noises!!!	C	98	Teacher's Choice Series	Dominie
Now We Can Go	C		Jonas, Ann	Greenwillow
Octopus Goes to School	C	42	Bordelon, Carolyn	Seedling
Oh, No!	C	53	Joy Readers	Dominie
Old and New	C	50	Interaction	Rigby
Old Tuatara	C	33	Ready to Read	Pacific Learning

Title	Level	Words	Author/Series	Publisher/Distributor
Old Tuatara	C	33	Pacific Literacy	Pacific Learning
On a Chair	C	30	Story Box	Wright Group
On a Cold, Cold Day	C	33	Tadpoles	Rigby
On the Farm	C	18	Literacy 2000	Rigby
On the Go	C	43	Learn to Read	Creative Teaching Press
On the Ground	C	40	Sunshine	Wright Group
On the Road	C	47	Teacher's Choice Series	Dominie
One Bee Got on the Bus	C	43	Ready Readers	Pearson Learning
One Bird Sat on the Fence	C	40	Wonder World	Wright Group
One for You and One for Me	C	27	Blaxland, Wendy	Scholastic
Orchestra, The	C	33	Foundations	Wright Group
Our Car	C	32	Sunshine	Wright Group
Our Dog Sam	C	56	Literacy 2000	Rigby
Our Grandad	C	30	Sunshine	Wright Group
Our Granny	C	41	Sunshine	Wright Group
Our School	C	46	Twig	Wright Group
Our Street	C	40	Sunshine	Wright Group
Our Week	C	37	Storyteller-First Snow	Wright Group/ McGraw-Hill
Outside and Inside	C	43	Twig	Wright Group
Painting	C	24	Story Box	Wright Group
Pam & Sam at the Park	C	108	Carousel Earlybirds	Dominie
Pam & Sam at the Zoo	C	84	Carousel Earlybirds	Dominie
Pam & Sam Fly Over the City	C	80	Carousel Earlybirds	Dominie
Pancakes for Breakfast	C	108	Emergent	Pioneer Valley
Pancakes, Crackers and Pizza	C	63	Rookie Readers	Children's Press
Parades!	C	24	Pair-It Books	Steck-Vaughn
Parents	C	60	Pebble Books	Grolier, Capstone
Pass the Present	C	86	Storyteller-First Snow	Wright Group/ McGraw-Hill
Pat's Perfect Pizza	C	37	Ready Readers	Pearson Learning
Patterns	C	35	Discovery Links	Newbridge
Patty and Pop's Picnic	C	57	Little Books	Sadlier-Oxford
Pedal Power	C	22	Pacific Literacy	Pacific Learning
Pet for Me, A	C	73	Early Emergent	Pioneer Valley
Pet Parade	C	33	Literacy 2000	Rigby
Pet Shop, The	C	32	Oxford Reading Tree	Oxford University Press
Photo Book, The	C	50	PM Story Books	Rigby
Pick a Pet	C		Little Celebrations	Pearson Learning
Picnic, The	C	48	Teacher's Choice Series	Dominie
Picture, A	C	58	Storyteller-First Snow	Wright Group/ McGraw-Hill
Pigs Peek	C	28	Books for Young Learners	Richard C. Owen
Pitty Pitty Pat	C	45	Little Celebrations	Pearson Learning
Places	C	88	Little Red Readers	Sundance
Play Dough	C	63	Foundations	Wright Group
Playground, The	C	108	Early Emergent	Pioneer Valley
Playhouse for Monster	C		Mueller, Virginia	Whitman
Playing in the Snow	C	61	Early Emergent	Pioneer Valley
Playtime	C		Voyages	SRA/McGraw-Hill
Plop!	C	30	Story Box	Wright Group

Title	Level	Words	Author/Series	Publisher/Distributor
Pond, The	C	25	Books for Young Learners	Richard C. Owen
Pond, The	C	54	Joy Readers	Dominie
Pop...Pop...Popcorn	C	40	Home Connection Collection	Rigby
Potatoes on Tuesday	C	28	Little Celebrations	Pearson Learning
Puppet Play, A	C	54	Storyteller-First Snow	Wright Group/ McGraw-Hill
Python Caught the Eagle, The	C	60	Voyages	SRA/McGraw-Hill
Queen on a Quilt	C	26	Ready Readers	Pearson Learning
Quilts	C	35	Foundations	Wright Group
Race, The	C	25	Sunshine	Wright Group
Rain	C	56	Kalan, Robert	Greenwillow
Rain or Shine?	C	21	Twig	Wright Group
Rainbow of My Own	C	268	Freeman, Don	The Penguin Group
Raindrop, A	C	41	Teacher's Choice Series	Dominie
Raindrops	C	66	Gay, Sandy	Scholastic
Rat's Funny Story	C	39	Story Box	Wright Group
Reaching the Sky	C	46	Sunshine	Wright Group
Ready for School	C	41	Teacher's Choice Series	Dominie
Red Balloon, The	C	34	Joy Readers	Dominie
Ribbon, The	C	46	Rise & Shine	Hampton-Brown
Riding	C	67	Foundations	Wright Group
Rita Rolls	C	36	Little Celebrations	Pearson Learning
Roberto's Smile	C	43	Story Box	Wright Group
Rockets	C		Little Celebrations	Pearson Learning
Rockity Rock	C	36	KinderReaders	Rigby
Roll Over!	C	201	Peek, Merle	Clarion
Roller Coaster	C	45	Joy Readers	Dominie
Round	C	40	Windmill Books	Rigby
Round and Round	C	38	Story Box	Wright Group
Row Your Boat	C	18	Literacy 2000	Rigby
Rules for Pets	C	54	Joy Readers	Dominie
Run! Run!	C	64	Book Shop	Mondo Publishing
Running	C	39	Foundations	Wright Group
Safety	C	35	Interaction	Rigby
Safety First	C	131	Twig	Wright Group
Sally and the Daisy	C	60	PM Story Books	Rigby
Sally and the Elephant	C	45	Wonder World	Wright Group
Sam	C	17	KinderReaders	Rigby
Same Team	C	44	The Candid Collection	Dominie
Sammy at the Farm	C	83	Urmston, Kathleen & Evans, Karen	Kaeden Books
Sandwich, The	C	68	Carousel Earlybirds	Dominie
Sandy	C	32	Ready Readers	Pearson Learning
Scarecrow	C	31	Literacy 2000	Rigby
Scarecrow's Friends	C	56	Start to Read	School Zone
Scaredy Cat	C	85	Learn to Read	Creative Teaching Press
Scary Monster	C	19	Eifrig, Kate	Kaeden Books
Seasons	C	28	Discovery World	Rigby
Seesaw, The	C	46	Voyages	SRA/McGraw-Hill
Seesaw, The	C	100	Emergent	Pioneer Valley
Shape Walk	C	25	Little Celebrations	Pearson Learning
Shapes	C	30	Rise & Shine	Hampton-Brown

Title	Level	Words	Author/Series	Publisher/Distributor
Shapes	C	31	Visions	Wright Group
Sharing	C	24	Literacy 2000	Rigby
Shark in a Sack	C	65	Sunshine	Wright Group
She Said	C	35	Ready Readers	Pearson Learning
Sheep's Bell	C	37	Ready Readers	Pearson Learning
Shoo!	C	37	Sunshine	Wright Group
Shopping	C	41	Interaction	Rigby
Shopping	C	78	Little Red Readers	Sundance
Shopping for School	C	33	Visions	Wright Group
Shopping with Dad	C	43	Home Connection Collection	Rigby
Signs	C	35	Little Celebrations	Pearson Learning
Signs	C	40	Carousel Earlybirds	Dominie
Silly Old Possum	C	41	Story Box	Wright Group
Six Cats	C	50	Joy Readers	Dominie
Six Go By	C	24	Ready Readers	Pearson Learning
Sizes	C	32	Discovery World	Rigby
Skating	C	52	Story Box	Wright Group
Smiling Salad, A	C	32	Pair-It Books	Steck-Vaughn
Smokie	C	47	Carousel Readers	Dominie
Snap! Splat!	C	25	Sunshine	Wright Group
Snip-Snap, Clickety-Click	C		Little Celebrations	Pearson Learning
Snow Cover	C	29	Little Celebrations	Pearson Learning
Snowman	C	21	Sunshine	Wright Group
Snowman, A	C	59	Foundations	Wright Group
Sometimes I'm Silly	C	24	Visions	Wright Group
Speed Boat, The	C	170	Sunshine	Wright Group
Splash	C	34	Foundations	Wright Group
Splashing Dad	C	37	Early Emergent	Pioneer Valley
Splosh	C	47	Story Box	Wright Group
Sports Day	C	24	Home Connection Collection	Rigby
Spots	C	41	Sunshine	Wright Group
Spots, Feathers and Curly Tails	C		Tafuri, Nancy	Morrow
Spring	C	47	Carousel Readers	Dominie
Squares Everywhere	C	26	Discovery Links	Newbridge
Sssh!	C	49	Book Bank	Wright Group
Stepping Stones	C	42	Sunshine	Wright Group
Stop	C	54	Story Box	Wright Group
Stop That	C	41	Ready Readers	Pearson Learning
Stop That Noise!	C	41	Pacific Literacy	Pacific Learning
Stop!	C	31	Wonder World	Wright Group
Stores	C	66	Carousel Readers	Dominie
Storm, The	C	28	Voyages	SRA/McGraw-Hill
Storm, The	C	29	Story Box	Wright Group
Story Time	C	32	Ready Readers	Pearson Learning
Strawberries	C	37	Little Books for Early Readers	University of Maine
Strings	C	53	Storyteller-First Snow	Wright Group/ McGraw-Hill
Sunrise	C	46	Literacy 2000	Rigby
Surprise Cake	C	32	Literacy 2000	Rigby
Swimming	C	65	Carousel Readers	Dominie
Swimming Pool, The	C	29	Visions	Wright Group

Title	Level	Words	Author/Series	Publisher/Distributor
Swing, Swing, Swing	C	93	Tuchman, G. & Dieterichs, S.	Scholastic
Tails and Claws	C	65	Wonder World	Wright Group
Take a Bite	C	19	Little Celebrations	Pearson Learning
Take a Guess	C	45	Little Celebrations	Pearson Learning
Talk, Talk, Talk	C	56	Literacy 2000	Rigby
Taxi, The	C	45	Joy Readers	Dominie
Tea Party	C	38	Carousel Readers	Dominie
Tea Party, The	C	76	Storyteller-First Snow	Wright Group/ McGraw-Hill
Tee-Ball	C	53	Little Celebrations	Pearson Learning
Teeny Tiny Tina	C	34	Literacy 2000	Rigby
Teeter-Totter, The	C	35	Joy Readers	Dominie
Teeth	C	26	Wonder World	Wright Group
Ten Crazy Caterpillars	C	40	Voyages	SRA/McGraw-Hill
Terrific Shoes	C	19	Ready Readers	Pearson Learning
That Fly	C	26	Ready Readers	Pearson Learning
There Is a Planet	C	52	Sunshine	Wright Group
These Legs	C	42	Foundations	Wright Group
Things I Like	C	42	Carousel Earlybirds	Dominie
Things I Like to Do	C	58	Foundations	Wright Group
Things I Like to Do	C	63	Carousel Earlybirds	Dominie
Things on Wheels	C	69	Little Red Readers	Sundance
Things That Help Me	C	18	Pacific Literacy	Pacific Learning
This Is My Friend	C	77	Foundations	Wright Group
This Is My Home	C	51	Joy Readers	Dominie
Tick-Tock	C	53	Story Box	Wright Group
Tiger, Tiger	C	55	PM Story Books	Rigby
Time for a Change	C	31	Pacific Literacy	Pacific Learning
Time for Bed	C	28	Smart Starts	Rigby
Timmy Tries	C	22	Little Celebrations	Pearson Learning
To the Ocean	C	26	Twig	Wright Group
To Work	C	43	Sunshine	Wright Group
Together	C	37	Sunshine	Wright Group
Tom and His Tractor	C	27	Cat on the Mat	Oxford University Press
Tommy's Tummy Ache	C	20	Literacy 2000	Rigby
Too Many Clothes	C	24	Literacy 2000	Rigby
Toot! Toot!	C	21	Joy Readers	Dominie
Toot, Toot	C	47	Wildsmith, Brian	Oxford University Press
Tossed Salad	C	28	Twig	Wright Group
Touch	C	39	Twig	Wright Group
Toy Town	C	36	Home Connection Collection	Rigby
Toys with Wheels	C	41	Home Connection Collection	Rigby
Tracks	C	25	Sunshine	Wright Group
Tracks	C	49	Twig	Wright Group
Train Ride, The	C	29	Literacy 2000	Rigby
Train, The	C	27	Visions	Wright Group
Transportation Museum, The	C	79	Little Red Readers	Sundance
Traveling	C	86	Foundations	Wright Group
Traveling Ted's Postcards	C		Little Celebrations	Pearson Learning
Tree Fell Over the River, A	C	72	Little Red Readers	Sundance
Trip to the Aquarium, A	C	18	Kloes, Carol	Kaeden Books

Title	Level	Words	Author/Series	Publisher/Distributor
Trip to the Zoo, A	C	78	Carousel Readers	Dominie
Trolley Ride, The	C	87	Tadpoles	Rigby
Truck Stop, The	C	25	Kloes, Carol	Kaeden Books
Trucks	C	24	Twig	Wright Group
Trucks	C	27	Pebble Books	Grolier, Capstone
Trucks	C	38	Literacy 2000	Rigby
Two Little Chicks	C	32	KinderReaders	Rigby
Tyler's Train	C		Little Celebrations	Pearson Learning
Umbrella	C	73	Story Box	Wright Group
Uncle Buncle's House	C	56	Sunshine	Wright Group
Under My Bed	C	49	Little Celebrations	Pearson Learning
Under the Ground	C	42	Foundations	Wright Group
Underground	C	31	Twig	Wright Group
Up in a Tree	C	47	Sunshine	Wright Group
Up Went the Goat	C	38	Gregorich, Barbara	School Zone
Using Tools	C	30	Discovery Links	Newbridge
Vacation, The	C	94	Emergent	Pioneer Valley
Valentine's Checkup	C	45	Little Books	Sadlier-Oxford
Valentine's Day	C	49	Story Box	Wright Group
Vultures on Vacation	C	36	Ready Readers	Pearson Learning
Wait for Me	C	75	Little Books	Sadlier-Oxford
Wake Up Mom!	C	94	Sunshine	Wright Group
Wake Up, Dad	C	67	PM Story Books	Rigby
Walking to School	C	38	Voyages	SRA/McGraw-Hill
Walking, Walking	C	32	Twig	Wright Group
Warm Clothes	C	51	Pebble Books	Grolier, Capstone
Watch Me Zoom	C	45	Windmill Books	Rigby
Watch Out!	C	27	Literacy 2000	Rigby
Water	C	20	Carousel Readers	Dominie
Water! Water!	C	33	Sunshine	Wright Group
We All Play Sports	C	26	Pacific Literacy	Pacific Learning
We Can Run	C	77	PM Starters	Rigby
We Dance	C	30	Pacific Literacy	Pacific Learning
We Like	C	42	Foundations	Wright Group
We Like the Sun	C	30	Pair-It Books	Steck-Vaughn
We Like to Graph	C	48	Coulton, Mia	Kaeden Books
We Love Recess	C	63	Fiesta Series	Dominie
We Make Pizza	C	37	Carousel Readers	Dominie
We Need Trees	C	33	Hoenecke, Karen	Kaeden Books
We Use Water	C	48	Early Connections	Benchmark Education
We Went Flying	C	40	Carousel Earlybirds	Dominie
Weather	C	54	Chanko, P. & Morton, D.	Scholastic
What a Mess!	C	51	Story Box	Wright Group
What a Tale!	C	38	Wildsmith, Brian	Oxford University Press
What a Week!	C	36	Home Connection Collection	Rigby
What Am I?	C	51	Williams, Deborah	Kaeden Books
What Animals Do You See?	C	50	Read-More Books	Dominie
What Are You Called?	C	66	Voyages	SRA/McGraw-Hill
What Can Float?	C	32	Windmill Books	Rigby
What Can Fly?	C	33	Joy Readers	Dominie
What Can Hurt?	C	30	Windmill Books	Rigby

Title	Level	Words	Author/Series	Publisher/Distributor
What Can I Do?	C	42	Read-More Books	Dominie
What Can I Do?	C	42	Foundations	Wright Group
What Can I See?	C	42	Foundations	Wright Group
What Can We Smell?	C	44	Windmill Books	Rigby
What Can You See?	C	25	Literacy 2000	Rigby
What Comes First?	C	56	Book Shop	Mondo Publishing
What Could I Be?	C	64	Foundations	Wright Group
What Did Kim Catch?	C	48	Literacy 2000	Rigby
What Did They Want?	C	28	Smart Starts	Rigby
What Do We Have?	C	28	Step-By-Step Series	Dominie
What Do You Have?	C	88	Windmill Books	Rigby
What Do You See at the Pet Store?	C	27	Read-More Books	Dominie
What Do You See?	C	35	Windmill Books	Rigby
What Do You Touch?	C	50	Windmill Books	Rigby
What Does Greedy Cat Like?	C	35	Pacific Literacy	Pacific Learning
What Floats?	C	16	Twig	Wright Group
What Goes in the Bathtub?	C	31	Literacy 2000	Rigby
What Goes into a Salad?	C	22	Home Connection Collection	Rigby
What Goes Up and Down	C	40	Windmill Books	Rigby
What Hangs from the Tree?	C	42	Questions & Answers	Dominie
What Has Stripes?	C	25	Ballinger, Margaret	Scholastic
What I Left on My Plate	C	54	Teacher's Choice Series	Dominie
What I Like at School	C	64	Little Red Readers	Sundance
What If?	C	41	Little Celebrations	Pearson Learning
What Is Blue?	C	31	Carousel Earlybirds	Dominie
What Is Delicious?	C	25	Windmill Books	Rigby
What Is Fun?	C	34	Windmill Books	Rigby
What Is in Space?	C	41	Science	Wright Group
What Is Old?	C	32	Windmill Books	Rigby
What Is Slow?	C	29	Windmill Books	Rigby
What Is Soft?	C	30	Windmill Books	Rigby
What Is That?	C	61	Ready Readers	Pearson Learning
What Is This Skeleton?	C	48	Science	Wright Group
What Is This?	C	28	Ready Readers	Pearson Learning
What Is Young?	C	31	Windmill Books	Rigby
What Kind of Dog Am I?	C	21	Twig	Wright Group
What Plays Music?	C	36	Questions & Answers	Dominie
What Season Is This?	C	24	Wonder World	Wright Group
What Smells Good?	C	26	Windmill Books	Rigby
What's for Lunch?	C	48	Carle, Eric	Scholastic
What's Inside?	C	47	Hoenecke, Karen	Kaeden Books
What's on Your T-Shirt?	C	64	Carousel Readers	Dominie
What's That?	C	27	Carousel Earlybirds	Dominie
What's the Time Mr Wolf?	C	49	Windmill	Wright Group
What's Under My Bed?	C	18	Visions	Wright Group
Wheel, The	C	102	Joy Readers	Dominie
Wheels	C	27	Literacy 2000	Rigby
Wheels	C	29	Discovery Links	Newbridge
Wheels	C	39	Sunshine	Wright Group
When Do Cars Stop?	C	62	Questions & Answers	Dominie
When I Grow Up	C	38	Rise & Shine	Hampton-Brown

Title	Level	Words	Author/Series	Publisher/Distributor
When I Play	C	31	Literacy 2000	Rigby
When I Pretend	C	40	Literacy 2000	Rigby
When It Rains	C	39	Foundations	Wright Group
When It Snowed	C	33	Home Connection Collection	Rigby
When Itchy Witchy Sneezes	C	39	Sunshine	Wright Group
When Mr. Quinn Snored	C	31	Little Books	Sadlier-Oxford
Where Are They Going?	C	42	Story Box	Wright Group
Where Do I Live?	C	29	Visions	Wright Group
Where Do Monsters Live?	C	56	Learn to Read	Creative Teaching Press
Where Do They Live?	C	45	Ready Readers	Pearson Learning
Where Does a Leopard Hide?	C	108	Foundations	Wright Group
Where Does It Go?	C	61	Questions & Answers	Dominie
Where Does the Teacher Sleep?	C	50	Gibson, Kathleen	Seedling
Where Is Happy Monkey?	C	46	Joy Readers	Dominie
Where Is My Bone?	C	42	Sunshine	Wright Group
Where Is My Grandma?	C	74	Foundations	Wright Group
Where Is My Pencil?	C	34	Little Celebrations	Pearson Learning
Where Is the Cat?	C	28	Read-More Books	Dominie
Where Is Water?	C	36	Twig	Wright Group
Where Will You Sleep Tonight?	C	77	Foundations	Wright Group
Where's Bear?	C	41	Windmill	Wright Group
Where's Little Mole?	C	43	Little Celebrations	Pearson Learning
Where's My Backpack?	C	27	Little Celebrations	Pearson Learning
Where's the Halloween Treat?	C	102	Ziefert, Harriet	The Penguin Group
Where's Tim?	C	38	Sunshine	Wright Group
Where's Your Tooth?	C	53	Learn to Read	Creative Teaching Press
Which Clothes Do You Wear?	C	49	Foundations	Wright Group
Which Juice Would You Like?	C	28	Step-By-Step Series	Dominie
Which Way Home?	C	26	Little Celebrations	Pearson Learning
Whisper and Shout	C	92	Twig	Wright Group
White Paw, Black Paw	C	41	KinderReaders	Rigby
Who Are We?	C	30	Home Connection Collection	Rigby
Who Are You?	C	55	Book Bank	Wright Group
Who Ate the Pizza?	C	59	Foundations	Wright Group
Who Came By Here?	C	31	Rise & Shine	Hampton-Brown
Who Can Hop?	C	35	Questions & Answers	Dominie
Who Can See the Camel?	C	70	Story Box	Wright Group
Who Has Wings?	C	30	Questions & Answers	Dominie
Who Is Ready?	C	36	Ready Readers	Pearson Learning
Who Is the Robot?	C	67	Pacific Literacy	Pacific Learning
Who Lives Here?	C	28	Story Box	Wright Group
Who Lives Here?	C	42	Questions & Answers	Dominie
Who Lives Here?	C	62	Learn to Read	Creative Teaching Press
Who Lives in a Tree?	C	43	Discovery Links	Newbridge
Who Lives in this Hole?	C	25	Twig	Wright Group
Who Made That?	C	31	Ready Readers	Pearson Learning
Who Rides the Bus?	C	19	Little Celebrations	Pearson Learning
Who Says?	C	49	Twig	Wright Group
Who Will Help Me?	C	53	Home Connection Collection	Rigby
Who's Going to Lick the Bowl?	C	18	Story Box	Wright Group
Whose Birthday Is It Today?	C	50	Book Bank	Wright Group

Title	Level	Words	Author/Series	Publisher/Distributor
Whose Forest Is It?	C	45	Learn to Read	Creative Teaching Press
Whose List Is This?	C		Little Celebrations	Pearson Learning
Winter	C	49	Carousel Readers	Dominie
Winter	C	54	Foundations	Wright Group
Winter Fun	C	13	Teacher's Choice Series	Dominie
With My Mom and Dad	C	63	Early Connections	Benchmark Education
Wizard of Earthsea, The	C		Voyages	SRA/McGraw-Hill
Woof!	C	40	Literacy 2000	Rigby
Work	C	65	TOTTS	Tott Publications
Working Together	C	50	Early Connections	Benchmark Education
Would You Like to Fly?	C	52	Twig	Wright Group
Wrinkles	C	32	Literacy 2000	Rigby
Yes, I Can	C	30	Teacher's Choice Series	Dominie
You	C	20	Carousel Earlybirds	Dominie
Yummy, Tum, Tum	C		Little Celebrations	Pearson Learning
Zebra's Yellow Van	C	31	Ready Readers	Pearson Learning
Zippers	C	21	Books for Young Learners	Richard C. Owen
Zoo Food	C	58	Reading Corners	Dominie
Zoo, The	C	33	Carousel Readers	Dominie
Zoom! Zoom!	C	43	Joy Readers	Dominie
Accidents	D	35	Visions	Wright Group
After School	D	58	Sunshine	Wright Group
Ali's Story	D	236	Sunshine	Wright Group
All Join In	D	38	Literacy 2000	Rigby
All Kinds of Food	D	72	Learn to Read	Creative Teaching Press
All Pull Together	D	69	Home Connection Collection	Rigby
Along Comes Jake	D	86	Sunshine	Wright Group
Animal Shapes	D	14	Wildsmith, Brian	Oxford University Press
Animal Tracks	D	152	Wonder World	Wright Group
Animals	D	70	Foundations	Wright Group
Animals and Their Babies	D	166	Early Connections	Benchmark Education
Animals at the Mall	D	39	Teacher's Choice Series	Dominie
Animals Hide	D	55	Discovery Links	Newbridge
Animals in the Desert	D	31	Carousel Readers	Dominie
Apple Trees	D	62	Pebble Books	Grolier, Capstone
As Fast as a Fox	D	69	Ready Readers	Pearson Learning
At Grandma's House	D	66	Teacher's Choice Series	Dominie
At Night	D	21	Literacy 2000	Rigby
At the Fair	D	116	Little Red Readers	Sundance
At the Fair	D	175	Sunshine	Wright Group
At the Horse Show	D	24	Books for Young Learners	Richard C. Owen
At the Park	D	37	Hoenecke, Karen	Kaeden Books
At the Park	D	74	Teacher's Choice Series	Dominie
At the Park	D	91	Little Red Readers	Sundance
At the Supermarket	D	29	Read-More Books	Dominie
At the Toyshop	D	41	Home Connection Collection	Rigby
At the Zoo	D	37	Little Celebrations	Pearson Learning
At the Zoo	D	116	Predictable Storybooks	SRA/McGraw-Hill
Auntie Maria and the Cat	D	215	Sunshine	Wright Group
Aunts	D	49	Pebble Books	Grolier, Capstone

Title	Level	Words	Author/Series	Publisher/Distributor
Baby Animals	D	41	Discovery Links	Newbridge
Baby Animals	D	78	Foundations	Wright Group
Baby Birds	D	51	Pebble Books	Grolier, Capstone
Baby Elephant Gets Lost	D	90	Foundations	Wright Group
Baby Hippo	D	117	PM Extensions-Yellow	Rigby
Baby's Birthday	D	53	Literacy 2000	Rigby
Bad Day, The	D	93	Teacher's Choice Series	Dominie
Baked Potatoes	D	73	Book Bank	Wright Group
Ball Bounced, The	D	33	Tafuri, Nancy	Morrow
Ball Game, A	D	72	Carousel Readers	Dominie
Ballerina Girl	D	77	My First Reader	Grolier Press
Balloon, The	D	64	Carousel Readers	Dominie
Balloons!	D	56	Storyteller-First Snow	Wright Group/ McGraw-Hill
Banana Monster, The	D	54	Joy Readers	Dominie
Bath for a Beagle	D	102	First Start	Troll
Bats at Bat	D	36	Pair-It Books	Steck-Vaughn
Beach, The	D	38	Book Bank	Wright Group
Bear Escape, The	D	42	Pair-It Books	Steck-Vaughn
Bear Lived in a Cave, A	D	102	Little Red Readers	Sundance
Bears	D	56	Joy Readers	Dominie
Bears in the Night	D	108	Berenstain, Stan & Jan	Random House
Bears on Wheels	D	89	Berenstain, Stan & Jan	Random House
Bears' Picnic, The	D	61	Story Box	Wright Group
Bears, Bears Everywhere	D	52	Rookie Readers	Children's Press
Bears, Bears, Bears	D	76	Step-By-Step Series	Dominie
Beat This	D	79	Ready Readers	Pearson Learning
Beetles	D	39	Pebble Books	Grolier, Capstone
Ben's Fun Box	D	63	New Way Red	Steck-Vaughn
Ben's Teddy Bear	D	68	PM Story Books	Rigby
Ben's Treasure Hunt	D	72	PM Story Books	Rigby
Best Friends	D	68	Little Readers	Houghton Mifflin
Best Places, The	D	68	Ready Readers	Pearson Learning
Big and Green	D	12	Wonder World	Wright Group
Big and Little	D	92	Joy Readers	Dominie
Big Cat, The	D	41	Ready Readers	Pearson Learning
Big Hill, The	D	19	Story Box	Wright Group
Big Sneeze, The	D	112	Foundations	Wright Group
Bigger Than? Smaller Than?	D	123	Early Connections	Benchmark Education
Bike Ride, The	D	100	Emergent	Pioneer Valley
Bikes	D	156	Foundations	Wright Group
Bill and Ted at the Store	D	50	Joy Readers	Dominie
Bird Feeder, The	D	55	Coulton, Mia	Kaeden Books
Birds Need Trees	D	63	Teacher's Choice Series	Dominie
Birthday Book, The	D	86	Book Bank	Wright Group
Birthday Cake	D	27	Literacy 2000	Rigby
Black and White	D	77	Storyteller Nonfiction	Wright Group/ McGraw-Hill
Blackberries	D	107	PM Story Books	Rigby
Blue Bug and the Bullies	D	18	Poulet, Virginia	Children's Press
Blue Bug Goes to School	D	57	Poulet, Virginia	Children's Press

Title	Level	Words	Author/Series	Publisher/Distributor
Blue Bug's Vegetable Garden	D	27	Poulet, Virginia	Children's Press
Blueberry Muffins	D	191	Story Box	Wright Group
Boat Trip, The	D	70	Carousel Earlybirds	Dominie
Boats	D	57	Twig	Wright Group
Boats, Boats, Boats	D	44	My First Reader	Grolier Press
Boogie-Woogie Man, The	D	101	Story Box	Wright Group
Braids	D	24	Visions	Wright Group
Bread	D	69	Sunshine	Wright Group
Breakfast on the Farm	D	73	Storyteller Nonfiction	Wright Group/ McGraw-Hill
Brushing Well	D	42	Pebble Books	Grolier, Capstone
Bubble Gum Can Be Trouble	D	147	Visions	Wright Group
Bulldozer, The	D	48	Sunshine	Wright Group
Bumble Bee	D	53	Ready to Read	Pacific Learning
Bumble Bee	D	53	Pacific Literacy	Pacific Learning
Bump, Bump, Bump	D	51	Cat on the Mat	Oxford University Press
Bunny, Bunny	D	40	My First Reader	Grolier Press
Busy Week, A	D	49	Pair-It Books	Steck-Vaughn
But Granny Did	D	58	Voyages	SRA/McGraw-Hill
By the Tree	D	75	Ready Readers	Pearson Learning
Cake for Mom, A	D	63	Home Connection Collection	Rigby
Camping	D	64	Hooker, Karen	Kaeden Books
Can a Cow Hop?	D	40	Ready Readers	Pearson Learning
Can You Find the Pattern?	D	113	Visions	Wright Group
Can't You See We're Reading?	D	71	Stepping Stones	Nelson/Michaels Assoc.
Carry-Out Food	D	56	Tadpoles	Rigby
Cat and the King	D	30	Literacy 2000	Rigby
Cat Tails	D	40	Books for Young Learners	Richard C. Owen
Cat Traps	D	93	Coxe, Molly	Random House
Cat Who Loved Red, The	D	63	Salem, Lynn & Stewart, J.	Seedling
Chick and the Duckling, The	D	112	Ginsburg, Mirra	Macmillan
Chickens	D	23	Books for Young Learners	Richard C. Owen
Chinese New Year	D	33	Pacific Literacy	Pacific Learning
Circus Clown, The	D	31	Literacy 2000	Rigby
Circus, The	D	42	Wonder World	Wright Group
City Mouse and Country Mouse	D	87	Learn to Read	Creative Teaching Press
Clever Little Bird	D	73	Storyteller-Setting Sun	Wright Group/ McGraw-Hill
Closet in the Hall, The	D	84	Wonder World	Wright Group
Clothes	D	63	Voyages	SRA/McGraw-Hill
Clown in the Well, The	D	140	Story Box	Wright Group
Colors	D	198	Foundations	Wright Group
Come and Play, Sarah!	D	49	Sunshine	Wright Group
Come on Mom	D		New Way	Steck-Vaughn
Communities	D	42	Pebble Books	Grolier, Capstone
Cookies	D	18	Little Celebrations	Pearson Learning
Cooling Off	D	104	Reading Corners	Dominie
Cousins	D	41	Pebble Books	Grolier, Capstone
Cracker Jack, The	D	25	Sunshine	Wright Group
Crickets	D	48	Pebble Books	Grolier, Capstone
Crickets on the Go	D	56	Little Celebrations	Pearson Learning

Title	Level	Words	Author/Series	Publisher/Distributor
Daddy Works Out	D	39	Visions	Wright Group
Dad's Garden	D	25	Literacy 2000	Rigby
Danny's Dollars	D	88	Reading Corners	Dominie
Day and Night	D	102	Twig	Wright Group
Definitely, Positively, Absolutely NO!	D	147	Story Basket	Wright Group
Detective Max	D	32	Pair-It Books	Steck-Vaughn
Dinosaur Times	D	43	Sunshine	Wright Group
Dinosaurs Galore	D	34	Eaton, Audrey & Kennedy, Jane	Seedling
Dirty Larry	D	53	Rookie Readers	Children's Press
Do You Remember When?	D	198	Visions	Wright Group
Dog Called Mischief, A	D	42	Cat on the Mat	Oxford University Press
Dog Went for a Walk	D	51	Voyages	SRA/McGraw-Hill
Dress Up	D	80	Carousel Readers	Dominie
Ducks	D	94	Story Box	Wright Group
Early in the Morning	D	55	Rise & Shine	Hampton-Brown
Ebenezer and the Sneeze	D	77	Story Box	Wright Group
Eggs for Breakfast	D	126	PM Nonfiction-Red	Rigby
Eight Friends in All	D	64	Ready Readers	Pearson Learning
Elevator	D	90	Story Box	Wright Group
Everyday Math	D	102	Early Connections	Benchmark Education
Fabulous Fruits	D	121	Fiesta Series	Dominie
Face in the Dark, The	D	64	Storyteller-Setting Sun	Wright Group/ McGraw-Hill
Faces	D		Little Celebrations	Pearson Learning
Families	D	60	Pebble Books	Grolier, Capstone
Family Names	D	36	Visions	Wright Group
Family Soccer	D	55	Geddes, Diana	Kaeden Books
Fantail, Fantail	D	67	Ready to Read	Pacific Learning
Fantail, Fantail	D	67	Pacific Literacy	Pacific Learning
Farm Concert, The	D	74	Story Box	Wright Group
Farm Day	D	36	Little Celebrations	Pearson Learning
Farm in Spring, The	D	69	PM Starters	Rigby
Fast Draw Freddie	D	50	Rookie Readers	Children's Press
Fast Food	D	112	Foundations	Wright Group
Fast Machines	D	146	Foundations	Wright Group
Father Bear Goes Fishing	D	98	PM Story Books	Rigby
Feeding Time at the Zoo	D	73	Windmill Books	Rigby
Feelings	D	39	Rise & Shine	Hampton-Brown
Feet	D	18	Story Box	Wright Group
Festival, The	D	146	Fiesta Series	Dominie
First Day of School	D	60	Carousel Readers	Dominie
First in Line	D	77	Teacher's Choice Series	Dominie
Fish	D	58	Wonder World	Wright Group
Fishing	D	48	Yukish, Joe	Kaeden Books
Fishy Color Story	D	142	Wylie, Joanne & David	Children's Press
Five Ducks	D	89	Joy Readers	Dominie
Five Little Monsters	D		Learn to Read	Creative Teaching Press
Follow the Leader	D	75	Teacher's Choice Series	Dominie
Food from the Farm	D	78	Home Connection Collection	Rigby
Footprints in the Snow	D		Benjamin, Cynthia	Scholastic
Fred Said	D	35	Sunshine	Wright Group

Title	Level	Words	Author/Series	Publisher/Distributor
Freddie the Frog	D	132	First Start	Troll
Friends	D	57	Book Shop	Mondo Publishing
Friends	D	134	Fiesta Series	Dominie
Friends Go Together	D	36	Pair-It Books	Steck-Vaughn
Frito Jumps In	D	34	Step-By-Step Series	Dominie
Frog and the Fly, The	D	33	Cat on the Mat	Oxford University Press
Frogs	D	28	Pebble Books	Grolier, Capstone
Frogs on a Log	D	75	Teacher's Choice Series	Dominie
From Bud to Blossom	D	40	Pebble Books	Grolier, Capstone
Fruit Salad	D	18	Hoenecke, Karen	Kaeden Books
Fruit Salad	D	37	Wonder World	Wright Group
Fun	D	45	Yannone, Deborah	Kaeden Books
Funny Faces and Funny Places	D	45	Ready Readers	Pearson Learning
Fur	D		Mark, Jan	Harper & Row
Gardening	D	77	Foundations	Wright Group
Geoffrey the Dinosaur	D	36	Sunshine	Wright Group
Ghosts' Secret, The	D	79	TOTTS	Tott Publications
Gingerbread Men, The	D	37	Sunshine	Wright Group
Glasses	D	19	Visions	Wright Group
Go to Bed	D	45	Joy Readers	Dominie
Gobble, Gobble, Gone	D	58	Little Celebrations	Pearson Learning
Going Out	D	94	Foundations	Wright Group
Going Shopping	D	92	Carousel Readers	Dominie
Going to the Pool	D	55	Pair-It Books	Steck-Vaughn
Going to the Vet	D	46	Sunshine	Wright Group
Good Bad Cat	D	65	Start to Read	School Zone
Good Bad Cat, The	D	65	Little Readers	Houghton Mifflin
Good for You	D	44	Sunshine	Wright Group
Good Night, Little Bug	D	54	Ready Readers	Pearson Learning
Good Night, Little Kitten	D	78	My First Reader	Grolier Press
Goodbye, Lucy	D	60	Sunshine	Wright Group
Good-bye, Zoo	D	48	Ready Readers	Pearson Learning
Goodnight!	D	61	Joy Readers	Dominie
Goose Chase	D	43	Ready Readers	Pearson Learning
Grandma's Letter	D	67	Foundations	Wright Group
Grass Is for Goats	D	84	Joy Readers	Dominie
Gravity	D	33	Wonder World	Wright Group
Greedy Cat Is Hungry	D	103	Ready to Read	Pacific Learning
Greedy Cat Is Hungry	D	103	Pacific Literacy	Pacific Learning
Green Snake, The	D	131	Twig	Wright Group
Green, Green	D	114	Little Readers	Houghton Mifflin
Grocery Shopping	D	34	Yannone, Deborah	Kaeden Books
Gulp!	D	103	Story Box	Wright Group
Haddie's Caps	D	90	Ready Readers	Pearson Learning
Haircut, The	D	27	Hartley, S. & Armstrong, Shane	Scholastic
Halloween	D	32	Visions	Wright Group
Happy Birthday, Danny and the Dinosaur	D	250+	Little Readers	Houghton Mifflin
Happy Birthday, Danny and the Dinosaur!	D	250+	Hoff, Syd	HarperTrophy
Happy Birthday, Estela!	D	30	Pacific Literacy	Pacific Learning
Happy Monkey's Peanuts	D	63	Joy Readers	Dominie
Harry's Hats	D	49	Teacher's Choice Series	Dominie

Title	Level	Words	Author/Series	Publisher/Distributor
Have You Seen Joe?	D	57	Home Connection Collection	Rigby
Hello, Dad!	D	16	Pacific Literacy	Pacific Learning
Help Me	D	107	Emergent	Pioneer Valley
Helping	D	79	Joy Readers	Dominie
Helping My Dad	D	90	Teacher's Choice Series	Dominie
Helping You	D	53	Interaction	Rigby
Henry and the Helicopter	D	58	Literacy 2000	Rigby
Here We Go Round the Mulberry Bush	D	187	Little Readers	Houghton Mifflin
Hey, Diddle, Diddle!	D	30	Sunshine	Wright Group
Hi Dog	D	137	Ready Readers	Pearson Learning
Hide and Seek	D	49	New Way Red	Steck-Vaughn
Hide and Seek	D	63	Brown, R. & Carey, S.	Scholastic
Hide and Seek	D	108	PM Extensions-Red	Rigby
Hiding	D	97	Foundations	Wright Group
Hogboggit, The	D	65	Ready to Read	Pacific Learning
Hogboggit, The	D	65	Pacific Literacy	Pacific Learning
Hoiho's Chicks	D	38	Ready to Read	Pacific Learning
Home for Little Teddy, A	D	53	PM Extensions-Red	Rigby
Homes	D	42	Rise & Shine	Hampton-Brown
Honey Bees	D	41	Pebble Books	Grolier, Capstone
Hoofprints	D	62	Teacher's Choice Series	Dominie
Hope Not	D	83	Salem, Lynn & Stewart, J.	Seedling
Horace	D	56	Story Box	Wright Group
Horrible Big Black Bug, The	D	50	Tadpoles	Rigby
Horse Feathers	D	41	Pair-It Books	Steck-Vaughn
How Are We the Same?	D	100	Teacher's Choice Series	Dominie
How Can I Help?	D	65	Questions & Answers	Dominie
How Do I Feel?	D	64	Questions & Answers	Dominie
How Machines Help	D	143	Sunshine	Wright Group
How Many Bugs in a Box?	D	126	Carter, David	Simon & Schuster
How Many Pets?	D	37	Book Shop	Mondo Publishing
Humpty Dumpty	D		Peppe, Rodney	The Penguin Group
Hungry Kitten, The	D	95	PM Story Books	Rigby
Hurricane	D	36	Joy Readers	Dominie
Hurry Up	D	49	Voyages	SRA/McGraw-Hill
I Am	D	27	Rookie Readers	Children's Press
I Am a Fireman	D	45	Read-More Books	Dominie
I Am a Train Driver	D	32	Read-More Books	Dominie
I Am an Explorer	D	32	Rookie Readers	Children's Press
I Can Help	D	65	Teacher's Choice Series	Dominie
I Can Swim	D	61	Ready Readers	Pearson Learning
I Can Use a Computer	D	52	Teacher's Choice Series	Dominie
I Can't Sleep	D	71	Learn to Read	Creative Teaching Press
I Do Not Like Peas	D	32	Visions	Wright Group
I Like Books	D		Browne, Anthony	Random House
I Like My Picture!	D	160	Teacher's Choice Series	Dominie
I Like Worms!	D	213	Sunshine	Wright Group
I Live in a House	D	51	Read-More Books	Dominie
I Live in an Apartment	D	41	Read-More Books	Dominie
I Love Chickens	D	67	Story Box	Wright Group
I Love Fishing	D	37	Rookie Readers	Children's Press

Title	Level	Words	Author/Series	Publisher/Distributor
I Love Mud and Mud Loves Me	D	121	Stephens, Vicki	Scholastic
I Love My Grandma	D	36	Rise & Shine	Hampton-Brown
I Want to be a Ballerina	D	66	Teacher's Choice Series	Dominie
I Wish I Had a Dinosaur	D	46	Little Celebrations	Pearson Learning
Ice Is ... Whee!	D	59	Rookie Readers	Children's Press
If Germs Were Purple	D	53	Carousel Readers	Dominie
I'll Run Away	D	53	Home Connection Collection	Rigby
I'm a Little Seed	D	30	Pair-It Books	Steck-Vaughn
I'm Bigger Than You!	D	48	Sunshine	Wright Group
I'm Brave	D	51	Sunshine	Wright Group
I'm Hungry	D	84	Tuer, Judy	Scholastic
In My Desert	D	24	Little Celebrations	Pearson Learning
In Nonna's Kitchen	D	32	Home Connection Collection	Rigby
In Summer	D	36	Discovery Links	Newbridge
In the Chicken Coop	D	56	Twig	Wright Group
In the Desert	D	62	Sunshine	Wright Group
In the Garden	D	90	Literacy 2000	Rigby
In the Park	D	65	Foundations	Wright Group
Insects That Bother Us	D	87	Foundations	Wright Group
International Day	D	47	Home Connection Collection	Rigby
Is a Dollar Enough?	D	75	Visions	Wright Group
Island, The	D	24	Wildsmith, Brian	Oxford University Press
It Didn't Frighten Me	D	387	Book Shop	Mondo Publishing
It Sounds Like Music	D	56	Pair-It Books	Steck-Vaughn
It's Game Day	D	65	Salem, Lynn & Stewart, J.	Seedling
It's Hot	D	54	Ready Readers	Pearson Learning
Jack-O-Lantern	D	47	Pebble Books	Grolier, Capstone
Jimmy	D	83	Foundations	Wright Group
Jolly Roger, the Pirate	D	138	PM Extensions-Yellow	Rigby
Julia's Lists	D	47	Little Celebrations	Pearson Learning
Jump Right In	D	50	Ready Readers	Pearson Learning
Jump Rope	D	31	Visions	Wright Group
Jungle Parade: A Singing Game	D	105	Little Celebrations	Pearson Learning
Just Like Dad	D	44	Hiris, Monica	Kaeden Books
Just Like Me!	D	62	Sunshine	Wright Group
Just Like My Grandpa	D	48	Rise & Shine	Hampton-Brown
Kangaroo in the Kitchen	D	72	Ready Readers	Pearson Learning
Karina	D	40	Step-By-Step Series	Dominie
Keep the Beat	D	48	Little Celebrations	Pearson Learning
Keeping Cool	D	84	Foundations	Wright Group
Kindergarten	D	118	Carousel Readers	Dominie
King's Surprise, The	D	54	Stewart, J. & Salem, Lynn	Seedling
Kitchen Tools	D	104	Foundations	Wright Group
Kite, The	D	59	My First Reader	Grolier Press
Ladybugs	D	42	Pebble Books	Grolier, Capstone
Late One Night	D	97	Mader, Jan	Kaeden Books
Later	D	106	Teacher's Choice Series	Dominie
Laundromat, The	D	50	Sunshine	Wright Group
Lazy Mary	D	191	Read-Togethers	Wright Group
Legs	D	21	Literacy 2000	Rigby
Let's Be Friends	D	23	Pair-It Books	Steck-Vaughn

Title	Level	Words	Author/Series	Publisher/Distributor
Let's Celebrate	D	33	Rise & Shine	Hampton-Brown
Library, The	D	96	Emergent	Pioneer Valley
Like Me	D	20	Book Bank	Wright Group
Like My Daddy	D	129	Visions	Wright Group
Listen	D	35	Visions	Wright Group
Little Bear	D	77	My First Reader	Grolier Press
Little Boy Blue	D	32	Sunshine	Wright Group
Little Hen, The	D	107	Ready Readers	Pearson Learning
Little Meanie's Lunch	D	90	Story Box	Wright Group
Little Rabbit Is Sad	D	97	Williams, Deborah	Kaeden Books
Lizard Loses His Tail	D	54	PM Story Books	Rigby
Long Ago	D	105	Early Connections	Benchmark Education
Longest Noodle in the World, The	D	66	Joy Readers	Dominie
Look at Me	D	67	Carousel Readers	Dominie
Look for Me	D	71	Story Box	Wright Group
Look in Mom's Purse	D	60	Carousel Readers	Dominie
Look into Space, A	D	71	Discovery World	Rigby
Look Out!	D	53	Sunshine	Wright Group
Look Up, Look Down	D	165	PM Nonfiction-Red	Rigby
Looking After Grandpa	D	91	Foundations	Wright Group
Lost and Found	D	55	New Way Red	Steck-Vaughn
Lost and Found	D	64	Carousel Readers	Dominie
Lost in the Fog	D	59	Ready Readers	Pearson Learning
Lump in My Bed, A	D	48	Book Bank	Wright Group
Make It Spin	D	18	Pacific Literacy	Pacific Learning
Making a Memory	D	53	Ballinger, Margaret	Scholastic
Making Pancakes	D	39	Carousel Readers	Dominie
Making Things	D	64	Foundations	Wright Group
Mama Goes to School	D	47	Visions	Wright Group
Many Friends, Many Languages	D	98	Fiesta Series	Dominie
March Along with Me	D	56	Literacy 2000	Rigby
March, March, Marching	D	60	Teacher's Choice Series	Dominie
Maria Goes to School	D	174	Foundations	Wright Group
Market, The	D	48	Joy Readers	Dominie
Mary Wore Her Red Dress	D	170	Peek, Merle	Clarion
Maybe I'll Be	D	49	Carousel Readers	Dominie
Mess, A	D	34	Ready Readers	Pearson Learning
Mess, The	D	55	My First Reader	Grolier Press
Migration, The	D	45	Wonder World	Wright Group
Mirror, The	D	112	Story Box	Wright Group
Miss Geeta's Hair	D	44	Joy Readers	Dominie
Mom Can Fix Anything	D	74	Learn to Read	Creative Teaching Press
Mom's New Car	D	116	Foundations	Wright Group
Monkey Bridge, The	D	66	Sunshine	Wright Group
Monster and the Baby	D		Mueller, Virginia	Puffin Books
Monster Can't Sleep	D		Mueller, Virginia	Puffin Books
Monsters!	D	45	My First Reader	Grolier Press
Moon, The	D	139	Joy Readers	Dominie
Moonlight	D	48	Literacy 2000	Rigby
More and More Clowns	D	249	Allen, R. V.	SRA/McGraw-Hill
Mother Hippopotamus's Dry Skin	D	201	Foundations	Wright Group

Title	Level	Words	Author/Series	Publisher/Distributor
Mouse Finds a House	D	72	Start to Read	School Zone
Mouse's Baby Blanket	D	68	Swerdlow Brown, Beverly	Seedling
Mouse's House	D	70	New Way Red	Steck-Vaughn
Moving In	D	82	Foundations	Wright Group
Mr. Grump	D	73	Sunshine	Wright Group
Mr. Noisy	D	90	Learn to Read	Creative Teaching Press
Mr. Wolf	D	48	Joy Readers	Dominie
Mrs. Sato's Hens	D	51	Little Readers	Houghton Mifflin
Mud	D		Lewison, Wendy	Random House
Mumps	D	108	Carousel Readers	Dominie
Mumps	D	112	PM Story Books	Rigby
Museum, The	D	41	Sunshine	Wright Group
My Baby	D	64	Storyteller-First Snow	Wright Group/ McGraw-Hill
My Big Box	D	94	Voyages	SRA/McGraw-Hill
My Bike	D	38	Storyteller-First Snow	Wright Group/ McGraw-Hill
My Bike	D	108	Ready to Read	Pacific Learning
My Bike	D	108	Pacific Literacy	Pacific Learning
My Brother	D	51	Rise & Shine	Hampton-Brown
My Brother Wants to Be Like Me	D	62	Mader, Jan	Kaeden Books
My Brother's Motorcycle	D	45	Visions	Wright Group
My Brown Cow	D	62	Story Box	Wright Group
My Buddy, My Friend	D	33	Visions	Wright Group
My Cat	D	40	Ready Readers	Pearson Learning
My Cat	D	42	Sunshine	Wright Group
My Cat's Surprise	D	71	New Way Blue	Steck-Vaughn
My Clock Is Sick	D	45	Ready Readers	Pearson Learning
My Dog	D	38	Visions	Wright Group
My Dog	D	51	Sunshine	Wright Group
My Friend Alan	D	65	Carousel Readers	Dominie
My Friends	D	58	Little Celebrations	Pearson Learning
My Little Brother Ben	D	35	Books for Young Learners	Richard C. Owen
My Little Sister	D	44	Joy Readers	Dominie
My Messy Room	D		Packard, Mary	Scholastic
My Mom and Dad	D	86	Story Box	Wright Group
My Nest Is Best	D	92	Foundations	Wright Group
My Pet	D	65	Salem, Lynn & Stewart, J.	Seedling
My Skateboard	D	89	Carousel Readers	Dominie
My Skin	D	64	Wonder World	Wright Group
Naughty Patch	D	74	Foundations	Wright Group
Neep, Beep, Beep	D	86	Foundations	Wright Group
Never Be	D	73	Salem, Lynn & Stewart, J.	Seedling
New Dog, A	D	52	Oxford Reading Tree	Oxford University Press
New Road, The	D	49	Joy Readers	Dominie
Night Animals	D	56	Ready Readers	Pearson Learning
Night in the Desert	D	69	Carousel Readers	Dominie
No One Else Like Me	D	129	Early Connections	Benchmark Education
No, No	D	91	Story Box	Wright Group
No, You Can't	D	52	Sunshine	Wright Group
Noisy Breakfast	D		Blonder, Ellen	Scholastic

Title	Level	Words	Author/Series	Publisher/Distributor
Not Enough Water	D	84	Armstrong, Shane & Hartley, S.	Scholastic
Now I Ride	D	63	Carousel Readers	Dominie
Nut Pie for Jud, A	D	46	Ready Readers	Pearson Learning
Off to Grandma's House	D	80	Little Celebrations	Pearson Learning
Old MacDonald Had a Farm	D	505	Rounds, Glen	Holiday House
Old MacDonald Had a Farm	D		Jones, Carol	Houghton Mifflin
On a Hill	D	53	Start to Read	School Zone
On the Computer	D	67	Twig	Wright Group
On the Move	D	26	Wonder World	Wright Group
On This Earth	D	71	Rise & Shine	Hampton-Brown
On Vacation	D	88	Little Red Readers	Sundance
One Chick, One Egg	D	64	Step-By-Step Series	Dominie
One Cold, Wet Night	D	134	Read-Togethers	Wright Group
One Happy Classroom	D	49	Rookie Readers	Children's Press
One, Two, Three, Four	D	89	Rise & Shine	Hampton-Brown
Oops!	D		Mayer, Mercer	The Penguin Group
Open It!	D	27	Pacific Literacy	Pacific Learning
Our Baby	D	70	Voyages	SRA/McGraw-Hill
Our Chore Chart	D	65	Storyteller-First Snow	Wright Group/ McGraw-Hill
Our Earth	D	33	Discovery Links	Newbridge
Our Playhouse	D	46	Voyages	SRA/McGraw-Hill
Our Senses	D	39	Rise & Shine	Hampton-Brown
Our Teacher, Miss Pool	D	62	Ready to Read	Pacific Learning
Our Teacher, Miss Pool	D	62	Pacific Literacy	Pacific Learning
Outside, Inside	D	97	Teacher's Choice Series	Dominie
Over the Oregon Trail	D	131	Twig	Wright Group
Pajama Party, The	D	46	Sunshine	Wright Group
Pam & Sam on the Beach	D	94	Carousel Earlybirds	Dominie
Party, The	D	26	Ready Readers	Pearson Learning
Pass the Pasta, Please	D	63	Storyteller-Setting Sun	Wright Group/ McGraw-Hill
Pat's Train	D	22	KinderReaders	Rigby
Paul the Pitcher	D	86	Rookie Readers	Children's Press
Penguin's Chicks	D	38	Pacific Literacy	Pacific Learning
People Who Help Us	D	62	Foundations	Wright Group
Peppers	D	32	Rise & Shine	Hampton-Brown
Pet for Pat, A	D	45	Rookie Readers	Children's Press
Pet Shop	D	167	Story Box	Wright Group
Picnic in the Sky, The	D	80	Foundations	Wright Group
Pinata Time	D	71	Teacher's Choice Series	Dominie
Pippa's Pet Pest	D	35	Home Connection Collection	Rigby
Pizza, The	D	100	Foundations	Wright Group
Play Ball!	D	30	Books for Young Learners	Richard C. Owen
Playground Fun	D	127	Early Connections	Benchmark Education
Pockets	D	32	Visions	Wright Group
Pond Party	D	33	Little Celebrations	Pearson Learning
Porcupine, A	D	49	Wonder World	Wright Group
Practice Makes Perfect	D	111	Teacher's Choice Series	Dominie
Praying Mantis, The	D	46	Ready to Read	Pacific Learning
Praying Mantis, The	D	46	Pacific Literacy	Pacific Learning

Title	Level	Words	Author/Series	Publisher/Distributor
Presents	D	43	Storyteller-First Snow	Wright Group/ McGraw-Hill
Puppets for a Play	D	45	Home Connection Collection	Rigby
Push!	D	21	Oxford Reading Tree	Oxford University Press
Quack, Quack, Quack	D	97	Carousel Readers	Dominie
Race Is On, The	D	45	New Way Red	Steck-Vaughn
Rain	D	45	Step-By-Step Series	Dominie
Rain in the Hills	D	41	Book Bank	Wright Group
Rain! Rain!	D	29	Rookie Readers	Children's Press
Rainy Day, A	D	105	New Way Blue	Steck-Vaughn
Reading Is Everywhere	D	53	Sunshine	Wright Group
Reading Under the Covers	D	25	Visions	Wright Group
Ready Steady Jump	D	25	Ready to Read	Pacific Learning
Ready, Steady, Jump!	D	25	Pacific Literacy	Pacific Learning
Recycling Dump	D	48	Little Celebrations	Pearson Learning
Red and Blue and Yellow	D	100	PM Nonfiction-Red	Rigby
Ride in the Country, A	D	83	Carousel Readers	Dominie
River, The	D	42	Foundations	Wright Group
Rocks	D	49	Voyages	SRA/McGraw-Hill
Roof and a Door, A	D	93	PM Nonfiction-Red	Rigby
Rosie the Nosy Goat	D	56	Sunshine	Wright Group
Roy G. Biv	D	68	Story Box	Wright Group
Rumble, Rumble, Boom!	D	26	Pacific Literacy	Pacific Learning
Salad Feast, A	D	57	Little Readers	Houghton Mifflin
Sally's Beans	D	123	PM Story Books	Rigby
Sam Writes	D	62	Book Bank	Wright Group
Sammy's Sneeze	D	69	Home Connection Collection	Rigby
Sam's Ball	D	64	Lindgren, Barbro	Morrow
Sam's Cookie	D	52	Lindgren, Barbro	Morrow
Sam's Teddy Bear	D	60	Lindgren, Barbro	Morrow
Sam's Wagon	D	83	Lindgren, Barbro	Morrow
Sandwiches	D		New Way	Steck-Vaughn
Sandwiches, Sandwiches	D	54	Pair-It Books	Steck-Vaughn
Saturday Mornings	D	63	Book Shop	Mondo Publishing
Scarecrow, The	D	97	Little Red Readers	Sundance
Scarecrows	D	39	Pebble Books	Grolier, Capstone
Scared	D	59	Twig	Wright Group
Scaredy Cat Runs Away	D		Learn to Read	Creative Teaching Press
Scat! Said the Cat	D	33	Sunshine	Wright Group
School Bus	D	51	Crews, Donald	Morrow
Scissors	D	51	Storyteller-Setting Sun	Wright Group/ McGraw-Hill
Scratch My Back	D	66	Foundations	Wright Group
Screech!	D	43	Literacy 2000	Rigby
Seed, The	D	51	Sunshine	Wright Group
Shadow Dance	D	66	Little Celebrations	Pearson Learning
Shadows	D	35	Literacy 2000	Rigby
Shapes	D	98	Carousel Readers	Dominie
Shapes in My World	D	47	Visions	Wright Group
Sharing Time	D	113	Carousel Readers	Dominie
Shoes	D	79	Book Bank	Wright Group

Title	Level	Words	Author/Series	Publisher/Distributor
Shopping	D	26	Literacy 2000	Rigby
Shopping	D	41	Sunshine	Wright Group
Shush!	D	29	Pacific Literacy	Pacific Learning
Shut the Door	D	46	Visions	Wright Group
Sick Bear, The	D	61	Joy Readers	Dominie
Sid and Sam	D	120	Buck, Nola	HarperTrophy
Silly Cat Tricks	D	83	Teacher's Choice Series	Dominie
Sky Is Falling Down, The	D	101	Joy Readers	Dominie
Sleeping Out	D	49	Story Box	Wright Group
Sleep-Over Mouse	D	63	My First Reader	Grolier Press
Sleepy Dog	D	118	Ziefert, Harriet	Random House
Smile! Said Dad	D	66	Pacific Literacy	Pacific Learning
Smile, The	D	53	Ready to Read	Pacific Learning
Smile, The	D	53	Pacific Literacy	Pacific Learning
Snacks	D	19	Joy Readers	Dominie
Snow Joe	D	59	Rookie Readers	Children's Press
Snow Walk	D	32	Reading Corners	Dominie
Snow, The	D	36	Sunshine	Wright Group
Snowball Fight!	D	35	Wonder World	Wright Group
Snowflakes	D	49	Urmston, Kathleen & Evans, Karen	Kaeden Books
So Do I	D	49	Teacher's Choice Series	Dominie
Some Days Are Like That	D	69	Teacher's Choice Series	Dominie
Some People	D	50	Reading Corners	Dominie
Something New	D	72	Little Celebrations	Pearson Learning
Something to Share	D	98	Carousel Readers	Dominie
Space Aliens in Our School	D	45	Joy Readers	Dominie
Space Shuttle, The	D	45	Sunshine	Wright Group
Spider	D	43	Sunshine	Wright Group
Spider Legs	D	52	Twig	Wright Group
Spider, Spider	D	70	Sunshine	Wright Group
Spiders Everywhere	D	36	Books for Young Learners	Richard C. Owen
Spiders, Spiders Everywhere!	D		Learn to Read	Creative Teaching Press
Splash!	D	63	New Way Red	Steck-Vaughn
Splish! Splash!	D	45	Little Celebrations	Pearson Learning
Staircase to the Sky	D	133	Visions	Wright Group
Storm, The	D	71	Foundations	Wright Group
Sunflower Seeds	D	48	Story Box	Wright Group
Sunflowers	D	35	Pebble Books	Grolier, Capstone
Surfer, The	D	40	Wonder World	Wright Group
Surprise!	D	28	My First Reader	Grolier Press
Swans	D	53	Joy Readers	Dominie
Swat it!	D	46	Bauer, Roger	Kaeden Books
Tails	D	52	Wonder World	Wright Group
Take a Bow, Jody	D	78	Eaton, Audrey & Kennedy, Jane	Seedling
Taking Care of Our World	D	137	Visions	Wright Group
Tall Things	D	83	PM Nonfiction-Red	Rigby
Taste Sensation	D	115	Visions	Wright Group
Tasty Bug, A	D	50	Little Celebrations	Pearson Learning
T-Ball	D	35	Visions	Wright Group
Ted's Red Sled	D	69	Ready Readers	Pearson Learning
Teeth	D	71	Story Box	Wright Group

Title	Level	Words	Author/Series	Publisher/Distributor
That's Dangerous	D	71	Voyages	SRA/McGraw-Hill
There Is a Town	D	116	Heiman, Gail	Random House
There Was a Mouse	D	77	Books for Young Learners	Richard C. Owen
There's No One Like Me!	D	80	Sunshine	Wright Group
They Call Me...	D	31	The Candid Collection	Dominie
Things I Like	D		Browne, Anthony	Random House
Things That Drag Behind	D	42	Teacher's Choice Series	Dominie
Things That Protect You	D	51	Foundations	Wright Group
This Hat	D	52	Little Celebrations	Pearson Learning
This Is My Family	D	36	Read-More Books	Dominie
This Is the Plate	D		Little Celebrations	Pearson Learning
This Mouth	D	64	Wonder World	Wright Group
Three Silly Monkeys	D	150	Foundations	Wright Group
Thumbprint Critters	D	27	Little Celebrations	Pearson Learning
Time for a Bath	D	60	Mader, Jan	Kaeden Books
Time for Sleep!	D	62	Sunshine	Wright Group
Tiny Little Woman, The	D	74	Joy Readers	Dominie
To New York	D	32	Story Box	Wright Group
To the Beach	D	43	Urmston, Kathleen & Evans, Karen	Kaeden Books
Toby Tomato	D	54	Little Celebrations	Pearson Learning
Tom Gets Fit	D	150	New Way Red	Steck-Vaughn
Tom Is Brave	D	57	PM Story Books	Rigby
Too Big for Me	D	70	Story Box	Wright Group
Too High!	D	66	Ready Readers	Pearson Learning
Too Many Balloons	D	182	Rookie Readers	Children's Press
Too Much Ketchup	D	30	Ready Readers	Pearson Learning
Tooth Fairy, The	D	57	My First Reader	Grolier Press
Treehouse, The	D	43	Hoenecke, Karen	Kaeden Books
Try It!	D	49	Reading Corners	Dominie
Turtle, The	D	68	Foundations	Wright Group
Two Crazy Pigs	D	250+	Nagel, Karen Berman	Scholastic
Two Eyes, Two Ears	D	83	PM Nonfiction-Red	Rigby
Uncle Elephant and Uncle Tiger	D	77	Joy Readers	Dominie
Uncles	D	36	Pebble Books	Grolier, Capstone
Uncle's Clever Tricks	D	61	Joy Readers	Dominie
Up and Down	D	92	New Way Red	Steck-Vaughn
Up the Tree	D	41	New Way Red	Steck-Vaughn
Up Went Edmond	D	26	Pacific Literacy	Pacific Learning
Very Big	D	49	Ready Readers	Pearson Learning
Wait for Me	D	185	Visions	Wright Group
Wake Up, Wake Up!	D		Wildsmith, B. & R.	Scholastic
Watching TV	D	89	Foundations	Wright Group
Water Changes	D	36	Discovery Links	Newbridge
Water Falling	D	41	Literacy 2000	Rigby
Watermelon, The	D	80	Joy Readers	Dominie
We Like Fish	D	109	PM Starters	Rigby
We Make Music	D	44	Literacy 2000	Rigby
Week with Aunt Bea, A	D	62	Book Shop	Mondo Publishing
What a Bad Dog!	D	52	Oxford Reading Tree	Oxford University Press
What Are You Doing?	D	101	Foundations	Wright Group
What Comes in Twos?	D	125	Early Connections	Benchmark Education

Title	Level	Words	Author/Series	Publisher/Distributor
What Did I Forget?	D	43	Teacher's Choice Series	Dominie
What Did I Use?	D	65	Discovery World	Rigby
What Do You Hear?	D	60	Windmill Books	Rigby
What Do You Like to Eat?	D	99	Foundations	Wright Group
What Do You Like to Wear?	D	50	Read-More Books	Dominie
What Fell Out?	D	32	Carousel Readers	Dominie
What I Like to Wear	D	93	Home Connection Collection	Rigby
What Is Big?	D	72	Armstrong, Shane & Hartley, S.	Scholastic
What Is It Called?	D		Reading Unlimited	Pacific Learning
What Lays Eggs?	D	56	Storyteller Nonfiction	Wright Group/ McGraw-Hill
What People Do	D	113	Early Connections	Benchmark Education
What Would the Zoo Do?	D	59	Salem, Lynn	Seedling
What Would You Like?	D	52	Sunshine	Wright Group
What's Alive?	D	53	Discovery Links	Newbridge
What's for Lunch?	D	49	Rise & Shine	Hampton-Brown
What's It For?	D	47	Visions	Wright Group
Wheels	D	49	Rise & Shine	Hampton-Brown
Wheels	D	69	Cobb, Annie	Random House
Where Are My Socks?	D	42	Ready to Read	Pacific Learning
Where Are My Socks?	D	42	Pacific Literacy	Pacific Learning
Where Are the Seeds?	D	67	Wonder World	Wright Group
Where Are the Sunhats?	D	130	PM Story Books	Rigby
Where Are You Going, Aja Rose?	D	100	Sunshine	Wright Group
Where Are You Going?	D	66	Learn to Read	Creative Teaching Press
Where Can a Hippo Hide?	D	41	Ready Readers	Pearson Learning
Where Did They Go?	D	102	Teacher's Choice Series	Dominie
Where Do Bugs Live?	D	33	Pair-It Books	Steck-Vaughn
Where Do You Play?	D	131	Twig	Wright Group
Where Is Hannah?	D	141	PM Extensions-Red	Rigby
Where Is Kate's Skate?	D	46	KinderReaders	Rigby
Where Is Miss Pool?	D	55	Ready to Read	Pacific Learning
Where Is Miss Pool?	D	55	Pacific Literacy	Pacific Learning
Where Is Skunk?	D	65	Story Box	Wright Group
Where Is the Milk?	D	87	Foundations	Wright Group
Where Is the School Bus?	D	40	Carousel Readers	Dominie
Where's Al?	D	49	Barton, Byron	Houghton Mifflin
Where's Baby Tom?	D	91	Book Bank	Wright Group
Where's Cupcake?	D	71	Little Readers	Houghton Mifflin
Where's the Frog?	D	46	Discovery Links	Newbridge
Where's the Puppy?	D		Dwight, Laura	Checkerboard
Which Egg Is Mine?	D	65	Rise & Shine	Hampton-Brown
Which Is Heavier	D	51	Questions & Answers	Dominie
Which Toys?	D	40	Home Connection Collection	Rigby
Whistle Like a Bird	D	53	Pair-It Books	Steck-Vaughn
Who Am I ?	D	81	Rise & Shine	Hampton-Brown
Who Cried for Pie?	D	86	First Start	Troll
Who Is the Tallest?	D	46	Sunshine	Wright Group
Who Is Who?	D	115	Rookie Readers	Children's Press
Who Likes to Swim?	D	100	Teacher's Choice Series	Dominie
Who Made These Tracks?	D	45	Teacher's Choice Series	Dominie
Who Says?	D	36	My First Reader	Grolier Press

Title	Level	Words	Author/Series	Publisher/Distributor
Who Wants to Live in My House?	D	60	Book Bank	Wright Group
Who Will Help?	D	93	Learn to Read	Creative Teaching Press
Who Will Win the Race?	D	53	Sunshine	Wright Group
Who Works Here?	D	57	Questions & Answers	Dominie
Who's Hiding?	D	51	Learn to Read	Creative Teaching Press
Whose Shoes?	D	84	Twig	Wright Group
Why Do I Feel Safe?	D	61	Questions & Answers	Dominie
Why?	D	68	Twig	Wright Group
Will You Play with Us?	D	62	Book Shop	Mondo Publishing
Willy the Helper	D	79	Little Readers	Houghton Mifflin
Wilma's Wagon	D	48	Ready Readers	Pearson Learning
Wind Surfing	D	224	Sunshine	Wright Group
Wind, The	D	34	Wonder World	Wright Group
Winter Is Here	D	55	Weinberger, Kimberly	Scholastic
Wishing for a Horse	D	105	Carousel Earlybirds	Dominie
Wobbly Tooth, The	D	102	Literacy 2000	Rigby
Word Machine, The	D	33	Sunshine	Wright Group
Working for Dad	D	31	Visions	Wright Group
Worms	D	39	Literacy 2000	Rigby
Yes, I Can!	D	45	Ready Readers	Pearson Learning
Yes, It Does	D	91	Teacher's Choice Series	Dominie
Zoe's Birthday Presents	D	83	Emergent	Pioneer Valley
1 Is for One	E	82	Book Shop	Mondo Publishing
20 Pennies	E	212	Teacher's Choice Series	Dominie
Alien at the Zoo	E	85	Sunshine	Wright Group
All By Myself	E	105	Foundations	Wright Group
All By Myself	E	157	Mayer, Mercer	Golden
All Kinds of Wheels	E	76	Pair-It Books	Steck-Vaughn
All Night Long	E	65	Visions	Wright Group
All Over the World	E	82	Jones, D.	Seedling
Angry Old Woman, The	E	126	Adventures in Reading	Dominie
Animal Babies	E	114	Rookie Readers	Children's Press
Animal Coverings	E	153	Early Connections	Benchmark Education
Animals in the Fall	E	34	Pebble Books	Grolier, Capstone
Animals Love the Fair	E	43	Literacy 2000	Rigby
Ant, The	E	97	Ready Readers	Pearson Learning
Ants	E	50	Pebble Books	Grolier, Capstone
Ants, Ants, Ants	E	131	Sunshine	Wright Group
Apple Farm, The	E	95	Ready Readers	Pearson Learning
Apple Pie Family, The	E	72	Pair-It Books	Steck-Vaughn
Apples and More Apples	E	97	Pair-It Books	Steck-Vaughn
Are You the New Principal?	E	120	Teacher's Choice Series	Dominie
Around My School	E	60	Exploring History & Geography	Rigby
Around the Neighborhood	E	74	Pair-It Books	Steck-Vaughn
At the Barbershop	E	179	Visions	Wright Group
At the Beach	E	85	Oxford Reading Tree	Oxford University Press
At the Car Wash	E	143	Visions	Wright Group
At the Park	E	29	Oxford Reading Tree	Oxford University Press
At the Seaside	E	85	Oxford Reading Tree	Oxford University Press
At the Track	E	122	Ready Readers	Pearson Learning
Baby Bear Goes Fishing	E	112	PM Story Books	Rigby

Title	Level	Words	Author/Series	Publisher/Distributor
Baby, The	E	60	Burningham, John	Crowell
Baby's Dinner	E	26	Literacy 2000	Rigby
Baby-Sitter, The	E	69	Oxford Reading Tree	Oxford University Press
Bad Dream, The	E	88	Teacher's Choice Series	Dominie
Bad Hair Day	E	113	Teacher's Choice Series	Dominie
Baseball Fun	E	51	Geddes, Diana	Kaeden Books
Bath for Patches, A	E	89	Carousel Readers	Dominie
Bats, Bats, Bats	E	33	Pair-It Books	Steck-Vaughn
Bear Facts	E	41	Pair-It Books	Steck-Vaughn
Beaver Tale, A	E	228	Twig	Wright Group
Behind the Rocks	E	50	Wonder World	Wright Group
Ben Ate It	E	130	Teacher's Choice Series	Dominie
Benny's Baby Brother	E	89	Start to Read	School Zone
Ben's Dad	E	102	PM Story Books	Rigby
Best Birthday Mole Ever Had, The	E	252	Ready Readers	Pearson Learning
Best Friends	E	31	Fitros, Pamela	Kaeden Books
Between the Tides	E	52	Wonder World	Wright Group
Biff's Aeroplane	E	64	Oxford Reading Tree	Oxford University Press
Big and Little Dinosaurs	E	50	Planet Earth	Rigby
Big Eggs	E	103	Coxe, Molly	Random House
Big Friend, Little Friend	E		Greenfield, Eloise	Houghton Mifflin
Big Pig, Little Pig	E	54	Little Celebrations	Pearson Learning
Big Rocks, Little Rocks	E	180	Early Connections	Benchmark Education
Big Seed, The	E	83	New Way	Steck-Vaughn
Big Toe, The	E	123	Read-Togethers	Wright Group
Big, Brown Box, The	E	93	Voyages	SRA/McGraw-Hill
Biggest Sandwich Ever, The	E	87	Pair-It Books	Steck-Vaughn
Bike That Spike Likes, The	E	91	Ready Readers	Pearson Learning
Bill's Baby	E	41	Tadpoles	Rigby
Birthday Celebrations	E	111	Early Connections	Benchmark Education
Black Bears	E	50	Pebble Books	Grolier, Capstone
Blanket, The	E	65	Burningham, John	Crowell
Blue Bug's Book of Colors	E	49	Poulet, Virginia	Children's Press
Bobbie's Airplane	E	64	Oxford Reading Tree	Oxford University Press
Bobby's Zoo	E	54	Rookie Readers	Children's Press
Boogly, The	E	61	Literacy 2000	Rigby
Boo-Hoo	E	149	Story Box	Wright Group
Book Week	E	71	Oxford Reading Tree	Oxford University Press
Boots and Shoes	E	68	Cooper, Anne	Kaeden Books
Bottle Garden, A	E	52	Wonder World	Wright Group
Box Can Be Many Things, A	E	51	Rookie Readers	Children's Press
Boxes	E	103	Foundations	Wright Group
Boxes, Boxes, Boxes	E	63	Stewart, J. & Salem, Lynn	Seedling
Brave Father Mouse	E	92	PM Story Books	Rigby
Brothers	E	65	Talk About Books	Dominie
Brown Bears	E	45	Pebble Books	Grolier, Capstone
Bruno's Birthday	E	32	Literacy 2000	Rigby
Bumble Bees	E	56	Pebble Books	Grolier, Capstone
Burrows	E	51	Storyteller-Setting Sun	Wright Group/ McGraw-Hill
Buster McCluster	E	71	Wonder World	Wright Group
Busy Street	E	67	Traditional Tales & More	Rigby

Title	Level	Words	Author/Series	Publisher/Distributor
Butch, the Outdoor Cat	E	65	Carousel Readers	Dominie
Butterflies	E	41	Pebble Books	Grolier, Capstone
Buzz Is Part of a Bee, A	E	56	Rookie Readers	Children's Press
By the Stream	E	73	Oxford Reading Tree	Oxford University Press
Calico Cat's Rainbow	E		Charles, Donald	Children's Press
Camping	E	264	Sunshine	Wright Group
Camping Out	E	141	Visions	Wright Group
Castle	E	37	Exploring History & Geography	Rigby
Catch It, Marvin	E	61	Windmill Books	Rigby
Catch That Frog	E	131	Reading Unlimited	Pacific Learning
Catherine the Counter	E	86	Sunshine	Wright Group
Cats	E	137	Wonder World	Wright Group
Chicken Feed	E	67	Joy Readers	Dominie
Chocolate, Chocolate, Chocolate	E	106	Visions	Wright Group
Chook, Chook	E	42	Sunshine	Wright Group
Choosing a Puppy	E	158	PM Extensions-Yellow	Rigby
Christmas Shopping	E	48	Literacy 2000	Rigby
Cinco de Mayo	E	120	Fiesta Holiday Series	Dominie
City Cat and the Country Cat, The	E	152	Ready Readers	Pearson Learning
City Scenes	E	24	Pacific Literacy	Pacific Learning
City Storm	E	180	Twig	Wright Group
Click	E	41	Books for Young Learners	Richard C. Owen
Close Your Eyes	E	131	Foundations	Wright Group
Colorful Ghost, The	E	135	TOTTS	Tott Publications
Communities	E	59	Wonder World	Wright Group
Cookies to Share	E	45	Pair-It Books	Steck-Vaughn
Cook-Out, The	E	78	Oxford Reading Tree	Oxford University Press
Covers	E	30	Little Celebrations	Pearson Learning
Cow in the Garden, The	E	158	New Way Green	Steck-Vaughn
Crabs	E	46	Pebble Books	Grolier, Capstone
Creepy Caterpillar	E	118	Little Readers	Houghton Mifflin
Curious Cat	E	95	Little Celebrations	Pearson Learning
Custard	E	82	Wonder World	Wright Group
Dad's Bike	E	52	Literacy 2000	Rigby
Dan Goes Home	E	153	Story Basket	Wright Group
Dancing Dinosaurs	E	45	Little Celebrations	Pearson Learning
Dandelion, The	E	99	Sunshine	Wright Group
Daniel's Basketball Team	E	80	Carousel Readers	Dominie
Day Shopping, A	E	157	Foundations	Wright Group
Days of Adventure	E	47	Book Shop	Mondo Publishing
Deep in the Woods	E	164	Carousel Readers	Dominie
Diana Made Dinner	E	81	Carousel Readers	Dominie
Dinosaur Fun Facts	E	84	Pair-It Books	Steck-Vaughn
Dinosaurs Dance	E	17	Rookie Readers	Children's Press
Dishy-Washy	E	92	Story Basket	Wright Group
Dizzy Lizzy	E	37	Literacy 2000	Rigby
Do Ladybugs Go to School?	E	75	Visions	Wright Group
Dog and Cat	E	62	My First Reader	Grolier Press
Dog and Cat	E	62	Fehner, C.	Children's Press
Dog and Cat	E	73	Story Basket	Wright Group
Don't Be Silly	E	76	Teacher's Choice Series	Dominie
Don't Panic!	E	122	Book Bank	Wright Group

Title	Level	Words	Author/Series	Publisher/Distributor
Don't You Laugh at Me!	E	167	Sunshine	Wright Group
Double Dutch	E	191	Visions	Wright Group
Down at the River	E	51	Pacific Literacy	Pacific Learning
Down By the Bay	E	121	Little Celebrations	Pearson Learning
Down the Street	E	66	Little Celebrations	Pearson Learning
Dragon!	E	68	Wonder World	Wright Group
Dragonflies	E	39	Pebble Books	Grolier, Capstone
Drawbridge	E	29	Books for Young Learners	Richard C. Owen
Dreams	E	93	Book Bank	Wright Group
Dressed Up Sammy	E	91	Urmston, Kathleen & Evans, Karen	Kaeden Books
Duck, Duck, Goose!	E	92	My First Reader	Grolier Press
Ear Book	E		Perkins, Al	Random House
Earthquake	E	40	Wonder World	Wright Group
Easter	E	112	Fiesta Holiday Series	Dominie
Eat Your Peas, Louise	E	83	Rookie Readers	Children's Press
Elephants Are Coming, The	E	138	Little Readers	Houghton Mifflin
Engelbert's Exercises	E	23	Little Celebrations	Pearson Learning
Engines	E	81	Sunshine	Wright Group
Every Bird Has a Beak	E	49	Birds Series	Dominie
Every Bird Has Feathers	E	50	Birds Series	Dominie
Every Bird has Two Feet	E	46	Birds Series	Dominie
Every Day But Sunday	E	83	Home Connection Collection	Rigby
Every Mother Bird Builds a Nest	E	62	Birds Series	Dominie
Excuses, Excuses	E	104	Tadpoles	Rigby
Eyes are Everywhere	E	131	Ready Readers	Pearson Learning
Fall	E	73	Sunshine	Wright Group
Fall Harvest	E	39	Pebble Books	Grolier, Capstone
Family, The	E	55	Sunshine	Wright Group
Fans and Umbrellas	E	107	Joy Readers	Dominie
Fantastic Cake, The	E	169	Story Box	Wright Group
Farmer in the Dell	E		Parkinson, Kathy	Whitman
Fastest Gazelle, The	E	146	Literacy 2000	Rigby
Find a Caterpillar	E	102	Book Bank	Wright Group
Fire and Water	E	127	Story Box	Wright Group
Fire, Fire	E	164	PM Story Books	Rigby
Fireflies	E	49	Pebble Books	Grolier, Capstone
Fishing	E	47	Wonder World	Wright Group
Five Little Dinosaurs	E	113	Ready Readers	Pearson Learning
Five Little Monkeys Going to the Zoo	E	201	Cutteridge's, V's First Grade	Seedling
Five Little Monkeys Jumping on the Bed	E	200	Christelow, Eileen	Houghton Mifflin
Five Silly Fishermen	E	250+	Edwards, Roberta	Random House
Fix It, Fox	E	62	Ready Readers	Pearson Learning
Fizz and Splutter	E	92	Story Box	Wright Group
Floppy's Bath	E	55	Oxford Reading Tree	Oxford University Press
Flowers for Mom	E	88	Carousel Readers	Dominie
Fluffy Chicks	E	50	Book Bank	Wright Group
Food for Healthy Teeth	E	40	Pebble Books	Grolier, Capstone
Foot Book	E		Seuss, Dr.	Random House
Forgetful Fred	E	78	Tadpoles	Rigby
Free to Fly	E	96	Gibson, Kathleen	Seedling
Friend for Little White Rabbit	E	113	PM Story Books	Rigby
From Blossom to Fruit	E	44	Pebble Books	Grolier, Capstone

Title	Level	Words	Author/Series	Publisher/Distributor
From the Air	E	107	Wonder World	Wright Group
Fun Place to Eat, A	E	90	Ready Readers	Pearson Learning
Funny Fish Story	E	152	Rookie Readers	Children's Press
Funny Man, A	E	244	Jensen, Patricia	Scholastic
Fuzz, Feathers, Fur	E	131	Twig	Wright Group
Get Lost Becka!	E	102	Start to Read	School Zone
Getting Ready for School	E	109	Foundations	Wright Group
Giggle Box, The	E	176	Story Box	Wright Group
Glenda the Lion	E	88	Ready Readers	Pearson Learning
Gloves	E	103	Story Box	Wright Group
Go Back to Sleep	E	74	Literacy 2000	Rigby
Go Dog Go	E		Eastman, Philip D.	Random House
Go-cart, The	E	47	Oxford Reading Tree	Oxford University Press
Going Fishing	E	26	Literacy 2000	Rigby
Going to Lucy's House	E	151	Sunshine	Wright Group
Goldilocks & the Three Bears	E		Hunia, Fran	Ladybird Books
Good Boy, Andrew!	E	85	Literacy 2000	Rigby
Good Catch!, A	E	191	New Way Red	Steck-Vaughn
Good-bye Perky	E	54	Twig	Wright Group
Grandma's Present	E	191	Foundations	Wright Group
Grandmother	E	60	Joy Readers	Dominie
Grandpa	E	70	Sunshine	Wright Group
Grandpa Knits Hats	E	55	Wonder World	Wright Group
Great Car Race, The	E	162	Carousel Readers	Dominie
Greedy Cat's Breakfast	E	53	Story Basket	Wright Group
Green Footprints	E	42	Literacy 2000	Rigby
Grow, Seed, Grow	E	36	Discovery Links	Newbridge
Grumpy Elephant	E	100	Story Box	Wright Group
Guess What Kind of Ball	E	219	Urmston, Kathleen & Evans, Karen	Kaeden Books
Guess What!	E	28	Literacy 2000	Rigby
Guess What?	E	120	Foundations	Wright Group
Gum on the Drum	E	41	Gregorich, Barbara	School Zone
Halloween	E	128	Fiesta Holiday Series	Dominie
Happy Egg	E	210	Kraus, Robert	Scholastic
Haunted House, The	E	77	Story Box	Wright Group
Have You Seen the Tooth Fairy?	E	187	Visions	Wright Group
Healthy Visit, A	E	44	New Way Red	Steck-Vaughn
Hello, Hello, Hello	E	56	Sunshine	Wright Group
Henry	E	77	Books for Young Learners	Richard C. Owen
Henry's Busy Day	E		Campbell, Rod	The Penguin Group
Here Comes Annette!	E	143	Voyages	SRA/McGraw-Hill
Herman the Helper	E	94	Kraus, Robert	Simon & Schuster
Hermit Crab	E	111	PM Story Books	Rigby
Hide and Seek	E	215	Foundations	Wright Group
Hi-De-Hi	E	110	Little Celebrations	Pearson Learning
Home Run, The	E	92	Teacher's Choice Series	Dominie
Home Sweet Home	E		Roffey, Maureen	Bodley
Honey Bees and Hives	E	58	Pebble Books	Grolier, Capstone
Honey, My Rabbit	E	56	Voyages	SRA/McGraw-Hill
Hot Rod Harry	E	66	Rookie Readers	Children's Press
How Many Ants?	E	35	Rookie Readers	Children's Press
How Many Hot Dogs?	E	115	Story Box	Wright Group

Title	Level	Words	Author/Series	Publisher/Distributor
How Many Seeds?	E	42	Pair-It Books	Steck-Vaughn
How Many?	E	147	Early Connections	Benchmark Education
How to Grow a Plant	E	172	Visions	Wright Group
How to Make a Sun Hat	E	87	Home Connection Collection	Rigby
Howie Has a Stomachache	E	100	Moore, J. R.	Seedling
Humpback Whales	E	48	Pair-It Books	Steck-Vaughn
Hungry Happy Monkey	E	77	Joy Readers	Dominie
Hungry Horse	E	35	Literacy 2000	Rigby
Hurry Squirrel!	E	72	Start to Read	School Zone
I Am a Photographer	E	32	Read-More Books	Dominie
I Am Cold	E	136	Foundations	Wright Group
I Am Hot	E	123	Foundations	Wright Group
I Am King!	E	57	My First Reader	Grolier Press
I Can Be Anything	E	242	Pair-It Books	Steck-Vaughn
I Can Do It Myself	E	150	Visions	Wright Group
I Can Squeak	E	154	Windmill	Wright Group
I Got a Goldfish	E	92	Ready Readers	Pearson Learning
I Have a Home	E	79	Sunshine	Wright Group
I Love Camping	E	83	Carousel Readers	Dominie
I Love Cats	E	116	Rookie Readers	Children's Press
I Love You	E	121	Teacher's Choice Series	Dominie
I Smell Smoke!	E	49	Sunshine	Wright Group
I Wonder Why	E	73	Foundations	Wright Group
If Horses Could Talk!	E	32	Teacher's Choice Series	Dominie
If I Were You	E	77	Wildsmith, Brian	Oxford University Press
I'll Be a Pirate	E	53	Eifrig, Kate	Kaeden Books
I'm Telling	E	71	Teacher's Choice Series	Dominie
In a Dark, Dark Wood	E	81	Read-Togethers	Wright Group
In a Town	E	47	Little Celebrations	Pearson Learning
In My Pocket	E	195	Carousel Readers	Dominie
In the Rain Forest	E	57	Twig	Wright Group
Inside or Outside?	E	57	Literacy 2000	Rigby
Inside Story, The	E	43	Teacher's Choice Series	Dominie
Inside, Outside, Upside Down	E		Berenstain, Stan & Jan	Random House
Is It Floating?	E	146	Sunshine	Wright Group
Is Tomorrow My Birthday?	E	87	Blaxland, Wendy	Scholastic
It Could Be Worse	E	108	Home Connection Collection	Rigby
It Looked Like Split Milk	E	172	Shaw, Charles	Harper & Row
It's Noisy at Night	E	80	Wonder World	Wright Group
It's Raining	E	86	Teacher's Choice Series	Dominie
It's Time for Bed	E	126	Visions	Wright Group
It's Time to Get Up	E	143	Visions	Wright Group
Jack and Jill	E	51	Sunshine	Wright Group
Jan and the Jacket	E	74	Oxford Reading Tree	Oxford University Press
Jigaree, The	E	128	Story Box	Wright Group
Jimmy's Goal	E	159	Foundations	Wright Group
Jobs	E	112	Benger, Wendy	Kaeden Books
Jock Jerome	E	99	Voyages	SRA/McGraw-Hill
Joe and the BMX Bike	E	91	Oxford Reading Tree	Oxford University Press
Joe's Father	E	138	Book Bank	Wright Group
Jolly Jumping Jelly Beans	E	121	Sunshine	Wright Group

Title	Level	Words	Author/Series	Publisher/Distributor
Jumble Sale, The	E	81	Oxford Reading Tree	Oxford University Press
Just a Seed	E	74	Blaxland, Wendy	Scholastic
Just Like Grandpa	E	81	Literacy 2000	Rigby
Just Like Me	E	138	Rookie Readers	Children's Press
Just Like Us	E	55	Ready Readers	Pearson Learning
Just Right for the Night	E		Voyages	SRA/McGraw-Hill
Katydids	E	20	Books for Young Learners	Richard C. Owen
Keeping Fit!	E	36	Little Celebrations	Pearson Learning
Kipper's Birthday	E	64	Oxford Reading Tree	Oxford University Press
Koalas	E	36	Literacy 2000	Rigby
Larry and the Cookie	E	56	Rookie Readers	Children's Press
Let's Eat	E	63	Teacher's Choice Series	Dominie
Let's Go Marching	E	94	Ready Readers	Pearson Learning
Let's Play Basketball	E	46	Geddes, Diana	Kaeden Books
Little Bird	E	42	Sunshine	Wright Group
Little Bulldozer Man	E	170	PM Story Books	Rigby
Little Frog's Monster Story	E	144	Ready Readers	Pearson Learning
Little Monkey Is Stuck	E	251	Foundations	Wright Group
Little Zoot	E	33	Little Celebrations	Pearson Learning
Lizard	E	80	Foundations	Wright Group
Lonely Bull, The	E	116	Pacific Literacy	Pacific Learning
Long Walk, A	E	131	Twig	Wright Group
Look Here!	E	67	Wonder World	Wright Group
Look Up	E	44	Little Celebrations	Pearson Learning
Looking After Baby	E	143	Storyteller Nonfiction	Wright Group/ McGraw-Hill
Looking at Baby Animals	E	54	Teacher's Choice Series	Dominie
Looking Down	E	130	Early Connections	Benchmark Education
Lucky Duck, The	E	73	Ready Readers	Pearson Learning
Lucky Goes to Dog School	E	127	PM Story Books	Rigby
Lunch at the Pond	E	146	Foundations	Wright Group
Machines	E	44	Twig	Wright Group
Magic Wand, The	E	100	Start to Read	School Zone
Magnets	E	52	Discovery Links	Newbridge
Mail Myself to You	E	60	Little Celebrations	Pearson Learning
Making Oatmeal	E	38	Interaction	Rigby
Marketplace, The	E	58	Visions	Wright Group
Martian Goo	E	65	Salem, Lynn & Stewart, J.	Seedling
Marvin's Manners	E	32	Pair-It Books	Steck-Vaughn
Mask, The	E	45	Pair-It Books	Steck-Vaughn
Masks	E	62	Wonder World	Wright Group
May I Stay Home Today?	E	73	Tadpoles	Rigby
Meanies Came to School, The	E	135	Story Basket	Wright Group
Meanie's Trick, The	E	93	Story Box	Wright Group
Meanies' Trick, The	E	158	Story Basket	Wright Group
Measuring Time	E	217	Early Connections	Benchmark Education
Meet Mr. Cricket	E	86	Carousel Readers	Dominie
Mia's Sun Hat	E	32	Start to Read	School Zone
Michael in the Hospital	E	91	Oxford Reading Tree	Oxford University Press
Midge in the Hospital	E	91	Oxford Reading Tree	Oxford University Press
Milwaukee Cows	E	79	Story Box	Wright Group

Title	Level	Words	Author/Series	Publisher/Distributor
Mmm...Very Nice	E	91	Home Connection Collection	Rigby
Monkey Tricks	E	81	Joy Readers	Dominie
Monster at the Beach, The	E	82	Storyteller-Moon Rising	Wright Group/ McGraw-Hill
Moon Cake, The	E	127	Joy Readers	Dominie
More or Less Fish Story	E		Wylie, Joanne & David	Children's Press
Morris the Moose	E	250+	Wiseman, Bernard	HarperTrophy
Mosquito Buzzed, A	E	133	Little Readers	Houghton Mifflin
Mosquitoes	E	39	Pebble Books	Grolier, Capstone
Move it	E	58	Wonder World	Wright Group
Move Over!	E	118	Story Basket	Wright Group
Moving Day	E		Sunshine	Wright Group
Moving to America	E	81	Carousel Readers	Dominie
Mr. Bumbleticker's Birthday	E	110	Foundations	Wright Group
Mr. Crawford	E	119	Foundations	Wright Group
Mr. Cricket Takes a Vacation	E	165	Carousel Readers	Dominie
Mr. Egg	E	22	Pair-It Books	Steck-Vaughn
Mr. Fin's Trip	E	130	Ready Readers	Pearson Learning
Mr. Wink	E	86	Ready Readers	Pearson Learning
Mrs. Wishy Washy	E	102	Story Box	Wright Group
Mud Pies	E	143	Start to Read	School Zone
My Big Brother	E	103	PM Nonfiction-Yellow	Rigby
My Body Works	E	131	Twig	Wright Group
My Brother, the Brat	E		Hall, Kirsten	Scholastic
My Bug Box	E	99	Books for Young Learners	Richard C. Owen
My Dad	E	114	PM Nonfiction-Yellow	Rigby
My Dad Lost His Job	E	76	Carousel Readers	Dominie
My Dad's Truck	E	57	Costain, Meredith	Scholastic
My Doll	E	86	Yukish, Joe	Kaeden Books
My Fish Does Not Chirp	E	77	Ready Readers	Pearson Learning
My Five Senses Education	E	142	Early Connections	Benchmark
My Friend	E	95	Foundations	Wright Group
My Grandma and Grandpa	E	130	PM Nonfiction-Yellow	Rigby
My Hamster, Van	E	73	Ready Readers	Pearson Learning
My Little Sister	E	120	PM Nonfiction-Yellow	Rigby
My Lost Top	E	70	Ready Readers	Pearson Learning
My Old Cat	E	110	Foundations	Wright Group
My Pet Bobby	E	150	Little Readers	Houghton Mifflin
My Pony Minnie	E	59	Sunshine	Wright Group
My Shadow	E	46	Pacific Literacy	Pacific Learning
My Special Job	E	110	Pacific Literacy	Pacific Learning
My Special Place	E	116	Teacher's Choice Series	Dominie
My Tiger Cat	E	76	Frankford, Marilyn	Kaeden Books
My Two Homes	E	69	Carousel Readers	Dominie
Nana's Sweet Potato Pie	E	233	Visions	Wright Group
Nests	E	58	Literacy 2000	Rigby
New Baby, The	E	133	PM Story Books	Rigby
New Balloon, A	E	36	Pacific Literacy	Pacific Learning
New Nest, The	E	207	Foundations	Wright Group
Nibbly Mouse	E		Voyages	SRA/McGraw-Hill
Nick's Glasses	E	51	Ready to Read	Pacific Learning

Title	Level	Words	Author/Series	Publisher/Distributor
Nickels and Pennies	E	53	Williams, Deborah	Kaeden Books
Nick's Glasses	E	51	Pacific Literacy	Pacific Learning
Nick's Pet	E	119	Teacher's Choice Series	Dominie
Night and Day	E	112	Ready Readers	Pearson Learning
Night Train, The	E	65	Story Box	Wright Group
Night Walk	E	47	Prokopchak, Ann	Kaeden Books
Nine Days of Camping, The	E	254	Twig	Wright Group
Noggin and Bobbin in the Garden	E	57	Little Celebrations	Pearson Learning
Noises	E	49	Literacy 2000	Rigby
Noisy Toys	E	77	Home Connection Collection	Rigby
Nose Book	E		Perkins, Al	Random House
Noses	E	56	Literacy 2000	Rigby
Numbers Are Everywhere	E	125	Early Connections	Benchmark Education
Numbers Are Everywhere	E	131	Twig	Wright Group
Oh a Hunting We Will Go	E	346	Langstaff, John	Macmillan
Oh No Otis!	E	45	Rookie Readers	Children's Press
Oh No!	E	127	Book Shop	Mondo Publishing
Oh, Cats!	E	93	Buck, Nola	HarperTrophy
Oh, Jump in a Sack	E	130	Story Box	Wright Group
Oh, No, Sherman	E	66	Erickson, Betty	Seedling
One Sun in the Sky	E	120	Windmill	Wright Group
Our Baby	E	90	PM Nonfiction-Yellow	Rigby
Our Cat	E	99	Foundations	Wright Group
Our House Had a Mouse	E	102	Worthington, Denise	Seedling
Our Mom	E	107	PM Nonfiction-Yellow	Rigby
Our Tree House	E	144	Twig	Wright Group
Out the Door	E	150	Rookie Readers	Children's Press
Outing, An	E	68	Sunshine	Wright Group
Over the Marble Mountain	E	92	Voyages	SRA/McGraw-Hill
Over-Under	E	29	Rookie Readers	Children's Press
Package, The	E	35	Bauer, Roger	Kaeden Books
Paper Bag Trail	E	67	Schreiber, Anne & Doughty, A.	Scholastic
Parts of a Whole	E	165	Early Connections	Benchmark Education
Pat's New Puppy	E	88	Reading Unlimited	Pacific Learning
Patterns	E	57	Literacy 2000	Rigby
Peaches the Pig	E	120	Little Readers	Houghton Mifflin
Peanut Butter	E	60	Little Celebrations	Pearson Learning
Peanut Butter and Jelly	E	164	Little Readers	Houghton Mifflin
People Can Build	E	46	Sunshine	Wright Group
People Dance	E	46	Wonder World	Wright Group
Pet That I Want, The	E		Packard, Mary	Scholastic
Pictures	E	76	Teacher's Choice Series	Dominie
Pirate's Treasure, The	E	63	Joy Readers	Dominie
Planting a Garden	E	62	Ready Readers	Pearson Learning
Polly's Shop	E	130	Ready Readers	Pearson Learning
POP Pops the Popcorn	E	60	Ready Readers	Pearson Learning
Present, The	E	30	Literacy 2000	Rigby
Pumpkin, The	E	56	Story Box	Wright Group
Puppet Show, The	E	25	Literacy 2000	Rigby
Purple Is Part of a Rainbow	E	131	Rookie Readers	Children's Press
Quack!	E	48	Ready Readers	Pearson Learning
Quarter Story, The	E	99	Williams, Deborah	Kaeden Books

Title	Level	Words	Author/Series	Publisher/Distributor
Quick, Go Peek!	E	83	Little Celebrations	Pearson Learning
Quilts	E	131	Twig	Wright Group
Race, The	E	30	Little Celebrations	Pearson Learning
Rain and the Sun, The	E	45	Wonder World	Wright Group
Rat-a-tat-tat	E	107	Literacy 2000	Rigby
Rattlesnake Looks for Food, The	E	105	Foundations	Wright Group
Ready for School	E	77	Windmill Books	Rigby
Red Rose, The	E	127	Read-Togethers	Wright Group
Rex's Dance	E	103	Little Readers	Houghton Mifflin
Riddles	E	51	Literacy 2000	Rigby
River Grows, The	E	70	Ready Readers	Pearson Learning
Roll Out the Red Rug	E	68	Ready Readers	Pearson Learning
Rope Swing, The	E	77	Oxford Reading Tree	Oxford University Press
Rosie's Party	E	111	Little Readers	Houghton Mifflin
Roy and the Parakeet	E	74	Oxford Reading Tree	Oxford University Press
Rummage Sale, The	E	81	Oxford Reading Tree	Oxford University Press
Rum-Tum-Tum	E	62	Story Box	Wright Group
Rush, Rush, Rush	E	52	Ready Readers	Pearson Learning
Sack Race, A	E	106	New Way Blue	Steck-Vaughn
Saguaro	E	44	Books for Young Learners	Richard C. Owen
Sally and the Sparrows	E	151	PM Extensions-Yellow	Rigby
Sally's Red Bucket	E	127	PM Story Books	Rigby
Sally's Spaceship	E	86	Ready Readers	Pearson Learning
Sam's Mask	E	36	Pacific Literacy	Pacific Learning
Sam's Mask	E	41	Ready to Read	Pacific Learning
Sam's Seasons	E	143	Pair-It Books	Steck-Vaughn
Sand Castle Contest, The	E	173	Pair-It Books	Steck-Vaughn
Sand Picnic, The	E	123	New Way White	Steck-Vaughn
Sarah Snail	E	55	Voyages	SRA/McGraw-Hill
Saturday Morning Breakfast	E	65	Teacher's Choice Series	Dominie
School Bus, The	E	60	Sunshine	Wright Group
School, The	E	27	Burningham, John	Crowell
Schools Around the World	E	78	Pair-It Books	Steck-Vaughn
Sea Star, A	E	82	Ready Readers	Pearson Learning
Sea Stars	E	63	Pebble Books	Grolier, Capstone
Seagull Is Clever	E	98	PM Story Books	Rigby
Secret Friend, The	E	189	Little Readers	Houghton Mifflin
Secret Friend, The	E	196	Little Celebrations	Pearson Learning
Secret Soup	E	51	Literacy 2000	Rigby
Seeds, Seeds, Seeds	E	96	Sunshine	Wright Group
Senses	E	66	Voyages	SRA/McGraw-Hill
Shadows	E	190	Visions	Wright Group
Shane and Ned	E	52	Windmill Books	Rigby
Shopping	E	45	Read-More Books	Dominie
Shopping	E	101	Storyteller-Setting Sun	Wright Group/ McGraw-Hill
Signs	E	131	Twig	Wright Group
Simply Sam	E	69	Voyages	SRA/McGraw-Hill
Sing a Song	E	154	Read-Togethers	Wright Group
Sisters	E	77	Talk About Books	Dominie
Sitting	E	46	Literacy 2000	Rigby
Skating Whiz	E	40	Visions	Wright Group

Title	Level	Words	Author/Series	Publisher/Distributor
Skin, Skin	E	44	Wonder World	Wright Group
Skipper's Balloon	E	62	Oxford Reading Tree	Oxford University Press
Skipper's Birthday	E	64	Oxford Reading Tree	Oxford University Press
Skipper's Idea	E	81	Oxford Reading Tree	Oxford University Press
Skipper's Laces	E	66	Oxford Reading Tree	Oxford University Press
Sleeping	E	43	Literacy 2000	Rigby
Sleepy Bear	E	153	Foundations	Wright Group
Smarty Pants	E	116	Read-Togethers	Wright Group
Smiles	E	366	Visions	Wright Group
Smiling Stan, the Pedicab Man	E	121	Joy Readers	Dominie
Snails	E	67	Foundations	Wright Group
Snakes	E	37	Visions	Wright Group
Snowman, The	E	76	Oxford Reading Tree	Oxford University Press
Something to Munch	E	58	Ready Readers	Pearson Learning
Sounds in the Night	E	126	Visions	Wright Group
Spiders	E	53	Discovery Links	Newbridge
Spiders	E	75	Wonder World	Wright Group
Splash!	E	85	Joy Readers	Dominie
Splishy-Sploshy	E	127	Story Basket	Wright Group
Spots	E	48	Literacy 2000	Rigby
Spots!	E	55	Oxford Reading Tree	Oxford University Press
Spring	E	58	Sunshine	Wright Group
Stallion's Call, The	E	77	Salem, Lynn & Stewart, J.	Seedling
Stan Packs	E	84	Ready Readers	Pearson Learning
Starting School	E		Voyages	SRA/McGraw-Hill
Stella	E	57	Storyteller-Moon Rising	Wright Group/ McGraw-Hill
Storm!	E	49	Wonder World	Wright Group
Storm, The	E	33	Literacy 2000	Rigby
Strange Plants	E	30	Books for Young Learners	Richard C. Owen
Strawberry Jam	E	77	Oxford Reading Tree	Oxford University Press
Stuck in the Muck	E	139	Spinelle, Nancy Louise	Kaeden Books
Summer	E	73	Sunshine	Wright Group
Summer Fun	E	30	Literacy 2000	Rigby
Sun, The	E	42	Discovery Links	Newbridge
Sunflowers	E	33	Books for Young Learners	Richard C. Owen
Sunshine, Moonshine	E	128	Armstrong, Jennifer	Random House
Super Pig's Adventures	E	133	New Way Blue	Steck-Vaughn
Surprise for Mom	E	101	Urmston, Kathleen & Evans, Karen	Kaeden Books
Sweet Potato Pie	E	72	Rockwell, Anne	Random House
Tails	E	59	Discovery Links	Newbridge
Taking Care of Rosie	E	61	Salem Lynn & Stewart, J.	Seedling
Taking Our Photos	E	132	Voyages	SRA/McGraw-Hill
Ten Little Men	E	38	Literacy 2000	Rigby
Terrible Twos	E	86	Tadpoles	Rigby
That Dog!	E	213	Foundations	Wright Group
There Was a Crooked Man	E	40	Sunshine	Wright Group
Things People Do for Fun	E	124	Foundations	Wright Group
Three Little Ducks	E	102	Read-Togethers	Wright Group
Three Little Monkeys	E	36	Sunshine	Wright Group
Three Little Pigs and One Big Pig	E	123	Ready Readers	Pearson Learning
Timmy	E	54	Literacy 2000	Rigby

Title	Level	Words	Author/Series	Publisher/Distributor
Tires	E	180	Foundations	Wright Group
Tittle-Tattle Goose	E	117	Story Box	Wright Group
Toenails	E	83	Voyages	SRA/McGraw-Hill
Tomatoes and Bricks	E	126	Windmill	Wright Group
Tom's Rubber Band	E	82	Sunshine	Wright Group
Too Little	E	119	Foundations	Wright Group
Tornado	E	37	Spinelle, Nancy Louise	Kaeden Books
Tortillas	E	71	Gonzalez-Jensen	Scholastic
Toys	E	76	Talk About Books	Dominie
Traffic Jam	E	133	Harper, Leslie	Kaeden Books
Tree Can Be, A	E	74	Nayer, Judy	Scholastic
Trip, The	E	108	Ready Readers	Pearson Learning
Trouble	E	113	Teacher's Choice Series	Dominie
Trucks	E	196	Foundations	Wright Group
Two	E	84	Carousel Readers	Dominie
Two Is a Pair	E	78	Teacher's Choice Series	Dominie
Two Little Dogs	E	74	Story Box	Wright Group
Two Plus Two	E	44	Teacher's Choice Series	Dominie
Under the Big Top	E	103	Twig	Wright Group
Until We Got Princess	E	94	Book Shop	Mondo Publishing
Up and Down	E	79	Storyteller-Setting Sun	Wright Group/ McGraw-Hill
Valentine's Day	E	132	Fiesta Holiday Series	Dominie
Very Strong Baby, The	E	74	Joy Readers	Dominie
Visit to the Library, A	E	109	Foundations	Wright Group
Visitors	E	46	Literacy 2000	Rigby
Wagon Ride, The	E	115	Teacher's Choice Series	Dominie
Waiting	E	75	Voyages	SRA/McGraw-Hill
Wake Up, Sun!	E	250+	Harrison, David	Random House
Water Fight, The	E	64	Oxford Reading Tree	Oxford University Press
Watermelon	E	81	Rise & Shine	Hampton-Brown
Waves	E	70	Voyages	SRA/McGraw-Hill
We Can Play	E	58	TOTTS	Tott Publications
We Make Cookies	E	48	Pair-It Books	Steck-Vaughn
Weather	E	138	Early Connections	Benchmark Education
Well-fed Bear, The	E	35	Literacy 2000	Rigby
Wet Paint	E	92	Storyteller-Setting Sun	Wright Group/ McGraw-Hill
Whale Watchers, The	E	63	Windmill Books	Rigby
What Animals Eat	E	75	Little Red Readers	Sundance
What Do We Have to Get?	E	117	Ready Readers	Pearson Learning
What Grows on Trees?	E	49	Start to Read	School Zone
What If...	E	57	Teacher's Choice Series	Dominie
What Is at the Top?	E	197	Ready Readers	Pearson Learning
What Is in the Closet?	E	107	Story Box	Wright Group
What Is It?	E	69	Storyteller-First Snow	Wright Group/ McGraw-Hill
What Shall I Wear?	E	58	Book Bank	Wright Group
What Things Go Together	E	26	Literacy 2000	Rigby
What Tommy Did	E	125	Literacy 2000	Rigby
Whatever Will These Become	E	47	Literacy 2000	Rigby
What's Black and White and Moos?	E	78	Twig	Wright Group

Title	Level	Words	Author/Series	Publisher/Distributor
What's for Dinner?	E	112	Salem, Lynn & Stewart, J.	Seedling
What's for Lunch	E	91	New Way Red	Steck-Vaughn
What's in the Bag?	E	98	Visions	Wright Group
When It Rains	E	36	Voyages	SRA/McGraw-Hill
When We Are Big	E	123	Ready Readers	Pearson Learning
Where Can It Be?	E	83	Jonas, Ann	Morrow
Where Can Teddy Go?	E	141	Foundations	Wright Group
Where Does the Rabbit Hop?	E	71	Ready Readers	Pearson Learning
Where Is Daniel?	E	135	Carousel Readers	Dominie
Where Is Jake?	E	35	My First Reader	Grolier Press
Where Is Nancy?	E	56	Literacy 2000	Rigby
Where's Spot?	E	65	Hill, Eric	Putnam
Which Hat Today?	E	94	Ballinger, Margaret & Gossett, R.	Scholastic
Who Am I?	E		Christensen, Nancy	Scholastic
Who Ate the Broccoli?	E	42	Little Readers	Houghton Mifflin
Who Is Coming?	E	28	Rookie Readers	Children's Press
Who Spilled the Beans?	E	87	Story Basket	Wright Group
Who Will Be My Mother?	E	156	Read-Togethers	Wright Group
Who?	E	46	Storyteller-Setting Sun	Wright Group/ McGraw-Hill
Whoops!	E	49	Little Celebrations	Pearson Learning
Who's in the Nest?	E	75	Start to Read	School Zone
Who's There?	E	92	Story Box	Wright Group
Whose Eggs Are These?	E	125	Sunshine	Wright Group
Wide-mouthed Frog, The	E	121	Literacy 2000	Rigby
Wiggly, Jiggly, Joggly, Tooth, A	E	61	Little Celebrations	Pearson Learning
Willy's Hats	E	65	Stewart, J. & Salem, Lynn	Seedling
Wind Blows Strong, The	E	114	Sunshine	Wright Group
Wind, The	E	36	Discovery Links	Newbridge
Wind, The	E	64	Ready to Read	Pacific Learning
Wind, The	E	64	Pacific Literacy	Pacific Learning
Winter	E	56	Discovery Links	Newbridge
Wishy-Washy Day	E	65	Story Basket	Wright Group
Wooly, Wooly	E	136	Literacy 2000	Rigby
Woosh!	E	124	Read-Togethers	Wright Group
Words are Everywhere	E	46	Literacy 2000	Rigby
World's Greatest Juggler, The	E	105	Little Readers	Houghton Mifflin
Yippy-Day-Yippy-Doo!	E	117	Sunshine	Wright Group
You Should Try That with a Rhino	E	123	Home Connection Collection	Rigby
Ziggy and the Cat	E	72	Windmill Books	Rigby
Zip-Zip, Rattle-Bang!	E	141	Story Basket	Wright Group
Zoo in Willy's Bed, The	E	81	Sturnman Gorman, Kate	Seedling
Above and Below	F	128	Sunshine	Wright Group
Across the Stream	F	94	Ginsburg, Mirra	Morrow
Airplanes	F	60	Pebble Books	Grolier, Capstone
Alexander Ant Cools Off	F	76	Little Books	Sadlier-Oxford
All Through the Year	F	261	Visions	Wright Group
Amy Loves the Snow	F	127	Hoban, Julia	Scholastic
Amy Loves the Sun	F	122	Hoban, Julia	Scholastic
Amy Loves the Wind	F	116	Hoban, Julia	Scholastic
Animal Babies	F	131	Twig	Wright Group

Title	Level	Words	Author/Series	Publisher/Distributor
Animals at the Zoo	F	158	First Start	Troll
Are We There Yet?	F	127	Teacher's Choice Series	Dominie
Are You a Ladybug?	F	116	Sunshine	Wright Group
Are You My Mommy?	F	112	Dijs, Carla	Simon & Schuster
Are You There, Bear?	F		Maris, Ron	Greenwillow
Artist, The	F	83	Books for Young Learners	Richard C. Owen
Ask Nicely	F	110	Literacy 2000	Rigby
Astronauts, The	F	112	Foundations	Wright Group
At the Library	F	31	Little Celebrations	Pearson Learning
At the Pool	F	87	Oxford Reading Tree	Oxford University Press
Baby Bear's Present	F	206	PM Story Books	Rigby
Baby Elephant's Sneeze	F	78	Foundations	Wright Group
Ballyhoo!	F	124	Story Basket	Wright Group
Bandages	F	139	Moskowitz, Ellen	Kaeden Books
Bang	F	55	Literacy 2000	Rigby
Be Careful, Matthew!	F	80	Sunshine	Wright Group
Beep, Beep	F	51	Gregorich, Barbara	School Zone
Ben's New Trick	F	219	Ready Readers	Pearson Learning
Best Cake, The	F	162	PM Story Books	Rigby
Best Children in the World, The	F	148	Story Box	Wright Group
Best Thing About Food, The	F	132	Twig	Wright Group
Betsy the Babysitter	F	115	First Start	Troll
Big Bird's Copycat Day	F	232	Lerner, Sharon	Random House
Bigger or Smaller?	F	112	Sunshine	Wright Group
Biggest Cake in the World, The	F	120	Ready to Read	Pacific Learning
Biggest Cake in the World, The	F	120	Pacific Literacy	Pacific Learning
Bikes	F	133	Discovery Links	Newbridge
Billie's Book	F	110	Sunshine	Wright Group
Billy Goats Gruff	F	381	Hunia, Fran	Ladybird Books
Bird Eggs	F	50	Pebble Books	Grolier, Capstone
Bird Families	F	60	Pebble Books	Grolier, Capstone
Bird Nests	F	78	Pebble Books	Grolier, Capstone
Birds	F	50	Literacy 2000	Rigby
Birds	F	54	Birds Series	Dominie
Birthday Balloons	F	182	PM Extensions-Blue	Rigby
Birthday Bird, The	F	82	Books for Young Learners	Richard C. Owen
Birthday in the Woods, A	F	199	Salem, Lynn & Stewart, J.	Seedling
Blast Off!	F	95	Ready Readers	Pearson Learning
Blue Bug Goes to the Library	F		Poulet, Virginia	Children's Press
Bossy Bettina	F	97	Literacy 2000	Rigby
Bread, Bread, Bread	F	95	Morris, Ann	Scholastic
Bug Party	F	131	Twig	Wright Group
Bug, a Bear, and a Boy, A	F	250+	McPhail, David	Random House
Building Things	F	24	Sunshine	Wright Group
Buildings on My Street	F	109	Foundations	Wright Group
Bull's-eye!	F	87	Oxford Reading Tree	Oxford University Press
Bumpity, Bumpity, Bump	F	62	Parker, C.	Seedling
Bus Ride, The	F	99	Storyteller-Setting Sun	Wright Group/ McGraw-Hill
Butterfly Colors	F	52	Pebble Books	Grolier, Capstone
Butterfly Eggs	F	57	Pebble Books	Grolier, Capstone
Calico Cat at the Zoo	F		Charles, Donald	Children's Press

Title	Level	Words	Author/Series	Publisher/Distributor
Calico the Cat	F		Charles, Donald	Children's Press
Camping Outside	F	95	Book Bank	Wright Group
Car Accident, The	F	161	Foundations	Wright Group
Carnival, The	F	82	Oxford Reading Tree	Oxford University Press
Carrots, Peas, and Beans	F	142	Sunshine	Wright Group
Cars	F	72	Rockwell, Anne	Dutton
Cat Chat	F	85	Ready Readers	Pearson Learning
Cat Goes Fiddle-i-fee	F	333	Galdone, Paul	Houghton Mifflin
Cat in the Tree, A	F	79	Oxford Reading Tree	Oxford University Press
Caterpillars	F	54	Pebble Books	Grolier, Capstone
Caterpillar's Adventure	F	69	Story Box	Wright Group
Cats and Kittens	F	51	Reading Unlimited	Pacific Learning
Chase, The	F	85	Oxford Reading Tree	Oxford University Press
Christmas Tree, The	F	163	PM Books	Dominie
Chug the Tractor	F	203	PM Extensions-Blue	Rigby
Clothes	F	103	Talk About Books	Dominie
Cock-A-Doodle Do	F		Brandenberg, Franz	Greenwillow
Cold Day, The	F	80	Oxford Reading Tree	Oxford University Press
Come for a Swim!	F	129	Sunshine	Wright Group
Come to My House!	F	131	Sunshine	Wright Group
Cookie's Week	F	84	Ward, Cindy	Putnam
Cooking Pot, The	F	132	Sunshine	Wright Group
Dad Didn't Mind at All	F	134	Literacy 2000	Rigby
Dad's Headache	F	86	Sunshine	Wright Group
Dad's New Path	F	218	Foundations	Wright Group
Dad's Shirt	F	38	Joy Readers	Dominie
Dark, Dark Tale, A	F	115	Brown, Ruth	The Penguin Group
Dear Zoo	F	115	Campbell, Rod	Macmillan
Dinner by Five	F	215	Ready Readers	Pearson Learning
Dinosaur Fan, The	F	125	Windmill Books	Rigby
Dinosaur, The	F	131	Joy Readers	Dominie
Dive In!	F	133	Ready Readers	Pearson Learning
Do Not Open This Book!	F	134	Story Basket	Wright Group
Dog Show, The	F	131	Foundations	Wright Group
Dogs at School	F	94	Books for Young Learners	Richard C. Owen
Don't Throw It Away!	F	90	Wonder World	Wright Group
Down at the Billabog	F	93	Voyages	SRA/McGraw-Hill
Down by the Swamp	F	50	Little Celebrations	Pearson Learning
Dozen Dogs, A	F	228	Ziefert, Harriet	Random House
Dragon Hunt,The	F	53	New Way Red	Steck-Vaughn
Dragon's Lunch	F	85	Ready Readers	Pearson Learning
Dream, The	F	54	Oxford Reading Tree	Oxford University Press
Duck with the Broken Wing, The	F	189	PM Extensions-Blue	Rigby
Eve Shops	F	146	Ready Readers	Pearson Learning
Families	F	132	Twig	Wright Group
Family on Lake Street, The	F	159	Teacher's Choice Series	Dominie
Family Photos	F	106	Literacy 2000	Rigby
Farms	F	102	Sunshine	Wright Group
Farms	F	153	Foundations	Wright Group
Feisty Old Woman Who Lived in the Cozy Cave, The	F	301	Foundations	Wright Group
Find Yourself a Friend	F	261	Visions	Wright Group
Firehouse Sal	F	52	Rookie Readers	Children's Press

Title	Level	Words	Author/Series	Publisher/Distributor
Fishy Alphabet Story	F	126	Wylie, Joanne & David	Children's Press
Five Little Monkeys	F	81	Book Shop	Mondo Publishing
Flies	F	56	Pebble Books	Grolier, Capstone
Floppy the Hero	F	74	Oxford Reading Tree	Oxford University Press
Fly, Butterfly	F	49	Discovery Links	Newbridge
Flying High	F	250+	Predictable Storybooks	SRA/McGraw-Hill
Fourth of July, The	F	153	Ready Readers	Pearson Learning
Freddie's Spaghetti	F	250+	Doyle, R. H.	Random House
Friendly Snowman	F	134	First Start	Troll
Friendly Snowman	F		Joyce, William	Scholastic
Frog's Lunch	F	89	Lillgard, Dee & Zimmerman, J.	Scholastic
Gecko's Story	F	61	Books for Young Learners	Richard C. Owen
Get Lost!	F	219	Foundations	Wright Group
Gingerbread Boy	F	137	New Way Red	Steck-Vaughn
Gingerbread Man, The	F	180	Little Readers	Houghton Mifflin
Going Fishing	F	26	Voyages	SRA/McGraw-Hill
Going Shopping	F	112	Book Shop	Mondo Publishing
Going to School	F	171	Foundations	Wright Group
Going to the Dentist	F	122	Pebble Books	Grolier, Capstone
Goldilocks Comes back	F	134	Pair-It Books	Steck-Vaughn
Good Night, Little Brother	F	69	Literacy 2000	Rigby
Grandma and the Pirate	F		Lloyd, David	Crown
Grandma's Memories	F	102	Literacy 2000	Rigby
Grandpa Snored	F	51	Literacy 2000	Rigby
Grandpa's Candy Store	F	65	Books for Young Learners	Richard C. Owen
Grandpa's Cookies	F	193	Little Readers	Houghton Mifflin
Grasshoppers	F	50	Pebble Books	Grolier, Capstone
Great White Sharks	F	98	Pair-It Books	Steck-Vaughn
Green Banana	F	49	Tadpoles	Rigby
Green Eyes	F	111	Literacy 2000	Rigby
Gregory's Garden	F	70	Cat on the Mat	Oxford University Press
Growing Up, Up, Up Book	F	120	First Start	Troll
Grumbles, Growls, and Roars	F	133	Twig	Wright Group
Grump, The	F	73	Literacy 2000	Rigby
Guess Who's Coming to Dinner?	F	130	Literacy 2000	Rigby
Habitat Is Where We Live, A	F	132	Twig	Wright Group
Hands, Hands, Hands	F	85	Book Shop	Mondo Publishing
Happy Jack	F	99	First Start	Troll
Harry Takes Bath	F	132	Ziefert, Harriet	The Penguin Group
Harry's House	F	83	Medearis, Angela & Keeter, S.	Scholastic
Hats	F	88	Talk About Books	Dominie
Hats	F	114	Wonder World	Wright Group
Have You Seen the Crocodile?	F	150	West, Colin	Harper & Row
Hay Making	F	62	Wonder World	Wright Group
Helping	F	64	Book Shop	Mondo Publishing
Here Comes a Bus	F	171	Ziefert, Harriet	The Penguin Group
Herman the Helper Lends a Hand	F		Kraus, Robert	Windmill
Herman's Tooth	F	210	Foundations	Wright Group
Hole in the Hedge, The	F	188	Sunshine	Wright Group
Honey Bees and Honey	F	57	Pebble Books	Grolier, Capstone
Honey for Baby Bear	F	200	PM Story Books	Rigby
Hooray for Snail	F	102	Stadler, John	HarperCollins

Title	Level	Words	Author/Series	Publisher/Distributor
Horses	F	131	Twig	Wright Group
Horse's Hiccups	F	83	Storyteller-Moon Rising	Wright Group/ McGraw-Hill
House in the Tree, The	F	202	PM Story Books	Rigby
How Animals Hide	F	98	Wonder World	Wright Group
How Far Will I Fly?	F	94	Oyama, Sachi	Scholastic
How Spiders Live	F	145	Sunshine	Wright Group
Hug Bug	F	65	Start to Read	School Zone
Humpback Whales	F	72	Ready Readers	Pearson Learning
Hungry Giant	F	183	Read-Togethers	Wright Group
Hungry Giant, The	F	183	Story Box	Wright Group
Hungry Giant's Lunch, The	F	140	Story Box	Wright Group
Huzzard Buzzard	F		Reese, Bob	Children's Press
I Can Fly	F	107	Carousel Readers	Dominie
I Can Spell Dinosaur	F		Predictable Storybooks	SRA/McGraw-Hill
I Can!	F	131	Twig	Wright Group
I Know That Tune!	F	201	Foundations	Wright Group
I Need a Book	F	113	Sunshine	Wright Group
I Need a Rest	F	119	Home Connection Collection	Rigby
I Want to Be a Clown	F	82	Start to Read	School Zone
I Went to Visit a Friend One Day	F		Voyages	SRA/McGraw-Hill
I Wonder	F	67	Sunshine	Wright Group
I Wonder Why?	F	95	Wonder World	Wright Group
If I Had an Elephant	F	90	Teacher's Choice Series	Dominie
I'm Glad I'm Me	F	147	Windmill Books	Rigby
I'm King of the Castle	F		Watanabe, Shigeo	Philomel
I'm Looking for My Hat	F	89	Book Bank	Wright Group
In My Bucket	F	94	Carousel Readers	Dominie
In the Park	F	96	Literacy 2000	Rigby
In-Line Skates, The	F	137	Foundations	Wright Group
Interruptions	F	81	Book Shop	Mondo Publishing
Is Anyone Home?	F	65	Maris, Ron	Greenwillow
Is This You?	F	250+	Krauss, Ruth	Scholastic
Itchy, Itchy Chicken Pox	F	131	Maccarone, Grace	Scholastic
It's Alright to Cry	F	138	Teacher's Choice Series	Dominie
It's Not Fair	F	51	Tadpoles	Rigby
Jackie's New Friend	F	168	O'Connor, C. M.	Seedling
Jacks and More Jacks	F	79	Little Celebrations	Pearson Learning
Jane's Car	F	121	PM Story Books	Rigby
Jeremy's Cake	F	97	Storyteller-Moon Rising	Wright Group/ McGraw-Hill
Jessica's Dress Up	F	130	Voyages	SRA/McGraw-Hill
Jimmy's Birthday Balloon	F	95	Foundations	Wright Group
Jip the Pirate	F	142	New Way Blue	Steck-Vaughn
Joe and the Mouse	F	138	Oxford Reading Tree	Oxford University Press
Jog, Frog, Jog	F	72	Gregorich, Barbara	School Zone
Johnny Lion's Rubber Boots	F		Hurd, Edith Thacher	HarperCollins
Just Like Daddy	F	93	Asch, Frank	Simon & Schuster
Just Like Me	F		First Start	Troll
Katie Couldn't	F	176	Rookie Readers	Children's Press
Koalas	F	45	Pebble Books	Grolier, Capstone
Late for Soccer (Football)	F	185	PM Story Books	Rigby

Title	Level	Words	Author/Series	Publisher/Distributor
Leaf Rain	F	82	Book Bank	Wright Group
Let's Get a Pet	F	22	Jellybeans	Rigby
Lightning Liz	F	41	Rookie Readers	Children's Press
Lili's Breakfast	F	156	Storyteller-Setting Sun	Wright Group/ McGraw-Hill
Lion and the Mouse, The	F	115	New Way Red	Steck-Vaughn
Lion and the Rabbit, The	F	99	PM Story Books	Rigby
Lion's Tail, The	F	147	Reading Unlimited	Pacific Learning
Little Bulldozer Helps Again	F	197	PM Extensions-Blue	Rigby
Little Car	F	181	Sunshine	Wright Group
Little Miss Muffet	F		Literacy 2000	Rigby
Little Overcoat, The	F	237	Book Shop	Mondo Publishing
Little Yellow Chicken's House, The	F	287	Story Basket	Wright Group
Look at Me	F	48	Literacy 2000	Rigby
Looking for a Letter	F	223	New Way Green	Steck-Vaughn
Lost at the Fun Park	F	192	PM Extensions-Blue	Rigby
Lucky Day for Little Dinosaur, A	F	135	PM Extensions-Yellow	Rigby
Lucky We Have a Station Wagon	F	259	Foundations	Wright Group
Lucy's Sore Knee	F	93	Windmill	Wright Group
Lunch	F	156	Urmston, Kathleen & Evans, Karen	Kaeden Books
Lydia and the Present Press	F	77	Oxford Reading Tree	Oxford University
Magpie's Baking Day	F	132	PM Story Books	Rigby
Mai Li's Surprise	F	63	Books for Young Learners	Richard C. Owen
Make a Lei	F	39	Pacific Literacy	Pacific Learning
Making Movies	F	43	Sunshine	Wright Group
Map Book, The	F	144	Sunshine	Wright Group
Maple Trees	F	118	Pebble Books	Grolier, Capstone
Marmalade's Nap	F	57	Wheeler, Cindy	Alfred A. Knopf, Inc.
Marmalade's Snowy Day	F		Wheeler, Cindy	Alfred A. Knopf, Inc.
Marvella and the Moon	F	303	Book Shop	Mondo Publishing
Marvelous Me	F	29	Literacy 2000	Rigby
Math Is Everywhere	F	95	Sunshine	Wright Group
Me and My Dog	F	115	Sunshine	Wright Group
Meanies	F	158	Read-Togethers	Wright Group
Melting	F	69	Book Shop	Mondo Publishing
Messy Mark	F	180	First Start	Troll
Mike Ghost's Delicious Rainbow	F	157	TOTTS	Tott Publications
Mike's New Bike	F	183	First Start	Troll
Milking	F	67	Wonder World	Wright Group
Molly's Mailbox	F	122	Teacher's Choice Series	Dominie
Monkey See, Monkey Do	F	89	Gave, Marc	Scholastic
Moose Is Loose, A	F	120	Little Readers	Houghton Mifflin
Mother's Day	F	128	Fiesta Holiday Series	Dominie
Mr. Cricket's New Home	F	121	Carousel Readers	Dominie
Mr. Rabbit and the Moon	F	137	New Way Red	Steck-Vaughn
Mr. Smarty Loves to Party	F	101	Storyteller-Moon Rising	Wright Group/ McGraw-Hill
Mr. Wind	F	37	Literacy 2000	Rigby
Mrs. Bold	F	94	Literacy 2000	Rigby
Mrs. Tuck's Little Tune	F	195	Ready Readers	Pearson Learning
Muffy and Fluffy	F	155	First Start	Troll

Title	Level	Words	Author/Series	Publisher/Distributor
Mural, The	F	262	Visions	Wright Group
My Cat	F		My World	Steck-Vaughn
My Computer	F	76	Wonder World	Wright Group
My Dad	F	79	Talk About Books	Dominie
My Dog's the Best!	F	175	Calmenson, Stephanie	Scholastic
My Friend Goes Left	F	72	Gregorich, Barbara	School Zone
My Grandpa	F	75	Book Shop	Mondo Publishing
My Hard-Boiled Egg	F	94	Windmill Books	Rigby
My Holiday Diary	F	95	Stepping Stones	Nelson/Michaels Assoc.
My House	F	52	Cat on the Mat	Oxford University Press
My House	F	79	My First Reader	Grolier Press
My House	F	126	Literacy 2000	Rigby
My Kitchen	F		Rockwell, Harlow	Morrow
My Mom	F	91	Talk About Books	Dominie
My Monster Friends	F	94	Literacy 2000	Rigby
My Native American School	F	86	Gould, Carol	Kaeden Books
My New Pet	F	105	Little Readers	Houghton Mifflin
My Old Cat and the Computer	F	81	Foundations	Wright Group
My Shadow	F	116	Ready Readers	Pearson Learning
My Very Hungry Pet	F	334	Reading Corners	Dominie
My Wonderful Chair	F	109	Windmill	Wright Group
Name Garden, A	F	125	Sunshine	Wright Group
Nana's Orchard	F	92	Gould, Carol	Kaeden Books
Neighborhood Picnic, The	F	157	Visions	Wright Group
New Gym Shoes	F	175	Yukish, Joe	Kaeden Books
New Sneakers	F	34	Oxford Reading Tree	Oxford University Press
New York City Buildings	F	59	Books for Young Learners	Richard C. Owen
Night Walk	F	51	Books for Young Learners	Richard C. Owen
Niles Likes to Smile	F	80	Little Books	Sadlier-Oxford
No Dogs Allowed	F	73	Books for Young Learners	Richard C. Owen
No Extras	F	90	Literacy 2000	Rigby
No Luck	F	120	Stewart, J. & Salem, Lynn	Seedling
Notes from Mom	F	99	Salem, Lynn & Stewart, J.	Seedling
Notes to Dad	F	114	Stewart, J. & Salem, Lynn	Seedling
Nothing in the Mailbox	F	73	Books for Young Learners	Richard C. Owen
Oak Trees	F	132	Pebble Books	Grolier, Capstone
Oatmeal	F	96	Wonder World	Wright Group
Oh Dear	F		Campbell, Rod	Macmillan
Oh No!	F	122	Traditional Tales & More	Rigby
Old Car, The	F	135	Voyages	SRA/McGraw-Hill
Old Oak Tree, The	F	108	Little Celebrations	Pearson Learning
Old Steam Train, The	F	43	Literacy 2000	Rigby
Old Teeth, New Teeth	F	53	Wonder World	Wright Group
Old Train, The	F	68	Books for Young Learners	Richard C. Owen
On the School Bus	F	62	Little Readers	Houghton Mifflin
One Stormy Night	F	165	Story Basket	Wright Group
Our Garage	F	80	Urmston, Kathleen & Evans, Karen	Kaeden Books
Our Senses	F	182	Discovery Links	Newbridge
Pancakes!	F	106	Ready Readers	Pearson Learning
Paper Patchwork	F	54	Pacific Literacy	Pacific Learning
Pardon? Said the Giraffe	F	123	West, Colin	Harper & Row
Paul	F	54	Ready to Read	Pacific Learning

Title	Level	Words	Author/Series	Publisher/Distributor
Paulo the Pilot	F	131	Windmill Books	Rigby
Pea or the Flea?, The	F	66	Start to Read	School Zone
People on the Beach	F	87	Carousel Readers	Dominie
Pete the Parakeet	F	133	First Start	Troll
Peter's Painting	F	147	Book Shop	Mondo Publishing
Pets	F	56	Literacy 2000	Rigby
Picking Apples	F	53	Pebble Books	Grolier, Capstone
Picnic, The	F	122	Wonder World	Wright Group
Pip and the Little Monkey	F	112	Oxford Reading Tree	Oxford University Press
Pip at the Zoo	F	70	Oxford Reading Tree	Oxford University Press
Pizza Party!	F		Maccarone, Grace	Scholastic
Plane Ride, The	F	68	Little Red Readers	Sundance
Play Ball, Sherman	F	88	Erickson, Betty	Seedling
Playing It Safe	F	135	Early Connections	Benchmark Education
Playing with Dad	F	146	Foundations	Wright Group
Polar Bears	F	77	Pebble Books	Grolier, Capstone
Polka Dots!	F		Little Celebrations	Pearson Learning
Pollution	F	46	Wonder World	Wright Group
Poor Old Polly	F	111	Read-Togethers	Wright Group
Poor Polly Pig	F	57	Start to Read	School Zone
Processed Food	F	54	Wonder World	Wright Group
Puppet Show	F	105	First Start	Troll
Pussy Cat	F	143	Literacy 2000	Rigby
Questions, Questions, Questions	F	190	Visions	Wright Group
Race, The	F	145	Little Readers	Houghton Mifflin
Rap Party, The	F	300	Foundations	Wright Group
Red and I Visit the Vet	F	196	Ready Readers	Pearson Learning
Riddle Book	F		Reading Unlimited	Pacific Learning
Rocks	F	112	Discovery Links	Newbridge
Roll Over	F	220	Gerstein, Mordicai	Crown
Roller Blades, The	F	137	Foundations	Wright Group
Rose	F		Wheeler, Cindy	Alfred A. Knopf, Inc.
Rosie's Button Box	F	233	Stepping Stones	Nelson/Michaels Assoc.
Rosie's Walk	F	32	Hutchins, Pat	Macmillan
Running	F	185	Visions	Wright Group
Sally's Friends	F	128	PM Story Books	Rigby
Sam the Scarecrow	F	143	First Start	Troll
Sammy Gets a Ride	F	91	Evans, Karen & Urmston, Kathleen	Kaeden Books
Sammy's Moving	F	166	Urmston, Kathleen & Evans, Karen	Kaeden Books
Samuel's Sprout	F	194	Little Celebrations	Pearson Learning
Say Cheese!	F	128	Storyteller-Moon Rising	Wright Group/ McGraw-Hill
Scit, Scat, Scaredy Cat!	F	59	Sunshine	Wright Group
Scrubbing Machine, The	F	148	Story Box	Wright Group
Sea Horses	F	67	Pebble Books	Grolier, Capstone
Season to Season	F	113	Pair-It Books	Steck-Vaughn
Shadows	F	130	Wonder World	Wright Group
Shell Shopping	F	145	Ready Readers	Pearson Learning
SHHH	F	66	Henkes, Kevin	Greenwillow
Shine Sun	F		Rookie Readers	Children's Press
Shoes	F	73	Talk About Books	Dominie
Shoveling Snow	F	109	Cummings, Pat	Scholastic

Title	Level	Words	Author/Series	Publisher/Distributor
Sick in Bed	F	109	Little Red Readers	Sundance
Silvia's Soccer Game	F	138	Ready Readers	Pearson Learning
Six Empty Pockets	F	85	Rookie Readers	Children's Press
Six Fine Fish	F	252	Ready Readers	Pearson Learning
Skin	F	97	Literacy 2000	Rigby
Sleepy Bear	F	80	Literacy 2000	Rigby
Sly Fox and Red Hen	F	314	Hunia, Fran	Ladybird Books
Smile, Baby!	F	165	Little Readers	Houghton Mifflin
Snake's Sore Head	F	139	Storyteller-Moon Rising	Wright Group/ McGraw-Hill
Sneezes	F	36	Literacy 2000	Rigby
Snowy Gets a Wash	F	181	PM Extensions-Yellow	Rigby
Snuggle Up	F	125	Harrison, P. & Worthington, Denise	Seedling
Soccer at the Park	F	131	PM Extensions-Yellow	Rigby
Soccer Game!	F	63	Maccarone, Grace	Scholastic
Sparky's Bone	F	273	Ready Readers	Pearson Learning
Sparrows, The	F	60	Books for Young Learners	Richard C. Owen
Speak Up!	F	194	Sunshine	Wright Group
Special Friend, A	F	80	Carousel Readers	Dominie
Spinning Snake, A	F	156	Sunshine	Wright Group
Squirrels	F	109	Ready Readers	Pearson Learning
Ssh, Don't Wake the Baby	F	135	Voyages	SRA/McGraw-Hill
Staying with Grandma Norma	F	168	Salem Lynn & Stewart, J.	Seedling
Sticky Stanley	F	97	First Start	Troll
Strongest Animal, The	F	58	Books for Young Learners	Richard C. Owen
Susie Goes Shopping	F	194	First Start	Troll
Swamp Hen	F	59	Pacific Literacy	Pacific Learning
T Shirts	F	112	Pacific Literacy	Pacific Learning
Tabby in the Tree	F	200	PM Story Books	Rigby
Tails	F	47	Literacy 2000	Rigby
Tails	F	65	Book Shop	Mondo Publishing
Taking Jason to Grandma's	F	118	Book Bank	Wright Group
Tarantulas are Spiders	F	39	Book Shop	Mondo Publishing
Teasing Dad	F	158	PM Extensions-Blue	Rigby
Teeny Tiny Woman, The	F	250+	O'Connor, Jane	Random House
Ten Little Caterpillars	F	102	Literacy 2000	Rigby
Thank You, Nicky!	F	119	Ziefert, Harriet	The Penguin Group
Thanksgiving	F	75	Urmston, Kathleen & Evans, Karen	Kaeden Books
That Pig Can't Do a Thing	F	83	Ready Readers	Pearson Learning
Three Goats, The	F	128	Storyteller-Setting Sun	Wright Group/ McGraw-Hill
Three Muddy Monkeys	F	180	Foundations	Wright Group
Tiger Is a Scaredy Cat	F	220	Phillips, Joan	Random House
Tiger Runs Away	F	213	PM Extensions-Blue	Rigby
Time for a Party	F	111	Discovery World	Rigby
Tim's Favorite Toy	F	202	PM Extensions-Blue	Rigby
Tiny and the Big Wave	F	163	PM Extensions-Yellow	Rigby
To Town	F	148	Read-Togethers	Wright Group
Toys' Party, The	F	48	Oxford Reading Tree	Oxford University Press
Tree, The	F	101	Sunshine	Wright Group
Treehouse Club, The	F	158	Home Connection Collection	Rigby

Title	Level	Words	Author/Series	Publisher/Distributor
Trick or Treat Halloween	F	131	First Start	Troll
Trick, The	F	65	New Way Red	Steck-Vaughn
Tricking Tracy	F	125	Tadpoles	Rigby
Trip to the Park, The	F	277	Foundations	Wright Group
Trouble in the Sandbox	F	318	Foundations	Wright Group
Try to Be a Brave Girl, Sarah	F	102	Windmill	Wright Group
T-Shirts	F	112	Ready to Read	Pacific Learning
Two Ogres, The	F	116	Joy Readers	Dominie
Under My Sombrero	F	79	Books for Young Learners	Richard C. Owen
Underwater Journey	F	60	Sunshine	Wright Group
Use Your Beak!	F	106	Erickson, Betty	Seedling
Victor and the Kite	F	84	Oxford Reading Tree	Oxford University Press
Wake Up, Sleepyheads!	F	35	Little Books	Sadlier-Oxford
Washing	F	150	Foundations	Wright Group
Water Boatman, The	F	44	Ready to Read	Pacific Learning
Water Boatman, The	F	94	Pacific Literacy	Pacific Learning
Water! Water!	F	186	Story Basket	Wright Group
We Want That	F	158	Visions	Wright Group
Wedding, The	F	50	Literacy 2000	Rigby
What a Dog!	F	134	First Start	Troll
What a School	F	100	Salem, Lynn & Stewart, J.	Seedling
What Are You Going to Buy?	F	180	Read Alongs	Rigby
What Can It Be?	F	113	Storyteller-First Snow	Wright Group/ McGraw-Hill
What Dinosaurs Ate	F	44	Planet Earth	Rigby
What Do I See in the Garden?	F	108	Wonder World	Wright Group
What Helps a Bird to Fly?	F	95	Birds Series	Dominie
What I'd Like to Be	F	112	Little Red Readers	Sundance
What Is It?	F	135	Foundations	Wright Group
What Is That? Said the Cat	F	118	Maccarone, Grace	Scholastic
What Makes Light?	F	119	Sunshine	Wright Group
What Mynah Bird Saw	F	90	Sunshine	Wright Group
What Next?	F	277	Story Basket	Wright Group
What Was This?	F	53	Wonder World	Wright Group
When Dad Came Home	F	46	Literacy 2000	Rigby
When Do You Feel	F	132	Twig	Wright Group
When Goldilocks Went to the House of the Bears	F	156	Book Shop	Mondo Publishing
When I Was Sick	F	53	Literacy 2000	Rigby
When I'm Older	F	156	Literacy 2000	Rigby
When It Rains	F	106	Frankford, Marilyn	Kaeden Books
When Lana Was Absent	F	78	Tadpoles	Rigby
When Lincoln Was a Boy	F	132	Twig	Wright Group
Where Are the Eggs?	F	152	Discovery Links	Newbridge
Where Can We Go from Here?	F	54	Spinelle, Nancy Louise	Kaeden Books
Where Will I Sit?	F	78	Teacher's Choice Series	Dominie
Where's My Daddy?	F		Watanabe, Shigeo	Putnam
Where's Sylvester's bed?	F	78	Wonder World	Wright Group
Who Came Out?	F	45	Ready Readers	Pearson Learning
Who Lives Here?	F	185	Storyteller Nonfiction	Wright Group/ McGraw-Hill
Who Lives in the Woods?	F	110	Pair-It Books	Steck-Vaughn

Title	Level	Words	Author/Series	Publisher/Distributor
Who Wants to See the Doctor?	F	116	Adventures in Reading	Dominie
Who Will Be My Friends?	F	205	Hoff, Syd	HarperTrophy
Who Will Help?	F	74	New Way Red	Steck-Vaughn
Who's in the Jungle?	F	116	Ready Readers	Pearson Learning
William, Where Are You?	F	239	Gerstein, Mordicai	Crown
Wind, The	F	84	Voyages	SRA/McGraw-Hill
Winter Sleeps	F	158	Reading Corners	Dominie
Wobbly Tooth, The	F	74	Oxford Reading Tree	Oxford University Press
Wolves	F	132	Twig	Wright Group
Wool	F	91	Sunshine	Wright Group
Worker's Tools, A	F	93	Discovery World	Rigby
Youngest in the Family	F	144	Visions	Wright Group
Yummy, Yummy	F		Grey, Judith	Troll
Zoo Babies	F		Little Celebrations	Pearson Learning
Addition Annie	G	30	Rookie Readers	Children's Press
After the Flood	G	210	PM Extensions-Green	Rigby
All About You	G	250+	Anholt, Catherine & Laurence	Scholastic
All Mixed Up	G	105	Little Books	Sadlier-Oxford
Alligator Shoes	G	122	Dorros, Arthur	Dutton
Along Came Greedy Cat	G	166	Pacific Literacy	Pacific Learning
Amanda's Bear	G	154	Reading Corners	Dominie
Amazing Fish, The	G	167	Pair-It Books	Steck-Vaughn
Amazing Popple Seed, The	G	113	Read Alongs	Rigby
Animal Inventions	G	80	Sunshine	Wright Group
Animals from Long Ago	G	141	Discovery Links	Newbridge
Ants	G	94	Wonder World	Wright Group
Ants and Grasshoppers, The	G	144	New Way Blue	Steck-Vaughn
Apple Tree Apple Tree	G	340	Blocksma, Mary	Children's Press
At the Playground	G	151	Discovery Links	Newbridge
Aunt Jessie	G	114	Literacy 2000	Rigby
Aunt Louisa Is Coming for Lunch	G	118	Windmill Books	Rigby
Awful Waffles	G	296	Williams, D. H.	Seedling
Baby Elephant's New Bike	G	187	Foundations	Wright Group
Backyard Zoo	G	167	Ready Readers	Pearson Learning
Balcony Garden	G	258	Storyteller Nonfiction	Wright Group/ McGraw-Hill
Barnaby's New House, The	G	135	Literacy 2000	Rigby
Batter Up	G	183	Adventures in Reading	Dominie
Beaks	G	125	Discovery Links	Newbridge
Benny's School Trip	G	217	Pair-It Books	Steck-Vaughn
Big Box, The	G	183	New Way Green	Steck-Vaughn
Big Crocodile, The	G	61	Little Celebrations	Pearson Learning
Big Fat Worm, The	G	250+	Van Laan, Nancy	Random House
Big Red Fire Engine	G	158	First Start	Troll
Big Roundup, The	G	121	Wonder World	Wright Group
Biscuit	G		Capucilli, Alyssa Satin	HarperTrophy
Biscuit Finds a Friend	G	114	Capucilli, Alyssa Satin	HarperTrophy
Black Swan's Breakfast	G	147	Book Bank	Wright Group
Blackbird's Nest	G	71	Ready to Read	Pacific Learning
Blackbird's Nest	G	71	Pacific Literacy	Pacific Learning
Blue Lollipops	G	250	Stepping Stones	Nelson/Michaels Assoc.
Blue Sue	G	121	Ready Readers	Pearson Learning

Title	Level	Words	Author/Series	Publisher/Distributor
BMX Billy	G	93	Literacy 2000	Rigby
Boats	G	84	Rockwell, Anne	The Penguin Group
Boris Bad Enough	G		Kraus, Robert	Simon & Schuster
Brave Triceratops	G	178	PM Story Books	Rigby
Breakfast in Bed	G	36	Tadpoles	Rigby
Broken Window	G	136	New Way Blue	Steck-Vaughn
Buffy's Tricks	G	97	Literacy 2000	Rigby
Bus Stop, The	G		Hellen, Nancy	Orchard
Buzz Said the Bee	G	62	Lewison, Wendy	Scholastic
Calico Cat at School	G		Charles, Donald	Children's Press
Calico Cat Meets Bookworm	G		Charles, Donald	Children's Press
Candle-Light	G	231	PM Story Books	Rigby
Captain B's Boat	G	158	Sunshine	Wright Group
Carla's Breakfast	G	225	Harper, Leslie	Kaeden Books
Carla's Ribbons	G	212	Harper, Leslie	Kaeden Books
Carrot Seed, The	G	101	Krauss, Ruth	Harper & Row
Case of the Furry Thing, The	G	267	Ready Readers	Pearson Learning
Cat and Dog	G		Minarik, Else H.	HarperCollins
Cat That Broke the Rules, The	G	192	Ready Readers	Pearson Learning
Cat's Trip	G	158	Ready Readers	Pearson Learning
Cats, Cats, Cats	G	217	Story Basket	Wright Group
Celebrations	G	107	Storyteller-Moon Rising	Wright Group/ McGraw-Hill
Cement Tent	G	358	First Start	Troll
Changing Caterpillar, The	G	56	Books for Young Learners	Richard C. Owen
Chickens	G	105	Book Shop	Mondo Publishing
Christmas Santa Almost Missed, The	G	158	First Start	Troll
Christmas Surprise	G	145	First Start	Troll
Circus Fun	G	219	Momentum Literacy Program	Troll
City Buildings	G	133	Discovery Links	Newbridge
City Sounds	G	142	Marzollo, Jean	Scholastic
Clever Penguins, The	G	174	PM Story Books	Rigby
Click	G	288	Foundations	Wright Group
Coat Full of Bubbles, A	G	72	Books for Young Learners	Richard C. Owen
Come and See!	G	134	Foundations	Wright Group
Come On, Tim	G	198	PM Story Books	Rigby
Coo Coo Caroo	G	57	Books for Young Learners	Richard C. Owen
Cookie Jar, The	G	106	Sunshine	Wright Group
Cooking at School	G	68	City Kids	Rigby
Corals	G	51	Pebble Books	Grolier, Capstone
Cows in the Garden	G	163	PM Story Books	Rigby
Crazy Quilt, The	G	148	Little Readers	Houghton Mifflin
Crazy Quilt, The	G	148	Little Celebrations	Pearson Learning
Critter Race	G		Reese, Bob	Children's Press
Crunchy Munchy	G	189	Book Shop	Mondo Publishing
Dances We Do, The	G	131	Twig	Wright Group
Day and Night	G	115	Discovery Links	Newbridge
Day I Had to Play with My Sister, The	G	139	Bonsall, Crosby	HarperCollins
Dee and Me	G	189	Ready Readers	Pearson Learning
Deep Sea, The	G	152	Ready Readers	Pearson Learning
Deer and the Crocodile, The	G	178	Literacy 2000	Rigby
Dentist, The	G	201	PM Nonfiction-Blue	Rigby

Title	Level	Words	Author/Series	Publisher/Distributor
Did you Say "Fire?"	G	158	Ready to Read	Pacific Learning
Did you say, "Fire"?	G	158	Pacific Literacy	Pacific Learning
Dinosaur Hunt, The	G	131	Windmill Books	Rigby
Dinosaur in Trouble	G	121	First Start	Troll
Dinosaur Show and Tell	G	212	Pair-It Books	Steck-Vaughn
Dinosaurs, Dinosaurs	G	96	Barton, Byron	HarperCollins
Doctor Green	G	141	Little Readers	Houghton Mifflin
Doctor, The	G	179	PM Nonfiction-Blue	Rigby
Dog, The	G		Burningham, John	Crowell
Donkey in the Lion's Skin, The	G	56	Aesop	Wright Group
Don't Cut Down This Tree	G	129	Voyages	SRA/McGraw-Hill
Don't Tell!	G	82	Little Books	Sadlier-Oxford
Dragonflies	G	53	Books for Young Learners	Richard C. Owen
Dreams	G	98	Sunshine	Wright Group
Dry and Snug and Warm	G	64	Book Bank	Wright Group
Each Peach Pear Plum	G	115	Ahlberg, Allan & Janet	The Penguin Group
Eagle Flies High, An	G	142	Ready Readers	Pearson Learning
Earth and Moon	G	250	Sunshine	Wright Group
Easter Bunny's Lost Egg	G	174	First Start	Troll
Eat Up!	G	95	Sunshine	Wright Group
Elephant and Envelope	G	158	Gregorich, Barbara	School Zone
Every Shape and Size	G	97	Wonder World	Wright Group
Everybody Says	G	70	Rookie Readers	Children's Press
Face Painting	G	90	Wonder World	Wright Group
Family Reunion	G	243	Visions	Wright Group
Family Tree, The	G	213	Ready Readers	Pearson Learning
Far Away Moon	G	80	Pacific Literacy	Pacific Learning
Fat Cat Sat on the Mat, The	G	250+	Karlin, Nurit	HarperTrophy
Fishing	G	180	Foundations	Wright Group
Flip Flop	G	70	Books for Young Learners	Richard C. Owen
Four Getters and Arf, The	G	123	Little Celebrations	Pearson Learning
Fourth of July, The	G	120	Fiesta Holiday Series	Dominie
Friend, A	G	57	Literacy 2000	Rigby
Friends	G	195	Reading Unlimited	Pacific Learning
Frogs	G	100	Storyteller-First Snow	Wright Group/McGraw-Hill
Fun at the Amusement Park	G	176	Frankford, Marilyn	Kaeden Books
Fun in the Mud	G	182	Foundations	Wright Group
Getting Glasses	G	82	Wonder World	Wright Group
Getting the Mail	G	213	Voyages	SRA/McGraw-Hill
Giant Pandas	G	72	Pebble Books	Grolier, Capstone
Going to the Symphony	G	132	Twig	Wright Group
Goldilocks	G	244	Sunshine	Wright Group
Goldilocks and the Three Bears	G	265	Storyteller Nonfiction	Wright Group/McGraw-Hill
Gone Fishing	G	180	Long, Erlene	Houghton Mifflin
Goodnight Peter	G	107	Windmill	Wright Group
Goose That Laid the Golden Egg, The	G	73	Aesop	Wright Group
Grandma's Bicycle	G	74	Read-Togethers	Wright Group
Grandma's Bicycle	G	74	Read Alongs	Rigby
Grandpa, Grandpa	G	122	Read-Togethers	Wright Group

Title	Level	Words	Author/Series	Publisher/Distributor
Grandpa's Lemonade	G	138	Storyteller Nonfiction	Wright Group/ McGraw-Hill
Great Bug Hunt, The	G	96	Rookie Readers	Children's Press
Great Race, The	G	250+	McPhail, David	Scholastic
Great-Grandpa	G	130	Voyages	SRA/McGraw-Hill
Greedy Cat	G	166	Ready to Read	Pacific Learning
Greedy Gray Octopus, The	G	195	Tadpoles	Rigby
Gregor the Grumblesome Giant	G	212	Literacy 2000	Rigby
Growing a Plant	G	115	Discovery World	Rigby
Grumputer, The	G	235	Story Basket	Wright Group
Guard the House, Sam!	G	46	Rookie Readers	Children's Press
Hairdresser, The	G	164	PM Nonfiction-Blue	Rigby
Hairy Bear	G	109	Read-Togethers	Wright Group
Hand Me Downs, The	G	156	Little Readers	Houghton Mifflin
Hannah's Hiccups	G	196	Home Connection Collection	Rigby
Hansel and Gretel	G	451	Hunia, Fran	Ladybird Books
Happy Birthday	G	130	First Start	Troll
Happy Mother's Day!	G	101	Teacher's Choice Series	Dominie
Harold's Flyaway Kite	G	166	First Start	Troll
Hay for Ambrosia	G	86	Pacific Literacy	Pacific Learning
Here Comes Winter	G	134	First Start	Troll
Hermit Crab, The	G	119	Sunshine	Wright Group
Hide, Spider!	G	179	Momentum Literacy Program	Troll
Hippo's Hiccups	G	208	Literacy 2000	Rigby
Hockey Practice	G	134	Geddes, Diana	Kaeden Books
Home for a Puppy	G	194	First Start	Troll
Honey Bees and Flowers	G	67	Pebble Books	Grolier, Capstone
Horrible Urktar of Or, The	G	143	Sunshine	Wright Group
House-Hunting	G	223	PM Story Books	Rigby
How Animals Move	G	132	Discovery Links	Newbridge
How Do Frogs Grow?	G	42	Discovery Links	Newbridge
How Do You Make a Bubble?	G	250+	Hooks, William H.	Bantam Doubleday Dell
How Have I Grown	G	235	Reid, Mary	Scholastic
How the Chick Tricked the Fox	G	167	Ready Readers	Pearson Learning
How to Clean a Dinosaur	G	208	Windmill Books	Rigby
How to Make a Card	G	69	Urmston, Kathleen & Evans, Karen	Kaeden Books
Hungry Animals	G	127	Little Readers	Houghton Mifflin
Hungry Giant's Birthday Cake, The	G	241	Story Basket	Wright Group
Hungry Giant's Soup, The	G	42	Story Basket	Wright Group
Hunt for Clues, A	G	157	Ready Readers	Pearson Learning
I Can Do It, I Really Can	G	195	Teacher's Choice Series	Dominie
I Don't Think It's Fair	G	147	Teacher's Choice Series	Dominie
I Have a Question, Grandma	G	124	Literacy 2000	Rigby
I Saw a Dinosaur	G	55	Literacy 2000	Rigby
I Shop with My Daddy	G	131	Maccarone, Grace	Scholastic
I Wish I Was Sick Too	G		Brandenburg, Franz	Morrow
I'm a Caterpillar	G	169	Marzollo, Jean	Scholastic
I'm King of the Mountain	G	285	Ready to Read	Pacific Learning
I'm King of the Mountain	G	285	Pacific Literacy	Pacific Learning
In My Head	G	74	Voyages	SRA/McGraw-Hill
In the Forest	G	95	Voyages	SRA/McGraw-Hill
In the Hen House	G	82	Oppenlander, Meredith	Kaeden Books

Title	Level	Words	Author/Series	Publisher/Distributor
In the Woods	G	304	Reading Corners	Dominie
Is It Time Yet?	G	162	Foundations	Wright Group
It's a Bit Tricky	G	250+	Home Connection Collection	Rigby
Jack DePert at the Supermarket	G	188	Wonder World	Wright Group
Jason's Bus Ride	G	117	Ziefert, Harriet	The Penguin Group
Jeb's Barn	G	86	Little Celebrations	Pearson Learning
Jessie's Flower	G	132	Read Alongs	Rigby
Jim's Visit to Kim	G	149	Ready Readers	Pearson Learning
Joey	G	243	PM Extensions-Green	Rigby
Jungle Tiger Cat	G	120	Frankford, Marilyn	Kaeden Books
Just Enough	G	107	Salem, Lynn & Stewart, J.	Seedling
Just for You	G	160	Mayer, Mercer	Donovan
Just My Luck	G	136	Literacy 2000	Rigby
Just Right!	G	105	Sunshine	Wright Group
Katie Did It	G	105	Rookie Readers	Children's Press
Kittens	G	107	Discovery Links	Newbridge
Kitzikuba	G	198	Story Basket	Wright Group
Laughing Cake, The	G	89	Reading Corners	Dominie
Left, Right	G	182	Sunshine	Wright Group
Let's Bake	G	195	Discovery Links	Newbridge
Let's Make Something New	G	116	Discovery Links	Newbridge
Lift Off!	G	121	Pair-It Books	Steck-Vaughn
Light and Shadow	G	138	Discovery Links	Newbridge
Lion and the Mouse, The	G	125	PM Story Books	Rigby
Lion and the Mouse, The	G	250	Traditional Tales & More	Rigby
Listen to Me	G	47	Rookie Readers	Children's Press
Little Danny Dinosaur	G	195	First Start	Troll
Little Elephant	G	192	New Way Blue	Steck-Vaughn
Little Ghost Goes to School	G	210	TOTTS	Tott Publications
Little Ghost's Baby Brother	G	221	TOTTS	Tott Publications
Little Ghost's Vacation	G	118	TOTTS	Tott Publications
Little Red Hen	G	255	New Way Green	Steck-Vaughn
Little Red Hen, The	G	256	Storyteller-Moon Rising	Wright Group/ McGraw-Hill
Little Red Pig, The	G	214	Ready Readers	Pearson Learning
Locked Out	G	195	PM Story Books	Rigby
Lollipop	G		Watson, Wendy	Crowell
Look for Me	G	208	Little Readers	Houghton Mifflin
Lydia and Her Cat	G	77	Oxford Reading Tree	Oxford University Press
Lydia and Her Garden	G	88	Oxford Reading Tree	Oxford University Press
Lydia and Her Kitten	G	77	Oxford Reading Tree	Oxford University Press
Lydia and the Ducks	G	87	Oxford Reading Tree	Oxford University Press
Make a Glider	G	57	Storyteller-Setting Sun	Wright Group/ McGraw-Hill
Malcolm Magpie	G	126	Storyteller-Setting Sun	Wright Group/ McGraw-Hill
March for Freedom	G	132	Twig	Wright Group
Mess Monster	G	179	Literacy 2000	Rigby
Messy Monsters, The	G	167	Carousel Readers	Dominie
Mice and Max	G	169	Carousel Readers	Dominie
Michael and the Eggs	G	154	Oxford Reading Tree	Oxford University Press
Mike and Tony: Best Friends	G	171	Ziefert, Harriet	The Penguin Group

Title	Level	Words	Author/Series	Publisher/Distributor
Mike's First Haircut	G	136	First Start	Troll
Mine's the Best	G	104	Bonsall, Crosby	HarperCollins
Monarch Butterflies	G	56	Pebble Books	Grolier, Capstone
Money in My Pocket	G	133	Twig	Wright Group
Monkeys	G		Reading Unlimited	Pacific Learning
Monster Math School Time	G	120	Maccarone, Grace	Scholastic
More Spaghetti I Say	G	340	Gelman, Rita	Scholastic
Mother Hen	G	205	Book Bank	Wright Group
Moving Day	G	215	Momentum Literacy Program	Troll
Mr. Cricket Finds a Friend	G	134	Carousel Readers	Dominie
Mrs. Pomelili's Wet Week	G	215	Book Bank	Wright Group
Mudskipper	G	132	Twig	Wright Group
Munching Mark	G	88	Tadpoles	Rigby
Mushrooms for Dinner	G	177	PM Story Books	Rigby
My Birthday Surprise	G	153	Foundations	Wright Group
My Boat	G	133	Sunshine	Wright Group
My Dog	G	72	Taylor, Judy	Macmillan
My Dog	G		My World	Steck-Vaughn
My Feet Are Just Right	G	220	Sunshine	Wright Group
My Friends	G	152	Gomi, Taro	Scholastic
My Home Is Just Right for Me	G	250+	Momentum Literacy Program	Troll
My Secret Hiding Place	G	155	First Start	Troll
My Secret Place	G	121	Wonder World	Wright Group
My Skin Looks After Me	G	82	Pacific Literacy	Pacific Learning
Name Is the Same, The	G	115	Ready Readers	Pearson Learning
Naughty Ann, The	G	159	PM Story Books	Rigby
Neighborhood Clubhouse, The	G	474	Visions	Wright Group
Never Say Never	G	225	Ready Readers	Pearson Learning
New House for Mole and Mouse, A	G	223	Ziefert, Harriet	The Penguin Group
New Paper, Everyone!	G	53	Pacific Literacy	Pacific Learning
New Puppy, A	G	250+	Momentum Literacy Program	Troll
Newspaper for Dad, A	G	192	New Way Green	Steck-Vaughn
Newspaper, The	G	132	Twig	Wright Group
Nicky Upstairs and Downstairs	G	179	Ziefert, Harriet	The Penguin Group
Night Noises	G	97	Storyteller-Moon Rising	Wright Group/ McGraw-Hill
Night Noises	G	107	Sunshine	Wright Group
Night Sky, The	G	226	Ready Readers	Pearson Learning
Nine Men Chase a Hen	G	74	Gregorich, Barbara	School Zone
No Mail for Mitchell	G	250+	Siracusa, Catherine	Random House
Nobody Knew My Name	G	276	Foundations	Wright Group
Noise	G	138	Sunshine	Wright Group
Not Me, Said the Monkey	G	118	West, Colin	Harper & Row
Oak Tree and Fir Tree	G	102	New Way Red	Steck-Vaughn
Obadiah	G	105	Read-Togethers	Wright Group
Octopuses	G	47	Pebble Books	Grolier, Capstone
Odd Socks	G	83	Literacy 2000	Rigby
Oh, No!	G	128	Little Celebrations	Pearson Learning
Old Cat, New Cat	G	169	Wonder World	Wright Group
On Top of Spaghetti	G	105	Little Celebrations	Pearson Learning
One Monday Morning	G	180	Shulevitz, Uri	Scribner
Open Wide	G	189	Home Connection Collection	Rigby

Title	Level	Words	Author/Series	Publisher/Distributor
Optometrist, The	G	191	PM Nonfiction-Blue	Rigby
Our Car	G	94	Book Shop	Mondo Publishing
Our Parents	G	142	PM Nonfiction-Blue	Rigby
Over in the Meadow	G	242	Little Readers	Houghton Mifflin
P.J. Funnybunny Camps Out	G	250+	Sadler, Marilyn	Random House
Paco's Garden	G	118	Books for Young Learners	Richard C. Owen
Pancakes	G	181	Foundations	Wright Group
Papa's Spaghetti	G	248	Literacy 2000	Rigby
Parrotfish	G	51	Pebble Books	Grolier, Capstone
Patchwork Patterns	G		Little Celebrations	Pearson Learning
Peanut Butter and Jelly	G	156	Wescott, Nadine B.	The Penguin Group
Pete Little	G	222	PM Story Books	Rigby
Peter and the Pennytree	G	119	First Start	Troll
Pete's Bad Day	G	164	Ready Readers	Pearson Learning
Pete's New Shoes	G	91	Literacy 2000	Rigby
Philippa and the Dragon	G	137	Literacy 2000	Rigby
Picnic, The	G	151	Home Connection Collection	Rigby
Pond for Tim, A	G		Counters & Seekers	Steck-Vaughn
Princess Who Couldn't Cry, The	G	300	Ready Readers	Pearson Learning
Printing Machine, The	G	102	Literacy 2000	Rigby
Pukeko Morning	G		Ready to Read	Pacific Learning
Rabbit's Party	G	351	Bunting, Eve & Sloan-Childers, E.	Scholastic
Rain	G	68	Literacy 2000	Rigby
Rain, Rain	G	58	Ready to Read	Pacific Learning
Rain, The	G	171	Foundations	Wright Group
Rainbow Somewhere, A	G	201	Ready Readers	Pearson Learning
Ready, Get Set, Go!	G	137	First Start	Troll
Recycle It!	G	118	Discovery Links	Newbridge
Red Socks and Yellow Socks	G	155	Sunshine	Wright Group
Rhyme Game, The	G	159	Storyteller-Setting Sun	Wright Group/ McGraw-Hill
Roler Coaster Ride, The	G	106	Carousel Readers	Dominie
Rosie's Pool	G	130	Little Readers	Houghton Mifflin
Rotten Reggie	G	232	TOTTS	Tott Publications
Roy at the Fun Park	G	111	Oxford Reading Tree	Oxford University Press
Sally's Picture	G	125	Literacy 2000	Rigby
Salmon Story, A	G	132	Twig	Wright Group
Sam and Dasher	G	53	Rookie Readers	Children's Press
Sam the Garbage Hound	G	53	Rookie Readers	Children's Press
Sand Castles	G	80	Wonder World	Wright Group
Sandwich Person, A	G	63	Wonder World	Wright Group
Saturday Morning	G	180	Ready to Read	Pacific Learning
Save That Trash!	G	181	Ready Readers	Pearson Learning
Say Goodnight	G		Gregorich, Barbara	School Zone
Say It Sign It	G	169	Epstein, Elaine	Scholastic
Scary Larry	G		Rookie Readers	Children's Press
Scientist, The	G	195	Adventures in Reading	Dominie
Scruffy Messed It Up	G	105	Literacy 2000	Rigby
Sea Anemones	G	58	Pebble Books	Grolier, Capstone
Sea Urchins	G	51	Pebble Books	Grolier, Capstone
Secret Code, The	G	69	Rookie Readers	Children's Press
Secret Valentine	G	223	First Start	Troll

Title	Level	Words	Author/Series	Publisher/Distributor
Shaggy Sheep, The	G	301	Wonders	Hampton-Brown
Sharing Danny's Dad	G	89	Little Celebrations	Pearson Learning
Sheep in a Jeep	G	83	Shaw, Nancy	Houghton Mifflin
Shhhh!	G		Kline, Suzy	Whitman
Shopping at the Mall	G	145	Urmston, Kathleen & Evans, Karen	Kaeden Books
Show and Tell	G	190	First Start	Troll
Skating on Thin Ice	G	130	First Start	Troll
Small Baby Raccoon, A	G	104	Ready Readers	Pearson Learning
Snack Time	G	59	City Kids	Rigby
Snail Saves the Day	G		Stadler, John	HarperCollins
Snap! Splash!	G	48	Pacific Literacy	Pacific Learning
Snow, The	G		Burningham, John	Crowell
So, So Sam	G	107	TOTTS	Tott Publications
Sometimes Things Change	G		Rookie Readers	Children's Press
Sounds all Around	G	153	Discovery Links	Newbridge
Spaghetti! Spaghetti!	G	85	Book Bank	Wright Group
Special Things	G	128	Literacy 2000	Rigby
Spicy-Herby Day, A	G	117	Evangeline Nicholas Collection	Wright Group
Spider Can't Fly	G	149	Book Bank	Wright Group
Spot's First Walk	G	63	Hill, Eric	Putnam
Squeaky Car, The	G	200	New Way Green	Steck-Vaughn
Stamps	G	58	Wonder World	Wright Group
Stars	G	105	Sunshine	Wright Group
Steve's Room	G	171	Ready Readers	Pearson Learning
Stew for Egor's Mom, A	G	162	Ready Readers	Pearson Learning
Stop That Rabbit	G	168	First Start	Troll
Storm, The	G	75	Books for Young Learners	Richard C. Owen
Sue Likes Blue	G	131	Gregorich, Barbara	School Zone
Summer at Cove Lake	G	288	Ready Readers	Pearson Learning
Summer Trips	G	272	Visions	Wright Group
Sunshine, the Black Cat	G	143	Carousel Readers	Dominie
Surprise Visit, The	G	23	New Way Blue	Steck-Vaughn
T. J.'s Tree	G	77	Literacy 2000	Rigby
Taking Care of Baby	G	159	Discovery Links	Newbridge
Teacher, The	G	155	PM Nonfiction-Blue	Rigby
Teddy Bear for Sale	G	152	Herman, Gail	Scholastic
Ten Bears in My Bed	G	252	Mack, Stan	Pantheon
Ten Little Bears	G	211	Reading Unlimited	Pacific Learning
Ten Sleepy Sheep	G		Keller, Holly	Greenwillow
Terrible Tiger, The	G	140	Sunshine	Wright Group
That Cat!	G	146	Ready Readers	Pearson Learning
That's Not All	G	105	Start to Read	School Zone
Three Billy Goats Gruff, The	G	140	Little Readers	Houghton Mifflin
Three Billy Goats Gruff, The	G		New Way Green	Steck-Vaughn
Three Cheers for Hippo	G	90	Stadler, John	HarperCollins
Three Kittens	G	116	Ginsburg, Mirra	Crown
Three Little Pigs, The	G	250+	Little Readers	Houghton Mifflin
Three Little Witches	G	189	First Start	Troll
Thumpety-Rah!	G	98	Sunshine	Wright Group
Tiger Dave	G	33	Books for Young Learners	Richard C. Owen
Tiny Christmas Elf, The	G	173	First Start	Troll
Titch	G	121	Hutchins, Pat	The Penguin Group

Title	Level	Words	Author/Series	Publisher/Distributor
Tom's Trousers	G	173	Storyteller-Night Crickets	Wright Group/ McGraw-Hill
Too Late!	G	226	Foundations	Wright Group
Too Many Bones	G	125	New Way Blue	Steck-Vaughn
Toothbrush Tale	G	117	New Way Blue	Steck-Vaughn
Tree House Fun	G	165	First Start	Troll
True or False?	G	119	Ready Readers	Pearson Learning
Try Again, Hannah	G	228	PM Extensions-Green	Rigby
TweedledeDee Tumbleweed	G		Reese, Bob	Children's Press
Two Stupid Cats	G	140	Sunshine	Wright Group
Uncle Jim	G	127	Windmill Books	Rigby
Uncle Timi's Sleep	G		Ready to Read	Pacific Learning
Up Close	G	123	Discovery Links	Newbridge
Using Wheels	G	115	Little Red Readers	Sundance
Victor the Champion	G	102	Oxford Reading Tree	Oxford University Press
Visiting Grandma and Grandpa	G	136	Carousel Readers	Dominie
Wait Skates	G	58	Rookie Readers	Children's Press
Waiting	G	59	Literacy 2000	Rigby
Waiting for a Frog	G	124	Coats, Glenn	Kaeden Books
Walk	G		Reading Unlimited	Pacific Learning
Washing the Dog	G	84	Little Red Readers	Sundance
Washing the Dog	G	84	Little Readers	Houghton Mifflin
Watching the Game	G	210	Momentum Literacy Program	Troll
Watching the Weather	G	142	Discovery Links	Newbridge
Whales	G	150	Foundations	Wright Group
What a Mess	G	124	New Way Blue	Steck-Vaughn
What Am I?	G	124	Sunshine	Wright Group
What Can Change?	G	96	Discovery Links	Newbridge
What Can We Do Today?	G	146	Carousel Readers	Dominie
What Can You Do with a Ball of String?	G	250+	Home Connection Collection	Rigby
What Comes from a Cow?	G	85	Sunshine	Wright Group
What Do You Do?	G	125	Little Celebrations	Pearson Learning
What Does a Garden Need?	G	118	Discovery Links	Newbridge
What Is Bat?	G	136	Literacy 2000	Rigby
What Would You Do?	G	272	Book Bank	Wright Group
What's Inside?	G	50	Foundations	Wright Group
When Bob Woke Up Late	G	139	Ready Readers	Pearson Learning
When I Go See Gram	G	123	Ready Readers	Pearson Learning
When Jose Hits That Ball	G	45	Pacific Literacy	Pacific Learning
When the Sun Goes Down	G	109	Wonder World	Wright Group
When You Were a Baby	G	104	Jonas, Ann	Morrow
Which One Is Which?	G	187	Sunshine	Wright Group
Who Goes Out on Halloween?	G		Alexander, Sue	Bantam Doubleday Dell
Who Has a Tail?	G	186	Ready Readers	Pearson Learning
Who Lays Eggs?	G	132	Twig	Wright Group
Why Can't I Fly	G	449	Gelman, Rita	Scholastic
Why Cry?	G	121	Sunshine	Wright Group
Why Do I Need to Know When?	G	198	Visions	Wright Group
Why Elephants Have Long Noses	G	175	Literacy 2000	Rigby
Wiggly Worm	G	115	Literacy 2000	Rigby
Wildlife Helpers	G	132	Twig	Wright Group
William's Skateboard	G	100	Windmill	Wright Group

Title	Level	Words	Author/Series	Publisher/Distributor
Willie the Slowpoke	G	125	First Start	Troll
Wind and Sun	G	170	Literacy 2000	Rigby
Witch's Haircut, The	G	135	Windmill	Wright Group
Women at Work	G	112	Foundations	Wright Group
Wood and Other Materials	G	97	Discovery World	Rigby
You Can Make Skittles	G	128	Sunshine	Wright Group
You Did It!	G	246	Sunshine	Wright Group
You Look Funny	G	180	First Start	Troll
Yo-yos	G	62	City Kids	Rigby
Zoo-Looking	G	149	Book Shop	Mondo Publishing
Day Buzzy Stopped Being Busy, The	G	147	First Start	Troll
Desert Dance	G	184	Little Celebrations	Pearson Learning
Accident, The	H	313	Foundations	Wright Group
After School	H	199	Foundations	Wright Group
Agua, Agua, Agua	H	94	Little Celebrations	Pearson Learning
Alien, The	H	177	Windmill Books	Rigby
Aliens on the Lawn	H	175	Windmill Books	Rigby
All Dressed Up	H	137	Voyages	SRA/McGraw-Hill
Alphabet Game, The	H	272	Story Basket	Wright Group
And the Teacher Got Mad	H	109	City Kids	Rigby
And the Teacher Smiled	H	86	City Kids	Rigby
Andi's Wool	H	107	Books for Young Learners	Richard C. Owen
Animals Build	H	129	Discovery Links	Newbridge
Annabel	H	251	Story Basket	Wright Group
At the Science Center	H	158	Discovery Links	Newbridge
Awful Mess, The	H		Rockwell, Anne	Four Winds
Baby at Our House, The	H	93	Foundations	Wright Group
Babysitter, The	H	243	PM Extensions-Green	Rigby
Barry and Bennie	H		Little Celebrations	Pearson Learning
Beach Creatures	H	231	Pair-It Books	Steck-Vaughn
Bee My Valentine!	H	250+	Cohen, Miriam	Bantam Doubleday Dell
Ben's Tooth	H	197	PM Story Books	Rigby
Big Chief of the Neverwoz, The	H		Little Celebrations	Pearson Learning
Big Game, The	H	69	Pacific Literacy	Pacific Learning
Big Red Apple, The	H	250+	Momentum Literacy Program	Troll
Big Surprise, The	H	123	Pacific Literacy	Pacific Learning
Bird Table, The	H	166	Book Bank	Wright Group
Birthday Cake, The	H	201	Story Box	Wright Group
Blue Jay, The	H	173	Little Readers	Houghton Mifflin
Bogle's Card	H	244	Sunshine	Wright Group
Bonnie on the Beach	H	198	Little Readers	Houghton Mifflin
Boxes	H	153	Literacy 2000	Rigby
Boy and the Lion, The	H	166	Aesop	Wright Group
Boy Who Cried Wolf, The	H	324	Sunshine	Wright Group
Bozo	H	94	Wonder World	Wright Group
Bubble Gum	H	66	City Kids	Rigby
Building a House	H	83	Barton, Byron	Morrow
But I Knew Better	H	242	Home Connection Collection	Rigby
Buzz, Buzz, Buzz	H	162	Barton, Byron	Macmillan
Cake That Mack Ate, The	H	189	Robart, Rose & Kovalski, Maryann	Little, Brown & Co.
Can I Play Outside?	H	121	Literacy 2000	Rigby

Title	Level	Words	Author/Series	Publisher/Distributor
Captain Cat	H	250+	Hoff, Syd	HarperTrophy
Cats and Mice	H	51	Gelman, Rita	Scholastic
Caught in the Storm	H	250+	Home Connection Collection	Rigby
Chicken Pox	H	220	Little Readers	Houghton Mifflin
Choose Me	H	204	Reading Corners	Dominie
Clean House for Mole and Mouse, A	H	201	Ziefert, Harriet	Scholastic
Cleaning Up the Park	H	153	Home Connection Collection	Rigby
Clock That Couldn't Tell Time	H	310	Carousel Readers	Dominie
Clouds	H	108	Sunshine	Wright Group
Clouds	H	132	Twig	Wright Group
Come Out and Play Little Mouse	H	198	Kraus, Robert	Morrow
Come! Sit! Speak!	H	57	Rookie Readers	Children's Press
Coral Reef, The	H	186	Discovery Links	Newbridge
Corn: From Table to Table	H	171	Discovery Links	Newbridge
Cow Up a Tree	H	215	Read Alongs	Rigby
Crab at the Bottom of the Sea, The	H	141	Literacy 2000	Rigby
Cross Country Race, The	H	246	PM Story Books	Rigby
Dad Cooks Breakfast	H	195	Windmill Books	Rigby
Danny and the Dinosaur Go to Camp	H	250+	Hoff, Syd	HarperTrophy
Daughter of the Sun	H	210	Storyteller-Night Crickets	Wright Group/ McGraw-Hill
Day at the Races, A	H	85	Bauer, Roger	Kaeden Books
Dear Mabel!	H		Little Celebrations	Pearson Learning
Dear Tom	H	153	Wonder World	Wright Group
Debra's Dog	H	157	Tadpoles	Rigby
Digging to China	H	108	Books for Young Learners	Richard C. Owen
Dinosaurs	H	117	Sunshine	Wright Group
Doctor Has the Flu, The	H	106	Ready Readers	Pearson Learning
Donkey Work	H	129	Wonder World	Wright Group
Do-Whacky-Do	H	249	Read Alongs	Rigby
Dragon's Coming After You, The	H		Voyages	SRA/McGraw-Hill
Dream in the Wishing Well	H	250+	Allen, R. V.	SRA/McGraw-Hill
Dressing Up	H	222	Stepping Stones	Nelson/Michaels Assoc.
Dress-Up Corner, The	H	68	City Kids	Rigby
Drummers, The	H	80	Gould, Carol	Kaeden Books
Dumpsideary Jelly	H	250+	Momentum Literacy Program	Troll
Earthworm, The	H	157	Wonder World	Wright Group
Elephant in Trouble	H	98	First Start	Troll
Elephants	H	224	Foundations	Wright Group
Emma's Problem	H	190	Literacy 2000	Rigby
Engelbert the Hero	H		Little Celebrations	Pearson Learning
Enormous Turnip	H	431	Hunia, Fran	Ladybird Books
Enormous Watermelon, The	H	304	Traditional Tales & More	Rigby
Erik and the Three Goats	H	257	Ready Readers	Pearson Learning
Families	H	160	Early Connections	Benchmark Education
Fancy Dress Parade, The	H	171	Stepping Stones	Nelson/Michaels Assoc.
Farmyard Fiasco, A	H	186	Book Bank	Wright Group
Father Bear's Surprise	H	224	PM Extensions-Green	Rigby
Fern and Burt	H	250+	Ready Readers	Pearson Learning
First Day Back at School	H	132	City Kids	Rigby
Flip's Trick	H	134	Ready Readers	Pearson Learning

Title	Level	Words	Author/Series	Publisher/Distributor
Floating and Sinking	H	168	Sunshine	Wright Group
Flood, The	H	237	PM Story Books	Rigby
Flying Fish, The	H	215	PM Extensions-Green	Rigby
Football Fever	H	51	Pacific Literacy	Pacific Learning
Fox and the Stork	H	149	New Way Blue	Steck-Vaughn
Fox Who Was Foxed, The	H	212	PM Story Books	Rigby
Freddy Frog's Note	H	253	Ready Readers	Pearson Learning
Frog Prince, The	H	526	Sunshine	Wright Group
From Sky to Sea	H	40	Pacific Literacy	Pacific Learning
Fun at Camp	H	178	First Start	Troll
Fur, Feathers, Scales, Skin	H	173	Discovery Links	Newbridge
George Shrinks	H	114	Joyce, William	Scholastic
Getting Around	H	211	Momentum Literacy Program	Troll
Giant in the Bed, The	H	253	New Way Green	Steck-Vaughn
Giant's Boy, The	H	89	Sunshine	Wright Group
Giant's Cake, The	H	162	Literacy 2000	Rigby
Giant's Job, The	H	180	Stewart, J. & Salem, Lynn	Seedling
Gifts for Dad	H	178	Urmston, Kathleen & Evans, Karen	Kaeden Books
Gigantic George	H		Little Celebrations	Pearson Learning
Gingerbread Man, The	H	197	Sunshine	Wright Group
Goes to the Races	H	158	The Monster Bus Series	Dominie
Goggly Gookers	H	100	Story Basket	Wright Group
Going to the Hospital	H	335	Foundations	Wright Group
Golden Lasso, The	H	250+	Home Connection Collection	Rigby
Goldilocks and the Three Bears	H	250+	Traditional Tales & More	Rigby
Gonna Bird, The	H	209	Storyteller-Night Crickets	Wright Group/ McGraw-Hill
Good Sports	H	206	Foundations	Wright Group
Good-bye Summer, Hello Fall	H	169	Ready Readers	Pearson Learning
Goodnight, Moon	H	130	Brown, Margaret Wise	HarperCollins
Grandpa, Grandma, and the Tractor	H	220	Ready Readers	Pearson Learning
Granny Bundle's Boring Walk	H	250+	Stepping Stones	Nelson/Michaels Assoc.
Great Big Enormous Turnip, The	H	317	Reading Unlimited	Pacific Learning
Great Big Enormous Turnip, The	H	250+	Tolstoi, Aleksei & Nikolaevich, Graf	Watts
Greedy Dog, The	H	148	New Way Blue	Steck-Vaughn
Green Plants	H	213	Foundations	Wright Group
Hamburger	H	49	City Kids	Rigby
Handy Dragon, A	H	159	Literacy 2000	Rigby
Happy Faces	H	210	Reading Unlimited	Pacific Learning
Hatching Chickens at School	H	94	City Kids	Rigby
Help Me	H	196	Story Box	Wright Group
Henny Penny	H	292	New Way Green	Steck-Vaughn
Here are My Hands	H		Bobber Book	SRA/McGraw-Hill
Hiccups Would Not Stop, The	H	177	Ready Readers	Pearson Learning
Hide & Seek	H	138	Wonder World	Wright Group
Hide-and-Seek	H	250+	Momentum Literacy Program	Troll
Hiking with Dad	H	189	Wonder World	Wright Group
Hippo in June's Tub, A	H	85	Little Books	Sadlier-Oxford
Hobson Family Vacation, The	H	250+	Momentum Literacy Program	Troll
Horrible Thing with Hairy Feet	H	208	Read Alongs	Rigby
House for Hickory, A	H	174	Book Shop	Mondo Publishing

Title	Level	Words	Author/Series	Publisher/Distributor
How Bat Learned to Fly	H	168	Storyteller-Night Crickets	Wright Group/ McGraw-Hill
How Do I Put It On?	H		Watanabe, Shiego	The Penguin Group
How to Make a Crocodile	H	62	Little Books	Sadlier-Oxford
How to Make a Mud Pie	H	127	Little Readers	Houghton Mifflin
I Can't Wait to Read	H	185	Adventures in Reading	Dominie
I Don't Care!	H	250	TOTTS	Tott Publications
I Fixed Breakfast	H	176	Teacher's Choice Series	Dominie
I Was Walking Down the Road	H	299	Barchas, Sarah	Scholastic
Ice Fishing	H	140	Ready Readers	Pearson Learning
If	H	83	Sunshine	Wright Group
If I Had an Alligator	H		Mayer, Mercer	Dial
If I Were a Penguin	H	159	Goeneil, Heidi	Little, Brown & Co.
If You Like Strawberries, Don't Read this Book	H	101	Literacy 2000	Rigby
I'm a Good Reader	H	188	Carousel Readers	Dominie
I'm Glad to Say	H	165	Sunshine	Wright Group
I'm Sick Today	H	150	Carousel Readers	Dominie
In the Afternoon	H	156	PM Nonfiction-Green	Rigby
In the Backyard	H		Little Celebrations	Pearson Learning
In the Morning	H	218	PM Nonfiction-Green	Rigby
Island Picnic, The	H	236	PM Story Books	Rigby
It Takes Time to Grow	H	57	Sunshine	Wright Group
It's George!	H		Cohen, Miriam	Bantam Doubleday Dell
I've Got New Sneakers	H	111	City Kids	Rigby
Jace, Mace, and the Big Race	H		Gregorich, Barbara	School Zone
Jack and the Beanstalk	H	170	Sunshine	Wright Group
Jellybean Tree, The	H	231	Sunshine	Wright Group
Jenny Lives on Hunter Street	H	141	Book Bank	Wright Group
Jim's Trumpet	H	304	Sunshine	Wright Group
Joey's Rowboat	H	83	Little Books	Sadlier-Oxford
Joke, The	H	186	Little Readers	Houghton Mifflin
Juan	H	77	City Kids	Rigby
Jumbaroo, The	H	173	Story Basket	Wright Group
Just Me and My Babysitter	H	182	Mayer, Mercer	Donovan
Just Me and My Dad	H	161	Mayer, Mercer	Donovan
Just Me and My Puppy	H	190	Mayer, Mercer	Donovan
Just This Once	H	252	Sunshine	Wright Group
Kangaroo from Wooloomooloo	H	254	Jellybeans	Rigby
Kick-a-Lot Shoes, The	H	433	Story Box	Wright Group
Kiss for Little Bear, A	H	250+	Hoban, Tana	Scholastic
Kite That Flew Away, The	H	279	Ready Readers	Pearson Learning
Learning New Things	H	156	Foundations	Wright Group
Letters for Mr. James	H	203	Sunshine	Wright Group
Lift the Sky Up	H	133	Little Readers	Houghton Mifflin
Lift the Sky Up	H	133	Little Celebrations	Pearson Learning
Lilly-Lolly-Little-Legs	H	129	Literacy 2000	Rigby
Little Brown House	H	266	Jellybeans	Rigby
Little Kid	H	169	Literacy 2000	Rigby
Little Red Bus, The	H	222	PM Story Books	Rigby
Little Red Hen, The	H	375	Traditional Tales	Dominie
Little Red Riding Hood	H	250+	Hunia, Fran	Ladybird Books

Title	Level	Words	Author/Series	Publisher/Distributor
Lola and Miss Kitty	H	250+	Little Readers	Houghton Mifflin
Lollipop Please, A	H	73	Literacy 2000	Rigby
Looking for Angus	H	99	Ready Readers	Pearson Learning
Lottie Goat & Donny Goat	H	145	Ready Readers	Pearson Learning
Lunchbox, The	H	90	Pacific Literacy	Pacific Learning
Machines at Work	H	101	Little Red Readers	Sundance
Maggie Moves Away	H	327	Adventures in Reading	Dominie
Make a "Talking" Card	H	165	Sunshine	Wright Group
Making a Plate	H	183	Ready Readers	Pearson Learning
Man in the Moon, The	H	173	Pair-It Books	Steck-Vaughn
Me and My Shadow	H	247	Momentum Literacy Program	Troll
Meet Me at the Water Hole	H	144	Storyteller-Night Crickets	Wright Group/ McGraw-Hill
Meet My Mouse	H	135	Little Celebrations	Pearson Learning
Mice	H	143	Literacy 2000	Rigby
Missing Necklace, The	H	231	Reading Unlimited	Pacific Learning
Misty's Mischief	H	61	Campbell, Rod	Viking
Mom Paints the House	H	220	Foundations	Wright Group
Mom's Haircut	H	99	Literacy 2000	Rigby
Monster Bus	H	103	The Monster Bus Series	Dominie
Most Scary Ghost	H	355	Jellybeans	Rigby
Mother Sun's Rest Day	H	250+	Momentum Literacy Program	Troll
Move Like Us!	H	250+	Home Connection Collection	Rigby
Mr. Beekman's Deli	H	96	Story Basket	Wright Group
Mr. Bitter's Butter	H	231	Story Basket	Wright Group
Mr. Clutterbus	H		Voyages	SRA/McGraw-Hill
Mr. Fixit	H	196	Sunshine	Wright Group
Mr. McCready's Cleaning Day	H	119	Shilling, Tracy	Scholastic
Mr. McGrah's New Car	H	119	Book Bank	Wright Group
Mr. Whisper	H	325	Sunshine	Wright Group
Mrs. McNosh Hangs Up Her Wash	H		Little Celebrations	Pearson Learning
Mrs. Murphy's Crows	H	120	Books for Young Learners	Richard C. Owen
Mrs. Spider's Beautiful Web	H	250+	PM Story Books	Rigby
My Brown Bear Barney	H		Butler, Dorothy	Morrow
My Cat	H	79	Taylor, Judy	Macmillan
My Family Split Up	H	85	City Kids	Rigby
My Friend Jess	H	124	Wonder World	Wright Group
My Friend Trent	H	186	Foundations	Wright Group
My Sister June	H	182	Ready Readers	Pearson Learning
Mystery of the Missing Red Mitten, The	H	246	Little Readers	Houghton Mifflin
Name for Rabbit, A	H	94	Pacific Literacy	Pacific Learning
New Baby Calf, The	H	240	Chase, Edith & Reid, Barbara	Scholastic
New Building, The	H	78	Sunshine	Wright Group
Night the Lights Went Out, The	H	155	Little Readers	Houghton Mifflin
No Ball Games Here	H		Ziefert, Harriet	The Penguin Group
No Singing Today	H	419	Book Shop	Mondo Publishing
Obstacle Course, The	H	211	Foundations	Wright Group
Off to the Shop	H	323	Storyteller-Night Crickets	Wright Group/ McGraw-Hill
Old Grizzly	H	185	Sunshine	Wright Group
Old Hat, New Hat	H		Berenstain, Stan & Jan	Random House
Old Mother Hubbard	H	117	Literacy 2000	Rigby

Title	Level	Words	Author/Series	Publisher/Distributor
Old Woman, The	H	69	Sunshine	Wright Group
Oliver	H		Kraus, Robert	Simon & Schuster
On My Street	H	292	Visions	Wright Group
Once Upon a Time	H	243	Ready Readers	Pearson Learning
One Bear All Alone	H	107	Bucknall, Caroline	Dial
One Little Elephant	H	174	Sunshine	Wright Group
One Sock, Two Socks	H	285	Reading Corners	Dominie
One Thousand Currant Buns	H	213	Sunshine	Wright Group
Only an Octopus	H	236	Literacy 2000	Rigby
Our School	H	98	City Kids	Rigby
Out After Dark	H	114	Book Bank	Wright Group
Pancakes for Supper	H	96	Literacy 2000	Rigby
Panda's Surprise	H	242	Little Readers	Houghton Mifflin
Pepper Goes to School	H	125	Foundations	Wright Group
Pepper's Adventure	H	250+	PM Story Books	Rigby
Pesky Paua, The	H	267	Book Bank	Wright Group
Peter's Move	H	224	Little Readers	Houghton Mifflin
Pick Up Nick!	H	219	Ready Readers	Pearson Learning
Picture for Harold's Room, A	H	550	Johnson, Crockett	HarperCollins
Pig William's Midnight Walk	H	354	Book Bank	Wright Group
Pine Trees	H	138	Pebble Books	Grolier, Capstone
Pirate Feast, The	H	172	Story Basket	Wright Group
Pizza for Dinner	H	164	Literacy 2000	Rigby
Planning Dinner	H	260	Urmston, Kathleen & Evans, Karen	Kaeden Books
Pond Where Harriet Lives, The	H	151	Storyteller-Night Crickets	Wright Group/ McGraw-Hill
Potatoes, Potatoes	H	91	Wonder World	Wright Group
Pumpkin That Kim Carved, The	H	149	Little Readers	Houghton Mifflin
Put Me in the Zoo	H	250+	Lopshire, Robert	Random House
Quack, Said the Billy Goat	H	88	Causley, Charles	Harper & Row
Quiet in the Library!	H	113	Sunshine	Wright Group
Rabbit, The	H	59	Burningham, John	Crowell
Rain, Rain, and More Rain	H	250+	Momentum Literacy Program	Troll
Rainy Days at School	H	118	City Kids	Rigby
Rapid Robert Roadrunner	H	125	Reese, Bob	Children's Press
Ratty Tatty	H	181	Sunshine	Wright Group
Reading Robot, The	H	224	Sunshine	Wright Group
Ready, Set, Go	H	250+	Stadler, John	HarperTrophy
Real-Skin Rubber Monster Mask, The	H		Cohen, Miriam	Bantam Doubleday Dell
Rescue, The	H	155	PM Extensions-Green	Rigby
Rice Cakes	H	332	Literacy 2000	Rigby
Riding	H	210	Wonder World	Wright Group
Robert Makes a Graph	H	160	Coulton, Mia	Kaeden Books
Rock Garden, The	H	139	Windmill Books	Rigby
Rock-a-Bye Moon	H	107	Pair-It Books	Steck-Vaughn
Rooster and the Weather Vane, The	H	235	First Start	Troll
Rosa at the Zoo	H	135	Pacific Literacy	Pacific Learning
Rosie at the Zoo	H	135	Ready to Read	Pacific Learning
Royal Goose, The	H	198	Ready Readers	Pearson Learning
Safe Place, The	H	147	Ready to Read	Pacific Learning
Safe Place, The	H	147	Pacific Literacy	Pacific Learning

Title	Level	Words	Author/Series	Publisher/Distributor
Sally the Great	H	250+	Home Connection Collection	Rigby
Sammy the Seal	H	250+	Hoff, Syd	HarperTrophy
Sam's Big Day	H	74	Cat on the Mat	Oxford University Press
Seven Little Monsters	H	55	Sendak, Maurice	HarperCollins
Sharks	H	155	Ready Readers	Pearson Learning
Ski Lesson, The	H	155	Storyteller-Moon Rising	Wright Group/ McGraw-Hill
Slippery, Sloppery Spaghetti	H	250+	Home Connection Collection	Rigby
Slugs and Snails	H	132	Wonder World	Wright Group
Small Rabbit Goes Visiting	H	445	Book Bank	Wright Group
Small World, A	H	146	Sunshine	Wright Group
Snail Girl	H	250+	Momentum Literacy Program	Troll
Snails in School	H	181	Discovery Links	Newbridge
Snake Slithers, A	H		Reading Unlimited	Pacific Learning
Snow	H	217	Stepping Stones	Nelson/Michaels Assoc.
Snow on the Hill	H	213	PM Extensions-Green	Rigby
Sophie's Chicken	H	107	Tadpoles	Rigby
Space	H	100	Sunshine	Wright Group
Stars	H	181	Discovery Links	Newbridge
Starshine	H	224	Sunshine	Wright Group
Story of Corn, The	H	171	Ready Readers	Pearson Learning
Stuck on an Island	H	181	Sunshine	Wright Group
Sunshine Street	H	110	Sunshine	Wright Group
Super Smile Shop, The	H	254	Story Basket	Wright Group
Superkids	H	165	Sunshine	Wright Group
Surfing the Information Highway	H	137	Wonder World	Wright Group
Surprise, The	H	124	Literacy 2000	Rigby
Tale of Cowboy Roy, The	H	185	Ready Readers	Pearson Learning
Tale of the Christmas Mouse	H	97	First Start	Troll
Ten Little Garden Snails	H	101	PM Story Books	Rigby
Ten Traveling Tigers	H	165	Little Readers	Houghton Mifflin
Thing in the Log, The	H		Reading Unlimited	Pacific Learning
This Old Car	H		Voyages	SRA/McGraw-Hill
Three Little Kittens	H	164	Ready Readers	Pearson Learning
Three Little Pigs	H	392	New Way Blue	Steck-Vaughn
Three Little Pigs	H		Hunia, Fran	Ladybird Books
Three Little Pigs, The	H	276	Reading Unlimited	Pacific Learning
Three Little Pigs, The	H	346	Reading Corners	Dominie
Three Silly Cowboys	H	213	Ready Readers	Pearson Learning
Three Wishes	H	250+	Ready Readers	Pearson Learning
Three-Legged Race, The	H	202	Windmill Books	Rigby
Tiny Woman's Coat, The	H	147	Sunshine	Wright Group
Tommy Snake's Problem	H	328	TOTTS	Tott Publications
Too Much Noise	H	340	Literacy 2000	Rigby
Tool Box	H	144	Rockwell, Anne	Macmillan
Traffic Light Sandwich	H	87	Wonder World	Wright Group
Trash	H	130	Sunshine	Wright Group
Trees	H	194	Momentum Literacy Program	Troll
Tricky Sticky Problem, The	H	71	Pacific Literacy	Pacific Learning
Trip to the Video Store, A	H	203	Foundations	Wright Group
Turtle Nest	H	85	Books for Young Learners	Richard C. Owen

Title	Level	Words	Author/Series	Publisher/Distributor
Two Bear Cubs	H		Jonas, Ann	Morrow
Uncle Carlos's Barbecue	H	207	Foundations	Wright Group
Uncle Joe	H	149	Pacific Literacy	Pacific Learning
Under a Microscope	H	254	Sunshine	Wright Group
Up the Haystack	H	251	Book Shop	Mondo Publishing
Very Funny Act, A	H	181	Home Connection Collection	Rigby
Very Greedy Dog, The	H	228	Aesop's Fables	Dominie
Victor and the Martian	H	109	Oxford Reading Tree	Oxford University Press
Victor and the Sail-cart	H	94	Oxford Reading Tree	Oxford University Press
Victor Makes a TV	H	85	Reading Unlimited	Pacific Learning
Victor the Hero	H	103	Oxford Reading Tree	Oxford University Press
Visiting the Vet	H	259	Foundations	Wright Group
Wagon, The	H		Reading Unlimited	Pacific Learning
Wait for Your Turn!	H	141	Teacher's Choice Series	Dominie
Walking in the Autumn	H	206	PM Nonfiction-Green	Rigby
Walking in the Spring	H	168	PM Nonfiction-Green	Rigby
Walking in the Summer	H	233	PM Nonfiction-Green	Rigby
Walking in the Winter	H	251	PM Nonfiction-Green	Rigby
Water	H	94	Wonder World	Wright Group
Waving Sheep, The	H	252	PM Story Books	Rigby
We Are Best Friends	H	629	Aliki	Morrow
We Can Share It	H	140	Little Celebrations	Pearson Learning
We Wrote to Grandma	H	239	Momentum Literacy Program	Troll
Wee Whopper	H	181	Windmill Books	Rigby
Wet Grass	H	188	Story Box	Wright Group
What a Dog!	H	223	Story Basket	Wright Group
What Am I Going to Be?	H	111	Storyteller-Moon Rising	Wright Group/ McGraw-Hill
What Are Purple Elephants Good For?	H	136	Reading Corners	Dominie
What Came Out of My Bean?	H	158	Book Bank	Wright Group
What Do Scientists Do?	H	79	Discovery Links	Newbridge
What Game Shall We Play?	H	306	Hutchins, Pat	Sundance
What Gives You Goose Bumps?	H	140	Home Connection Collection	Rigby
What Has Wings?	H	250+	Momentum Literacy Program	Troll
What Is a Park?	H	138	Discovery World	Rigby
What Is the Weather Today?	H	250+	Momentum Literacy Program	Troll
What People Do	H	148	Little Red Readers	Sundance
What's Cooking	H	287	Book Shop	Mondo Publishing
What's for Lunch?	H	169	Ready Readers	Pearson Learning
What's That Smell?	H	56	Pacific Literacy	Pacific Learning
What's Under the Ocean	H		Now I Know	Troll
When Dad Went to Daycare	H	211	Sunshine	Wright Group
When Robins Sing	H	238	Twig	Wright Group
Where Are You Going, Little Mouse?	H	148	Kraus, Robert	Greenwillow
Where Does Breakfast Come From?	H	170	Discovery World	Rigby
Where Is My Caterpillar?	H	277	Wonder World	Wright Group
Where Is the Queen?	H	109	Ready Readers	Pearson Learning
Whistle Tooth, The	H	188	Storyteller-Night Crickets	Wright Group/ McGraw-Hill
White Wednesday	H	321	Literacy 2000	Rigby
Who's Looking After the Baby?	H	127	Foundations	Wright Group

Title	Level	Words	Author/Series	Publisher/Distributor
Whose Mouse Are You?	H	98	Kraus, Robert	Macmillan
Wibble Wobble, Albatross	H	101	Ready to Read	Pacific Learning
Wibble Wobble, Albatross!	H	101	Pacific Literacy	Pacific Learning
Wibble-Wobble	H	263	Storyteller-Night Crickets	Wright Group/ McGraw-Hill
Wilbert Took a Walk	H	216	Ready Readers	Pearson Learning
Will It Rain on the Parade?	H	102	Wonder World	Wright Group
Winter	H	172	Storyteller-Setting Sun	Wright Group/ McGraw-Hill
Winter Wind, The	H	250+	Momentum Literacy Program	Troll
Winter's Song	H	233	Ready Readers	Pearson Learning
World's Biggest Baby, The	H	239	Ready Readers	Pearson Learning
Yes Ma'am	H	125	Read-Togethers	Wright Group
You Do Ride Well	H	165	Windmill Books	Rigby
You Might Fall	H	180	Stepping Stones	Nelson/Michaels Assoc.
You'll Soon Grow into Them Titch	H	191	Hutchins, Pat	Morrow
You're So Clever	H	188	Voyages	SRA/McGraw-Hill
Zithers	H	55	Little Celebrations	Pearson Learning
Zoo Party, A	H	134	Book Bank	Wright Group
Ah-choo!	I	291	Little Books	Sadlier-Oxford
Airport	I	116	Barton, Byron	HarperCollins
Albert the Albatross	I	191	Hoff, Syd	HarperCollins
All Kinds of Eyes	I	128	Pacific Literacy	Pacific Learning
All Tutus Should Be Pink	I	243	Brownrigg, Sheri	Scholastic
Alligators All Around	I	59	Sendak, Maurice	HarperCollins
Ambulance	I	116	Pebble Books	Grolier, Capstone
Anansi's Narrow Waist	I	157	Little Readers	Houghton Mifflin
Anansi's Narrow Waist	I	157	Little Celebrations	Pearson Learning
And Billy Went Out to Play	I	227	Book Shop	Mondo Publishing
Angus and the Cat	I	250+	Flack, Marjorie	Viking
Animal Actions	I	190	Home Connection Collection	Rigby
Animal Builders	I	148	Little Celebrations	Pearson Learning
Animal Fibers	I	440	Science	Wright Group
Animal Messengers	I	116	Discovery Links	Newbridge
Animals at Night	I	215	First Start	Troll
Animals Grow	I	152	Wonder World	Wright Group
Anna's Tree	I	213	Windmill Books	Rigby
Ant and the Dove, The	I	173	New Way Blue	Steck-Vaughn
Ant and the Grasshopper, The	I	231	Aesop's Fables	Dominie
Apple Tree	I	110	Book Bank	Wright Group
Apples and Pumpkins	I	185	Rockwell, Ann	Scholastic
Are You My Mother?	I	250+	Eastman, Philip D.	Random House
Astronauts	I	171	Wonder World	Wright Group
At the Pet Store	I	177	Foundations	Wright Group
Away Went the Hat	I	260	New Way Green	Steck-Vaughn
Baby Monkey, The	I	250+	Reading Unlimited	Pacific Learning
Baby Writer	I	182	Stepping Stones	Nelson/Michaels Assoc.
Barney's Horse	I	250+	Hoff, Syd	HarperTrophy
Baseball Game, The	I	211	Foundations	Wright Group
Basketball	I	159	Ready Readers	Pearson Learning

Title	Level	Words	Author/Series	Publisher/Distributor
Bean Bag That Mom Made, The	I	270	Tadpoles	Rigby
Bear's Bicycle, The	I	185	McLeod, Emilie	Little, Brown & Co.
Bears, Bears, Bears	I	250+	Little Readers	Houghton Mifflin
Because a Little Bug Went Ka-Choo	I	250+	Stone, Rosetta	Random House
Because Daddy Did My Hair	I	214	Teacher's Choice Series	Dominie
Ben and the Bear	I	250+	Riddell, Chris	Harper & Row
Benji's Pup	I	439	Evangeline Nicholas Collection	Wright Group
Benny Bakes a Cake	I		Rice, Eve	Greenwillow
Bertie the Bear	I	250+	Allen, Pamela	Coward
Best Guess, The	I	241	Foundations	Wright Group
Big Bad Rex	I	176	Erickson, Betty	Seedling
Big Bed, The	I	346	Pacific Literacy	Pacific Learning
Big Dog, Little Dog	I	265	Eastman, Philip D.	Random House
Big Hungry Bear, The	I	148	Wood, Don & Audrey	Scholastic
Big Laugh, The	I	152	Sunshine	Wright Group
Biggest Fish, The	I	254	PM Story Books-Orange	Rigby
Bike Lesson	I	250+	Berenstain, Stan & Jan	Random House
Bird Barn, The	I	241	Foundations	Wright Group
Bird Beaks	I	180	Wonder World	Wright Group
Bird Song	I	99	Storyteller-Night Crickets	Wright Group/ McGraw-Hill
Birds, Bees, and Sailing Ships	I	243	Sunshine	Wright Group
Birthdays	I	147	Sunshine	Wright Group
Boggywooga	I	274	Sunshine	Wright Group
Bogle's Feet	I	280	Sunshine	Wright Group
Bookstore Cat	I	207	Little Readers	Houghton Mifflin
Boring Old Bed	I	211	Sunshine	Wright Group
Boy and the Wolf, The	I	200	Book Bank	Wright Group
Boy Who Tried to Hide, The	I	219	Storyteller-Night Crickets	Wright Group/ McGraw-Hill
Broken Plate, The	I	198	Foundations	Wright Group
Buggy Riddles	I	221	Little Books	Sadlier-Oxford
Bun, The	I	421	Storyteller-Moon Rising	Wright Group/ McGraw-Hill
Bunny Hop, The	I		Slater, Teddy	Scholastic
Busy Beavers, The	I	362	PM Story Books-Orange	Rigby
Busy Buzzing Bumblebees	I	250+	Schwartz, Alvin	HarperTrophy
Busy Buzzing Bumblebees and Other Tongue Twisters	I	250+	Schwartz, Alvin	HarperTrophy
Cabbage Caterpillar	I	221	Sunshine	Wright Group
Careful Crocodile, The	I	271	PM Story Books-Orange	Rigby
Carla Gets a Pet	I	250+	Ready Readers	Pearson Learning
Cat and the Mice, The	I	526	Book Bank	Wright Group
Cat Came Back, The	I		Little Celebrations	Pearson Learning
Cat with No Tail, The	I	137	Books for Young Learners	Richard C. Owen
Cats	I	250+	PM Animal Facts: Pets-Orange	Rigby
Changing Land, The	I	64	Pacific Literacy	Pacific Learning
Chicken Licken	I	346	Sunshine	Wright Group
Chicken Little	I	250+	PM Traditional Tales-Orange	Rigby
Cinderella	I	580	Traditional Tales	Dominie
Cinderella	I	250+	PM Traditional Tales & Plays	Rigby
Cleaning My Room	I	189	Early Connections	Benchmark Education

Title	Level	Words	Author/Series	Publisher/Distributor
Clouds	I	249	Pebble Books	Grolier, Capstone
Clyde Klutter's Room	I	146	Sunshine	Wright Group
Coconut Lunches	I	564	Sunshine	Wright Group
Collecting Cones	I	127	Wonder World	Wright Group
Come and Have Fun	I		Hurd, Edith Thacher	HarperCollins
Come Meet Some Seals	I	118	Little Books	Sadlier-Oxford
Community Jobs	I	207	Early Connections	Benchmark Education
Cooking Spaghetti	I	150	City Kids	Rigby
Cowboy Jake	I	174	Sunshine	Wright Group
Coyote Plants a Peach Tree	I	233	Books for Young Learners	Richard C. Owen
Crabbing Time	I	75	Books for Young Learners	Richard C. Owen
Crow and the Pitcher, The	I	265	Aesop's Fables	Dominie
Dad and the Mosquito	I	246	Sunshine	Wright Group
Dancin' Down	I	193	Evangeline Nicholas Collection	Wright Group
Dancing Dragon, The	I	236	Book Shop	Mondo Publishing
Day I Tore My Shorts, The	I	209	City Kids	Rigby
Day the Gorilla Came to School, The	I	293	Sunshine	Wright Group
Digby	I	250+	Little Readers	Houghton Mifflin
Dinosaur Chase, The	I	240	PM Story Books-Orange	Rigby
Dinosaur Who Lived in My Backyard, The	I	250+	Hennessy, Brendan G.	Scholastic
Dinosaurs & Other Reptiles	I	123	Planet Earth	Rigby
Dogs	I	116	Hutchins, Pat	Wright Group
Dogs	I	250+	PM Animal Facts: Pets-Orange	Rigby
Don't Interrupt!	I	225	Windmill Books	Rigby
Don't Touch	I	250+	Kline, Suzy	The Penguin Group
Down in the Woods	I	155	Storyteller-Moon Rising	Wright Group/ McGraw-Hill
Dragon	I	161	Pacific Literacy	Pacific Learning
Dragon	I	250+	Story Box	Wright Group
Dragon Gets By	I	250+	Pilkey, Dav	Orchard
Dragon's Fat Cat	I	250+	Pilkey, Dav	Orchard
Dragon's Halloween	I	250+	Pilkey, Dav	Orchard
Dragon's Merry Christmas	I	250+	Pilkey, Dav	Orchard Paperbacks
Eat Up, Gemma	I	463	Hayes, Sarah	Sundance
Eating Lunch at School	I	170	City Kids	Rigby
Elephant for the Holidays, An	I	118	Sunshine	Wright Group
Emily Loved Yellow	I	99	Sunshine	Wright Group
Farm, The	I	228	Pebble Books	Grolier, Capstone
Fasi Sings and Fasi's Fish	I	204	Ready to Read	Pacific Learning
Fast Food for Butterflies	I	170	Storyteller-Moon Rising	Wright Group/ McGraw-Hill
Fat Cat	I	250+	Kent, Jack	Scholastic
Fat Cat Tompkin	I	196	Voyages	SRA/McGraw-Hill
Father Bear Comes Home	I	331	Minarik, Else H.	HarperCollins
Feathers and Flight	I	790	Sunshine	Wright Group
Fibers from Plants	I	392	Sunshine	Wright Group
Finger Puppets, Finger Plays	I	268	Storyteller-Night Crickets	Wright Group/ McGraw-Hill
Fire at the Zoo, A	I	229	Sunshine	Wright Group
Fire Boats	I	188	Pebble Books	Grolier, Capstone
Fire Engines	I	184	Pebble Books	Grolier, Capstone

Title	Level	Words	Author/Series	Publisher/Distributor
Fish from the Rainbow	I	239	Sunshine	Wright Group
Fix It	I	171	McPhail, David	The Penguin Group
Flood, The	I	138	Wonder World	Wright Group
Fly Away Home	I	250+	Wonder World	Wright Group
Food Around the World	I	298	Early Connections	Benchmark Education
Food Trappers	I	165	Wonder World	Wright Group
Fox and the Crow, The	I	250+	Aesop	Wright Group
Fox and the Goat, The	I	365	Aesop's Fables	Dominie
Fox Lives Here, A	I	160	Ready Readers	Pearson Learning
Friend for Dragon, A	I	250+	Pilkey, Dav	Orchard Paperbacks
Friendly Crocodile, The	I	218	Hiris, Monica	Kaeden Books
Friends	I	313	Early Connections	Benchmark Education
Friends Forever	I	250+	Ready Readers	Pearson Learning
Frog or Toad?	I	241	Ready Readers	Pearson Learning
Frog Prince, The	I	572	Traditional Tales	Dominie
Froggy Tale, The	I	250+	Literacy 2000	Rigby
Fun Things to Make and Do	I	250+	Discovery World	Rigby
Funny Talk and More	I	250+	Book Shop	Mondo Publishing
Gardens on Green Street, The	I	174	TOTTS	Tott Publications
Geraldine's Big Snow	I	250+	Keller, Holly	Scholastic
Giant -Sized Day, A	I	245	Ready Readers	Pearson Learning
Giant's Stew, The	I	259	Sunshine	Wright Group
Ginger	I	232	Little Readers	Houghton Mifflin
Gingerbread Man	I	250+	Hunia, Fran	Ladybird Books
Gingerbread Man, The	I	544	Traditional Tales	Dominie
Gingerbread Man, The	I	250+	Rose, Rita	Scholastic
Go Away Dog	I	250+	Nodset, Joan	HarperCollins
Goha and His Donkey	I	114	Books for Young Learners	Richard C. Owen
Going Fishing	I	250+	Momentum Literacy Program	Troll
Going on a Field Trip	I	288	Visions	Wright Group
Going to a Football Game	I	131	City Kids	Rigby
Goldfish	I	250+	PM Animal Facts: Pets-Orange	Rigby
Good Knee for a Cat, A	I	205	Pacific Literacy	Pacific Learning
Good Luck Elephant	I	171	Sunshine	Wright Group
Good News	I	250+	Brenner, Barbara	Bantam Doubleday Dell
Goodness Gracious	I	190	Literacy 2000	Rigby
Goodnight, Owl!	I	196	Hutchins, Pat	Macmillan
Graffiti	I	168	Sunshine	Wright Group
Grandma Carol's Plant	I	250+	Home Connection Collection	Rigby
Grandpa's Special Present	I	286	Foundations	Wright Group
Green Dragon, The	I	131	Sunshine	Wright Group
Griffin, the School Cat	I	160	Sunshine	Wright Group
Grizzwold	I	250+	Hoff, Syd	HarperTrophy
Growing Older	I	216	Early Connections	Benchmark Education
Growing Radishes and Carrots	I	125	Book Shop	Mondo Publishing
Gruff Brothers, The	I	250+	Hooks, William H.	Bantam Doubleday Dell
Guinea Pig Grass	I	140	Literacy 2000	Rigby
Guinea Pigs	I	250+	PM Animal Facts: Pets-Orange	Rigby
Gumby Shop, The	I	359	Read Alongs	Rigby
Happy Birthday, Sam	I	213	Hutchins, Pat	Greenwillow
Hattie and the Fox	I	321	Fox, Mem	Bradbury/Trumpet

Title	Level	Words	Author/Series	Publisher/Distributor
Having My Hair Washed	I	171	City Kids	Rigby
Heat	I	203	Early Connections	Benchmark Education
Hello, Cat You Need a Hat	I		Gelman, Rita	Scholastic
Hello, First Grade	I		Ryder, Joanne	Troll
Henny Penny	I	582	Galdone, Paul	Scholastic
Herman Henry's Dog	I	250+	Little Readers	Houghton Mifflin
Hiccups	I	268	Book Shop	Mondo Publishing
Hiccups for Elephant	I	250+	Preller, James	Scholastic
Hiccups for Hippo	I	100	Sunshine	Wright Group
Hide-and-Seek with Grandpa	I	250+	Lewis, Rob	Mondo Publishing
Hoketichee and the Manatee	I	113	Books for Young Learners	Richard C. Owen
Hole in Harry's Pocket, The	I	250+	Little Readers	Houghton Mifflin
Horse and the Donkey, The	I	382	New Way Green	Steck-Vaughn
Hot Dogs	I	196	City Kids	Rigby
House that Jack Built, The	I		Cat on the Mat	Oxford University Press
How Birds Live	I	1090	Sunshine	Wright Group
How Do Fish Live?	I	1242	Sunshine	Wright Group
How Flies Live	I	448	Sunshine	Wright Group
How Many Are Left?	I	225	Early Connections	Benchmark Education
How Owl Changed His Hoot	I	227	Sunshine	Wright Group
How the Mouse Got Brown Teeth	I	460	Book Shop	Mondo Publishing
How to Ride a Giraffe	I	191	Little Readers	Houghton Mifflin
Hundred Hugs, A	I	229	Sunshine	Wright Group
Hungry Monster	I	241	Story Box	Wright Group
Hungry Sea Star, The	I	69	Books for Young Learners	Richard C. Owen
I Bought My Lunch Today	I	90	City Kids	Rigby
I Can Do It	I	200	Book Shop	Mondo Publishing
I Did That!	I	250+	Momentum Literacy Program	Troll
I Have a Paper Route	I	90	City Kids	Rigby
I Know That!	I	99	Sunshine	Wright Group
I Live in an Apartment Building	I	111	City Kids	Rigby
I Love Cats	I	104	Book Shop	Mondo Publishing
I Spy a Fly	I	132	Wonder World	Wright Group
If I Were an Ant	I	51	Rookie Readers	Children's Press
In My Garden	I	250+	Momentum Literacy Program	Troll
Invisible	I	111	Read Alongs	Rigby
Is This My Dinner?	I		Black/Fry	Whitman
It's Not Easy Being a Bunny	I		Sadler, Marilyn	Random House
Jack and Chug	I	337	PM Story Books-Orange	Rigby
Jack and the Beanstalk	I	777	Traditional Tales & More	Rigby
Jackson's Monster	I	250+	Little Readers	Houghton Mifflin
Jennifer Pockets	I	205	Book Bank	Wright Group
Jessica in the Dark	I	362	PM Story Books-Orange	Rigby
Jim Meets the Thing	I	250+	Cohen, Miriam	Bantam Doubleday Dell
Jim's Dog Muffins	I	250+	Cohen, Miriam	Bantam Doubleday Dell
Josie Cleans Up	I	213	Little Readers	Houghton Mifflin
Just a Mess	I	206	Mayer, Mercer	Donovan
Just Grandma and Me	I	186	Mayer, Mercer	Donovan
Just Like Everyone Else	I		Kuskin, Karla	HarperCollins
Just One Fish Would Do	I	250+	Home Connection Collection	Rigby
Just One Guinea Pig	I	339	PM Story Books-Orange	Rigby

Title	Level	Words	Author/Series	Publisher/Distributor
Kids at Our School	I	107	City Kids	Rigby
Kite and the Butterflies, The	I	364	Book Bank	Wright Group
Learning to Swim	I	234	My World	Steck-Vaughn
Leaves	I	250+	Momentum Literacy Program	Troll
Leo the Late Bloomer	I	164	Kraus, Robert	Simon & Schuster
Let Me In	I	1814	Story Box	Wright Group
Liar, Liar Pants on Fire	I	250+	Cohen, Miriam	Bantam Doubleday Dell
Life in the Mangroves	I	172	Home Connection Collection	Rigby
Lift-off!	I	141	Pacific Literacy	Pacific Learning
Lighthouse Children, The	I	250+	Hoff, Syd	HarperTrophy
Lion Roars, The	I	270	Ready Readers	Pearson Learning
Lion Talk	I	216	Storyteller-Night Crickets	Wright Group/ McGraw-Hill
Litle Mouse's Trail Tale	I	349	Book Shop	Mondo Publishing
Little Chick's Friend Duckling	I	572	Kwitz, Mary Deball	HarperTrophy
Little Fish that Got Away	I	250+	Cook, Bernadine	Scholastic
Little Girl and Her Beetle, The	I	250+	Literacy 2000	Rigby
Little House, The	I	391	Pacific Literacy	Pacific Learning
Little Leaf's Journey, The	I	564	New Way Orange	Steck-Vaughn
Little Puppy Rap	I	211	Sunshine	Wright Group
Little Red and the Wolf	I	316	Pair-It Books	Steck-Vaughn
Little Red Hen	I	250+	Hunia, Fran	Ladybird Books
Little Red Hen, The	I	226	Sunshine	Wright Group
Little Red Hen, The	I	416	Traditional Tales & More	Rigby
Little Tuppen	I	250+	Galdone, Paul	Houghton Mifflin
Little Yellow Chicken, The	I	322	Sunshine	Wright Group
Lobster Fishing at Dawn	I	194	Ready Readers	Pearson Learning
Lost in the Forest	I	298	PM Story Books-Orange	Rigby
Lost in the Museum	I	250+	Cohen, Miriam	Bantam Doubleday Dell
Lost Sheep, The	I	219	Little Readers	Houghton Mifflin
Lot Happened Today, A	I	193	Ready Readers	Pearson Learning
Lots of Caps	I	205	New Way Blue	Steck-Vaughn
Lunch Bunch, The	I	169	Storyteller-Moon Rising	Wright Group/ McGraw-Hill
Magic Pear Tree, The	I		Little Celebrations	Pearson Learning
Magic Porridge Pot, The	I	321	New Way Orange	Steck-Vaughn
Magician's Lunch	I	272	Jellybeans	Rigby
Magnets	I	79	Sunshine	Wright Group
Make a Boat That Floats	I	126	Book Bank	Wright Group
Make Dinosaur Eggs	I	188	Sunshine	Wright Group
Make Mini Movies	I	309	Sunshine	Wright Group
Make Your Own Party	I	314	Sunshine	Wright Group
Making Caterpillars and Butterflies	I	162	Literacy 2000	Rigby
Manners of a Pig, The	I	299	Book Shop	Mondo Publishing
Marco Saves Grandpa	I	232	Foundations	Wright Group
Maria	I	72	City Kids	Rigby
Mark's Monster	I		Reading Unlimited	Pacific Learning
McBungle's African Safari	I	336	Traditional Tales & More	Rigby
Meet Tom Paxton	I		Little Celebrations	Pearson Learning
Meet William Joyce	I		Little Celebrations	Pearson Learning
Messy Bessey	I	63	Rookie Readers	Children's Press

©1999 by I. C. Fountas & G. S. Pinnell from *Matching Books to Readers*. Portsmouth, NH: Heinemann. May not be reproduced without written permission of the publisher.

Title	Level	Words	Author/Series	Publisher/Distributor
Messy Bessey's Garden	I	60	Rookie Readers	Children's Press
Mice	I	250+	PM Animal Facts: Pets-Orange	Rigby
Mice at Bat	I	250+	Oechsli, Kelly	HarperTrophy
Mishi-Na	I	217	Sunshine	Wright Group
Miss Muffett and the Spider	I	270	Ready Readers	Pearson Learning
Mitch to the Rescue	I	302	PM Story Books-Orange	Rigby
Molly's Bracelet	I	250+	Voyages	SRA/McGraw-Hill
Molly's Broccoli	I	233	Ready Readers	Pearson Learning
Mom's Birthday	I	229	Sunshine	Wright Group
Mom's Diet	I	228	Sunshine	Wright Group
Monarch Butterfly, The	I	152	Foundations	Wright Group
Monster	I	201	Read Alongs	Rigby
Monster Bus Goes on a Hot Air Balloon Trip	I	254	The Monster Bus Series	Dominie
Monster Bus Goes to Yellowstone Park	I	259	The Monster Bus Series	Dominie
Mother Hippopotamus's Hiccups	I	162	Foundations	Wright Group
Mr. Bumbleticker Likes to Cook	I	196	Foundations	Wright Group
Mr. Bumbleticker Likes to Fix Machines	I	142	Foundations	Wright Group
Mr. Bumbleticker's Apples	I	338	Foundations	Wright Group
Mr. Fizzle, the Man Who Went "Boo!"	I	250+	Home Connection Collection	Rigby
Mr. Sun and Mr. Sea	I	202	Little Celebrations	Pearson Learning
Mr. Verdi's New Path	I	250+	Home Connection Collection	Rigby
Mr. Wumple's Travels	I	259	Read Alongs	Rigby
Mrs. Brice's Mice	I	250+	Hoff, Syd	HarperTrophy
Mrs. Grindy's Shoes	I	211	Sunshine	Wright Group
Mrs. Muddle's Mud-Puddle	I	181	Sunshine	Wright Group
Mrs. Murphy's Bears	I	188	Little Readers	Houghton Mifflin
Munching Monster	I	261	Storyteller-Moon Rising	Wright Group/ McGraw-Hill
My Best Friend	I		Hutchins, Pat	Greenwillow
My Brother, Owen	I	150	Book Bank	Wright Group
My Dad Has Asthma	I	138	Wonder World	Wright Group
My Skateboard	I	81	City Kids	Rigby
My Sloppy Tiger	I	211	Sunshine	Wright Group
My Teacher's Leaving	I	154	City Kids	Rigby
Mystery Box, The	I	326	New Way Orange	Steck-Vaughn
Name for a Dog, A	I	258	Windmill Books	Rigby
Nana's Place	I	211	Gibson, Akimi & Meyer, K.	Scholastic
Napping House, The	I	268	Wood, Don & Audrey	Harcourt
Nick Goes Fishing	I	123	Yukish, Joe	Kaeden Books
Night Walk, The	I	667	PM Story Books-Gold	Rigby
No Good in Art	I	250+	Cohen, Miriam	Bantam Doubleday Dell
Nobody Listens to Andrew	I	250+	Little Readers	Houghton Mifflin
Noggin and Bobbin By the Sea	I		Little Celebrations	Pearson Learning
Noisy Nora	I	204	Wells, Rosemary	Scholastic
Not-So-Scary-Scarecrow, The	I	166	Ready Readers	Pearson Learning
Now I Am Five	I	582	Sunshine	Wright Group
Nowhere and Nothing	I	143	Sunshine	Wright Group
Old Man's Mitten, The	I	378	Book Shop	Mondo Publishing
One for You and One for Me	I	354	Early Connections	Benchmark Education
One Hot Summer Night	I	126	Book Shop	Mondo Publishing
Our Eyes	I	869	Sunshine	Wright Group

Title	Level	Words	Author/Series	Publisher/Distributor
Our Polliwogs	I	91	Books for Young Learners	Richard C. Owen
Palm Trees	I	123	Pebble Books	Grolier, Capstone
Paper Trail, The	I	253	Windmill Books	Rigby
Parakeets	I	250+	PM Animal Facts: Pets-Orange	Rigby
Party Time at the Milky Way	I	160	Sunshine	Wright Group
Percival	I	303	Literacy 2000	Rigby
Pet Day at School	I	198	City Kids	Rigby
Pet Tarantula, The	I	208	Storyteller Nonfiction	Wright Group/ McGraw-Hill
Picnic Tea	I	224	Stepping Stones	Nelson/Michaels Assoc.
Piece of Cake	I	250+	Home Connection Collection	Rigby
Pig That Learned to Jig, The	I	140	Wonder World	Wright Group
Pizza Pokey	I	280	Pair-It Books	Steck-Vaughn
Plants	I	250+	Momentum Literacy Program	Troll
Plants and Seeds	I	148	Sunshine	Wright Group
Play It Again Sam	I	139	Literacy 2000	Rigby
Playing Soccer	I	123	Foundations	Wright Group
Please, Do Not Drop Your Jelly Beans	I	180	Storyteller-Night Crickets	Wright Group/ McGraw-Hill
Police Cars	I	177	Pebble Books	Grolier, Capstone
Poor Sore Paw, The	I	244	Sunshine	Wright Group
Pot of Gold, The	I	266	Reading Unlimited	Pacific Learning
Potato Chips	I	101	City Kids	Rigby
Princess and the Pea, The	I	304	Traditional Tales	Dominie
Princess, the Mud Pies, and the Dragon, The	I	250+	Little Readers	Houghton Mifflin
Pterosaur's Long Flight	I	301	PM Story Books-Orange	Rigby
Quack, Quack, Quack!	I	219	Sunshine	Wright Group
Queen and the Dragon, The	I	243	New Way Green	Steck-Vaughn
Quilt, The	I	165	Jonas, Ann	Morrow
Race, The	I	451	New Way Green	Steck-Vaughn
Rebecca and the Concert	I	374	PM Story Books-Orange	Rigby
Rebus Bears, The	I	250+	Reit, Seymour	Bantam Doubleday Dell
Reflections	I		Jonas, Ann	Morrow
Richie the Greedy Mouse	I	179	Sunshine	Wright Group
Road Work Ahead	I	207	Little Readers	Houghton Mifflin
Robert the Rose Horse	I		Heilbroner, Joan	Random House
Rock Pools	I	250+	Momentum Literacy Program	Troll
Rocking and Rolling Along	I	73	Evangeline Nicholas Collection	Wright Group
Roller Coaster, The	I	194	Sunshine	Wright Group
Roly-Poly	I	1227	Story Box	Wright Group
Sacks of Gold	I	263	Sunshine	Wright Group
Same But Different	I	184	Sunshine	Wright Group
Sammy's Supper	I	293	Reading Unlimited	Pacific Learning
Sarah and the Barking Dog	I	328	PM Story Books-Orange	Rigby
Sara's Lovely Songs	I	250+	Ready Readers	Pearson Learning
Saturday Sandwiches	I	154	Evangeline Nicholas Collection	Wright Group
Sea Turtle Night	I	200	Ready Readers	Pearson Learning
Secret Lives of Mr. And Mrs. Smith, The	I	395	Sunshine	Wright Group
Seven Foolish Fishermen	I	250+	PM Traditional Tales & Plays	Rigby
Shintaro's Umbrellas	I	95	Books for Young Learners	Richard C. Owen
Shoe Grabber, The	I	260	Read Alongs	Rigby

Title	Level	Words	Author/Series	Publisher/Distributor
Shots	I	90	City Kids	Rigby
Show and Tell	I		Little Celebrations	Pearson Learning
Silly Times with Two Silly Trolls	I	250+	Jewell, Nancy	HarperTrophy
Sione Went Fishing	I	225	Sunshine	Wright Group
Skates for Luke	I	346	PM Story Books-Orange	Rigby
Sky Is Falling, The	I	181	Storyteller-Setting Sun	Wright Group/ McGraw-Hill
Sleeping	I	114	Book Bank	Wright Group
Slithery Snakes and Unicorns	I	289	Sunshine	Wright Group
Sloppy Tiger and the Party	I	293	Sunshine	Wright Group
Sloppy Tiger Bedtime	I	320	Sunshine	Wright Group
Small Pig	I	250+	Lobel, Arnold	HarperTrophy
Snakes	I	208	Momentum Literacy Program	Troll
Snickers	I	250+	Momentum Literacy Program	Troll
Snow Day	I	250+	Bliss, Corinne Demas	Random House
Snow White and the Seven Dwarfs	I	250+	Enrichment	Wright Group
So Many Birthdays	I	250+	Momentum Literacy Program	Troll
So What?	I	250+	Cohen, Miriam	Bantam Doubleday Dell
Soup Can Telephone	I	190	Wonder World	Wright Group
Spiders in Space	I	242	Sunshine	Wright Group
Spinning Top	I	182	Wonder World	Wright Group
Spooky Riddles	I		Brown, Marc	Random House
Spot's Birthday Party	I	97	Hill, Eric	Putnam
Spring	I	142	Pebble Books	Grolier, Capstone
Stables Are for Horses	I	66	Windmill	Wright Group
Stanley	I	250+	Hoff, Syd	HarperTrophy
Stingrays	I	126	Wonder World	Wright Group
Stop Knitting, Nina!	I	250+	Home Connection Collection	Rigby
Storm on the Beach, A	I	72	Book Bank	Wright Group
Story of Chicken Licken	I	250+	Ormerod, Jan	Lothrop
Strings, Ropes, and Cables	I	250+	Home Connection Collection	Rigby
Summer	I	178	Pebble Books	Grolier, Capstone
Super-Duper Sunflower Seeds, The	I	389	Book Bank	Wright Group
Surprise from the Sky	I	295	Windmill Books	Rigby
Surprise Party, The	I	192	New Way Green	Steck-Vaughn
Surprise!	I		Little Celebrations	Pearson Learning
Sweet or Sour?	I	177	Sunshine	Wright Group
Sweet to Eat	I	105	Pacific Literacy	Pacific Learning
Swimming Lessons	I	200	Storyteller Nonfiction	Wright Group/ McGraw-Hill
Tails	I	170	Sunshine	Wright Group
Tails Can Tell	I	346	Wonder World	Wright Group
Tale of the Turnip, The	I	250+	PM Traditional Tales-Orange	Rigby
Talking Yam, The	I	340	Little Readers	Houghton Mifflin
Tallest Sunflower, The	I		Counters & Seekers	Steck-Vaughn
Tania's Tooth	I	131	Sunshine	Wright Group
Teachers at Our School	I	115	City Kids	Rigby
Teeny Tiny	I	250+	Bennett, Jill	Putnam
Ten Happy Elephants	I	201	Sunshine	Wright Group
Ten Loopy Caterpillars	I	191	Jellybeans	Rigby
Tents	I	175	Reading Unlimited	Pacific Learning

Title	Level	Words	Author/Series	Publisher/Distributor
Termites	I	130	Books for Young Learners	Richard C. Owen
Terrible Armadillo	I	229	Jellybeans	Rigby
There are Mice in Our School	I	95	City Kids	Rigby
There Is No Water	I	250+	Home Connection Collection	Rigby
There's a Dog in the Yard	I	119	City Kids	Rigby
There's a Nightmare in My Closet	I	153	Mayer, Mercer	The Penguin Group
This Is the Bear	I	211	Hayes, Sarah & Craig, H.	Harper & Row
This Is the Place for Me	I	250+	Cole, Joanna	Scholastic
This Is the Seed	I	171	Little Celebrations	Pearson Learning
This Room Is a Mess!	I	250+	Ready Readers	Pearson Learning
Three Billy Goats Gruff	I	536	Traditional Tales	Dominie
Three Billy Goats Gruff, The	I	450	PM Traditional Tales-Orange	Rigby
Three Billy Goats Gruff, The	I	549	Brown, Marcia	Harcourt Brace
Three Little Pigs, The	I	523	PM Traditional Tales-Orange	Rigby
Three Little Pigs, The	I	568	Traditional Tales	Dominie
Three Silly Monkeys Go Fishing	I	163	Foundations	Wright Group
Tides	I	210	Wonder World	Wright Group
Tidy Titch	I	231	Hutchins, Pat	Morrow
Tiger's Tummy Ache	I	220	Ready Readers	Pearson Learning
Time for Bed, Little Bear	I	303	Story Basket	Wright Group
Tim's Pumpkin	I	250+	Home Connection Collection	Rigby
To Market, to Market	I	393	Read-Togethers	Wright Group
Toast for Mom	I	250+	Ready Readers	Pearson Learning
Toby and B.J.	I	307	PM Story Books-Orange	Rigby
Toby and the Big Red Van	I	291	PM Story Books-Orange	Rigby
Toby and the Big Tree	I	298	PM Story Books-Orange	Rigby
Tommy's Treasure	I		Literacy 2000	Rigby
Tooth Race, The	I	250+	Little Readers	Houghton Mifflin
Too-Tight Shoes	I	170	Evangeline Nicholas Collection	Wright Group
Town Mouse and Country Mouse, The	I	172	Aesop	Wright Group
Toy Farm, The	I	311	PM Story Books-Orange	Rigby
Train that Ran Away	I	32	Jellybeans	Rigby
Travel Money, U.S.A.	I	245	Early Connections	Benchmark Education
Tree Is a Home, A	I	135	Pacific Literacy	Pacific Learning
Trees Are Special	I	85	Sunshine	Wright Group
Trek, The	I	158	Jonas, Ann	Greenwillow
Trip into Space, A	I	129	Little Red Readers	Sundance
Trucks	I	38	Literacy 2000	Rigby
Tug of War	I	250+	Folk Tales	Wright Group
Turtle Talk	I	217	Storyteller-Setting Sun	Wright Group/ McGraw-Hill
Two Little Goldfish	I	344	PM Story Books-Orange	Rigby
Two Little Mice, The	I	163	Literacy 2000	Rigby
Very Busy Spider, The	I	263	Carle, Eric	Philomel
Warming Up! Cooling Off!	I	553	Sunshine	Wright Group
We Care for Our School	I	134	Wonder World	Wright Group
We Just Moved!	I	250+	Krensky, Stephen	Scholastic
We're Going on a Bear Hunt	I	363	Rosen, Michael	Macmillan
We're in Big Trouble, Black Board Bear	I	250+	Alexander, Martha	Dial
What a Noise!	I	165	Pacific Literacy	Pacific Learning
What Am I?	I	100	Foundations	Wright Group

Title	Level	Words	Author/Series	Publisher/Distributor
What Bear Cubs Like to Do	I	83	Little Books	Sadlier-Oxford
What Else?	I	154	Sunshine	Wright Group
What I Would Do	I	173	Read Alongs	Rigby
What Lays Eggs?	I	216	Momentum Literacy Program	Troll
What on Earth?	I	133	Sunshine	Wright Group
Wheels on the Bus	I	362	Kovalski, Mary Ann	Little, Brown & Co.
When the Moon Was Blue	I	174	Literacy 2000	Rigby
When Will I Read?	I	250+	Cohen, Miriam	Bantam Doubleday Dell
Where's Lulu?	I	250+	Hooks, William H.	Bantam Doubleday Dell
Which Animal Is That?	I	250+	Momentum Literacy Program	Troll
Who Lives Here?	I	230	Little Readers	Houghton Mifflin
Who Loves Getting Wet?	I	204	Sunshine	Wright Group
Who Took the Farmer's Hat	I	340	Nodset, Joan	Scholastic
Who Wants One?	I		Serfozo, Mary	Macmillan
Who's Afraid of the Dark?	I	250+	Bonsall, Crosby	HarperTrophy
Who's Afraid?	I		Reading Unlimited	Pacific Learning
Who's in the Shed?	I	202	Traditional Tales & More	Rigby
Why Cats Wash After Dinner	I	128	Pacific Literacy	Pacific Learning
Wicked Pirates, The	I	226	Sunshine	Wright Group
Wild Wet Wellington Wind	I	104	Ready to Read	Pacific Learning
Willie's Wonderful Pet	I	315	Cebulash, Mel	Scholastic
Wind and Sun	I	238	Sunshine	Wright Group
Winter	I	240	Pebble Books	Grolier, Capstone
Wolves	I	188	Pair-It Books	Steck-Vaughn
Wonderful Ears	I	1017	Science	Wright Group
Woolly Sally	I		Ready to Read	Pacific Learning
Working with Animals	I	250+	Home Connection Collection	Rigby
Worms for Breakfast	I	250+	Little Readers	Houghton Mifflin
Yard Sale, The	I	250+	Little Readers	Houghton Mifflin
Year with Mother Bear, A	I	164	Storyteller Nonfiction	Wright Group/ McGraw-Hill
Yoo Hoo, Moon!	I	250+	Blocksma, Mary	Bantam Doubleday Dell
You and Your Teeth	I	1009	Sunshine	Wright Group
Yukadoos	I	121	Jellybeans	Rigby
Yum and Yuk	I	125	Story Box	Wright Group
Addie's Bad Day	J	566	Robins, Joan	HarperTrophy
Adventures of Snail at School	J		Stadler, John	HarperTrophy
Ah Liang's Gift	J	352	Sunshine	Wright Group
Aladdin & the Magic Lamp	J	851	Traditional Tales	Dominie
Alison Wendlebury	J	250+	Literacy 2000	Rigby
All About Bats	J	250+	Ready Readers	Pearson Learning
Allie's Basketball Dream	J	250+	Barber, Barbara & Ligasan, Darryl	Scholastic
Amazing Eggs	J	250+	Discovery World	Rigby
Amazing Maze, The	J	334	Foundations	Wright Group
And I Mean It Stanley	J	184	Bonsall, Crosby	HarperCollins
Annie's Pet	J	250+	Brenner, Barbara	Bantam Doubleday Dell
Ant City	J	393	PM Story Books-Turquoise	Rigby
Apple Tree, The	J	160	Sunshine	Wright Group
Art Around the World	J	239	Early Connections	Benchmark Education
Ask Mr. Bear	J	613	Flack, Marjorie	Macmillan

Title	Level	Words	Author/Series	Publisher/Distributor
Autumn	J	225	Pebble Books	Grolier, Capstone
Bear Shadow	J	489	Asch, Frank	Simon & Schuster
Bear's Bargain	J	250+	Asch, Frank	Scholastic
Beautiful Pig	J	423	Read Alongs	Rigby
Beauty and the Beast	J	250+	PM Traditional Tales-Orange	Rigby
Beavers	J	1193	Book Shop	Mondo Publishing
Best Little Monkeys in the World, The	J	250+	Standiford, Natalie	Random House
Best Nest	J	250+	Eastman, Philip D.	Random House
Better Than TV	J	250+	Miller, Sara Swan	Bantam Doubleday Dell
Big Green Caterpillar, The	J	161	Literacy 2000	Rigby
Big Mama and Grandma Ghana	J	250+	Shelf Medearis, Angela	Scholastic
Big Max	J	250+	Platt, Kin	HarperTrophy
Bill	J	166	Sunshine	Wright Group
Billy Magee's New Car	J	391	Foundations	Wright Group
Bird's-Eye View	J	393	PM Story Books-Turquoise	Rigby
Birds' Nests	J	111	Wonder World	Wright Group
Blackboard Bear	J	117	Alexander, Martha	The Penguin Group
Boy Who Cried Wolf, The	J	140	Littledale, Freya	Scholastic
Bush Bunyip, The	J	396	Book Shop	Mondo Publishing
Buzby	J	250+	Hoban, Julia	HarperTrophy
Cabin in the Hills, The	J	349	PM Story Books-Turquoise	Rigby
Camouflage	J	154	Sunshine	Wright Group
Camp Big Paw	J	250+	Cushman, Doug	HarperTrophy
Carrots Don't Talk!	J	250+	Ready Readers	Pearson Learning
Cat Concert	J	250+	Literacy 2000	Rigby
Cat in the Hat	J	250+	Seuss, Dr.	Random House
Catch the Cookie	J		Little Celebrations	Pearson Learning
Cells	J	96	Wonder World	Wright Group
Charlie Needs a Cloak	J	187	DePaola, Tomie	Prentice-Hall
Chicken in the Middle of the Road	J	478	Book Shop	Mondo Publishing
Children of Sierra Leone, The	J	142	Books for Young Learners	Richard C. Owen
Chocolate-Chip Muffins	J	204	Sunshine	Wright Group
City Mouse-Country Mouse	J	198	Aesop	Scholastic
City Mouse-Country Mouse	J	250+	Wallner, John	Scholastic
Class Play, The	J	250+	Little Readers	Houghton Mifflin
Clocks and More Clocks	J	374	Hutchins, Pat	Scholastic
Clouds	J	246	Early Connections	Benchmark Education
Collecting Badges	J	250+	Stepping Stones	Nelson/Michaels Assoc.
Collecting Shapes	J	250+	Stepping Stones	Nelson/Michaels Assoc.
Color Wizard, The	J	250+	Brenner, Barbara	Bantam Doubleday Dell
Coral	J	253	Marine Life for Young Readers	Dominie
Costume Party, The	J	145	City Kids	Rigby
Could It Be?	J	250+	Oppenheim, Joanne	Bantam Doubleday Dell
Cubby's Gum	J	250+	Ready Readers	Pearson Learning
Cupboard Full of Summer, A	J	234	Pacific Literacy	Pacific Learning
Curious George and the Ice Cream	J	250+	Rey, Margaret	Scholastic
Dad's Surprise	J	202	Foundations	Wright Group
Daisy	J	250+	Stepping Stones	Nelson/Michaels Assoc.
Dan the Dunce	J	539	Tales from Hans Andersen	Wright Group
Danny and the Dinosaur	J	250+	Hoff, Syd	Scholastic
Day I Lost My Bus Pass, The	J	131	City Kids	Rigby

Title	Level	Words	Author/Series	Publisher/Distributor
Days with Frog and Toad	J	250+	Lobel, Arnold	HarperTrophy
Detective Dinosaur	J	250+	Skofield, James	HarperTrophy
Difficult Day, The	J	304	Read Alongs	Rigby
Ditching School	J	128	City Kids	Rigby
Dogs at Work	J	250+	Little Readers	Houghton Mifflin
Dogstar	J		Literacy 2000	Rigby
Dolphins	J	111	Wonder World	Wright Group
Donkey's Tale, The	J	250+	Oppenheim, Joanne	Bantam Doubleday Dell
Don't Be My Valentine-A Classroom Mystery	J	250+	Lexau, Joan M.	HarperTrophy
Don't Eat Too Much Turkey	J	250+	Cohen, Miriam	Bantam Doubleday Dell
Don't Worry	J	339	Literacy 2000	Rigby
Doorbell Rang, The	J	283	Hutchins, Pat	Greenwillow
Dragon Who Had the Measles,The	J	250+	Literacy 2000	Rigby
Drummer, Hoff	J	173	Emberly, Ed	Prentice-Hall
Egg to Chick OP	J	250+	Selsam, Millicent	HarperTrophy
Eggs, Eggs, Eggs	J	188	Wonder World	Wright Group
Elaine	J	250+	Stepping Stones	Nelson/Michaels Assoc.
Elephant and the Bad Baby, The	J	250+	Hayes, Sarah	Sundance
Elephant in the House, An	J	546	Read Alongs	Rigby
Emil	J	250+	Stepping Stones	Nelson/Michaels Assoc.
Emperor's New Clothes, The	J	571	Tales from Hans Andersen	Wright Group
Everybody Eats Bread	J	241	Literacy 2000	Rigby
Fair Day	J	184	City Kids	Rigby
Families	J	184	Storyteller-Night Crickets	Wright Group/ McGraw-Hill
Farmer and His Two Lazy Sons, The	J	250+	Aesop's Fables	Dominie
Farmer Joe's Hot Day	J	406	Richards, Nancy W.	Scholastic
Fight on the Hill, The	J	336	Read Alongs	Rigby
Fire Cat, The	J	250+	Averill, Esther	HarperTrophy
Fire Station, The	J	237	Pebble Books	Grolier, Capstone
First Grade Takes a Test	J	250+	Cohen, Miriam	Bantam Doubleday Dell
Floating and Sinking	J	279	Book Shop	Mondo Publishing
Flora, a Friend for the Animals	J	337	Sunshine	Wright Group
Fox All Week	J	250+	Marshall, Edward	Puffin Books
Fox and His Friends	J	250+	Marshall, Edward	Puffin Books
Fox and the Crow, The	J	250+	Aesop's Fables	Dominie
Fox at School	J	250+	Marshall, Edward	Puffin Books
Fox Be Nimble	J	250+	Marshall, James	Puffin Books
Fox in Love	J	250+	Marshall, Edward	Puffin Books
Fox on Stage	J	250+	Marshall, James	Puffin Books
Fox on the Job	J	250+	Marshall, James	Puffin Books
Fox on Wheels	J	250+	Marshall, Edward	Puffin Books
Fox Outfoxed	J	250+	Marshall, James	Puffin Books
Fraidy Cats	J	250+	Krensky, Stephen	Scholastic
Franklin Plays the Game	J	250+	Bourgeois, Paulette & Clark, Brenda	Scholastic
Froggy Learns to Swim	J	250+	London, Jonathan	Scholastic
From Rocks to Sand: The Story of a Beach	J	224	Wonder World	Wright Group
From the Earth	J	186	Discovery Links	Newbridge
Funny Bones	J	250+	Ahlberg, Allan & Janet	Viking
Gallo and Zorro	J	369	Literacy 2000	Rigby
Get-Up Machine, The	J	115	Sunshine	Wright Group

Title	Level	Words	Author/Series	Publisher/Distributor
Ghosts!	J	250+	Schwartz, Alvin	HarperTrophy
Ghosts! Ghostly Tales from Folklore	J	250+	Schwartz, Alvin	HarperTrophy
Giant in the Forest, A	J	250+	Reading Unlimited	Pacific Learning
Giant Soup	J	419	Pacific Literacy	Pacific Learning
Gingerbread Man, The	J	535	Traditional Tales & More	Rigby
Going Swimming	J	210	City Kids	Rigby
Going to the Bank	J	317	Foundations	Wright Group
Going to the Hairdresser	J	227	Foundations	Wright Group
Grandad's Mask	J	446	PM Story Books-Turquoise	Rigby
Grandma Mixup, The	J	250+	Little Readers	Houghton Mifflin
Grandma Mix-Up, The	J	250+	McCully, Emily Arnold	HarperTrophy
Grandma's at Bat	J	250+	McCully, Emily Arnold	HarperTrophy
Grandma's Pictures of the Past	J	250+	Home Connection Collection	Rigby
Granny and the Desperadoes	J	250+	Parish, Peggy	Simon & Schuster
Great Day for Up	J	180	Seuss, Dr.	Random House
Great Snake Escape, The	J	250+	Coxe, Molly	HarperTrophy
Green Eggs and Ham	J	250+	Seuss, Dr.	Random House
Ha-Ha Party, The	J	250	Sunshine	Wright Group
Hailstorm, The	J	386	PM Story Books-Turquoise	Rigby
Hair Party, The	J	250+	Literacy 2000	Rigby
Hand, Hand, Fingers, Thumb	J	250+	Perkins, Al	Random House
Hannah	J	250+	Stepping Stones	Nelson/Michaels Assoc.
Harry and the Lady Next Door	J	250+	Zion, Gene	HarperTrophy
Having a Haircut	J	298	City Kids	Rigby
He Bear, She Bear	J	250+	Berenstain, Stan & Jan	Random House
Hedgehog Bakes a Cake	J	250+	McDonald, Maryann	Bantam Doubleday Dell
Help! I'm Stuck!	J	250+	Little Celebrations	Pearson Learning
Henry and Mudge and the Bedtime Thumps	J	250+	Rylant, Cynthia	Aladdin
Henry and Mudge and the Best Day of All	J	250+	Rylant, Cynthia	Aladdin
Henry and Mudge and the Careful Cousin	J	250+	Rylant, Cynthia	Aladdin
Henry and Mudge and the Forever Sea	J	250+	Rylant, Cynthia	Aladdin
Henry and Mudge and the Happy Cat	J	250+	Rylant, Cynthia	Aladdin
Henry and Mudge and the Long Weekend	J	250+	Rylant, Cynthia	Aladdin
Henry and Mudge and the Wild Wind	J	250+	Rylant, Cynthia	Aladdin
Henry and Mudge Get the Cold Shivers	J	250+	Rylant, Cynthia	Aladdin
Henry and Mudge Get the Cold Shivers	J	250+	Little Readers	Houghton Mifflin
Henry and Mudge in Puddle Trouble	J	250+	Rylant, Cynthia	Aladdin
Henry and Mudge in the Family Trees	J	250+	Rylant, Cynthia	Aladdin
Henry and Mudge in the Green Time	J	250+	Rylant, Cynthia	Aladdin
Henry and Mudge in the Sparkle Days	J	250+	Rylant, Cynthia	Aladdin
Henry and Mudge Take the Big Test	J	250+	Rylant, Cynthia	Aladdin
Henry and Mudge Under the Yellow Moon	J	250+	Rylant, Cynthia	Aladdin
Henry and Mudge: The First Book	J	250+	Rylant, Cynthia	Aladdin
Henry and Mudge: The First Book	J	250+	Little Readers	Houghton Mifflin
Heroes	J	250+	Wildcats	Wright Group
Hiding Places	J	250+	Storyteller-Night Crickets	Wright Group/ McGraw-Hill
Hippopotamus Ate the Teacher, A	J	250+	Thaler, Mike	Avon Books
His Majesty the King	J	250+	Little Celebrations	Pearson Learning
Hop on Pop	J	250+	Seuss, Dr.	Random House
Horse in Harry's Room, The	J	425	Hoff, Syd	HarperCollins

Title	Level	Words	Author/Series	Publisher/Distributor
House that Jack Built, The	J	250+	Peppe, Rodney	Delacorte
House That Jack's Friends Built, The	J	254	Pair-It Books	Steck-Vaughn
House that Stood on Booker Hill, The	J	250+	Ready Readers	Pearson Learning
How Grandmother Spider Got the Sun	J	115	Little Readers	Houghton Mifflin
How Kittens Grow	J	250+	Selsam, Millicent	Scholastic
How to Cook Scones	J		Book Shop	Mondo Publishing
How to Make Salsa	J	192	Book Shop	Mondo Publishing
How Turtle Raced Beaver	J	182	Literacy 2000	Rigby
I Can Read with My Eyes Shut	J	250+	Seuss, Dr.	Random House
I Love to Sneeze	J	250+	Schecter, Ellen	Bantam Doubleday Dell
I Play Soccer	J	97	City Kids	Rigby
I Saw You in the Bathtub	J	250+	Schwartz, Alvin	HarperTrophy
I Was So Mad	J	232	Mayer, Mercer	Donovan
I Went to the Movies	J	120	City Kids	Rigby
Imagine That	J	250+	Story Box	Wright Group
In a Dark, Dark Room	J	250+	Schwartz, Alvin	HarperTrophy
Insects	J	171	MacLulich, Carolynn	Scholastic
Into Space	J	250+	Momentum Literacy Program	Troll
Invisible Spy, The	J	227	Foundations	Wright Group
Jack and the Magic Harp	J	250+	PM Traditional Tales & Plays	Rigby
Jake and the Copycats	J	250+	Rocklin, Joanne	Bantam Doubleday Dell
Jamberry	J	111	Degen, Bruce	Harper & Row
Jillian Jiggs	J	250+	Gilman, Phoebe	Scholastic
Jimmy Lee Did It	J	250+	Cummings, Pat	Lothrop
Job for Giant Jim, A	J	298	Sunshine	Wright Group
Joe and Betsy the Dinosaur	J	250+	Hoban, Lillian	HarperTrophy
Johnny Lion's Book	J	250+	Hurd, Edith Thacher	HarperCollins
Jonathan Buys a Present	J	353	PM Story Books-Turquoise	Rigby
Jordan's Lucky Day	J	466	PM Story Books-Turquoise	Rigby
Just for Fun	J	250+	Literacy 2000	Rigby
Just Hanging Around	J	223	Storyteller-Night Crickets	Wright Group/ McGraw-Hill
Just Like Me	J	2154	Story Box	Wright Group
Keeping Score	J	240	Early Connections	Benchmark Education
Kenny and the Little Kickers	J	250+	Mareollo, Claudio	Scholastic
Kick, Pass, and Run	J	250+	Kessler, Leonard	HarperTrophy
King Midas & the Golden Touch	J	562	Traditional Tales	Dominie
Kiss for Little Bear	J	250+	Minarik, Else H.	HarperTrophy
Knit, Knit, Knit, Knit	J	250+	Literacy 2000	Rigby
Lad Who Went to the North Wind, The	J	796	Book Shop	Mondo Publishing
Last One in Is a Rotten Egg	J	250+	Kessler, Leonard	HarperTrophy
Let's Be Enemies	J	250+	Sendak, Maurice	Harper & Row
License Plates	J	411	PM Story Books-Turquoise	Rigby
Life in the City	J	307	Early Connections	Benchmark Education
Light	J	250+	Momentum Literacy Program	Troll
Lion and the Mouse, The	J	285	Sunshine	Wright Group
Lion and the Mouse, The	J	325	Little Books	Sadlier-Oxford
Lion in the Night, The	J	250+	Momentum Literacy Program	Troll
Little Bear	J	1664	Minarik, Else H.	HarperCollins
Little Bear's Friend	J	250+	Minarik, Else H.	HarperTrophy
Little Bear's Visit	J	250+	Minarik, Else H.	HarperTrophy

Title	Level	Words	Author/Series	Publisher/Distributor
Little Black, a Pony	J	250+	Farley, Walter	Random House
Little Blue and Little Yellow	J	250+	Lionni, Leo	Scholastic
Little Dinosaur Escapes	J	389	PM Story Books-Turquoise	Rigby
Little Fireman	J	250+	Brown, Margaret Wise	HarperCollins
Little Gorilla	J	167	Bornstein, Ruth	Clarion
Little Red Hen, The	J	250+	Galdone, Paul	Viking
Little Red Riding Hood	J	250+	PM Trad. Tales & Plays-Turq.	Rigby
Lizard's Grandmother	J	336	Sunshine	Wright Group
Lonely Dragon, The	J	250+	Momentum Literacy Program	Troll
Look Inside	J	168	Storyteller Nonfiction	Wright Group/ McGraw-Hill
Look Out for Your Tail	J	250+	Literacy 2000	Rigby
Looking for Patterns	J	160	Early Connections	Benchmark Education
Lost Tooth, The	J	632	New Way Orange	Steck-Vaughn
Lulu Goes to Witch School	J	250+	O'Connor, Jane	HarperTrophy
Magic Fish, The	J	250+	Rylant, Cynthia	Scholastic
Magic Store, The	J	203	Sunshine	Wright Group
Make a Bottle Orchestra	J	250	Sunshine	Wright Group
Make a Guitar	J	540	Sunshine	Wright Group
Make Masks for a Play	J	540	Sunshine	Wright Group
Making Friends	J	214	Foundations	Wright Group
Marigold and Grandma on the Town	J	250+	Calmenson, Stephanie	HarperTrophy
Matthew Likes to Read	J	144	Ready to Read	Pacific Learning
Matthew's Tantrum	J	250+	Literacy 2000	Rigby
Max	J	234	Isadora, Rachel	Macmillan
Meg and Mog	J	236	Nicoll, Helen	Viking
Messy Bessey's School Desk	J	104	Rookie Readers	Children's Press
Mike Swam, Sink or Swim	J	250+	Heiligman, Deborah	Bantam Doubleday Dell
Milton the Early Riser	J	148	Kraus, Robert	Simon & Schuster
Miss McKenzie Had a Farm	J	515	Pair-It Books	Steck-Vaughn
Missing Tooth, The	J	250+	Cole, Joanna	Random House
Mix, Make and Munch	J	245	Home Connection Collection	Rigby
Monkey and Fire	J	372	Literacy 2000	Rigby
Monkey Tricks	J	328	PM Story Books-Turquoise	Rigby
Monster Manners	J	250+	Cole, Joanna	Scholastic
Moon Boy	J	250+	Brenner, Barbara	Bantam Doubleday Dell
Moon Stories	J	250+	Ready Readers	Pearson Learning
Morning Star	J	250+	Literacy 2000	Rigby
Morning, Noon, and Night: Poems to Fill Your Day	J	1132	Book Shop	Mondo Publishing
Morris and Boris at the Circus	J	250+	Wiseman, Bernard	HarperTrophy
Morris Goes to School	J	250+	Wiseman, Bernard	HarperTrophy
Mother Hippopotamus Gets Wet	J	421	Foundations	Wright Group
Mouse and the Elephant, The	J	250+	Little Readers	Houghton Mifflin
Mouse Monster	J	302	Jellybeans	Rigby
Mouse Soup	J	1350	Lobel, Arnold	HarperCollins
Mouse Tales	J	1519	Lobel, Arnold	HarperCollins
Mouse Who Wanted to Marry, The	J	250+	Orgel, Doris	Bantam Doubleday Dell
Mr. Bumbleticker Goes Shopping	J	391	Foundations	Wright Group
Mr. Putter and Tabby Bake the Cake	J	250+	Rylant, Cynthia	Harcourt Brace
Mr. Putter and Tabby Fly the Plane	J	250+	Rylant, Cynthia	Harcourt Brace
Mr. Putter and Tabby Pick the Pears	J	250+	Rylant, Cynthia	Harcourt Brace

Title	Level	Words	Author/Series	Publisher/Distributor
Mr. Putter and Tabby Pour the Tea	J	250+	Rylant, Cynthia	Harcourt Brace
Mr. Putter and Tabby Walk the Dog	J	250+	Rylant, Cynthia	Harcourt Brace
Mrs. Barnett's Birthday	J	135	Sunshine	Wright Group
My Brother, Ant	J	250+	Byars, Betsy	Viking
My Father	J	194	Mayer, Laura	Scholastic
My Sloppy Tiger Goes to School	J	217	Sunshine	Wright Group
My Treasure Garden	J	134	Book Bank	Wright Group
Mystery of the Missing Dog, The	J	250+	Levy, Elizabeth	Scholastic
Nelson the Baby Elephant	J	350	PM Story Books-Turquoise	Rigby
Nesting Place, The	J	356	PM Story Books-Turquoise	Rigby
New Bike, The	J	526	Sunshine	Wright Group
New School, The	J	210	City Kids	Rigby
Newborn Animals	J	250+	Momentum Literacy Program	Troll
Newt	J	250+	Novak, Matt	HarperTrophy
Nightingale, The	J	563	Tales from Hans Andersen	Wright Group
No Dinner for Sally	J	340	Literacy 2000	Rigby
No More Monsters for Me!	J	250+	Parish, Peggy	HarperTrophy
Norma Jean, Jumping Bean	J	250+	Cole, Joanna	Random House
Not Now! Said the Cow	J	250+	Demares, Chris	Bantam Doubleday Dell
Number One	J	170	Ready to Read	Pacific Learning
Ocean Animals	J	204	Early Connections	Benchmark Education
On the Open Plains	J	250+	Momentum Literacy Program	Troll
Oscar Otter	J	250+	Benchley, Nathaniel	HarperTrophy
Otto the Cat	J	250+	Herman, Gail	Grosset & Dunlap
Our Baby	J	128	Foundations	Wright Group
Our Money	J	255	Early Connections	Benchmark Education
Owl at Home	J	1488	Lobel, Arnold	HarperCollins
Pack 109	J	164	Thaler, Mike	Scholastic
Parachutes	J	145	Storyteller-Moon Rising	Wright Group/ McGraw-Hill
Party Games	J	399	Foundations	Wright Group
Paru Has a Bath	J	242	Ready to Read	Pacific Learning
Paru Has a Bath	J	242	Pacific Literacy	Pacific Learning
Paul and Lucy	J	250+	Stepping Stones	Nelson/Michaels Assoc.
People at Work	J	250+	Momentum Literacy Program	Troll
Peter's Chair	J	250+	Keats, Ezra Jack	HarperTrophy
Pets	J	90	Ready to Read	Pacific Learning
Pets	J	90	Pacific Literacy	Pacific Learning
Planets, The	J	101	Wonder World	Wright Group
Plants of My Aunt	J	429	Jellybeans	Rigby
Popcorn Shop, The	J	250+	Low, Alice	Scholastic
Poppleton	J	250+	Rylant, Cynthia	Scholastic
Poppleton and Friends	J	250+	Rylant, Cynthia	Blue Sky Press
Poppleton and Friends	J	250+	Rylant, Cynthia	Scholastic
Poppleton Everyday	J	250+	Rylant, Cynthia	Scholastic
Poppleton Forever	J	250+	Rylant, Cynthia	Scholastic
Poppleton in Spring	J	250+	Rylant, Cynthia	Scholastic
Porcupine's Pajama Party	J	250+	Harshman, Terry Webb	HarperTrophy
Postman Pete	J	285	Book Shop	Mondo Publishing
Pretty Good Majic	J	250+	Dubowski, Cathy	Random House
Pumpkin House, The	J	250+	Literacy 2000	Rigby

Title	Level	Words	Author/Series	Publisher/Distributor
Puppets	J	250+	Little Celebrations	Pearson Learning
Queen's Parrot, The: A Play	J	365	Literacy 2000	Rigby
Rabbit's Birthday Kite	J	250+	McDonald, Maryann	Bantam Doubleday Dell
Race to Green End, The	J	506	PM Story Books-Turquoise	Rigby
Rain Puddle OP	J		Holl, Adelaide	Morrow
Rain, Snow, and Hail	J	`250+	Discovery World	Rigby
Rescue!	J	295	Sunshine	Wright Group
Rescuing Nelson	J	369	PM Story Books-Turquoise	Rigby
Riding to Craggy Rock	J	386	PM Story Books-Turquoise	Rigby
Ripeka's Carving	J	250+	Literacy 2000	Rigby
Road Goes By, A	J	250+	Momentum Literacy Program	Troll
Rocks in the Road, The	J	457	Pacific Literacy	Pacific Learning
Roller Skates!	J	250+	Calmenson, Stephanie	Scholastic
Roses for Renee	J	395	Evangeline Nicholas Collection	Wright Group
Row, Row, Row Your Boat	J	250+	O'Malley, Kevin	Bantam Doubleday Dell
Royal Baby-Sitters, The	J	435	Sunshine	Wright Group
Rules	J	265	Early Connections	Benchmark Education
Rumpelstilskin	J	940	Traditional Tales	Dominie
Rumpelstiltskin	J	250+	PM Traditional Tales & Plays	Rigby
Rumpelstltskin	J	855	Book Shop	Mondo Publishing
Sam and the Firefly	J	250+	Eastman, Philip D.	Random House
Sam the Minuteman	J	250+	Benchley, Nathaniel	HarperTrophy
Scary Spiders!	J	198	Sunshine	Wright Group
School Vacation	J	113	City Kids	Rigby
Seat Belt Song, The	J	505	PM Story Books-Turquoise	Rigby
Secret of Spooky House, The	J	352	Sunshine	Wright Group
See You in Second Grade	J	250+	Cohen, Miriam	Bantam Doubleday Dell
See You Tomorrow, Charles	J	250+	Cohen, Miriam	Bantam Doubleday Dell
Seeds	J	210	Pebble Books	Grolier, Capstone
Selena Who Speaks in Silence	J	311	Evangeline Nicholas Collection	Wright Group
Show-and-Tell	J	220	Foundations	Wright Group
Show-and-Tell Frog, The	J	250+	Oppenheim, Joanna	Bantam Doubleday Dell
Silly Tilly's Valentine	J	250+	Hoban, Lillian	HarperTrophy
Silly Willy and Silly Billy	J	221	Foundations	Wright Group
Skeleton on the Bus, The	J	250+	Literacy 2000	Rigby
SkyFire	J	250+	Asch, Frank	Scholastic
Slugs and Snails	J	426	Book Shop	Mondo Publishing
Small Wolf	J	250+	Benchley, Nathaniel	HarperTrophy
Snakes	J	448	Sunshine	Wright Group
Snow White and the Seven Dwarfs	J	250+	PM Traditional Tales & Plays	Rigby
Snowy Day, The	J	319	Keats, Ezra Jack	Scholastic
Some Machines are Enormous	J	337	Book Shop	Mondo Publishing
Something Everyone Needs	J	250+	Ready Readers	Pearson Learning
Something Noise, The	J	276	Windmill Books	Rigby
Somewhere	J	93	Book Shop	Mondo Publishing
Sophie's Singing Mother	J	313	Jellybeans	Rigby
Sounds	J	200	Early Connections	Benchmark Education
Space Race	J	213	Sunshine	Wright Group
Starring First Grade	J	250+	Cohen, Miriam	Bantam Doubleday Dell
Stone Soup	J	932	McGovern, Ann	Scholastic
Stone Soup	J	250+	PM Trad. Tales & Plays-Turq.	Rigby

Title	Level	Words	Author/Series	Publisher/Distributor
Straight Line Wonder, The	J	464	Book Shop	Mondo Publishing
Street Musicians	J	283	Sunshine	Wright Group
String Performers	J	250+	Home Connection Collection	Rigby
Sulky Simon	J	246	Windmill Books	Rigby
Summer Camp	J	182	City Kids	Rigby
Sun, The	J	219	Wonder World	Wright Group
Sunburn	J	176	City Kids	Rigby
Super Supermarket Plan, The	J	250+	Home Connection Collection	Rigby
Surprise Party, The	J	250+	Proger, Annabelle	Random House
Sword in the Stone, The	J	250+	Maccarone, Grace	Scholastic
Teeny Tiny Woman, The	J	369	Seuling, Barbara	Scholastic
Ten Apples Up on Top	J	250+	LaSieg, Theo	Random House
Tess and Paddy	J	242	Sunshine	Wright Group
Then and Now	J	250+	Discovery World	Rigby
There's a Hippopotamus Under My Bed	J	250+	Thaler, Mike	Avon Books
There's An Alligator Under My Bed	J	250+	Mayer, Mercer	The Penguin Group
There's Something in My Attic	J	258	Mayer, Mercer	The Penguin Group
Things with Wings	J	267	Storyteller Nonfiction	Wright Group/ McGraw-Hill
Tickle-Bugs, The	J		Literacy 2000	Rigby
Tiny Creatures	J	250+	Discovery World	Rigby
Toby and the Accident	J	329	PM Story Books-Turquoise	Rigby
Today I Got Yelled At	J	174	City Kids	Rigby
Tom the TV Cat	J	250+	Heilbroner, Joan	Random House
Tongue Twister Prize, The	J	331	Little Books	Sadlier-Oxford
Too Many Mice	J	250+	Brenner, Barbara	Bantam Doubleday Dell
Too Many Rabbits	J	250+	Parish, Peggy	Bantam Doubleday Dell
Too Many Steps	J	424	Foundations	Wright Group
Too Much Noise	J	250+	McGovern, Ann	Scholastic
Too Small Jill	J	306	Little Books	Sadlier-Oxford
Trash Can Band, The	J	252	Little Books	Sadlier-Oxford
Trees	J	124	Literacy 2000	Rigby
Tummy Ache	J	104	Sunshine	Wright Group
Two Silly Trolls	J	250+	Jewell, Nancy	HarperTrophy
Ugly Duckling, The	J	558	Tales from Hans Andersen	Wright Group
Uh-Oh! Said the Crow	J	250+	Oppenheim, Joanna	Bantam Doubleday Dell
Uncle Elephant	J	1784	Lobel, Arnold	HarperCollins
Unusual Machines	J	229	Little Red Readers	Sundance
Vagabond Crabs	J	117	Literacy 2000	Rigby
Very Hungry Caterpillar, The	J	237	Carle, Eric	Philomel
Waiting for the Rain	J	307	Foundations	Wright Group
Wake Me in Spring	J	301	Preller, James	Scholastic
Wake-Up, Baby!	J	209	Oppenheim, Joanna	Bantam Doubleday Dell
Water	J	250+	Momentum Literacy Program	Troll
Waves: The Changing Surface of the Sea	J	204	Wonder World	Wright Group
We Use Numbers	J	298	Early Connections	Benchmark Education
Wet Day at School, A	J	130	Sunshine	Wright Group
What Are My Chances	J	393	Early Connections	Benchmark Education
What Do You Hear When Cows Sing?	J	250+	Maestro, Marco & Giulio	HarperTrophy
What Would You Do?	J	160	Sunshine	Wright Group
When the King Rides By	J	247	Book Shop	Mondo Publishing

Title	Level	Words	Author/Series	Publisher/Distributor
When the Volcano Erupted	J	262	PM Story Books-Turquoise	Rigby
Where People Live	J	259	Early Connections	Benchmark Education
Where the Wild Things Are	J	339	Sendak, Maurice	Harper & Row
Where's Tony?	J	114	City Kids	Rigby
Who's a Pest?	J	250+	Bonsall, Crosby	HarperTrophy
Why the Bear's Tail Is Short	J	431	Sunshine	Wright Group
Wild, Wooly Child, The	J	315	Read Alongs	Rigby
Wind and the Sun, The	J	250+	New Way Orange	Steck-Vaughn
Wind Power	J	103	Ready to Read	Pacific Learning
Wind Power	J	103	Pacific Literacy	Pacific Learning
Wizard and Wart at Sea	J	250+	Smith, Janice Lee	HarperTrophy
Worst Show-and-Tell Ever, The	J	250+	Walsh, Rita	Troll
Wow! What a Week!	J	364	Wonders	Hampton-Brown
Wrong Way Reggie	J		Little Celebrations	Pearson Learning
Wrong-Way Rabbit, The	J		Slater, Teddy	Scholastic
You Are Much Too Small	J	250+	Boegehold, Betty	Bantam Doubleday Dell
You Can't Catch Me	J	250+	Oppenheim, Joanne	Houghton Mifflin
Your Teeth	J	131	Pebble Books	Grolier, Capstone
Zoe at the Fancy Dress Ball	J		Literacy 2000	Rigby
Zunid	J	250+	Stepping Stones	Nelson/Michaels Assoc.
Alison's Puppy	K	250+	Bauer, Marion Dane	Hyperion
Alison's Wings	K	250+	Bauer, Marion Dane	Hyperion
All About Things People Do	K	250+	Rice, Melanie & Chris	Scholastic
All Kinds of Eyes	K	250+	Discovery World	Rigby
Amalia and the Grasshopper	K	392	Tello, Jerry & Krupinski, Loretta	Scholastic
And Grandpa Sat on Friday	K	250+	Marshall & Tester	SRA/McGraw-Hill
Animal Homes	K	257	Pair-It Books	Steck-Vaughn
Animals and Their Teeth	K	510	Sunshine	Wright Group
Animals' Eyes and Ears	K	411	Early Connections	Benchmark Education
Animals on the Move	K	145	Planet Earth	Rigby
Are We Hurting the Earth?	K	363	Early Connections	Benchmark Education
Arguments	K	398	Read Alongs	Rigby
Arthur's Back to School Day	K	250+	Hoban, Lillian	HarperTrophy
Arthur's Camp-Out	K	250+	Hoban, Lillian	HarperTrophy
Arthur's Christmas Cookies	K	250+	Hoban, Lillian	HarperTrophy
Arthur's Funny Money	K	250+	Hoban, Lillian	HarperTrophy
Arthur's Great Big Valentine	K	250+	Hoban, Lillian	HarperTrophy
Arthur's Honey Bear	K	250+	Hoban, Lillian	HarperCollins
Arthur's Loose Tooth	K	250+	Hoban, Lillian	HarperCollins
Arthur's Pen Pal	K	250+	Hoban, Lillian	HarperCollins
Arthur's Prize Reader	K	250+	Hoban, Lillian	HarperTrophy
At the Water Hole	K	236	Foundations	Wright Group
Aunt Eater Loves a Mystery	K	250+	Cushman, Doug	HarperTrophy
Aunt Eater's Mystery Christmas	K	250+	Cushman, Doug	HarperTrophy
Aunt Eater's Mystery Vacation	K	250+	Cushman, Doug	HarperTrophy
Baba Yaga	K	250+	Literacy 2000	Rigby
Baby Sister for Frances, A	K	250+	Hoban, Lillian	Scholastic
Bargain for Frances, A	K	250+	Hoban, Russell	HarperTrophy
Barney's Lovely Lunch	K	330	Windmill Books	Rigby
Barrel of Gold, A	K	251	Story Box	Wright Group

Title	Level	Words	Author/Series	Publisher/Distributor
Baseball Ballerina	K	250+	Cristaldi, Kathryn	Random House
Bat Bones and Spider Stew	K	250+	Poploff, Michelle	Bantam Doubleday Dell
Bath Day for Brutus	K	347	Little Red Readers	Sundance
Bats	K	250+	PM Animal Facts-Gold	Rigby
Be Ready at Eight	K	250+	Parish, Peggy	Simon & Schuster/Aladdin
Bear at the Beach	K	250+	Carmichael, Clay	North-South Books
Bear for Miguel, A	K	250+	Alphin, Elaine Marie	HarperTrophy
Bear Goes to Town	K	250+	Browne, Anthony	Doubleday
Beauty and the Beast	K	250+	Sunshine	Wright Group
Beavers Beware!	K	250+	Brenner, Barbara	Bantam Doubleday Dell
Bedtime at Aunt Carmen's	K	250	Ready Readers	Pearson Learning
Bedtime for Frances	K	250+	Hoban, Russell	Scholastic
Bedtime Story, A	K	335	Book Shop	Mondo Publishing
Best Birthday Present, The	K	250+	Literacy 2000	Rigby
Best Friends for Frances	K	250+	Hoban, Russell	Scholastic
Best Teacher in the World, The	K	250+	Chardiet, Bernice & Maccarone, Grace	Scholastic
Best Way to Play, The	K	250+	Cosby, Bill	Scholastic
Big Balloon Race, The	K	250+	Coerr, Eleanor	HarperTrophy
Big Fish Little Fish	K	250+	Folk Tales	Wright Group
Big Prize, The	K	401	Adventures in Reading	Dominie
Big Sneeze, The	K	131	Brown, Ruth	Lothrop
Biggest Bear in the Woods, The	K	250+	Little Celebrations	Pearson Learning
Birthday Bike for Brimhall, A	K	250+	Delton, Judy	Bantam Doubleday Dell
Birthday for Frances, A	K	250+	Hoban, Russell	Scholastic
Blind Man and the Elephant, The	K	250+	Backstein, Karen	Scholastic
Body Numbers	K	250+	Discovery World	Rigby
Bony-Legs	K	250+	Cole, Joanna	Scholastic
Bootsie Barker Ballerina	K	250+	Bottner, Barbara	HarperTrophy
Boy and His Donkey, A	K	250+	Literacy 2000	Rigby
Boy Named Boomer, A	K	250+	Esiason, Boomer	Scholastic
Boy Who Cried Wolf, The	K	460	Aesop's Fables	Dominie
Brave Ben	K	162	Literacy 2000	Rigby
Brave Little Tailor, The	K	250+	PM Trad. Stories & Tales	Rigby
Bread and Jam for Frances	K	250+	Hoban, Russell	Scholastic
Bremen Town Musicians, The	K	863	Gross & Kent	Scholastic
Brenda's Private Swing	K	250+	Chardiet, Bernice & Maccarone, Grace	Scholastic
Brown Bears	K	250+	PM Animals in the Wild-Yellow	Rigby
Bubbling Crocodile	K	250+	Ready to Read	Pacific Learning
Buffalo Bill and the Pony Express	K	250+	Coerr, Eleanor	HarperTrophy
Bumps in the Night	K	250+	Allard, Harry	Bantam Doubleday Dell
Bunny Runs Away	K	250+	Chardiet, Bernice & Maccarone, Grace	Scholastic
Busy Guy, A	K	72	Rookie Readers	Children's Press
Button Soup	K	250+	Orgel, Doris	Bantam Doubleday Dell
Cabbage Princess, The	K	250+	Literacy 2000	Rigby
Camel Called Bump-Along, A	K	373	Evangeline Nicholas Collection	Wright Group
Camp Knock Knock	K	250+	Douglas, Ann	Bantam Doubleday Dell
Camp Knock Knock Mystery, The	K	250+	Douglas, Ann	Bantam Doubleday Dell
Camping with Claudine	K	250+	Literacy 2000	Rigby
Caps for Sale	K	675	Slobodkina, Esphyr	Harper & Row
Case of the Cat's Meow, The	K	250+	Bonsall, Crosby	HarperTrophy

Title	Level	Words	Author/Series	Publisher/Distributor
Case of the Double Cross, The	K	250+	Bonsall, Crosby	HarperTrophy
Case of the Dumb Bells, The	K	250+	Bonsall, Crosby	HarperTrophy
Case of the Scaredy Cats, The	K	250+	Bonsall, Crosby	Harper & Row
Case of the Two Masked Robbers, The	K	250+	Hoban, Lillian	HarperTrophy
Cats' Burglar, The	K		Parish, Peggy	Hearst Corp.
Cats of the Night	K	379	Book Bank	Wright Group
Catten	K	769	Jellybeans	Rigby
Change for Zoe, A	K	250+	Home Connection Collection	Rigby
Cheerful King, The	K	351	Little Books	Sadlier-Oxford
Chicago Winds	K	173	Evangeline Nicholas Collection	Wright Group
Chickens Aren't the Only Ones	K	250+	Heller, Ruth	Scholastic
Children as Young Scientists	K	393	Early Connections	Benchmark Education
Chipmunk at Hollow Tree Lane	K	250+	Sherrow, Victoria	Scholastic
Cinderella	K	250+	Once Upon a Time	Wright Group
Clara and the Bookwagon	K	250+	Levinson, Nancy Smiler	HarperTrophy
Clever Bird	K	250+	Little Celebrations	Pearson Learning
Clever Hamburger	K	560	Jellybeans	Rigby
Clever Mr. Brown	K	397	Story Box	Wright Group
Clifford, the Big Red Dog	K	241	Bridwell, Norman	Scholastic
Clifford, the Small Red Puppy	K	499	Bridwell, Norman	Scholastic
Clouds, Rain and Fog	K	488	Sunshine	Wright Group
Clubhouse, The	K	659	PM Story Books-Gold	Rigby
Collecting Leaves	K	250+	Stepping Stones	Nelson/Michaels Assoc.
Commander Toad and the Big Black Hole	K	250+	Yolen, Jane	Putnam & Grosset
Commander Toad and the Dis-Asteroid	K	250+	Yolen, Jane	Putnam & Grosset
Commander Toad and the Intergalactic Spy	K	250+	Yolen, Jane	Putnam & Grosset
Commander Toad and the Planet of the Grapes	K	250+	Yolen, Jane	Putnam & Grosset
Commander Toad and the Space Pirates	K	250+	Yolen, Jane	Putnam & Grosset
Commander Toad and the Voyage Home	K	250+	Yolen, Jane	Putnam & Grosset
Computers Are for Everyone	K	464	Sunshine	Wright Group
Concert Night	K	250+	Literacy 2000	Rigby
Corduroy	K	250+	Freeman, Don	Scholastic
Counting Insects	K	230	Early Connections	Benchmark Education
Crocodile Lake	K	322	Pacific Literacy	Pacific Learning
Crosby Crocodile's Disguise	K	250+	Literacy 2000	Rigby
Cunning Creatures	K	250+	Home Connection Collection	Rigby
Dabble Duck	K	250+	Leo Ellis, Anne	HarperTrophy
Dancing with the Manatees	K	250+	McNulty, Faith	Scholastic
Daniel's Duck	K	250+	Bulla, Clyde Robert	HarperTrophy
Darcy and Gran Don't Like Babies	K	250+	Cutler, Jane	Scholastic
Day Jimmy's Boa Ate the Wash, The	K	250+	Noble, Trinka, H.	Scholastic
Dede and the Dinosaur	K	232	Wonders	Hampton-Brown
Desert Machine, The	K	202	Sunshine	Wright Group
Dinosaur Days	K	250+	Ready Readers	Pearson Learning
Dinosaur on the Motorway	K	231	Wesley & the Dinosaurs	Wright Group
Dinosaur Time	K	250+	Parish, Peggy	Harper & Row
Dinosaurs	K	193	Book Shop	Mondo Publishing
Diplidocus in the Garden, A	K	210	Wesley & the Dinosaurs	Wright Group
Discovering Dinosaurs	K	335	Little Books	Sadlier-Oxford
Do You Like Cats?	K	250+	Oppenheim, Joanne	Bantam Doubleday Dell
Doctor's Office, The	K	272	Pebble Books	Grolier, Capstone

Title	Level	Words	Author/Series	Publisher/Distributor
Donald's Garden	K	250+	Reading Unlimited	Pacific Learning
Dragon Feet	K	153	Books for Young Learners	Richard C. Owen
Dragons Galore	K	250+	Wildcats	Wright Group
Effie	K	250+	Allinson, Beverly	Scholastic
Egg	K	250+	Logan, Dick	Cypress
Eggs, Larvae and Flies	K	450	Sunshine	Wright Group
Elaine and the Flying Frog	K	250+	Chang, Heidi	Scholastic
Elephants	K	250+	PM Animals in the Wild-Yellow	Rigby
Elves and the Shoemaker, The	K	300	PM Trad. Tales & Plays-Turq.	Rigby
Elves and the Shoemaker, The	K	622	New Way Orange	Steck-Vaughn
Everything Changes	K	250+	Discovery World	Rigby
Fables by Aesop	K	250+	Reading Unlimited	Pacific Learning
Fabulous Animal Families	K	250+	Home Connection Collection	Rigby
Fabulous Freckles	K	250+	Literacy 2000	Rigby
Families Are Different	K	250+	Pellegrini, Nina	Scholastic
Farmer in the Soup, The	K	250+	Littledale, Freya	Scholastic
Fast and Funny	K	1499	Story Box	Wright Group
Father Who Walked on Hands	K	344	Literacy 2000	Rigby
Fergus and Bridey	K	250+	Little Celebrations	Pearson Learning
Fight in the Schoolyard, The	K	129	City Kids	Rigby
Fire! Fire!	K	250+	Wildcats	Wright Group
First Fire, The	K	250+	Little Celebrations	Pearson Learning
First Flight	K	250+	Shea, George	HarperTrophy
Five Funny Frights	K	250+	Stamper, Judith Bauer	Scholastic
Flour	K	174	Wonder World	Wright Group
Flows & Quakes and Spinning Winds	K	250+	Home Connection Collection	Rigby
Flying Fingers	K	250+	Literacy 2000	Rigby
Follow That Fish	K	250+	Oppenheim, Joanne	Bantam Doubleday Dell
Food Journey, The	K	116	Home Connection Collection	Rigby
Forty-Three Cats	K	232	Sunshine	Wright Group
Four on the Shore	K	250+	Marshall, Edward	Puffin Books
Fox and the Crow, The	K	250+	Ready Readers	Pearson Learning
Foxes	K	250+	PM Animal Facts-Gold	Rigby
Franklin Goes to School	K	250+	Bourgeois, Paulette & Clark, Brenda	Scholastic
Freddy's Train Ride	K	573	Pair-It Books	Steck-Vaughn
Friends are Forever	K	585	Literacy 2000	Rigby
Friendship Garden, The	K	250+	Little Celebrations	Pearson Learning
Frog and Toad All Year	K	250+	Little Readers	Houghton Mifflin
Frog and Toad are Friends	K	250+	Lobel, Arnold	Harper & Row
Frog and Toad Together	K	1927	Lobel, Arnold	HarperCollins
Frog and Toad Together	K	250+	Little Readers	Houghton Mifflin
Frog Prince, The	K	250+	Tarcov, Edith H.	Scholastic
Frog Princess, The	K	206	Literacy 2000	Rigby
Frogs	K	311	Wonder World	Wright Group
Frown, The	K	228	Read Alongs	Rigby
George the Drummer Boy	K	250+	Benchley, Nathaniel	HarperTrophy
Getting Cold! Getting Hot!	K	753	Sunshine	Wright Group
Getting to Know Sharks	K	379	Little Books	Sadlier-Oxford
Giant Jam Sandwich, The	K	250+	Vernon Lord, John	Houghton Mifflin
Gift to Share, A	K	544	Pair-It Books	Steck-Vaughn
Gifts to Make	K	509	Pair-It Books	Steck-Vaughn

Title	Level	Words	Author/Series	Publisher/Distributor
Gluepots	K	205	Book Bank	Wright Group
Go and Hush the Baby	K	250+	Byars, Betsy	Viking
Go-cart Day	K	165	City Kids	Rigby
Going Places	K	410	Early Connections	Benchmark Education
Goldilocks and the Three Bears	K	250+	Once Upon a Time	Wright Group
Golly Sisters Go West, The	K	250+	Byars, Betsy	HarperTrophy
Golly Sisters Ride Again, The	K	250+	Byars, Betsy	HarperTrophy
Good Morning Mrs. Martin	K	156	Book Bank	Wright Group
Grandfather Horned Toad	K	250+	Little Celebrations	Pearson Learning
Grandma's Heart	K	90	Wonder World	Wright Group
Grandma's at the Lake	K	250+	McCully, Emily Arnold	HarperTrophy
Grandpa Comes to Stay	K	1083	Lewis, Rob	Mondo Publishing
Grasshopper and the Ants	K	452	Sunshine	Wright Group
Great Bean Race, The	K	295	Pacific Literacy	Pacific Learning
Greg's Microscope	K	250+	Selsam, Millicent	HarperTrophy
Guide Dog, The	K	338	Foundations	Wright Group
Half for You, Half for Me	K	399	Literacy 2000	Rigby
Hansel and Gretel	K	250+	Enrichment	Wright Group
Happy Birthday, Dear Duck	K	250+	Bunting, Eve	Clarion
Hare and the Tortoise, The	K	250+	Literacy 2000	Rigby
Harold and the Purple Crayon	K	660	Johnson, Crockett	Harper & Row
Harry Hates Shopping!	K	250+	Armitage, Ronda & David	Scholastic
Hat Came Back, The	K	250+	Literacy 2000	Rigby
Have You Seen a Javelina?	K	250+	Literacy 2000	Rigby
He Who Listens	K	250+	Literacy 2000	Rigby
Heather's Book	K	250+	Ready Readers	Pearson Learning
Hello Creatures!	K	250+	Literacy 2000	Rigby
Here Comes the Strike Out	K	250+	Little Readers	Houghton Mifflin
Here Comes the Strike Out	K	250+	Kessler, Leonard	HarperTrophy
Hippos	K	250+	PM Animals in the Wild-Yellow	Rigby
Home in the Sky	K	250+	Baker, Jeannie	Scholastic
Hooray for the Golly Sisters!	K	250+	Byars, Betsy	HarperTrophy
Hot and Cold Weather	K	922	Sunshine	Wright Group
How Does It Breathe?	K	250+	Home Connection Collection	Rigby
How Fire Came to Earth	K	250+	Literacy 2000	Rigby
How Much Does This Hold?	K	179	Coulton, Mia	Kaeden Books
How to Weigh an Elephant	K	390	Pacific Literacy	Pacific Learning
Hugo Hogget	K	528	Wonders	Hampton-Brown
I Am a Gypsy Pot	K	220	Evangeline Nicholas Collection	Wright Group
I Am Not Afraid	K	250+	Mann, Kenny	Bantam Doubleday Dell
I Can See the Leaves	K	368	Pacific Literacy	Pacific Learning
I Dream	K	583	Sunshine	Wright Group
I Get the Creeps	K	250+	Reading Corners	Dominie
I Went to the Dentist	K	152	City Kids	Rigby
Ibis: A True Whale Story	K	250+	Himmelman, John	Scholastic
If You Give a Moose a Muffin	K	250+	Numeroff, Laura Joffe	HarperCollins
If You Give a Mouse a Cookie	K	291	Numeroff, Laura Joffe	HarperCollins
In a Faraway Forest	K	347	Wonders	Hampton-Brown
Insects All Around	K	229	Early Connections	Benchmark Education
Is It a Fish?	K	606	Sunshine	Wright Group
It's Halloween	K	250+	Prelutsky, Jack	Scholastic

Title	Level	Words	Author/Series	Publisher/Distributor
It's Valentine's Day	K	250+	Prelutsky, Jack	Scholastic
Jack and the Beanstalk	K	901	Hunia, Fran	Ladybird Books
Jack and the Beanstalk	K	250+	Weisner, David	Scholastic
Jamaica and Brianna	K	250+	Little Readers	Houghton Mifflin
Jamaica's Find	K	250+	Havill, Juanita	Scholastic
Johnny Appleseed	K	250+	Moore, Eva	Scholastic
Julie's Mornings	K	250+	Ready Readers	Pearson Learning
Just Us Women	K	250+	Caines, Jeannette	Scholastic
Kangaroos	K	250+	PM Animals in the Wild-Yellow	Rigby
Keep the Lights Burning Abbie	K	250+	Roop, Peter & Connie	Scholastic
Keeping Warm! Keeping Cool!	K	946	Sunshine	Wright Group
King, the Mice and the Cheese	K	250+	Gurney, Nancy	Random House
King Midas and the Golden Touch	K	721	PM Story Books-Gold	Rigby
Knock! Knock!	K	250+	Carter, Jackie	Scholastic
Know-Nothing Birthday, A	K	250+	Spirn, Michelle Sobel	HarperTrophy
Know-Nothings, The	K	250+	Spirn, Michelle Sobel	HarperTrophy
Kwanzaa	K	225	Visions	Wright Group
Last Puppy, The	K	244	Asch, Frank	Simon & Schuster
Leaves	K	236	Pebble Books	Grolier, Capstone
Legend of the Red Bird, The	K	389	Sunshine	Wright Group
Letter to Amy, A	K	250+	Keats, Ezra Jack	Harper & Row
Lion and the Mouse, The	K	557	Pair-It Books	Steck-Vaughn
Lionel and Louise	K	250+	Krensky, Stephen	Puffin Books
Lionel at Large	K	250+	Krensky, Stephen	Puffin Books
Lions & Tigers	K	250+	PM Animals in the Wild-Yellow	Rigby
Little Chief	K	250+	Hoff, Syd	HarperCollins
Little Hawk's New Name	K	250+	Bolognese, Don	Scholastic
Little Knight, The	K	250+	Reading Unlimited	Pacific Learning
Little One Inch	K	384	Gibson, A. & Akiyam, M.	Scholastic
Little Polar Bear and the Brave Little Hare	K	250+	DeBeer, Hans	North-South Books
Little Red Hen	K	558	Galdone, Paul	Clarion
Little Red Riding Hood	K	250+	Enrichment	Wright Group
Little Runner of the Longhouse	K	250+	Baker, Betty	HarperTrophy
Little Soup's Birthday	K	250+	Peck, Robert	Bantam Doubleday Dell
Little Walrus Rising	K	250+	Young, Carol	Scholastic
Little Witch Goes to School	K	250+	Hautzig, Deborah	Random House
Little Witch's Big Night	K	250+	Hautzig, Deborah	Random House
Living in the Sky	K	328	Sunshine	Wright Group
Lonely Giant, The	K	449	Literacy 2000	Rigby
Looking for Shapes	K	289	Early Connections	Benchmark Education
M & M and the Bad News Babies	K	250+	Ross, Pat	The Penguin Group
M & M and the Big Bag	K	250+	Ross, Pat	The Penguin Group
M & M and the Halloween Monster	K	250+	Ross, Pat	The Penguin Group
M & M and the Haunted House Game	K	250+	Ross, Pat	The Penguin Group
M & M and the Mummy Mess	K	250+	Ross, Pat	The Penguin Group
M & M and the Santa Secrets	K	250+	Ross, Pat	Puffin Chapters
M & M and the Super Child Afternoon	K	250+	Ross, Pat	The Penguin Group
Madeline	K	250+	Bemelmans, Ludwig	Scholastic
Madeline's Rescue	K	250+	Bemelmans, Ludwig	Scholastic
Magic Box, The	K	250+	Brenner, Barbara	Bantam Doubleday Dell
Make Prints and Patterns	K	454	Sunshine	Wright Group

Title	Level	Words	Author/Series	Publisher/Distributor
Malawi-Keeper of the Trees	K	250+	Little Celebrations	Pearson Learning
Manatee Winter	K	250+	Zoehfeld, Kathleen Weidnetz	Scholastic
Market Day for Mrs. Wordy	K	177	Sunshine	Wright Group
Martin and the Teacher's Pets	K	250+	Chardiet, Bernice & Maccarone, Grace	Scholastic
Martin and the Tooth Fairy	K	250+	Chardiet, Bernice & Maccarone, Grace	Scholastic
Matchbox Collection, A	K	250+	Stepping Stones	Nelson/Michaels Assoc.
Me Too	K	136	Mayer, Mercer	Donovan
Meanest Thing to Say, The	K	250+	Cosby, Bill	Scholastic
Measure Up!	K	303	Early Connections	Benchmark Education
Meat Eaters, Plant Eaters	K	156	Planet Earth	Rigby
Meet M & M	K	250+	Ross, Pat	Puffin Chapters
Meet the Octopus	K	701	Book Shop	Mondo Publishing
Meet the Villarreals	K	387	Wonders	Hampton-Brown
Messy Bessey's Closet	K	92	Rookie Readers	Children's Press
Mile High, A	K	331	Book Bank	Wright Group
Misha Disappears	K	250+	Literacy 2000	Rigby
Miss Mouse Gets Married	K	250+	Folk Tales	Wright Group
Missing Pet, The	K	618	Pair-It Books	Steck-Vaughn
Mollie Whuppie	K	250+	New Way Orange	Steck-Vaughn
Molly the Brave and Me	K	250+	O'Connor, Jane	Random House
Mom's Getting Married	K	376	Sunshine	Wright Group
Monkeys & Apes	K	250+	PM Animals in the Wild-Yellow	Rigby
Monster from the Sea, The	K	250+	Hooks, William H.	Bantam Doubleday Dell
Monster Movie	K	250+	Cole, Joanna	Scholastic
Monster of Mirror Mountain, The	K	250+	Literacy 2000	Rigby
Monster Under the Bed, The	K	250+	Ready Readers	Pearson Learning
More Tales of Amanda Pig	K	1939	Van Leeuwen, Jean	The Penguin Group
More Tales of Oliver Pig	K	2052	Van Leeuwen, Jean	The Penguin Group
Morning Dance, The	K	268	Jellybeans	Rigby
Mother Sea Turtle	K	240	Foundations	Wright Group
Mother's Helpers	K	250+	Ready Readers	Pearson Learning
Mr. and Mrs. Murphy and Bernard	K	250+	Little Celebrations	Pearson Learning
Mr. Gumpy's Motor Car	K	250+	Burningham, John	HarperCollins
Mr. Pepperpot's Pet	K	250+	Literacy 2000	Rigby
Mrs. Huggins and Her Hen Hannah	K	250+	Dabcovich, Lydia	Dutton
My New Mom	K	282	Sunshine	Wright Group
My Scrapbook	K	312	Storyteller Nonfiction	Wright Group/ McGraw-Hill
My Sister's Getting Married	K	300	Foundations	Wright Group
Nate the Great	K	250+	Sharmat, M. Weinman	Bantam Doubleday Dell
Nate the Great and the Boring Beach Bag	K	250+	Sharmat, M. Weinman	Bantam Doubleday Dell
Nate the Great and the Crunchy Christmas	K	250+	Sharmat, M. Weinman	Bantam Doubleday Dell
Nate the Great and the Fishy Prize	K	250+	Sharmat, M. Weinman	Bantam Doubleday Dell
Nate the Great and the Halloween Hunt	K	250+	Sharmat, M. Weinman	Bantam Doubleday Dell
Nate the Great and the Lost List	K	250+	Sharmat, M. Weinman	Bantam Doubleday Dell
Nate the Great and the Missing Key	K	250+	Sharmat, M. Weinman	Bantam Doubleday Dell
Nate the Great and the Mushy Valentine	K	250+	Sharmat, M. Weinman	Bantam Doubleday Dell
Nate the Great and the Musical Note	K	250+	Sharmat, M. Weinman	Bantam Doubleday Dell
Nate the Great and the Phony Clue	K	250+	Sharmat, M. Weinman	Bantam Doubleday Dell
Nate the Great and the Pillowcase	K	250+	Sharmat, M. Weinman	Bantam Doubleday Dell
Nate the Great and the Snowy Trail	K	250+	Sharmat, M. Weinman	Bantam Doubleday Dell

Title	Level	Words	Author/Series	Publisher/Distributor
Nate the Great and the Sticky Case	K	250+	Sharmat, M. Weinman	Bantam Doubleday Dell
Nate the Great and the Stolen Base	K	250+	Sharmat, M. Weinman	Bantam Doubleday Dell
Nate the Great and the Tardy Tortoise	K	250+	Sharmat, M. Weinman	Bantam Doubleday Dell
Nate the Great Goes Down in the Dumps	K	250+	Sharmat, M. Weinman	Bantam Doubleday Dell
Nate the Great Goes Undercover	K	250+	Sharmat, M. Weinman	Bantam Doubleday Dell
Nate the Great Saves the King of Sweden	K	250+	Sharmat, M. Weinman	Bantam Doubleday Dell
Nate the Great Stalks Stupidweed	K	250+	Sharmat, M. Weinman	Bantam Doubleday Dell
Nathan and Nicholas Alexander	K	250+	Delacre, Lulu	Scholastic
Natural History Museum, The	K	250+	Stepping Stones	Nelson/Michaels Assoc.
Next Time I Will	K	250+	Orgel, Doris	Bantam Doubleday Dell
Nice New Neighbors	K	250+	Brandenberg, Franz	Scholastic
No Fighting, No Biting!	K	250+	Minarik, Else H.	HarperTrophy
No Tooth, No Quarter!	K	250+	Buller, Jon	Random House
Nothing to Be Scared About	K	343	Sunshine	Wright Group
Now Listen, Stanley	K		Literacy 2000	Rigby
On Friday the Giant	K	240	The Giant	Wright Group
On Monday the Giant	K	250+	The Giant	Wright Group
On Sunday the Giant	K	250+	The Giant	Wright Group
On Thursday the Giant	K	250+	The Giant	Wright Group
On Tuesday the Giant	K	250+	The Giant	Wright Group
On Wednesday the Giant	K	250+	The Giant	Wright Group
One Drop of Water and a Million More	K	156	Book Bank	Wright Group
Oogly Gum Chasing Game, The	K	250+	Literacy 2000	Rigby
Opposite of Pig, The	K	250+	Little Celebrations	Pearson Learning
Orca Song	K	250+	Armour, Michael C.	Scholastic
Our Busy Bodies	K	144	Home Connection Collection	Rigby
Our New Principal	K	149	City Kids	Rigby
Out in the Big Wild World	K	430	Jellybeans	Rigby
Outside Dog, The	K	250+	Pomerantz, Charlotte	HarperTrophy
Owls	K	250+	PM Animal Facts-Gold	Rigby
Pancake, The	K	250+	Lobel, Anita	Bantam Doubleday Dell
Paper Birds, The	K	363	Foundations	Wright Group
Paper Route, The	K	314	New Way Green	Steck-Vaughn
Parents' Night Fright	K	250+	Levy, Elizabeth	Scholastic
Peanut Butter Gang, The	K	250+	Siracusa, Catherine	Hyperion
People Are Living Things	K	250+	Home Connection Collection	Rigby
Pet for You, A	K	531	Pair-It Books	Steck-Vaughn
Peter and the North Wind	K	250+	Littledale, Freya	Scholastic
Picking Up Papers	K	161	City Kids	Rigby
Pied Piper of Hamelin, The	K	250+	Hautzig, Deborah	Random House
Piggle	K	250+	Bonsall, Crosby	HarperCollins
Pile in Pete's Room, The	K	745	Sunshine	Wright Group
Pizza for Everyone	K	251	Pair-It Books	Steck-Vaughn
Playhouse, The	K	197	Pacific Literacy	Pacific Learning
Pocket for Corduroy, A	K	250+	Freeman, Don	Scholastic
Polar Bears	K	276	Wonder World	Wright Group
Pookie and Joe	K	250+	Literacy 2000	Rigby
Popcorn Book, The	K	208	Reading Unlimited	Pacific Learning
Poppy, The	K	152	Pacific Literacy	Pacific Learning
Power of Nature, The	K	274	Early Connections	Benchmark Education
Princess and the Peas, The	K	250+	Enrichment	Wright Group

Title	Level	Words	Author/Series	Publisher/Distributor
Princess and the Wise Woman, The	K	250+	Ready Readers	Pearson Learning
Prize for Purry, A	K	250+	Literacy 2000	Rigby
Pterodactyl at the Airport	K	185	Wesley & the Dinosaurs	Wright Group
Public Library, The	K	250+	Stepping Stones	Nelson/Michaels Assoc.
Purple Walrus and Other Perfect Pets	K	250+	Wildcats	Wright Group
Quilt for Kiri, A	K	367	Pacific Literacy	Pacific Learning
Raccoons	K	250+	PM Animal Facts-Gold	Rigby
Rain	K	263	Pebble Books	Grolier, Capstone
Rats, Bats, and Black Puddings	K	714	Pacific Literacy	Pacific Learning
Reduce, Reuse, and Recycle	K	326	Early Connections	Benchmark Education
Riches from Nature	K	382	Early Connections	Benchmark Education
Rise and Shine, Mariko-chan	K		Tomioka, Chiyoko	Scholastic
Rollo and Tweedy and the Ghost at Dougal Castle	K	250+	Allen, Laura Jean	HarperTrophy
Rosa's Tonsils	K	337	Foundations	Wright Group
Rose Rest Home, The	K	304	Sunshine	Wright Group
Rosie's House	K		Literacy 2000	Rigby
Ruby the Copycat	K	250+	Rathman, Peggy	Scholastic
Sam Who Never Forgets	K	281	Rice, Eve	Morrow
Sam's Big Clean-up	K	287	Windmill Books	Rigby
Sam's Solution	K		Literacy 2000	Rigby
Sandy's Suitcase	K		Edwards, Elsy	SRA/McGraw-Hill
Scaredy Dog	K	250+	Thomas, Jane Resh	Hyperion
Scare-Kid	K		Literacy 2000	Rigby
Scruffy	K	250+	Parish, Peggy	HarperTrophy
Sea Turtles	K	296	Marine Life for Young Readers	Dominie
Sea Wall, The	K	251	Foundations	Wright Group
Seashells	K	186	Marine Life for Young Readers	Dominie
Secret Hideaway, The	K	618	PM Story Books-Gold	Rigby
Secret of Foghorn Island, The	K	250+	Hayes, Geoffrey	Random House
Seeing the School Doctor	K	167	City Kids	Rigby
Sheila Rae, the Brave	K	250+	Henkes, Kevin	Scholastic
Shingo's Grandfather	K	370	Sunshine	Wright Group
Shipwreck Saturday	K	250+	Cosby, Bill	Scholastic
Shortest Kid in the World	K	250+	Bliss, Corinne Demas	Random House
Show and Tell	K	201	City Kids	Rigby
Sidetrack Sam	K	250+	Literacy 2000	Rigby
Sing to the Moon	K	2448	Story Box	Wright Group
Skunks	K	250+	PM Animal Facts-Gold	Rigby
SkyScraper, The	K	252	Little Red Readers	Sundance
Sleeping Beauty	K	250+	Enrichment	Wright Group
Smallest Cow in the World, The	K	250+	Paterson, Katherine	HarperTrophy
Smallest Tree, The	K		Literacy 2000	Rigby
Smile, The	K	253	Read Alongs	Rigby
Snakes	K	259	Foundations	Wright Group
Sneakers	K	388	Sunshine	Wright Group
Snow White and Rose Red	K	250+	Hunia, Fran	Ladybird Books
Snowball War, The	K	250+	Chardiet, Bernice	Scholastic
Snowshoe Thompson	K	250+	Smiler Levinson, Nancy	HarperTrophy
Soap Soup and Other Verses	K	250+	Kuskin, Karla	HarperTrophy
Soccer Cousins	K	250+	Marzollo, Jean	Scholastic
Souvenirs	K	179	Literacy 2000	Rigby
Space Rock	K	250+	Buller, Jon	Random House

Title	Level	Words	Author/Series	Publisher/Distributor
Special Ride, The	K	647	PM Story Books-Gold	Rigby
Stan the Hot Dog Man	K	250+	Kessler, Ethel & Leonard	HarperTrophy
Starfish & Urchins	K	322	Marine Life for Young Readers	Dominie
Stems	K	231	Pebble Books	Grolier, Capstone
Stone Works	K	124	Wonder World	Wright Group
Story of Hungbu and Nolbu, The	K	802	Book Shop	Mondo Publishing
Strawberry Pop And Soda Crackers	K		Little Celebrations	Pearson Learning
Street Action	K	250+	Wildcats	Wright Group
String Food	K	250+	Home Connection Collection	Rigby
Suki and the Case of the Lost Bunnies	K	250+	Ready Readers	Pearson Learning
Supermarket, The	K	255	Pebble Books	Grolier, Capstone
Surprise Party	K	333	Hutchins, Pat	Macmillan
Tasmanian Devils	K	250+	PM Animal Facts-Gold	Rigby
Tea	K	267	Wonder World	Wright Group
Teddy Bears Cure a Cold	K		Gretz, Susanna	Scholastic
Teeth	K	470	Sunshine	Wright Group
Terrible Fright, A	K	291	Story Box	Wright Group
That Fat Hat	K	250+	Barkan, Joanne	Scholastic
That's Really Weird!	K	129	Read Alongs	Rigby
Three Bears	K	873	Galdone, Paul	Clarion
Three Billy Goats Gruff	K	478	Stevens, Janet	Harcourt Brace
Three By the Sea	K	250+	Marshall, Edward	Puffin Books
Three Days on a River in a Red Canoe	K	250+	Williams, Vera B.	Scholastic
Three Ducks Went Wandering	K	250+	Roy, Ron	Clarion
Three Magicians, The	K		Literacy 2000	Rigby
Three Stories You Can Read to Your Cat	K	250+	Miller, Sara Swan	Houghton Mifflin
Three Stories You Can Read to Your Dog	K	250+	Miller, Sara Swan	Houghton Mifflin
Three Wishes, The	K	501	Sunshine	Wright Group
Thumbelina	K	807	Tales from Hans Andersen	Wright Group
Too Busy for Pets!	K	472	Sunshine	Wright Group
Too Many Babas	K	250+	Little Readers	Houghton Mifflin
Too Many Babas	K	250+	Croll, Carolyn	HarperTrophy
Treasure of the Lost Lagoon	K	250+	Hayes, Geoffrey	Random House
Trees	K	388	Early Connections	Benchmark Education
Tubes in My Ears: My Trip to the Hospital	K	658	Book Shop	Mondo Publishing
Turtle Flies South	K		Literacy 2000	Rigby
Two Foolish Cats	K		Literacy 2000	Rigby
Ugly Duckling, The	K	452	Traditional Tales & More	Rigby
Under the City	K	206	Sunshine	Wright Group
Vicky the High Jumper	K		Literacy 2000	Rigby
Wagon Wheels	K	250+	Brenner, Barbara	HarperTrophy
Water Goes Up! Water Goes Down!	K	299	Early Connections	Benchmark Education
Waterhole	K	149	Planet Earth	Rigby
We Scream for Ice Cream	K	250+	Chardiet, Bernice & Maccarone, Grace	Scholastic
Well I Never	K	2517	Story Box	Wright Group
What a Funny Thing to Do	K	236	Stepping Stones	Nelson/Michaels Assoc.
What Happens When You Recycle?	K	215	Discovery World	Rigby
What's for Dinner, Dad?	K	459	Sunshine	Wright Group
What's Inside?	K	238	Wonder World	Wright Group
What's Missing?	K	252	Book Bank	Wright Group
What's Underneath?	K	200	Discovery World	Rigby

Title	Level	Words	Author/Series	Publisher/Distributor
When I Get Bigger	K	205	Mayer, Mercer	Donovan
When Will We Be Sisters?	K	250+	Kroll, Virginia	Scholastic
Where Are the Bears?	K	250+	Winters, Kay	Bantam Doubleday Dell
Where Is the Bear?	K	250+	Nims, Bonnie	Whitman
Where Jeans Come From	K	250+	Ready Readers	Pearson Learning
White Horse, The	K		Literacy 2000	Rigby
Who Pushed Humpty?	K		Literacy 2000	Rigby
Who Sank the Boat?	K	219	Allen Pamela	Coward
Who's Afraid of the Big, Bad Bully?	K	250+	Slater, Teddy	Scholastic
Why Coyote Howls at Night	K	274	Little Books	Sadlier-Oxford
Why the Kangaroo Hops	K	391	Sunshine	Wright Group
Why There Are Shooting Stars	K	362	Pacific Literacy	Pacific Learning
Wide Street Club and Molly, The	K	965	Sunshine	Wright Group
William's Wheelchair Race	K	279	Sunshine	Wright Group
Wind and Storms	K	868	Sunshine	Wright Group
Wind Eagle, The	K	370	Wonders	Hampton-Brown
Winter Woollies	K	289	Storyteller Nonfiction	Wright Group/ McGraw-Hill
You Can Always Tell Cathy from Caitlin	K	583	Sunshine	Wright Group
Zack's Alligator	K	250+	Mozelle, Shirley	HarperTrophy
Zack's Alligator	K	250+	Little Readers	Houghton Mifflin
Zack's Alligator Goes to School	K	250+	Mozelle, Shirley	HarperTrophy
Daniel's Dog	K	250+	Bogart, Jo Allen	Scholastic
Abracadabra	L	372	Reading Unlimited	Pacific Learning
Abraham Lincoln	L	235	Pebble Books	Grolier, Capstone
Acid Rain	L	368	Wonder World	Wright Group
Adventures of a Kite	L	33	Jellybeans	Rigby
Adventures of the Buried Treasure, The	L	250+	McArthur, Nancy	Scholastic
Afternoon on the Amazon	L	250+	Osborne, Mary Pope	Random House
Alexander and the Wind-Up Mouse	L	250+	Lionni, Leo	Scholastic
Alfie's Gift	L	250+	Literacy 2000	Rigby
All About Plants	L	250+	Home Connection Collection	Rigby
All About Stacy	L	250+	Giff, Patricia Reilly	Bantam Doubleday Dell
Amanda Pig and Her Big Brother Oliver	L	250+	Van Leeuwen, Jean	Puffin Books
Amazing Trains	L	482	Pair-It Books	Steck-Vaughn
Amelia Bedelia	L	250+	Parish, Peggy	Harper & Row
Amelia Bedelia and the Baby	L	250+	Parish, Peggy	Harper & Row
Amelia Bedelia and the Surprise Shower	L	250+	Parish, Peggy	Harper & Row
Amelia Bedelia and the Surprise Shower	L	250+	Little Readers	Houghton Mifflin
Amelia Bedelia Goes Camping	L	250+	Parish, Peggy	Avon Camelot
Amelia Bedelia Helps Out	L	250+	Parish, Peggy	Avon Camelot
Amelia Bedelia's Family Album	L	250+	Parish, Peggy	Avon Books
Animal Reports	L	277	Little Red Readers	Sundance
Animal Tracks	L	250+	Dorros, Arthur	Scholastic
Annie Bananie Moves to Barry Avenue	L	250+	Komaiko, Leah	Bantam Doubleday Dell
Another Day, Another Challenge	L	250+	Literacy 2000	Rigby
Ant and the Grasshopper, The	L	250+	Little Celebrations	Pearson Learning
Ashes for Gold	L	250+	Folk Tales	Mondo Publishing
Ashley's World Record	L		Little Celebrations	Pearson Learning
Bad Day for Benjamin, A	L	250+	Reading Unlimited	Pacific Learning
Bad-Luck Penny, The	L	250+	O'Connor, Jane	Grosset & Dunlap

Title	Level	Words	Author/Series	Publisher/Distributor
Beans on the Roof	L	250+	Byars, Betsy	Bantam Doubleday Dell
Bear's Diet	L	652	PM Story Books-Gold	Rigby
Best Older Sister, The	L	250+	Choi, Sook Nyul	Bantam Doubleday Dell
Best Worst Day, The	L	250+	Graves, Bonnie	Hyperion
Best-Loved Doll, The	L	250+	Caudill, Rebecca	Henry Holt & Co.
Big Al	L	250+	Yoshi, Andrew C.	Scholastic
Big Balloon Festival, The	L	625	PM Story Books-Gold	Rigby
Big Beet, The	L	250+	Ready Readers	Pearson Learning
Billy the Ghost and Me	L	250+	Greer, Greg & Ruddick, Bob	HarperTrophy
Bobo's Magic Wishes	L	250+	Little Readers	Houghton Mifflin
Boy Who Cried Wolf, The	L	250+	Literacy 2000	Rigby
Boy Who Turned into a T.V. Set, The	L	250+	Manes, Stephen	Avon Camelot
Boy Who Went to the North Wind, The	L	250+	Literacy 2000	Rigby
Brachiosaurus in the River	L	200	Wesley & the Dinosaurs	Wright Group
Brand New Butterfly, A	L	186	Literacy 2000	Rigby
Bravo Amelia Bedelia!	L	250+	Parish, Herman	Avon Books
Breathing	L	106	Book Shop	Mondo Publishing
Brigid Beware	L	250+	Leverich, Kathleen	Random House
Brigid Bewitched	L	250+	Leverich, Kathleen	Random House
Brigid the Bad	L	250+	Leverich, Kathleen	Random House
Bringing the Sea Back Home	L	250+	Literacy 2000	Rigby
Bug Off!	L	250+	Dussling, Jennifer	Grosset & Dunlap
Cam Jansen and the Chocolate Fudge Mystery	L	250+	Adler, David	Puffin Books
Cam Jansen and the Ghostly Mystery	L	250+	Adler, David	Puffin Books
Cam Jansen and the Mystery at the Haunted House	L	250+	Adler, David	Puffin Books
Cam Jansen and the Mystery at the Monkey House	L	250+	Adler, David	Puffin Books
Cam Jansen and the Mystery of Flight 54	L	250+	Adler, David	Puffin Books
Cam Jansen and the Mystery of the Babe Ruth Baseball	L	250+	Adler, David	Puffin Books
Cam Jansen and the Mystery of the Carnival Prize	L	250+	Adler, David	Puffin Books
Cam Jansen and the Mystery of the Circus Clown	L	250+	Adler, David	Puffin Books
Cam Jansen and the Mystery of the Dinosaur	L	250+	Adler, David	Puffin Books
Cam Jansen and the Mystery of the Dinosaur Bones	L	250+	Adler, David	Puffin Books
Cam Jansen and the Mystery of the Gold Coins	L	250+	Adler, David	Puffin Books
Cam Jansen and the Mystery of the Monster Movie	L	250+	Adler, David	Puffin Books
Cam Jansen and the Mystery of the Stolen Corn Popper	L	250+	Adler, David	Puffin Books
Cam Jansen and the Mystery of the Stolen Diamonds	L	250+	Adler, David	Puffin Books
Cam Jansen and the Mystery of the Television Dog	L	250+	Adler, David	Puffin Books
Cam Jansen and the Mystery of the U.F.O.	L	250+	Adler, David	Puffin Books
Cam Jansen and the Triceratops Pops Mystery	L	250+	Adler, David	Puffin Books
Can I Have a Dinosaur?	L	250+	Literacy 2000	Rigby
Candy Corn Contest, The	L	250+	Giff, Patricia Reilly	Bantam Doubleday Dell
Cannonball Chris	L	250+	Marzollo, Jean	Random House
Captain Bumble	L	510	Story Box	Wright Group
Carlita Ropes the Twister	L	363	Pair-It Books	Steck-Vaughn
Car Trouble	L	724	PM Story Books-Gold	Rigby
Case of the Cool-Itch Kid, The	L	250+	Giff, Patricia Reilly	Bantam Doubleday Dell
Cass Becomes a Star	L	250+	Literacy 2000	Rigby
Cesar Chavez	L	262	Pebble Books	Grolier, Capstone
Chang's Paper Pony	L	250+	Coerr, Eleanor	HarperTrophy

Title	Level	Words	Author/Series	Publisher/Distributor
Charlie	L	250+	Literacy 2000	Rigby
Chicken Little	L	587	Traditional Tales & More	Rigby
Claudine's Concert	L	250+	Literacy 2000	Rigby
Clouds of Terror	L	250+	Welsh, Catherine A.	Carolrhoda Books
Clue at the Zoo, The	L	250+	Giff, Patricia Reilly	Bantam Doubleday Dell
Come Back, Amelia Bedelia	L	250+	Parish, Peggy	Harper & Row
Conversation Club, The	L	250+	Stanley, Diane	Aladdin
Could We Be Friends? Poems for Pals	L	1717	Book Shop	Mondo Publishing
Crafty Jackal	L	250+	Folk Tales	Wright Group
Creep Show	L	250+	Dussling, Jennifer	Grosset & Dunlap
Curse of the Cobweb Queen, The	L	250+	Hayes, Geoffrey	Random House
Daniel	L	161	Literacy 2000	Rigby
Day in Space, A	L	250+	Lord, Suzanne & Epstein, Jolie	Scholastic
Day in Town, A	L	206	Story Box	Wright Group
Day of the Rain, The	L	250+	Cowley, Joy	Dominie
Day of the Snow, The	L	250+	Cowley, Joy	Dominie
Day of the Wind, The	L	250+	Cowley, Joy	Dominie
December Secrets	L	250+	Giff, Patricia Reilly	Bantam Doubleday Dell
Deputy Dan and the Bank Robbers	L	250+	Rosenbloom, Joseph	Random House
Deputy Dan Gets His Man	L	250+	Rosembloom, Joseph	Random House
Desert Giant: The World of the Saguaro Cactus	L	250+	Bash, Barbara	Scholastic
Diary of a Honeybee	L	250+	Literacy 2000	Rigby
Diego Rivera: An Artist's Life	L	250+	Pair-It Books	Steck-Vaughn
Dinosaur Babies	L	250+	Penner, Lucille Recht	Random House
Dinosaur Days	L	250+	Milton, Joyce	Random House
Dinosaur Hunters	L	250+	McMullan, Kate	Random House
Dinosaur Reports	L	324	Little Red Readers	Sundance
Dog That Pitched a No-Hitter, The	L	250+	Christopher, Matt	Little, Brown & Co.
Dog That Stole Football Plays, The	L	250+	Christopher, Matt	Little, Brown & Co.
Dog That Stole Home, The	L	250+	Christopher, Matt	Little, Brown & Co.
Dog-Gone Hollywood	L	250+	Sharmat, M. Weinman	Random House
Doing the Dishes	L	136	City Kids	Rigby
Dolphin	L	250+	Morris, Robert A.	HarperTrophy
Dolphins, The	L	721	PM Story Books-Gold	Rigby
Dom's Handplant	L	250+	Literacy 2000	Rigby
Don't Forget Fun	L	250+	Little Celebrations	Pearson Learning
Dragon Breath	L	250+	O'Connor, Jane	Grosset & Dunlap
Dragon's Birthday, The	L	250+	Literacy 2000	Rigby
Dragons of Blueland, The	L	250+	Gannett, Ruth Stiles	Random House
Eagle in the Sky	L	250+	Little Celebrations	Pearson Learning
Edgar Badger's Balloon Day	L	864	Book Shop	Mondo Publishing
Everyone Knows About Cars	L	176	Book Shop	Mondo Publishing
Farm Life Long Ago	L	436	Pair-It Books	Steck-Vaughn
Finding Providence: The Story of Roger Williams	L	250+	Avi	HarperTrophy
Fish	L	298	Marine Life for Young Readers	Dominie
Flea Story, A	L	250+	Lionni, Leo	Scholastic
Flight of the Union, The	L	250+	White, Tekla	Carolrhoda Books
Flower Girls #1: Violet	L	250+	Leverich, Kathleen	HarperTrophy
Flower Girls #2: Daisy	L	250+	Leverich, Kathleen	HarperTrophy
Flower Girls #3: Heather	L	250+	Leverich, Kathleen	HarperTrophy
Flower Girls #4: Rose	L	250+	Leverich, Kathleen	HarperTrophy
Flower of Sheba, The	L	250+	Orgel, Doris & Schecter, Ellen	Bantam Doubleday Dell

Title	Level	Words	Author/Series	Publisher/Distributor
Flowers	L	270	Pebble Books	Grolier, Capstone
Fly Trap	L	250+	Anastasio, Dina	Grosset & Dunlap
Football Friends	L	250+	Marzollo, Jean, Dan, & Dave	Scholastic
Fox and the Little Red Hen	L	400	Traditional Tales & More	Rigby
Frog Who Thought He Was a Horse, The	L	250+	Literacy 2000	Rigby
Gail & Me	L	250+	Literacy 2000	Rigby
Gail Devers: A Runner's Dream	L	250+	Pair-It Books	Steck-Vaughn
Gasp!	L	529	Book Shop	Mondo Publishing
Gator Girls Book 2, The: Rockin Reptiles	L	250+	Calmenson, Stephanie & Cole	Beech Tree Books
Gator Girls, The	L	250+	Calmenson, Stephanie & Cole	Beech Tree Books
George and Martha	L	250+	Marshall, James	Houghton Mifflin
George and Martha Back in Town	L	250+	Marshall, James	Houghton Mifflin
George and Martha Encore	L	250+	Marshall, James	Houghton Mifflin
George and Martha One Fine Day	L	250+	Marshall, James	Houghton Mifflin
George and Martha Rise and Shine	L	250+	Marshall, James	Houghton Mifflin
George and Martha Round and Round	L	250+	Marshall, James	Houghton Mifflin
George Washington	L	270	Pebble Books	Grolier, Capstone
Ginger Brown: The Nobody Boy	L	250+	Wyeth, Sharon	Random House
Ginger Brown: Too Many Houses	L	250+	Wyeth, Sharon	Random House
Gingerbread Boy, The	L	1097	Galdone, Paul	Clarion
Girl Who Climbed to the Moon, The	L	604	Sunshine	Wright Group
Golden Goose, The	L	731	Sunshine	Wright Group
Goldsworthy and Mort Blast Off	L	250+	Little Celebrations	Pearson Learning
Goliath and the Burglar	L	250+	Dicks, Terrance	Barron's Educational
Goliath and the Buried Treasure	L	250+	Dicks, Terrance	Barron's Educational
Goliath and the Cub Scouts	L	250+	Dicks, Terrance	Barron's Educational
Goliath at the Dog Show	L	250+	Dicks, Terrance	Barron's Educational
Goliath at the Seaside	L	250+	Dicks, Terrance	Barron's Educational
Goliath Goes to Summer School	L	250+	Dicks, Terrance	Barron's Educational
Goliath on Vacation	L	250+	Dicks, Terrance	Barron's Educational
Goliath's Birthday	L	250+	Dicks, Terrance	Barron's Educational
Goliath's Christmas	L	250+	Dicks, Terrance	Barron's Educational
Goliath's Easter Parade	L	250+	Dicks, Terrance	Barron's Educational
Good As New	L	250+	Douglass, Barbara	Scholastic
Good Driving, Amelia Bedelia	L	250+	Parish, Peggy	Harper & Row
Good Work, Amelia Bedelia	L	250+	Parish, Peggy	Avon Camelot
Grandad	L	250+	Literacy 2000	Rigby
Grasshopper on the Road	L	250+	Lobel, Arnold	HarperTrophy
Great Ghosts	L	250+	Cohen, Daniel	Scholastic
Greedy Goat, The	L	451	Book Shop	Mondo Publishing
Gregory, the Terrible Eater	L	250+	Sharmat, M. Weinman	Scholastic
Guess Who?	L	250+	Home Connection Collection	Rigby
Happy Birthday, Martin Luther King	L	250+	Marzollo, Jean	Scholastic
Happy Birthday, Moon	L	345	Asch, Frank	Simon & Schuster
Happy Birthday, Mrs. Boedecker	L	250+	Little Celebrations	Pearson Learning
Harry and Willy and Carrothead	L	250+	Caseley, Judith	Scholastic
Haunted Bike, The	L	250+	Herman, Gail	Grosset & Dunlap
Headless Horseman, The	L	250+	Standiford, Natalie	Random House
Hello, Peter-Bonjour, Remy	L	250+	Little Celebrations	Pearson Learning
Here's Bobby's World! How a TV Cartoon Is Made	L	250+	Little Celebrations	Pearson Learning
Hide to Survive	L	250+	Home Connection Collection	Rigby
Hill of Fire	L	1099	Lewis, Thomas P.	HarperCollins

Title	Level	Words	Author/Series	Publisher/Distributor
Honey Bees	L	250+	Kahkonen, Sharon	Steck-Vaughn
Horrible Harry and the Ant Invasion	L	250+	Kline, Suzy	Scholastic
Horrible Harry and the Christmas Surprise	L	250+	Kline, Suzy	Scholastic
Horrible Harry and the Dungeon	L	250+	Kline, Suzy	Puffin Books
Horrible Harry and the Green Slime	L	250+	Kline, Suzy	Puffin Books
Horrible Harry and the Kickball Wedding	L	250+	Kline, Suzy	Puffin Books
Horrible Harry and the Purple People	L	250+	Kline, Suzy	Puffin Books
Horrible Harry in Room 2B	L	250+	Kline, Suzy	Puffin Books
Horrible Harry's Secret	L	250+	Kline, Suzy	Puffin Books
Hospitals	L	177	Book Shop	Mondo Publishing
Hot Air Balloons	L	479	Pair-It Books	Steck-Vaughn
How Animals Move	L	250+	Discovery World	Rigby
How Do Plants Get Food?	L	250+	Goldish, Meish	Steck-Vaughn
How Does It Grow?	L	250+	Home Connection Collection	Rigby
How Much Is That Guinea Pig in the Window?	L	250+	Rocklin, Joanne	Scholastic
How Spiders Got Eight Legs	L	884	Pair-It Books	Steck-Vaughn
How the Rattlesnake Got Its Rattle	L	1006	Pair-It Books	Steck-Vaughn
How the Water Got to the Plains	L	250+	Home Connection Collection	Rigby
How to Choose a Pet	L	250+	Discovery World	Rigby
Huberta the Hiking Hippo	L	250+	Literacy 2000	Rigby
Hungry, Hungry Sharks	L	250+	Cole, Joanna	Random House
Hush Up!	L		Little Celebrations	Pearson Learning
I Can Read! I Can Read!	L	250+	Little Celebrations	Pearson Learning
I Hate English	L	250+	Levine, Ellen	Scholastic
I Hate My Best Friend	L	250+	Rosner, Ruth	Hyperion
I Know a Lady	L	221	Zolotow, Charlotte	Puffin Books
In a New Land	L	378	Sunshine	Wright Group
In City Gardens	L		Little Celebrations	Pearson Learning
Jane Goodall and the Wild Chimpanzees	L	250+	Birnbaum, Bette	Steck-Vaughn
Jennifer, Too	L	250+	Havill, Juanita	Hyperion
Jenny and the Cornstalk	L	890	Pair-It Books	Steck-Vaughn
Joey's Head	L	250+	Cretan, Gladys	Simon & Schuster
Josefina Story Quilt	L	250+	Coerr, Eleanor	HarperTrophy
Jump the Broom	L	119	Books for Young Learners	Richard C. Owen
Junkpile Robot, The	L	250+	Ready Readers	Pearson Learning
Katy and the Big Snow	L	250+	Burton, Virginia L.	Scholastic
Kerri Strug: Heart of Gold	L	250+	Strug, Kerri & Brown, Greg	Scholastic
Kilmer's Pet Monster	L	250+	Dadey, Debbie & Jones, Marcia	Scholastic
King Beast's Birthday	L	250+	Literacy 2000	Rigby
Kyle's First Kwanzaa	L		Little Celebrations	Pearson Learning
Laura Ingalls Wilder: An Author's Story	L	250+	Pair-It Books	Steck-Vaughn
Lightning	L	279	Pebble Books	Grolier, Capstone
Lilacs, Lotuses, and Ladybugs	L	402	Evangeline Nicholas Collection	Wright Group
Lionel and Amelia	L	702	Book Shop	Mondo Publishing
Lions	L	644	Pair-It Books	Steck-Vaughn
Little Brown Jay, The: A Tale from India	L	366	Folk Tales	Mondo Publishing
Little Penguin's Tale	L	250+	Wood, Audrey	Scholastic
Little Spider, The	L	250+	Literacy 2000	Rigby
Little Vampire and the Midnight Bear	L	250+	Kwitz, Mary Deball	Puffin Books
Lizards	L	356	Wonder World	Wright Group
Lizzie's Lizard	L	289	Storyteller Nonfiction	Wright Group/ McGraw-Hill

Title	Level	Words	Author/Series	Publisher/Distributor
Long Way to a New Land, A	L	250+	Sandin, Joan	HarperTrophy
Long Way Westward, The	L	250+	Sandin, Joan	HarperTrophy
Looking at Insects	L	250+	Discovery World	Rigby
Looking into Space	L	345	Early Connections	Benchmark Education
Loose Laces	L	209	Reading Unlimited	Pacific Learning
Lost at the White House: A 1909 Easter Story	L	250+	Griest, Lisa	Carolrhoda Books
Lucky Feather, The	L	250+	Literacy 2000	Rigby
Lucky Stars	L	250+	Adler, David	Random House
Lucy Meets a Dragon	L	250+	Literacy 2000	Rigby
Luke's Go-Cart	L	656	PM Story Books-Gold	Rigby
Made's Birthday	L	250+	Little Celebrations	Pearson Learning
Magic All Around	L	250+	Literacy 2000	Rigby
Magic Fish	L	870	Littledale, Freya	Scholastic
Magic Money	L	250+	Adler, David	Random House
Magic Porridge Pot, The	L	497	Sunshine	Wright Group
Magpie's Tail, The	L	543	Pacific Literacy	Pacific Learning
Make Way for Ducklings	L	250+	McCloskey, Robert	Puffin Books
Manly Ferry Pigeon, The	L	375	Sunshine	Wright Group
Maple Thanksgiving, The	L		Little Celebrations	Pearson Learning
Marcella	L	250+	Literacy 2000	Rigby
Mare for Young Wolf, A	L	250+	Shefelman, Janice	Random House
Margarito's Carvings	L	250+	Little Celebrations	Pearson Learning
Martin Luther King Day	L	250+	Lowery, Linda	Scholastic
Martin Luther King, Jr.	L	290	Pebble Books	Grolier, Capstone
Marvin Redpost: Alone in His Teacher's House	L	250+	Sachar, Louis	Random House
Marvin Redpost: Is He a Girl?	L	250+	Sachar, Louis	Random House
Marvin Redpost: Kidnapped at Birth?	L	250+	Sachar, Louis	Random House
Marvin Redpost: Why Pick on Me?	L	250+	Sachar, Louis	Random House
Mary Maroney Hides Out	L	250+	Kline, Suzy	Bantam Doubleday Dell
Mary Marony and the Chocolate Surprise	L	250+	Kline, Suzy	Bantam Doubleday Dell
Mary Marony and the Snake	L	250+	Kline, Suzy	Bantam Doubleday Dell
Mary Marony, Mummy Girl	L	250+	Kline, Suzy	Bantam Doubleday Dell
Materials	L	250+	Discovery World	Rigby
Meet the Molesons	L	250+	Bos, Burny	North-South Books
Mermaid Island	L	250+	Frith, Margaret	Grosset & Dunlap
Miss Nelson Has a Field Day	L	250+	Allard, Harry	Scholastic
Miss Nelson Is Missing	L	598	Allard, Harry	Houghton Mifflin
Missing Fossil Mystery, The	L	250+	Herman, Emily	Hyperion
Mog at the Zoo	L	250+	Nicoll, Helen	The Penguin Group
Mog's Mumps	L	250+	Nicoll, Helen	The Penguin Group
Monsters Next Door, The	L	250+	Dadey, Debbie & Jones, Marcia	Scholastic
Mr. Gumpy's Outing	L	283	Burningham, John	Holt, Henry & Co.
Mr. Sun and Mr. Sea	L	506	Sunshine	Wright Group
Mrs. Jeepers' Batty Vacation	L	250+	Dadey, Debbie & Jones, Marcia	Scholastic
Mud Pony, The	L	764	Sunshine	Wright Group
Mummy's Gold, The	L	250+	McMullan, Kate	Grosset & Dunlap
My Wonderful Aunt, Story One	L	193	Sunshine	Wright Group
My Wonderful Aunt, Story Two	L	199	Sunshine	Wright Group
Mystery of the Blue Ring, The	L	250+	Giff, Patricia Reilly	Bantam Doubleday Dell
...of the Pirate Ghost, The	L	250+	Hayes, Geoffrey	Random House
...Tooth Gremlin	L	250+	Graves, Bonnie	Hyperion

Title	Level	Words	Author/Series	Publisher/Distributor
Mystery Seeds	L	250+	Reading Unlimited	Pacific Learning
Nine Lives of Adventure Cat, The	L	250+	Clymer, Susan	Scholastic
No Copycats Allowed!	L	250+	Graves, Bonnie	Hyperion
Octopuses, Squid, & Cuttlefish	L	231	Marine Life for Young Readers	Dominie
Oh, What a Daughter!	L	250+	Literacy 2000	Rigby
Old Enough for Magic	L	250+	Pickett, A.	HarperTrophy
Oliver and Amanda's Halloween	L	250+	Van Leeuwen, Jean	Puffin Books
Once When I Was Shipwrecked	L	250+	Literacy 2000	Rigby
Other Side of the Lake, The	L	250+	Little Celebrations	Pearson Learning
Over in the Meadow	L	375	Galdone, Paul	Simon & Schuster
Owl and the Pussy Cat	L	215	Lear, Edward	Scholastic
Owls in the Garden	L	670	PM Story Books-Gold	Rigby
Paloma's Party	L	250+	Little Celebrations	Pearson Learning
Partners	L	159	Home Connection Collection	Rigby
Pedro's Journal: A Voyage with Christopher Columbus	L	250+	Conrad, Pam	Scholastic
Pee Wee Scouts: A Pee Wee Christmas	L	250+	Delton, Judy	Bantam Doubleday Dell
Pee Wee Scouts: Blue Skies, French Fries	L	250+	Delton, Judy	Bantam Doubleday Dell
Pee Wee Scouts: Bookworm Buddies	L	250+	Delton, Judy	Bantam Doubleday Dell
Pee Wee Scouts: Computer Clues	L	250+	Delton, Judy	Bantam Doubleday Dell
Pee Wee Scouts: Cookies and Crutches	L	250+	Delton, Judy	Bantam Doubleday Dell
Pee Wee Scouts: Eggs with Legs	L	250+	Delton, Judy	Bantam Doubleday Dell
Pee Wee Scouts: Fishy Wishes	L	250+	Delton, Judy	Bantam Doubleday Dell
Pee Wee Scouts: Greedy Groundhogs	L	250+	Delton, Judy	Bantam Doubleday Dell
Pee Wee Scouts: Grumpy Pumpkins	L	250+	Delton, Judy	Bantam Doubleday Dell
Pee Wee Scouts: Halloween Helpers	L	250+	Delton, Judy	Bantam Doubleday Dell
Pee Wee Scouts: Lights, Action, Land-Ho!	L	250+	Delton, Judy	Bantam Doubleday Dell
Pee Wee Scouts: Lucky Dog Days	L	250+	Delton, Judy	Bantam Doubleday Dell
Pee Wee Scouts: Moans & Groans & Dinosaur Bones	L	250+	Delton, Judy	Bantam Doubleday Dell
Pee Wee Scouts: Pedal Power	L	250+	Delton, Judy	Bantam Doubleday Dell
Pee Wee Scouts: Pee Wee Pool Party	L	250+	Delton, Judy	Bantam Doubleday Dell
Pee Wee Scouts: Piles of Pets	L	250+	Delton, Judy	Bantam Doubleday Dell
Pee Wee Scouts: Planet Pee Wee	L	250+	Delton, Judy	Bantam Doubleday Dell
Pee Wee Scouts: Rosy Noses, Freezing Toes	L	250+	Delton, Judy	Bantam Doubleday Dell
Pee Wee Scouts: Send in the Clowns	L	250+	Delton, Judy	Bantam Doubleday Dell
Pee Wee Scouts: Sky Babies	L	250+	Delton, Judy	Bantam Doubleday Dell
Pee Wee Scouts: Sonny's Secret	L	250+	Delton, Judy	Bantam Doubleday Dell
Pee Wee Scouts: Spring Sprouts	L	250+	Delton, Judy	Bantam Doubleday Dell
Pee Wee Scouts: Stage Frightened	L	250+	Delton, Judy	Bantam Doubleday Dell
Pee Wee Scouts: Super Duper Pee Wee!	L	250+	Delton, Judy	Bantam Doubleday Dell
Pee Wee Scouts: Teeny Weeny Zucchinis	L	250+	Delton, Judy	Bantam Doubleday Dell
Pee Wee Scouts: That Mushy Stuff	L	250+	Delton, Judy	Bantam Doubleday Dell
Pee Wee Scouts: The Pee Wee Jubilee	L	250+	Delton, Judy	Bantam Doubleday Dell
Pee Wee Scouts: Trash Bash	L	250+	Delton, Judy	Bantam Doubleday Dell
Pee Wee Scouts: Tricks and Treats	L	250+	Delton, Judy	Bantam Doubleday Dell
Pee Wee Scouts: Wild, Wild West	L	250+	Delton, Judy	Bantam Doubleday Dell
Pee Wees on First	L	250+	Delton, Judy	Bantam Doubleday Dell
Pee Wees on Parade	L	250+	Delton, Judy	Bantam Doubleday Dell
Pee Wees on Skis	L	250+	Delton, Judy	Bantam Doubleday Dell
PeeWee Scouts	L	250+	Delton, Judy	Yearling
PeeWee's on First	L	250+	Delton, Judy	Yearling
Perfect the Pig	L	250+	Jeschke, Susan	Scholastic
Pet Sitters Plus Five	L	250+	Springstubb, Tricia	Scholastic

Title	Level	Words	Author/Series	Publisher/Distributor
Pete's Story	L	250+	Literacy 2000	Rigby
Pheasant and Kingfisher	L	910	Book Shop	Mondo Publishing
Photos, Photos	L	250+	Wildcats	Wright Group
Picked for the Team	L	709	PM Story Books-Gold	Rigby
Picking Apples and Pumpkins	L	250+	Hutchings, A. & R.	Scholastic
Pickle Puss	L	250+	Giff, Patricia Reilly	Bantam Doubleday Dell
Pied Piper	L	250+	Hunia, Fran	Ladybird Books
Pignocchio	L	250+	Pair-It Books	Steck-Vaughn
Pinky and Rex	L	250+	Howe, James	Simon & Schuster
Pinky and Rex and the Bully	L	250+	Howe, James	Simon & Schuster
Pinky and Rex and the Double-Dad Weekend	L	250+	Howe, James	Simon & Schuster
Pinky and Rex and the Mean Old Witch	L	250+	Howe, James	Simon & Schuster
Pinky and Rex and the New Baby	L	250+	Howe, James	Simon & Schuster
Pinky and Rex and the New Neighbors	L	250+	Howe, James	Simon & Schuster
Pinky and Rex and the Perfect Pumpkin	L	250+	Howe, James	Simon & Schuster
Pinky and Rex and the School Play	L	250+	Howe, James	Simon & Schuster
Pinky and Rex and the Spelling Bee	L	250+	Howe, James	Simon & Schuster
Pinky and Rex Get Married	L	250+	Howe, James	Simon & Schuster
Pioneer Bear	L	250+	Sandin, Joan	Random House
Play Ball, Amelia Bedelia	L	250+	Parish, Peggy	Harper & Row
Pony Trouble	L	250+	Gasque, Dale Blackwell	Hyperion
Pooped Troop, The	L	250+	Delton, Judy	Bantam Doubleday Dell
Pot of Stone Soup, A	L	250+	Ready Readers	Pearson Learning
Powder Puff Puzzle, The	L	250+	Giff, Patricia Reilly	Bantam Doubleday Dell
Power of Water, The	L	250+	Home Connection Collection	Rigby
Princess Josie's Pets	L	250+	Macdonald, Maryann	Hyperion
Priscilla and the Dinosaurs	L	340	Sunshine	Wright Group
Puppy Who Wanted a Boy, The	L	250+	Thayer, Jane	Scholastic
Quilt Story, The	L	250+	Johnston, Tony & DePaola, Tomie	Scholastic
Rabbit Stew	L	250+	Literacy 2000	Rigby
Rain Forest Adventure	L	482	Pair-It Books	Steck-Vaughn
Rapunzel	L	250+	Literacy 2000	Rigby
Raven's Gift	L	160	Books for Young Learners	Richard C. Owen
Red-Tailed Hawk, The	L	197	Books for Young Learners	Richard C. Owen
Rescue, The	L	176	Ready to Read	Pacific Learning
Riddle of the Red Purse, The	L	250+	Giff, Patricia Reilly	Bantam Doubleday Dell
River Rapids Ride, The	L	283	Sunshine	Wright Group
Rosie's Story	L	840	Book Shop	Mondo Publishing
Royal Drum, The	L	526	Book Shop	Mondo Publishing
Sadie and the Snowman	L	250+	Morgan, Allen	Scholastic
Say "Cheese	L	250+	Giff, Patricia Reilly	Bantam Doubleday Dell
School Mural, The	L	250+	Pair-It Books	Steck-Vaughn
Schoolyard Mystery, The	L	250+	Levy, Elizabeth	Scholastic
Science-Just Add Salt	L	250+	Markle, Sandra	Scholastic
Sculpture	L		Little Celebrations	Pearson Learning
Sea Otters	L	406	Storyteller Nonfiction	Wright Group/ McGraw-Hill
Secondhand Star	L	250+	Macdonald, Maryann	Hyperion
Secret Soldier, The	L	250+	McGovern, Ann	Scholastic
Giant, The	L		Literacy 2000	Rigby
	L	238	Wonder World	Wright Group
	L	284	Marine Life for Young Readers	Dominie

Title	Level	Words	Author/Series	Publisher/Distributor
Ships	L	275	Wonder World	Wright Group
Silent World, A	L		Literacy 2000	Rigby
Six Foolish Fishermen	L	715	Elkin, Benjamin	Children's Press
Six Things to Make	L	987	Book Shop	Mondo Publishing
Sky High	L	619	Pair-It Books	Steck-Vaughn
Slim Shorty and the Mules	L	411	Reading Unlimited	Pacific Learning
Snakes	L	252	Wonder World	Wright Group
Snow Daughter, The	L	505	Sunshine	Wright Group
Snow Goes to Town	L		Literacy 2000	Rigby
Solo Flyer	L	605	PM Story Books-Gold	Rigby
Sound, Heat & Light: Energy at Work	L	250+	Berger, Melvin	Scholastic
Space Dog and Roy	L	250+	Standiford, Natalie	Random House
Space Dog and the Pet Show	L	250+	Standiford, Natalie	Random House
Space Dog in Trouble	L	250+	Standiford, Natalie	Random House
Space Dog the Hero	L	250+	Standiford, Natalie	Random House
Spider and the King, The	L		Literacy 2000	Rigby
Spider's Web, A	L	323	Wonder World	Wright Group
Spoiled Rotten	L	250+	DeClements, Barthe	Hyperion
Squanto and the First Thanksgiving	L	250+	Celsi, Teresa	Steck-Vaughn
Statue of Liberty, The	L	250+	Penner, Lucille Recht	Random House
Storms!	L	359	Pair-It Books	Steck-Vaughn
Storytellers	L	506	Storyteller Nonfiction	Wright Group/ McGraw-Hill
Strike Me Down with a Stringbean	L	404	Read Alongs	Rigby
Sun, the Wind, & Tashira, The	L	371	Folk Tales	Mondo Publishing
Sunflower That Went Flop, The	L	637	Story Box	Wright Group
Sunshine	L	307	Pebble Books	Grolier, Capstone
Supermarket Chase, The	L	438	Sunshine	Wright Group
Surprise Dinner, The	L	680	PM Story Books-Gold	Rigby
Surprises	L	250+	Hopkins, Lee Bennett	HarperTrophy
Table for Two	L		Little Celebrations	Pearson Learning
Tale of Peter Rabbit, The	L	250+	Potter, Beatrix	Scholastic
Tales of Amanda Pig	L	250+	Van Leeuwen, Jean	Puffin Books
Teach Us, Amelia Bedelia	L	250+	Parish, Peggy	Scholastic
Teacher's Pet	L	250+	Dicks, Terrance	Scholastic
Tell Me a Story, Grandpa	L		Little Celebrations	Pearson Learning
Thank You, Amelia Bedelia	L	250+	Parish, Peggy	Harper & Row
Thank You, Amelia Bedelia	L	250+	Little Readers	Houghton Mifflin
There's a Rainbow in the River	L	250+	Home Connection Collection	Rigby
Things That Go: A Traveling Alphabet	L	250+	Reit, Seymour	Bantam Doubleday Dell
Thinking About Ants	L	662	Book Shop	Mondo Publishing
This Is My House	L	250+	Dorros, Arthur	Scholastic
Three Blind Mice Mystery, The	L	250+	Krensky, Stephen	Bantam Doubleday Dell
Three Little Pigs	L	919	Galdone, Paul	Houghton Mifflin
Three Little Pigs	L	250+	Once Upon a Time	Wright Group
Three Little Pigs, The	L	250+	Marshall, James	Scholastic
Three Sillies, The	L		Literacy 2000	Rigby
Three Smart Pals	L	250+	Rocklin, Joanne	Scholastic
Three Wishes, The	L	717	Book Shop	Mondo Publishing
Through Grandpa's Eyes	L	250+	MacLachlan, Patricia	HarperTrophy
Tongues Are for Tasting, Licking, Tricking	L		Literacy 2000	Rigby
Trees Belong to Everyone	L		Literacy 2000	Rigby

Title	Level	Words	Author/Series	Publisher/Distributor
Triceratops on the Farm	L	208	Wesley & the Dinosaurs	Wright Group
Triplet Trouble and the Bicycle Race	L	250+	Dadey, Debbie & Jones, Marcia	Scholastic
Triplet Trouble and the Class Trip	L	250+	Dadey, Debbie & Jones, Marcia	Scholastic
Triplet Trouble and the Cookie Contest	L	250+	Dadey, Debbie & Jones, Marcia	Scholastic
Triplet Trouble and the Field Day	L	250+	Dadey, Debbie & Jones, Marcia	Scholastic
Triplet Trouble and the Field Day Disaster	L	250+	Dadey, Debbie & Jones, Marcia	Scholastic
Triplet Trouble and the Pizza Party	L	250+	Dadey, Debbie & Jones, Marcia	Scholastic
Triplet Trouble and the Red Heart Race	L	250+	Dadey, Debbie & Jones, Marcia	Scholastic
Triplet Trouble and the Runaway Reindeer	L	250+	Dadey, Debbie & Jones, Marcia	Scholastic
Triplet Trouble and the Talent Show	L	250+	Dadey, Debbie & Jones, Marcia	Scholastic
Triplet Trouble and the Talent Show Mess	L	250+	Dadey, Debbie & Jones, Marcia	Scholastic
Trouble with Herbert, The	L	1830	Book Shop	Mondo Publishing
True Story of Balto, The	L	250+	Standiford, Natalie	Random House
True Story of Balto: The Bravest Dog Ever	L	250+	Standiford, Natalie	Random House
T-Shirt Triplets, The	L	344	Literacy 2000	Rigby
Twiddle Twins' Haunted House, The	L	1141	Book Shop	Mondo Publishing
Two Plus One Goes A.P.E.	L	250+	Springstubb, Tricia	Scholastic
Tyrannosaurus the Terrible	L	182	Wesley & the Dinosaurs	Wright Group
Upside-Down Reader, The	L	250+	Gruber, Wolfram	North-South Books
Using the Library	L	291	Wonder World	Wright Group
Vampire Trouble	L	250+	Dadey, Debbie & Jones, Marcia	Scholastic
Very Strange Dollhouse, A	L	250+	Dussling, Jennifer	Grosset & Dunlap
Very Thin Cat of Alloway Road, The	L		Literacy 2000	Rigby
Wacky Jacks	L	250+	Adler, David	Random House
Walk with Grandpa, A	L	388	Read Alongs	Rigby
Watch Out! Man-eating Snake	L	250+	Giff, Patricia Reilly	Bantam Doubleday Dell
Watching the Whales	L	267	Foundations	Wright Group
Wax Museum	L	250+	Cook, Donald	Grosset & Dunlap
Weather Poems for All Seasons	L	250+	Hopkins, Lee Bennett	HarperTrophy
We're Off to Thunder Mountain	L	270	Book Shop	Mondo Publishing
Whales-The Gentle Giants	L	250+	Milton, Joyce	Random House
What Do You Think?	L	250+	Wildcats	Wright Group
What Joy Found	L	250+	Ready Readers	Pearson Learning
What Keeps Them Warm?	L	156	Pacific Literacy	Pacific Learning
What Kind of Babysitter Is This?	L	250+	Johnson, Dolores	Scholastic
What Next, Baby Bear?	L	313	Murphy, Jill	Dial
What's It Like to Be a Fish?	L	250+	Little Readers	Houghton Mifflin
When I Broke the Office Window	L	257	City Kids	Rigby
When the Giants Came to Town	L	250+	Leonard, Marcia	Scholastic
When Tony Got Lost at the Zoo	L	122	City Kids	Rigby
Whistle for Willie	L	380	Keats, Ezra Jack	The Penguin Group
Whizz! Click!	L	285	Pacific Literacy	Pacific Learning
Why the Leopard Has Spots	L	250+	Pair-It Books	Steck-Vaughn
Why the Sea Is Salty	L		Literacy 2000	Rigby
Wide Street Club and the Duck Man, The	L	1057	Sunshine	Wright Group
Wild Swans, The	L	754	Tales from Hans Andersen	Wright Group
Wind Blew, The	L	169	Hutchins, Pat	Puffin Books
Wizard of Oz, The	L	903	Hunia, Fran	Ladybird Books
Wolf and the Seven Little Kids	L	250+	Hunia, Fran	Ladybird Books
...s of Willoughby Chase	L	250+	Aiken, Joan	Bantam Doubleday Dell
...n Water	L	250+	Home Connection Collection	Rigby
...lls	L		Literacy 2000	Rigby

Title	Level	Words	Author/Series	Publisher/Distributor
Young Arthur Ashe: Brave Champion	L	250+	First-Start Biography	Troll
Young Clara Barton: Battlefield Nurse	L	250+	First-Start Biography	Troll
Young Davy Crockett: Frontier Fighter	L	250+	First-Start Biography	Troll
Young Helen Keller: Woman of Courage	L	250+	First-Start Biography	Troll
Young Jackie Robinson: Baseball Hero	L	250+	First Start Biography	Troll
Young Jim Thorpe: All-American Athlete	L	250+	First-Start Biography	Troll
Young Orville and Wilbur Wright: First to Fly	L	250+	First-Start Biography	Troll
Young Reggie Jackson: Hall of Fame Champion	L	250+	First-Start Biography	Troll
Young Rosa Parks: A Civil Rights Heroine	L	250+	First-Start Biography	Troll
Young Squanto: The First Thanksgiving	L	250+	First-Start Biography	Troll
Young Thurgood Marshall: Fighter for Equality	L	250+	First-Start Biography	Troll
Young Tom Edison: Great Inventor	L	250+	First-Start Biography	Troll
Abby	M	250+	Hanel, Wolfram	North-South Books
Abe Lincoln's Hat	M	250+	Brenner, Martha	Random House
Adventures of Ratman	M	250+	Weiss & Freidman	Random House
Aliens Don't Wear Braces	M	250+	Dadey, Debbie & Jones, Marcia	Scholastic
Aliens for Breakfast	M	250+	Etra, Jonathan & Spinner, Stephanie	Random House
Aliens for Dinner	M	250+	Spinner, Stephanie	Random House
Aliens for Lunch	M	250+	Spinner, Stephanie & Etra, Jonathan	Random House
All Star Fever	M	250+	Christopher, Matt	Little, Brown & Co.
Angels Don't Know Karate	M	250+	Dadey, Debbie & Jones, Marcia	Scholastic
Animals in Danger	M	250+	Pair-It Books	Steck-Vaughn
Annie's Secret Diary	M	250+	Little Celebrations	Pearson Learning
Art Around the World	M	250+	Discovery World	Rigby
Art Lesson, The	M	246	DePaola, Tomie	Putnam
Arthur Accused!	M	250+	Brown, Marc	Little, Brown & Co.
Arthur and the Crunch Cereal Contest	M	250+	Brown, Marc	Little, Brown & Co.
Arthur and the Lost Diary	M	250+	Brown, Marc	Little, Brown & Co.
Arthur and the Popularity Test	M	250+	Brown, Marc	Little, Brown & Co.
Arthur and the Scare-Your-Pants-Off Club	M	250+	Brown, Marc	Little, Brown & Co.
Arthur Makes the Team	M	250+	Brown, Marc	Little, Brown & Co.
Arthur Rocks with BINKY	M	250+	Brown, Marc	Little, Brown & Co.
Arthur's Mystery Envelope	M	250+	Brown, Marc	Little, Brown & Co.
Asteroid, The	M	752	PM Story Books-Gold	Rigby
At the Edge of the Sea	M	693	Sunshine	Wright Group
Aunt Flossie's Hats (and Crab Cakes Later)	M	250+	Howard, Elizabeth	Scholastic
Back to the Dentist	M	199	City Kids	Rigby
Ballad of Robin Hood, The	M	250+	Literacy 2000	Rigby
Baseball Flyhawk	M	250+	Christopher, Matt	Little, Brown & Co.
Baseball Heroes, The	M	250+	Schultz, Irene	Wright Group
Baseball Pals	M	250+	Christopher, Matt	Little, Brown & Co.
Basket Counts, The	M	250+	Christopher, Matt	Little, Brown & Co.
Bats	M	250+	Literacy 2000	Rigby
Bears' Picnic	M	250+	Berenstain, Stan & Jan	Random House
Bears' Christmas	M	250+	Berenstain, Stan & Jan	Random House
Bears on Hemlock Mountain, The	M	250+	Dalgliesh, Alice	Aladdin
Beast and the Halloween Horror	M	250+	Giff, Patricia Reilly	Bantam Doubleday Dell
Beast in Ms. Rooney's Room, The	M	250+	Giff, Patricia Reilly	Bantam Doubleday Dell
Beauregard the Cat	M	876	Book Shop	Mondo Publishing
Beekeeper, The	M	250+	Literacy 2000	Rigby
Berenstain Bears & the Missing Honey	M	531	Berenstain, Stan & Jan	Random House

Title	Level	Words	Author/Series	Publisher/Distributor
Big Bulgy Fat Black Slugs	M	250+	Stepping Stones	Nelson/Michaels Assoc.
Big Fish, The	M	301	Yukish, Joe	Kaeden Books
Bigfoot Doesn't Square Dance	M	250+	Dadey, Debbie & Jones, Marcia	Scholastic
Bird Behavior: Living Together	M	631	Sunshine	Wright Group
Birds of the City	M	840	Sunshine	Wright Group
Blue Ribbon Blues	M	250+	Spinelli, Jerry	Random House
Blueberries for Sal	M	250+	McCloskey, Robert	Scholastic
Boats Afloat	M	752	Sunshine	Wright Group
Bogeymen Don't Play Football	M	250+	Dadey, Debbie & Jones, Marcia	Scholastic
Book About Your Skeleton, A	M	250+	Gross, Ruth Belov	Scholastic
Boundless Grace	M	250+	Hoffman, Mary	Scholastic
Boy Who Stretched to the Sky, The	M	463	Book Bank	Wright Group
Brad and Butter Play Ball!	M	250+	Hughes, Dean	Random House
Brain-in-a-Box	M	250+	Matthews, Steve	Sundance
Brave Maddie Egg	M	250+	Standiford, Natalie	Random House
Brith the Terrible	M	250+	Literacy 2000	Rigby
Build, Build, Build	M	470	Sunshine	Wright Group
Buried Eye, The	M	250+	Schultz, Irene	Wright Group
Buster's Dino Dilemma	M	250+	Brown, Marc	Little, Brown & Co.
Cake, The	M	250+	Read Alongs	Rigby
Camp Sink or Swim	M	250+	Davis, Gibbs	Random House
Can Do, Jenny Archer	M	250+	Conford, Ellen	Random House
Case for Jenny Archer, A	M	250+	Conford, Ellen	Random House
Case of the Elevator Duck, The	M	250+	Brends, Polly Berrien	Random House
Case of the Hungry Stranger, The	M	1358	Bonsall, Crosby	HarperTrophy
Cat Burglar, The	M	250+	Krailing, Tessa	Barron's Educational
Catch That Pass!	M	250+	Christopher, Matt	Little, Brown & Co.
Catcher with a Glass Arm	M	250+	Christopher, Matt	Little, Brown & Co.
Catcher's Mask, The	M	250+	Christopher, Matt	Little, Brown & Co.
Caterpillars	M	114	Book Shop	Mondo Publishing
Caves	M	250+	Discovery World	Rigby
Center Court Sting	M	250+	Christopher, Matt	Little, Brown & Co.
Centerfield Ballhawk	M	250+	Christopher, Matt	Little, Brown & Co.
Chair for My Mother, A	M	250+	Williams, Vera B.	Scholastic
Challenge at Second Base	M	250+	Christopher, Matt	Little, Brown & Co.
Cherries and Cherry Pits	M	250+	Williams, Vera B.	Houghton Mifflin
Chester the Wizard	M	250+	Reading Unlimited	Pacific Learning
Chicken Soup with Rice	M	310	Sendak, Maurice	HarperCollins
Chicken Sunday	M	250+	Polacco, Patricia	Scholastic
Circus Mystery, The	M	250+	Schultz, Irene	Wright Group
Cities Around the World	M	250+	Pair-It Books	Steck-Vaughn
Clouds	M	250+	Literacy 2000	Rigby
Cloudy with a Chance of Meatballs	M	250+	Barrett, Judi	Atheneum
Clue in the Castle, The	M	250+	Schultz, Irene	Wright Group
Cobwebs, Elephants, and Stars	M	779	Sunshine	Wright Group
Comeback Challenge, The	M	250+	Christopher, Matt	Little, Brown & Co.
Connie's Dance	M	361	Windmill Books	Rigby
Copper Lady, The	M	250+	Ross, Alice & Kent	Carolrhoda Books
Corn: An American Indian Gift	M	690	Pair-It Books	Steck-Vaughn
Count Your Money with the Polk Street School	M	250+	Giff, Patricia Reilly	Bantam Doubleday Dell
Counterfeit Tackle, The	M	250+	Christopher, Matt	Little, Brown & Co.
Crabs	M	272	Wonder World	Wright Group

Title	Level	Words	Author/Series	Publisher/Distributor
Crabs	M	501	Sunshine	Wright Group
Crabs, Shrimp, & Lobsters	M	322	Marine Life for Young Readers	Dominie
Crackerjack Halfback	M	250+	Christopher, Matt	Little, Brown & Co.
Crane Wife, The	M	620	Pair-It Books	Steck-Vaughn
Crinkum Crankum	M	250+	Ready to Read	Pacific Learning
Crocodile in the Library	M	250+	Ready to Read	Pacific Learning
Crocodile's Christmas Jandles	M	250+	Ready to Read	Pacific Learning
Cupid Doesn't Flip Hamburgers	M	250+	Dadey, Debbie & Jones, Marcia	Scholastic
Curse of the Squirrel, The	M	250+	Yep, Laurence	Random House
Cyclops Doesn't Roller-Skate	M	250+	Dadey, Debbie & Jones, Marcia	Scholastic
Dancing with the Indians	M	250+	Medearis, Angela	Scholastic
Day for J.J. and Me, A	M	371	Evangeline Nicholas Collection	Wright Group
Day of Ahmed's Secret, A	M	250+	Heide, Florence & Gilliland, Judith	Scholastic
Day of the Dragon King	M	250+	Osborne, Mary Pope	Random House
Dayton and the Happy Tree	M	1237	Sunshine	Wright Group
Deadly Dungeon, The	M	250+	Roy, Ron	Random House
Dear Grandma	M	264	Storyteller Nonfiction	Wright Group/ McGraw-Hill
Desert Treasure	M	250+	Pair-It Books	Steck-Vaughn
Diamond Champs, The	M	250+	Christopher, Matt	Little, Brown & Co.
Diamond of Doom, The	M	250+	Schultz, Irene	Wright Group
Did You Carry the Flag Today, Charley	M	250+	Caudill, Rebecca	Bantam Doubleday Dell
Dinosaurs Before Dark	M	250+	Osborne, Mary Pope	Random House
Dirt Bike Racer	M	250+	Christopher, Matt	Little, Brown & Co.
Dirt Bike Runaway	M	250+	Christopher, Matt	Little, Brown & Co.
Dog Who Wanted to Be a Tiger!, The	M		Little Celebrations	Pearson Learning
Dog's Best Friend, A	M	647	Pair-It Books	Steck-Vaughn
Dolphins at Daybreak	M	250+	Osborne, Mary Pope	Random House
Donkey	M	250+	Literacy 2000	Rigby
Donkey Rescues	M	250+	Krailing, Tessa	Barron's Educational
Don't Forget the Bacon	M	174	Hutchins, Pat	Puffin Books
Double Play at Short	M	250+	Christopher, Matt	Little, Brown & Co.
Double Trouble	M	250+	Literacy 2000	Rigby
Dr. Jekyll, Orthodontist	M	250+	Greenburg, Dan	Grosset & Dunlap
Dracula Doesn't Drink Lemonade	M	250+	Dadey, Debbie	Scholastic
Dragons Don't Cook Pizza	M	250+	Dadey, Debbie & Jones, Marcia	Scholastic
Dream Catchers	M	176	Storyteller-Night Crickets	Wright Group/ McGraw-Hill
Drinking Gourd	M	250+	Monjo, Ferdinand N.	HarperTrophy
Drought Marker, The	M	250+	Literacy 2000	Rigby
Duck in the Gun, The	M	250+	Literacy 2000	Rigby
Earthquake	M	415	Jellybeans	Rigby
Eat!	M	250+	Kroll, Steven	Hyperion
Edward's Night Light	M	622	Reading Corners	Dominie
Eggs and Baby Birds	M	539	Sunshine	Wright Group
Eliza the Hypnotizer	M	250+	Granger, Michelle	Scholastic
Elmer and the Dragon	M	250+	Gannett, Ruth Stiles	Random House
Elves Don't Wear Hard Hats, The	M	250+	Dadey, Debbie & Jones, Marcia	Scholastic
Elvis the Turnip…And Me	M	250+	Greenburg, Dan	Grosset & Dunlap
Emilio and the River	M	403	Sunshine	Wright Group
Emily Arrow Promises to Do Better This Year	M	250+	Giff, Patricia Reilly	Bantam Doubleday Dell
Emily Eyefinger	M	250+	Ball, Duncan	Aladdin

Title	Level	Words	Author/Series	Publisher/Distributor
Emma, the Birthday Clown	M	1887	Sunshine	Wright Group
Er-Lang and the Suns: A Tale from China	M	250+	Folk Tales	Mondo Publishing
Everybody Cooks Rice	M	250+	Dooley, Norah	Scholastic
Everyday Forces	M	250+	Discovery World	Rigby
Explorers: Searching for Adventure	M	250+	Pair-It Books	Steck-Vaughn
Expressway Jewels	M	368	Evangeline Nicholas Collection	Wright Group
Fancy Feet	M	250+	Giff, Patricia Reilly	Bantam Doubleday Dell
Farmer's Journey, The	M	250+	Little Celebrations	Pearson Learning
Fibers Made by People	M	442	Sunshine	Wright Group
Fiddle and the Gun, The	M	250+	Literacy 2000	Rigby
Fighting Tackle	M	250+	Christopher, Matt	Little, Brown & Co.
Fiji Flood, The	M	250+	Schultz, Irene	Wright Group
Fish Face	M	250+	Giff, Patricia Reilly	Bantam Doubleday Dell
Fishing Off the Wharf	M	274	Pacific Literacy	Pacific Learning
Five True Dog Stories	M	250+	Davidson, Margaret	Scholastic
Five True Horse Stories	M	250+	Davidson, Margaret	Scholastic
Flowers for Mrs. Falepau	M	857	Book Bank	Wright Group
Flying Trunk, The	M	644	Tales from Hans Andersen	Wright Group
Football Fugitive	M	250+	Christopher, Matt	Little, Brown & Co.
Fox Steals Home, The	M	250+	Christopher, Matt	Little, Brown & Co.
Frankenstein Doesn't Plant Petunias	M	250+	Dadey, Debbie	Scholastic
Frankenstein Doesn't Slam Hockey Pucks	M	250+	Dadey, Debbie & Jones, Marcia	Scholastic
Frankenstein Moved on to the 4th Floor	M	250+	Levy, Elizabeth	Harper & Row
Freckle Juice	M	250+	Blume, Judy	Bantam Doubleday Dell
Frog Who Would Be King, The	M	250+	Walker, Kate	Mondo
Funny Old Man and the Funny Old Woman, The	M	562	Book Shop	Mondo Publishing
Game for Jamie, A	M	572	Sunshine	Wright Group
Gargoyles Don't Drive School Buses	M	250+	Dadey, Debbie & Jones, Marcia	Scholastic
Gaston the Giant	M	331	New Way Orange	Steck-Vaughn
Genies Don't Ride Bicycles	M	250+	Dadey, Debbie & Jones, Marcia	Scholastic
George Washington's Mother	M	250+	Fritz, Jean	Scholastic
Ghost in Tent 19, The	M	250+	O'Connor, Jim & Jane	Random House
Ghost Named Wanda, A	M	250+	Greenburg, Dan	Grosset & Dunlap
Ghost Town at Sundown	M	250+	Osborne, Mary Pope	Random House
Ghost Town Treasure	M	250+	Bulla, Clyde Robert	The Penguin Group
Ghosts Don't Eat Potato Chips	M	250+	Dadey, Debbie & Jones, Marcia	Scholastic
Ghouls Don't Scoop Ice Cream	M	250+	Dadey, Debbie & Jones, Marcia	Scholastic
Giant Jack's Boots	M	420	Book Bank	Wright Group
Giant's Cake	M	250+	Learning Media	Mondo Publishing
Giants Don't Go Snowboarding	M	250+	Dadey, Debbie & Jones, Marcia	Scholastic
Gladys and Max Love Bob	M	459	Book Bank	Wright Group
Golden Goose, The	M	250+	Literacy 2000	Rigby
Good-for-Nothing Dog, The	M	250+	Schultz, Irene	Wright Group
Great Dinosaur Hunt, The	M	250+	Schultz, Irene	Wright Group
Great Grumbler and the Wonder	M	250+	Ready to Read	Pacific Learning
Greatest Binnie in the World, The	M	709	Sunshine	Wright Group
Great-Grandpa's in the Litter Box	M	250+	Greenburg, Dan	Grosset & Dunlap
Gremlins Don't Chew Bubble Gum	M	250+	Dadey, Debbie & Jones, Marcia	Scholastic
Hand Tools	M	367	Wonder World	Wright Group
Hard Drive to Short	M	250+	Christopher, Matt	Little, Brown & Co.
Haunted Halloween, The	M	250+	Schultz, Irene	Wright Group
Helen Keller	M	250+	Davidson, Margaret	Scholastic

Title	Level	Words	Author/Series	Publisher/Distributor
Henry's Choice	M	527	Reading Unlimited	Pacific Learning
Hercules Doesn't Pull Teeth	M	250+	Dadey, Debbie & Jones, Marcia	Scholastic
Hidden Hand, The	M	250+	Schultz, Irene	Wright Group
Hippo from Another Planet	M	250+	Little Celebrations	Pearson Learning
Hit-Away Kid, The	M	250+	Christopher, Matt	Little, Brown & Co.
Hoopstars: Go to the Hoop!	M	250+	Hughes, Dean	Random House
Horrakapotchkin	M	250+	Ready to Read	Pacific Learning
Hour of the Olympics	M	250+	Osborne, Mary Pope	Random House
House of the Horrible Ghosts	M	250+	Hayes, Geoffrey	Random House
Houses	M	279	Wonder World	Wright Group
How a Volcano Is Formed	M	135	Wonder World	Wright Group
How Do You Measure a Dinosaur?	M	257	Pacific Literacy	Pacific Learning
How the Giraffe Became a Giraffe	M	648	Sunshine	Wright Group
Howling at the Hauntly's	M	250+	Dadey, Debbie & Jones, Marcia	Scholastic
Hunt for Pirate Gold, The	M	250+	Schultz, Irene	Wright Group
I Can't Said the Ant	M	250+	Cameron, Polly	Scholastic
I Hate Camping	M	250+	Petersen, P. J.	The Penguin Group
I Like Shopping	M	287	Sunshine	Wright Group
I Love the Beach	M	250+	Literacy 2000	Rigby
Ice Magic	M	250+	Christopher, Matt	Little, Brown & Co.
I'm No One Else But Me	M	1010	Book Bank	Wright Group
I'm Out of My Body…Please Leave a Message	M	250+	Greenburg, Dan	Grosset & Dunlap
In Danger	M	250+	Home Connection Collection	Rigby
In the Clouds	M	250+	Literacy 2000	Rigby
In the Dinosaur's Paw	M	250+	Giff, Patricia Reilly	Bantam Doubleday Dell
Inside a Rain Forest	M	353	Pair-It Books	Steck-Vaughn
Inventor's Diary, The	M	271	Pacific Literacy	Pacific Learning
Inventors: Making Things Better	M	250+	Pair-It Books	Steck-Vaughn
Invisible Dog, The	M	250+	King-Smith, Dick	Alfred A. Knopf, Inc.
Invisible in the Third Grade	M	250+	Cuyler, Margery	Scholastic
Island Baby	M	250+	Keller, Holly	Scholastic
It's About Time	M	481	Storyteller Nonfiction	Wright Group/ McGraw-Hill
Japan	M	488	Pair-It Books	Steck-Vaughn
Jenny Archer to the Rescue	M	250+	Conford, Ellen	Little, Brown & Co.
Jenny Archer, Author	M	250+	Conford, Ellen	Little, Brown & Co.
Jilly the Kid	M	250+	Krailing, Tessa	Barron's Educational
Job for Jenny Archer, A	M	250+	Conford, Ellen	Little, Brown & Co.
Johnny Long Legs	M	250+	Christopher, Matt	Little, Brown & Co.
Junie B. Jones and a Little Monkey Business	M	250+	Park, Barbara	Random House
Junie B. Jones and Her Big Fat Mouth	M	250+	Park, Barbara	Random House
Junie B. Jones and Some Sneaky Peeky Spying	M	250+	Park, Barbara	Random House
Junie B. Jones and that Meanie Jim's Birthday	M	250+	Park, Barbara	Random House
Junie B. Jones and the Stupid Smelly Bus	M	250+	Park, Barbara	Random House
Junie B. Jones and the Yucky Blucky Fruitcake	M	250+	Park, Barbara	Random House
Junie B. Jones Has a Monster Under Her Bed	M	250+	Park, Barbara	Random House
Junie B. Jones Is a Beauty Shop Guy	M	250+	Park, Barbara	Random House
Junie B. Jones Is a Party Animal	M	250+	Park, Barbara	Random House
Junie B. Jones Is Not a Crook	M	250+	Park, Barbara	Random House
Junie B. Jones Loves Handsome Warren	M	250+	Park, Barbara	Random House
Junie B. Jones Smells Something Fishy	M	250+	Park, Barbara	Random House
Junior Gymnasts: #2 Katie's Big Move	M	250+	Slater, Teddy	Scholastic

Title	Level	Words	Author/Series	Publisher/Distributor
Kate Shelley and the Midnight Express	M	250+	Wetterer, Margaret	Carolrhoda Books
Kid Who Only Hit Homers, The	M	250+	Christopher, Matt	Little, Brown & Co.
Kids in Ms. Colman's Class: Author Day	M	250+	Martin, Ann M.	Scholastic
King Arthur	M	250+	Brown, Marc	Little, Brown & Co.
Knight at Dawn, The	M	250+	Osborne, Mary Pope	Random House
Knights Don't Teach Piano	M	250+	Dadey, Debbie & Jones, Marcia	Scholastic
Korky Paul	M	250+	Discovery World	Rigby
Lavender the Library Cat	M	418	Jellybeans	Rigby
Lazy Jackal, The	M	561	Sunshine	Wright Group
Lazy Lions, Lucky Lambs	M	250+	Giff, Patricia Reilly	Bantam Doubleday Dell
Legend of the Hummingbird, The	M	250+	Folk Tales	Mondo Publishing
Leprechauns Don't Play Basketball	M	250+	Dadey, Debbie & Jones, Marcia	Scholastic
Let's Get Moving	M	250+	Literacy 2000	Rigby
Let's Go, Philadelphia!	M	250+	Giff, Patricia Reilly	Bantam Doubleday Dell
Life in the Desert	M	250+	Pair-It Books	Steck-Vaughn
Lighthouse Mermaid, The	M	250+	Karr, Kathleen	Hyperion
Lily and Miss Liberty	M	250+	Stephens, Carla	Scholastic
Lion and the Mouse, The	M	499	Aesop's Fables	Dominie
Lions at Lunchtime	M	250+	Osborne, Mary Pope	Random House
Listening in Bed	M	116	Book Bank	Wright Group
Little Firefighter, The	M	867	Sunshine	Wright Group
Little Lefty	M	250+	Christopher, Matt	Little, Brown & Co.
Little Old Lady Who Danced on the Moon, The	M	711	Sunshine	Wright Group
Little Swan	M	250+	Geras, Adele	Random House
Little Tin Soldier,The	M	766	Tales from Hans Andersen	Wright Group
Little Whale, The	M	1057	Sunshine	Wright Group
Little Women	M	250+	Bullseye	Random House
Little, Little Man, The	M	741	Book Bank	Wright Group
Littles and the Great Halloween Scare, The	M	250+	Peterson, John	Scholastic
Littles and the Lost Children, The	M	250+	Peterson, John	Scholastic
Littles and the Terrible Tiny Kid, The	M	250+	Peterson, John	Scholastic
Littles and the Trash Tinies, The	M	250+	Peterson, John	Scholastic
Littles Give a Party, The	M	250+	Peterson, John	Scholastic
Littles Go Exploring, The	M	250+	Peterson, John	Scholastic
Littles Go to School, The	M	250+	Peterson, John	Scholastic
Littles Have a Wedding, The	M	250+	Peterson, John	Scholastic
Littles Take a Trip, The	M	250+	Peterson, John	Scholastic
Littles to the Rescue, The	M	250+	Peterson, John	Scholastic
Littles, The	M	250+	Peterson, John	Scholastic
Lizards and Salamanders	M	250+	Reading Unlimited	Pacific Learning
Locked in the Library!	M	250+	Brown, Marc	Little, Brown & Co.
Long Grass of Tumbledown Road	M	283	Read Alongs	Rigby
Long Shot for Paul	M	250+	Christopher, Matt	Little, Brown & Co.
Look at Dogs, A	M	551	Pair-It Books	Steck-Vaughn
Look at Spiders, A	M	785	Pair-It Books	Steck-Vaughn
Look of Snakes, A	M	784	Pair-It Books	Steck-Vaughn
Look Who's Playing First Base	M	250+	Christopher, Matt	Little, Brown & Co.
Lucky Baseball Bat, The	M	250+	Christopher, Matt	Little, Brown & Co.
Lucky Last Luke	M	250+	Clark, Margaret	Sundance
Mad Scientist, the Mountain Gorillas	M	250+	Schultz, Irene	Wright Group
Magic Ride, The	M	170	Book Bank	Wright Group
Making Friends on Beacon Street	M	250+	Literacy 2000	Rigby

Title	Level	Words	Author/Series	Publisher/Distributor
Man Out at First	M	250+	Christopher, Matt	Little, Brown & Co.
Martians Don't Take Temperatures	M	250+	Dadey, Debbie & Jones, Marcia	Scholastic
Martin's Mighty Hit	M	390	Windmill Books	Rigby
Marvelous Treasure, The	M	481	Sunshine	Wright Group
Maui and the Sun	M	359	Pacific Literacy	Pacific Learning
Maui and the Sun	M	250+	Ready to Read	Pacific Learning
Maybe Yes, Maybe No, Maybe Maybe	M	250+	Patron, Susan	Bantam Doubleday Dell
Medal for Nickie, A	M	262	Sunshine	Wright Group
Mermaids Don't Run Track	M	250+	Dadey, Debbie & Jones, Marcia	Scholastic
Michael Jordan	M	250+	Edwards, Nick	Scholastic
Midnight on the Moon	M	250+	Osborne, Mary Pope	Random House
Milo's Great Invention	M	250+	Pair-It Books	Steck-Vaughn
Minerva's Dream	M	250+	Pair-It Books	Steck-Vaughn
Miracle at the Plate	M	250+	Christopher, Matt	Little, Brown & Co.
Misfortune Cookie, The	M	250+	Greenburg, Dan	Grosset & Dunlap
Mitten, The	M	250+	Brett, Jan	Scholastic
Moana's Island	M	450	Sunshine	Wright Group
Molly's Pilgrim	M	250+	Cohen, Barbara	Bantam Doubleday Dell
Momotaro	M	631	Sunshine	Wright Group
Monster for Hire	M	250+	Wilson, Trevor	Mondo Publishing
Monster Rabbit Runs Amuck!	M	250+	Giff, Patricia Reilly	Bantam Doubleday Dell
Monsters Don't Scuba Dive	M	250+	Dadey, Debbie & Jones, Marcia	Scholastic
Most Terrible Creature in the World, The	M	340	Pacific Literacy	Pacific Learning
Mouse Party!	M		Little Celebrations	Pearson Learning
Mr. Beep	M	250+	Read Alongs	Rigby
Mrs. Always Goes Shopping	M	423	Sunshine	Wright Group
Mrs. Bubble's Baby	M	250+	Ready to Read	Pacific Learning
Mummies Don't Coach Softball	M	250+	Dadey, Debbie & Jones, Marcia	Scholastic
Mummies in the Morning	M	250+	Osborne, Mary Pope	Random House
Mutt and the Lifeguards	M	754	Sunshine	Wright Group
My Father's Dragon	M	250+	Gannett, Ruth Stiles	Random House
My Prairie Summer	M	250+	Pair-It Books	Steck-Vaughn
My Son, the Time Traveler	M	250+	Greenburg, Dan	Grosset & Dunlap
My Wonderful Aunt, Story Five	M	493	Sunshine	Wright Group
My Wonderful Aunt, Story Four	M	436	Sunshine	Wright Group
My Wonderful Aunt, Story Six	M	432	Sunshine	Wright Group
My Wonderful Aunt, Story Three	M	392	Sunshine	Wright Group
Mystery in the Night Woods	M	250+	Peterson, John	Scholastic
Mystery of the Dark Old House, The	M	250+	Schultz, Irene	Wright Group
Mystery of the Missing Dog, The	M	250+	Schultz, Irene	Wright Group
Mystery of the Stolen Bike, The	M	250+	Brown, Marc	Little, Brown & Co.
Mystery of the Talking Tail, The	M	250+	Clark, Margaret	Sundance
Nana's in the Plum Tree	M	250+	Ready to Read	Pacific Learning
Nannies for Hire	M	250+	Hest, Amy	William Morrow & Co.
Nature's Celebration	M	250+	Literacy 2000	Rigby
Never Trust a Cat Who Wears Earrings	M	250+	Greenburg, Dan	Grosset & Dunlap
Night of the Ninjas	M	250+	Osborne, Mary Pope	Random House
Night Owls, The	M	368	Wonder World	Wright Group
Nine True Dolphin Stories	M	250+	Davidson, Margaret	Scholastic
No Arm in Left Field	M	250+	Christopher, Matt	Little, Brown & Co.
Now You See Me…Now You Don't	M	250+	Greenburg, Dan	Grosset & Dunlap
Old Bones	M	848	Sunshine	Wright Group

Title	Level	Words	Author/Series	Publisher/Distributor
Old Friends	M	345	Literacy 2000	Rigby
Old Man and the Bear, The	M	250+	Hanel, Wolfram	North-South Books
Old Rocking Chair, The	M	250+	Root, Phyllis	Scholastic
Old Woman Who Lived in a Vinegar Bottle, The	M	1161	Book Shop	Mondo Publishing
On with the Show!	M	250+	Pair-It Books	Steck-Vaughn
One Bad Thing About Father, The	M	250+	Monjo, Ferdinand N.	HarperTrophy
One- Eyed Jake	M	547	Hutchins, Pat	Morrow
One in the Middle Is the Green Kangaroo, The	M	250+	Blume, Judy	Bantam Doubleday Dell
Onion Sundaes	M	250+	Adler, David	Random House
Paint Brush Kid, The	M	250+	Bulla, Clyde Robert	Random House
Pajama Party	M	250+	Hest, Amy	William Morrow & Co.
Pandas in the Mountains	M	735	PM Story Books-Gold	Rigby
Patches	M	250+	Szymanski, Lois	Avon Camelot
Patrick and the Leprechaun	M	677	PM Story Books-Gold	Rigby
Phantoms Don't Drive Sports Cars	M	250+	Dadey, Debbie & Jones, Marcia	Scholastic
Picture Book of Hellen Keller, A	M	250+	Little Readers	Houghton Mifflin
Pied Piper, The	M	585	Sunshine	Wright Group
Pirates Don't Wear Pink Sunglasses	M	250+	Dadey, Debbie & Jones, Marcia	Scholastic
Pirates Past Noon	M	250+	Osborne, Mary Pope	Random House
Polar Bears Past Bedtime	M	250+	Osborne, Mary Pope	Random House
Postcard Pest, The	M	250+	Giff, Patricia Reilly	Bantam Doubleday Dell
Present from Aunt Skidoo, The	M	250+	Literacy 2000	Rigby
Purple Climbing Days	M	250+	Giff, Patricia Reilly	Bantam Doubleday Dell
Rabbit Catches the Sun	M	621	Sunshine	Wright Group
Rabbits	M	250+	Literacy 2000	Rigby
Rashee and the Seven Elephants	M	250+	Little Celebrations	Pearson Learning
Rats on the Range	M	250+	Marshall, James	Puffin Books
Rats on the Range and Other Stories	M	250+	Marshall, James	The Penguin Group
Rats on the Roof	M	250+	Marshall, James	Troll
Rats on the Roof and Other Stories	M	250+	Marshall, James	The Penguin Group
Red and Blue Mittens	M	250+	Reading Unlimited	Pacific Learning
Red Ribbon Rosie	M	250+	Marzollo, Jean	Random House
Return of Rinaldo, the Sly Fox	M	250+	Scheffler, Ursel	North-South Books
Return of the Third-Grade Ghost Hunters	M	250+	Maccarone, Grace	Scholastic
Rinaldo the Sly Fox	M	250+	Scheffler, Ursel	North-South Books
Rip-Roaring Russell	M	250+	Hurwitz, Johanna	The Penguin Group
Robber Pig and the Ginger Bear	M	403	Read Alongs	Rigby
Robber Pig and the Green Eggs	M	250+	Read Alongs	Rigby
Robber, The	M	1255	Sunshine	Wright Group
Rumpelstiltskin	M	250+	Once Upon a Time	Wright Group
Russell and Elisa	M	250+	Hurwitz, Johanna	The Penguin Group
Russell Rides Again	M	250+	Hurwitz, Johanna	Puffin Books
Russell Sprouts	M	250+	Hurwitz, Johanna	Puffin Books
Sable	M	250+	Hesse, Karen	Henry Holt & Co.
Sam's Glasses	M	250+	Literacy 2000	Rigby
Santa Claus Doesn't Mop Floors	M	250+	Dadey, Debbie	Scholastic
Save the River!	M	250+	Pair-It Books	Steck-Vaughn
Scrunder Goes Wandering	M	250+	Krailing, Tessa	Barron's Educational
Search for the Lost Cave, The	M	250+	Schultz, Irene	Wright Group
Second Grade-Friends Again!	M	250+	Cohen, Miriam	Scholastic
Secret at the Polk Street School, The	M	250+	Giff, Patricia Reilly	Bantam Doubleday Dell
Secret of the Monster Book, The	M	250+	Schultz, Irene	Wright Group

Title	Level	Words	Author/Series	Publisher/Distributor
Secret of the Old Oak Trunk, The	M	250+	Schultz, Irene	Wright Group
Secret of the Song, The	M	250+	Schultz, Irene	Wright Group
Selli and Kana' Ti	M	250+	Folk Tales	Mondo Publishing
Shadow Over Second	M	250+	Christopher, Matt	Little, Brown & Co.
Shooting Star, The	M	661	PM Story Books-Gold	Rigby
Shopping with a Crocodile	M	250+	Ready to Read	Pacific Learning
Shortstop from Tokyo	M	250+	Christopher, Matt	Little, Brown & Co.
Shorty	M	250+	Literacy 2000	Rigby
Show Time at the Polk Street School	M	250+	Giff, Patricia Reilly	Bantam Doubleday Dell
Shy People's Picnic, The	M	250+	Little Celebrations	Pearson Learning
Si Won's Victory	M	250+	Little Celebrations	Pearson Learning
Silly Willy	M	500	Book Shop	Mondo Publishing
Skateboard Tough	M	250+	Christopher, Matt	Little, Brown & Co.
Skeletons Don't Play Tubas	M	250+	Dadey, Debbie & Jones, Marcia	Scholastic
Slam Dunk Saturday	M	250+	Marzollo, Jean	Random House
Snaggle Doodles	M	250+	Giff, Patricia Reilly	Bantam Doubleday Dell
Snake Alarm	M	250+	Krailing, Tessa	Barron's Educational
Snake!	M	641	Sunshine	Wright Group
So You Want to Move a Building?	M	380	Pacific Literacy	Pacific Learning
Soccer	M		Little Celebrations	Pearson Learning
Soccer Mania	M	250+	Tamar, Erika	Random House
Soccer Sam	M	250+	Marzollo, Jean	Random House
Solo Girl	M	250+	Pinkey, Andrea Davis	Hyperion
Something Soft for Danny Bear	M	493	Literacy 2000	Rigby
Spectacular Stone Soup	M	250+	Giff, Patricia Reilly	Yearling
Spider Man	M	250+	Literacy 2000	Rigby
Spiders	M	447	Book Shop	Mondo Publishing
Spy Down the Street, The	M	250+	Schultz, Irene	Wright Group
Spy in the Attic, The	M	250+	Scheffler, Ursel	North-South Books
Spy on Third Base, The	M	250+	Christopher, Matt	Little, Brown & Co.
Stacy Says Good-Bye	M	250+	Giff, Patricia Reilly	Bantam Doubleday Dell
Star	M	250+	Simon, Jo Ann	Random House
Stop, Stop	M	250+	Hurd, Edith Thacher	HarperCollins
Stories in Stone	M	250+	Pacific Literacy	Pacific Learning
Story of Jeans, The	M	250+	Discovery World	Rigby
Story of You, The	M	482	Sunshine	Wright Group
Strike Out!	M	250+	Howard, Tristan	Scholastic
Summer Sands	M	839	Evangeline Nicholas Collection	Wright Group
Sunny-Side Up	M	250+	Giff, Patricia Reilly	Bantam Doubleday Dell
Sunset of the Sabertooth	M	250+	Osborne, Mary Pope	Random House
Supercharged Infield	M	250+	Christopher, Matt	Little, Brown & Co.
Survival of Fish, The	M	946	Science	Wright Group
Take Care of Our Earth	M	250+	Pair-It Books	Steck-Vaughn
Tale of Veruschka Babuschka, The	M	250+	Literacy 2000	Rigby
That's a Laugh: Four Funny Fables	M	250+	Literacy 2000	Rigby
These Old Rags	M	352	Evangeline Nicholas Collection	Wright Group
Through the Medicine Cabinet	M	250+	Greenburg, Dan	Grosset & Dunlap
Tight End	M	250+	Christopher, Matt	Little, Brown & Co.
Timber Box, The	M	250+	Enrichment	Wright Group
Time Capsule, The	M	257	Book Bank	Wright Group
Timothy's Five-City Tour	M	250+	Pair-It Books	Steck-Vaughn
Tin Lizzy	M	425	Windmill Books	Rigby

Title	Level	Words	Author/Series	Publisher/Distributor
Tom Edison's Bright Idea	M	250+	Keller, Jack	Steck-Vaughn
Tom, the Dragon	M	522	New Way Orange	Steck-Vaughn
Too Hot to Handle	M	250+	Christopher, Matt	Little, Brown & Co.
Totara Tree, The	M	391	Book Bank	Wright Group
Touchdown for Tommy	M	250+	Christopher, Matt	Little, Brown & Co.
Treasure Hunting	M	250+	Literacy 2000	Rigby
Trixie and the Cyber Pet	M	250+	Krailing, Tessa	Barron's Educational
Trog	M	432	Sunshine	Wright Group
Trolls Don't Ride Roller Coasters	M	250+	Dadey, Debbie & Jones, Marcia	Scholastic
True Stories About Abraham Lincoln	M	250+	Gross, Ruth Belov	Scholastic
Turkey Trouble	M	250+	Giff, Patricia Reilly	Bantam Doubleday Dell
Turkeys' Side of it, The	M	250+	Smith, Janice Lee	HarperTrophy
Twelve Dancing Princesses	M	250+	Enrichment	Wright Group
Two Runaways, The	M	250+	Schultz, Irene	Wright Group
Tyler Toad and Thunder	M	250+	Crowe, Robert	Dutton
Umbrellas	M	430	Sunshine	Wright Group
Unicorns Don't Give Sleigh Rides	M	250+	Dadey, Debbie & Jones, Marcia	Scholastic
Vacation Journal, A	M	250+	Discovery World	Rigby
Vacation Under the Volcano	M	250+	Osborne, Mary Pope	Random House
Valentine Star, The	M	250+	Giff, Patricia Reilly	Bantam Doubleday Dell
Vampires Don't Wear Polka Dots	M	250+	Dadey, Debbie & Jones, Marcia	Scholastic
Very Happy Birthday, A	M	1017	Jellybeans	Rigby
Viking Ships at Sunrise	M	250+	Osborne, Mary Pope	Random House
Volcano Goddess Will See You Now, The	M	250+	Greenburg, Dan	Grosset & Dunlap
Voyage, The	M	250+	Pair-It Books	Steck-Vaughn
Wake Up, Emily, It's Mother's Day	M	250+	Giff, Patricia Reilly	Yearling
Walter the Warlock	M	250+	Hautzig, Deborah	Random House
Watching Every Drop	M	250+	Home Connection Collection	Rigby
Water for the World	M	250+	Home Connection Collection	Rigby
Werewolves Don't Go to Summer Camp	M	250+	Dadey, Debbie & Jones, Marcia	Scholastic
What Is a Fly?	M	561	Sunshine	Wright Group
What Is a Reptile?	M	183	Now I Know	Troll
What Made Teddalik Laugh	M	250+	Folk Tales	Wright Group
What Shall I Do?	M	584	Sunshine	Wright Group
Whatever Am I Going to Do Now?	M	250+	Little Celebrations	Pearson Learning
What's Cooking, Jenny Archer?	M	250+	Conford, Ellen	Little, Brown & Co.
When My Dad Came to School	M	230	City Kids	Rigby
Where Does the Wind Go?	M	95	Book Shop	Mondo Publishing
Who's in Love with Arthur?	M	250+	Brown, Marc	Little, Brown & Co.
Why Crocodiles Live in Rivers	M	415	Sunshine	Wright Group
Wingman on Ice	M	250+	Christopher, Matt	Little, Brown & Co.
Winklepoo the Wicked	M	1614	Sunshine	Wright Group
Witches Don't Do Backflips	M	250+	Dadey, Debbie & Jones, Marcia	Scholastic
Wizards Don't Need Computers	M	250+	Dadey, Debbie & Jones, Marcia	Scholastic
Wolf's First Deer	M	434	Book Bank	Wright Group
Wonder Kid Meets the Evil Lunch Snatcher	M	250+	Duncan, Lois	Little, Brown & Co.
Wonderful Eyes	M	1070	Science	Wright Group
Words	M	578	Pacific Literacy	Pacific Learning
Words	M	250+	Ready to Read	Pacific Learning
World's Greatest Toe Show, The	M	250+	Lamb, Nancy & Singer, Muff	Troll
Write Up a Storm with the Polk Street School	M	250+	Giff, Patricia Reilly	Bantam Doubleday Dell
Year Mom Won the Pennant, The	M	250+	Christopher, Matt	Little, Brown & Co.

©1999 by I. C. Fountas & G. S. Pinnell from Matching Books to Readers. Portsmouth, NH: Heinemann. May not be reproduced without written permission of the publisher.

Title	Level	Words	Author/Series	Publisher/Distributor
Young Wolf's First Hunt	M	250+	Shefelman, Janice	Random House
Zap! I'm a Mind Reader	M	250+	Greenburg, Dan	Grosset & Dunlap
Zero's Slider	M	250+	Christopher, Matt	Little, Brown & Co.
Zombies Don't Play Soccer	M	250+	Dadey, Debbie & Jones, Marcia	Scholastic
Abraham Lincoln: President of a Divided Country	N	250+	Rookie Biographies	Children's Press
Absent Author, The	N	250+	Roy, Ron	Random House
Adam Joshua Capers, The: Halloween Monster	N	250+	Smith, Janice Lee	HarperTrophy
Adam Joshua Capers, The: Monster in the Third	N	250+	Smith, Janice Lee	HarperTrophy
Adam Joshua Capers, The: Nelson in Love	N	250+	Smith, Janice Lee	HarperCollins
Adam Joshua Capers, The: Superkid!	N	250+	Smith, Janice Lee	HarperTrophy
Adam Joshua Capers, The: Turkey Trouble	N	250+	Smith, Janice Lee	HarperTrophy
Adios, Anna	N	250+	Giff, Patricia Reilly	Bantam Doubleday Dell
Adventures of Max and Ned, The	N	250+	Little Celebrations	Pearson Learning
Alroy's Very Nearly Clean Bedroom	N	250+	Orr, Wendy	Sundance
Amber Brown Goes Fourth	N	250+	Danziger, Paula	Scholastic
Amber Brown Is Feeling Blue	N	250+	Danziger, Paula	Scholastic
Amber Brown Is Not a Crayon	N	250+	Danziger, Paula	Scholastic
Amber Brown Sees Red	N	250+	Danziger, Paula	Scholastic
Amber Brown Wants Extra Credit	N	250+	Danziger, Paula	Scholastic
Animal Shelters	N	586	Book Shop	Mondo Publishing
Animals and Their Young	N	484	Wonders	Hampton-Brown
Animals of the Tundra	N	250+	Little Celebrations	Pearson Learning
Anna, Grandpa, and the Big Storm	N	250+	Stevens, Carla	The Penguin Group
Archaeologists Dig for Clues	N	250+	Duke, Kate	Scholastic
Baba Yaga: A Russian Folktale	N	250+	Phinney, Margaret Y.	Mondo
Bald Bandit, The	N	250+	Roy, Ron	Random House
Behind the Couch	N	250+	Gerstein, Mordicai	Hyperion
Behind the Scenes with Sammy	N	250+	Little Celebrations	Pearson Learning
Benjamin Franklin: A Man with Many Jobs	N	250+	Rookie Biographies	Children's Press
Berlioz the Bear	N	250+	Brett, Jan	Scholastic
Bill Clinton: Forty-Second President of the U.S.	N	250+	Rookie Biographies	Children's Press
Black Elk: A Man with a Vision	N	250+	Rookie Biographies	Children's Press
Blackberries in the Dark	N	250+	Jukes, Mavis	Alfred A. Knopf, Inc.
Boonsville Bombers, The	N	250+	Herzig, Alison	Puffin Books
Boy in the Doghouse, A	N	250+	Douglas, Ann	Simon & Schuster
Bozo the Clone	N	250+	Greenburg, Dan	Grosset & Dunlap
Busybody Nora	N	250+	Hurwitz, Johanna	The Penguin Group
Canary Caper, The	N	250+	Roy, Ron	Random House
Case of Hermie the Missing Hamster, The	N	250+	Preller, James	Scholastic
Case of the Christmas Snowman, The	N	250+	Preller, James	Scholastic
Case of the Secret Valentine, The	N	250+	Preller, James	Scholastic
Case of the Spooky Sleepover, The	N	250+	Preller, James	Scholastic
Cat Who Wore a Pot on Her Head, The	N	250+	Slepian, Jon & Seidler, A.	Scholastic
Chalk Box Kid, The	N	250+	Bulla, Clyde Robert	Random House
Christopher Columbus: A Great Explorer	N	250+	Rookie Biographies	Children's Press
Cloud Book, The	N	250+	DePaola, Tomie	Scholastic
Dance with Rosie	N	250+	Giff, Patricia Reilly	The Penguin Group
Danger Guys	N	250+	Abbott, Tony	HarperTrophy
Danger Guys Blast Off	N	250+	Abbott, Tony	HarperTrophy
Danger Guys on Ice	N	250+	Abbott, Tony	HarperTrophy
Daniel Boone: Man of the Forests	N	250+	Rookie Biographies	Children's Press

Title	Level	Words	Author/Series	Publisher/Distributor
Did You Hear Wind Sing Your Name?	N	182	Book Shop	Mondo Publishing
Dolphin's First Day	N	250+	Zoehfeld, Kathleen W.	Scholastic
Donovan's Word Jar	N	250+	DeGross, Monalisa	HarperTrophy
Don't Call Me Beanhead!	N	250+	Wojciechowski, Susan	Candlewick Press
Elizabeth Blackwell: First Woman Doctor	N	250+	Rookie Biographies	Children's Press
Elizabeth the First: Queen of England	N	250+	Rookie Biographies	Children's Press
Emily Dickinson: American Poet	N	250+	Rookie Biographies	Children's Press
Empty Envelope, The	N	250+	Roy, Ron	Random House
Enormous Crocodile, The	N	250+	Dahl, Roald	Puffin Books
Eureka! It's an Airplane	N	250+	Bendick, Jeanne	Scholastic
Experiment with Movement	N	250+	Murphy, Bryan	Scholastic
Experiment with Water	N	250+	Murphy, Bryan	Scholastic
Falcon's Feathers, the	N	250+	Roy, Ron	Random House
Farms	N	606	Wonders	Hampton-Brown
Favorite Greek Myths	N	250+	Osborne, Mary Pope	Scholastic
First Things	N	250+	Stepping Stones	Nelson/Michaels Assoc.
Flat Stanley	N	250+	Brown, Jeff	HarperTrophy
Flunking of Joshua T. Bates, The	N	250+	Shreve, Susan	Scholastic
Forever Amber Brown	N	250+	Danziger, Paula	Scholastic
Frogs	N	1440	Book Shop	Mondo Publishing
Gadget War, the	N	250+	Douglas, Ann	The Penguin Group
George Washington Carver: Scientist and Teacher	N	250+	Rookie Biographies	Children's Press
George Washington: First President of the U.S.	N	250+	Rookie Biographies	Children's Press
Ghost Dog	N	250+	Allen, Eleanor	Scholastic
Gift for Mama, A	N	250+	Hautzig, Esther	The Penguin Group
Glass Slipper for Rosie, A	N	250+	Giff, Patricia Reilly	The Penguin Group
Good Dog, Bonita	N	250+	Giff, Patricia Reilly	Bantam Doubleday Dell
Gooey Chewy Contest, The	N	1512	Book Shop	Mondo Publishing
Goose's Gold, The	N	250+	Roy, Ron	Random House
Grain of Rice, A	N	250+	Pittman, Helena Clare	Bantam Doubleday Dell
Green Thumbs, Everyone	N	250+	Giff, Patricia Reilly	Bantam Doubleday Dell
Hannah	N	250+	Whelan, Gloria	Random House
Hans Christian Andersen: Prince of Storytellers	N	250+	Rookie Biographies	Children's Press
Happy Birthday, Anna, Sorpresa!	N	250+	Giff, Patricia Reilly	Bantam Doubleday Dell
Helen Keller's Teacher	N		Davidson, Margaret	Scholastic
Hey, New Kid!	N	250+	Douglas, Ann	The Penguin group
Ho, Ho, Benjamin, Feliz Navidad	N	250+	Giff, Patricia Reilly	Bantam Doubleday Dell
Homes Are for Living	N	417	Wonders	Hampton-Brown
Horses of the Air	N	250+	Little Celebrations	Pearson Learning
House on Walenska Street, The	N	250+	Herman, Charlotte	The Penguin Group
How Is a Crayon Made?	N	250+	Charles, Oz	Scholastic
How to Be Cool in the Third Grade	N	250+	Douglas, Ann	The Penguin Group
How to Speak Dolphin in Three Easy Lessons	N	250+	Greenburg, Dan	Grosset & Dunlap
Invisible Stanley	N	250+	Brown, Jeff	HarperTrophy
It Takes a Village	N	250+	Cowen-Fletcher, Jane	Scholastic
It's a Fiesta, Benjamin	N	250+	Giff, Patricia Reilly	Bantam Doubleday Dell
Jackie Robinson and the Story of All-Black Baseball	N	250+	O'Connor, Jim	Random House
Jackie Robinson: Baseball's First Black Major Leaguer	N	250+	Rookie Biographies	Children's Press
Jenius-The Amazing Guinea Pig	N	250+	King-Smith, Dick	Hyperion
Johann Sebastian Bach: Great Man of Music	N	250+	Rookie Biographies	Children's Press
John Chapman: The Man Who Was Johnny Appleseed	N	250+	Rookie Biographies	Children's Press

Title	Level	Words	Author/Series	Publisher/Distributor
John Muir: Man of the Wild Places	N	250+	Rookie Biographies	Children's Press
John Philip Sousa: The March King	N	250+	Rookie Biographies	Children's Press
Julian, Dream Doctor	N	250+	Cameron, Ann	Random House
Julian, Secret Agent	N	250+	Cameron, Ann	Random House
Julian's Glorious Summer	N	250+	Cameron, Ann	Random House
Katherine Dunham, Black Dancer	N	250+	Rookie Biographies	Children's Press
Keelboat Annie	N	250+	Johnson, Janet P.	Troll
Keeping Tadpoles	N	250+	Discovery World	Rigby
Key to the Treasure	N	250+	Parish, Peggy	Yearling
Kid Next Door, The	N	250+	Smith, Janice Lee	HarperTrophy
Laura Ingalls Wilder: Author of the Little House Books	N	250+	Rookie Biographies	Children's Press
Leftovers, The: Catch Flies!	N	250+	Howard, Tristan	Scholastic
Leftovers, The: Fast Break!	N	250+	Howard, Tristan	Scholastic
Leftovers, The: Get Jammed!	N	250+	Howard, Tristan	Scholastic
Leftovers, The: Reach Their Goal!	N	250+	Howard, Tristan	Scholastic
Leftovers, The: Strike Out!	N	250+	Howard, Tristan	Scholastic
Leftovers, The: Use Their Heads!	N	250+	Howard, Tristan	Scholastic
Leotyne Price: Opera Superstar	N		Williams, Sylvia	Children's Press
Lili the Brave	N	250+	Armstrong, Jennifer	Random House
Lion Dancer: Ernie Wan's Chinese New Year	N	250+	Waters, Kate & Slovenz-Low, Madeline	Scholastic
Llama Pajamas	N	250+	Clymer, Susan	Scholastic
Look at the Moon	N	405	Book Shop	Mondo Publishing
Louis Braille: The Boy Who Invented Books for the Blind	N		Davidson, Margaret	Scholastic
Ludwig van Beethoven: Musical Pioneer	N	250+	Rookie Biographies	Children's Press
Luke's Bully	N	250+	Winthrop, Elizabeth	Puffin Books
Magic Finger, The	N	250+	Dahl, Roald	Puffin Books
Margaret Wise Brown	N	250+	Rookie Biographies	Children's Press
Martin Luther King, Jr., a Man Who Changed Things	N	250+	Rookie Biographies	Children's Press
Max Malone and the Great Cereal Rip-off	N	250+	Herman, Charlotte	Henry Holt & Co.
Max Malone Makes a Million	N	250+	Herman, Charlotte	Henry Holt & Co.
Max Malone the Magnificent	N	250+	Herman, Charlotte	Scholastic
Max Malone, Superstar	N	250+	Herman, Charlotte	Scholastic
More Stories Huey Tells	N	250+	Cameron, Ann	Alfred A. Knopf, Inc.
More Stories Julian Tells	N	250+	Cameron, Ann	Random House
Mountain Gorillas	N	250+	Connal, Julie	Wright Group
My Name Is Maria Isabel	N	250+	Ada, Alma Flor	Aladdin
Mystery of Pony Hollow, The	N	250+	Hall, Lynn	Random House
Mystery of the Phantom Pony, The	N	250+	Hall, Lynn	Random House
New Kid in Town	N	250+	Kroll, Stephen	Avon Camelot
Next Spring an Oriole	N	250+	Whelan, Gloria	Random House
No Room for a Dog	N	250+	Kane Nichols, Joan	Avon Books
Not-So-Perfect Rosie	N	250+	Giff, Patricia Reilly	The Penguin Group
Ocean by the Lake, The	N	250+	Little Celebrations	Pearson Learning
Octopuses and Squids	N	328	Wonder World	Wright Group
Off to Squintums/The Four Musicians	N	1268	Book Shop	Mondo Publishing
Our Book of Maps	N	250+	Discovery World	Rigby
Pasta	N	250+	Little Celebrations	Pearson Learning
Phyllis Wheatley: First African-American Poet	N	250+	Rookie Biographies	Children's Press
Pioneer Cat	N	250+	Hooks, William H.	Random House
Pirate's Promise	N	250+	Bulla, Clyde Robert	HarperTrophy

Title	Level	Words	Author/Series	Publisher/Distributor
Pitching Trouble	N	250+	Kroll, Stephen	Avon Camelot
Planning a Birthday Party	N	1455	Book Shop	Mondo Publishing
Platypus	N	1098	Book Shop	Mondo Publishing
Playing Favorites	N	250+	Kroll, Stephen	Avon Camelot
Pocahontas: Daughter of a Chief	N	250+	Rookie Biographies	Children's Press
Pompeii…Buried Alive!	N	250+	Kunhardt, Edith	Random House
Prehistoric Record Breakers	N	250+	Discovery World	Rigby
Pride of the Rockets	N	250+	Kroll, Stephen	Avon Camelot
Puppy Love	N	250+	Duffy, Betsy	Puffin Books
Rachel Carson: Friend of Nature	N	250+	Rookie Biographies	Children's Press
Return of the Home Run Kid	N	250+	Christopher, Matt	Scholastic
Roald Dahl's Revolting Rhymes	N	250+	Dahl, Roald	Puffin Books
Roberto Clemente: Baseball Superstar	N	250+	Rookie Biographies	Children's Press
Rollerama	N	250+	Hinchliffe, Jo	Sundance
Rosie's Big City Ballet	N	250+	Giff, Patricia Reilly	The Penguin Group
Rosie's Nutcracker Dreams	N	250+	Giff, Patricia Reilly	The Penguin Group
Rumpelstiltskin	N	250+	Zelinsky, Paul O.	Scholastic
Save the Manatee	N	250+	Friesinger, Alison	Random House
Say Hola, Sarah	N	250+	Giff, Patricia Reilly	Bantam Doubleday Dell
School's Out	N	250+	Hurwitz, Johanna	Scholastic
Second Chance	N	250+	Kroll, Stephen	Avon Camelot
Shadow of the Wolf	N	250+	Whelan, Gloria	Random House
Shark in School	N	250+	Giff, Patricia Reilly	Bantam Doubleday Dell
Shark Lady: The Adventures of Eugenie Clark	N	250+	McGovern, Ann	Scholastic
Shoeshine Girl	N	250+	Bulla, Clyde Robert	HarperTrophy
Show-and-Tell War, The	N	250+	Smith, Janice Lee	HarperTrophy
Sidewalk Story	N	250+	Mathis, Sharon Bell	The Penguin Group
Silver	N	250+	Whelan, Gloria	Random House
Simon and the Aliens	N	250+	Mills, Eva	Sundance
Slump, The	N	250+	Kroll, Stephen	Avon Camelot
Someone Is Following Pip Ramsey	N	250+	Roy, Ron	Random House
Something Queer at the Ball Park	N	250+	Levy, Elizabeth	Bantam Doubleday Dell
Something Queer at the Haunted School	N	250+	Levy, Elizabeth	Bantam Doubleday Dell
Something Queer at the Lemonade Stand	N	250+	Levy, Elizabeth	Bantam Doubleday Dell
Something Queer at the Library	N	250+	Levy, Elizabeth	Hyperion
Something Queer at the Scary Movie	N	250+	Levy, Elizabeth	Hyperion
Something Queer in Outer Space	N	250+	Levy, Elizabeth	Hyperion
Something Queer in the Cafeteria	N	250+	Levy, Elizabeth	Hyperion
Something Queer in the Wild West	N	250+	Levy, Elizabeth	Hyperion
Something Queer Is Going On	N	250+	Levy, Elizabeth	Bantam Doubleday Dell
Something Queer on Vacation	N	250+	Levy, Elizabeth	Bantam Doubleday Dell
Song Lee and the Hamster Hunt	N	250+	Kline, Suzy	The Penguin Group
Song Lee and the Leech Man	N	250+	Kline, Suzy	The Penguin Group
Song Lee in Room 2B	N	250+	Kline, Suzy	The Penguin Group
Spirit of Hope	N	878	Book Shop	Mondo Publishing
Squanto: Friend of the Pilgrims	N	250+	Bulla, Clyde Robert	Scholastic
Squirrels	N	460	Storyteller Nonfiction	Wright Group/ McGraw-Hill
Stanley and the Magic Lamp	N	250+	Brown, Jeff	HarperTrophy
Starring Rosie	N	250+	Giff, Patricia Reilly	The Penguin Group
Stories Huey Tells, The	N	250+	Cameron, Ann	Alfred A. Knopf, Inc.
Stories Julian Tells, The	N	250+	Cameron, Ann	Alfred A. Knopf, Inc.

Title	Level	Words	Author/Series	Publisher/Distributor
Streak, The	N	250+	Kroll, Stephen	Avon Camelot
Striped Ice Cream	N	250+	Lexau, Joan M.	Scholastic
Sugar Cakes Cyril	N	4022	Book Shop	Mondo Publishing
Talk! Talk! Talk!	N	50	Little Celebrations	Pearson Learning
Things Change	N	569	Wonders	Hampton-Brown
Third Grade Bullies	N	250+	Levy, Elizabeth	Hyperion
Thomas Jefferson: Author, Inventor, President	N	250+	Rookie Biographies	Children's Press
Throw-Away Pets	N	250+	Duffy, Betsy	Puffin Books
Thurgood Marshall: First Black Supreme Court Justice	N	250+	Rookie Biographies	Children's Press
Titanic, The	N	250+	Donnelly, Judy	Random House
Titanic, the Lost…and Found	N	250+	Donnelly, Judy	Random House
To the Top!	N	250+	Kramer, Sydelle A.	Random House
Toad for Tuesday, A	N	250+	Erickson, Russell	Beech Tree Books
Trojan Horse, The: How the Greeks Won the War	N	250+	Little, Emily	Random House
Trouble with Buster, The	N	250+	Lorimer, Janet	Scholastic
True-Life Treasure Hunts	N	250+	Donnelly, Judy	Random House
Up and Away! Taking a Flight	N	1195	Book Shop	Mondo Publishing
Walking the Road to Freedom	N	250+	Ferris, Jeri	Carolrhoda
Wayside School Gets a Little Stranger	N	250+	Sachar, Louis	Avon Camelot
Weather Watch	N	624	Wonders	Hampton-Brown
Whales	N	1617	Book Shop	Mondo Publishing
Whales on the Move	N	250+	Little Celebrations	Pearson Learning
What Am I Made Of?	N	250+	Bennett, David	Scholastic
What Makes a Bird a Bird?	N	250+	Garelick, May	Mondo
What's the Matter, Kelly Beans?	N	250+	Enderle, Judith & Tessler, Stephanie	Candlewick Press
White Bird	N	250+	Bulla, Clyde Robert	Random House
Wild Baby Animals	N	250+	Little Celebrations	Pearson Learning
Wild Willie and King Kyle Detectives	N	250+	Joosse, Barbara M.	Bantam Doubleday Dell
Witch Hunt: It Happened in Salem Village	N	250+	Krensky, Stephen	Random House
Wolfgang Amadeus Mozart: Musical Genius	N	250+	Rookie Biographies	Children's Press
Writer's Work, A	N	481	Wonder World	Wright Group
Wrong Way Around Magic	N	250+	Chew, Ruth	Scholastic
You Can't Eat Your Chicken Pox, Amber Brown	N	250+	Danziger, Paula	Scholastic
You're Out	N	250+	Kroll, Stephen	Avon Camelot
89th Kitten, The	O	250+	Nilsson, Eleanor	Scholastic
Adventures of Ali Baba Bernstein, The	O	250+	Hurwitz, Johanna	Scholastic
Aldo Ice Cream	O	250+	Hurwitz, Johanna	The Penguin Group
Aldo Peanut Butter	O	250+	Hurwitz, Johanna	The Penguin Group
All About Sam	O	250+	Lowry, Lois	Houghton Mifflin
Allen Jay and the Underground Railroad	O	250+	Brill, Marlene Targ	Carolrhoda Books
And Then What Happened, Paul Revere?	O	250+	Fritz, Jean	Scholastic
Angel Park Hoopstars: Nothing but Net	O	250+	Hughes, Dean	Alfred A. Knopf, Inc.
Angel Park Hoopstars: Point Guard	O	250+	Hughes, Dean	Alfred A. Knopf, Inc.
Angel Park Soccer Stars: Backup Goalie	O	250+	Hughes, Dean	Random House
Angel Park Soccer Stars: Defense!	O	250+	Hughes, Dean	Alfred A. Knopf, Inc.
Angel Park Soccer Stars: Psyched!	O	250+	Hughes, Dean	Random House
Angel Park Soccer Stars: Total Soccer	O	250+	Hughes, Dean	Alfred A. Knopf, Inc.
Angel Park Soccer Stars: Victory Goal	O	250+	Hughes, Dean	Alfred A. Knopf, Inc.
Angry Bull and Other Cases, The	O	250+	Simon, Seymour	Avon Books
Armies of Ants	O	250+	Retan, Walter	Scholastic
Baby Animal Zoo	O	250+	Martin, Ann M.	Scholastic

Title	Level	Words	Author/Series	Publisher/Distributor
Baby-Sitter's Club Mystery, #2 Beware Dawn!	O	250+	Martin, Ann M.	Scholastic
Baby-Sitter's Club, #110 Abby the Bad Sport	O	250+	Martin, Ann M.	Scholastic
Baby-Sitter's Club, #116 Abby and the Best Kid	O	250+	Martin, Ann M.	Scholastic
Baby-Sitter's Club, #128 Claudia and the Little Liar	O	250+	Martin, Ann M.	Scholastic
Baby-Sitter's Club, #14 Hello, Mallory	O	250+	Martin, Ann M.	Scholastic
Baby-Sitter's Club, #19 Claudia and the Bad Joke	O	250+	Martin, Ann M.	Scholastic
Baby-Sitter's Club, #27 Jessi and the Superbrat	O	250+	Martin, Ann M.	Scholastic
Baby-Sitter's Club, #31 Dawn's Wicked Stepsister	O	250+	Martin, Ann M.	Scholastic
Baby-Sitter's Club, #67 Dawn's Big Move	O	250+	Martin, Ann M.	Scholastic
Baby-Sitter's Club, #68 Jessi and the Bad Baby-Sitter	O	250+	Martin, Ann M.	Scholastic
Baby-Sitter's Club, #98 Dawn and Too Many Sitters	O	250+	Martin, Ann M.	Scholastic
Baby-Sitter's Little Sister, #107 Karen's Copycat	O	250+	Martin, Ann M.	Scholastic
Baby-Sitter's Little Sister, #69 Karen's Big Sister	O	250+	Martin, Ann M.	Scholastic
Baby-Sitter's Little Sister, #73 Karen's Dinosaur	O	250+	Martin, Ann M.	Scholastic
Baby-Sitter's Little Sister, #79 Karen's Big Fight	O	250+	Martin, Ann M.	Scholastic
Baby-Sitter's Little Sister, #81 Karen's Accident	O	250+	Martin, Ann M.	Scholastic
Baseball Fever	O	250+	Hurwitz, Johanna	William Morrow & Co.
Baseball Megastars	O	250+	Weber, Bruce	Scholastic
Baseball Pitching Challenge and Other Cases, The	O	250+	Simon, Seymour	Avon Books
Baseball Saved Us	O	250+	Mochizuki, Ken	Scholastic
Baseball's Best, Five True Stories	O	250+	Gutelle, Andrew	Random House
Beezus and Ramona	O	250+	Cleary, Beverly	Avon Books
Birds of Prey	O	250+	Woolley, M. & Pigdon, K.	Mondo
Blind Pony, The	O	250+	Betancourt, Jeanne	Scholastic
Book About Planets and Stars, A	O	250+	Reigot, Betty P.	Scholastic
Borreguita and the Coyote	O	250+	Aardema, Verna	Scholastic
Boxcar Children Return, The	O	250+	Warner, Gertrude Chandler	Scholastic
Boxcar Children, The	O	250+	Warner, Gertrude Chandler	Scholastic
Boxcar Children: Benny Uncovers a Mystery	O	250+	Warner, Gertrude Chandler	Albert Whitman & Co.
Boxcar Children: The Amusement Park Mystery	O	250+	Warner, Gertrude Chandler	Albert Whitman & Co.
Boxcar Children: The Animal Shelter Mystery	O	250+	Warner, Gertrude Chandler	Albert Whitman & Co.
Boxcar Children: The Bicycle Mystery	O	250+	Warner, Gertrude Chandler	Albert Whitman & Co.
Boxcar Children: The Black Pearl Mystery	O	250+	Warner, Gertrude Chandler	Albert Whitman & Co.
Boxcar Children: The Blue Bay Mystery	O	250+	Warner, Gertrude Chandler	Albert Whitman & Co.
Boxcar Children: The Bus Station Mystery	O	250+	Warner, Gertrude Chandler	Albert Whitman & Co.
Boxcar Children: The Camp-Out Mystery	O	250+	Warner, Gertrude Chandler	Albert Whitman & Co.
Boxcar Children: The Canoe Trip Mystery	O	250+	Warner, Gertrude Chandler	Albert Whitman & Co.
Boxcar Children: The Castle Mystery	O	250+	Warner, Gertrude Chandler	Albert Whitman & Co.
Boxcar Children: The Cereal Box Mystery	O	250+	Warner, Gertrude Chandler	Albert Whitman & Co.
Boxcar Children: The Deserted Library Mystery	O	250+	Warner, Gertrude Chandler	Albert Whitman & Co.
Boxcar Children: The Dinosaur Mystery	O	250+	Warner, Gertrude Chandler	Albert Whitman & Co.
Boxcar Children: The Disappearing Friend Mystery	O	250+	Warner, Gertrude Chandler	Albert Whitman & Co.
Boxcar Children: The Firehouse Mystery	O	250+	Warner, Gertrude Chandler	Albert Whitman & Co.
Boxcar Children: The Ghost Ship Mystery	O	250+	Warner, Gertrude Chandler	Albert Whitman & Co.
Boxcar Children: The Growling Bear Mystery	O	250+	Warner, Gertrude Chandler	Scholastic
Boxcar Children: The Haunted Cabin Mystery	O	250+	Warner, Gertrude Chandler	Albert Whitman & Co.
Boxcar Children: The Lighthouse Mystery	O	250+	Warner, Gertrude Chandler	Albert Whitman & Co.
Boxcar Children: The Mountain Top Mystery	O	250+	Warner, Gertrude Chandler	Albert Whitman & Co.
Boxcar Children: The Mystery at the Dog Show	O	250+	Warner, Gertrude Chandler	Albert Whitman & Co.
Boxcar Children: The Mystery at the Fair	O	250+	Warner, Gertrude Chandler	Albert Whitman & Co.
Boxcar Children: The Mystery Bookstore	O	250+	Warner, Gertrude Chandler	Scholastic

Title	Level	Words	Author/Series	Publisher/Distributor
Boxcar Children: The Mystery Cruise	O	250+	Warner, Gertrude Chandler	Albert Whitman & Co.
Boxcar Children: The Mystery in the Cave	O	250+	Warner, Gertrude Chandler	Scholastic
Boxcar Children: The Mystery in the Old Attic	O	250+	Warner, Gertrude Chandler	Scholastic
Boxcar Children: The Mystery in the Sand	O	250+	Warner, Gertrude Chandler	Albert Whitman & Co.
Boxcar Children: The Mystery of the Hidden Beach	O	250+	Warner, Gertrude Chandler	Albert Whitman & Co.
Boxcar Children: The Mystery of the Lost Mine	O	250+	Warner, Gertrude Chandler	Scholastic
Boxcar Children: The Mystery of the Lost Village	O	250+	Warner, Gertrude Chandler	Scholastic
Boxcar Children: The Mystery of the Missing Cat	O	250+	Warner, Gertrude Chandler	Albert Whitman & Co.
Boxcar Children: The Mystery of the Mixed-Up Zoo	O	250+	Warner, Gertrude Chandler	Albert Whitman & Co.
Boxcar Children: The Mystery of the Stolen Boxcar	O	250+	Warner, Gertrude Chandler	Scholastic
Boxcar Children: The Mystery of the Stolen Music	O	250+	Warner, Gertrude Chandler	Scholastic
Boxcar Children: The Mystery on Stage	O	250+	Warner, Gertrude Chandler	Albert Whitman & Co.
Boxcar Children: The Mystery on the Train	O	250+	Warner, Gertrude Chandler	Scholastic
Boxcar Children: The Outer Space Mystery	O	250+	Warner, Gertrude Chandler	Scholastic
Boxcar Children: The Pizza Mystery	O	250+	Warner, Gertrude Chandler	Albert Whitman & Co.
Boxcar Children: The Schoolhouse Mystery	O	250+	Warner, Gertrude Chandler	Albert Whitman & Co.
Boxcar Children: The Snowbound Mystery	O	250+	Warner, Gertrude Chandler	Albert Whitman & Co.
Boxcar Children: The Soccer Mystery	O	250+	Warner, Gertrude Chandler	Scholastic
Boxcar Children: The Surprise Island	O	250+	Warner, Gertrude Chandler	Scholastic
Broken Window and Other Cases, The	O	250+	Simon, Seymour	Avon Books
Bugs	O	250+	Parker, N. & Wright, R.	Scholastic
Can't You Make Them Behave, King George?	O	250+	Fritz, Jean	Scholastic
Case of the Dirty Bird, The	O	250+	Paulsen, Gary	Bantam Doubleday Dell
Cat's Meow, The	O	250+	Soto, Gary	Scholastic
Chocolate Fever	O	250+	Smith, Robert	Bantam Doubleday Dell
Class Clown	O	250+	Hurwitz, Johanna	Scholastic
Class President	O	250+	Hurwitz, Johanna	Scholastic
Cloak of the Wind	O	250+	Voyages in…	Wright Group
Clothes	O	386	Wonder World	Wright Group
Cowpokes and Desperadoes	O	250+	Paulsen, Gary	Bantam Doubleday Dell
Creature from Beneath the Ice and Other Cases, The	O	250+	Simon, Seymour	Avon Books
Creatures of the Night	O	250+	Murdoch, K. & Ray, S.	Mondo
Crowded Dock and Other Cases, The	O	250+	Simon, Seymour	Avon Books
Crying Rocks and Other Cases, The	O	250+	Simon, Seymour	Avon Books
Culpepper's Canyon	O	250+	Paulsen, Gary	Bantam Doubleday Dell
Dangerous Comet and Other Cases, The	O	250+	Simon, Seymour	Avon Books
Different Dragons	O	250+	Little, Jean	The Penguin Group
Dirty Beasts	O	250+	Dahl, Roald	The Penguin Group
Disappearing Cookies and Other Cases, The	O	250+	Simon, Seymour	Avon Books
Disappearing Ice Cream and Other Cases, The	O	250+	Simon, Seymour	Avon Books
Disappearing Snowball and Other cases, The	O	250+	Simon, Seymour	Avon Books
Distant Stars and Other Cases, The	O	250+	Simon, Seymour	Avon Books
Dragon Bones	O	250+	Hindman, Paul & Evans, Nate	Random House
E Is for Elisa	O	250+	Hurwitz, Johanna	The Penguin Group
Electric Spark and Other Cases, The	O	250+	Simon, Seymour	Avon Books
Electrifying Cows and Other Cases, The	O	250+	Simon, Seymour	Avon Books
Eleven Kids, One Summer	O	250+	Martin, Ann M.	Scholastic
Elisa in the Middle	O	250+	Hurwitz, Johanna	The Penguin Group
Face-Off	O	250+	Christopher, Matt	Little, Brown & Co.
Fantastic Water Pot and Other Cases, The	O	250+	Simon, Seymour	Avon Books
Far-Out Frisbee and Other Cases, The	O	250+	Simon, Seymour	Avon Books

Title	Level	Words	Author/Series	Publisher/Distributor
Fastest Ketchup in the Cafeteria and Other Cases, The	O	250+	Simon, Seymour	Avon Books
Finches' Fabulous Furnace, The	O	250+	Drury, Roger	Scholastic
Flossie and the Fox	O	250+	McKissack, Patricia	Scholastic
Flying-Saucer People and Other Cases, The	O	250+	Simon, Seymour	Avon Books
Foolish Gretel	O	250+	Armstrong, Jennifer	Random House
George Washington's Socks	O	250+	Woodruff, Elvira	Scholastic
Ghost Pony, The	O	250+	Betancourt, Jeanne	Scholastic
Gigantic Ants and Other Cases, The	O	250+	Simon, Seymour	Avon Books
Ginger Pye	O	250+	Estes, Eleanor	Scholastic
Give Me Back My Pony	O	250+	Betancourt, Jeanne	Scholastic
Godzilla Ate My Homework	O	250+	Jones, Marcia	Scholastic
Good Grief Third Grade	O	250+	O'Shaughnessy, Colleen	Scholastic
Gorganzola Zombies in the Park	O	250+	Levy, Elizabeth	HarperTrophy
Grace the Pirate	O	250+	Lasky, Kathryn	Hyperion
Great Little Madison, The	O	250+	Fritz, Jean	Scholastic
Grizzly Bears	O	250+	Woolley, M. & Pigdon, K.	Mondo
Grizzly Mistake and Other Cases, The	O	250+	Simon, Seymour	Avon Books
Halloween Horror and Other Cases, The	O	250+	Simon, Seymour	Avon Books
Happily Ever After	O	250+	Quindlen, Anna	The Penguin Group
Haunting of Grade Three, The	O	250+	Maccarone, Grace	Scholastic
Heavy Weight and Other Cases, The	O	250+	Simon, Seymour	Avon Books
Henry and Beezus	O	250+	Cleary, Beverly	Avon Books
Henry and Ribsy	O	250+	Cleary, Beverly	Avon Books
Henry and the Clubhouse	O	250+	Cleary, Beverly	Avon Books
Henry and the Paper Route	O	250+	Cleary, Beverly	Avon Books
Henry Huggins	O	250+	Cleary, Beverly	Avon Books
Herbie Jones	O	250+	Kline, Suzy	Puffin Books
Herbie Jones and Hamburger Head	O	250+	Kline, Suzy	Puffin Books
Herbie Jones and the Birthday Showdown	O	250+	Kline, Suzy	Puffin Books
Herbie Jones and the Class Gift	O	250+	Kline, Suzy	Puffin Books
Herbie Jones and the Dark Attic	O	250+	Kline, Suzy	Puffin Books
Herbie Jones and the Monster Ball	O	250+	Kline, Suzy	Puffin Books
Here Comes McBroom	O	250+	Fleischman, Sid	Beech Tree Books
Howling Dog and Other Cases, The	O	250+	Simon, Seymour	Avon Books
Hundred Dresses, The	O	250+	Estes, Eleanor	Scholastic
Hurray for Ali Baba Bernstein	O	250+	Hurwitz, Johanna	Scholastic
Hurricane Machine and Other Cases, The	O	250+	Simon, Seymour	Avon Books
Hypnotized Frog and Other Cases, The	O	250+	Simon, Seymour	Avon Books
I Want a Pony	O	250+	Betancourt, Jeanne	Scholastic
I Wonder Why Snakes Shed their Skins	O	250+	O'Neill, Amanda	Scholastic
Icy Question and Other Cases, The	O	250+	Simon, Seymour	Avon Books
Impossible Bend and Other Cases, The	O	250+	Simon, Seymour	Avon Books
In the Treetops	O	250+	Woolley, M. & Pigdon, K.	Mondo
Incredible Shrinking Machine and Other Cases, The	O	250+	Simon, Seymour	Avon Books
Indian-Head Pennies and Other Cases, The	O	250+	Simon, Seymour	Avon Books
It Came Through the Wall	O	1182	Book Shop	Mondo Publishing
Jason and the Aliens Down the Street	O	250+	Greer, Greg & Ruddick, Bob	HarperTrophy
Key to the Playhouse, The	O	250+	York, Carol	Scholastic
King's Equal, The	O	250+	Paterson, Katherine	HarperTrophy
Kristy and the Walking Disaster	O	250+	Martin, Ann M.	Scholastic
Lake Critter Journal	O		Little Celebrations	Pearson Learning

Title	Level	Words	Author/Series	Publisher/Distributor
Lavender	O	250+	Hesse, Karen	Henry Holt & Co.
Legend of the Bluebonnet, The	O	250+	DePaola, Tomie	Scholastic
Lightweight Rocket and Other Cases, The	O	250+	Simon, Seymour	Avon Books
Little Icicle	O	250+	Szymanski, Lois	Avon Camelot
Little Miss Stoneybrook and Dawn	O	250+	Martin, Ann M.	Scholastic
Look Out, Washington D.C.!	O	250+	Giff, Patricia Reilly	Bantam Doubleday Dell
Lost Continent and Other Cases, The	O	250+	Simon, Seymour	Avon Books
Lost Hikers and Other Cases, The	O	250+	Simon, Seymour	Avon Books
Ma and Pa Dracula	O	250+	Martin, Ann M.	Scholastic
Make a Wish, Molly	O	250+	Cohen, Barbara	Bantam Doubleday Dell
Make Room for Elisa	O	250+	Hurwitz, Johanna	Puffin Books
McBroom's Wonderful One-Acre Farm	O	250+	Fleischman, Sid	Beech Tree Books
Meg Mackintosh and the Case of the Curious Whale	O	250+	Landon, Lucinda	Secret Passage Press
Meg Mackintosh and the Case of the Missing Babe Ruth	O	250+	Landon, Lucinda	Secret Passage Press
Meg Mackintosh and the Myst. at the Medieval Castle	O	250+	Landon, Lucinda	Secret Passage Press
Meg Mackintosh and the Mystery at Camp Creepy	O	250+	Landon, Lucinda	Secret Passage Press
Meg Mackintosh and the Mystery at the Soccer Match	O	250+	Landon, Lucinda	Secret Passage Press
Meg Mackintosh and the Mystery in the Locked Library	O	250+	Landon, Lucinda	Secret Passage Press
Melting Snow Sculptures and Other Cases, The	O	250+	Simon, Seymour	Avon Books
Mieko and the Fifth Treasure	O	250+	Coerr, Eleanor	Bantam Doubleday Dell
Moonwalk-The First Trip to the Moon	O	250+	Donnelly, Judy	Random House
Most Beautiful Place in the World, The	O	250+	Cameron, Ann	Alfred A. Knopf, Inc.
Most Wonderful Doll in the World	O	250+	McGinley, Phyllis	Scholastic
Mouse and the Motorcycle, The	O	250+	Cleary, Beverly	Avon Camelot
Mr. Popper's Penguins	O	250+	Atwater, Richard & Florence	Little, Brown & Co.
Much Ado About Aldo	O	250+	Hurwitz, Johanna	Puffin Books
Muggie Maggie	O	250+	Cleary, Beverly	Avon Camelot
Mysterious Green Swimmer and Other Cases, The	O	250+	Simon, Seymour	Avon Books
Mysterious Tracks and Other Cases, The	O	250+	Simon, Seymour	Avon Books
Mystery on October Road	O	250+	Herzig, Alison C. & Mali, Jane	Scholastic
Next Stop, New York City!	O	250+	Giff, Patricia Reilly	Bantam Doubleday Dell
Night Crossing, The	O	250+	Ackerman, Karen	Alfred A. Knopf, Inc.
No One Is Going to Nashville	O	250+	Jukes, Mavis	Alfred A. Knopf, Inc.
Not-So-Dead Fish and Other Cases, The	O	250+	Simon, Seymour	Avon Books
Oh Boy, Boston!	O	250+	Giff, Patricia Reilly	Bantam Doubleday Dell
On-Line Spaceman and Other Cases, The	O	250+	Simon, Seymour	Avon Books
Owl Moon	O	250+	Yolen, Jane	Scholastic
Patrick Doyle Is Full of Blarney	O	250+	Armstrong, Jennifer	Random House
Penguins	O	250+	Woolley, M. & Pigdon, K.	Mondo
Penguins on Parade	O	250+	Little Celebrations	Pearson Learning
Perfect Pony, A	O	250+	Szymanski, Lois	Avon Camelot
Pet Parade	O	250+	Giff, Patricia Reilly	Bantam Doubleday Dell
Pony for Keeps, A	O	250+	Betancourt, Jeanne	Scholastic
Pony in Trouble, A	O	250+	Betancourt, Jeanne	Scholastic
Pony to the Rescue	O	250+	Betancourt, Jeanne	Scholastic
Ralph S. Mouse	O	250+	Cleary, Beverly	Avon Books
Ramona and Her Father	O	250+	Cleary, Beverly	Avon Books

Title	Level	Words	Author/Series	Publisher/Distributor
Ramona and Her Mother	O	250+	Cleary, Beverly	Avon Books
Ramona Forever	O	250+	Cleary, Beverly	Avon Books
Ramona Quimby, Age 8	O	250+	Cleary, Beverly	Avon Books
Ramona the Brave	O	250+	Cleary, Beverly	Avon Books
Ramona the Pest	O	250+	Cleary, Beverly	Avon Books
Rent a Third Grader	O	250+	Hiller, Bonnie Bryant	Scholastic
Rescue	O	250+	Wildcats	Wright Group
Ribsy	O	250+	Cleary, Beverly	Avon Books
Rotating Rollerblades and Other Cases, The	O	250+	Simon, Seymour	Avon Books
Runaway Pony	O	250+	Betancourt, Jeanne	Scholastic
Runaway Ralph	O	250+	Cleary, Beverly	Hearst
San Francisco Exploratorium, The	O	250+	Little Celebrations	Pearson Learning
Shining Blue Planet and Other Cases, The	O	250+	Simon, Seymour	Avon Books
Sideways Stories from Wayside School	O	250+	Sachar, Louis	Avon Books
Smasher	O	250+	King-Smith, Dick	Random House
Socks	O	250+	Cleary, Beverly	Avon Books
Space Quest	O	250+	Discovery World	Rigby
Space Station Plot and Other Cases, The	O	250+	Simon, Seymour	Avon Books
Speeding Sleigh and Other Cases, The	O	250+	Simon, Seymour	Avon Books
Speedy Pasta and Other Cases, The	O	250+	Simon, Seymour	Avon Books
Speedy Snake and Other Cases, The	O	250+	Simon, Seymour	Avon Books
Speedy Soapbox Car and Other Cases, The	O	250+	Simon, Seymour	Avon Books
Stacey and the Haunted Masquerade	O	250+	Martin, Ann M.	Scholastic
Stacey and the Missing Ring	O	250+	Martin, Ann M.	Scholastic
Stacey and the Mystery at the Mall	O	250+	Martin, Ann M.	Scholastic
Stacey and the Mystery Money	O	250+	Martin, Ann M.	Scholastic
Stay Away from Simon!	O	250+	Carrick, Carol	Clarion
Story of Benjamin Franklin, The	O		Davidson, Margaret	Gareth Stevens
Story of Ruby Bridges, The	O	250+	Coles, Robert	Scholastic
Strange Clues and Other Cases, The	O	250+	Simon, Seymour	Avon Books
Strange Museum and Other cases, The	O	250+	Simon, Seymour	Avon Books
Swamp of the Hideous Zombies	O	250+	Hayes, Geoffrey	Random House
Tall Tale and Other Cases, The	O	250+	Simon, Seymour	Avon Books
Tamika and the Wisdom Rings	O	250+	Yarbrough, Camille	Random House
Teacher's Pet	O	250+	Hurwitz, Johanna	Scholastic
Ten True Animal Rescues	O	250+	Betancourt, Jeanne	Scholastic
Terrible Test Mark and Other Cases, The	O	250+	Simon, Seymour	Avon Books
They Led the Way: 14 American Women	O	250+	Johnston, Joanna	Scholastic
Tiger Tales	O		Little Celebrations	Pearson Learning
Time Machine and Other Cases, The	O	250+	Simon, Seymour	Avon Books
Too Many Ponies	O	250+	Betancourt, Jeanne	Scholastic
Tornado	O	250+	Byars, Betsy	The Penguin Group
Trapped!	O	250+	Small, Mary	Sundance
Trickster Ghost, The	O	250+	Showell, Ellen	Scholastic
Universal Solvent and Other Cases, The	O	250+	Simon, Seymour	Avon Books
Vicar of Nibbleswick, The	O	250+	Dahl, Roald	Puffin Books
Virtual Fred	O	250+	Courtney, Vincent	Random House
Wall of Names: The Story of the Viet Vets Memorial	O	250+	Donnelly, Judy	Random House
Whales	O	333	Wonder World	Wright Group
What Animal Lives Here?	O	250+	Woolley, M. & Pigdon, K.	Mondo
What's the Big Idea, Ben Franklin?	O	250+	Fritz, Jean	Scholastic
What's the Matter with Herbie Jones?	O	250+	Kline, Suzy	Puffin Books

Title	Level	Words	Author/Series	Publisher/Distributor
Whipping Boy, The	O	250+	Fleischman, Sid	Troll
Wild Culpepper Cruise, The	O	250+	Paulsen, Gary	Bantam Doubleday Dell
Wild Pony, The	O	250+	Betancourt, Jeanne	Scholastic
Wingman	O	250+	Pinkwater, Daniel	Bantam Skylark
Against the Odds	P	250+	Layden, Joe	Scholastic
All-Pro Biographies: Dan Marino	P		Stewart, Mark	Children's Press
All-Pro Biographies: Gwen Torrence	P		Stewart, Mark	Children's Press
Amazing But True Sports Stories	P	250+	Hollander, Phyllis & Zander	Scholastic
Amelia Earhart	P	250+	Parlin, John	Bantam Doubleday Dell
Another Point of View	P	250+	Wildcats	Wright Group
Appointment with Action	P	250+	Wildcats	Wright Group
Attaboy Sam	P	250+	Lowry, Lois	Bantam Doubleday Dell
Baby Island	P	250+	Brink, Carol R.	Simon & Schuster
Bad Spell for the Worst Witch, A	P	250+	Murphy, Jill	Puffin Books
Baseball's Greatest Pitchers	P	250+	Kromer, S. A.	Random House
Berenstain Bear Scouts Ghost Versus Ghost, The	P	250+	Berenstain, Stan & Jan	Scholastic
Best Enemies	P	250+	Leverich, Kathleen	Beech Tree Books
Best Enemies Again	P	250+	Leverich, Kathleen	Alfred A. Knopf, Inc.
Best Enemies Forever	P	250+	Leverich, Kathleen	William Morrow & Co.
Body Battles	P	250+	Gelman, Rita G.	Scholastic
Book of Black Heroes from A to Z	P	250+	Hudson, Wade & Wilson	Scholastic
Bunnicula	P	250+	Howe, James	Avon Camelot
Burning Questions of Bingo Brown	P	250+	Byars, Betsy	Scholastic
Circle of Gold	P	250+	Boyd Dawson, Candy	Scholastic
Cyberspace	P	250+	Wildcats	Wright Group
Dancing with Jacques	P	250+	Voyages in…	Wright Group
Daring Rescue of Marlon the Swimming Pig, The	P	250+	Saunders, Susan	Random House
Dinosaur Detective	P	250+	Wildcats	Wright Group
Dolphin Adventure	P	250+	Grover, Wayne	Beech Tree Books
Dolphin Treasure	P	250+	Grover, Wayne	Beech Tree Books
Dragon in the Family, A	P	250+	Koller, Jackie French	Pocket Books
Dragon Quest	P	250+	Koller, Jackie French	Pocket Books
Dragon Trouble	P	250+	Koller, Jackie French	Pocket Books
Dragonling, The	P	250+	Koller, Jackie French	Pocket Books
Dragons and Kings	P	250+	Koller, Jackie French	Pocket Books
Dragons of Krad	P	250+	Koller, Jackie French	Pocket Books
Dynamic Duos	P	250+	Moore, David	Scholastic
Eddie and the Fire Engine	P	250+	Haywood, Carolyn	Beech Tree Books
Ellen Tebbits	P	250+	Cleary, Beverly	Avon Camelot
Emily's Runaway Imagination	P	250+	Cleary, Beverly	Avon Camelot
Encyclopedia Brown & Case of Mysterious Handprint	P	250+	Sobol, Donald & Rose	Bantam Doubleday Dell
Encyclopedia Brown & Case of the Disgusting Sneakers	P	250+	Sobol, Donald & Rose	Bantam Doubleday Dell
Encyclopedia Brown Boy Detective	P	250+	Sobol, Donald & Rose	Bantam Doubleday Dell
Encyclopedia Brown Case of the Dead Eagles	P	250+	Sobol, Donald & Rose	Bantam Doubleday Dell
Encyclopedia Brown Case of the Midnight Visitor	P	250+	Sobol, Donald & Rose	Bantam Doubleday Dell
Encyclopedia Brown Case of the Secret Pitch	P	250+	Sobol, Donald & Rose	Bantam Doubleday Dell
Encyclopedia Brown Case of the Treasure Hunt	P	250+	Sobol, Donald & Rose	Bantam Doubleday Dell
Encyclopedia Brown Case of the Two Spies	P	250+	Sobol, Donald & Rose	Bantam Doubleday Dell
Encyclopedia Brown Finds the Clues	P	250+	Sobol, Donald & Rose	Bantam Doubleday Dell
Encyclopedia Brown Gets His Man	P	250+	Sobol, Donald & Rose	Bantam Doubleday Dell

Title	Level	Words	Author/Series	Publisher/Distributor
Encyclopedia Brown Keeps the Peace	P	250+	Sobol, Donald & Rose	Bantam Doubleday Dell
Encyclopedia Brown Lends a Hand	P	250+	Sobol, Donald & Rose	Bantam Doubleday Dell
Encyclopedia Brown Saves the Day	P	250+	Sobol, Donald & Rose	Bantam Doubleday Dell
Encyclopedia Brown Shows the Way	P	250+	Sobol, Donald & Rose	Bantam Doubleday Dell
Encyclopedia Brown Solves Them All	P	250+	Sobol, Donald & Rose	Bantam Doubleday Dell
Encyclopedia Brown Takes the Case	P	250+	Sobol, Donald & Rose	Bantam Doubleday Dell
Encyclopedia Brown Tracks Them Down	P	250+	Sobol, Donald & Rose	Bantam Doubleday Dell
Encyclopedia Brown's Book of Strange But True Crimes	P	250+	Sobol, Donald & Rose	Scholastic
Eruption	P	250+	Wildcats	Wright Group
Exploring Freshwater Habitats	P	250+	Snowball, Diane	Mondo
Exploring Land Habitats	P	250+	Phinney, Margaret Y.	Mondo
Exploring Saltwater Habitats	P	250+	Smith, Sue	Mondo
Exploring Tree Habitats	P	250+	Seifert, Patti	Mondo
Eye Spy	P	250+	Wildcats	Wright Group
Fantastic Mr. Fox	P	250+	Dahl, Roald	The Penguin Group
Felicia the Critic	P	250+	Conford, Ellen	Little, Brown & Co.
Finding the Titanic	P	250+	Ballard, Robert D.	Scholastic
Fire at the Triangle Factory	P	250+	Littlefield, Holly	Carolrhoda Books
Five Brave Explorers	P	250+	Hudson, Wade	Scholastic
Five Notable Inventors	P	250+	Hudson, Wade	Scholastic
Florence Kelley	P	250+	Saller, Carol	Carolrhoda Books
Forgotten Door, The	P	250+	Key, Alexander	Scholastic
Four A's, The	P	250+	Wildcats	Wright Group
George's Marvelous Medicine	P	250+	Dahl, Roald	Puffin Books
Gerbilitis	P	250+	Spinner, Stephanie & Weiss, E.	HarperTrophy
Ghost Fox, The	P	250+	Yep, Laurence	Scholastic
Giraffe and the Pelly and Me, The	P	250+	Dahl, Roald	Puffin Books
Girl Called Al, A	P	250+	Greene, Constance C.	The Penguin Group
Glenda	P	250+	Udry, Janice	HarperTrophy
Grace's Letter to Lincoln	P	250+	Roop, Peter and Connie	Hyperion
Hare and the Tortoise, The	P	587	Aesop's Fables	Dominie
Head Full of Notions: A Story About Robert Fulton	P	250+	Russell Bowen, Andy	Carolrhoda Books
Helen Keller	P	250+	Graff, Stewart & Polly Anne	Bantam Doubleday Dell
Hercules and Other Greek Legends	P	250+	Wildcats	Wright Group
Hot Fudge Hero	P	250+	Brink, Carol R.	Henry Holt & Co.
How the Crystals Grow	P	1234	Book Shop	Mondo Publishing
Hurricanes!	P	250+	Hopping, Jean	Scholastic
If You Grew Up with Abraham Lincoln	P	250+	McGovern, Ann	Scholastic
If You Lived at the Time of the Civil War	P	250+	Moore, Kay	Scholastic
If You Lived at the Time of the Great San Francisco Earthquake	P	250+	Levine, Ellen	Scholastic
If You Lived in Colonial Times	P	250+	McGovern, Ann	Scholastic
If You Lived in the Time of Martin Luther King	P	250+	Levine, Ellen	Scholastic
If You Lived with the Sioux Indians	P	250+	McGovern, Ann	Scholastic
If You Sailed on the Mayflower in 1620	P	250+	McGovern, Ann	Scholastic
If You Traveled on the Underground Railroad	P	250+	Levine, Ellen	Scholastic
If You Were There When They Signed the Constitution	P	250+	Levy, Elizabeth	Scholastic
If Your Name Was Changed at Ellis Island	P	250+	Levine, Ellen	Scholastic
In the Rain Forest	P	250+	Wildcats	Wright Group
Incredible Places	P	250+	Wildcats	Wright Group

Title	Level	Words	Author/Series	Publisher/Distributor
Indian School, The	P	250+	Whelan, Gloria	HarperTrophy
It's Mine!	P	250+	Lionni, Leo	Scholastic
Jacob Two-Two Meets the Hooded Fang	P	250+	Richler, Mordecai	Seal Books
Jason Kidd Story, The	P	250+	Moore, David	Scholastic
Jazz Pizzazz and the Silver Threads	P	250+	Quattlebaum, Mary	Bantam Doubleday Dell
Jesse Owens: Olympic Hero	P	250+	Sabin, Francene	Troll
Joyful Noise: Poems for Two Voices	P	250+	Fleischman, Paul	HarperTrophy
Justin and the Best Biscuits in the World	P	250+	Pitts, Walter & Mildred	Random House
Koi's Python	P	250+	Moore, Miriam	Hyperion
Koya Delaney and the Good Girl Blues	P	250+	Greenfield, Eloise	Scholastic
Last Chance for Magic	P	250+	Chew, Ruth	Scholastic
Last Look	P	250+	Bulla, Clyde Robert	Puffin Books
Lion to Guard Us, A	P	250+	Bulla, Clyde Robert	HarperTrophy
Little Sea Pony, The	P	250+	Cresswell, Helen	Simon & Schuster
Long Ago and Far Away	P	250+	Wildcats	Wright Group
Lucky Stone, The	P	250+	Clifton, Lucille	Bantam Doubleday Dell
Magic School Bus and the Electric Field Trip	P	250+	Cole, Joanna & Degen, Bruce	Scholastic
Magic School Bus at the Waterworks	P	250+	Cole, Joanna & Degen, Bruce	Scholastic
Magic School Bus Blows Its Top	P	250+	Cole, Joanna	Scholastic
Magic School Bus Gets All Dried Up	P	250+	Cole, Joanna & Degen, Bruce	Scholastic
Magic School Bus Gets Ants in Its Pants	P	250+	Cole, Joanna & Degen, Bruce	Scholastic
Magic School Bus Gets Baked in a Cake	P	250+	Cole, Joanna & Degen, Bruce	Scholastic
Magic School Bus Goes Upstream	P	250+	Cole, Joanna & Degen, Bruce	Scholastic
Magic School Bus in the Haunted Museum	P	250+	Cole, Joanna	Scholastic
Magic School Bus in the Time of the Dinosaurs	P	250+	Cole, Joanna & Degen, Bruce	Scholastic
Magic School Bus Inside a Beehive	P	250+	Cole, Joanna & Degen, Bruce	Scholastic
Magic School Bus Inside a Hurricane	P	250+	Cole, Joanna & Degen, Bruce	Scholastic
Magic School Bus Inside Ralphie	P	250+	Cole, Joanna & Degen, Bruce	Scholastic
Magic School Bus Inside the Earth	P	250+	Cole, Joanna & Degen, Bruce	Scholastic
Magic School Bus Inside the Human Body	P	250+	Cole, Joanna & Degen, Bruce	Scholastic
Magic School Bus Lost in the Solar System	P	250+	Cole, Joanna & Degen, Bruce	Scholastic
Magic School Bus on the Ocean Floor	P	250+	Cole, Joanna & Degen, Bruce	Scholastic
Magic School Bus Plants Seeds	P	250+	Cole, Joanna & Degen, Bruce	Scholastic
Magic School Bus Spins a Web	P	250+	Cole, Joanna	Scholastic
Magic Squad and the Dog of Great Potential	P	250+	Quattlebaum, Mary	Bantam Doubleday Dell
Maps and Codes	P	250+	Wildcats	Wright Group
Mario's Mayan Journey	P	1021	Book Shop	Mondo Publishing
Minpins, The	P	250+	Dahl, Roald	The Penguin Group
Miss Geneva's Lantern	P	1691	Book Shop	Mondo Publishing
Mixed-Up Max	P	250+	King-Smith, Dick	Troll
Mountain Gorillas	P	330	Wonder World	Wright Group
Mythical Beasts	P	250+	Wildcats	Wright Group
New Kind of Magic, The	P	250+	Szymanski, Lois	Avon Camelot
Night Music	P	250+	Voyages in…	Wright Group
No Way, Winky Blue!	P	4053	Book Shop	Mondo Publishing
Nose for Trouble, A	P	250+	Wilson, Nancy	Avon Camelot
Not What It Seems	P	250+	Wildcats	Wright Group
Odds on Oliver	P	250+	Greene, Carol	Puffin Books
Oh, Brother	P	250+	Wilson, Johnnice M.	Scholastic
One Day in the Tropical Rain Forest	P	250+	Craighead George, Jean	HarperTrophy
One Day in the Woods	P	250+	Craighead George, Jean	HarperTrophy
Owls in the Family	P	250+	Mowat, Farley	Bantam Doubleday Dell

Title	Level	Words	Author/Series	Publisher/Distributor
Piglet in a Playpen	P	250+	Daniels, Lucy	Barron's Educational
Pony Named Shawney, A	P	3075	Book Shop	Mondo Publishing
Potter in Fiji, A	P	453	Wonder World	Wright Group
Private Notebook of Katie Roberts, Age 11, The	P	250+	Hest, Amy	Candlewick Press
Revolting Rhymes	P	250+	Dahl, Roald	The Penguin Group
Rising Stars of the NBA	P	250+	Layden, Joe	Scholastic
Shoebag	P	250+	James, Mary	Scholastic
Skates of Uncle Richard, The	P	250+	Fenner, Carol	Random House
Sky's the Limit, The	P	250+	Wildcats	Wright Group
Special Effects	P	250+	Wildcats	Wright Group
Sports Bloopers	P	250+	Hollander, Phyllis & Zander	Scholastic
Spray-Paint Mystery, The	P	250+	Medearis, Angela	Scholastic
Spreading the Word	P	250+	Wildcats	Wright Group
Stone Fox	P	250+	Gardiner, John Reynolds	HarperTrophy
Story of Alexander Graham Bell, The	P		Davidson, Margaret	Gareth Stevens
Story of George Washington Carver, The	P	250+	Moore, Eva	Scholastic
Story of Harriet Tubman, The	P	250+	McMullen, Kate	Dell Publishing
Story of Jackie Robinson, Bravest Man in Baseball	P	250+	Davidson, Margaret	Dell Publishing
Story of Thomas Alva Edison, Inventor, The	P	250+	Davidson, Margaret	Scholastic
Story of Walt Disney, Maker of Magical Worlds, The	P	250+	Selden, Bernice	Bantam Doubleday Dell
Sub, The	P	250+	Peterson, P. J.	Puffin Books
Surf's Up	P	250+	Wildcats	Wright Group
Tales of Olga da Polga, The	P	250+	Bond, Michael	Houghton Mifflin
Third Grade Stars	P	250+	Ransom, Candice	Troll
Time Warp Trio, The: 2095	P	250+	Scieszka, Jon	The Penguin Group
Time Warp Trio, The: The Not-So-Jolly Roger	P	250+	Scieszka, Jon	The Penguin Group
Time Warp Trio, The: Tut Tut	P	250+	Scieszka, Jon	The Penguin Group
Time Warp Trio, The: Your Mother Was a Neanderthal	P	250+	Scieszka, Jon	The Penguin Group
Time Warp Trio, The: The Good, the Bad, and the Goofy	P	250+	Scieszka, Jon	The Penguin Group
Time Warp Trio, The: The Knights of the Kitchen Table	P	250+	Scieszka, Jon	The Penguin Group
Tornadoes!	P	250+	Hopping, Lorraine	Scholastic
Transportation Time Line, A	P	250+	Discovery World	Rigby
Tut's Mummy: Lost and Found	P	250+	Donnelly, Judy	Random House
Twisters and Other Wind Storms	P	250+	Wildcats	Wright Group
Twits, The	P	250+	Dahl, Roald	Puffin Books
Up in the Air	P	250+	Wildcats	Wright Group
Wanted Dead or Alive: The True Story of H. Tubman	P	250+	McGovern, Ann	Scholastic
Where in the World Is the Perfect Family?	P	250+	Hest, Amy	The Penguin Group
Who Shot the President?	P	250+	Donnelly, Judy	Random House
Witch's Cat	P	250+	Chew, Ruth	Scholastic
Woods, Irons, and Greens	P	250+	Wildcats	Wright Group
Worst Witch at Sea, The	P	250+	Murphy, Jill	Candlewick Press
Worst Witch Strikes Again, The	P	250+	Murphy, Jill	Candlewick Press
Worst Witch, The	P	250+	Murphy, Jill	Puffin Books
Writer of the Plains: A Story About Willa Cather	P	250+	Streissguth, Tom	Carolrhoda Books
Yang the Second and Her Secret Admirers	P	250+	Namiaka, Lensey	Bantam Doubleday Dell
Yang the Third & Her Impossible Family	P	250+	Namiaka, Lensey	Bantam Doubleday Dell
Yang the Youngest & His Terrible Ear	P	250+	Namiaka, Lensey	Bantam Doubleday Dell

Bibliography

Adams, M. 1990. *Beginning to Read: Thinking and Learning About Print.* Cambridge, MA: MIT Press.

Allington, R. L. 1983. "The Reading Instruction Provided Readers of Differing Ability." *Elementary School Journal* 83, 548–559.

Clay, M. M. 1991. *What Did I Write?* Portsmouth, NH: Heinemann.

———. 1993a. *An Observation Survey of Early Literacy Achievement.* Portsmouth, NH: Heinemann.

———. 1993b. *Reading Recovery: A Guidebook for Teachers in Training.* Portsmouth, NH: Heinemann.

Collard , S. B. III. 1997. *Animal Dads.* Boston: Houghton Mifflin.

Durkin, D. 1996. *Children Who Read Early.* New York: Teachers College Press.

Holdaway, D. 1979. *The Foundations of Literacy.* Sydney, Australia: Ashton Scholastic.

Johnston, P. H. 1997. *Knowing Literacy: Constructive Literacy Assessment.* York, ME: Stenhouse.

Fountas, I. C., and G. S. Pinnell. 1996. *Guided Reading: Good First Teaching for All Children.* Portsmouth, NH: Heinemann.

———. 2000. *Guiding Readers and Writers, Grades 3–6.* Portsmouth, NH: Heinemann.

———, eds. 1999. *Voices on Word Matters: Learning About Phonics and Spelling in the Literacy Classroom.* Portsmouth, NH: Heinemann.

Pinnell, G. S., and I. C. Fountas. 1998. *Word Matters: Teaching Phonics and Spelling in the Reading/Writing Classroom.* Portsmouth, NH: Heinemann.

Pinnell, G. S., J. J. Pikulski, K. K. Wixson, J. R. Campbell, P. B. Gough, and A. S. Beatty. 1995. *Listening to Children Read Aloud: Data from NAEP's Integrated Reading Performance Record (IRPR) at Grade 4.* Report No. 23-FR-04, prepared by the Educational Testing Service. Washington, DC: Office of Educational Research and Improvement. U.S. Department of Education.

Index